VOLUME 4

"BEHIND" THE TEXT:

History and Biblical Interpretation

The Scripture and Hermeneutics Series

SCRIPTURE AND HERMENEUTICS SERIES

VOLUME 4

"BEHIND" THE TEXT:

History and Biblical Interpretation

editors

CRAIG BARTHOLOMEW • C. STEPHEN EVANS
MARY HEALY • MURRAY RAE

PATERNOSTER PRESS

UNIVERSITY OF
GLOUCESTERSHIRE

BAYLOR
UNIVERSITY

bible society

ZONDERVAN™

GRAND RAPIDS, MICHIGAN 49530 USA

First published 2003 jointly
in the UK by Paternoster Press, an imprint of Authentic Media,
P.O. Box 300, Carlisle, Cumbria, CA3 0QS
Website: www.paternoster-publishing.com
and in the United States of America by Zondervan
5300 Patterson Ave SE, Grand Rapids, Michigan 49530
www.zondervan.com

08 07 06 05 04 03 02   7 6 5 4 3 2 1

British Library Cataloguing in Publication Data
A catalogue record for this book is available from the British Library
ISBN 1-84227-068-0

Library of Congress Cataloguing in Publication Data
"Behind" the text : history and biblical interpretation / edited by
Craig Bartholomew ... [et al.].
     p. cm. — (The scripture and hermeneutics series ; v. 4)
Includes bibliographical references and indexes.
ISBN 1-84227-068-0 (U.K. : alk. paper) —
ISBN 0-310-23414-X (U.S. : alk. paper)
   1. Bible—Historiography—Congresses. 2. Bible—Hermeneutics—Congresses.
I. Bartholomew, Craig G., 1961- II. Series.
   BS635.3.B44 2003
   220.6'7—dc21
2003010322

Cover Design by Gert Swart and Zak Benjamin, South Africa
Typeset by WestKey Ltd, Falmouth, Cornwall
Printed in the United States of America
Printed on acid free paper

This volume well illustrates the Christian adage that faith pushes reason to achieve goals previously unsuspected but still proper to itself. The last few centuries have seen the development of an epistemology and an understanding of history that never leave the closed system thinking of both modernism and post-modernism. In biblical studies their child is the historical-critical method. The essays presented here respect the need and fruitfulness of a critical historiography while beginning the much-needed process of correcting the philosophical tenets that underlie much modern and post-modern biblical research. The result is a book that mediates a faith understanding, both theoretical and practical, of how to read the Bible authentically as a Christian today. I recommend it to both professors and students of theology and philosophy.

Fr. Francis Martin,
Chair, Catholic-Jewish Theological Studies,
John Paul II Cultural Center, Washington D.C.

This volume of excellent essays brings together eminent scholars from several disciplines, representing various theological positions, to focus on the subject of history and biblical interpretation. The book breaks new ground in its interdisciplinary examination of the methodology, the presuppositions, the practices, and the purposes of biblical hermeneutics, with a special emphasis on the relation of faith and history. It is requisite reading for anyone interested in the subject, from historical biblical critics and philosophical theologians to educated laity concerned to understand trends in the field.

Eleonore Stump,
Robert J. Henle Professor of Philosophy,
Saint Louis University, USA

There are few topics more central to the task of biblical interpretation than history, and not many become so multi-faceted as soon as they are examined in depth. Equally, few books open up the topic in such an illuminating and thought-provoking manner as this splendid collection of essays and responses.

Hugh Williamson,
Regius Professor of Hebrew,
University of Oxford, UK

This latest volume in the excellent Scripture and Hermeneutics Series showcases a high-level dialogue about the stubborn reality of history in the Bible and its contemporary interpretation. It is unique in bringing together leading representatives from a wide range of disciplines (notably philosophy, theology, biblical studies, and literature) who engage each other, not only with great sophistication and expertise, but also with a seriousness of purpose and an overt faith commitment which is rare in academic discourse today. In my view, this volume represents the initial stages of a conversation which is long overdue, and which holds great promise for the full-fledged academic recovery of the Bible as Scripture. It embodies an unusual combination of world-class scholarship, historic Christian orthodoxy, bold challenges to conventional wisdom, and the launching of fresh new ideas.

Al Wolters,
Professor of Religion and Theology,
Redeemer University College, Ontario, Canada

Contents

Rethinking History

Tradition and History

History and Narrative

History and Biblical Interpretation

Contributors

William P. Alston is Professor Emeritus of Philosophy at Syracuse University, where he has been on the faculty since 1980. Before that he was on the faculty of the University of Michigan, Rutgers University, and the University of Illinois. His main work has been in philosophy of religion, epistemology, and philosophy of language. Among his most recent books are *Illocutionary Acts and Sentence Meaning*; *A Realist Conception of Truth* and *Perceiving God*.

Craig G. Bartholomew is Senior Research Fellow at the University of Gloucestershire. He is the author of *Reading Ecclesiastes: Old Testament Exegesis and Hermeneutical Theory*. He has also edited *In the Fields of the Lord: A Calvin Seerveld Reader* and co-edited *Christ and Consumerism: A Critical Analysis of the Spirit of the Age*. He is the Series Editor for the Scripture and Hermeneutics Series.

C. Stephen Evans is University Professor of Philosophy and Humanities at Baylor University. Prior to coming to Baylor in 2001, he taught philosophy at Calvin College, St. Olaf College, and Wheaton College. His published works include fifteen books, among which are *The Historical Christ and the Jesus of Faith* and *Why Believe?*

Robert P. Gordon is Regius Professor of Hebrew, University of Cambridge, and Fellow of St Catharine's College, Cambridge. He is the author/editor of several books, including commentaries on 1 and 2 Samuel and Hebrews. He is Review Editor of *Vetus Testamentum* and Secretary 2001–4 of the International Organisation for the Study of the Old Testament.

Joel B. Green is Dean of Academic Affairs at Asbury Theological Seminary, as well as Dean of the School of Theology and Professor of New Testament Interpretation. He has written numerous books, the most recent being *Introducing the New Testament: Its Literature and Theology* (co-authored); *Beginning with Jesus: Christ in Scripture, the Church, and Discipleship*; *Recovering the Scandal of the Cross: Atonement in New Testament and Contemporary Contexts* (co-authored) and *The Gospel of Luke* in the New International Commentary on the New Testament Series. He is now in his twenty-second year of editing *Catalyst*.

Colin J.D. Greene is Dean of the School of Theology and Professor of Systematic Theology at Seattle Pacific University. He is the author of *Christology and Atonement in Historical Context* and *Christology in Cultural Perspective: Marking Out the Horizons*. He is the Consultant Editor for the Scripture and Hermeneutics Series, and the Public Theology in Cultural Engagement Series.

Mary E. Healy is lecturer in Sacred Scripture at the Notre Dame Graduate School of Christendom College in Alexandria, VA, and Council Chairman of Mother of God Community. She completed a doctorate in biblical theology at the Gregorian University in Rome in 2000.

David Lyle Jeffrey is Provost and Vice President for Academic Affairs at Baylor University. He is General Editor and co-author of *A Dictionary of Biblical Tradition in English Literature*. Among his other books are *The Early English Lyric and Franciscan Spirituality*; *By Things Seen: Reference and Recognition in Medieval Thought*; *Chaucer and Scriptural Tradition*; *English Spirituality in the Age of Wesley*; *English Spirituality in the Age of Wyclif* and *People of the Book: Christian Identity and Literary Culture*. His most recent book is *Houses of the Interpreter: Reading Scripture, Reading Culture*.

Gregory L. Laughery is associated with L'Abri Fellowship, Switzerland. He received his doctorate from the University of Fribourg, Switzerland, and is the author of *Living Hermeneutics in Motion: An Analysis and Evaluation of Paul Ricoeur's Contribution to Biblical Hermeneutics* and *The Apocalypse*.

Neil Beaton MacDonald is Senior Lecturer in Theology at the University of Surrey Roehampton. He has previously taught systematic theology at the Universities of Aberdeen, St Andrews and Edinburgh and has been visiting scholar at the Center of Theological Inquiry, Princeton, USA. He is the author of *Karl Barth and the Strange New World within the Bible: Barth, Wittgenstein, and the Metadilemmas of the Enlightenment* and *Metaphysics and the God of Israel* and the co-editor of *Barth, Calvin and Reformed Theology*.

Karl Möller is Lecturer in Theology and Religious Studies at the University College of St Martin, Lancaster. He is the author of *A Prophet in Debate: The Rhetoric of Persuasion in the Book of Amos*. He has also co-edited *Renewing Biblical Interpretation* and *After Pentecost: Language and Biblical Interpretation*.

Alvin Plantinga is John A. O'Brien Professor of Philosophy at the University of Notre Dame where he has taught philosophy for twenty years. Prior to that he taught at Calvin College for nineteen years. Among his many books are *God and Other Minds*; *The Nature of Necessity*; *God, Freedom and Evil*; *Does God Have a*

Nature?; *Warrant: The Current Debate*; *Warrant and Proper Function* and *Warranted Christian Belief.*

Iain W. Provan is the Marshall Sheppard Professor of Biblical Studies at Regent College, Vancouver. He is an ordained minister in the Presbyterian Church of Scotland. He has written numerous articles and several books – *Hezekiah and the Books of Kings*; *Lamentations* (New Century Bible Commentary); *1 and 2 Kings* (New International Biblical Commentary); *1 and 2 Kings* (Old Testament Guides) and *Ecclesiastes and Song of Songs* (NIV Application Commentary).

Murray A. Rae is Lecturer in Systematic Theology at King's College, London. He is the author of *Kierkegaard's Vision of the Incarnation* and has co-edited *The Practice of Theology* and *More Than a Single Issue: Theological Considerations Concerning the Ordination of Practising Homosexuals*. He is also the co-director of a research colloquium on Theology and the Built Environment.

Christopher R. Seitz is Professor of Old Testament and Theological Studies at the University of St Andrews. An Episcopal Priest (USA), he is the author of commentaries on Isaiah, and most recently, *Word Without End* and *Figured Out*. He is the President of a Society for Ecumenical and Anglican Doctrine (SEAD).

Walter Sundberg is Professor of Church History at Luther Seminary. He is co-author of *The Bible in Modern Culture: Baruch Spinoza to Brevard Childs*.

Peter van Inwagen is John Cardinal O'Hara Professor of Philosophy at The University of Notre Dame. He previously taught at Syracuse University and has been Visiting Professor of the Universities of Rochester, Arizona and Rutgers. He is the author of *An Essay on Free Will*; *Material Beings*; *Metaphysics*; *God, Knowledge, and Mystery: Essays in Philosophical Theology*; *The Possibility of Resurrection and Other Essays in Christian Apologetics*; *Ontology, Identity, and Modality: Essays in Metaphysics*; *Being: A Study in Ontology* (forthcoming) and is the author of over one hundred articles in professional journals.

Peter S. Williamson is Assistant Dean and Assistant Professor of Theology at the Sacred Heart Seminary in Detroit. He is the author of *Catholic Principles for Interpreting Scripture: A Study of the Pontifical Biblical Commission's 'The Interpretation of the Bible in the Church'* and co-editor of *John Paul II and the New Evangelization*.

Stephen I. Wright is an Anglican priest who served in parishes in the north of England from 1986 to 1998. Since 1998 he has been Director of the College of Preachers at Spurgeon's College, London. He is the author of *The Voice of Jesus: Studies in the Interpretation of Six Gospel Parables* and *Tales Jesus Told*.

Acknowledgements

Marc Chagall's painting, *Exodus 1952–66* (*L'exode*), is used by permission. © ADAGP, Paris and DACS, London, 2002. Cnac – Mnam/Dist RMN, Philippe Migest.

Alvin Plantinga's chapter (ch. 1) was originally published as 'Two (or More) Kinds of Scripture Scholarship', in *Modern Theology* 14.2 (April 1998), 243–77, and is used by permission of Blackwell Publishing. Nowhere in Blackwell's press is there acknowledged a previously published source for all or part of the material in question.

Extensive sections of Iain Provan's chapter (ch. 11) are reproduced from *A Biblical History of Israel* by Iain Provan, Phil Long, and Tremper Longman, to be published by Westminster John Knox Press, copyright 2003. Used by permission of Westminster John Knox Press.

Abbreviations

AB	Anchor Bible
ABD	*Anchor Bible Dictionary*
ABRL	Anchor Bible Reference Library
AGJU	Arbeiten zur Geschichte des antiken Judentums und des Urchristentums
AnBib	Analecta biblica
AOAT	Alter Orient und Altes Testament
ATD	Das Alte Testament Deutsch
BA	*Biblical Archaeologist*
BBB	Bonner biblische Beiträge
BibInt	*Biblical Interpretation*
BibSem	The Biblical Seminar
BIS	Biblical Interpretation Series
BKAT	Biblischer Kommentar, Altes Testament
BN	*Biblische Notizen*
BO	*Bibliotheca orientalis*
BVC	*Bible et vie chrétienne*
BZAW	Beihefte zur Zeitschrift für die alttestamentliche Wissenschaft
CBQ	*Catholic Biblical Quarterly*
ChrCent	*Christian Century*
ChrLit	*Christianity and Literature*
Comm	*Communio*
CRBS	*Currents in Research: Biblical Studies*
CS	*Chicago Studies*
EvQ	*Evangelical Quarterly*
EuroJTh	*European Journal of Theology*
EvT	*Evangelische Theologie*
FAT	Forschungen zum Alten Testament
FRLANT	Forschungen zur Religion und Literatur des Alten und Neuen Testaments
GBS	Guides to Biblical Scholarship
HKAT	Handkommentar zum Alten Testament
HvTSt	*Hervormde teologiese studies*
ICC	International Critical Commentary
IJST	*International Journal of Systematic Theology*
JAAR	*Journal of the American Academy of Religion*
JBL	*Journal of Biblical Literature*

JETh	*Jahrbuch für evangelikale Theologie*
JR	*Journal of Religion*
JSNTSup	Journal for the Study of the New Testament: Supplement Series
JSOT	*Journal for the Study of the Old Testament*
JSOTSup	Journal for the Study of the Old Testament: Supplement Series
KAT	Kommentar zum Alten Testament
KHAT	Kurzer Hand-Commentar zum Alten Testament
LTQ	*Lexington Theological Quarterly*
NPNF[1]	*Nicene and Post-Nicene Fathers*, Series 1
OBO	Orbis biblicus et orientalis
OBS	The Oxford Bible Series
OBT	Overtures to Biblical Theology
OTL	Old Testament Library
OTS	Old Testament Studies
RSR	*Recherches de science religieuse*
SBET	*Scottish Bulletin of Evangelical Theology*
SBLDS	Society of Biblical Literature Dissertation Series
SBLRBS	Society of Biblical Literature Resources for Biblical Study
SBLSP	*Society of Biblical Literature Seminar Papers*
SBLSS	Society of Biblical Literature Symposium Series
SBT	Studies in Biblical Theology
SEÅ	*Svensk exegetisk årsbok*
SHANE	Studies in the History of the Ancient Near East
SHS	Scripture and Hermeneutics Series
SJT	*Scottish Journal of Theology*
StPat	*Studia patavina*
SubBi	*Subsidia biblica*
TCW	*Tydskrif Vir Christelike Wetenskap*
TJ	*Trinity Journal*
TS	*Theological Studies*
TRE	*Theologische Realenzyklopädie*
TV	*Teología y vida*
TZ	*Theologische Zeitschrift*
UTB	Uni-Taschenbücher
VT	*Vetus Testamentum*
VTSup	Supplements to Vetus Testamentum
WCB	Alvin Plantinga, *Warranted Christian Belief* (New York: OUP, 2000)
WMANT	Wissenschaftliche Monographien zum Alten und Neuen Testament
WUNT	Wissenschaftliche Untersuchungen zum Neuen Testament
WW	*Word and World*
ZAW	*Zeitschrift für die alttestamentliche Wissenschaft*

The Artists

Zak Benjamin, Painter and Printmaker

Calvin Seerveld has thus characterized his style: '... bright gaiety and humour combined with ethereal seriousness. Like the unusual world of *One Hundred Years of Solitude* (Gabriel García Márquez), the paintings hold together, as natural, the most outlandish realities. Bold naiveté of forms and colours, stories of mysteries and conflict, trouble and healing – with a difference: friendly, zany, readable, provoking the viewer to look again ... a wholesome pleasure in the grit of life.'

Benjamin's friendship with sculptor Gert Swart is grounded in their mutual struggle to discover what it means to make contemporary art as Christians in post-apartheid South Africa.

His work is represented in collections internationally. He is married and lives in Vereeniging, South Africa, and has two daughters and two granddaughters.

<http://zakbenjaminartist.homestead.com/index.html>

Gert Swart

Gert Swart was born in Durban, South Africa, where he qualified and worked as a public health inspector before studying fine art for two years at the Natal Technikon. He now resides and works as a sculptor in Pietermaritzburg, South Africa. He is married to Istine Rodseth.

His most important exhibition of this period was staged at the Tatham Art Gallery in 1997. This exhibition, titled 'Contemplation: a body of work by Gert Swart', expressed the redemption of an individual as a metamorphosis from the curse of death to the hope of resurrection and how this transition affects the individual's relationship to society, nature and God.

One of Swart's most significant commissions of the past decade was a monument erected on the battlefield at Isandlwana in 1999. Although the battle of Isandlwana is known for its stunning defeat of a colonial army by an unconventional army, only monuments to fallen British soldiers had been erected on it in the past. It was a privilege to be involved in redressing this injustice and a challenge to design a monument that honours the fallen Zulu warriors but does not glorify war.

Recently Gert was commissioned by the Evangelical Seminary of Southern Africa (ESSA) to make a cross that would reflect the violence and suffering experienced in Southern Africa, particularly in the province of KwaZulu-Natal, RSA. While being a stark depiction of the cross as a brutal means of execution, the ESSA Cross is primarily a powerful symbol of hope: of the saving grace of God.

Gert met Zak Benjamin at a Christian Arts Festival over a decade ago. He and Benjamin were among the founder members of the Christian Worldview Network initiated by Craig Bartholomew. They enjoy a rich friendship that is currently finding expression in the joint design of book covers for this series in collaboration with Craig. This design project is the fruit of Craig's concern for Christian artists and his friendship with Gert and Zak.

<http://gertswartsculptor.homestead.com/index.html>

Marc Chagall's painting, *Exodus 1952–66 (L'exode)*, is used by permission.
© ADAGP, Paris and DACS, London, 2002.
Cnac – Mnam/Dist RMN, Philippe Migest.

Introduction

Craig G. Bartholomew

Introduction: Chagall's *Exodus* and the Swart–Benjamin Reworking

Chagall's *Exodus*, and even more so Swart and Benjamin's reworking of it, alert us to the centrality of story and event to the Bible. Chagall juxtaposes the exodus from Egypt with the cross. Swart and Benjamin introduce a river running through time and connecting Moses with his tablets of the law to the culmination of the river in Jesus, the crucified one. These are powerful visual reminders that at the heart of Christianity are the facts that God immersed himself in the life of an ancient Near Eastern nation, Israel, and that that immersion found its fulfilment in Jesus of Nazareth.

The events of God's involvement with Israel always have to be explained with words, but such words – 'I am the LORD your God who brought you out of the land of Egypt' – inevitably refer to actual deeds. God's revelation of himself is *in* history, and the scandal of this particularity is unavoidable. There may be more to the Bible than history, but what Goldingay says of the Old Testament is surely true of the Bible as a whole: 'Yet it remains true that the major overt emphasis of much of the OT is that Yahweh has acted, acts and will act in Israel's history for her salvation. The importance of this emphasis should not be lost in the course of emphasising complementary features of OT faith.'[1]

Swart and Benjamin introduce a contemporary dimension into their reworking of Chagall, namely the clock and boats in the top right-hand side, and the rocket and peaceful houses in the upper left-hand side. This is a vital addition, for it links the particularity of the biblical story – Israel and Jesus – with today and thus with universal history. This alerts us to the fact that not only are events an important part of the biblical story, but also that God's revelation of himself in those events is the key to the whole of history. Few make this point as clearly as Lesslie Newbigin:

---

[1] Goldingay, *Approaches*, 69.

What is unique about the Bible is the story which it tells, with its climax in the story of the incarnation, ministry, death and resurrection of the Son of God. If that story is true, then it is unique and also universal in its implications for all human history. It is in fact the true outline of world history.[2]

In its narrative from creation to new creation, the Bible tells us the story of the whole of history so that we know the goal towards which history is headed. Christ is the clue to the whole of this history, and this clue illumines our present with all of its technological and other challenges pointed to by Swart and Benjamin.

Swart and Benjamin's painting thus focuses our attention on two aspects in relation to the Bible and history. Firstly that actual event is fundamental to the biblical story, and secondly that the biblical story is the key to history as a whole. Now, of course, this is where the debate begins rather than ends. History has been, and continues to be, a hotly contested area in biblical studies, and theologians and biblical scholars express a diversity of views on these issues.[3]

Historical method has preoccupied biblical scholars for over a century now, and amidst the challenges of postmodernism not only does traditional historical criticism continue, but new concerns with history such as reception history and *Wirkungsgeschichte* are emerging. What lies 'behind the biblical text' will not go away as an important topic for biblical interpretation,[4] and in this volume we seek to identify key issues in that respect and to suggest ways forward towards a renewal of the interpretation of the Bible as Scripture.

The Twists and Turns to the Present

When I try and initiate students into the wide range of interpretative possibilities in biblical studies today, I suggest that a helpful way of visualizing the larger context is to think in terms of several *turns*:[5]

---

[2] Newbigin, *Gospel*, 97; see also chs. 6–9.

[3] For a useful introduction to the debate about faith and history see Michalson, 'Faith and History'. For an influential view that history is not as central to the Bible as my comments above suggest, see Barr, 'Concepts of History and Revelation'. On history and Scripture see also Goldingay, *Models*, part 1; and Long, *Art*. N.T. Wright's work is well known for its emphasis on the importance of history for NT theology. See ch. 9, 'History and Theology', in Neill and Wright, *Interpretation*, and in particular Wright, *New Testament*.

[4] On the metaphor of 'behind the text' see Thiselton, 'Behind', 97–102; and Ricœur, *Hermeneutics*, 142–44. In the title of this volume we are using 'behind' in a general sense to refer to the history that underlies the biblical text.

[5] The metaphor of a 'turn' has become commonplace in scientific and philosophical literature. See Botha, 'Understanding'.

- the historical turn
  - the literary turn
    - the postmodern turn
      - a theological turn

As a model, this has its limitations. For example, it is vital to note that one turn does not cancel out an earlier one. Nor are the turns monochrome in the sense that, for example, one philosophy of history governs the historical turn. Furthermore, there are no doubt other turns that could be included. However, the model *is* helpful in alerting us to the way in which 'history' has dominated biblical interpretation for the last century or so, and for flagging up ways in which the historical emphasis has had to readjust to other emphases. In this way the model helps us to glimpse the challenges of addressing history and biblical interpretation today.

The historical turn

Thiselton suggests that there have been two great paradigm shifts in NT interpretation. The first shift, which took place in the eighteenth century onwards, was '*toward a single preoccupation with historical method*, and the second, in the late twentieth century, has been toward a methodological pluralism'.[6] Thiselton locates an originating point for the first in the work of Semler, in which he discerns two strands – one struggling to be free of manipulation and illegitimate constraint in his scholarship and the other a tendency to succumb to a deistic world-view. In his assessment of the history of NT interpretation Thiselton is concerned not to lose sight of the positive, former strand while being rightly critical of the latter tendency.

A similar preoccupation with historical method developed in Old Testament study. De Wette was the first scholar to radically rewrite the history of Israelite religion. His approach to the OT was deeply influenced by Kantian thought, which was mediated inter alia through Fries. A critical approach to the OT demonstrated, according to de Wette, that it has little to offer in terms of authentic history. Through his exposure to Fries, de Wette arrived at an articulate view of religion, and in his study of the OT he brought this to bear on it comprehensively.[7]

As Thiselton notes,

de Wette's reconstructed history of Israelite religion and the development of New Testament theologies (plural) steadily became institutionalised as a basis for new theological evaluations. What began as a search for freedom from whatever might

---

[6] Thiselton, 'New Testament Interpretation', 10 (emphasis mine).
[7] On de Wette see Rogerson, *W.M.L. de Wette*.

inhibit inquiry, namely church dogma or manipulative ecclesial interests, itself became transformed into a new institutional structure. So monolithic does this structure at times appear to have become that some writers speak, though questionably, of '*the* historical-critical method'.[8]

There is much debate about the origins and nature of historical criticism and about precisely what is involved in the historical turn.[9] Krentz, as Thiselton notes, presents historical criticism as a single entity. Krentz argues that 'historical' and 'critical' both identify key elements of the historical-critical method of biblical interpretation. *Critical* signifies the subjection of the biblical tradition to examination on the basis of the modern world-view. *Historical* indicates that it is particularly Enlightenment *historical* method that is applied to the Bible by the historical-critical method, especially as it came to maturity in the nineteenth century in Germany. Krentz points out that

> it is difficult to overestimate the significance the nineteenth century has for biblical interpretation. It made historical criticism *the* approved method of interpretation. The result was a revolution of viewpoint in evaluating the Bible. The Scriptures were, so to speak, secularized.... The Bible was no longer the criterion for the writing of history; rather history had become the criterion for understanding the Bible.... The Bible stood before criticism as defendant before judge. The criticism was largely positivist in orientation, immanentist in its explanations, and incapable of appreciating the category of revelation.[10]

Thiselton acknowledges the preoccupation with historical method that developed, but he urges us not to lose sight of the variegated nature of the history of modern interpretation. Postmodernism has alerted us to the problems of viewing modernity monolithically. 'A plea must be made for the application of hermeneutics to the history of interpretation with no less rigor and sensitivity than is invited by the study of biblical texts.'[11] It seems to me that both Krentz and Thiselton have important points to make in this respect. The story of the historical turn is not simple, and we need to learn to tell that story in a way that does justice to the historical particularities.[12] At the same time we do

---

[8] Thiselton, 'New Testament Interpretation', 17.

[9] See the essays by Bartholomew, Sundberg, Riches, Wolters, Mason, Greene and Möller in Bartholomew, Greene and Möller, *Renewing*.

[10] Krentz, *Historical-Critical Method*, 30.

[11] Thiselton, 'New Testament Interpretation', 36.

[12] New Testament studies are well served by several expositions of the way in which NT interpretation has developed. For example, Kümmel, *New Testament;* Neill and Wright, *Interpretation;* Riches, *Century*. Old Testament study is, I think, less well served in this respect. Kraus, *Geschichte*, is an important volume, and John Rogerson has done very important work on the history of OT interpretation. There remains

need to recognize the overarching patterns that emerge in this story and its close link with modernity. Krentz rightly flags up the secularization of biblical interpretation that took place through the historical turn, and Christian reflection on historical criticism must take this critically into account, albeit not simplistically.

The main methods that the historical turn yielded in biblical interpretation are well known: source criticism, form criticism, tradition criticism and redaction criticism. These have been applied rigorously to the Scriptures with varying results. In terms of both Testaments, historical criticism has resulted in radical scepticism about the historical accuracy of the biblical narratives in some quarters, but Old Testament study has generally been more polarized in this respect than New Testament studies. Westcott, Hort and Lightfoot played a major role in developing a moderate, believing New Testament criticism,[13] a tradition sustained through the work of scholars such as F.F. Bruce, C.E.B. Cranfield, I.H. Marshall and N.T. Wright. There was no such equivalent movement in Old Testament studies, which have as a result been far more polarized between radical and conservative approaches to historical issues.[14]

The sort of challenge that historical reconstruction of the history of Israel presented to Christian scholars is well captured in von Rad's statement that:

> These two pictures of Israel's history lie before us – that of modern critical scholarship and that which the faith of Israel constructed – and for the present, we must reconcile ourselves to both of them … The one is rational and 'objective' … The other … is confessional … The fact that these two views of Israel's history are so divergent is one of the most serious burdens imposed upon Biblical scholarship.[15]

Christians have responded to the gap between these two histories in different ways. Some have tried to close the gap. Others have argued that history is not as central to Old Testament theology as is sometimes thought.[16] In this context the minimalist–maximalist distinction should be noted.[17] For some, God's revelation in Israel and Christ makes the historical accuracy of the biblical narratives vital – such scholars tend towards a maximalist view of the historical accuracy of the Bible. Minimalists, by comparison, ask what the minimum of

---

    scope for some major work on the history of OT interpretation that explores the philosophical and theological dimensions of the story.

[13] See Neill and Wright, *Interpretation*, ch. 3.

[14] I am indebted to Brevard Childs for this point.

[15] Von Rad, *Old Testament Theology*, I, 108.

[16] Barr, 'Concepts of History and Revelation'.

[17] Note that I am referring to this distinction among *Christian* scholars and not just biblical scholars in general, where it is also often applied.

historical truth is that is required for the Bible to continue to be taken seriously as Scripture.

In the second half of the twentieth century, the preoccupation with historical method was increasingly challenged in biblical studies. In his inaugural lecture at Oxford University,[18] Ernest Nicholson wondered aloud whether historical criticism might be a Sisyphean toil, and then dismissed the thought. It simply cannot be that all this historical-critical effort is of no avail! As time has passed, however, the challenge has grown stronger, and it has become harder to dismiss that thought so easily. Simultaneously, in New Testament studies scholars such as N.T. Wright have creatively and rigorously revived the notion of history as of fundamental importance for New Testament theology. According to Wright, 'we go back to the past because this is where God acted decisively and uniquely'.[19]

The literary turn

At the end of the nineteenth century and the start of the twentieth, positivism was the dominant philosophy in Europe. In literary studies this manifested itself in a concern with questions of genesis, context and authorial intent. What such an approach neglected was the *literary text* itself, and this neglect is paralleled in historical criticism's concern with questions of origin and what lies behind the text, and consequent neglect of the literary shape of the text itself. Alter and Kermode perceptively say of historical criticism:

> This 'scientific' criticism was of great cultural and doctrinal importance; but, as we have said, it diverted attention from biblical narrative, poetry, and prophecy as literature, treating them instead as more or less distorted historical records. The characteristic move was to infer the existence of some book that preceded the one we have – the lost documents that were combined to make Genesis as it has come down to us, the lost Aramaic Gospel, the lost 'sayings-source' used by Matthew and Luke, and so on. The effect of this practice was curious: one spoke of the existing books primarily as evidence of what must once have been available in an original closer to what actually happened. That was their real value – as substitutes for what had unfortunately been lost.[20]

In literary studies, New Criticism developed in response to this neglect of the literary text and, somewhat later, the literary turn developed in biblical studies to fill the parallel gap. Alter and Kermode identify Erich Auerbach's *Mimesis* (1946, ET 1953) as a landmark in this literary turn. The literary turn in biblical

---

[18] *Interpreting the Old Testament*, published in 1981.
[19] 'Interview', 132.
[20] Alter and Kermode, *Literary Guide*, 3.

studies has been traced from the growing awareness of the limitations of the historical-critical method through Canon Criticism[21] and New Criticism (including Muilenberg's rhetorical criticism) to the narratology of Alter, Berlin and Sternberg[22] and parallel developments in New Testament studies.

In 1981, Alter was able to write that 'over the last few years, there has been growing interest in literary approaches among the younger generation of biblical scholars ... but, while useful explications of particular texts have begun to appear, there have been as yet no major works of criticism, and certainly no satisfying overview of the poetics of the Hebrew Bible'.[23] Alter's *The Art of Biblical Narrative* is such an overview, but Sternberg's *The Poetics of Biblical Narrative* is the major work on OT narrative. Gunn rightly noted that 'Sternberg's recent book on poetics moves such a narratology into a whole new dimension of discrimination and sophistication and will be fundamental to the emerging generation of narrative critics'.[24]

The literary turn has radical implications for historical criticism. What was a doublet, thereby signalling a source, is now an example of careful, artistic repetition. Some have practised literary analysis of the Bible without concerning themselves much with historical issues.[25] But clearly the historical turn is not unaffected by the literary turn. Sternberg, Wright,[26] Thiselton[27] and others rightly argue for a careful integration of the historical and literary dimensions of the Bible, as well as the ideological or theological.

For Sternberg, seeing narrative technique as part of the text itself means taking the historical construction of the text seriously if one is going to come to grips with the functional purpose of biblical narrative. Sternberg is highly critical of the tendency to categorize Old Testament narratives as fiction. Fiction and history cannot, in Sternberg's view, be distinguished by form but only in terms of overall purpose. When the Old Testament narratives are assessed by this criterion, 'the product is neither historicized fiction nor fictionalised history, but historiography pure and uncompromising'.[28] Everything, in Sternberg's view, points in this direction. The Israelite obsession with

---

[21] Barton, *Reading*, notes the similarities between New Criticism and Childs's canonical approach, but Childs insists that his is a theological hermeneutic.

[22] Gunn, 'New Directions', 65–68.

[23] Alter, *Art*, 15.

[24] Gunn, 'New Directions', 68.

[25] This is a real danger in our postmodern context. As Wright, *New Testament*, 13, points out, 'while history and theology work at their stormy relationship, there is always a danger, particularly in postmodernism, that literary study will get on by itself, without impinging on, or being affected by, either of the others'.

[26] Wright, *New Testament*.

[27] Thiselton, 'Models'.

[28] Sternberg, *Poetics*, 35.

memory of the past and its significance for the present; Israel's uniqueness in this respect in the ancient Near East – these factors all confirm that the Old Testament narratives are making a strong historical truth-claim. 'Were the narrative written or read as fiction, then God would turn from the lord of history into a creature of the imagination, with the most disastrous results.'[29] Sternberg's approach is, of course, not uncontested. But it indicates well the way in which the literary turn complicates the historical turn.

The postmodern turn

So-called 'postmodernism' began in literary studies and was then extended to a critique of Western culture as a whole in the 1980s. It has impacted on biblical studies from both these places. Norris argues that 'literary theory, through its colonizing drive into other disciplines, bids fair to reverse that entire move-ment of progressive or enlightened critique which has sought to establish adequate protocols for the discrimination of truth from falsehood, of factual from fictive or historical from mythic modes of utterance'.[30] Whether we agree with Norris's articulation of the dangers of postmodernism or not, the postmodern debate has questioned central assumptions of modernity, includ-ing its notions of history, and it was inevitable that such questioning would eventually threaten the dominance of that quintessentially modern method in biblical studies, namely historical criticism.

Interwoven with this is the fact that since the literary turn in biblical studies, biblical scholars have kept an eye on developments in literary studies and the door open to importing their methods. Thus it is no surprise that literary theory's colonizing drive should find a receptive audience in biblical studies. By the late 1960s, New Criticism was being replaced by structuralism, and then came the post-structuralist developments, and it was only a matter of time before Fish, Rorty, Derrida, Barthes, Foucault and the like were being applied in biblical studies.[31]

The contours of the postmodern landscape are not always easily identifi-able. Postmodernism is synonymous with diversity and pluralism, and one needs to take care not to impose contours on diverse positions. Thus Rorty is to be distinguished from Derrida, and Derrida from Baudrillard, and so on. Nevertheless, it is clear that in its more extreme forms, postmodernism consti-tutes a radical challenge to biblical studies, whether historical or literary. With its wild pluralism, its view of texts as radically indeterminate and its suspicion of

---

[29] Sternberg, *Poetics*, 32.
[30] Norris, *Truth*, 114.
[31] See, e.g., Adams, *Handbook*.

getting behind texts, much postmodernism renders the historical-critical enterprise deeply problematic. If 'the past is not discovered or found ... [but] is created and represented by the historian as a text, which in turn is consumed by the reader',[32] where does this leave the enterprise of historical criticism?

The depth of the postmodern challenge in this respect should be noted. Postmodernism questions the foundational assumptions of modernity so that its challenge to an enterprise like historical criticism is not always immediately obvious but at a deep, *philosophical* level. As long as the standard narrative of modernity as rational progress was assumed, historical criticism did not have to worry too much about its philosophical presuppositions. Indeed, to this day the myth continues to be entertained that historical criticism has no philosophical presuppositions.[33] But postmodernism queries such objective neutrality and insists that particular epistemologies and views of history underlie the practice of historical criticism. If such views are to be maintained, then their basis must be argued for – it cannot just be assumed.[34]

It is particularly via postmodern views of history that historical criticism, and any view of the biblical narratives as accurately representing what happened, are challenged. Munslow, in his *Deconstructing History*, discerns three current options in historiography; firstly reconstructionism, secondly constructionism and thirdly deconstructionism. Reconstructionism believes that the more carefully we write history, the closer we will get to what actually happened. Constructionism refers to the approaches to history that invoke general laws, Marxism being the most well-known example. Munslow gathers postmodern approaches together under the label of 'deconstructionism', and this includes authors such as Hayden White and Keith Jenkins. Such approaches stress the fact that history writing is always an example of literary production, with all the attendant complexities that brings.

Central to postmodern debates about history is the question of the extent to which history can accurately represent the past through narrative. Scholars

---

[32] Munslow, *Deconstructing*, 178.

[33] In my 'Uncharted Waters' I trace this obscuring of the philosophical presuppositions of historical criticism to Wellhausen. Quite remarkably, James Barr, *History and Ideology*, 26, 27, still asserts that 'the typical biblical scholarship of modern times has been rather little touched by philosophy – certainly much less than it has been touched by theology. Going back to the last century, one remembers Vatke and his Hegelianism, and it has long been customary to accuse Wellhausen of the same thing though the accusation has long been proved to be an empty one. And after that we do have an influence of philosophy, but mostly on the theological use of the Bible rather than on biblical scholarship in the narrower sense.'

[34] Levenson's *Hebrew Bible* is an important text in terms of the current status of historical criticism.

point to the unavoidable interpretative and hermeneutical element in all history writing, and many draw radical conclusions from this.[35] This postmodern emphasis on the linguistic and narrative nature of history raises profound questions about historiography, whether one agrees with the likes of Hayden White or not. What kind of knowledge production is history writing? History always brings a narrative grid to bear on its telling of the past and Munslow, for example, suggests that 'history is best viewed epistemologically as a form of literature producing knowledge as much by its aesthetic or narrative structure as by any other criteria'.[36] History is a form of narrative and as such is part of the historical process: 'All such narratives make over events and explain why they happened, but are overlaid by the assumptions held by the historian about the forces influencing the nature of causality.'[37]

The postmodern turn thus problematizes the literary and historical turn in biblical studies. It questions the very foundations of the discipline and alerts us to the inevitability of a plurality of views in biblical interpretation. At the same time, its emphasis on plurality opens up the possibility of a re-engagement of biblical studies with theology.

A theological turn?

In his inaugural lecture at Oxford University, John Barton noted the crisis in Old Testament studies and that an emerging response is to call for a *religious* hermeneutic.[38] Barton is suspicious of this move and argues for a recovery of Enlightenment values as the centre of OT studies. Barton is right in noting that an increasing number of scholars are arguing, in response to the postmodern turn, that we need a *theological* hermeneutic in biblical studies.

Karl Barth, Childs's canonical approach and Yale's postliberal theology are major ingredients in this renewed interest in theological interpretation. Childs has long argued that the goal of the interpretation of Christian Scripture must be to understand both Testaments as witness to the self-same divine reality, namely the God and Father of Jesus Christ. Although this theological turn is now gathering momentum in response to the pluralism and nihilistic direction of (some) postmodernism, Childs's extensive corpus has played a major role in the twentieth century in laying the foundation for a theological, canonical hermeneutic in biblical studies. The theological turn is nevertheless in its early days in biblical studies. Inevitably, as with Childs, a theological turn will

---

[35] For a taste of the radicality of this see Burnett, 'Historiography'.

[36] Munslow, *Deconstructing*, 5.

[37] Munslow, *Deconstructing*, 10.

[38] Barton, *Future*.

involve going back to premodern readings of OT texts and finding traditions that can be re-appropriated and developed in our day.

There are (at least) two elements to this theological turn. One aspect is that of simply getting on with reading the Bible theologically. Scholars such as Christopher Seitz invoke in this respect the plain sense of Scripture, allow a limited role for historical criticism (canonical-historical, see below), and get on with interpretation in relation to the church and Christian doctrine.[39] A somewhat different approach is to argue that we need a theology of history (and literature, etc.) to fund biblical interpretation. Neill and Wright express this as follows:

> Similarly, there has, alas, been little progress in the areas of a theology of history, or of New Testament ecclesiology. It is an exciting idea, as was mooted in the first edition of this work, that 'An understanding of history which is incompatible with a Christian doctrine of revelation is bound to land the New Testament scholar in grave perplexities; a true theological understanding of history would not of itself solve any New Testament problems, but it would, so to speak, hold the ring within which a solution can be found.' But where are the scholars sufficiently familiar with actual history-writing, sufficiently at home in philosophy and the history of ideas, and sufficiently committed to the study of the New Testament, to undertake the task?[40]

Wright himself makes considerable progress in this direction in his *The New Testament and the People of God*.[41] Kevin Vanhoozer argues that 'the *best general hermeneutics is a trinitarian hermeneutics*. Yes, the Bible should be interpreted "like any other book"; but *every* book should be interpreted with norms that we derive and establish from trinitarian theology'.[42] Clearly there are different emphases among proponents of theological interpretation. Whatever the precise view, theological interpretation undoubtedly impacts upon how we think about history and biblical interpretation.

Thus, as we reopen the discussion between history and biblical interpretation in our attempt to renew biblical interpretation, it is important to think carefully about the historical turn in relation to the other three turns. There is also the question of how these turns relate to more fundamental philosophical or paradigm shifts. Indeed the postmodern turn, as we noted, forces the depth

---

[39] Seitz, *Word*.

[40] Neill and Wright, *Interpretation*, 366.

[41] Not uncontroversially, of course. See, inter alia, Newman (ed.), *Jesus and the Restoration of Israel*. In terms of a theology of history, Pannenberg's work remains very important. See Thiselton, *Two Horizons*, 74–84.

[42] Vanhoozer, *Meaning*, 456 (emphasis original).

issue of philosophical presuppositions to the surface. In a different context, Botha notes that

> the question I found intriguing was whether these 'turns' were representative of fundamental philosophical or epistemological revolutions, gestalt shifts, 'metaphoric revolutions' in the history and philosophy of science or whether they were in fact no more than manifestations and variations of one overall epistemological root metaphor or basic metaphor, characteristic of the epistemology of the twentieth century.[43]

So too with history and biblical interpretation; the relationship between historical approaches and underlying paradigms must be borne in mind.

In this way a model of turns, for all its limitations, helps us to start to get at the variety of factors involved in any attempt to reassess history and biblical interpretation today. There are complex archaeological layers to the concern with history in modern biblical interpretation, and this history is in turn connected with broader philosophical, theological and cultural issues.

Content of this Volume

This volume sets out to address many of the key issues in this complex re-assessment of history and biblical interpretation. Our aim is not to solve all of the problems, but rather to foreground the issues and to work away at them with a view to a renewal of biblical interpretation. The presence of several top (Christian) philosophers at our Boston consultation on history and biblical interpretation was a rich ingredient in our discussions. This ensured that sustained attention was given to the *philosophical issues* that are crucial to historiography today.

Historical criticism – Critical assessments

Alvin Plantinga brings his work on *epistemology* to bear on historical biblical criticism in his *Warranted Christian Belief*. Robert Gordon and Craig Bartholomew, both biblical scholars, respond to Plantinga's chapter on 'Two (or More) Kinds of Scripture Scholarship'. Bartholomew focuses on the importance of epistemology for biblical interpretation today, whereas Gordon attends closely to the role of historical criticism. Plantinga then responds to the responses.

How seriously should ordinary Christians take the sceptical results of some biblical criticism? Peter van Inwagen argues that ordinary Christians are

---

[43] Botha, 'Understanding', 16.

justified in ignoring the sceptical claims of New Testament scholars. Colin Greene (a theologian) and Joel Green (a New Testament scholar) interact with and respond critically to Van Inwagen's paper.

William Alston examines rigorously certain lines of argument still used by many New Testament scholars to support a negative view of the historicity of reports of sayings of Jesus and of events in the Synoptic Gospels, and finds them wanting.

Mary Healy revisits the philosophical problems with historical criticism and invokes the Christological analogy of Christ's two natures as a means of developing a narrative biblical hermeneutic that takes biblical narrative seriously as the means by which we discern the interior and divine meaning of real events.

Peter Williamson unpacks and examines the approach of the Pontifical Biblical Commission's *The Interpretation of the Bible in the Church* to the relationship between exegesis and history and its view of historical criticism.

Rethinking history

Iain Provan recognizes that progress in the area of history and the Bible requires attending to the nature of history and history writing. He looks in this respect at how modern understandings of history have developed and attends in particular to the role of testimony in history writing. Provan brings his conclusions from these foundational explorations to bear on the controversial contemporary debate about the history of Israel.

Murray Rae explores the disengagement with history in modernity and the effect of this upon biblical interpretation, and then against this backdrop he articulates the contours of a theology of history. He concludes by reflecting upon the implications of such a theology for the interpretation of the Bible.

Tradition and history

Walter Sundberg and Stephen Evans both address the issue of tradition and history. Sundberg highlights the importance of tradition for Christianity and then outlines the conflict that developed between tradition and history. He finds in Kierkegaard an exemplary way of facing this conflict. Evans explores the question of whether or not biblical interpretation that is guided by 'the rule of faith' can possibly arrive at historical truth. He argues that, whether one adopts an 'evidentialist' or a 'non-evidentialist' epistemology, such an interpretive practice can indeed lead to genuine historical knowledge. Along the way Evans also argues that such an interpretive practice is open to Protestants, and not just to Catholics.

History and narrative

Gregory Laughery attends to the radical historiographical challenge of postmodernism and draws on Paul Ricœur's work on narrative to answer these challenges and thereby to find fruitful approaches to history for biblical interpretation.

David Lyle Jeffrey revisits the issue of grand narrative and the Bible, arguing by means of fascinating literary and cultural examples for the ongoing relevance of grand narrative, not least with respect to the Bible. In relation to Galatians and Hebrews in particular, he explores the destination of the biblical story. His concern is with both the importance of remembering history in the biblical story and the implications of the story for historiography.

History and biblical interpretation

Historical criticism continues to dominate biblical studies in all sorts of ways. Karl Möller puts the redaction-critical reconstruction of Amos's literary pre-history under the microscope, looking at how it continues to influence the study of Amos, and he assesses its strengths and weaknesses.

Two essays in this volume develop the canonical approach associated with Brevard Childs in relation to issues of history and interpretation, albeit in quite different ways. Christopher Seitz explores the implications of reading the Book of the Twelve (the minor prophets) in their final form and order as a unity. Seitz describes his approach as canonical-historical. Neil Beaton MacDonald, drawing on Childs's canonical interpretation of the Old Testament, attends to the notion of divine speaking and the relationship between this and a theology of history.

Stephen Wright argues that attention to what is behind the text must not ignore our responsibility to indwell the biblical story, as the centre from which we can interpret history. Wright describes his approach in this respect as figural interpretation.

Bibliography

Adams, A.K.M. (ed.), *Handbook of Postmodern Biblical Interpretation* (St. Louis: Chalice Press, 2000)

Alter, R., *The Art of Biblical Narrative* (New York: Basic Books, 1981)

——, and F. Kermode (eds.), *The Literary Guide to the Bible* (London: Fontana, 1987)

Auerbach, E., *Mimesis: The Representation of Reality in Western Literature* (Princeton: Princeton University Press, 1953)

Barr, J., 'The Concepts of History and Revelation', in *Old and New in Interpretation: A Study of the Two Testaments* (London: SCM Press, 2nd edn, 1982), 65–102

——, *History and Ideology in the Old Testament: Biblical Studies at the End of a Millennium* (Oxford: OUP, 2000)

Bartholomew, C.G., 'Uncharted Waters: Philosophy, Theology and the Crisis in Biblical Interpretation', in *Renewing Biblical Interpretation* (ed. C.G. Bartholomew, C. Greene and K. Möller; SHS 1; Carlisle: Paternoster; Grand Rapids: Zondervan, 2000), 1–39

Bartholomew, C.G., C. Greene and K. Möller (eds.), *Renewing Biblical Interpretation* (SHS 1; Carlisle: Paternoster; Grand Rapids: Zondervan, 2000)

Barton, J., *The Future of Old Testament Study* (Oxford: Clarendon Press, 1993)

——, *Reading the Old Testament: Method in Biblical Study* (London: Darton, Longman & Todd, 2nd edn, 1996)

Botha, M.E., 'Understanding Our Age: Philosophy at a Turning Point of the "Turns"? – The Endless Search for the Elusive Universal', *TCW* 30.2 (1994), 16–31

Burnett, F.W., 'Historiography', in *Handbook of Postmodern Biblical Interpretation* (ed. A.K.M. Adam; St. Louis: Chalice Press, 2000), 106–12

Goldingay, J., *Approaches to Old Testament Interpretation* (Leicester: Inter-Varsity Press, 1981)

——, *Models for Scripture* (Grand Rapids: Eerdmans; Carlisle: Paternoster, 1994)

Gunn, D.M., 'New Directions in the Study of Biblical Hebrew Narrative', *JSOT* 39 (1987), 65–75

Kraus, H-J., *Geschichte der historisch-kritischen Erforschung des Alten Testaments* (Neukirchen-Vluyn: Neukirchener Verlag, 4th edn, 1988)

Krentz, E., *The Historical-Critical Method* (London: SPCK, 1975)

Kümmel, W.G., *The New Testament: The History of the Interpretation of its Problems* (London: SCM Press, 1973)

Levenson, J., *The Hebrew Bible, the Old Testament, and Historical Criticism: Jews and Christians in Biblical Studies* (Louisville, KY: Westminster / John Knox Press, 1993)

Long, V.P., *The Art of Biblical History* (Leicester: Apollos, 1994)

Michalson, G.E., 'Faith and History', in *The Blackwell Encyclopedia of Modern Christian Thought* (ed. A.E. McGrath; Oxford: Basil Blackwell, 1993), 210–14

Munslow, A., *Deconstructing History* (London: Routledge, 1997)

Neill, S., and T. Wright, *The Interpretation of the New Testament 1861–1986* (Oxford: OUP, 1988)

Newbigin, L., *The Gospel in a Pluralist Society* (Grand Rapids: Eerdmans; Geneva: WCC, 1989)

Newman, C.C. (ed.), *Jesus and the Restoration of Israel: A Critical Assessment of N.T. Wright's* Jesus and the Victory of God (Carlisle: Paternoster, 1999)

Nicholson, E., *Interpreting the Old Testament: A Century of the Oriel Professorship* (Oxford: Clarendon Press, 1981)

Norris, C., *Truth and the Ethics of Criticism* (Manchester: Manchester University Press, 1994)

Riches, J.K., *A Century of New Testament Study* (Valley Forge, PA: Trinity Press International, 1993)

Ricœur, P., *Hermeneutics and the Human Sciences* (Cambridge: CUP, 1981)

Rogerson, J., and W.M.L. de Wette, *Founder of Modern Biblical Criticism: An Intellectual Biography* (JSOTSup 26; Sheffield: Sheffield Academic Press, 1992)

Seitz, C.R., *Word Without End: The Old Testament as Abiding Theological Witness* (Grand Rapids: Eerdmans, 1998)

Sternberg, M., *The Poetics of Biblical Narrative: Ideological Literature and the Drama of Reading* (Bloomington: Indiana University Press, 1985)

Thiselton, A.C., *The Two Horizons: New Testament Hermeneutics and Philosophical Description with Special Reference to Heidegger, Bultmann, Gadamer and Wittgenstein* (Grand Rapids: Eerdmans; Carlisle: Paternoster, 1980)

——, 'On Models and Methods: A Conversation with Robert Morgan', in *The Bible in Three Dimensions* (ed. D.J.A. Clines, et al.; JSOTSup 87; Sheffield: JSOT, 1990), 337–56

——, 'New Testament Interpretation in Historical Perspective', in *Hearing the New Testament: Strategies for Interpretation* (ed. J.B. Green; Grand Rapids: Eerdmans; Carlisle: Paternoster, 1995), 10–36

——, ' "Behind" and "In Front of " the Text: Language, Reference and Indeterminacy', in *After Pentecost: Language and Biblical Interpretation* (ed. C.G. Bartholomew, C. Greene and K. Möller; SHS 2; Carlisle: Paternoster; Grand Rapids: Zondervan, 2001), 97–120

Vanhoozer, K., *Is There a Meaning in This Text? The Bible, The Reader, and the Morality of Literary Knowledge* (Grand Rapids: Zondervan, 1998)

Von Rad, G., *Old Testament Theology*, I (Edinburgh: Oliver & Boyd, 1973)

Wright, N.T., *The New Testament and the People of God* (Minneapolis: Fortress Press, 1992)

——, 'A Reformation and Revival Journal Interview with N.T. Wright', in - *Reformation and Revival Journal* 11.1 (2002), 117–39

Historical Criticism – Critical Assessments

1

Two (or More) Kinds of Scripture Scholarship[*]

Alvin Plantinga

The serious and scholarly study of the Bible is of first importance for the Christian community. The roll call of those who have pursued this project is maximally impressive: Chrysostom, Augustine, Aquinas, Calvin, Jonathan Edwards and Karl Barth, just for starters. These people and their successors begin from the idea that Scripture is indeed divinely inspired (however exactly they understand this claim); they then try to ascertain the Lord's teaching in the whole of Scripture or (more likely) a given bit. Since the Enlightenment, however, another kind of Scripture scholarship has also come into view. Variously called 'higher criticism', 'historical criticism', 'biblical criticism', or 'historical critical scholarship', this variety of Scripture scholarship *brackets* or *prescinds from* what is known by faith and aims to proceed 'scientifically', strictly on the basis of reason. I shall call it 'Historical Biblical Criticism' – HBC for short. Scripture scholarship of this sort also brackets the belief that the Bible is a special word from the Lord, as well as any other belief accepted on the basis of faith rather than reason.

Now it often happens that the declarations of those who pursue this latter kind are in apparent conflict with the main lines of Christian thought; one who pursues this sort of scholarship is quite unlikely to conclude, for example, that Jesus was really the pre-existent second person of the divine trinity who was crucified, died, and then literally rose from the dead the third day. As Van Harvey says, 'So far as the biblical historian is concerned, ... there is scarcely a popularly held traditional belief about Jesus that is not regarded with considerable skepticism.'[1] I shall try to describe both of these kinds of Scripture scholarship. Then I shall ask the following question: how should a traditional

---

[*] Originally published in *Modern Theology* 14.2 (1998), 243–77. Used by permission of Blackwell Publishers and reprinted with some minor modifications.
[1] 'New Testament Scholarship and Christian Belief' (hereafter 'NTS'), in *Jesus in History and Myth* (Buffalo, NY: Prometheus Books, 1986), p. 193.

Christian, one who accepts 'the great things of the gospel', respond to the deflationary aspects of HBC? How should she think about its apparently corrosive results with respect to traditional Christian belief? I shall argue that she need not be disturbed by the conflict between alleged results of HBC and traditional Christian belief.[2] Indeed, that conflict should not defeat her acceptance of the great things of the gospel – nor, to the degree that those alleged results rest upon epistemological assumptions she does not share, of anything else she accepts on the basis of Biblical teaching.

Scripture Divinely Inspired

At millions of worship services every week Christians all over the world hear passages of Scripture and respond by saying, 'This is the Word of the Lord.' Suppose we begin, therefore, by inquiring into the epistemology of the belief that the Bible is divinely inspired in a special way, and in such a way as to constitute divine discourse. How *does* a Christian come to believe that the gospel of Mark, or the book of Acts, or the entire New Testament is authoritative, because divinely inspired? What (if anything) is the source of its warrant?[3] There are several possibilities. For many, it will be by way of ordinary teaching and testimony. Perhaps I am brought up to believe the Bible is indeed the Word of God (just as I am brought up thinking that thousands perished in the American Civil War), and I have never encountered any reason to doubt this. But an important feature of warrant is that if I accept a belief *B* just on testimony, then *B* has warrant for me only if it had warrant for the testifier as well: the warrant a belief has for the testifiee is derivative from the warrant it has for the testifier.[4] Our question, therefore, becomes this: what is the epistemological status of this belief for those members of the community who do not accept it on the testimony of other members? What is the source of the warrant (if any) this belief has for the Christian community? Well, perhaps a Christian might come to think something like the following:

---

[2] I therefore concur (for the most part) both with C. Stephen Evans in his excellent *The Historical Christ and the Jesus of Faith: the Incarnational Narrative as History* (Oxford: Clarendon Press, 1996), and with Peter van Inwagen in 'Critical Studies of the New Testament and the User of the New Testament', *God, Knowledge, and Mystery* (Ithaca, NY: Cornell University Press, 1995), pp. 163–190.

[3] For an account of warrant, that property which distinguishes knowledge from mere true belief (a lucky guess, for example), see my *Warrant: The Current Debate* and *Warrant and Proper Function* (New York, NY: Oxford University Press, 1993).

[4] See *Warrant and Proper Function*, pp. 34–35.

Suppose the apostles were commissioned by God through Jesus Christ to be witnesses and representatives (deputies) of Jesus. Suppose that what emerged from their carrying out this commission was a body of apostolic teaching which incorporated what Jesus taught them and what they remembered of the goings-on surrounding Jesus, shaped under the guidance of the Spirit. And suppose that the New Testament books are all either apostolic writings, or formulations of apostolic teaching composed by close associates of one or another apostle. Then it would be correct to construe each book as a medium of divine discourse. And an eminently plausible construal of the process whereby these books found their way into a single canonical text, would be that by way of that process of canonization, God was authorizing these books as together constituting a single volume of divine discourse.[5]

So a Christian might come to think something like the above: she believes

(1) that the apostles were commissioned by God through Jesus Christ to be witnesses and deputies,

(2) that they produced a body of apostolic teaching which incorporates what Jesus taught, and

(3) that the New Testament books are all either apostolic writings or formulations of apostolic teaching composed by close associates of one or another apostle. She also believes

(4) that the process whereby these books found their way into a single canon is a matter of God's authorizing these books as constituting a single volume of divine discourse. She therefore concludes that indeed

(5) the New Testament is a single volume of divine discourse.

But of course our question then would be: how does she know, why does she believe each of (1)–(4)? What is the source of these beliefs?

Could it be, perhaps, by way of ordinary historical investigation? I doubt it. The problem is the Principle of Dwindling Probabilities. Suppose a Christian proposes to give a historical argument for the divine inspiration and consequent authority of the New Testament; and suppose we think of her as already knowing or believing the central truths of Christianity. She already knows that there is such a person as God, that the man Jesus is also the divine Son of God, that through his ministry, passion, death and resurrection we sinners can have life. These constitute part of her background information, and can be employed in the historical argument in question. Her body of background information B with respect to which she estimates the probability of (1)–(4), includes the main lines of Christian teaching. And of course she knows that the books of the New Testament – some of them, anyway – apparently teach or

---

[5] Nicholas Wolterstorff, *Divine Discourse: Philosophical Reflections on the Claim that God Speaks* (Cambridge: Cambridge University Press, 1995), p. 295.

presuppose these things. With respect to B, therefore, perhaps each of (1)–(4) could be considered at least quite plausible and perhaps even likely to be true.

Still, each is only probable. Perhaps, indeed, each is *very* likely and has a probability as high as .9 with respect to that body of belief B.[6] Even so, we can conclude only that the probability of their conjunction, on B, is somewhat more than .5. In that case, *belief* that the New Testament is the Word of God would not be appropriate; what would be appropriate is the belief that it is fairly *likely* that the New Testament is the Word of God. (The probability that the next throw of this die will not come up either 1 or 2 is greater than .5; that is nowhere nearly sufficient for my *believing* that it will not come up 1 or 2.) Of course, we could quibble about these probabilities – no doubt they could sensibly be thought to be greater than I suggested. No doubt; but they could also sensibly be thought to be less than I suggested. The historical argument for (1) to (4) will at best yield probabilities, and at best only a fairly insubstantial probability of (5) itself. The estimates of the probabilities involved, furthermore, will be vague, variable and not really well founded. If the belief in question is to have *warrant* for Christians, its epistemic status for them must be something different from that of a conclusion of ordinary historical investigation.

Now, of course, most Christian communities have taught that the warrant enjoyed by this belief is *not* conferred on it just by way of ordinary historical investigation. The Belgic Confession, one of the most important confessions of the Reformed churches, gives a list (the Protestant list) of the canonical books of the Bible (Article 5); it then goes on:

> And we believe without a doubt all things contained in them – not so much because the church receives them and approves them as such, but above all because the Holy Spirit testifies in our hearts that they are from God, and also because they prove themselves to be from God.

There is a possible ambiguity here; 'we believe all things contained in them not so much because the church receives them, but …' – but to what does this last 'them' refer? The teachings contained in the books, or the books themselves? If the former, then what we have here is the claim that the Holy Spirit is leading us to see, not that a given *book* is from God, but that some *teaching* – e.g., that God in Christ was reconciling the world to himself – is indeed true. If the latter, however, what we would be led to believe is such propositions as *The gospel of John is from God*. I think it is at least fairly clear that the latter is what the

---

[6] More exactly, perhaps the probability of (1) on B is as high as .9, the probability of (2) on (1)&B as high as .9, and the same for $P((3)/(B\&(1)\&(2)))$ and $P((4)/(B\&(1)\&(2)\&(3)))$. For more on this form of argument, see *Warranted Christian Belief*, chapter 8, 'The Extended A/C Model: Revealed to our Minds.'

Confession intends. According to the Confession, then, there are two sources for the belief that (e.g.) the gospel of John is from God. The first is that the Holy Spirit testifies in our hearts that this book is indeed from God; the Holy Spirit does not merely impel us to believe, with respect to a given teaching of the gospel of John, that it is from God, but also impels us to believe that the gospel of John itself is from God. The second is that the book 'proves itself' to be from God. Perhaps here the idea is that the believer first comes to think, with respect to many of the specific teachings of that book, that they are indeed from God; that is, the Holy Spirit causes her to believe this with respect to many of the teachings of the book. She then infers (with the help of other premises) that the whole book has that same status.[7]

This is only *one* way in which this belief could have warrant; there are other possibilities. Perhaps the believer knows by way of the internal invitation of the Holy Spirit that the Holy Spirit has guided and preserved the Christian church, making sure that its teachings on important matters are in fact true; then the believer would be warranted in believing, at any rate of those books of the Bible endorsed by all or nearly all traditional Christian communities, that they are from God. Or perhaps, guided by the Holy Spirit, she recapitulates the process whereby the canon was originally formed, paying attention to the original criteria of apostolic authorship, consistency with apostolic teaching, and the like, and relying on testimony for the propositions such and such books were indeed composed by apostles. There are also combinations of these ways. However precisely this belief receives its warrant, then, traditional Christians have accepted the belief that the Bible is indeed the Word of God and that in it the Lord intends to teach us truths.[8]

Traditional Christian Biblical Commentary

Of course, it is not always easy to tell what the Lord *is* teaching us in a given passage: what he teaches is indeed true, but sometimes it is not clear just what his teaching is. Part of the problem is the fact that the Bible contains material of so many different sorts; it is not in this respect like a contemporary book on

---

[7] Jonathan Edwards: 'And the opening to view with such clearness, such a world of wonderful and glorious truth in the gospel, that before was unknown, being quite above the view of a natural eye, but appearing so clear and bright, has a powerful and invincible influence on the soul to persuade of the divinity of the gospel.' *The Religious Affections* (New Haven, CT: Yale University Press, 1959), p. 303.

[8] I do not for a moment mean to suggest that teaching us truths is *all* that the Lord intends in Scripture: there is also raising affection, teaching us how to praise, how to pray, how to see the depth of our own sin, how marvelous the gift of salvation is, and a thousand other things.

theology or philosophy. It is not a book full of declarative sentences, with proper analysis and logical development and all the accoutrements academics have come to know and love and demand. The Bible does indeed contain sober assertion; but there is also exhortation, expression of praise, poetry, the telling of stories and parables, songs, devotional material, history, genealogies, lamentations, confession, prophecy, apocalyptic material, and much else besides. Some of these (apocalyptic, for example) present real problems of interpretation (for us, at present): what exactly is the Lord teaching in Daniel, or Revelation? That is not easy to say.

And even if we stick to straightforward assertion, there are a thousand questions of interpretation. Here are just a couple of examples. In Matthew 5:17–20, Jesus declares that not a jot or a tittle of the Law shall pass away and that '… unless your righteousness surpasses that of the Pharisees and the teachers of the law, you will certainly not enter the kingdom of heaven', but in Galatians Paul seems to say that observance of the Law does not count for much; how can we put these together? How do we understand Colossians 1:24: 'Now I rejoice in what was suffered for you, and I fill up in my flesh what is still lacking in regard to Christ's afflictions, for the sake of his body which is the church'? Is Paul suggesting that Christ's sacrifice is incomplete, insufficient, that it requires additional suffering on the part of Paul and/or the rest of us? That seems unlikely. Is it that our suffering can be a *type* of Christ's, thus standing to the latter in the relation in which a type stands to the reality it typifies? Or shall we understand it like this: we must distinguish between two kinds of Christ's suffering, the redemptive suffering, the expiatory and vicarious atonement to which nothing can be added or taken away, on the one hand, and another kind, also 'for the sake of his body', in which we human beings can genuinely participate? Perhaps it is suffering which can build up, edify the body of Christ, even as our response to Christ can be deepened by our meditating on Christ's sacrifice for us and the amazing selfless love displayed in it? Or what? Do Paul and James contradict each other on the relation between faith and works? Or rather, since God is the author of Scripture, is he proposing an inconsistent or self-contradictory teaching for our belief? Well no, surely not, but then how shall we understand the two in relation to each other? More generally, given that God is the principal author of Scripture, how shall we think about the apparent tensions the latter displays?

Scripture, therefore, is indeed inspired: what it teaches is indeed true; but it is not always trivial to tell what it *does* teach. Indeed, many of the sermons and homilies preached in a million churches every Sunday morning are devoted in part to bringing out what might otherwise be obscure in Scriptural teaching. Given that the Bible is a communication from God to humankind, a divine revelation, there is much about it that requires deep and perceptive reflection, much that taxes our best scholarly and spiritual resources. Of course, this fact was not lost on, for example, Chrysostom, Augustine, Aquinas, Calvin, and the others I mentioned earlier on; between them they wrote an impressive number of volumes devoted to powerful reflection on the meaning and teachings of Scripture. (Calvin's commentaries alone run to some twenty-two volumes.) Their aim was to try to determine as accurately as possible just what the Lord proposes to teach us in the Bible. Call this enterprise 'traditional biblical commentary', and note that it displays at least the following three features.

First, Scripture itself is taken to be a wholly authoritative and trustworthy guide to faith and morals; it is authoritative and trustworthy, because it is a revelation from God, a matter of God's speaking to us. Once it is clear, therefore, what the teaching of a given bit of Scripture is, the question of the truth and acceptability of that teaching is settled. In a commentary on Plato, we might decide that what Plato really meant to say was XYZ; we might then go on to consider and evaluate XYZ in various ways, asking whether it is true, or close to the truth, or true in principle, or superseded by things we have learned since Plato wrote, and the like; we might also ask whether Plato's grounds or arguments for XYZ are slight, or acceptable, or substantial, or compelling. These questions are out of place in the kind of Scripture scholarship under consideration. Once convinced that God *is* proposing XYZ for our belief, we do not go on to ask whether it is true, or whether God has made a good case for it. God is not required to make a case.

Secondly, an assumption of the enterprise is that the principal author of the Bible – the entire Bible – is God himself. Of course, each of the books of the Bible has a human author or authors as well; but the principal author is God. This impels us to treat the whole more like a unified communication than a miscellany of ancient books. Scripture is not so much a library of independent books as itself a book with many subdivisions but a central theme: the message of the gospel. By virtue of this unity, furthermore (by virtue of the fact that there is just one principal author), it is possible to 'interpret Scripture with Scripture'. If a given passage from one of Paul's epistles is puzzling, it is perfectly proper to try to come to clarity as to what God's teaching in this passage is by appealing, not only to what Paul himself says elsewhere in other epistles (his own or others), but also to what is taught elsewhere in Scripture (for example, the gospel of John[9]). Passages in Psalms or Isaiah can be interpreted in terms of

---

[9] See, for example, Richard Swinburne (*Revelation* [Oxford: Clarendon Press, 1992], p. 192), who suggests that Paul's Christology at Romans 1:4 should be understood in terms of the 'high' Christology of the first chapter of John's gospel. We could say the same for Paul's Christology in his speech in Acts 13, where he seems to suggest that a special status was *conferred* on Jesus, as opposed to John 1, according to which Jesus is the incarnation of the preexistent Word. See also Raymond Brown, *New Testament Christology* (New York, NY: Paulist Press, 1994), pp. 133ff.

the fuller, more explicit disclosure in the New Testament; the serpent elevated on a pole to save the Israelites from disaster can be seen as a type of Christ (and thus as getting some of its significance by way of an implicit reference to Christ, whose being raised on the cross averted a greater disaster for the whole human race). A further consequence: we can quite properly accept propositions that are inferred from premises coming from different parts of the Bible: once we see what God intends to teach in a given passage A and what he intends to teach in a given passage B, we can put the two together, and treat a consequence of these propositions as itself divine teaching.[10]

Thirdly (and connected with the second point), the fact that the principal author of the Bible is God himself means that one cannot always determine the meaning of a given passage by discovering what the human author had in mind. Of course, various post-modern hermeneuticists aim to amuse by telling us that in this case, as in all others, the author's intentions have nothing whatever to do with the meaning of a passage, that the reader herself confers upon it whatever meaning the passage has, or perhaps that even entertaining the idea of a text having meaning is to fall into 'hermeneutical innocence' – innocence, oddly enough, which (as they insist) is ineradicably sullied by its inevitable association with oppressive, racist, sexist, homophobic and other offensive modes of thought. This is indeed amusing. Returning to serious business, however, it is obvious (given that the principal author of the Bible is God) that the meaning of a biblical passage will be given by what it is that the Lord intends to teach in that passage, and it is precisely this that biblical commentary tries to discern. But we aren't just given that what the Lord intends to teach us is identical with what the human author had in mind;[11] the latter may not so much as have thought of what is in fact the teaching of the passage in question. Thus, for example, Christians take the suffering servant passages in Isaiah to be references to Jesus; Jesus himself says (Luke 4:18–21) that the prophecy in Isaiah 61:1–2 is fulfilled in him; John (19:36) takes passages from Exodus, Numbers, Psalms and Zechariah to be references to Jesus and the events of his life and death; Matthew and John take it that Zechariah 9:9 is a reference to Jesus' triumphal entry into Jerusalem (Matthew 21:5 and John 12:15); Hebrews 10 takes passages from Psalms, Jeremiah, and Habakkuk to be references to Christ and events in his career, as does Paul for passages from Psalms and Isaiah in his speech in Acts 13. Indeed, Paul refers to the Old Testament on nearly every

---

[10] Of course this procedure, like most others, can be and has been abused; that possibility in itself, however, is nothing against it, though it should serve as a salutary caution.

[11] A further complication: we cannot simply assume that there is some one thing, the same for everyone, that the Lord intends to teach in a given passage; perhaps what he intends to teach me, or my relevant sociological group, is not the same as what he intended to teach a fifth century Christian.

page of Romans and both Corinthian epistles, and frequently in other epistles. There is no reason to suppose the human authors of Exodus, Numbers, Psalms, Isaiah, Jeremiah, or Habakkuk had in mind Jesus' triumphal entry, or his incarnation, or other events of Jesus' life and death, or indeed anything else explicitly about Jesus. But the fact that it is God who is the principal author here makes it quite possible that what we are to learn from the text in question is something rather different from what the human author proposed to teach.

Historical Biblical Criticism

For at least the last couple of hundred years there has also been a quite different kind of Scripture scholarship variously called 'higher criticism', 'historical criticism', 'biblical criticism', or 'historical critical scholarship'; I will call it 'historical biblical criticism' (HBC). Clearly, we are indebted to HBC; it has enabled us to learn a great deal about the Bible we otherwise might not have known. Furthermore, some of the methods it has developed can be and have been employed to excellent effect in various studies of interest and importance, including traditional Biblical commentary. It differs importantly from the latter, however. HBC is fundamentally an enlightenment project; it is an effort to try to determine from the standpoint of reason alone what the Scriptural teachings are and whether they are true. Thus HBC eschews the authority and guidance of tradition, magisterium, creed, or any kind of ecclesial or 'external' epistemic authority. The idea is to see what can be established (or at least made plausible) using only the light of what we could call 'natural empirical reason'. (So, of course, not everyone who uses the methods of textual criticism commonly employed in HBC is involved in the project of HBC as I am thinking of it; to take part in that project one must aim to discover the truth about Scripture and its teachings from the standpoint of reason alone.) The faculties or sources of belief invoked, therefore, would be those that are employed in ordinary history: perception, testimony, reason taken in the sense of *a priori* intuition together with deductive and probabilistic reasoning, Reid's sympathy, by which we discern the thoughts and feelings of another, and so on – but bracketing any proposition one knows by faith or by way of the authority of the church. Spinoza (1632–1677) already lays down the charter for this enterprise: 'The rule for [Biblical] interpretation should be nothing but the natural light of reason which is common to all – not any supernatural light nor any external authority.'[12]

---

[12] *Tractatus theologico-politicus*, 14. Of course, this method does not preclude a rational argument (an argument from reason alone) for the proposition that indeed there has been a divine revelation, and that the Bible (or some part of it) is precisely that revelation: exactly this was John Locke's project.

This project or enterprise is often thought of as part and parcel of the development of modern empirical science, and indeed practitioners of HBC often drape about their shoulders the mantle of modern science. The attraction is not just that HBC can perhaps share in the prestige of modern science, but also that it can share in the obvious epistemic power and excellence of the latter.[13] It is common to think of science itself as our best shot at getting to know what the world is really like; HBC is, among other things, an attempt to apply these widely approved methods to the study of Scripture and the origins of Christianity. Thus Raymond Brown, a Scripture scholar than whom none is more highly respected, believes that HBC is 'scientific biblical criticism';[14] it yields 'factual results' (p. 9); he intends his own contributions to be 'scientifically respectable' (p. 11): and practitioners of HBC investigate the Scriptures with 'scientific exactitude' (pp. 18–19).[15]

But what is it, exactly, to study the Bible scientifically? As we will see below there is more than one answer to this question. One theme that seems to command nearly universal assent, however, is that in working at this scientific project (however exactly it is to be understood) you do not invoke or employ any theological assumptions or presuppositions. You do not assume, for example, that the Bible is inspired by God in any special way, or contains anything like specifically divine discourse. You do not assume that Jesus is the divine Son of God, or that he arose from the dead, or that his suffering and death is in some way a propitiatory atonement for human sin, making it possible for us to get once more in the right relationship to God. You do not assume any of these things because in pursuing science, one does not assume or employ any proposition which one knows by faith.[16] (As a consequence, the

---

[13] To understand historical criticism and its dominance properly, says David Yeago, one must understand 'the historic coupling of historical criticism with a "project to the Enlightenment" aimed at liberating mind and heart from the shackles of ecclesiastical tradition. In the modern context, claims to "Enlightenment" must be backed up with the claim to have achieved a proper *method*, capable of producing real knowledge to replace the pre-critical confusion and arbitrariness of tradition.' 'The New Testament and the Nicene Dogma', *Pro Ecclesia* Vol. III, No. 2 (Spring, 1994), p. 162.

[14] *The Virginal Conception and Bodily Resurrection of Jesus* (New York, NY: Paulist Press, 1973), p. 6.

[15] See also John P. Meier, *A Marginal Jew: Rethinking the Historical Jesus* (New York, NY: Doubleday, 1991, two volumes), p. 1.

[16] Nor can you employ a proposition which is such that the warrant it has for you comes from some proposition you know or believe by faith; we might put this by saying that in doing science you cannot employ any proposition whose epistemic provenance, for you, includes a proposition you know or believe by faith.

But is this really true? Why should we believe it? What is the status of the claim that if what you are doing is science, then you cannot employ, in your work, any

meaning of a text will be what the human author intended to assert (if it is an assertive kind of text); divine intentions and teaching do not enter into the meaning.[17]) Thus the idea, says E. P. Sanders, is to rely only on 'evidence on which everyone can agree'.[18] According to Jon Levenson,

> Historical critics thus rightly insist that the tribunal before which interpretations are argued cannot be confessional or 'dogmatic'; the arguments offered must be historically valid, able, that is, to compel the assent of *historians* whatever their religion or lack thereof, whatever their backgrounds, spiritual experiences, or personal beliefs, and without privileging any claim of revelation.[19]

Barnabas Lindars explains that

> There are in fact two reasons why many scholars are very cautious about miracle stories ... The second reason is historical. The religious literature of the ancient world is full of miracle stories, and we cannot believe them all. It is not open to a scholar to decide that, just because he is a believing Christian, he will accept all the Gospel miracles at their face value, but at the same time he will repudiate miracles attributed to Isis. All such accounts have to be scrutinized with equal detachment.[20]

And even Luke Timothy Johnson, who is in general astutely critical of HBC:

---

proposition you believe or know by faith? Is this supposed to be true by definition? If so, whose definition? Is there a good argument for it? Or what? See my 'Methodological Naturalism?', *Facets of Faith and Science*, ed. J. van der Meer (Lanham, MD: University Press of America, 1996), pp. 177–222.

[17] Thus Benjamin Jowett (the 19th century Master of Balliol College and eminent translator of Plato): 'Scripture has one meaning – the meaning which it had to the mind of the prophet or evangelist who first uttered or wrote, to the hearers or readers who first received it.' 'On the Interpretation of Scripture', in *The Interpretation of Scripture and Other Essays* (London: George Routledge & Sons, 1906), p. 36. Quoted in Jon D. Levenson, *The Hebrew Bible, the Old Testament, and Historical Criticism* (Louisville, KY: Westminster/John Knox Press, 1993), p. 78. Jowett was not a paragon of intellectual modesty, which may explain a poem composed and circulated by undergraduates at Balliol:

> First come I, my name is Jowett.
> There's no knowledge but I know it.
> I am the master of the college.
> What I don't know isn't knowledge.

[18] E. P. Sanders, *Jesus and Judaism* (Philadelphia, PA: Fortress Press, 1985), p. 5.

[19] Levenson, p. 109.

[20] 'Jesus Risen: Bodily Resurrection But No Empty Tomb', *Theology* Vol. 89 No. 728 (March, 1986), p. 91.

It is obviously important to study Christian origins historically. And in such historical inquiry, faith commitments should play no role. Christianity is no more privileged for the historian than any other human phenomenon.[21]

In practice, this emphasis means that HBC tends to deal especially with questions of *composition* and *authorship*, these being the questions most easily addressed by the methods employed. When was the document in question composed – or more exactly, since we cannot assume that we are dealing with a single unified document here, when were its various parts composed? How was the gospel of Luke, for example, composed? Was it written by one person, relying on his memory of Jesus and his words and deeds, or was it assembled from various reports, alleged quotations, songs, poems and the like in the oral tradition? Was it dependent on one or more earlier written or oral sources? Why did the editor or redactor put the book together in just the way he did – was it to make a theological point in a current controversy? Where traditional Biblical commentary assumes that the entire Bible is really one book with a single principal author, HBC tends to give us a collection of books by many authors. And even within the confines of a single book, it may give us a collection of discontinuous sayings and episodes (pericopes), these having been stitched together by one or more redactors. How much of what is reported as the sayings and discourse of Jesus really was said by Jesus? Can we discern various strata in the book – perhaps a bottom stratum, including the actual sayings of Jesus himself, and then successive overlaying strata? As Robert Alter says, scholarship of this kind tends to be 'excavative'; the idea is to dig behind the document as we actually have it to see what can be determined of its history.[22]

Of course, the idea is also to see, as far as this is possible, whether the events reported – in the gospels, for example – really happened, and whether the picture they give of Jesus is in fact historically accurate. Did he say the things they say he said, and do the things they say he did? Here the assumption is that we cannot simply take at face value the gospels as we now have them. There may have been all sorts of additions and subtractions and alterations made in the interest of advancing theological points. Further, the New Testament books are written from the standpoint of faith – faith that Jesus really was the Christ, did indeed suffer and die and rise from the dead, and did accomplish our salvation. From the standpoint of reason alone, however, this faith must be

---

[21] *The Real Jesus: The Misguided Quest for the Historical Jesus and the Truth of the Traditional Gospels* (San Francisco, CA: HarperSanFrancisco, 1996), p. 172. The target of much of Johnson's criticism is the notorious 'Jesus Seminar'.

[22] I do not mean to suggest, of course, that the traditional Biblical commentator cannot also investigate these questions; if she does, however, it will be in the ultimate service of an effort to discern what the Lord is teaching in the passages in question.

bracketed; hence (from that standpoint) the hermeneutics of suspicion is appropriate here. (This suspicion is sometimes carried so far that it reminds one of the way in which the CIA's denial that Mr X is a spy is taken as powerful evidence that Mr X is indeed a spy.)

Varieties of HBC

Those who practice HBC, therefore, propose to proceed without employing theological assumptions or anything one knows by faith (if indeed there is anything one knows by faith); these things are to be bracketed. Instead, one proceeds scientifically, on the basis of reason alone. Beyond this, however, there is vastly less concord. What is to count as reason? Precisely what premises can be employed in an argument from reason alone? What exactly does it mean to proceed scientifically?

Troeltschian HBC

Here many contemporary biblical critics will appeal to the thought and teaching of Ernst Troeltsch.[23] Thus John Collins:

> Among theologians these principles received their classic formulation from Ernst Troeltsch in 1898. Troeltsch sets out three principles ...: (1) The principle of criticism or methodological doubt: since any conclusion is subject to revision, historical inquiry can never attain absolute certainty but only relative degrees of probability. (2) The principle of analogy: historical knowledge is possible because all events are similar in principle. We must assume that the laws of nature in biblical times were the same as now. Troeltsch referred to this as 'the almighty power of analogy.' (3) The principle of correlation: the phenomena of history are inter-related and inter-dependent and no event can be isolated from the sequence of historical cause and effect.[24]

Collins adds a fourth principle, this one taken from Van Harvey's *The Historian and the Believer*,[25] a more recent *locus classicus* for the proper method of historical criticism:

---

[23] See especially his 'Über historische und dogmatische Methode in der Theologie' in his *Gesammelte Schriften* (Tübingen: Mohr, 1913) Vol. 2, pp. 729–753, and his article 'Historiography' in James Hastings (ed.). *Encyclopedia of Religion and Ethics* Vol. VI (Edinburgh: T & T Clark, 1925), pp. 716–723.

[24] 'Is Critical Biblical Theology Possible?' in *The Hebrew Bible and its Interpreters*, eds. William Henry Propp, Baruch Halpern and David Freedman (Winona Lake, IN: Eisenbrauns, 1990), p. 2.

[25] Subtitled *The Morality of Historical Knowledge and Christian Belief* (New York, NY: Macmillan, 1966).

To these should be added the principle of autonomy, which is indispensable for any critical study. Neither church nor state can prescribe for the scholar which conclusions should be reached.[26]

Now the first thing to note is that each of these principles is multiply ambiguous. In particular, each (except perhaps for the second) has a non-controversial, indeed, platitudinous interpretation. The first principle seems to be a *comment on* historical inquiry rather than a principle for its practice: historical inquiry can never attain absolutely certain results. (Perhaps the implied methodological principle is that in doing historical criticism, you should avoid claiming absolute certainty for your results.) Fair enough, I suppose nearly everyone would agree that few historical results of any significance are as certain as, say, that $2 + 1 = 3$, but if so, they do not achieve absolute certainty. (The only reasonably plausible candidates for historical events that *are* absolutely certain, I suppose, would be such 'historical' claims as that either Caesar crossed the Rubicon or else he did not.)

The third also has a platitudinous interpretation. What Troeltsch says is, 'The sole task of history in its specifically theoretical aspect is to explain every movement, process, state and nexus of things by reference to the web of its causal relations.'[27] This too can be seen as toothless if not platitudinous. Every event is to be explained by reference to the web of its causal relations – which of course would also include the intentions and actions of persons. Well then, consider even such an event as the resurrection of Jesus from the dead: according to the principle at hand, this event too would have to be explained by reference to the web of its causal relations. No problem; on the traditional view, this event was caused by God himself, who caused it in order to achieve certain of his aims and ends, in particular making it possible for human beings to be reconciled with God. So taken, this principle would exclude very little.

I say the second principle is perhaps the exception to the claim that each has a banal, uncontroversial interpretation: that is because on any plausible interpretation the second principle seems to entail the existence of *natural laws*. That there *are* such things as natural laws was a staple of 17th and 18th century science and philosophy of science;[28] what science discovers (so they thought) is just these laws of nature.[29] Empiricists have always been dubious about natural laws,

---

[26] *loc. cit.*

[27] 'Historiography', p. 718.

[28] Thus Descartes (part 2 of *Principles of Philosophy*) in stating something like a law of conservation of momentum:

> xxvii. The first law of nature: that each thing as far as in it lies, continues always in the same state; and that which is once moved always continues so to move.

[29] An opinion preserved among such contemporary philosophers as David Armstrong (see his *What is a Law of Nature?* (Cambridge: Cambridge University Press, 1984))

however, and at present the claim that there are any such things is at best extremely controversial.[30]

So all but one of Troeltsch's principles have platitudinous interpretations; but these are not in fact the interpretations given to them in the community of HBC. Within that community those principles are understood in such a way as to preclude *direct divine action* in the world. Not that all in this community *accept* Troeltsch's principles in their nonplatitudinous interpretation; rather, those who think of themselves as accepting (or rejecting) those principles think of themselves as accepting or rejecting their nonplatitudinous versions. (Presumably *everyone* accepts them taken platitudinously.) So taken, these principles imply that God has not in fact specially inspired any human authors in such a way that what they write is really divine speech addressed to us; nor has he raised Jesus from the dead, or turned water into wine, or performed miracles of any other sorts.

Thus Rudolph Bultmann:

> The historical method includes the presupposition that history is a unity in the sense of a closed continuum of effects in which individual events are connected by the succession of cause and effect.

This continuum, furthermore,

> cannot be rent by the interference of supernatural, transcendent powers.[31]

Many other theologians, oddly enough, chime in with agreement: God cannot or at any rate would not and will not act directly in the world. Thus John Macquarrie:

> The way of understanding miracles that appeals to breaks in the natural order and to supernatural intervention belongs to the mythological outlook and cannot commend itself in a post-mythological climate of thought ... The traditional conception of miracle is irreconcilable with our modern understanding of both science and history. Science proceeds on the assumption that whatever events occur in the world

---

and David Lewis (see, e.g., his 'New Work for a Theory of Universals', *Australasian Journal of Philosophy* Vol. 61 No. 4 (December 1983), pp. 343ff.).

[30] See, in particular, Bas van Fraassen's *Laws and Symmetry* (Oxford: Clarendon Press, 1989) for an extended and powerful argument against the exercise of natural laws.

[31] *Existence and Faith*, ed. Schubert Ogden (New York, NY: Meridian Books, 1960), pp. 291–292. Writing 50 years before Troeltsch, David Strauss concurs: '... all things are linked together by a chain of causes and effects, which suffers no interruption.' *Life of Jesus Critically Examined* (Philadelphia, PA: Fortress Press, 1972), sec. 14. (Quoted in Harvey, *The Historian and the Believer*, p. 15.).

can be accounted for in terms of other events that also belong within the world; and if on some occasions we are unable to give a complete account of some happening … the scientific conviction is that further research will bring to light further factors in the situation, but factors that will turn out to be just as immanent and this-worldly as those already known.[32]

And Langdon Gilkey:

… contemporary theology does not expect, nor does it speak of, wondrous divine events on the surface of natural and historical life. The causal nexus in space and time which the Enlightenment science and philosophy introduced into the Western mind … is also assumed by modern theologians and scholars; since they participate in the modern world of science both intellectually and existentially, they can scarcely do anything else. Now this assumption of a causal order among phenomenal events, and therefore of the authority of the scientific interpretation of observable events, makes a great difference to the validity one assigns to biblical narratives and so to the way one understands their meaning. Suddenly a vast panoply of divine deeds and events recorded in scripture are no longer regarded as having actually happened … Whatever the Hebrews believed, *we* believe that the biblical people lived in the same causal continuum of space and time in which we live, and so one in which no divine wonders transpired and no divine voices were heard.[33]

Gilkey says no divine wonders have transpired and no divine voices have been heard; Macquarrie adds that in this post-mythological age, we cannot brook the idea of 'breaks in the natural order and supernatural intervention'. Each, therefore, is ruling out the possibility of miracle, including the possibility of special divine action in inspiring human authors in such a way that what they write constitutes an authoritative communication from God. Now, of course, it is far from easy to say just what a miracle is; this topic is connected with deep and thorny questions about occasionalism, natural law, natural potentialities, and so on. We need not get into all that, however. The Troeltschian idea is that there is a certain way in which things ordinarily go; there are certain regularities, whether or not due to natural law, and God can be counted on to act in such a way as never to abrogate those regularities. Of course, God *could* if he chose abrogate those regularities (after all, even those natural laws, if there are any, are his creatures); but we can be sure, somehow, that God will not abrogate those regularities. Troeltschian Scripture scholarship, therefore, will proceed on the basis of the assumption that God never does anything specially;

---

[32] *Principles of Christian Theology*, 2nd ed. (New York: Charles Scribner's Sons, 1977), p. 248.

[33] 'Cosmology, Ontology and the Travail of Biblical Language', reprinted in Owen C. Thomas, ed., *God's Activity* in *the World: the Contemporary Problem* (Chico, CA: Scholars Press, 1983), p. 31.

in particular, he neither raised Jesus from the dead nor specially inspired the Biblical authors.

Duhemian HBC

Not all who accept and practice HBC accept Troeltsch's principles, and we can see another variety of HBC by thinking about an important suggestion made by Pierre Duhem. Duhem was both a serious Catholic and a serious scientist; he was accused (as he thought) by Abel Rey[34] of allowing his religious and metaphysical views as a Christian to enter his physics in an improper way. Duhem repudiated this suggestion, claiming that his Christianity did not enter his physics in any way at all and *a fortiori* did not enter it in an improper way.[35] Furthermore, the *correct* or *proper* way to pursue physical theory, he said, was the way in which he had in fact done it; physical theory should be completely independent of religious or metaphysical views or commitments.

Why did he think so? What did he have against metaphysics? Here he strikes a characteristic Enlightenment note: if you think of metaphysics as ingressing into physics, he says, then your estimate of the worth of a physical theory will depend upon the metaphysics you adopt. Physical theory will be dependent upon metaphysics in such a way that someone who does not accept the metaphysics involved in a given physical theory cannot accept the physical theory either. And the problem with *that* is that the disagreements that run riot in metaphysics will ingress into physics, so that the latter cannot be an activity we can all work at together, regardless of our metaphysical views:

> Now to make physical theories depend on metaphysics is surely not the way to let them enjoy the privilege of universal consent ... If theoretical physics is subordinated to metaphysics, the divisions separating the diverse metaphysical systems will extend into the domain of physics. A physical theory reputed to be satisfactory by the sectarians of one metaphysical school will be rejected by the partisans of another school.[36]

Duhem's main point, I think, is that if a physical theorist employs metaphysical assumptions or other notions that are not accepted by other workers in the field, and employs them in such a way that those who do not accept them

---

[34] 'La Philosophie scientifique de M. Duhem', *Revue de Métaphysique et de Morale*, XII (July, 1904), pp. 699ff.

[35] See the appendix to Duhem's *The Aim and Structure of Physical Theory*, trans. Philip P. Wiener, foreword by Prince Louis de Broglie (Princeton, NJ: Princeton University Press, 1954) (the book was first published in 1906). The appendix is entitled 'Physics of a Believer' and is a reprint of Duhem's reply to Rey; it was originally in the *Annales de Philosophie chrétienne* Vol I (Oct. and Nov. 1905), pp. 44ff. and 133ff.

[36] Duhem, p. 10.

cannot accept his physical theory, then to that extent his work cannot be accepted by those others; to that extent, furthermore, the cooperation important to science will be compromised. He therefore proposes a conception of science (or physics in particular) according to which the latter is independent of metaphysics:

> ... I have denied metaphysical doctrines the right to testify for or against any physical theory. ... Whatever I have said of the method by which physics proceeds, or the nature and scope that we must attribute to the theories it constructs, does not in any way prejudice either the metaphysical doctrines or religious beliefs of anyone who accepts my words. The believer and the nonbeliever may both work in common accord for the progress of physical science such as I have tried to define it.[37]

Duhem's proposal, reduced to essentials, is that physicists should not make essential use of religious or metaphysical assumptions in doing their physics: in that way lies chaos and cacophony, as each of the warring sects does things its own way. If we want to have the sort of commonality and genuine dialogue that promotes progress in physics, we should avoid assumptions – metaphysical, religious or otherwise – that are not accepted by all parties to the discussion.[38]

Duhem's suggestion is interesting and important, and (although Duhem himself did not do so) can obviously be applied far beyond the confines of physical theory: for example, to Scripture scholarship. Suppose we say that *Duhemian* Scripture scholarship is Scripture scholarship that does not involve any theological, religious or metaphysical assumptions that are not accepted by everyone in the relevant community.[39] Thus the Duhemian Scripture scholar would not take for granted either that God is the principal author of the Bible or that the main lines of the Christian story are in fact true; these are not accepted by all who are party to the discussion. She would not take for granted that Jesus rose from the dead, or that any other miracle has occurred; she could not so much as take it for granted that miracles are possible, since these claims are rejected by many who are party to the discussion. On the other hand, of

---

[37] Ibid., pp. 274–275.

[38] Of course, this proposal must be qualified, nuanced, sophisticated. It makes perfect sense for me to continue to work on a hypothesis after others have decided it is a dead end; science has often benefited from such disagreements.

[39] To be sure, it may be difficult to specify the relevant community. Suppose I am a Scripture scholar at a denominational seminary: what is my relevant community? Scripture scholars of any sort, all over the world? Scripture scholars in my own denomination? In western academia? The people, academics or not, in my denomination? Christians generally? The first thing to see here is that our Scripture scholar clearly belongs to many different communities, and may accordingly be involved in several different scholarly projects.

course, Duhemian Scripture scholarship cannot take it for granted that Christ did *not* rise from the dead or that *no* miracles have occurred, or that miracles are *im*possible. Nor, of course, could it employ Troeltsch's principles (taken non-platitudinously); not everyone accepts them. Duhemian Scripture scholarship fits well with Sanders' suggestion that 'what is needed is more secure evidence, evidence on which everyone can agree' (above, p. 29). It also fits well with John Meier's fantasy of 'an unpapal conclave' of Jewish, Catholic, Protestant and agnostic scholars, locked in the basement of the Harvard Divinity School library until they come to consensus on what historical methods can show about the life and mission of Jesus.[40] Among the proposed benefits of Duhemian HBC, obviously, are just the benefits Duhem cites: people of very different religious and theological beliefs can cooperate in this enterprise. Furthermore, although in principle the traditional Biblical commentator and the Troeltschian Biblical scholar could discover whatever is unearthed by Duhemian means, it is in fact likely that much will be learned in this cooperative enterprise that would not be learned by either group working alone.

Spinozistic HBC

Troeltschian and Duhemian HBC do not exhaust HBC; one can be a practitioner of HBC and accept neither. You might propose to follow reason alone in Scripture scholarship, but think that the Troeltschian principles, taken in the strong version in which they imply that God never acts specially in the world, are not in fact deliverances of reason. Reason alone, you say, certainly cannot demonstrate that God never acts specially in the world, or that no miracles have ever occurred. If so, you would not be a Troeltschian. On the other hand, you might also reject Duhemianism as well: for you might think that, as a matter of fact, there are deliverances of reason not accepted by everyone party to the project of Scripture scholarship. (The deliverances of reason are indeed *open* to all, but impeding factors of one kind or another can sometimes prevent someone from seeing the truth of one or another of them.) But then you might yourself employ those deliverances of reason in pursuing Scripture scholarship, thereby employing assumptions not accepted by everyone involved in the project, and thereby rejecting Duhemianism. You might therefore propose to follow reason alone, but be neither a Troeltschian nor a Duhemian. Suppose we use the term 'Spinozistic HBC'[41] to denote this variety of HBC. The Spinozist concurs with the Troeltschian and Duhemian that no theological assumptions or beliefs are to be employed in HBC. She differs from the Troeltschian in paying the same compliment to Troeltsch's principles: they too are not

---

[40] *A Marginal Jew: Rethinking the Historical Jesus*, p. 1.

[41] According to Spinoza, as we saw, 'The rule for [Biblical] interpretation should be nothing but the natural light of reason ...' (above p. 27).

deliverances of reason and hence are not to be employed in HBC. And she differs from the Duhemian in holding that there are some deliverances of reason not accepted by all who are party to the project of Scripture scholarship; hence, she proposes to employ some propositions or beliefs rejected by the Duhemian.

A final point: It is not of course accurate to suppose that all who practice HBC fall neatly into one or another of these categories. There are all sorts of half-way houses, lots of haltings between two opinions, many who fall partly into one and partly into another, and many who have never clearly seen that there *are* these categories. A real live Scripture scholar may be unlikely to have spent a great deal of thought on the epistemological foundations of his or her discipline and is likely to straddle one or more of the categories I mention.

Tensions with Traditional Christianity

There has been a history of substantial tension between HBC and traditional Christians. Thus David Friedrich Strauss[42] in 1835: 'Nay, if we would be candid with ourselves, that which was once sacred history for the Christian believer is, for the enlightened portion of our contemporaries, only fable.' Of course, the unenlightened faithful were not so unenlightened that they failed to notice this feature of Biblical criticism. Writing ten years after the publication of Strauss's book, William Pringle complains that, 'In Germany, Biblical criticism is almost a national pursuit ... Unhappily, [the critics] were but too frequently employed in maintaining the most dangerous errors, in opposing every inspired statement which the mind of man is unable fully to comprehend, in divesting religion of its spiritual and heavenly character, and in undermining the whole fabric of revealed truth.'[43]

Perhaps among Pringle's complaints were the following. First, practitioners of HBC tend to treat the Bible as a set of separate books rather than a unified communication from God. Thus, they tend to reject the idea that Old Testament passages can be properly understood as making reference to Jesus Christ, or to events in his life: 'Critical scholars rule out clairvoyance as an explanation axiomatically. Instead of holding that the Old Testament predicts events in the life of Jesus, critical scholars of the New Testament say that each Gospel writer sought to exploit Old Testament passages in order to bolster his case for the messianic and dominical claims of Jesus or of the church on his

---

[42] The author of *The Life of Jesus, Critically Examined* (London: Sonnenschein, 1892), one of the earliest higher critical salvoes.

[43] 'Translator's Preface', *Calvin's Commentaries*, Vol. xvi, trans. the Rev. William Pringle (Grand Rapids, MI: Baker Book House, 1979), p. vi. Pringle's preface is dated at Auchterarder, Jan. 4, 1845.

behalf.'[44] More generally, Brevard Childs: 'For many decades the usual way of initiating entering students in the Bible was slowly to dismantle the church's traditional teachings regarding scripture by applying the acids of criticism.'[45]

Second, following Ernst Troeltsch HBC tends to discount miracle stories, taking it as axiomatic that miracles do not and did not really happen, or at any rate claiming that the proper method for HBC cannot admit miracles either as evidence or conclusions. Perhaps Jesus effected cures of some psychosomatic disorders, but nothing that modern medical science cannot explain. Many employing this method propose that Jesus never thought of himself as divine, or as the Messiah, or as capable of forgiving sin[46] – let alone as having died and then risen from the dead. 'The Historical Jesus researchers,' says Luke Timothy Johnson, 'insist that the "real Jesus" must be found in the facts of his life before his death. The resurrection is, when considered at all, seen in terms of visionary experience, or as a continuation of an "empowerment" that began before Jesus' death. Whether made explicit or not, the operative premise is that there is no "real Jesus" after his death' (Johnson, p. 144).

Those who follow these methods sometimes produce quite remarkable accounts – and accounts remarkably different from traditional Christian understanding. According to Barbara Thiering's *Jesus and the Riddle of the Dead Sea Scrolls*,[47] for example, Jesus was buried in a cave; he did not actually die and was revived by the magician Simon Magus, whereupon he married Mary Magdalene, settled down, fathered three children, was divorced and finally died in Rome. According to Morton Smith, Jesus was a practicing homosexual and conjurer.[48] According to German Scripture scholar Gerd Lüdemann: the Resurrection is 'an empty formula that must be rejected by anyone holding a

---

[44] John D. Levenson, 'The Hebrew Bible, the Old Testament, and Historical Criticism' in *The Hebrew Bible, the Old Testament, and Historical Criticism*, p. 9. (An earlier version of this essay was published under the same title in *Hebrew Bible or Old Testament? Studying the Bible* in *Judaism and Christianity*, eds. John Collins and Roger Brooks (Notre Dame, IN: University of Notre Dame Press, 1990).) Of course, *clairvoyance* is not at issue at all: the question is really whether the Scripture has one principal author, namely God. If it does, then it does not require clairvoyance on the part of a human author for a passage from a given time to refer to something that happens much later. All that is required is God's omniscience. [45] *The New Testament* as *Canon: An Introduction* (Valley Forge, PA: Trinity Press International, 1984, 1994), p. xvii.

[46] 'The crisis grows out of the fact now freely admitted by both Protestant and Catholic theologians and exegetes: that as far as can be discerned from the available historical data, Jesus of Nazareth did not think he was divine [and] did not assert any of the messianic claims that the New Testament attributes to him ...' Thomas Sheehan, *The First Coming* (New York, NY: Random House, 1986), p. 9.

[47] San Francisco: HarperSanFrancisco, 1992.

[48] *Jesus the Magician* (New York, NY: Harper and Row, 1978).

scientific world view'.[49] G. A. Wells goes so far as to claim that our name 'Jesus', as it turns up in the Bible, is empty: like 'Santa Claus', it does not trace back to or denote anyone at all.[50] John Allegro apparently thinks there was no such person as Jesus of Nazareth; Christianity began as a hoax designed to fool the Romans, and preserve the cult of a certain hallucinogenic mushroom *(Amanita muscaria)*. Still, the name 'Christ' is not empty: it is really a name of that mushroom.[51] As engaging a claim as any is that Jesus, while neither merely legendary, nor actually a mushroom, was in fact an atheist, the first Christian atheist.[52] And even if we set aside the lunatic fringe, Van Harvey is correct: 'So far as the biblical historian is concerned, ... there is scarcely a popularly held traditional belief about Jesus that is not regarded with considerable skepticism' (NTS, p. 193).

Why Are Not Most Christians More Concerned?

So HBC has not in general been sympathetic to traditional Christian belief; it has hardly been an encouragement to the faithful. But the faithful seem relatively unconcerned; of course, they find traditional biblical commentary of great interest and importance, but the beliefs and attitudes of HBC have not seemed to filter down to them, despite its dominance in mainline seminaries. According to Van Harvey, 'Despite decades of research, the average person tends to think of the life of Jesus in much the same terms as Christians did three centuries ago ...' Harvey finds this puzzling: 'Why is it that, in a culture so dominated by experts in every field, the opinion of New Testament historians has had so little influence on the public?'[53] Are traditional Christians just ignoring inconvenient evidence? In what follows I will try to answer these questions. Obviously, HBC has contributed greatly to our knowledge of the Bible, in particular the circumstances and conditions of its composition; it has given us new alternatives as to how to understand the human authors, and this has also given us new ideas as to how to understand the divine Author. Nevertheless, there are in fact excellent reasons for tending to ignore that 'considerable skepticism', of which Harvey speaks. I do not mean to claim that the ordinary person in the pew ignores it because she has these reasons clearly in mind; no doubt she does not. I say only that these reasons are *good reasons* for a traditional Christian to ignore the deflationary results of HBC.

---

[49] *What Really Happened to Jesus: A Historical Approach to the Resurrection* (Louisville, KY: Westminster / John Knox Press, 1995).

[50] 'The Historicity of Jesus' in *Jesus in History and Myth*, eds., R. Joseph Hoffman and Gerald A. Larue (Buffalo, NY: Prometheus Books, 1986), pp. 27ff.

[51] *The Sacred Mushroom and the Cross* (Garden City, NY: Doubleday and Co., 1970).

[52] Sheehan, *op. cit.*

[53] Ibid., p. 194.

What might these reasons be? Well of course one thing is that skeptical Scripture scholars display vast disagreement among themselves.[54] There is also the fact that quite a number of the arguments they propose seem at best wholly inconclusive. Perhaps the endemic vice or at any rate the perennial temptation of HBC is what we might call the Fallacy of Creeping Certitude. To practice this fallacy, you note that some proposition A is probable (to .9, say) with respect to your background knowledge k (what you know to be true); you therefore annex it to k. Then you note that a proposition B is probable with respect to k&A; you therefore annex it too to k. Then you note that C is probable to .9 with respect to A&B&k, and also annex it to k; similarly for (say) D, E, F and G. You then pronounce A&B&C&D&E&F&G highly probable with respect to k, our evidence. But the fact is (as we learn from the probability calculus) that these probabilities must be *multiplied* − so that in fact the probability of A&B&C&D&E&F&G is .9 to the 7th power, i.e., less than .5! But suppose we look into reasons or arguments for preferring the results of HBC to those of traditional commentary. Why should we suppose that the former take us closer to the truth than the latter? Troeltsch's principles are particularly important here. As understood in the interpretative community of HBC, they preclude special divine action including special divine inspiration of Scripture and the occurrence of miracles. As Gilkey says, 'Suddenly a vast panoply of divine deeds and events recorded in scripture are no longer regarded as having actually happened' (above, p. 34). Many academic theologians and Scripture scholars appear to believe that Troeltschian HBC is *de rigueur;* it is often regarded as the only intellectually respectable variety of Scripture scholarship, or the only variety that has any claim to the mantle of science. (And many who arrive at relatively traditional conclusions in Scripture scholarship nevertheless pay at least lip service to the Troeltschian ideal, somehow feeling in a semi-confused way that this is the epistemically respectable or privileged way of proceeding.) But why think Scripture scholarship should proceed in this specific way − as opposed both to traditional biblical commentary and varieties of HBC that do not accept Troeltsch's principles? Are there any reasons or arguments for those principles?

Force Majeure

If so, they are extraordinarily well hidden. One common suggestion, however, seems to be a sort of appeal to *force majeure:* we simply cannot help it. Given our historical position, there is nothing else we can do; we are all in the grip of historical forces beyond our control (this thing is bigger than either one of us).

---

[54] As we have just seen. This lack of accord is especially well documented by Stephen Evans (op. cit.), pp. 322ff.

This reaction is typified by those, who like Harvey, Macquarrie, Gilkey, and others claim that nowadays, given our cultural situation, we just do not have any options. There are potent historical forces that impose these ways of thinking upon us; like it or not, we are blown about by these powerful winds of doctrine. 'The causal nexus in space and time which the Enlightenment science and philosophy introduced into the Western mind ... is also assumed by modern theologians and scholars; since they participate in the modern world of science both intellectually and existentially, they can scarcely do anything else', says Gilkey (above, p. 34); another example is Bultmann's famous remark to the effect that 'it is impossible to use electrical light and the wireless and to avail ourselves of modern medical and surgical discoveries, and at the same time to believe in the New Testament world of spirits and miracles.'[55]

But is not this view – that we are all compelled by contemporary historical forces to hold the sort of view in question – historically naive? First, why think we proceed together in lockstep through history, all at any given time perforce holding the same views and making the same assumptions? Clearly we do not do any such thing. The contemporary intellectual world is much more like a horse race (or perhaps a demolition derby) than a triumphal procession, more like a battleground than a Democratic Party fund-raiser, where everyone can be counted on to support the same slate. At present, for example, there are many like Macquarrie, Harvey and Gilkey who accept the semi-deistic view that God (if there is any such person) could not or would not act miraculously in history. But this is not, of course, the view of nearly everyone at present; hundreds of millions would reject it. The fact is that far more people reject this view than accept it. (So even if Gilkey, *et al.*, were right about the inevitable dance of history, they would be wrong in their elitist notion to the effect that what *they* do is the current step.)

The utter obviousness of this fact suggests a second interpretation of this particular justification of Troeltschian HBC. Perhaps what the apologists really mean is not that *everyone* nowadays accepts this semi-deism (that is trivially

[55] *Kerygma and Myth* (New York, NY: Harper and Row, 1961), p. 5. Compare Marcus Borg's more recent comment: '... to a large extent, the defining characteristic of biblical scholarship in the modern period is the attempt to understand Scripture without reference to another world because in this period the visible world of space and time is the world we think of as "real." ' ('Root Images and the Way We See', *Fragments of Infinity* [Dorset, UK, & Lindfield, Australia, 1991]), p. 38. Quoted in Huston Smith's 'Doing Theology in the Global Village', *Religious Studies and Theology*, Vol. 13/14, No. 2/3 (December, 1995), p. 12. On the other side, note Abraham Kuyper (*To Be Near Unto God*, trans. John Hendrik de Vries (Grand Rapids, MI: Wm. B. Eerdmans Publishing Co., 1918), pp. 50–51; writing not long after the invention of the 'wireless', he saw it not as an obstacle to traditional faith but as a sort of electronic symbol of the way in which each of us can communicate instantaneously with God.

false), but that everyone *in the know* does. Everyone who is properly educated and has read his Kant and Hume (and Troeltsch) and reflected on the meaning of the wireless and electric light knows these things; as for the rest of humanity (including, I suppose, those of us who have read our Kant and Hume but are unimpressed), their problem is simple ignorance. Perhaps people generally do not march lockstep through history, but those in the know do; and right now they all or nearly all reject special divine action.

But even if we chauvinistically stick to educated Westerners, this is still doubtful *in excelsis*. 'The traditional conception of miracle', Macquarrie says, 'is irreconcilable with *our* modern understanding of both science and history' (above, p. 33; emphasis added): to whom does this 'our', here refer? To those who have gone to university, are well-educated, know at least a little science, and have thought about the bearing of these matters on the possibility of miracles? If so, the claim is once more whoppingly false. Very many well-educated people (including even some theologians) understand science and history in a way that is entirely compatible both with the possibility and with the actuality of miracles. Many physicists and engineers understand 'electrical light and the wireless' vastly better than Bultmann or his contemporary followers, but nonetheless hold precisely those New Testament beliefs Bultmann thinks incompatible with using electric lights and radios. There are large numbers of educated contemporaries (including even some with Ph.Ds!) who believe Jesus really and literally arose from the dead, that God performs miracles in the contemporary world, and even that there are both demons and spirits who are active in the contemporary world. As a matter of historical fact, there are any number of contemporaries, and contemporary intellectuals very well acquainted with science, who do not feel any problem at all in pursuing science and also believing in miracles, angels, Christ's resurrection, the lot.

Once more, however, Macquarrie, *et al.*, must know this as well as anyone else; so what do he and his friends really mean? How can they make these claims about what 'we'[56] – we who use the products of science and know a bit about it – can and cannot believe? How can they blithely exclude or ignore the thousands, indeed millions of contemporary Christians who do not think as they do? The answer must be that they think those Christians somehow do not count. What they really mean to say, I fear, is that they and their friends think this way, and anyone who demurs is so ignorant as to be properly ignored. But that is at best a bit slim as a *reason* for accepting the Troeltschian view; it is more like a nasty little piece of arrogance. Nor is it any better for being tucked away in the suggestion that somehow we just *cannot* help ourselves. Of course, it is

---

[56] We might call this the preemptive 'we': those who do not agree with us on the point in question are (by comparison with us) so unenlightened that we can properly speak as if they do not so much as exist.

possible that Gilkey and his friends cannot help themselves; in that case they can hardly be blamed for accepting the view in question.[57] This incapacity on their parts, however, is no recommendation of Troeltsch's principles.

So this is at best a poor reason for thinking serious Biblical scholarship must be Troeltschian. Is there a better reason? A second suggestion, perhaps connected with the plea of inability to do otherwise, is given by the suggestion that the very practice of science presupposes rejection of the idea of miracle or special divine action in the world. 'Science proceeds on the assumption that whatever events occur in the world can be accounted for in terms of other events that also belong within the world', says Macquarrie (above, p. 33); perhaps he means to suggest that the very practice of science requires that one reject (e.g.) the idea of God's raising someone from the dead. Of course, the argument form

if X were true, it would be inconvenient for science; therefore, X is false

is at best moderately compelling. We are not just given that the Lord has arranged the universe for the comfort and convenience of the American Academy of Science. To think otherwise is to be like the drunk who insisted on looking for his lost car keys under the streetlight, on the grounds that the light was better there. (In fact it would be to go the drunk one better: it would be to insist that since the keys would be hard to find in the dark, they must be under the light.)

But why think in the first place that we would have to embrace this semi-deism in order to do science?[58] Newton certainly did some sensible science, but he thought Jesus was raised from the dead, as do many contemporary physicists. But of course that is physics; perhaps the problem would be (as Bultmann suggests) with *medicine*. Is the idea that one could not do medical research, or prescribe medications, if one thought that God has done miracles in the past and might even occasionally do some nowadays? To put the suggestion explicitly is to refute it; there is not the faintest reason why I could not sensibly believe that God raised Jesus from the dead and also engage in medical research into, say, Usher's Syndrome or Multiple Sclerosis, or into ways of staving off

---

[57] Some, however, might see here little more than an effort to gain standing and respectability in a largely secular academia by adopting a stance that is, so to say, more Catholic than the Pope.

[58] Here I can be brief; William Alston has already proposed a compelling argument for the claim I propose to support, namely, that one can perfectly well do science even if one thinks God has done and even sometimes still does miracles. See his 'Divine Action: Shadow or Substance?' in *The God Who Acts: Philosophical and Theological Explorations*, ed. Thomas F. Tracy (University Park, PA: Penn State University Press, 1994), pp. 49–50.

the ravages of coronary disease. What would be the problem? That it is always *possible* that God should do something different, thus spoiling my experiment? But that *is* possible: God is omnipotent. (Or do we have here a new antitheistic argument? If God exists, he could spoil my experiment; but nothing can spoil my experiment; therefore ...) No doubt if I thought God *often* or *usually* did things in an idiosyncratic way, so that there really are not much by way of discoverable regularities to be found, *then* perhaps I could not sensibly engage in scientific research; the latter presupposes a certain regularity, predictability, stability in the world. But that is an entirely different matter. What I must assume in order to do science, is only that *ordinarily* and for the *most* part these regularities hold.[59] This reason, too, then, is monumentally insufficient as a reason for holding that we are somehow obliged to accept the principles underlying Troeltschian Biblical scholarship.

It is therefore difficult indeed to see any reason for supposing that Troeltschian Scripture scholarship is somehow *de rigueur* or somehow forced upon us by our history.

A Moral Imperative?

Van Harvey proposes another reason for pursuing Troeltschian scholarship and preferring it to traditional Biblical commentary;[60] his reason is broadly *moral* or *ethical*. He begins[61] by referring to a fascinating episode in Victorian intellectual history[62] in which certain Victorian intellectuals found themselves wrestling with a serious problem of intellectual integrity. As Harvey sees it, they 'believed that it was morally reprehensible to insist that these claims [Christian claims about the activities and teachings of Jesus] were true on faith while at the same time arguing that they were also the legitimate objects of historical inquiry'.[63] Now I think this is a tendentious account of the problem these intellectuals faced – tendentious, because it makes it look as if these intellectuals were endorsing, with unerring prescience, precisely the position Harvey himself proposes to argue for. The fact is, I think, their position was both less idiosyncratic and far more plausible. After all, why should anyone

---

[59] As Alston argues.

[60] I *think* the argument is intended to support Troeltschian HBC; it could also be used, however, to support Spinozistic or (less plausibly) Duhemian HBC.

[61] NTS, pp. 194ff.; a fuller (if older) and influential presentation of his views is to be found in his *The Historian and the Believer*.

[62] Described with insight and verve in James C. Livingston's monograph *The Ethics of Belief: An Essay on the Victorian Religious Conscience* in the American Academy of Religion's *Studies in Religion* (Tallahassee, FL, and Missoula, MT: Scholars Press, 1978). I thank Martin Cook for calling my attention to this monograph.

[63] Harvey, NTS, p. 195.

think it immoral to believe by faith what could also be investigated by other sources of belief or knowledge? I am curious about your whereabouts last Friday night: were you perhaps at The Linebacker's Bar? Perhaps I could find out in three different ways: by asking you, by asking your wife, and by examining the bar for your fingerprints (fortunately the bar is never washed). Would there be something immoral in using one of these methods when in fact the others were also available? That is not easy to believe.

It was not just *that* that troubled the Victorians. Had they been confident that both faith and historical investigation were reliable avenues to the truths in question, they surely would not have thought it immoral to believe on the basis of one of these as opposed to the other or both. Their problem was deeper. They were troubled (among other things) by the German Scripture scholarship about which they knew relatively little; but they did know enough to think (rightly or wrongly) that it posed a real threat to the Christian beliefs that for many of them were in any event already shaky. They suspected or feared that this Scripture scholarship could show or would show or already had shown that essential elements of the Christian faith were just false. They were also troubled by what many saw as the antisupernaturalistic and antitheistic bent of science: could one really believe in the New Testament world of spirits and miracles in the era of the steam engine and ocean liner? They were troubled by the advent of Darwinism, which seemed to many to contradict the Christian picture of human origins. They were convinced, following Locke and the whole classical foundationalist tradition, that the right way to hold beliefs on these topics is by following the (propositional) evidence wherever it leads; and they were deeply worried about where this evidence was in fact leading. They were troubled, in short, by a variety of factors all of which seemed to suggest that traditional Christian belief was really no more than a beautiful story: inspiring, uplifting, perhaps necessary to public morality, but just a story. Given our scientific coming of age, they feared, informed people would regretfully have to jettison traditional Christian belief, perhaps (especially on ceremonial occasions) with an occasional nostalgic backward look.

But many of them also longed for the comfort and security of serious Christian belief; to lose it was like being thrown out of our Father's house into a hostile or indifferent world. And, of course, many of the Victorians had strong moral opinions and a highly developed moral sense. They thought it weak, spineless, cowardly to refuse to face these specters, to hide them from oneself, to engage in self-deception and double-think. All of this, they thought, is unworthy of a serious and upright person. They abhorred the weakness and moral softness of the sort of stance in which you suspect the bitter truth, but refuse to investigate the matter, preferring to hide the truth from yourself, perhaps hoping it will somehow go away. Many of them thought this was pre-cisely what some of the clergy and other educators were doing, and despised them for it. Far better to face the sad truth with intellectual honesty, manly courage and a stiff upper lip. So it was not just that they thought it reprehensible to believe on faith what can also be addressed by reason or historical investigation. It was rather that they suspected and deeply feared that the latter (together with the other factors I mentioned) would undermine the former. And they scorned and detested a sort of willful head-in-the-sand attitude in which, out of timidity or fear or a desire for comfort, one refuses to face the facts. It is reasons such as these that account for the moral fervor (if not stridency) of W. K. Clifford's oft-anthologized 'The Ethics of Belief'.[64]

However things may have stood with the Victorians, Harvey proposes the following bit of moral dogma:

> The gulf separating the conservative Christian believer and the New Testament scholar can be seen as the conflict between two antithetical ethics of belief ... New Testament scholarship is now so specialized and requires so much preparation that the layperson has simply been disqualified from having any right to a judgment regarding the truth or falsity of certain historical claims. Insofar as the conservative Christian believer is a layperson who has no knowledge of the New Testament scholarship, he or she is simply not entitled to certain historical beliefs at all. Just as the average layperson is scarcely in a position to have an informed judgment about the seventh letter of Plato, the relationship of Montezuma to Cortez, or the authorship of the Donation of Constantine, so the average layperson has no right to an opinion about the authorship of the Fourth Gospel or the trustworthiness of the synoptics.[65]

'The layperson has simply been disqualified from having any right to a judgment regarding the truth or falsity of certain historical claims. ...' Strong words! In an earlier age, priests and ministers, often the only educated members of their congregations, would exercise a certain intellectual and spiritual leadership, hoping the flock would in fact come to see, appreciate, and of course believe the truth. On Harvey's showing, the flock does not so much as have a right to an opinion on these points – not even an opinion purveyed by the experts! Harvey complains that many students seem unreceptive to the results of Scripture scholarship.[66] But of course if he is right, the students do not have a right to believe the results of Scripture scholarship; they are therefore doing no more than their simple duty in refusing to believe them. One hopes Harvey remembers, when teaching his classes, not to put his views on these matters in an attractive and winsome fashion – after all, if he did so, some of the students

---

[64] First published in *The Contemporary Review* (XXIX, 1877); reprinted in Clifford's *Lectures and Essays* (London: Macmillan, 1879), pp. 354ff.

[65] Harvey, NTS, p. 197.

[66] Harvey, NTS, p. 193.

might *believe* them, in which case they would be sinning and he himself would be giving offense in the Pauline sense (Romans 14, not to mention I Cor. 8:9).

But suppose we sadly avert our gaze from this elitism run amok: why does Harvey think that only the historian has a right to hold an opinion on these matters? Clearly enough, because he thinks that the only way to achieve accurate and reliable information on these matters is by way of Troeltschian scholarship. And *that* opinion, obviously, presupposes the philosophical and theological opinion that there is not any *other* epistemic avenue to these matters; it presupposes that, for example, faith (and the internal instigation or testimony of the Holy Spirit) is not a source of warranted belief or knowledge on these topics. If the latter *were* a source of warranted belief, and if the 'average layperson' had access to this source (if the 'average layperson' could have faith), then presumably there would be nothing whatever wrong with her holding views on these matters on this basis. 'Just as the average layperson is scarcely in a position to have an informed judgment about the seventh letter of Plato, the relationship of Montezuma to Cortez, or the authorship of the Donation of Constantine, so the average layperson has no right to an opinion about the authorship of the Fourth Gospel or the trustworthiness of the synoptics,' says Harvey. The only way to determine the truth about the seventh letter of Plato is by way of ordinary historical investigation; the same goes, Harvey assumes, for questions about the life and ministry of Christ, whether he rose from the dead, whether he thought of himself as a Messiah, and the like. What lies at the bottom of this moral claim is really a philosophical/theological judgment: that traditional Christian belief is completely mistaken in taking it that faith is in fact a reliable source of true and warranted belief on these topics.

This view is not, of course, a result of historical scholarship, Troeltschian or otherwise; nor is it supported by arguments that will appeal to anyone who does not already agree with him – or indeed by any arguments at all. Harvey's view is rather a *presupposition*, a methodological prescription of the pursuit of Troeltschian historical criticism and proscription of traditional Biblical commentary. So it can hardly be thought of as an independent good reason for preferring the former to the latter. What we have are different philosophical/ theological positions that dictate different ways of pursuing Scripture scholarship. A way to show that the one really *is* superior to the other would be to give a good argument *for* the one philosophical/theological position, or *against* the other. Harvey does neither, simply assuming (uncritically, and without so much as mentioning the fact) the one position and rejecting the other. He assumes that there is no source of warrant or knowledge in addition to reason. This is not self-evident; millions, maybe billions of Christians and others reject it. Is it sensible, then, just to *assume* it, without so much as acknowledging this contrary opinion, without so much as a feeble gesture in the direction of argument or reason?

HBC more Inclusive?

John Collins recognizes that Troeltschian scholarship involves theological assumptions not nearly universally shared. He does not argue for the truth of these assumptions, but recommends them on a quite different basis. Criticizing Brevard Childs's proposal for a 'canonical' approach to Scripture scholarship,[67] he claims that the problem is that the former does not provide an *inclusive context* for the latter:

> If biblical theology is to retain a place in serious scholarship, it must be ... conceived broadly enough to provide a context for debate between different viewpoints. Otherwise it is likely to become a sectarian reservation, of interest only to those who hold certain confessional tenets that are not shared by the discipline at large. Childs's dogmatic conception of the canon provides no basis for advancing dialogue. In my opinion historical criticism still provides the most satisfactory framework for discussion.[68]

He adds that:

> One criterion for the adequacy of presuppositions is the degree to which they allow dialogue between differing viewpoints and accommodate new insights ... Perhaps the outstanding achievement of historical criticism in this century is that it has provided a framework within which scholars of different prejudices and commitments have been able to debate in a constructive manner.[69]

So why should we prefer Troeltschian Scripture scholarship over traditional Bible commentary? Because it offers a wider context, one in which people with conflicting theological opinions can all take part. We may be conservative Christians, theological liberals, or people with no theological views whatever: we can all take part in Troeltschian Scripture scholarship, provided we acquiesce in its fundamental assumptions. This is why it is to be preferred to the more traditional sort.

Now this would perhaps be a reason for practicing *Duhemian* Scripture scholarship, but of course Troeltschian Scripture scholarship is not Duhemian: the principles upon which it proceeds are not accepted by nearly everyone. They would be accepted by only a tiny minority of contemporary Christians,

---

[67] See, e.g., Childs's *The New Testament as Canon: An Introduction* (Valley Forge, PA: Trinity Press International, 1994), pp. 3–53.

[68] 'Is a Critical Biblical Theology Possible?' in *The Hebrew Bible and its Interpreters*, pp. 6–7. Collins speaks here not of Troeltschian HBC but of HBC simpliciter; a couple of pages earlier, however, he identifies HBC with Troeltschian HBC.

[69] Ibid., p. 8.

for example. And this shows a fundamental confusion, so it seems to me, in Collins's defense of Troeltschian scholarship. The defense he offers is appropriate for *Duhemian* scholarship; it is not at all appropriate for *Troeltschian* scholarship. The principles of Troeltschian historical scholarship, so interpreted as to preclude miracle, direct divine action, and special divine inspiration of the Bible, are extremely controversial philosophical and theological assumptions. Those who do not accept these controversial assumptions will not be inclined to take part in Troeltschian HBC, just as those who do not accept traditional Christian philosophical and theological views will not be likely to engage in traditional Biblical commentary. (If you do not think the Lord speaks in Scripture, you will be unlikely to spend a great deal of your time trying to figure out what it is God says there.) As John Levenson puts it, historical criticism 'does not facilitate communication with those outside its boundaries: it requires fundamentalists, for example, to be born again as liberals – or to stay out of the conversation altogether.' He adds that 'if inclusiveness is to be gauged quantitatively, then [Brevard] Childs would win the match hands down, for far more people with biblical interests share Christian faith than a thoroughgoing historicism. Were we historical critics to be classed as a religious body we should have to be judged a most minuscule sect indeed – and one with a pronounced difficulty relating to groups that do not accept our beliefs.'[70]

Nothing to Be Concerned *About*

We are now prepared to return to Harvey's original question: why is it that the person in the pew pays little attention to the contemporary HBC, and, despite those decades of research, retains rather a traditional picture of the life and ministry of Jesus? As to why *in actual historical fact* this is the case, this is a job for an intellectual historian. What we have seen so far, however, is that there is no compelling or even reasonably decent argument for supposing that the procedures and assumptions of HBC are to be preferred to those of traditional Biblical commentary. A little epistemological reflection enables us to see something further: the traditional Christian (whether in the pew or not) has a good reason to reject the skeptical claims of HBC and continue to hold traditional Christian belief despite the allegedly corrosive acids of HBC.

Troeltschian HBC Again

As we have seen, there are substantially three types of HBC. For present purposes, however, we can consider Duhemian and Spinozistic HBC

---

[70] Levenson, p. 120.

together. Let us say, therefore, that we have both Troeltschian and non-Troeltschian HBC. Consider the first. The Troeltschian Scripture scholar accepts Troeltsch's principles for historical research, under an interpretation according to which they rule out the occurrence of miracles and the divine inspiration of the Bible (along with the corollary that the latter enjoys the sort of unity accruing to a book that has one principal author). But then it is not at all surprising that the Troeltschian tends to come up with conclusions wildly at variance with those accepted by the traditional Christian. As Gilkey says, 'Suddenly a vast panoply of divine deeds and events recorded in scripture are no longer regarded as having actually happened' (above, p. 34). Now if (instead of tendentious claims about our inability to do otherwise) the Troeltschian offered some good reasons to think that in fact these Troeltschian principles are *true*, then the traditional Christian would certainly have to pay attention; then she might be obliged to take the skeptical claims of historical critics seriously. But Troeltschians apparently do not offer any such good reasons. They simply declare that nowadays we cannot think in any other way, or (following Harvey) that it is immoral to believe in, e.g., Christ's resurrection on other than historical grounds.

Neither of these is remotely persuasive as a reason for modifying traditional Christian belief in the light of Troeltschian results. As for the first, of course, the traditional Christian knows that it is quite false: she herself and many of her friends nowadays (and hundreds of millions of others) do think in precisely that proscribed way. And as far as the implicit claims for the superiority of these Troeltschian ways of thinking go, she will not be impressed by them unless some decent arguments of one sort or another are forthcoming, or some other good reason for adopting that opinion. The mere claim that this is what many contemporary experts think will not and should not intimidate her. And the second proposed reason (Harvey's reason) seems to be itself dependent on the very claim at issue. Clearly the critic thinks it immoral to form beliefs about historical facts on grounds other than historical research because he believes that the only reliable grounds for beliefs of the former type is research of the latter type. Again, however, he offers no argument for this assumption, merely announcing it as what those in the know believe, and perhaps also adopting an air of injured puzzlement about the fact that the person in the pew does not seem to pay much attention.

To see the point here, consider an analogy: suppose your friend is accused and convicted of stealing an ancient and valuable Frisian vase from the local museum. As it happens, you remember clearly that at the time this vase was stolen, your friend was in your office defending his eccentric views about the gospel of John. You have testified to this in court, but to no avail. I come along and offer to do a scientific investigation to see whether your view here is in fact correct. You are delighted, knowing as you think you do that your friend is innocent. When I explain my methods to you, however, your delight turns to dismay. For I refuse to accept the testimony of memory; I propose to ignore completely the fact that you *remember* your friend's being in your office. Further, my method precludes from the start the conclusion that your friend is innocent, even if he *is* innocent. Could I blame you for losing interest in my 'scientific' investigation? But the traditional Christian ought to view Troeltschian HBC with the same suspicion: it refuses to admit a source of warranted belief (the testimony of Scripture) the traditional Christian accepts, and is precluded in advance from coming to such conclusions as that Jesus really did arise from the dead and really is the divine Son of God.

Non-Troeltschian HBC

Troeltschian HBC, therefore, has no claim on a serious Christian; it is wholly reasonable for her to form and maintain her beliefs quite independently of it. How about non-Troeltschian (Duhemian and Spinozistic) HBC? This is, of course, a very different kettle of fish. The non-Troeltschian proposes to employ only assumptions that are clearly deliverances of reason (or accepted by everyone party to the project). She does not (for purposes of scholarship) accept the traditional Christian's views about the Bible or the life of Christ, but she also does not accept Troeltsch's principles. She does not assume that miracles did or could happen; but of course that is quite different from assuming that they did not or could not, and she does not assume that either. She does not assume that the Bible is in fact a word from the Lord and hence authoritative and reliable; but she also does not assume that it is not.

Of course, that may not leave her a lot to go on. The non-Troeltschian is handicapped in this area in a way in which she is not in such areas as physics or chemistry. In the latter, there is little by way of theological controversy that seems relevant to the pursuit of the subject. Not so for Scripture scholarship; here the very foundations of the subject are deeply disputed. Does the Bible have one principal author, namely God himself? If not, then perhaps Jowett – 'Scripture has one meaning – the meaning which it had to the mind of the prophet or evangelist who first uttered or wrote, to the hearers or readers who first received it' – is right; otherwise, he is wrong.[71] Is it divinely inspired, so that what it teaches is both true and to be accepted? If it reports miraculous happenings – risings from the dead, a virgin birth, the changing of water into wine, healings of people blind or lame from birth – are these to be taken more or less at face value, or dismissed as contrary to 'what we now know'? Is there an entry into the truth about these matters – faith or divine testimony by way of Scripture, for example – quite different from ordinary historical investigation?

---

[71] See note 16 above.

If we prescind from all these matters and proceed responsibly (remembering to shun the Fallacy of Creeping Certitude, for example), what we come up with is likely to be pretty slender.

A. E. Harvey, for example, proposes the following as beyond reasonable doubt from everyone's point of view, i.e., Duhemianly: 'that Jesus was known in both Galilee and Jerusalem, that he was a teacher, that he carried out cures of various illnesses, particularly demon-possession and that these were widely regarded as miraculous; that he was involved in controversy with fellow Jews over questions of the law of Moses: and that he was crucified in the governorship of Pontius Pilate.'[72] It is not even clear whether Harvey means that the *conjunction* of these propositions is beyond reasonable doubt, or only each of the conjuncts;[73] in either case what we have is pretty slim.

Or consider John Meier's monumental *A Marginal Jew: Rethinking the Historical Jesus*.[74] Meier aims to be Duhemian, or anyway Spinozistic: 'My method follows a simple rule: it prescinds from what Christian faith or later Church teaching says about Jesus, without either affirming or denying such claims'.[75] (I think he also means to eschew assumptions incompatible with traditional Christian belief.) Meier's fantasy of 'an unpapal conclave' of Jewish, Catholic, Protestant and agnostic scholars, locked in the basement of the Harvard Divinity School library until they come to consensus on what historical methods can show about the life and mission of Jesus, is thoroughly Duhemian. This conclave, he says, would yield '... a rough draft of what that will-o'-the-wisp "all reasonable people" could say about the historical Jesus.'[76] Meier sets out, judiciously, objectively, carefully, to establish that consensus.[77] What is striking about his conclusions, however, is how slender they are, and how tentative – and this despite the fact that on occasion he cannot himself resist building occasional towers of probability. About all that emerges from

---

[72] *Jesus and the Constraints of History* (London and Philadelphia: Westminster Press, 1982), p. 6.

[73] It could be that each of the conjuncts is beyond reasonable doubt but that their conjunction is not. Suppose (just to choose arbitrarily a number) what is probable to degree .95 or higher is beyond reasonable doubt. Then if each of the above is beyond reasonable doubt, their conjunction might still be little more than twice as probable as its denial.

[74] New York, NY: Doubleday, 1991, 1994. The first volume has 484 pages; the second has 1,055 pages; a third volume is currently expected.

[75] Meier, *A Marginal Jew*, p. 1.

[76] Ibid., p. 2.

[77] 'Meier's treatment, in short, is as solid and moderate and pious as Historical Jesus scholarship is ever likely to be. More important, Meier is a careful scholar. There is nothing hasty or slipshod in his analysis; he considers every opinion, weighs every option.' Johnson, p. 128.

Meier's painstaking work is that Jesus was a prophet, a proclaimer of an eschatological message from God, someone who performs powerful deeds, signs and wonders, that announce God's kingdom, and also ratify his message.[78] As Duhemian or Spinozist, of course, we cannot add that these signs and miracles involve special or direct divine action; nor can we say that they do not. We cannot say that Jesus rose from the dead, or that he did not; we cannot conclude that Scripture is specially inspired, or that it is not.

Now what is characteristic of non-Troeltschian HBC is just that it does not involve those Troeltschian principles: but of course it also rejects any alleged source of warranted belief in addition to reason (Spinozistic) and any theological assumptions not shared by everyone party to the discussion. Traditional Christians, rightly or wrongly, think they do have sources of warranted belief in addition to reason: faith and the work of the Holy Spirit, or divine testimony in Scripture, or the testimony of the Spirit-led church. They may of course be *mistaken* about that; but until someone gives a decent argument for the conclusion that they *are* mistaken, they need not be impressed by the result of scholarship that ignores this further source of belief. If you want to learn the truth about a given area, you should not restrict yourself to only *some* of the sources of warranted belief (as does the Spinozist), or only to beliefs accepted by everyone else (with the Duhemian); maybe you know something some of the others do not. Perhaps you remember that your friend was in your office expostulating about the errors of postmodernism at the very time he is supposed to have been stealing that Frisian vase; if no one else was there, then you know something the rest do not.

So the traditional Christian need not be fazed by the fact that non-Troeltschian HBC does not support her views about what Jesus did and said. She thinks she knows some things by faith – that Jesus arose from the dead, for example. She may concede that if you leave out of account all that she knows in this way, then with respect to the remaining body of knowledge or belief the resurrection is not particularly probable. But that does not present her with an intellectual or spiritual crisis. We can imagine a renegade group of whimsical physicists proposing to reconstruct physics, refusing to use belief that comes from memory, say, or perhaps memory of anything more than one minute ago. Perhaps something could be done along these lines, but it would be a poor, paltry, truncated, trifling thing. And now suppose that, say, Newton's Laws or Special Relativity turned out to be dubious and unconfirmed from this point of view: that would presumably give little pause to the more traditional physicists. This truncated physics could hardly call into question physics of the fuller variety.

---

[78] See Johnson, pp. 130–131.

Similarly here. The traditional Christian thinks she knows *by faith* that Jesus was divine and that he rose from the dead. But then she will be unmoved by the fact that these truths are not especially probable on the evidence to which non-Troeltschian HBC limits itself. Why should that matter to her? So this is the rest of the answer to Harvey's question: if the HBC in question is non-Troeltschian, then the fact it does not verify traditional Christian beliefs is due to its limiting itself in the way it does, to its refusing to use all the data or evidence the Christian thinks he has in his possession. For a Christian to confine himself to the results of non-Troeltschian HBC would be a little like trying to mow your lawn with nail scissors or paint your house with a toothbrush; it might be an interesting experiment if you have time on your hands, but otherwise why limit yourself in this way?

More generally, then: HBC is either Troeltschian or non-Troeltschian. If the former, then it begins from assumptions entailing that much of what the traditional Christian believes is false; but then it is no surprise that its conclusions are at odds with traditional belief. It is also of little direct interest to the traditional Christian. It offers her no reason at all for rejecting or modifying her beliefs; it also offers little promise of enabling her to achieve better or deeper insight into what actually happened. As for non-Troeltschian HBC, on the other hand, this variety of historical criticism omits a great deal of what she sees as relevant evidence and relevant considerations. It is therefore left with little to go on. But again, the fact that it fails to support traditional belief will be of little direct interest to the traditional believer; that is only to be expected, and casts no doubt at all upon that belief. Either way, therefore, the traditional Christian can rest easy with the claims of HBC; she need feel no obligation, intellectual or otherwise, to modify her beliefs in the light of its claims and alleged results.[79]

Concluding Coda

But is not all of this just a bit too sunny? Is not it a recipe for avoiding hard questions, for hanging onto belief no matter what, for guaranteeing that you will never have to face negative results, even if there *are* some? 'HBC is either Troeltschian or non-Troeltschian: in the first case it proceeds from assumptions I reject; in the second it fails to take account of all of what I take to be the evidence; either way, therefore, I need not pay attention to it.' Could not I say this *a priori*, without even examining the results of HBC? But then there

---

[79] *Alleged* results: because of the enormous controversy and disagreement among followers of HBC, it is very difficult to find anything one could sensibly call 'results' of this scholarship.

must be something defective in the line of thought in question. Is not it clearly *possible* that historians should discover facts that put Christian belief into serious question, count heavily against it? Well, maybe so. How could this happen? As follows. HBC limits itself to the deliverances of reason; it is possible, at any rate in the broadly logical sense, that just by following ordinary historical reason, using the methods of historical investigation endorsed or enjoined by the deliverances of reason, someone should find powerful evidence against central elements of the Christian faith;[80] if this happened, Christians would face a genuine faith–reason clash. A series of letters could be discovered, letters circulated among Peter, James, John and Paul, in which the necessity for the hoax and the means of its perpetration are carefully and seriously discussed; these letters might direct workers to archeological sites in which still more material of the same sort is discovered.[81] The Christian faith is a *historical* faith, in the sense that it essentially depends upon what did in fact happen: 'And if Christ has not been raised, your faith is futile' (I Cor. 15:17). It could certainly happen that by the exercise of reason we come up with powerful evidence[82] against something we take or took to be deliverance of the faith.[83] It is conceivable that the assured results of HBC should include such evidence. Then Christians would have a problem, a sort of conflict between faith and reason.

But, of course, nothing at all like this has emerged from HBC, whether Troeltschian or non-Troeltschian; indeed, there is little of any kind that can be considered its 'assured results', if only because of the wide-ranging disagreement among those who practice HBC.[84] We do not have anything like assured

---

[80] Or, less crucially, evidence against what appear to be the teaching of Scripture. For example, archeological evidence could undermine the traditional belief that there was such a city as Jericho.

[81] See Bas van Fraassen, 'Three-sided Scholarship: Comments on the Paper of John R. Donahue, S.J.', in *Hermes and Athena*, eds. Eleonore Stump and Thomas Flint (Notre Dame, IN: University of Notre Dame Press, 1993), p. 322. 'Finish it [the depressing scenario] yourself, if you have the heart to do it', says van Fraassen.

[82] Or *think* we come up with it; even if we are mistaken about the evidence in question, it could still precipitate this sort of problem for us.

[83] See my 'When Faith and Reason Clash: Evolution and the Bible' in *Christian Scholar's Review*, Vol. XXI No.1 (September, 1991), pp. 9–15.

[84] Thus Harold Attridge in 'Calling Jesus Christ' in *Hermes and Athena*, p. 211: 'There remains enormous diversity among those who attempt to describe what Jesus really did, taught, and thought about himself. For some contemporary scholars he was a Hellenistic magician; for others, a Galilean charismatic or rabbi; for yet others, a prophetic reformer; for others, a sly teller of wry and engaging tales; for some he had grandiose ideas; for others he eschewed them. In general, the inquirer finds the Jesus that her historical method allows her to see. It is as true today as it was at the end of the liberal quest for the historical Jesus catalogued by Albert Schweitzer that we

results (or even reasonably well-attested results) that conflict with traditional Christian belief in such a way that belief of that sort can continue to be accepted only at considerable cost; nothing like this has happened. What would be the appropriate response if it *did* happen, or rather if I came to be convinced that it had happened? Would I have to give up Christian faith, or else give up the life of the mind? What would be the appropriate response?

Well, what would be the appropriate response if I came to be convinced that someone had given a wholly rigorous, ineluctable disproof of the existence of God, perhaps something along the lines of J. N. Findlay's alleged ontological disproof?[85] Or what if, with David Hume (at least as understood by Thomas Reid), I come to think that my cognitive faculties are probably not reliable, and go on to note that I form this very belief on the basis of the very faculties whose reliability this belief impugns? If I did, what would or should I do – stop thinking about these things, immerse myself in practical activity (maybe playing a lot of backgammon, maybe volunteering to help build houses for Habitat for Humanity), commit intellectual suicide? I do not know the answer to any of these questions. There is no need to borrow trouble, however: we can think about crossing these bridges when (more likely, if) we come to them.[86]

---

moderns tend to make Jesus in our own image and likeness.' The Schweitzer reference is to his *Von Reimarus zu Wrede* (1906), translated by W. Montgomery under the title *The Quest of the Historical Jesus: A Critical Study of its Progress from Reimarus to Wrede* (New York, NY: Macmillan, 1956).

[85] 'Can God's Existence be Disproved?' *Mind* Vol. 57 No. 226 (April, 1948), pp. 176–183.

[86] My thanks to Mike Bergmann, John Cooper, Kevin Corcoran, Ronald Feenstra, Marie Pannier, Neal Plantinga, Tapio Puolimatka, David Vanderlaan, James VanderKam, Calvin Van Reken, and Henry Zwaanstra. A longer version of this paper appears as Chapter 12 of *Warranted Christian Belief* (New York, NY: Oxford University Press, 2000).

2

Warranted Biblical Interpretation

Alvin Plantinga's 'Two (or More) Kinds of Scripture Scholarship'

Craig G. Bartholomew

Introduction

As *Time* magazine reported in 1980, there has been a remarkable renaissance in religious (Christian) belief among philosophers in the United States. A key factor in this was the founding in 1978 of the Society of Christian Philosophers (SCP), in which Bill Alston and Alvin Plantinga played a central role. Another important factor was Plantinga's inaugural lecture at the University of Notre Dame.[1] 'Advice to Christian Philosophers' is a deeply moving lecture in which Plantinga encourages Christian philosophers to display more autonomy, integrity and Christian boldness. Christians must of course remain deeply engaged with the mainstream debates, but they also have their own agenda to pursue and their own, legitimate starting point in belief in God. Many have heeded this call and now the SCP is the largest interest group at the American Philosophical Association, and a growing corpus of Christian philosophy is emerging.

Plantinga himself has recently completed a three-volume work on epistemology. In the third volume, *Warranted Christian Belief* (*WCB*), he brings his work on warrant and epistemology to bear on biblical interpretation in the context of asking whether or not biblical criticism is a *defeater* to Christian belief.[2] This chapter is the basis of our discussion.[3] Both Robert Gordon and I

---

[1] Clark, 'Introduction', 10.
[2] See Plantinga, *WCB*, 357ff., for a discussion of defeaters.
[3] This material was also published in a slightly shorter version in *Modern Theology*, which is reproduced in this volume (Ch. 1).

respond to Plantinga's 'Two (or More) Kinds of Scripture Scholarship'. *My* aims in what follows, but not necessarily in this order, are to:

- Explain the contours of Plantinga's epistemology of religious belief, bearing in mind that not all of us are philosophers. I therefore range beyond Plantinga's chapter in order to set it in context.[4]
- Show that attention to epistemology is crucial if we are to understand biblical studies today and find ways forward.
- Demonstrate the relevance of Plantinga's work on epistemology for biblical hermeneutics and for issues of history and hermeneutics by showing how it illumines the state of biblical interpretation today. I do this by focusing on Philip Davies' request for biblical studies to confine itself to the 'discourse of the academy', the discourse that underlies Davies' recent, radical work on the history of Israel.
- Explore some of the implications of Plantinga's approach for biblical interpretation and history and hermeneutics.

Philip Davies and Epistemology and Biblical Interpretation

Long gone are the days when Bright's moderate *History of Israel* was a standard reconstruction of the history of Israel in the academy. In recent decades, mainstream views of the history of Israel have become much more radical.[5] Indeed, Philip Davies discerns something of a paradigm shift in scholarly approaches to ancient Israel:

> Recognizing that the biblical literature is, like any literature, a distorting product of human authors (and it would be distorting even if it were written by a deity, since deities have to use our language and have to have a point of view) lays the ground for what I hesitate to call a 'paradigm shift'. Something of the sort is indeed occurring. We are enjoying a climate in which a non-theological paradigm is beginning to claim a place alongside the long-dominant theological one. The new paradigm emerges by the simple effort of demonstrating that the old paradigm is a paradigm, sustained by consent and claiming a truth for itself to which it is not entitled. Being non-theological, this paradigm can renounce any stake in the

---

[4] For helpful introductions to Plantinga's thought see Plantinga, 'Christian Life', 'Self-Profile'; Hoitenga, *Faith and Reason*, esp. ch. 7; and Sennett, *Modality*. A Plantinga reader has been published, viz., *The Analytic Theist*, edited by Sennett, containing a useful cross-section of Plantinga's work.

[5] See, e.g., Thompson, *Early History;* Lemche, *Prelude;* and Davies, *Search.*

historicity or non-historicity of what the literature says, or in the literary or ethical value of what is said.[6]

Davies' use of paradigm is helpful insofar as it alerts us to the different frameworks within which historical studies of the Bible take place. Somewhat like Plantinga, Davies discerns two ways of approaching the history of Israel – one which is theological and one which is non-theological. The theological paradigm claimed a truth for itself to which it is not entitled; presumably the latter claims a truth for itself to which it is entitled.

Why the discourse of the non-theological paradigm should have a greater claim to truth becomes clearer in Davies' provocative *Whose Bible Is it Anyway?* In this book Davies argues for non-confessional biblical studies done according to the 'discourse of the academy'. He acknowledges the existence and legitimacy of *interpretation of the Bible as Scripture* – what Plantinga calls traditional Christian biblical commentary – but Davies carefully distinguishes this from *biblical studies*. 'The two disciplines are not contesting, and they do not have to try and blow the other off the map. There is a proper place for each, within society and within individuals'.[7] The latter and decidedly not the former, however, is what is appropriate in the academy and underlies the paradigm shift in studies of ancient Israel.

Davies characterizes the discourse of the academy as follows:

- The academy, unlike a confessional community, aims at inclusion and not exclusion.
- The discourse of the academy *is* value-laden (humanistic, rational presuppositions) but different in principle and intent from confessional discourse, for …
- It permits and stimulates criticism of its own practices and beliefs.
- It encourages the expression of any opinion or belief that is amenable to public scrutiny, evaluation, contradiction or confirmation.
- It does not deal in truths but in hypotheses and paradigms (or truth is expressed through these), which can and do change.
- It excludes opinions and theories and beliefs that cannot be challenged, tested, critiqued or that insist on an absolute and non-negotiable truth.
- It excludes *emic* discourses, but it does not reject the expression of any belief or value system that can be communicated and examined by outsiders, and thus it enables members of different confessing communities to communicate on terms of equal privilege.
- In this discourse, the Bible is judged by criteria other than its own – this is how it is able to contribute to the process of 'interpretation'. By contrast,

---

[6] Davies, *Search*, 15, 16.
[7] Davies, *Whose Bible?*, 55.

a confessional reading in principle denies the scriptural texts the possibility of behaving in a non-canonical manner, and thus, paradoxically, denies the authority of the text in favour of the authority of the reception-conscious and theologically informed reader. Such, at any rate, is the tendency.[8]

We should not, according to Davies, conclude that interpretation of the Bible as Scripture is inferior to interpretation according to the discourse of the academy. It is simply the case that

> there is a social world that the academy inhabits. … it is a social world in which gods cannot walk unchallenged around the vocabulary, nor where private beliefs of an unarguable kind can operate as working hypotheses without constant challenge. While individual academics can have such beliefs … the beliefs are no part of the social discourse and do not form part of the curriculum. The conflict is not about what you believe, but what you may be allowed to assume in your professional discourse.[9]

Does this mean that Christians are excluded from the academy? By no means, as long as the individual can separate the worlds in which he or she operates.

> I see no sound reason why individuals who work in a university in the week and go to church on Sunday or synagogue on Sabbath and conduct bible study in their church during the week should have trouble keeping their confessional discourse apart from the academic one in which the history of bibles is studied by a historical agenda, their language according to the methods of linguistics, and so on. … if it is realized that the two discourses are in fact separate, and even operate with separate notions of 'truth', it becomes easier to accept that indulging in both implies no contradiction. Many believing scholars affirm things in church that they doubt or even deny in the classroom; but if in different discourses there are different concepts of truth, it is possible, for instance, to affirm emically the resurrection of Christ in church while denying that the body of Jesus of Nazareth revived and left its tomb.[10]

An etic, not an emic, discourse is proper to the academic domain.

Not surprisingly, Davies also makes an *ethical argument* for restricting biblical studies to the discourse of the academy. Appealing to Jesus' exhortation to render to Caesar what is his, Davies argues that, since taxpayers pay for academic biblical interpretation, it should not be confessional. 'In spending taxpayer's money doing research that advances churchly or Christian interests and at the expense of the academy's interests one is behaving unethically. At

---

[8] Davies, *Whose Bible?*, 49.
[9] Davies, *Whose Bible?*, 51.
[10] Davies, *Whose Bible?*, 51.

least I make the suggestion.'[11] Public institutions nowadays preclude discrimination and 'it would therefore be unethical or unprofessional to conduct a confessional discourse in Sheffield'.[12] Emic discourses can't communicate with
each other and 'that, I think, rules them out of universities'.[13] Academic study
of the Bible must be inclusive:

> I do not want anyone to be excluded … from the type of discourse I practise as an
> academic. I hope I can write for Christians and non-Christians, and that we can
> agree about what the presuppositions and aims of our common (etic) discourse are. I
> do not require any kind of belief, except in the usefulness of universally agreed rules
> of evidence and argument so that we can genuinely seek to persuade or entertain
> each other.[14]

Of his exegetical essays in *Whose Bible Is it Anyway?*, Davies asks his readers not
to assess them so much in terms of orthodoxy but rather 'ask instead whether
the arguments are well conducted, whether the ideas stimulate thought,
whether the engagement gives enjoyment, and, of course, whether I clearly
misread the written words. Doing this you are entering into the same discourse
as myself.'[15]

We are indebted to Davies for such a clear statement of what he envisages as
appropriate for the academy vis-à-vis biblical interpretation. This is, I think, a
perspective that underlies the radical views of the history of the Old Testament
that have emerged – not least from Sheffield – in recent years,[16] and it is most
helpful to have described so clearly the boundaries of the discourse within
which such views are being articulated. This is not to suggest that all biblical
scholars would agree with Davies. Davies himself notes a tendency for some
believing scholars to 'confuse' the contexts in which they read the Bible/bibles.
Davies cites Barr,[17] and particularly Childs, as examples of such confusion:

> while Childs is apparently discoursing at the level of 'history', mimicking a critical
> approach, he is actually *uninterested* in historical processes, and unable or unconcerned
> to bother with historical argumentation. His 'canon' is not a historical product at all,
> but a confessional datum. Playing with two different disciplines allows Childs to get
> away with an entirely bogus claim: a dogma posing as a historical hypothesis.[18]

---

[11] Davies, *Whose Bible?*, 53.
[12] Davies, *Whose Bible?*, 52.
[13] Davies, *Whose Bible?*, 52.
[14] Davies, *Whose Bible?*, 53.
[15] Davies, *Whose Bible?*, 55.
[16] See Davies, *Search*.
[17] See Davies, *Search*, 18. Barr is distinguished from Christopher Evans, who wished to
protect academic biblical study from theological claims that cannot be tested.
[18] Davies, *Whose Bible?*, 31.

However, clear as he is in his description of the 'discourse of the academy', Davies never attempts to position it philosophically, or to argue for the appropriateness of such a discourse. Presumably the distinctives of such an approach speak for themselves. Perhaps ...

I am not aware of any empirical research done on the discourse or discourses within which most biblical study operates. Davies has a radical reputation, but I suspect that in fact many mainline scholars would feel under pressure to accept Davies' ground rules for scholarship within the academy. There is, however, much confusion when it comes to the issue of the appropriate ground rules or epistemology for academic biblical interpretation. Plantinga rightly notes that 'a real live Scripture scholar is unlikely to have spent a great deal of thought on the epistemological foundations of the discipline'.[19] When one thinks of the variety of ingredients involved in biblical scholarship nowadays, that is not surprising. Furthermore, it is appropriate that biblical scholars get on with *biblical* scholarship. However, any academic discipline has foundational philosophical elements which structure the paradigm, or paradigms, within which work takes place, and from time to time there is value in focusing on the foundations. To Davies' credit, he is seeking clarity in what have often been muddy waters. In my opinion there is particular value in this at present, with biblical studies in flux and badly fragmented. Indeed, failure to be epistemologically aware may leave us destined to reinforce some truly unhelpful trends in biblical study.

In his 'Communicative Action', Anthony Thiselton argues that biblical scholars urgently need to be more aware of developments in philosophy of religion:

> Curiously, the limits of scientific method to explain all of reality seem to be appreciated more readily in the philosophy of religion than in biblical studies. Views and methods that students in philosophy of religion recognize as 'positivist', 'reductionist', or even 'materialist' are often embraced quite uncritically in issues of judgment about, for example, acts of God in biblical narrative. In place of the more rigorous and judicious exploration of these issues in philosophical theology, biblical studies seems too readily to become polarized.[20]

It is a moot point whether greater awareness will defuse the polarizations in biblical studies. Plantinga's 'Two (or More) Kinds' seems to me to suggest that such awareness may expose and even catalyse polarity. More of that later. For the present, I do think that awareness of current developments in philosophy of religion, not least the work of scholars such as Plantinga, Wolterstorff and Alston, is very helpful in assessing Davies' plea for biblical study according to the discourse of the academy.

---

[19] *WCB*, 399.
[20] Thiselton, 'Communicative Action', 137.

Postmodernism, Classical Foundationalism and Biblical Interpretation

Davies' approach shows the inevitable signs of 'postmodernism'. He is aware that the 'academy' is a social construct and bends over backwards to insist that the academy is not necessarily a better social context than the church. Furthermore, he is quite relaxed about a biblical scholar also being part of the Christian community as long as he or she is able to distinguish carefully the contexts and the different sets of rules that apply. For all these postmodern signs, Davies remains resolutely committed to his 'discourse of the academy' and wants to argue that study of the Bible as Scripture should be exempt from biblical studies in the academy.

Can current developments in philosophy of religion help us to position Davies' view and to orient ourselves in relation to it? They certainly can. A most significant development in philosophical epistemology in recent decades has been the rise of *metaepistemology*.[21] Wolterstorff describes this as follows:

> Rather than just plunging ahead and developing epistemological theories, philosophers have stood back and reflected seriously on the structural options available to them in their construction of such theories.[22]

Having discerned the major options available, scholars have been interested to see which ones have dominated modern Western thought. Intriguingly, one theory, namely *classical foundationalism* (CF), has long been dominant.

CF is 'a picture or total way of looking at faith, knowledge, justified belief, rationality, and allied topics. This picture has been enormously popular in Western thought; and despite a substantial opposing groundswell, I think it remains the dominant way of thinking about these topics'.[23] CF goes back to Plato and Aristotle. In modern times, Descartes established CF in relation to *scientia* and Locke extended it to all knowledge.[24] 'In effect, what Locke did was take the classical foundationalist demands that Descartes had laid down for scientific belief and lay them down for rational belief in general.'[25]

CFs believe that our beliefs are of two sorts:

- Those that are foundational; these do not require arguments or evidence for one to be rational in believing them. In this sense they are *basic*.

---

[21] See here Wolterstorff, 'Introduction'.

[22] Wolterstorff, 'Introduction', 1.

[23] Plantinga, in Sennett (ed.), *Analytic Theist*, 129.

[24] Wolterstorff, 'Introduction', 6.

[25] Wolterstorff, 'Introduction', 6.

- Those that are not foundational but are believed on the basis of other beliefs which are foundational. In this sense they are non-basic.

Basic beliefs do not require evidence, while non-basic beliefs do. According to CFs, basic beliefs are:

- Self-evident beliefs – that is, beliefs that are seen to be true simply by understanding them. $2 + 1 = 3$ is an example of a self-evident belief; you only have to understand it to see that it is true.
- Incorrigible beliefs – these are beliefs which one could not be mistaken in holding.
- Some CFs have held that beliefs formed on the basis of sense experience are basic.[26]

How do theistic and Christian beliefs look in the context of CF? Beliefs about God are neither self-evident, nor incorrigible, nor evident to the senses. Thus, according to CF, religious beliefs are not properly basic and cannot be assumed without evidence. Consequently, for them to be warranted as knowledge they must be supported by arguments and evidence. This is famously summed up by W.K. Clifford: 'it is wrong always, everywhere, and for anyone to believe anything upon insufficient evidence'. Bertrand Russell replied similarly when asked what he would say if he got to heaven to discover that Christianity was true: 'I'd say, "Not enough evidence, God. Not enough evidence!"'[27]

How does this relate to biblical interpretation? My suggestion is that Davies' 'discourse of the academy' is in a major respect closely akin to CF. Davies never develops a precise philosophical defence or description of his discourse of the academy, but the indications that this is akin to CF are the following: the values of the discourse are humanistic and rational; public criteria available to all are crucial so that nothing should be believed apart from rational evidence; theological beliefs as properly basic are excluded, as is all emic discourse; the discourse of the academy is regarded as occupying the moral high ground.[28]

This CF strand in Davies' thought is, of course, in deep tension with the postmodern elements in his approach. Once one acknowledges that the

---

[26] On the historical relationship between incorrigible beliefs and sense experience see Plantinga, 'Self-Profile', 59, 60. I am grateful to Stephen Evans for pointing out to me that since almost all beliefs are in some way formed on the basis of sense experience, the idea here is that some beliefs are made obvious by sense experience in a way that is not the case for other beliefs.

[27] Plantinga, *Analytical Theist*, 104.

[28] The parallels to W.K. Clifford's 'The Ethics of Belief' are fascinating! See Plantinga, *Analytic Theist*, 110. Note that I am not suggesting that Davies' work is a developed version of philosophical classical foundationalism, but only that the epistemological stance is similar as regards the modernist strand in Davies.

academy is a construct and all its discourse value-laden, as Davies does, it is hard to see why confessional discourse should be excluded – the history of Christian thought shows quite clearly that it is capable of being critical and rigorous. To block this possibility Davies resorts to CF, a modernist strategy that takes back what he has already granted to postmodernism.[29] However, it surely is not possible to have one's cake and eat it in this respect. If confessional discourse, which can be as rigorous and critical as any other, is only different from but not inferior to the discourse of the academy, what possible reason can there be for continuing to exclude it from the academy? Either one must go with the postmodern emphasis and then allow confessional discourse its place in a genuinely pluralistic context, or one must resort to CF – but then one will have to argue for it and assert its superiority.

Now, where philosophy of religion is illuminating is that, as Wolterstorff says of CF, 'most philosophers who have seen clearly the structure of this particular option have rejected it. On close scrutiny they have found classical foundationalism untenable.'[30] Thus Davies' moral high ground could be sinking sand! We will explore this by examining Plantinga's epistemology of religious belief.

Plantinga and Warranted Christian Belief

What are the arguments against CF? Firstly, in response to CF Plantinga provides numerous counter-examples of beliefs that appear to be basic but are excluded by the criteria of CF. An example that Plantinga has developed in detail and at length is our belief in other minds. These and our memory beliefs appear to be genuinely basic but are neither self-evident nor incorrigible. Secondly, Plantinga argues that CF is self-referentially incoherent. The CF-ist has no right to the view that only self-evident and incorrigible propositions are properly basic on his own principles. Plantinga argues that CFs take this principle as part of their properly basic beliefs but, as it is neither self-evident nor incorrigible, such an assumption is unwarranted according to their own logic.[31]

---

[29] Modernism is closely linked with classical foundationalism. The modernist view that the academy must be a 'neutral' place where religious perspectives have no place stems from the view of the academy as a place where 'objective reason' reigns. The hegemony of classical foundationalism was rooted in its claim to provide a superior way to find truth.

[30] Wolterstorff, 'Introduction', 4.

[31] See Alston's discussion of this argument and Plantinga's response in *Alvin Plantinga*. Alston, 'Plantinga's Epistemology', 299, argues that 'I cannot agree that Plantinga has adequately supported the substantive claim that modern

On the back of this refutation of CF, Plantinga and others have argued that belief in God is a properly basic belief which, like other properly basic beliefs, does not require evidence before it can be taken as properly basic. Plantinga is not saying that there are no good arguments for belief in God – Plantinga himself is well known for arguing that the ontological argument for the existence of God works. What Plantinga *is* saying is that we must not make belief in God dependent for its warrant on such evidence. This is what C.S. Evans is getting at when he types Plantinga's view of the faith–reason relationship as 'Faith Without Reasons'.[32]

Plantinga does agree with CF that not just any belief can be properly basic, but he does not offer criteria for proper basicality – he argues that we must proceed *inductively* in this respect and 'assemble examples of beliefs and conditions such that the former are obviously properly basic in the latter, and examples of beliefs and conditions such that the former are obviously not properly basic in the latter'.[33] We must proceed in this regard from below rather than from above. But we should not assume that everyone will agree on the relevant examples:

> The Christian will of course suppose that belief in God is entirely proper and rational; if he does not accept this belief on the basis of other propositions, he will certainly conclude that it is basic for him and quite properly so. Followers of Bertrand Russell and Madelyn Murray O'Hare may disagree; but how is that relevant? Must my criteria or those of the Christian community, conform to their examples? Surely not. The Christian community is responsible to its set of examples, not to theirs.
>
> So, the Reformed epistemologist can properly hold that belief in the Great Pumpkin is not properly basic, even though he holds that belief in God is properly basic and even if he has no full-fledged criterion of proper basicality.[34]

Belief in God is properly basic, but this does not mean it is groundless. Belief in God is properly basic in the right circumstances. Such an approach is not a form of fideism that ignores reason or plays it down in the interests of faith. Belief in God, for Plantinga, *is* a deliverance of reason – just as much as any other properly basic belief.[35] Furthermore, belief in God as basic does not mean that it

---

foundationalism is "self-referentially incoherent". ... What he has done is to issue a fundamental challenge to the modern foundationalist. Whatever the possibilities might be for justifying (7) foundationalists of this stripe have signally failed to do so, or even attempted to do so. ... Plantinga's signal achievement on this point is to force the issue on our attention.'

32 Evans, *Faith Beyond Reason*, ch. 3.
33 Plantinga, in Sennett (ed.), *Analytic Theist*, 151.
34 Plantinga, in Sennett (ed.), *Analytic Theist*, 151.
35 See Plantinga, in Sennett (ed.), *Analytic Theist*, 157–61.

might not be wrong or that it cannot be argued against. Plantinga's discussion of biblical interpretation occurs precisely in the context of possible defeaters for his view of *warranted* Christian belief.

Plantinga uses the term 'warrant' to refer to that property enough of which makes the difference between knowledge and true belief. For a true belief to count as knowledge it must 'have more going for it than truth'.[36] Warrant is the additional factor that transforms true belief into knowledge, and Plantinga locates warrant in *proper function*. In *Warrant: The Current Debate* (*WCD*) and *Warrant and Proper Function* (*WPF*) Plantinga examines the alternatives in epistemology, namely, internalism, coherentism, reliabilism and externalism. In *WPF* Plantinga argues for an externalist epistemology[37] that locates warrant in proper function:

> a belief has warrant just if it is produced by cognitive processes or faculties that are functioning properly, in a cognitive environment that is propitious for that exercise of cognitive powers, according to a design plan that is successfully aimed at the production of true belief.[38]

In *WCB*, Plantinga brings his epistemology to bear on Christian belief. He develops a model – which he calls the Aquinas/Calvin model – for theistic beliefs that have warrant. He extends this to cover specifically Christian belief and argues that Christian belief is warranted; it is not just true belief but may be taken as knowledge. Part of the intellectual economy of Christian belief is the view that the Bible is perspicuous and that 'the whole Bible is a message from the Lord to humankind; this entire book is authoritative for Christian belief and practice'.[39] But how can and should this belief function in the context of biblical study?

Warranted Biblical Interpretation?

Plantinga notes that rigorous, academic biblical interpretation has a long and prestigious tradition in Christianity, aimed at discerning what the Lord says to us through the Bible. Plantinga calls this 'traditional biblical commentary' (TBC). However, out of the Enlightenment came another type of biblical

---

[36] *WCB*, xi. Plantinga uses the example of an ardent fan of the Detroit Tigers, who through her loyalty to the team believes they will win the pennant, despite their poor performances in the previous year. Contrary to all expectations, they do! Nevertheless her belief was a lucky guess, not knowledge. Knowledge is more than true belief.

[37] See Evans, *Faith Beyond Reason*, 41–43.

[38] *WCB*, xi.

interpretation, which Plantinga describes as 'historical biblical criticism' (HBC). The great characteristic of HBC is, according to Plantinga, that it insists on reading the Bible according to reason alone; it specifically excludes employing theological assumptions in its epistemology. One may argue towards theological beliefs, but not from them.[40] Plantinga discerns three types of HBC, namely Troeltschian HBC, which interprets Troeltsch's principles to preclude direct divine action in the world; Duhemian HBC, which aims to avoid all assumptions that are not common to parties in the dialogue; and Spinozistic HBC, which uses principles of reason that may not be agreed upon by all participants.

Plantinga examines Troeltschian HBC in particular. Arguments for its principles are noticeable by their absence. Perhaps our cultural situation simply forces them upon us in terms of the progress of modernity? One finds this sort of assumption all over the place – for example in Macquarrie, Harvey, Gilkey, Borg and Tracy,[41] and specifically in relation to historical criticism in Krentz.[42] It assumes a modern narrative of progress in the academy, and not only has postmodernism challenged this severely but 'the contemporary intellectual world is much more like a horse race (or perhaps a demolition derby) than a triumphal procession, more like a battleground than a Democratic party fund-raiser, where everyone can be counted on to support the same slate'.[43]

Perhaps everyone in the 'know' accepts Troeltschian principles, but this arrogantly ignores the millions of contemporary Christians. Harvey argues that *morally* we are compelled to accept these principles, but as Plantinga discerns, 'what lies at the bottom of this moral claim is really a philosophical-theological judgement: that traditional Christian belief is completely mistaken in taking it that faith is, in fact, a reliable source of true and warranted belief on these topics'.[44] Or should we accept Troeltschian principles because they are more inclusive? Plantinga cites Collin's critique of Childs in this respect, claiming that a canonical approach is not broad enough to allow debate between different viewpoints.[45] Not only does this confuse Troeltschian with Duhemian HBC but, as Levenson has noted, if *inclusiveness* is the criterion then Childs wins hands down.[46]

---

[39] *WCB*, 376.

[40] Plantinga, *WCB*, 388, refers to Levenson's description of HBC in *Hebrew Bible*, 109.

[41] The first four are examples Plantinga uses in his chapter. For his reference to Tracy see Sennett (ed.), *Analytic Theist*, 306, 307.

[42] See Bartholomew, *Reading Ecclesiastes*, 66–68.

[43] *WCB*, 404.

[44] *WCB*, 407.

[45] The similarity between Collins and Davies at this point is remarkable – see *WCB*, 411.

Thus, Plantinga is unable to find any compelling arguments for HBC as
opposed to TBC. Troeltschian HBC has thus no claim on Christians in biblical
studies and Duhemian or Spinozistic HBC have little to go on and yield slender
results. The latter types of HBC raise the important epistemological question of
why one should avoid employing *all* one's resources in the search for truth.
Unlike physics or chemistry, according to Plantinga, the very foundations of
Scripture scholarship are deeply influenced by theological issues.[47] In a review
of Thomas Sheehan's *The First Coming: How the Kingdom of God Became Christianity*, Plantinga presents a strong case for utilizing *all* of our theological
resources in the quest for true knowledge of the Bible. I quote him at length:

> The idea is that a proper Scripture scholar will be 'objective.' Objectivity is some-
> times represented as a matter of sticking to the objective facts, not bringing in any
> theological interpretation. What is really meant in this context, however, is that
> the objective scholar will not use any theological assumptions or knowledge in the
> attempt to determine what the objective facts are ...
>
>   The real question here is this: is it legitimate for a Christian scholar ... to employ
> assumptions or beliefs the source of which is her Christian faith? Can one properly
> employ, in scholarship, assumptions that aren't shared by all members of the scholarly
> community? Can you properly employ what you know by faith? ...
>
>   And isn't it simple common sense that a Christian scholar ... should use every-
> thing she knows in pursuing her discipline? ... If what you want, in scholarship, is to
> reach the truth about matters at hand, then why not use all that you know, regardless
> of its particular source? Isn't it merely perverse to limit yourself to only some of what
> you know, or only some sources of knowledge, if your aim is to reach the truth about
> the phenomenon in question? That would be like trying to do physics, say, without
> in any way relying upon your own memory or the memory of anyone else ... You
> might be able to do a bit of physics that way, but it would be pretty limited, a poor,
> paltry, truncated thing. And why would you want to do it? (Perhaps I could climb
> Devil's Tower with my feet tied together, but why would I want to?) If your aim is to
> reach as much as you can of the full-fledged, full-orbed truth about the matter at
> hand, then presumably the right way to proceed is to use all of your resources, every-
> thing you know, including what you know by faith ...
>
>   This claim – that one ought not to employ the view that Jesus was (is) divine in
> scholarship – rests on the assumption that the only way in which we could properly
> come to characteristically Christian beliefs is by way of ordinary scientific or histori-
> cal investigation. But this assumption is dubious *in excelsis;* it is part and parcel of clas-
> sical Foundationalism and shares its liabilities ...
>
>   What really is at issue here is a philosophical (epistemological) view about
> what constitutes correct or reasonable belief, about what constitutes proper or real
> knowledge.

---

[46] Levenson, *Hebrew Bible*, 120.
[47] *WCB*, 414.

… objectivism is an entirely unnatural position for a Christian to adopt. A more natural position is that if we employ all that we know … we stand a much better chance of getting close to the actual full-orbed truth. And isn't that what we are after in scholarship? So why should we handicap ourselves in the fashion suggested by the objectivist?[48]

Quo Vadis?

This long quote brings us back to where we started, namely with Davies discerning a paradigm shift in studies of the history of Israel and locating the shift in the role of theological beliefs. Davies' and Plantinga's assessments of two types of Scripture scholarship are not that dissimilar, but of course they recommend entirely different types. What can we learn from Plantinga's application of his epistemological insights to biblical interpretation, and do these help us with the issue of history and biblical hermeneutics?

First, it seems to me that Plantinga's work is extremely helpful in positioning Davies' discourse of the academy. Biblical scholars are not trained in epistemology, and in areas like this we are in danger of the one-eyed becoming king. It is very helpful to be able to name Davies' discourse, namely a confusing mix of postmodernism and CF, and to be aware that 'metaepistemology' has not only enabled us to see how dominant CF epistemology has been, but has also facilitated its demise. The boot is now on the other foot, as it were – if Davies and company are going to maintain a sort of CF as normative in the academy, then we need to hear some strong arguments for it; it cannot just be assumed to be *the* discourse of *the* academy. As we have seen, the sort of arguments that Davies, Collins and others do provide – such as it being open to argument and public assessment, it being the ethical option, its inclusiveness – either presuppose the truth of CF or do not hold up to scrutiny. Thus, for example, Childs' approach wins on the issue of inclusiveness. As for the ethical argument, it presupposes the moral rectitude of CF. The most basic consideration of taxation should alert us to the fact that not only CFs pay taxes – what of all the theists who pay taxes *and* send their children to Sheffield University – might that not merit a confessional discourse or two?

CF should thus *not* just be assumed, but I suspect it remains the basic paradigm within which many biblical scholars work, even if Davies' approach is Troeltschian in a way that many others are not. Davies cites James Barr as a scholar who tends to blur the boundaries between theology and biblical studies. Barr certainly retains a real interest in theology and resists Davies' type of policing of the biblical studies/theology border. Barr could not be classified under Troeltschian HBC. However, it seems to me that although Barr retains a

---

[48] Plantinga, in Sennett (ed.), *Analytic Theist*, 325–27.

theological interest, he does so within a CF framework. In *Holy Scripture* he argues that it is not so much in biblical criticism as in *modern critical theology* in which a major shift came about. What changed was '*the conditions under which people were prepared to believe*'.[49] Perhaps even more precisely, he could have said that peoples' *epistemology* changed. 'What made the difference in the eighteenth century was not biblical criticism as such, but a more critical theological attitude to the sources of all belief, of which the Bible was first or at least central.'[50] And what does Barr mean by 'critical'?

> By criticism, when used of theology, I mean this: that the establishment of theological truth does not take place by a mere passive acceptance of data given by the sources of revelation, but takes place through a critical and estimative weighing of these data. The theologian asks 'Is this true?' and in doing so he asks '*Why* is this true?' ... Theology itself therefore must be critical; and, seen from the side of theology, its own critical nature is a much more important matter than the so-called 'historical criticism' of the biblical books.[51]

Barr's description of 'critical' betrays the telltale signs of CF: 'critical' precludes passive acceptance of the data of revelation. Presumably this would cover and exclude Plantinga's notion of belief in God as properly basic. Data must be accepted only on the basis of adequate evidence – production of rational evidence is the only acceptable response to the question, '*Why* is this true?' And Barr understands theology as operating within this broader, critical production of knowledge. He describes theology as at the apex of the knowledge pyramid, deeply dependent upon the lower, largely non-theological levels.[52]

Looking at Davies' and Barr's work in this context indicates just how helpful epistemological awareness can be. I have drawn in my discussion not just on Plantinga's chapter on biblical interpretation, but also on his and others' work on CF. It strikes me on reflection that it is important to see Plantinga's three types of HBC in their *common* indebtedness to CF in order to discern the radicality of Plantinga's challenge. It is the philosophical commitments informing these types of biblical criticism, and *not* their use of biblical criticism per se, that is the problem. Indeed, HBC may not be the best name for these three types of biblical interpretation, as it suggests that Christian scholars will eschew (historical) biblical criticism, even though this is a point that Plantinga specifically denies.[53] Indeed Robert Gordon, Plantinga and myself all agree that there

---

[49] Barr, *Holy Scripture*, 121 (emphasis mine).

[50] Barr, *Holy Scripture*, 121.

[51] Barr, *Holy Scripture*, 121.

[52] Barr, *Holy Scripture*, 117.

[53] *WCB*, 386. In my own pilgrimage, G.E. Ladd's little book on criticism and C. Amerding's book on OT interpretation were great helps in coming to see just how helpful biblical criticism can be.

can be such a thing as historical, critical investigation of Scripture that is faithful to Christian convictions. One of the great challenges for biblical interpretation is to tease out what a healthy biblical criticism looks like when informed by appropriate philosophical commitments.

Secondly, does a recognition and critique of the dominance of CF in (post)modern biblical studies mean that we should reject its results *tout court?* By no means – many, many gains have been made in modern biblical study – but it *does* mean that we take careful note of what I heard described as Sheffield's 'unbelief seeking understanding'. Critical Christian scholarship will need to be aware of the epistemology undergirding Davies' approach to Israel in the OT, for example, and be cautious of its influence upon his reading of the Bible.[54]

It should also be noted that it would be quite wrong to assume that we will all necessarily agree with Plantinga's epistemology of religious belief. It is not the only brand on offer, and serious debates are taking place between him and other (Christian) scholars on these issues. Some, for example, are defending Aquinas's view of religious belief which is more in line with CF. Presumably this would yield a different assessment of contemporary biblical interpretation.[55]

Thirdly, if Plantinga is right, then we should not be afraid of putting our Christian beliefs to work in biblical studies, even though such an approach will inevitably draw forth the dreaded f-word![56] Childs's canonical approach to the Bible evoked a storm of criticism. It is not always easy to get to the bottom of this at times vitriolic response, but a recurring criticism is that Childs introduces *theology* into biblical studies. This, as we have seen, is at the heart of Davies' criticism of Childs – Childs's project is found to be not purely historical but tainted by confessional interests. Within the CF paradigm this is a damning indictment indeed – it is a case of introducing data for which there is no evidence, and the only category that CF seems to have for this is fundamentalism. However, once we reject the CF-ist paradigm and adopt an epistemology of religious belief such as that of Plantinga, the obstacle to introducing theological issues is removed. Thus, *an* important response to Davies' accusation of bringing theology into biblical studies would be to say, 'Yes, and so what?'

A major influence upon Childs's canonical approach is the theology of Karl Barth. Intriguingly, Plantinga suggests that his epistemology is in line with, and

---

[54] See Buckley, *Origins*, for the danger of Christians giving way on the epistemological ground rules. Buckley argues persuasively that the origins of modern atheism in the West resulted to a large extent from the self-alienation of religion in which religion looked to philosophy to establish the existence of God. 'In an effort to secure its basis, religion unknowingly fathered its own estrangement' (359).

[55] See Zagzebski (ed.), *Rational Faith*, for a series of Catholic responses to Plantinga.

[56] I.e., fundamentalism! See *WCB*, 244–46.

explains, the epistemology of Barth's opposition to natural theology.[57] And Barth's influence underlies to a significant extent the current, minority renewal in theological interpretation. An implication of Plantinga's work is that we should not regard this kind of *theological* interpretation as somehow marginal to the real work of biblical studies. Theological interpretation of the Bible as Scripture – whether it be the canonical interpretation of Childs, Seitz and Watson; or varieties of postliberal interpretation in the line of Frei and Lindbeck; or Brueggemann's style of theological interpretation; or traditional biblical commentary of an evangelical sort – has just as much right to be part of the discourse of the academy as Davies' a-theistic type of scholarship.

I understand Davies' desire to do non-theistic biblical studies. But surely a more *just* paradigm than the discourse of the academy for biblical studies would be a *genuine* pluralism in the academy, in which biblical studies could be done rigorously in the context of different academic discourses – of which Christian theism would be one – rather than the coercive insistence that only Davies' discourse of the academy is acceptable. This, I think, connects with my earlier query as to whether or not, as Thiselton suggests, greater awareness of philosophy of religion will defuse the polarizations in biblical studies. Awareness of Plantinga's work would subvert the view that what Davies does is 'knowledge' and appropriate to the academy, whereas what Brevard Childs and Gordon Wenham and Richard Hays do is 'belief' and not true, critical knowledge. If Davies can provide a defence of his epistemology, then it ought also to be taken seriously as *a* contender for knowledge. Such awareness would *refigure* the polarizations in biblical studies, but I'm not sure it would necessarily reduce them. Perhaps it would enable the real dialogue to begin?

Fourthly, I think Plantinga's work bears on *the nature of* theological interpretation of the Bible. I have tried to address some of the important differences among proponents of theological interpretation in an earlier volume,[58] in which I argued that biblical interpretation cannot and should not avoid general hermeneutics. Yes, we should make overtly theological issues a priority in biblical interpretation – these have been avoided for too long. But no, this cannot be at the expense of ignoring the broader hermeneutical issues. Plantinga, rightly in my opinion, alerts us to the fact that when we are thinking about history and the Bible, theology is powerfully present in the *roots* of this discussion. We need, I suggest, a theology of history to shape this discussion – one that impacts at the general hermeneutical level and not just at the level of theological interpretation. In this respect I think Barr is right to insist that theology and theological interpretation involve a variety of disciplines such as

---

[57] See Sennett (ed.), *Analytic Theist*, 143ff.
[58] Bartholomew, 'Uncharted Waters'.

language, philosophy and history. Where I disagree with Barr is concerning the extent to which these are non-theological. Theology is not just at the apex of Barr's pyramid, but it also informs the foundations, that is, *inter alia* the epistemology.

Fifthly, by far the most interesting question in my opinion is how the historical question of the Bible looks in the context of *faith* seeking understanding rather than in the context of unbelief seeking understanding. A quick read of Iain Provan's stimulating chapter in this volume foregrounds the following as key issues in discussions of the search for ancient Israel: epistemology, testimony, tradition, scientific, memory.[59] And these terms are major topics in the epistemological work of Plantinga, Alston, Wolterstorff and others. Can the work of these Christian philosophers help us towards a faith seeking understanding of the history of the Bible? I think it can, but in the following terms.

It is quite clear from Plantinga's work and Alston's and Wolterstorff's[60] that a theologically informed approach does not yield a fundamentalism in which all historical problems in the Bible disappear. Rather, it moves us in the direction that Stephen Neill identified years ago as a major requirement in NT scholarship, namely, a theology of history.[61] As Neill discerned, this will not solve the problems – but it will provide the ring within which solutions may be found. However, as long as all of our energies are directed towards analysing the historical problems of the Bible on the basis of ground rules established according to CF, it is hard to get too excited about the results. What we urgently need are studies of the history of the OT and NT that are framed in a perspective of faith seeking understanding, in the grip of such an epistemology – this will enable us to discern the real problems and to advance towards genuine solutions.[62]

Take the Ten Commandments, for example. David Clines says of them, 'Did God (if there is a God) actually speak audible words out of the sky over a mountain in the Arabian peninsula in the late second millennium BCE? … it will not shock many readers of these pages if I say I do not believe that any such thing ever happened, and that I would be surprised if any scholarly reader did either'.[63] Clines presents no arguments for this view but simply says that even commentators who pretend that the Ten Commandments contain divine words know full well that they are in fact thoroughly human. For all his postmodernism, Clines's view is deeply influenced by an approach that excludes the possibility of God acting and speaking in the world.[64] Without for a moment trying to argue that there is a one-to-one correspondence between

---

[59] 'Knowing and Believing: Faith in the Past', Ch. 11.
[60] See, e.g., his comments on the Gospels in *Divine Discourse*.
[61] Neill and Wright, *Interpretation*, 366.
[62] This is not to deny that we already have good examples of this!
[63] Clines, 'Ten Commandments', 27, 28.

the telling of the giving of the commandments in Exodus 20 and Deuteronomy 5 and what actually happened, from a theistic perspective there is nothing unbelievable about God speaking to a particular group in history so that the possibility of God speaking the Ten Commandments to the Israelites should not be ruled out. Indeed, I take it from Plantinga's epistemology that I do not need evidence of a foundationalist sort for such a belief to be ruled in, and that I may be warranted as a biblical scholar in taking this belief as knowledge.

The really interesting question for me that follows from this, is how to relate such a belief to the different versions of the Ten Commandments in Exodus and Deuteronomy, and to the diverse data of Old Testament law that we find in the Pentateuch. The development of hypotheses along these lines within the context of faith seeking understanding would, I suggest, produce creative scholarly proposals from a Christian perspective and make possible real dialogue with alternative approaches such as those of Davies and Clines, even if at points it enhances rather than reduces the polarity in biblical studies. It is greatly to the credit of Alvin Plantinga that he pushes us in this direction.

---

[64] Clines rightly notes that the texts of the Ten Commandments claim that God spoke the ten words, and he is also helpful in his analysis of four different ways in which scholars avoid this claim. Unfortunately, what is never in view is how an intelligent Christian approach might affirm that God spoke the Ten Commandments as well as the possibility of a complex relationship between that speech and the forms of the texts as we have them.

Bibliography

Alston, W.P., 'Plantinga's Epistemology of Religious Belief', in *Alvin Plantinga* (ed. J.E. Tomberlin and P. Van Inwagen; Profiles 5; Dordrecht: D. Reidel, 1985), 289–312

Armerding, C.E., *The Old Testament and Criticism* (Grand Rapids: Eerdmans, 1983)

Barr, J., *Holy Scripture: Canon, Authority, Criticism* (Oxford: Clarendon Press, 1983)

Bartholomew, C.G., *Reading Ecclesiastes: Old Testament Exegesis and Hermeneutical Theory* (Rome: Pontifical Biblical Institute, 1998)

——, 'Uncharted Waters: Philosophy, Theology and the Crisis in Biblical Interpretation', in *Renewing Biblical Interpretation* (ed. C.G. Bartholomew, C. Greene and K. Möller; SHS 1; Carlisle: Paternoster; Grand Rapids: Zondervan, 2000), 1–39

Bright, J., *A History of Israel* (Philadelphia: Westminster Press, 1972)

Buckley, M.J., *At the Origins of Modern Atheism* (New Haven: Yale University Press, 1987)

Clark, K.J., 'Introduction: The Literature of Confession', in *Philosophers Who Believe* (ed. K.J. Clarke; Downers Grove, IL: InterVarsity Press, 1993), 7–21

——, (ed.), *Philosophers Who Believe: The Spiritual Journey of 11 Leading Thinkers* (Downers Grove, IL: InterVarsity Press, 1993)

Clifford, W.K., 'The Ethics of Belief', in *Lectures and Essays* (London: Macmillan, 1879)

Clines, D.J.A., *Interested Parties: The Ideology of Writers and Readers of the Hebrew Bible* (JSOTSup 205; Sheffield: Sheffield Academic Press, 1995)

——, 'The Ten Commandments, Reading from Left to Right', in *Interested Parties: The Ideology of Writers and Readers of the Hebrew Bible* (ed. D.J.A. Clines; JSOTSup 205; Sheffield: Sheffield Academic Press, 1995), 26–45

Davies, P.R., *In Search of 'Ancient Israel'* (JSOTSup 148; Sheffield: Sheffield Academic Press, 1992, 1995)

——, *Whose Bible Is it Anyway?* (JSOTSup 204; Sheffield: Sheffield Academic Press, 1995)

Evans, C.S., *Faith Beyond Reason* (Reason and Religion; Edinburgh: Edinburgh University Press, 1998)

Hoitenga, D.J., Jr., *Faith and Reason from Plato to Plantinga: An Introduction to Reformed Epistemology* (Albany, NY: State University of New York Press, 1991)

Ladd, G.E., *The New Testament and Criticism* (London: Hodder & Stoughton, 1970)

Lemche, N.P., *Prelude to Israel's Past: Background and Beginnings of Israelite History and Identity* (Peabody, MA: Hendrickson, 1998)

Levenson, J.D., *The Hebrew Bible, the Old Testament, and Historical Criticism* (Louisville, KY: Westminster / John Knox Press, 1993)

Neill, S., and N.T. Wright, *The Interpretation of the New Testament 1861–1986* (Oxford: OUP), 366

Plantinga, A., 'Alvin Plantinga: Self-Profile', in *Alvin Plantinga* (ed. J.E. Tomberlin and P. Van Inwagen; Profiles 5; Dordrecht: D. Reidel, 1985), 3–97

——, *Warrant: The Current Debate* (New York: OUP, 1993)

——, *Warrant and Proper Function* (New York: OUP, 1993)

✓ ——, *Warranted Christian Belief* (New York: OUP, 2000)

——, 'A Christian Life Partly Lived', in *Philosophers Who Believe* (ed. K.J. Clarke; Downers Grove, IL: InterVarsity Press, 1993), 45–82

✓ ——, and N. Wolterstorff (eds.), *Faith and Rationality: Reason and Belief in God* (Notre Dame: University of Notre Dame Press, 1983)

Sennett, J.F., *Modality, Probability, and Rationality: A Critical Examination of Alvin Plantinga's Philosophy* (American University Studies; Bern: Peter Lang, 1992)

——, (ed.), *The Analytic Theist: An Alvin Plantinga Reader* (Grand Rapids: Eerdmans, 1998)

✓ Thiselton, A.C., 'Communicative Action and Promise in Interdisciplinary, Biblical, and Theological Hermeneutics', in *The Promise of Hermeneutics* (ed. R. Lundin, C. Walhout and A.C. Thiselton; Grand Rapids: Eerdmans; Carlisle: Paternoster, 1999), 133–239

Thompson, T.L., *Early History of the Israelite People: From the Written and Archaeological Sources* (SHANE 4; Leiden: Brill, 1992)

Tomberlin, J.E., and P. Van Inwagen (eds.), *Alvin Plantinga* (Profiles 5; Dordrecht: D. Reidel, 1985)

✓ Wolterstorff, N., 'Introduction' in *Faith and Rationality: Reason and Belief in God* (ed. A. Plantinga and N. Wolterstorff; Notre Dame: University of Notre Dame Press, 1983), 1–15

✓ ——, *Divine Discourse: Philosophical Reflections on the Claim that God Speaks* (Cambridge: CUP, 1995)

✓ Zagzebski, L. (ed.), *Rational Faith: Catholic Responses to Reformed Epistemology* (Notre Dame: University of Notre Dame Press, 1993)

3

A Warranted Version of Historical Biblical Criticism?

A Response to Alvin Plantinga

Robert P. Gordon

When, as a biblical exegete, I (but very rarely) engage with a philosopher or dogmatician on the nature of Scripture, my mind runs quickly to the story of Israel at Sinai. There on the mountain receiving the lively oracles is Moses (for whom read 'philosopher' or 'dogmatician'), while down on the plain are the Israelite exegetes under Aaron, fashioning the golden calf and giving up on Moses. It is good and helpful to have the philosopher and the dogmatician lay down the lines, and it is good and helpful for the exegete to check that the lines touch the ground. My chapter has much more to do with texts than with the high doctrines that Plantinga writes about, nevertheless there are various points of intersection at this lowlier level, and I am privileged to attempt a response to such a distinguished practitioner.

I find very much with which to agree in what Plantinga writes in Chapter 12 of *Warranted Christian Belief*. In particular, I too believe that the true and effective apprehension of what Scripture teaches about the 'good things' of the Gospel depends upon human receptivity to God through the divine Spirit. Otherwise the study of Scripture is a form of antiquarianism, much practised as such and well worth pursuing as such, but a totally different pursuit from what Scripture professes itself to be about and from what the faith of the church has always proclaimed – and always will so long as it merits recognition as Christ's body on earth. Moreover, if there were no 'divine voices' in biblical times, as some aver, there are none now, the attempt to read off messages of authority or special worth from, say, a 'demythologized' text scarce merits the bother. The reception and appropriation of a proposition such as that 'Christ died for our sins according to the Scriptures' (1 Cor. 15:3) is always going to lie beyond the reaches of historical quest and verification, no matter how sound or how consensually powerful our historical method. Even the best possible arguments in defence of such a central Christian dogma as Christ's resurrection will leave a mighty gulf between conviction about this as a historical event, or about the probability of it, and the conviction that underlies the confessional statement just quoted from 1 Corinthians 15:3. 'Ordinary' Christians recognize this instinctively, and this is one of the reasons why Van Harvey has to complain that, despite decades of biblical research, the average person thinks of the life of Jesus much as they did a few centuries ago.[1] In other words, even if they were convinced that historical-critical method could deliver secure(r) results at ground level – and they have been given good reason to doubt that much – they recognize that even this could lift the inquirer no higher than the ground.

In all this, Scripture provides the text for discussion, and the particular question that Plantinga raises and that I wish to pursue concerns the part that 'Historical Biblical Criticism' (HBC) should have in the Christian reception of, and response to, Scripture. For practical purposes, Plantinga accepts the definition of HBC put out by some of its most convinced practitioners, who also claim to be representative of the general tendency. Since their pronouncements on HBC are not only radical but demonstrably elitist, he remains hugely sceptical of the right of this intruder to be in the Lord's house. But he wishes to pay tribute where he can: HBC has taught us a great deal about the Bible that we might not otherwise have known, and some of its methods have been assimilated to good effect by traditional biblical commentary.[2] It has contributed greatly to our knowledge of the circumstances and conditions in which the biblical books were composed.[3] And yet it is judged to have little to offer the Christian believer as far as the appropriation of the 'good things' of the faith is concerned. As the first page of Chapter 12 makes clear,[4] it is not the serious and scholarly study of Scripture that causes this (quickly resolving) ambivalence on Plantinga's part, but the presuppositions that inform HBC, especially in what he calls its 'Troeltschian' form: it depends on reason alone, and allows nothing that traditional Christianity would associate with revelation and faith.[5] There are other problems with it, such as its dependence on the well-named 'fallacy of creeping certitude'[6] and its requirement, according to some of

---

[1] Plantinga, *WCB*, 401.

[2] *WCB*, 386.

[3] *WCB*, 401.

[4] *WCB*, 374.

[5] *WCB*, 386.

[6] *WCB*, 402.

its advocates, that even fundamentalists must be reborn as liberals in order to qualify for the pursuit of this 'science'.[7]

As I have indicated, and as we would assume, Plantinga is a strong advocate of traditional biblical scholarship, which he distinguishes clearly from HBC (in the forms that he attributes to it). I want to suggest in this response that there are good reasons for people of faith to lay claim to HBC, in some form or other, as a department of 'the scholarly study of the Bible' and as a legitimate and necessary tool of biblical research. As Plantinga notes, there is 'vast disagreement' within HBC as regards both method and conclusions,[8] and this alone suggests that it should be capacious enough to house the faith-based scholar. It is at root, after all, 'historical study',[9] and none should exclude themselves. Nor is anyone authorized to lay down the membership requirements.[10] Men and women of Christian (or, for that matter, Jewish) faith should not have to become honorary liberals or radicals in order to participate. Nor, if they participate, are they to be dismissed as 'feeling in a semi-confused way that this is the epistemically respectable or privileged way of proceeding'.[11]

In this short contribution I want to look first at a key concept that separates Plantinga from classic HBC, probably in any of its recognized forms. Then I shall suggest ways in which HBC, properly constituted, may help in the elucidation of Scripture. Finally, I offer some comment on why HBC has become so comfortably installed in Moses' seat.

The Principal Author

The 'principal author' concept is of front rank importance for Plantinga.[12] The recognition of God as 'principal author' of the Bible involves the corollary that only what the 'principal author' says through the medium of Scripture is of any consequence for the understanding of the ultimate ('Gospel') message of Scripture. And what God wishes to say through Scripture may be quite distinct from what the human author had in mind.[13] Now, it is clear from the context and from the list of examples cited that Plantinga has in mind those Old

---

[7] *WCB*, 412.

[8] *WCB*, 402.

[9] *WCB*, 374.

[10] *Pace* Troeltsch and followers, see *WCB*, 391.

[11] *WCB*, 403; cf. p. 399, where Plantinga waxes very bold and judges it unlikely that a 'real live Scripture scholar' will have reflected much on 'the epistemological foundations of the discipline'.

[12] E.g., *WCB*, 384.

[13] *WCB*, 385.

Testament references that are said in the New Testament to predict some aspect of the Christ event. The Old Testament writers, it is observed, may have had nothing explicitly about Christ in mind when they wrote as they did; they 'may not so much as have thought of what is, in fact, the teaching of the passage in question'.[14] Something of the sort may be implied in 1 Peter 1:10–12 where, however, the Hebrew prophets are envisaged as having some insight into the longer-term, and perhaps even messianic, nature of their prophesying.[15] What is not clear is whether Plantinga thinks that other types of messages unimagined by the original authors may also have been encoded in Scripture by the 'principal author'. His reference to 'what the Lord intends to teach us' could have a limited or a more extended reach, but the former is less likely in view of the footnoted suggestion that texts may have variable significance: a passage (which undoubtedly meant something to its first readers) could be intended to teach one thing to a fifth-century reader, and something else to a twenty-first century reader.[16]

On the face of it, this seems to invite a question about the location of the message: is it in the text or in the mind of the 'principal author'?[17] Of course, God could know how many ways he might intend a text to be taken, and how many ways a text might additionally be taken, but too much of this could begin to undermine the idea of proprietorial authorship, if we are not careful. Indeed, this variability of meaning (or message[18]) as envisaged by Plantinga opens up large vistas and encourages a further thought. If, for instance, we advert directly to HBC for a moment, we might also inquire whether an all-knowing God who provides such a multifaceted text in the form of Scripture might not also have taken account of the prevailing modes of thought in the several eras for which his word was cast. Since he appears to have been happy with allegory (for example) as a key to the profounder aspects of Scripture, might he not also be willing to conspire with, say, 'Duhemian' HBC in an age when his people find themselves as deep as ever in the epistemological mire?

---

[14] *WCB*, 385.

[15] One would very much have liked to hear Plantinga further on the status of the meaning available to the human author when God had something different in mind.

[16] *WCB*, 385, n. 12.

[17] When addressing the issue of 'clairvoyance' Plantinga may have answered my question. If God is 'principal author', then clairvoyance is not required on the part of a human author for his prophecy to refer to something happening much later than the prophet's own time, since all then depends on the omniscience of God (*WCB*, 400, n. 43). Still, as possible 'meanings' or 'messages' multiply, the question of location remains for consideration.

[18] In the original form of this chapter I picked up Plantinga's use of 'meaning', but graduated a few lines later to 'message', since (as he rightly noted in his response) 'meaning' is usually associated with texts in this kind of discussion.

At the risk of overlap with the next section, I also want to issue a couple of caveats on how an absolutist or exclusivist stance on 'principal author' could affect our appreciation of important aspects of Scripture. The first concerns the playing down of dialectical or developmental aspects of Scripture, which in important respects may fairly be described as being in dialogue with itself. As examples of topics on which the Old Testament is obviously 'dialogical' in this sense I would cite divine presence and afterlife. In either case a number of differing perspectives are represented, and it is important in exegesis not simply to override the partial insights of one or another text with the composite view derivable from the whole Hebrew or Christian canon. There is value in considering the literary and historical settings of texts that may strike us as partial in their insight or as transitional in form. If a psalmist holds out no hope of praising God in the afterlife, as in Psalm 115:17 ('It is not the dead who praise the LORD, those who go down into silence'; cf. Ps. 88:5, 10), we can certainly move to consideration of the rounded teaching of Scripture on the subject, but we may also find profit in letting the errant text have its voice. Evidently this particular psalmist believed and rejoiced in God without needing the prompt of the hope of an afterlife – rather as C.S. Lewis noted of the early days of his own spiritual pilgrimage.[19] To rewrite the psalmist on the point, as did the original *Living Bible*, is therefore doubly objectionable. In fact, the process that Plantinga describes for commentary work on Plato[20] has a lot in common with that required for the understanding of biblical texts, granted with Plantinga that, for the believing reader, the question of authority separates Plato and the Bible. The two appear so dissimilar[21] partly because of the telescoped account of the biblical exegetical process given there.

A second problem with the traditional scholarly study of Scripture and its emphasis on 'principal author' is that it also, like HBC, brackets out issues from discussion. In this case it is not, of course, the exclusion of what is deemed to be historically inaccessible, but of what is deemed to be theologically inadmissible. Yet given the extent to which the two Testaments co-inhere with the literary and cultural conventions of the worlds in which they were formed, there are categories and possibilities that serious biblical criticism should at least consider. The creative retelling of narratives, pseudonymity, *vaticinia ex eventu* and composite authorship are among the features of ancient Jewish (and more generally Near Eastern) literature that traditional scholarship has found difficult to embrace. Nor is the effect of such consorting always negative. For example, HBC makes it easier to understand why animals are created before humans in

---

[19] Quoted in Vanauken, *Severe Mercy*, 92.
[20] *WCB*, 383–84.
[21] See *WCB*, 383–84.

Genesis 1 but after Adam in Genesis 2.[22] It offers the possibility that the biblical text presents two creation narratives whose distinctive perspectives are preserved in the composite account of creation that now occupies Genesis 1 and 2. The alternative of a blatant contradiction within a single original composition actually fails to do justice to the biblical text. A similar point might be made about the appearance of vegetation in relation to the creation of humans, in Genesis 1:11–12 as compared with Genesis 2:4–7. All this, and more, escapes the attention of those who insist that 'Genesis 1 teaches' the creation of the universe – strictly, those parts mentioned or implied in the chapter – in six days of twenty-four hours each. For, by so arguing, they elevate one Genesis creation narrative above the other and turn narrative perspectival differences into outright contradictions. If, as is so often claimed, contrary 'non-creationist' positions are supported by bad science, the solution is not to be found in equally bad biblical exegesis.

Thus the concept of 'principal author', for all its obvious merit, needs careful handling. From a traditional Christian point of view it serves well in that it deals with both the particulars of Scripture and the overall authority that Christian believers acknowledge it to possess. Variations on the theme such as 'general editor', or even 'series editor', would also have analogical worth provided that, in highlighting the human factor in the composition of Scripture, including the 'library' aspect of both Testaments, they did not exclude the essential element represented in 'principal author'.

The Value of HBC

There are several reasons why a 'warranted' version of HBC might exercise a benevolent effect on biblical study. First, I would suggest that the dividing wall between traditional biblical scholarship and HBC is not as substantial as it may seem. Calvin may be called as witness in this regard. Plantinga very credibly lists him on the traditional side of the critical divide, yet Calvin is sufficiently aware of critical issues, and is sometimes sufficiently unorthodox in his handling of them, as to lead some later exponents of HBC to claim him as evincing early HBC sympathies. As is well known, he was quite relaxed on the inerrancy question.[23] If HBC is mainly concerned about authorship and composition, as

---

[22] Even the invocation of the pluperfect in 2:19 does not relieve the tension, since it does not prove that the animals were created before Adam.

[23] Calvin comments on the surprising attribution of a text to Jeremiah in Mt. 27:9: 'How the name "Jeremiah" crept in here I must confess I do not know and I do not much care. "Jeremiah" was certainly put in error for "Zechariah"' (cf. Parker, *Calvin*, 192).

Plantinga notes,[24] then scholars of all types should be interested in this aspect of the HBC agenda, even if presuppositions may vary somewhat.

Secondly, the usefulness of the results of interaction with HBC should not be underestimated. And if HBC in one of its less prescriptive (e.g. Plantinga's 'Duhemian') modes still cannot 'prove' the resurrection, it might nevertheless demonstrate (for example) that belief in the resurrection is present at all presumed levels of Gospel and New Testament tradition; and that would be a conclusion worth having. Study alone, it is true, will not substantiate the doctrine of the resurrection in the mind of a believer, but it could provide an important bridge to such conviction by establishing what is the univocal testimony of the New Testament. At the very least, an obstacle to faith could be unsettled.

Thirdly, HBC can act as a corrective against easy, traditional assumptions about the nature of the biblical text and its composition. It was not 'scholarly study of Scripture' in the non-HBC sense that opened up the possibility that 'pan-Mosaism' does not reflect the circumstances of the composition of the Pentateuch and may even go beyond what the Bible itself has to say on the subject. Nor was study of this sort able to suggest that the psalm titles might be secondary additions to the text, even though they occasionally fail to match psalm contents and are even contradictory of mainline Scripture in one or two cases. But here I fight with one hand tied behind my back, since non-HBC 'scholarly study of Scripture' tends to reject even those proposals of HBC that might have some solid basis to them.

Fourthly, and as a subjoinder to the point made in the preceding paragraph, HBC can contribute healthily on the complex issue of the relationship between the two Testaments. There is, admittedly, a great deal of doublethink among those Christian exponents of HBC who want to hold on to Christianity as in some sense a revelation from God and yet insist on treating the Old Testament as a self-contained, closed system which offers no bridges directly to the New Testament. But however exactly the relationship is to be defined, it would be the sublimest oddity were God to be involved revelatorily in the Hebrew era and then in the Christian, and for this reality not to be reflected in *both* Testaments. God as 'principal author' addresses this issue. However, the devil really is in the detail here, and this is where HBC or something remarkably like it can come to the rescue. For example, traditional biblical scholarship has not been successful in preserving the believing community from inventing a series of unlikely 'fulfilments' of the Old Testament in the New. The 'direct hit' approach has been the norm: the direct alignment of Old Testament 'predictions' with New Testament events.

Now, without at all ruling out the predictive in Scripture, we can still appreciate that there are problems with this approach. The Matthean nativity

---

[24] *WBC*, 389.

prooftexts, to take an obvious example, not only include one that is very difficult to track down in the Old Testament (see Mt. 2:23), but also one that works
only because it has been completely recontextualized. When Matthew relates
the Holy Family's flight into Egypt to Hosea 11:1 he can quote no more than
he does ('Out of Egypt have I called my son', Mt. 2:15), for the Hoseanic text is
talking about disobedient Israel, and continues with the christologically
incompatible observation that the calling had an opposite effect to what was
intended: 'they sacrificed to Baals and burnt incense to idols' (Hos. 11:2). Here
a question arises as to whether the Matthean meaning or 'message' is to be
regarded as implicit in the prophetic text (which is, of course, a historical statement rather than a prediction) and as, in any sense, a 'direct hit' fulfilment of it.
Or perhaps it is something else. Of course, one may have recourse to, say,
typology in order to explain the relevance of the Hoseanic text to the life of
Christ. One need not even limit oneself to atomistic prising of the text from its
original context, since, from a typological perspective, Hosea 11 could be
taken to imply a contrast between historical Israel and the 'true Israel' personi-
fied in Messiah. But immediately we set out on this track we are dealing with
something more complex (or even more sophisticated) than 'direct hit'
fulfilment.

Commitment to 'direct hit' prophecy has left some elements of evangelicalism in denial over such a text as Isaiah 7:14 where, against the evidence, the
word ʿalmah has been given the very specific sense of 'virgin' – though no-one
would suggest that when Saul uses the masculine equivalent in reference to
David he is asking 'Whose son is that virgin-lad?' (1 Sam. 17:55). Since, if ever
a prophetic text did, Isaiah 7:14 has as its first port of call the circumstances of
the prophet's own lifetime (see verse 16), it is as well that ʿalmah does not mean
'virgin'. Christian faith knows only one virginal conception (cf. Mt. 1:22–23).
One may briefly illustrate the problems of 'direct hit' from a couple of other
texts. Psalm 72 was early dubbed 'messianic' and so interpreted of the end-
time reign of Christ – this helped by the use of the future indicative in several
verses where perhaps the optative (e.g., 'may he endure', v. 5) would be at
least as appropriate (cf. NIV footnote). Famously, in verse 15, where the
Hebrew text has 'Prayer shall be made for him continually' / 'May prayer be
made for him continually', the Prayer Book version has 'prayer shall be made
ever *unto* him'; for it is inconceivable that prayer should be offered *on behalf of*
Christ ruling as the Davidic Messiah. And so also one version of a popular
Christian hymn has the line, 'To him shall endless prayer be made'. Again, the
traditional interpretation of the wounds 'between [the] hands' in Zechariah
13:6 in the light of the crucifixion of Christ runs against the plain sense of the
expression and of the passage, but still survives in a context of pietistic 'direct
hit' reading of the Old Testament. That the words are actually addressed to a

false prophet who apparently has been involved in orgiastic rites makes the messianic application all the more regrettable.[25]

This kind of 'direct hit' treatment of Old Testament texts belongs within a larger framework of what David Clines has dubbed 'Christomonism'. Many Christian readers and students of Scripture apply 'Christomonism' with the most honourable intent, but its effects are not all good. One of its chief weaknesses is that it rubs out many of the contour lines of the Old Testament which, under the worst excesses of this regime, is valued only insofar as it offers typological or allegorical illustration of the life and work of Christ. But 'Christ in all the Scriptures' is a slogan that has been misapplied by too many preachers and writers. It diverts attention from other lessons that the biblical text is intended to teach, creates an air of jejune sameness about an otherwise rich and varied text, and inevitably depends for credibility on a principle of selectivity, involving the highlighting of biddable elements in the narrative and the downplaying of others less so. For how otherwise could anyone in the Old Testament foreshadow in the detail of their life history the life, death and resurrection of a divine Messiah? Parallels can be drawn, as Stephen's speech illustrates in Acts 7, in its references to Joseph and Moses as (initially rejected) deliverers of their people; but there is an excess to be avoided that even traditional scholarly study of Scripture has not adequately monitored, and that the aims and methods of HBC can help check. There will also be the occasional exegetical gain, as in Hebrews 7:3, where 'direct hit' robs the New Testament of perhaps its most outstanding text on the eternal pre-existence of Christ. To remove the shadowy figure of Melchizedek, mentioned in Genesis 14 and Psalm 110, from the historical plane and then turn him into a pre-incarnate manifestation of Christ commits such a robbery – quite apart from the logical and exegetical entanglements that it introduces into the Hebrews passage.

I reserve for special mention the New Testament's use of Septuagintal (mis)interpretations or mistranslations in confirmation of Christian teaching (e.g., Acts 15:17 [Amos 9:12]; Heb. 10:5 [Ps. 40:6]; Heb. 10:37 [Hab. 2:3][26]). What these texts represent varies: the sense expounded by the New Testament writer may be reflected in the parent text independently of the mistranslated element, or the New Testament writer may develop an interpretative line that is already represented in the Septuagint but that is not in agreement with the standard Hebrew text. Is one required in certain circumstances to say that one of the meanings that God originally had in mind is represented in the

---

[25] The lack of a historical perspective is also, of course, one of the reasons why thoroughgoing dispensationalism still flourishes in many circles.

[26] 'Apostolus, articulo addito, verba prophetae eleganter flectit ad Christum' (Bengel on Heb. 10:37, quoted in Alford, *Greek Testament*, 205).

Septuagint (mis)translation? I do not overlook the possibility that the 'mistrans-lation' may reflect an early Jewish interpretative tradition, and is therefore not 'mistranslation' *tout simple*. Nevertheless, there is a point to be addressed here, and the view that the New Testament writers used such texts of Scripture as were available, and that this was a legitimate part of Scripture-making, seems the simple and safer solution.

Whence Came HBC?

Plantinga reports as a common explanation of much of modern academic dependence upon HBC the *force majeure* of 'our historical position': 'we are all in the grip of historical forces beyond our control'.[27] Thus does he summarize modernity's response to the supernatural elements in the biblical witness, and to the world-view that they reflect. And to the extent that the *force majeure* claim applies, Plantinga gives good reasons for dismissing it. I note with special sympathy his comments on arrogance dressed up as historical necessity.[28] I would, at the same time, want to suggest that some of the impetus for HBC comes from the Bible itself, and from the questions that it prompts in the mind of the attentive reader. This goes some way towards explaining why tradition-alists at heart are drawn into HBC-type scholarship; it is not just that they are a bit confused and take cover in a 'respectable' consensus as they do their biblical research.[29] Perhaps the Gospels themselves give rise to HBC-type questions. Did Jesus repeat many of his sayings and actions, and sometimes more than once, with variations usually of a minor sort? Or is something else going on in the Synoptics? For most readers of the Gospels the answer is obvious (in most cases), but we should not overlook the kinds of judgements that go to make up this 'obvious' decision.

Many and various are the remaining HBC-type issues raised in Scripture: the creation narratives in Genesis 1–2; the occurrence and the distribution of the divine name in Genesis (cf. Ex. 6:2–3); the large numbers in the Exodus (and other) narratives; the variant forms of such a foundational document as the Decalogue (see Ex. 20 and Deut. 5); the stances of Joshua and Judges on the 'conquest' of Canaan; the existence of a Qumran version of Judges 6 without the 'Deuteronomic' speech of verses 7–10; the synoptic-type questions posed by a comparison of Samuel–Kings with Chronicles; differences between the Hebrew and Greek texts of Old Testament books (including rival Hebrew and Greek texts of Samuel and Jeremiah); the psalm titles in relation to their psalms

---

[27] *WBC*, 403.
[28] *WBC*, 405.
[29] Cf. *WBC*, 403.

and to other Old Testament data; texts with Babylonian, Egyptian or Canaanite parallels (not to say prototypes); gospel genealogies; and the afore-mentioned Old Testament quotations in the New. These issues mostly tran-scend the concerns of 'mere' textual criticism, and each is capable of raising HBC-type questions. They also differ in kind from the sorts of debated issues of interpretation cited by Plantinga,[30] some of these latter of fundamental impor-tance to the faith and the perennial concern of traditional biblical scholarship. They have in some instances the appearance of bringing us near to that world where suspicion lurks that there are 'all sorts of additions and subtractions and alterations made in the interest of advancing theological points',[31] and for that reason they demand attention.

In Conclusion

In his response to this chapter, Plantinga has emphasized that his critique of HBC is not concerned with its subject matter, but with its a priori assumptions, and he suggests that my discussion of HBC is partly about its subject matter and therefore only partly about the underlying approach. This I happily recognize: my inclusion of subject matter is explained by the prominence of the 'principal author' concept in Plantinga's original presentation. It seems to me that the implications of this model need further attention. In particular, if HBC is mainly about matters of composition and authorship,[32] and if one may include what one knows by way of faith when deciding on such questions,[33] then it would be interesting to know how, or in regard to what precisely, such illumi-nation takes place. More concretely, it would be useful to be able to consider specific cases where such privileged information has led to secure conclusions on issues of composition and authorship.

In my biblical work, I myself operate on the understanding that there is a 'warranted' form of HBC that all students of Scripture may claim and apply. I would claim that my personal warrant comes to a significant extent from Scrip-ture itself, for one of the most formative factors in my approach to academic biblical study has been the observation, closely and at length, of what Scripture does to Scripture – on which subject enough has been said above.[34] Here, surely, may be found hints at the parameters that are appropriate to the discus-sion of what often comes under the heading of 'introduction' in biblical study.

---

[30] *WBC*, 381–82.

[31] *WBC*, 390.

[32] *WBC*, 389.

[33] See Plantinga, Ch. 4, 'Reason and Scripture Scholarship'.

[34] I have touched on some of these matters in 'Did Moses Write?'.

For if HBC tends, as Plantinga notes,[35] to bracket out the notion of Scripture as 'word from God', so too traditional biblical scholarship has been disinclined to exploit the full freedom of inquiry that Scripture itself, by both its procedures and its silences, appears to encourage.

The form of HBC that I favour is certainly non-Troeltschian, whatever else it is. While recognizing the supernatural and revelatory nature of Scripture, it acknowledges that the 'good things of the Gospel' have been communicated in the form of a literary tradition that is so much in keeping with the literary conventions of its time as to call out for the canons normally applied to literary works, and in particular to ancient Near Eastern texts, to be applied also to the biblical text. How this works out has, I think, been illustrated in the course of the foregoing discussion. It acts as a necessary corrective to well-intentioned piety that by its inattentiveness to salient matters of the biblical text has difficulty with its answers to the legitimate questions of the curious and the opposed. For while the 'ordinary' believer may claim the crucial aid of the Spirit in the understanding and appropriation of the biblical message, such spiritual enlightenment does not normally extend to questions that press more and more in the post-Enlightenment world of the West in particular. Moreover, the 'ordinary' believer's independence of biblical scholarship can be overstated,[36] for all are dependent on, at the least, the textual and translational labours of those who have prepared themselves by academic training for the study of the biblical text. That the dependence may be obscured by the antiquity of the Bible version used, or by the antiquity or multiplicity of the Bible aids consulted, does not alter the basic fact of dependence. We are all just a little closer together than sometimes we are willing to acknowledge. A narrowly defined Troeltschian HBC would certainly be thin on positive results, and compromise HBC positions might be thought to promise little more. Nevertheless, perhaps the long and extendable list of disputed doctrines[37] – after all, they include even the most basic things, like what makes a person a Christian – shows that thinness of results is not restricted to one side of the divide.

Finally, what is not in dispute between Plantinga and myself is that, whatever the exercise of non-Troeltschian HBC produces by way of results (information? knowledge?), there must in any case be a point at which faith takes over. That is because the co-ordinates of revelation and faith have to do with a far deeper kind of knowing than the mere assurance that events in human history took place in a certain way.

---

[35] *WBC*, 375, 387–88.

[36] Cf. *WBC*, 374 = 'Two (or More)'.

[37] See *WBC*, 381–82.

Bibliography

Alford, H., *The Greek Testament*, IV, I: *The Epistle to the Hebrews* (London: Rivingtons, 3rd edn, 1864)

Gordon, R., 'Did Moses Write "Second Isaiah"?', *Theological Students' Fellowship News and Prayer Letter* (summer 1983), 3–4

Parker, T.H.L. (ed.), *Calvin's Old Testament Commentaries* (Edinburgh: T. & T. Clark, 1986)

√ Plantinga, A., *Warranted Christian Belief* (New York: OUP, 2000)

√ Vanauken, S., *A Severe Mercy* (London: Hodder & Stoughton, 1977)

4

Reason and Scripture Scholarship

A Response to Robert Gordon and Craig Bartholomew

Alvin Plantinga

I'd like to thank Robert Gordon and Craig Bartholomew for their challenging responses to my chapter in *Warranted Christian Belief* on Scripture scholarship. But first I must make an apology. Robert Gordon takes a bit of umbrage at my saying that 'a real live Scripture scholar is unlikely to have spent a great deal of thought on the epistemological foundations of the discipline'[1] and that 'many Scripture scholars who arrive at relatively traditional conclusions nevertheless pay at least lip service to the Troeltschian ideal, somehow feeling in a semi-confused way that this is the epistemically respectable or privileged way of proceeding'.[2]

As to the first, I didn't mean to suggest that Scripture scholars warrant reproof or instruction for spending little time or energy on the epistemological foundations of their discipline. Indeed, given human limitations, too much thought on these foundations could seriously interfere with the main job of Scripture scholars, which, naturally enough, is Scripture scholarship. As Bartholomew says, 'it is appropriate that biblical scholars get on with *biblical* scholarship'. Furthermore, I should not have suggested that many Scripture scholars are semi-confused; how would I know a thing like that? If they *were* a bit confused on this point, however, it would certainly be understandable, given all those who trumpet that Troeltschian or Duhemian or Spinozistic ways of proceeding are in fact epistemically *de rigueur*, and that traditional biblical commentary is not respectably scientific because not properly objective and theologically committed.

---

[1] *WBC*, 399.
[2] *WBC*, 403.

Gordon tells us that when he talks with philosophers or dogmaticians about Scripture scholarship, he starts thinking about Moses coming down from Mt. Sinai. Well, I can't speak for dogmaticians, but I don't for a moment think of myself or philosophers generally as descending Mt. Sinai with the truth in hand (whether or not engraved on stone tablets) in order to dispense it to Scripture scholars, who are carrying on with that miserable Troeltschian golden calf. Quite the contrary. It goes without saying that I have far more to learn than to contribute in this area. So perhaps it is presumptuous of me even to think that philosophy, or I, might have something to contribute to that topic. Well, perhaps so; it's a risky world. In any event I hope my suggestion will be useful; but whether it actually turns out to be so is up to others to decide.

I doubt that Gordon and I have any real disagreement. I wanted first to distinguish two kinds of Scripture scholarship, traditional biblical commentary (TBC) and historical biblical criticism (HBC). The practitioner of TBC assumes the main lines of Christian belief and also assumes that God is the principal author of the Bible. HBC, by contrast, is an effort to study the Bible *scientifically*. Here the thought is that someone pursuing a scientific discipline can't properly assume, in the pursuit of that discipline, that Christian belief is true, or that God is the principal author of the Bible, or even that there is such a person as God. Rather, in pursuing a scientific study, you must be constrained by the requirements of methodological naturalism: you must bracket your theological or religious convictions, proceeding on the basis of reason alone; you can't properly appeal to anything you know by way of faith. I went on to distinguish three varieties of HBC: Troeltschian HBC, where you explicitly assume that God, if there is any such person, does nothing direct or special in the world; Duhemian HBC, where you employ no assumptions not accepted by the relevant community; and Spinozistic HBC, where you don't make the Troeltschian assumption but do employ assumptions you take to be deliverances of reason, even if these assumptions are not shared by all inquirers in the relevant community.

When I spoke of HBC, therefore, I had in mind a certain enterprise, but not one defined just by subject matter. I wasn't talking about just *any* effort to answer the questions that practitioners of HBC typically address – questions of composition and authorship, for example. One can address these questions from the perspective of HBC, but of course one can also address such questions from the standpoint of TBC – a perspective in which you employ all that you know, including what you know by way of faith. Thus John Calvin, as enthusiastic a practitioner of TBC as any, sometimes addresses these questions of composition and authorship (for example, in his commentary of Hebrews he argues that Paul could not have been the author of that book). As I'm thinking of it, that's not HBC. To engage in HBC is to carry on a program of investigation of the Bible in which at the least you set aside, for purposes of investigation, whatever you think you know by way of faith. So you don't assume, in this context, that the Bible is a special word from the Lord, or that Jesus is the incarnate second person of the Trinity, or that he died for our sins, rose from the dead and the like. To engage in HBC, as I'm using the term, involves bracketing anything you know or think you know by faith. One cannot employ any such beliefs as premises, or as part of the background information with respect to which you gauge the plausibility of the hypotheses you employ.

So we might define HBC in two different ways. On the one hand, we could think of it as the effort to answer a certain range of questions – questions about authorship, date and process of composition, cultural influences of various kinds, and the like – for present purposes we need not try to specify exactly what these questions are. On the other hand, we might define HBC as the effort to answer these or other questions from a certain standpoint or stance. I'm thinking of HBC in the second way – not the first way. Taken the first way, I would enthusiastically agree with Gordon that there is such a thing as warranted HBC: certainly it can be worthwhile investigating and trying to answer questions of the sort we're talking about. I am less enthusiastic, though, about a warranted HBC of the second kind for Christians. Even here, no doubt often something can be learned from an enterprise in which you bracket part of what you know. And perhaps work of this kind can be important from an apologetic point of view. What I really do want to suggest, however, is that Christians need not think they are somehow obliged to engage only in HBC of the second sort – as if science, or objectivity, or epistemic respectability, or something else to which we owe allegiance, requires this. So I have no quarrel at all with Gordon's suggestion that there is a warranted HBC, that 'there are good reasons for people of faith to lay claim to HBC, in some form or other, as a department of "the scholarly study of the Bible" and as a legitimate and necessary tool of biblical research'. Certainly so. I would add only that in addressing those questions, they need not eschew what they know by way of faith.

Finally, a couple of comments on the dangers or problems Gordon sees as inherent in TBC; some of these are connected with the idea of God as the principal author of the Scripture. One question he raises is this: if, as I suggest, God might intend, in a given passage, to teach us something the original authors didn't have in mind, where is the meaning located: in the text, or in the mind of the principal author? I'm not quite sure how to answer this, but I'd begin by suggesting that *meaning*, strictly speaking, is a property of words or sentences or other linguistic items. So I would say that the meaning is to be found in the text, not in the mind of the author. On the other hand, the divine Author has in mind the message he means to communicate. Is that message to be found in the text as well as in the Author's mind – for example, in those Old Testament texts that in the New Testament are said to be references to Christ?

That's a more difficult question, to which I don't really know the answer. Gordon also asks whether God might not intend us to learn something from HBC, and in fact intend us, who are acquainted with HBC, to learn from *Scripture* something we would not have learned had we not been thus acquainted. That certainly seems to be a live possibility; I can't see any reason for supposing that it couldn't be true.

Gordon points out several more possible pitfalls in the notion of God as primary author; in all these cases I think he's quite right. These pitfalls and dangers are indeed pitfalls and dangers, and it is important to point them out; it is also important to see, however, that taking God to be the principal author of Scripture doesn't automatically compel you to fall victim to them. It is important to eschew simplistic ideas of the way in which God is the principal author. For example, perhaps he's less like the author of a textbook in Greek history than like the author of a play: the latter may intend to teach us something important, but it may emerge only from a dialectical process involving what the various characters say and perhaps other kinds of interactions as well. In that sort of model, one doesn't take it that whatever any character in the play says is something the author intends to teach us: not at all. Clearly there is much to be thought about here.

Turning now to Craig Bartholomew's contribution, I very much appreciate his kind words for epistemology and for my own contributions to that subject. And even if it would be presumptuous of me to try to instruct Scripture scholars in the proper practice of their craft – that is, by suggesting that they take some epistemology to heart – I can gratefully agree with a real Scripture scholar when he says that he aims to 'show that attention to epistemology is crucial if we are to understand biblical studies today and find ways forward'.

First, a distinction. In *Warranted Christian Belief* and elsewhere I've argued that it is perfectly appropriate for Christian philosophers and scholars, including Scripture scholars, to carry on their discipline from a Christian perspective, assuming the main lines of the Christian story in their work, perhaps appealing to it for premises of the arguments they present, and also including Christian belief in the set of background beliefs against which they estimate the plausibility and probability of the hypotheses they propose. There is nothing in proper epistemology to suggest that the correct way to do Scripture scholarship is from the standpoint of Classical Foundationalism, or from a standpoint according to which, to pursue this discipline scientifically, one must pursue it in a Troeltschian or Duhemian or Spinozistic way. Now Bartholomew aims to focus his comments by considering some claims of Philip Davies. Davies' main claim is not that it is inappropriate for Christian Scripture scholars to assume Christian belief in doing their work, but rather that work of that sort, work with those presuppositions, or proceeding from those premises, doesn't belong in the academy. As Davies puts it, 'the conflict is not about what you believe, but what you may be allowed to assume in your professional discourse'. (What you may be *allowed* to assume? Bring on the premise police.) In any event, we have two questions here: 1) is it epistemically proper for Christian Scripture scholars to take for granted Christian belief in doing their work; and 2) should work with Christian or other committed presuppositions be allowed in the academy? These questions are, of course, connected.

Since all I can say about Bartholomew's paper is 'yea and amen', I'll make a couple of independent comments on what Davies says. First, there is more than a hint of postmodern excess in his claim that biblical literature is, like any literature, a distorting product of human authors 'and it would be distorting even if it were written by a deity, since deities have to use our language and have to have a point of view'. No doubt deities have to have a point of view, but why would it have to be a *distorting* point of view? Davies seems to think that just any point of view, even God's, would have to be distorting, a matter of failing to see things as they really are, if, indeed, there is any such thing as the way they really are. As far as I can see, there is nothing behind this but a postmodern penchant for excess. Of course human points of view are often distorting; but even they aren't *always* distorting. You can have a point of view on a given topic, and on a given question or issue within that topic. Some such points of view, I should think, aren't distorting at all. Our point of view on elementary arithmetic – I mean on which statements of elementary arithmetic are true – isn't, I should think, distorting, and neither is our shared point of view on whether London, England, is larger than London, Ontario. *A fortiori*, God's point of view, if indeed he has one, isn't distorting: on the contrary, he sees things exactly as they are. Of course Davies might just be *defining* the term 'point of view' in such a way that points of view are always partial, distorting, confused or whatever. But then, given that definition, there isn't any reason at all to think God has a point of view, and every reason to think he doesn't.

Now Davies apparently believes there is good reason to exclude 'confessional' Scripture scholarship from the academy. The first question is as to just what this means. What, exactly, is 'the academy' here? Does it include book publishers, for example, and is the suggestion that publishers shouldn't publish confessional Scripture scholarship? Or perhaps only explicitly ecclesiastical presses should be allowed to publish that kind of thing? That seems a bit strong. And do all universities and colleges belong to the academy? If so, should there be an embargo on confessional Scripture scholarship in all colleges and universities, including, for example, Calvin College and the University of Notre Dame? Again, that seems a bit strong. No doubt Davies would repudiate these suggestions – at least one hopes so. What he clearly *does* seem to think is that a public, state-supported university should not support confessional Scripture scholarship. He offers a moral argument: 'In spending taxpayer's money doing research that advances churchly or Christian interests and at the expense of the academy's interests one is behaving unethically'. Perhaps he thinks that confessional scholarship would be of no relevance to those who don't accept the confession in question, since many whose tax dollars go to support public, state-supported universities don't accept Christian beliefs; these people would be unfairly required to support and subsidize scholarship of a kind that is of no interest to them. Indeed, it may be worse yet: they may think the confession in question is a pernicious mistake, in which case confessional scholarship, from their perspective, would be not just a waste of time and money, but a dangerous error — one they shouldn't be required to subsidize.

So we should confine the academy to academic discourse, proscribing confessional discourse; and the academy, says Davies, is unlike a confessional community in that it 'aims at inclusion and not exclusion'. Of course this inclusion has limits: Davies proposes that confessional Scripture scholarship be excluded from the academy. How are we to understand this proposed exclusion, given that the aim of the academy is inclusion? That's not an easy question. A few years ago, a young Christian philosopher at a state university in the US wrote to me, saying he had been turned down for tenure. The reason given him was that the philosophy department in question aspired to be a *pluralistic* philosophy department; and he, or his behavior, or his way of thinking, or all three, were insufficiently pluralistic. One of the principle examples of this insufficient pluralism, they said, was that this philosopher, himself an Asiatic, gave lectures on Christian topics to groups of Asiatic Christians. Decidedly unpluralistic behavior. You might have thought a pluralistic philosophy department would be one in which a certain pluralism of points of view would be tolerated and even welcome. Not so. According to the perception of this department, there is a specifically pluralistic way of thinking; what they wanted was a department in which everyone thought that way; others were to be excluded. Davies seems to concur: for example, proper academicians don't believe in absolute truth, so those who think something or other absolutely true are to be excluded from the academy. Thus is exclusion practiced in the name of inclusion, uniformity in the name of diversity, dogmatism in the name of open-mindedness, intolerance in the name of tolerance (and so on).

It's worth noting what is, of course, wholly obvious — that this pattern of exclusion will proscribe a lot more than just confessional Scripture scholarship — at any rate if the point of the exclusion is that many or most supporting the relevant institutions with their tax money don't accept the point of view in question. Vast swatches of contemporary philosophy are devoted to giving naturalistic accounts of various phenomena. In philosophy of mind, for example, we have naturalistic accounts of intentionality, consciousness, belief and so on. There are also putative naturalistic accounts of the notion of proper function, of the right and the good, of epistemology, and much else besides. In psychology, anthropology and sociology departments there are attempts to give naturalistic, evolutionary accounts of altruism, humor, love, and even morality and religion. What is common to all of these enterprises is that they are carried on from a certain perspective or point of view – a perspective certainly not shared, at least in the United States, by the bulk of the taxpaying public. In fact, vastly more Americans endorse the starting point of traditional biblical commentary than endorse the starting point of these various naturalistic endeavors. That's naturalism. But, on the other side of the coin, many scholars in literary studies, history, music, art and the like apparently assume a postmodern anti-realist stance of one kind or another in pursuing their work – certainly not, once more, a perspective shared by the bulk of the taxpaying public. As far as I can see, if commitment to a stance most taxpayers don't support is what is at issue, all of these projects would also have to be excluded from the academy.

But of course this is sheer, high angle nonsense. A public university ought to support a wide variety of intellectual projects, not just projects whose presuppositions are endorsed by the bulk of the taxpaying public. Materialists, naturalists, postmodern anti-realists, theists of various colors and stripes – all ought to be able to carry on their projects in public universities. And what holds generally also holds more specifically: naturalistic Troeltschian Scripture scholarship ought to be supported by public universities, but also Duhemian Scripture scholarship, as well as Christian, Jewish and Islamic Scripture scholarship. This seems wholly obvious, even if not apparent to Davies.

But, in any event, the whole question may be less important than it appears. That is because there is an easy way to divest any confessional project of its presuppositions, an easy recipe for turning any piece of confessional discourse into academic discourse of the sort Davies favors. This is to *conditionalize* the project. Naturalists often assume the truth of naturalism in investigating a certain phenomenon X; Christians might sometimes assume the truth of Christian belief in investigating the same phenomenon. Both are then subject to Davies' strictures and, at least if Davies were running things, liable to exclusion from the academy. However, instead of proceeding in this way (risking the wrath of Davies and his cohorts), each might instead conditionalize. The Christian, then, can ask the following question: suppose Christian belief *were* in fact true (whether or not it actually is): then what would be the best way to think about that phenomenon X? And the naturalist can ask a similar question: suppose naturalism *were* true: what would then be the best way to think about X? Instead of investigating that *categorical* question from a certain perspective, each instead investigates a *hypothetical* or *conditional* question. The conclusions of such research, furthermore, would take a conditional form: if Christian belief were true, the best, right, most satisfactory way of thinking about phenomenon X would be so and so.

Consider, therefore, some question that a Christian biblical scholar wishes to investigate – perhaps the question whether a certain Old Testament prophecy is fulfilled in the New. The Christian biblical scholar may believe that God is the principal author of the Bible, and, being omniscient, would certainly know at the earlier time what was to happen at the latter. There would then be no obstacle in principle, at any rate, to the conclusion that the Old Testament prophecy is in fact fulfilled in that way. Of course this conclusion presupposes that in fact God is both omniscient and the principal author of the Bible. Presumably Davies would object that in making these assumptions the scholar in question is straying outside academic discourse; she should not draw this conclusion, at least within the hallowed halls of academia. But now suppose instead that the TBC conditionalizes; she asks whether, *given* the truth of Christian belief, including the propositions that God is omniscient and the principal author of Scripture, it is likely or certain that the Old Testament prophecy is fulfilled in the New. *Now* she is not assuming the truth of Christian belief. All she assumes (to oversimplify) are the premises and argument forms employed in seeing what the best way to think about this question would be, if in fact Christian belief were true. And if perchance Davies found even some of *those* premises and argument forms objectionable, our investigator could add them to the antecedent of the relevant conditional. Indeed, in principle she'd have to assume nothing but some principle of inference – *modus ponens*, for example.

The conclusion of her investigation, of course, will be a conditional proposition: if Christian belief is in fact true, then the best way to think about X is so and so. That the conclusion takes this conditional form, of course, is no real obstacle to the Christian intent on finding the best way to think about X; all she has to do is detach the consequent. The result of the investigation is the proposition that if Christian belief were true, the best way to think about X would be so and so. The Christian, thinking of course that Christian belief is indeed true, concludes that the best way to think about X is so and so.

So Davies' strictures, silly as they are, are easily sidestepped. But the main point here, I should think, would be twofold. First, the Christian Scripture scholar is in no way obliged to jump through these or similar hoops. She has a perfect right to assume Christian belief in pursuing her inquiries; doing so violates no correct epistemological prescriptions or proscriptions. She is not, in so doing, proceeding in an intellectually suspect or second-rate way, or in some other way violating proper epistemic procedure. This way of proceeding is every bit as epistemologically sound as is working at the topics in question assuming only the deliverances of reason, or in assuming those Troeltschian claims to the effect that God never does anything special and is not in any special way the author or inspirer of the Bible. Indeed, something stronger is true. Not only does she have a *right* to do this: it is, of course, crucially important to the

Christian community that it be done. This is not to say, obviously, that Christian Scripture scholars should work only at this particular task. It is also important for Christian Scripture scholars to join the world of secular Scripture scholarship, pointing out inadequacies and biases, and perhaps showing how certain conclusions are the correct ones from the standpoints – Troeltschian, Duhemian, Spinozistic or whatever – adopted by secular Scripture scholars. That is also important, if only for apologetic reasons. But certainly a central task of the Christian community of Scripture scholarship is that of approaching and inquiring into the topics in question from a Christian epistemic base.

5

Do You Want Us to Listen to You?

Peter van Inwagen

Introduction

This essay was originally published in 1993. I re-publish it now, with a new title and a new introductory section.[1] I have two reasons for doing this. First, few people seem to have read it the first time round, and I'd like to give it another chance at attracting people's attention. Secondly, a significant proportion of the people who did read it seem to have misunderstood it. The new title and the new introductory section are intended to make its point clear.

Let me begin with the new title. The 'you' of the title refers to scholars professionally engaged in New Testament studies and, especially, to those among them who believe that very little of what is said about the words and actions of Jesus in the Gospels (and elsewhere in the New Testament) is true. (And, I should add, to those among them who do not regard this belief of theirs as simply a personal opinion, as something that reasonable and informed people could disagree about.)

The 'us' of the title refers to a class of people to which I and almost all other believing Christians belong: those who regard the New Testament as (in a sense I will try to make clear in the sequel) historically reliable and who are not trained New Testament scholars. ('Regards the New Testament as historically reliable' is not, as one might suppose it was, implied by 'believing Christian'. There are apparently Christian New Testament scholars and systematic

---

[1] This essay was originally published as 'Critical Studies of the New Testament and the User of the New Testament', in *Hermes and Athena*. It is reprinted in my *God, Knowledge, and Mystery*.

    I have made a few small stylistic changes in the body of the essay and a few changes in the notes and have left it otherwise unchanged. It therefore says nothing about recent developments in NT scholarship. (From my perspective – the perspective of a 'user' of the NT – the most important recent development in NT scholarship is the vast amount of attention accorded the 'findings' of the 'Jesus Seminar' by the news media. I allude to the Jesus Seminar in note 11, but I do not discuss it.)

theologians who think the Gospels have little value as historical documents and who nevertheless recite the Nicene Creed with conviction every Sunday.)

This essay is addressed primarily to those of 'you' who are concerned about what 'we' think. In all probability, some of 'you' are *not* concerned about what 'we' think. It is entirely conceivable that a New Testament scholar should not care a fig for what people outside the academic field of New Testament studies think about the New Testament. But just as there are evolutionary biologists who care deeply about what non-scientists think about evolution, so there are New Testament scholars who care deeply about what 'the man on the Clapham omnibus' thinks about the New Testament. Among them are many of those scholars who deny that the Gospels have any value as historical documents. Some of them wish they had more influence in Clapham-omnibus circles. Van A. Harvey, for example, asks

> Why is it that, in a culture so dominated by experts in every field, the opinion of New Testament historians has had so little influence?[2]

Skeptical New Testament historians who wish to be complacent about their lack of influence outside the academy will find all the materials they need for complacency in an obvious analogy of proportion: the skeptical New Testament historian is to Christians who ignore the 'findings of biblical scholarship' as the geologist (or palaeontologist or evolutionary biologist) is to 'fundamentalists' – Christians who believe that six thousand years ago God created the earth in six days.

A lot could be said about this analogy. I will not discuss it in any detail.[3] But there are facts that seem to me to imply that the analogy is very weak.

First, all geologists, palaeontologists and evolutionary biologists agree that the earth is not merely thousands but thousands of millions of years old. And they agree that there have been fish (say) for hundreds of millions of years and human beings, by any definition of 'human being', for at least a hundred thousand years. No such agreement about the past is to be found among biblical historians. If geologists and the practitioners of the various life sciences disagreed among themselves to the extent that New Testament historians do, we should not call them experts.

Secondly, agreement about the essential[4] historicity of the gospel stories is common to the apostolic fathers, the Fathers, the scholastics and the reformers.

---

[2] Harvey, 'New Testament Scholarship', 194.

[3] Much of what I would say about it can be inferred from my essay 'Genesis and Evolution', which is also reprinted in *God, Knowledge, and Mystery*.

[4] 'Mark ... wrote down accurately all that [Peter] mentioned, whether sayings or doings of Christ; *not however in order*'. (This is Eusebius' paraphrase of what Papias

It is therefore plausible to contend that the thesis that these stories are essentially historical is 'mere Christianity' – *pace* certain 'New Testament scholars and systematic theologians' to whom I alluded a moment ago. No such claim can be made on behalf of the thesis that the creation story in Genesis is the literal truth. (See, e.g., St Augustine's *The Literal Meaning of Genesis*. Augustine's speculations about the sequence of events comprising the creation may strike us as quaint, but it is no more consistent with literalism about the first two chapters of Genesis than is the modern, scientific account of the origin of the earth and of terrestrial life.[5])

This chapter should be read as an answer to Harvey's question. That is, it should be regarded as a piece of information that skeptical New Testament scholars who want to convert the Christians on the Clapham omnibus to their views need to have in order to carry out this project. It should be read as advice on the best way for these scholars to present their case to Christians who are not professionally trained in New Testament studies. The essay takes the form of an argument for the following conclusions. First, 'ordinary' Christians (Christians not trained in New Testament scholarship) have grounds for believing that the gospel stories are (essentially) historical – grounds independent of the claims of historical scholarship. Secondly, New Testament scholars have established nothing that tells against the thesis that ordinary Christians have grounds independent of historical studies for believing in the essential historicity of the gospel stories. Thirdly, ordinary Christians may therefore ignore any skeptical historical claims made by New Testament scholars with a clear intellectual conscience.

One way to misunderstand this essay would be to regard it as an attempt to *prove* the conclusion that ordinary Christians may ignore the skeptical claims of New Testament scholars with a clear intellectual conscience. It is not an attempt at proof, however. It is no more than the presentation of an argument. Since this argument is logically valid (that is, since its conclusion follows logically from the five premises explicitly stated and labeled 'premises' in the essay), its conclusion – 'Ordinary Christians may therefore ignore any skeptical historical claims made by New Testament scholars with a clear intellectual conscience' – can be false only if at least one of the premises of the argument is false. To present a logically valid argument for a certain conclusion is not

---

said about Mark. See note 12 and the sentence in the text to which the note is appended.)

[5] I once met an atheist, a lapsed fundamentalist, who regarded the thesis that the earth was created in six days six thousand years ago as essential to Christianity. He maintained that any professed Christian who denied this thesis was a 'wishy-washy theological liberal', a Christian in name only. I asked him if he was willing to call St Augustine a wishy-washy theological liberal. 'Oh, certainly', he said.

necessarily to claim to prove or to have established that conclusion.[6] One *might* offer such an argument with that purpose in mind, but here is another purpose one might have in mind, and it is in fact the purpose *I* have in mind: to lay out the points at which those who deny the conclusion of the argument can attack the argument to some purpose – the points at which they can make *relevant* objections to the argument. The reason for this is simple: since the argument is logically valid, its conclusion must be true if its five premises are true. Therefore, no matter what 'you' say about the argument, what you say will not, as a matter of logic, have any tendency to show that the conclusion of the argument is false unless it has at least some tendency to show that at least one of its premises is false.

At the risk of belaboring the obvious, here is what I ask. What 'you' must do if you want 'us' to listen to you is to present some reason or reasons for thinking that at least one of the five premises of the argument is false.

Critical Studies of the New Testament and the User of the New Testament

By *users* of the New Testament I mean: 1) ordinary churchgoers who read the New Testament and hear it read in church and hear it preached on; 2) the pastors who minister to the ordinary churchgoers; and 3) theologians who regard the New Testament as an authoritative divine revelation.

By *critical studies of the New Testament* (hereinafter, 'critical studies'), I mean those historical studies that either deny the authority of the New Testament or else maintain a methodological neutrality on the question of its authority and which attempt, by methods that presuppose either a denial of, or neutrality about, its authority, to investigate such matters as the authorship, dates,

---

[6] The reader is asked to keep the above definition of 'logically valid' in mind. To call an argument logically valid in this technical sense is to make a rather weak claim on its behalf. The following (artificially simple) example illustrates this point. Every atheist who understands 'logically valid' will give his untroubled assent to the statement that the following argument is logically valid. The Bible is the word of God; if the Bible is the word of God, everything said in the Bible is true; therefore, everything said in the Bible is true. The atheist will, of course, reject the conclusion of this argument, but not on the ground that the argument contains some logical flaw (unlike the argument, 'Everything said in the Bible is true; if the Bible is the word of God, everything said in the Bible is true; therefore, the Bible is the word of God', which does contain a logical flaw). It is rather because the atheist *rejects its first premise* that he is in a position to reject its conclusion. An argument some of whose premises are false may well be logically valid. Indeed, an argument *all* of whose premises are *known to be* false may well be logically valid.

histories of composition, historical reliability and mutual dependency of the various books of the New Testament.[7] Source criticism, form criticism and redaction criticism provide many central examples of critical studies as I mean to use the term, but I do not mean to restrict its application to gospel studies. An author who contends that Paul did not write the Letter to the Ephesians or that 2 Peter was composed well into the second century is engaged in what I am calling critical studies. For that matter, so are authors who contend that Paul *did* write Ephesians, or who (like the late J.A.T. Robinson) contend that 2 Peter was probably composed in the early sixties of the first century – provided their arguments for those conclusions do not presuppose that the New Testament texts are authoritative or inspired.

I exclude from 'critical studies' all purely textual studies – studies that attempt to determine the original wording of the New Testament books by the comparative study of ancient manuscripts. Thus, the well-known arguments purporting to show that the last chapter of John was not a part of the original composition (arguments based mainly on a supposed discontinuity of sense in the text) belong to critical studies, while the well-known arguments purporting to show that the last twelve verses of Mark were not a part of the original composition (arguments based mainly on the fact that important early manuscripts do not contain those verses) do not belong to critical studies.

Again, a close study of a New Testament book or group of books or idea may not be an instance of what I am calling critical studies, for it may be that it does not raise questions of dates, authorship, historical reliability and so on, but, so to speak, takes the texts at face value. An example of such a study would be Oscar Cullmann's famous Ingersol Lecture.[8] But it is unusual for a book or article or lecture about the New Testament to be a 'pure' example of the *genre* critical studies, and it is even more unusual for a book or article or lecture on the New Testament to contain no material belonging to that *genre*. Most recent works on the New Testament (to judge from the very small sample of them I have read) are mixtures of critical studies with many other things. My term 'critical studies' should therefore be regarded as a name for an aspect of New Testament scholarship, and not for something that is a subject or discipline in its own right.

It is taken for granted in many circles that pastors and theologians must know a great deal about critical studies if they are to be responsible members of their professions, and it has been said that even ordinary churchgoers should know a lot more about critical studies than they usually do. My purpose in this chapter is to present an argument against this evaluation of the importance of

---

[7] This is a purely stipulatory definition. My conclusions about 'critical studies' apply only to those studies that meet the strict terms of this definition.

[8] 'Immortality of the Soul or Resurrection of the Body?'.

critical studies to users of the New Testament. I present this argument first in the form of a schematic outline and then proceed to fill in the detail of the argument by commentary on, and defense of, the premises.

> *Premise 1.* If a user of the New Testament has grounds for believing that the New Testament is historically and theologically reliable, grounds that are independent of critical studies, and if he has good reason to believe that critical studies do not undermine these grounds, then he need not attend further to critical studies – that is, once he has satisfied himself that critical studies do not undermine his reasons for believing in the historical and theological reliability of the New Testament, he need not attend further to critical studies.

Comment on Premise 1

The famous Rylands Papyrus, a fragment of the Fourth Gospel, has been dated to around AD 130 on palaeographic grounds. Clearly the methods by which this date was arrived at are *independent of* radiocarbon dating. But if radiocarbon dating of the fragment assigned it to the fourth century, this result would *undermine* – if it were incontrovertible, it would refute – the palaeographic arguments for the second-century date. (The radiocarbon dating would not, of course, show where the palaeographic arguments went wrong, but, if it were correct, it would show that they went wrong somewhere.)

> *Premise 2.* The liturgical, homiletic and pastoral use the church has made of the New Testament, and the church's attitude towards the proper use of the New Testament by theologians, presuppose that the New Testament is historically and theologically reliable.

> *Premise 3.* These presuppositions of reliability do not depend on accidents of history, in the sense that if history had been different, the church might have held different presuppositions and yet have been recognizably the same institution. If the church's use of the New Testament had not presupposed the historical and theological reliability of the New Testament, the church would have been a radically different sort of institution – or perhaps *it* would not have existed at all; perhaps what was called 'the Christian church' or 'the Catholic Church' would have been a numerically distinct institution.

First Comment on Premise 3

If the constitutional convention of 1787 had established a political entity called 'the United States of America' by uniting the thirteen former colonies under a hereditary monarchy and an established church, the United States would have been a radically different sort of political entity. Perhaps, indeed, the nation called 'the United States' would not have been the nation that is called that in fact.

If the New Testament books had never been collected into a canon and portions of this canon read at Mass and as part of the divine office; if preachers had not been assigned the task of preaching on New Testament texts; if Christians had not generally believed that the New Testament narratives presented a reasonably accurate account of Jesus' ministry, death and resurrection, and of the beginnings of the church; if Christians had not believed that God speaks to us in the pages of the New Testament on particular occasions (as in the story of Augustine's conversion); if theologians had not generally believed that their speculations must be grounded in the spirit of, and subject to correction by the letter of, the New Testament – then the church would have been a radically different institution. We might in fact wonder whether an institution that regarded what we call the New Testament as nothing more than twenty-seven venerable but non-authoritative books would really be the institution referred to in the Nicene Creed as the one, holy, catholic and apostolic church. I think we should have to say that if it *was* the same institution, it was that institution in a radically different form.

Second comment on Premise 3

One might wonder why I am conducting my argument in terms of what the church has presupposed about the New Testament, rather than in terms of what the church has *taught* about the New Testament. The answer is that it is much clearer what the practice of the church presupposes about the New Testament than it is what the church has taught about the New Testament. The main reason for this is that the church's practice as regards the New Testament has been much more uniform than its teaching. I grant that there can be disputes about what a given practice presupposes, but I prefer dealing with disputes of that sort to dealing with the disputes that would attend any very specific attempt to define the church's teaching about the New Testament.

> *Premise 4.* There are grounds, grounds independent of critical studies, for believing that whatever the church has presupposed is true – provided that presupposition is understood in the strong or 'essential' sense described above.

Comment on Premises 3 and 4

There are things the church has pretty uniformly presupposed in certain periods that are false. I would say, for example, that Paul, and probably all first-century Christians, presupposed that Christians would never be able to do much to change the large-scale features of what they called the world and what people today call 'society'. This was doubtless partly because they expected that the world was not going to last long enough to be changed by *anything*, but they seem also to have thought of Christians as necessarily held in contempt (if not actively persecuted) by those on whom the world has conferred power and prestige. Today we know that, for good or ill, it is possible for there to be a formally Christian society, and that even in a society not formally Christian, or formally anti-Christian, it is possible for Christians to exert significant influence on society as a whole.

No doubt there are false presuppositions that the church has held uniformly from the day of Pentecost to the present, though it is not for me, who do not claim to be a prophet, to say what they might be. The combined force of Premises 3 and 4 is this: Any such universally held but false presupposition of the church is not essential to the church's being what it is. And (the two premises imply) any presupposition of the church that is essential to the church's being what it is is true – or, more exactly, there are grounds for believing that it is true.

> *Premise 5.* Critical studies do not undermine these grounds, and there are good reasons for believing that they do not – reasons whose discovery requires no immersion in the minutiae of critical studies, but which can be grasped by anyone who attends to the most obvious features of critical studies.

These five premises entail the following conclusion:

> Once users of the New Testament have satisfied themselves that critical studies do not undermine their independent grounds for believing in the historical and theological reliability of the New Testament, they need not attend further to critical studies.

First Comment on the Argument

I have already said that by critical studies I do not mean just any historical studies of or related to the New Testament. I have explicitly excluded from the category of critical studies purely textual studies and studies of aspects of the New Testament that, as I said, take the texts at face value. Many other historical studies related to the New Testament are obviously essential to pastors and theologians, and advisable for ordinary churchgoers who have the education and leisure to be able to profit from them.

Pastors and theologians should obviously know something about the history and geography of the ancient Mediterranean world. They should know something about who the Pharisees, Sadducees and Zealots were, what the legal status of the Sanhedrin was, what the powers and responsibilities of a procurator were, what it meant to be a Roman citizen and how an appeal to the emperor worked. They should know something about the Jewish religion and the other religions of the Roman world. They should know something about second-century Gnosticism, and something about its probable first-century roots. They should know something about the social, agricultural and legal facts and customs of which knowledge is presupposed in the parables of Jesus. (I have found facts about fig trees to be enlightening.) All this is obvious, and a lot more that could be said in the same vein is obvious. I mention it only to show that I don't mean to deny the obvious.

It is also worth mentioning that there are historical studies that users of the New Testament need know little if anything about, but on which things they must know something about are based. (The painstaking comparisons of manuscripts by which our present New Testament texts have been established would be an example, but far from the only example, of what I mean.) It is my position not only that users of the New Testament need know little about critical studies, but also that nothing they need to know much about is so much as based upon critical studies.[9]

Second Comment on the Argument

The conclusion of the argument applies to users of the New Testament *qua* users of the New Testament. Consider, for example, theologians. The conclusion is consistent with the thesis that *some* theologians, by virtue of the particular theological vineyard in which they labor, may need to be well versed in critical studies. For example, a theologian trying to reconstruct Luke's theology from clues provided by the way Luke used his sources would obviously need to have an expert's knowledge of critical studies. This qualification is strictly parallel with the following statement: A physicist *qua* physicist need

---

[9] Many studies of the NT presuppose the results, or the alleged results, of critical studies. The conclusion of our argument applies to such studies to the extent that these presuppositions are essential to them. Consider, for example, the following quotation from Professor Adams's 'Role of Miracles': '... Luke's Gospel was written in the 80s C.E., and arguably reflects the conflict between Christian and non-Christian Jews over who is to blame for the destruction of Jerusalem' (258). The thesis that Luke's Gospel was written in the eighties is an alleged result of critical studies. To the extent, therefore, that this thesis is essential to her paper – I do not claim that this extent is very great; it seems to me that most of what Professor Adams says in her paper could be true even if Luke's Gospel was, as I myself believe it to have been, written in the early sixties – the conclusion of our argument applies to her paper. Any study of Luke that is *wholly* dependent on the thesis that Luke was written well after the destruction of Jerusalem is, if our argument is sound, a study users of the NT may, if they wish, ignore with a clear intellectual conscience.

have scant knowledge of biology, but a *bio*physicist has to know a great deal about biology.

Third Comment on the Argument

The conclusion of the argument is not that users of the New Testament must not or should not have an extensive acquaintance with critical studies, but that they need not. Biophysicists need to know a lot of biology, but it is not generally supposed that physicists working in the more abstract and general areas of physics need know much about biology. Erwin Schrödinger, however, set out to educate himself in biology because he thought that the observed stability of the gene was inexplicable in terms of known physics, and that the study of living systems therefore held important clues for the theoretical physicist. Well, he was wrong about the gene, but he was no fool, and the matter was certainly worth looking into. I want to say that something like that should be the case in respect of theology and critical studies: that critical studies are not, in general, particularly relevant to the theologian's task (except in the case in which the task is to reconstruct the theology of the writer of a New Testament book, or something of that sort); but a theologian may conclude at a certain point in his or her investigations that those investigations require a deep knowledge of critical studies. But this is no more than a special case of what I would suppose to be a wholly uncontroversial thesis: A theologian may conclude at a certain point in his or her investigations that those investigations require a deep knowledge of just about anything – physics, say, or formal logic or evolutionary biology. I am arguing that critical studies cannot be said *a priori* to be of any greater relevance to the concerns of the theologian (or the pastor or the ordinary churchgoer) than physics or formal logic or evolutionary biology.

Fourth Comment on the Argument

Users of any very recent edition or translation of the Bible are going to be exposed to the judgements of those engaged in critical studies and the corresponding historical studies of the Old Testament. I mention the Old Testament because my favorite example of the way in which one can be exposed to such a judgement is Genesis 1:2. If one's translation says, 'and a mighty wind swept over the face of the waters', instead of, 'and the Spirit of God moved over the face of the waters', one may want to know what the arguments in favor of the former reading are. Or if in one's Bible the twenty-first chapter of John has some such heading as 'An Ancient Appendix', one may want to know what the arguments are upon which this editorial comment rests. No such example as these is individually of any very great importance, but a large number of such translations and editorial comments may combine to produce an impression of the nature of the biblical texts – an impression that may be correct, but which certainly reflects views of editors and translators that are at least partly conditioned by critical studies. If one wants to make up one's own mind about the views that have shaped modern editions and translations of Scripture, one may have to devote more time to critical studies than the conclusion of my argument suggests – in self-defense, as it were. An analogy: in ideal circumstances, a student of Plato would not need to know much about nineteenth-century British idealism; but if the only available edition of Plato were Jowett, such knowledge would be prudent.

Fifth Comment on the Argument

The argument refers to critical studies as they actually are. For example, the thesis of Premise 5, that critical studies do not undermine the user's grounds for believing in the historical and theological reliability of the New Testament (the grounds alleged to exist in Premise 4), does not imply that critical studies could not possibly undermine these grounds, but only that they have not in fact done so.

Even when the qualifications contained in these five comments have been taken into account, the argument is unlikely to win immediate and unanimous approval. The place of critical studies in theological education is more eloquent testimony to the strength of the convictions opposing the conclusion of the argument than any chorus of dissent could be. In the seminaries maintained by my own denomination, for example, seminarians spend more time reading works that fall in the area I am calling critical studies, or works which are deeply influenced by the supposed results of critical studies, than they do reading the Fathers of the church. I doubt whether things are much different in typical Roman Catholic and 'mainline' Protestant seminaries. And, no doubt, any suggestion that critical studies should have at most a marginal role in doctoral programs in theology would be greeted with the same sort of incredulity that would attend a suggestion of a marginal role for the study of anatomy in the training of physicians. As to the laity (as opposed both to the ordained clergy and the theologically learned), probably no small number of diocesan vicars of education, and their Protestant counterparts, would agree with the proposal of Ellen Fleeseman-van Leer that the Bible be taught to the laity, '… in such a way that the question of its authority is for the time being left to one side and that modern biblical scholarship is taken into account at every step'.[10]

---

[10] From a sort of open letter written by Dr. Fleeseman-van Leer to the NT scholar Christopher Evans, 'Dear Christopher', in Hooker and Hickling (eds.), *What about the New Testament?*, 240.

The remainder of this chapter will be devoted to further clarification of some of the ideas contained in the argument, and to a defense of its premises. Unfortunately, I do not have the space to perform either of these tasks adequately. I must either touch on all the points that deserve consideration in a very sketchy way, or else be selective. I choose the latter course.

The ideas that figure in the argument that are most in need of clarification are the ideas of 'historical reliability' and 'theological reliability'. The premises most in need of defense are the fourth and the fifth.

Despite the fact that the idea of theological reliability is badly in need of clarification, I am not going to attempt to clarify it, because that would be too large a task. I could not even begin to explain what I mean by the words 'The New Testament is theologically reliable' in the one or two pages I could devote to the topic here. I shall, therefore, attempt to clarify only the idea of *historical* reliability. It is certainly true that the idea of historical reliability is more directly related to the topic of critical studies than is the idea of theological reliability. There are plenty of people who believe that critical studies have shown that the New Testament cannot be, in any sense that could reasonably be given to these words, theologically reliable. But the primary argument for this thesis would, surely, have to be that critical studies have shown that the New Testament is not theologically reliable *by* showing that it is not historically reliable. (After all, if we cannot believe the New Testament when it tells us of earthly things, how can we believe it when it tells us of heavenly things?)

But what thesis do I mean to express by the words 'The New Testament is historically reliable?' What is meant by historical reliability?

The concept of historical reliability, although it is much simpler than the concept of theological reliability, is sufficiently complex that I am going to have to impose two restrictions on my discussion of it. I hope that what I say within the scope of these restrictions will indicate to the reader what I would say about other aspects of the topic of historical reliability.

First, I am going to restrict my attention to the narrative passages of the New Testament: Passages written in the past tenses or the historical present, in which the author represents himself as narrating the course of past events (one typical sign of this being the frequent use of connecting and introductory phrases like 'in those days' and 'about that time'), passages in which what is presented is not represented as a dream or a vision, and in which the references to persons and places are in the main concrete and specific. Secondly, I am going to restrict my attention to descriptions of the words and actions of Jesus. I do this because there are certain stylistic and expository advantages to my focusing my discussion on a strictly delimited class of events, and this class of events has attracted more attention from those engaged in critical studies than any other strictly delimited class. I will attempt to explain what I mean by saying that the descriptions of the words and actions of Jesus in the narrative passages of the

New Testament are historically reliable. It should be kept in mind that in what immediately follows I am explaining what I mean by this thesis and not defending it. I give three explanations of historical reliability, which I believe are consistent and, in fact, mutually illuminating.

I begin with a formal explanation – roughly, an explanation in terms of how much of what is said in the texts is historically accurate – for obviously the notion of historical reliability must be closely related to the notion of historical accuracy. I mean by saying that the New Testament narratives are historically reliable (as regards the words and acts of Jesus) that (1) Jesus said and did at least most of the things ascribed to him in those narratives, and (2) any false statements the narratives may contain about what Jesus said and did will do no harm to those users of the New Testament who accept them as true because they occur in the New Testament. But clause (2) of this explanation is itself in need of an explanation.

I will explain the idea of 'doing no harm' by analogy. Suppose a general who is conducting a campaign in, say, Italy, is separated by some misadventure of battle from all his military maps and reference materials. Suppose he finds a pre-war guidebook to Italy with which he makes do. Suppose this guidebook is in some respects very accurate: its maps, tables of distances between towns, statements about the width of roads and so on, are all without error. On the other hand, it has wrong dates for lots of churches, contains much purely legendary material about Italian saints and has Garibaldi's mother's maiden name wrong. If the general, so to speak, treats the guidebook as gospel, and as a consequence believes all the legends and wrong dates and mistakenly concludes he is related to Garibaldi, it will probably do him no harm. At any rate, it will do him no military harm, and that kind of harm is the kind relevant in the present context. And if he later comes to believe that God providentially put the guidebook into his hands in his moment of greatest need, it is unlikely that he will be argued out of this belief by a skeptic who shows him that it contains a lot of misinformation about churches and saints and Italian patriots.

The false statements in our imaginary guidebook were militarily irrelevant. And it may be that there are false statements about the words and acts of Jesus in the New Testament that are irrelevant to the spiritual warfare. Let us examine this possibility.

Suppose Jesus never said, 'Blessed are the peacemakers, for they shall be called sons of God'.[11] Suppose, however, that this is something he might very

---

[11] I learn from reports in the press that the seventh Beatitude has been established as inauthentic by the majority vote of a group of biblical scholars and will be so marked in the group's forthcoming edition of the NT, in which the words the evangelists ascribe to Jesus are to be printed in four colours, signifying 'certainly said', 'probably said', 'probably didn't say', and 'certainly didn't say'.

well have said. Suppose it in no way misrepresents his teaching, and is in fact an excellent expression of something he believed. If these things are so, it is hard to see how anyone would be worse off for believing he said these words. We may contrast this case with the following case: If the early church had twisted the story of the widow's mite into an injunction to the poor to give to the church, even to the point of starvation, the changed version of the story would have done grave harm to those who believed it.

My explanation of the notion of historical reliability, therefore, is consistent with the supposition that Jesus did not say all the things ascribed to him in the gospel narratives. But this statement naturally raises the question, 'how much?' Is it possible that these narratives ascribe to him *lots* of things he never said or did, all of them being nevertheless things he might well have said or done? I think there is no contradiction in the idea that the narratives are perfect guides to what Jesus might well have said and done, even though they are most imperfect guides to what, in point of historical fact, he did say and do. I do not, however, regard their having this feature as a real possibility. I believe that if very *many* of the ascriptions of words and acts to Jesus in the New Testament narratives are historically false, then it is very unlikely that any significant *proportion* of those ascriptions attribute to him things he might well have said or done. I shall presently touch on my reasons for believing this.

We can see a second kind of 'harmless' historical inaccuracy if we consider the order in which events are narrated. Suppose that, as most scholars apparently believe, the things Jesus is represented as saying in Matthew 5, 6, and 7 (the Sermon on the Mount), are things that – assuming Jesus said all of them – he did not say on any single occasion. But it has certainly never done anyone any harm to believe that he did – not, at least, if he did say them all, and said them in contexts that give them the same significance the 'Sermon on the Mount' narrative framework gives them. It is not an altogether implausible thesis that the order in which many of the sayings and acts of Jesus are recorded is of no great importance to anyone but New Testament scholars trying to work out the relations among the Synoptic Gospels. If Mark, as Eusebius said Papias said, '… wrote down accurately all that [Peter] mentioned, whether sayings or doings of Christ; not however in order',[12] and if a simple reader of Mark believes X happened before Y because that's what it says in Mark, when in fact Y happened before X, it's hard to see how this could have done the simple reader any harm.[13]

---

[12] *Ecclesiastical History*, iii, 39 (as quoted in Bruce, *New Testament Documents*, 35).

[13] In correspondence, Harold W. Attridge has suggested that the various NT texts that have been used to justify persecution of the Jews pose a difficult problem for my thesis about historical reliability. In connection with this question, it is important to realize – I do not mean to imply that Professor Attridge is confused on this point –

This completes my formal explanation of what I mean by historical reliability. I now give a *functional* explanation of this notion.

As I have said, the church has made very extensive liturgical, homiletic and pastoral use of the New Testament, including the narrative portions thereof. These texts have been read to congregations and preached on for getting on toward a hundred thousand Sundays. My functional explanation of what is meant by the historical reliability of the New Testament narratives is this: the narratives are historically reliable if they are historically accurate to a degree consonant with the use the church has made of them. Again, the explanation needs to be explained. Let us consider a rather extreme suggestion. Suppose most of the New Testament stories about the sayings and actions of Jesus were made up in various communities of the early church in response to certain contemporary and local needs. (We suppose that when the evangelists eventually came to hear these stories, they took them for historical fact and incorporated them into their Gospels, adding, perhaps, various fictions of their own composition.) This suggestion is, I believe, *not* consonant with the use the church has made of the New Testament historical narratives. The church has caused these stories, these past-tense narratives bursting with concrete and specific historical reference, to be read, without any hint that they should not be taken at face value, to sixty generations of people the church knew full well *would* take them at face value. If these narratives were indeed largely a product of the imaginations of various people in the early church, then the church has, albeit unwittingly, been guilty of perpetrating a fraud. (We might compare the position of the church – if this suggestion is correct – with the position of the palaeoanthropological community in the thirties and forties in respect of

---

that my thesis does not entail that these texts, or any texts, have done no harm; it entails only that, if any of these texts is not historical, no one has come to any harm by believing it was historical. Nevertheless, I am willing to defend the strong thesis that Mt. 27:25; Jn. 8:44; 1 Thes. 2:14; and Rev. 2:9 have done no harm. These texts have indeed been used as prooftexts by persecutors of the Jews, but it seems wholly obvious to me that only people who were already dead to both reason and the gospel could use them for such a purpose. As to the masses who may have been swayed by such texts – well, they must have been pretty easy to sway. ('There are in England this day a hundred thousand men ready to die in battle against Popery, without knowing whether Popery be a man or a horse.') I doubt whether the devil needs to quote Scripture to get people to murder Jews or any other harmless and inoffensive people. At any rate, it would take a strong argument to convince me that any NT text has been anything more than a sort of theological ornament tacked on the racks and gas chambers, like a cross on a crusader's shield. The only harm involving these texts I'm willing to concede is this: to attempt to use Scripture to justify murder and oppression is blasphemy, and those who have done this may have been damned for six reasons rather than five.

Piltdown Man. The comparison is not an idle one: it would be hard to find a better case of a fraud that was accepted because it met the needs created by the *Sitz im Leben* of a community.)

What, then, is the degree of historical accuracy that is required of the New Testament narratives (as regards the words and actions of Jesus) if they are to satisfy the present functional characterization of historical reliability? Not surprisingly, I would identify it with the degree of accuracy that figured in our formal explanation of historical reliability. Last Sunday,[14] for example, many churchgoers heard a reading from the gospel according to John that began, 'There was a man of the Pharisees named Nicodemus, ... this man came to Jesus by night ...' The degree of historical accuracy exhibited by this passage is consonant with the use the church has made of it only if: (1) there was a Pharisee named Nicodemus who came to Jesus by night and had a certain conversation with him about being born again; or (2) the passage falls short of historical accuracy in ways that will do no harm to those who hear it read and accept it as a historically accurate narrative. As to the latter possibility – well, perhaps it isn't very important whether Jesus said those things to *Nicodemus*. Perhaps (despite Jesus' characteristic depreciation of the knowledge of 'the teachers of Israel') the passage has its historical roots in a conversation Jesus had with some wholly unimportant person, although he might well have said the same things to a distinguished Pharisee if the occasion had arisen. Perhaps the passage is woven together from things Jesus said on several different occasions, or perhaps it records a set speech he delivered many times with only minor variations. Perhaps the 'voice' Jesus is represented as using is to some degree a literary device of the Fourth Evangelist, or displays a way of speaking Jesus sometimes used in the presence of a few people like the Apostle John, but rarely if ever used in conversations with strangers. All this, and a great deal more in the same line, would be consonant with the church's use of John 3:1–17. If historical inaccuracies of all these kinds were present in that passage, and if someone heard or read the story and took it as unadorned historical fact, it would be a hard critic of the church indeed who accused her of deceiving that person.[15] If, on the other hand, Jesus never talked about being 'born again' at all, the charge of ecclesiastical deception would have considerable merit.

---

[14]   That is, the Sunday preceding the conference at the University of Notre Dame, the proceedings of which are printed in Stump and Flint, *Hermes and Athena* (the second Sunday in Lent, 1990).

[15]   I am myself inclined to take this passage as at least very close to unadorned historical fact. (This is, of course, merely one of my opinions – like my opinion that Anglican orders are valid – and not a part of my Christian faith.) If, on another shore, in a greater light, it should transpire that this opinion of mine had been incorrect, I should not regard the church as having deceived me.

The third explanation I shall give of the notion of historical reliability is *ontological*, an explanation that proceeds by describing the basis in reality of the fact (supposing it to be a fact) that the New Testament narratives possess the degree of historical accuracy I have characterized formally and functionally. In giving this explanation, I adapt to the New Testament narratives what I have said elsewhere about a very different part of the Bible, the creation narrative in Genesis.[16] What I said there had to do with the work of the Holy Spirit in the transformation of myth. What I say here pertains to the work of the Holy Spirit in the preservation of tradition.

It was natural for primitive Christian communities to tell stories about what Jesus had said and done. (I continue to restrict my discussion to this class of events. But what I shall say is applicable with no important modification to those parts of the gospel narratives about people other than Jesus, and to the Acts of the Apostles.) Every reporter, lawyer and historian knows that the stories people tell about past events are not always entirely consistent with one another – and therefore not entirely true. Intelligent, observant and wholly disinterested witnesses to a traffic accident will shortly afterwards give wildly different descriptions of the accident. The four ancient writers who provide our primary documentation of the life of Tiberius Caesar give accounts of his reign at least as hard to 'harmonize' as the four Gospels.[17]

Now let us assume that God was interested in Christians having an account of the things Jesus said and did during the years of his public ministry – an account conforming to the standard of 'historical reliability' described above. Let us in fact assume that he was sufficiently interested in there being such an account that he was willing to take some positive action to ensure its existence. (But let us put to one side the question of why God would have this interest.) Given the facts about the unreliability of witnesses briefly touched on in the last paragraph, and the many mischances a piece of information is subject to in the course of its oral transmission, what might God do to insure the existence of such an accurate account?

I suppose no one seriously thinks God might have chosen to achieve this end by dictating narratives of Jesus' ministry, Greek word by Greek word, to some terrified or ecstatic scribe. (People are often accused of believing that God did this, but I have never seen a case of anyone who admits to it.) Though I firmly believe in miracles, I do not believe – I expect no one believes – that God's governance of the world is entirely, or even largely, a matter of signs, wonders and powers. God created the natural processes whose activity constitutes the world. They are all expressions of his being, and he is continuously present in them. The natural process of story formation and transmission

---

[16] In 'Genesis and Evolution'.
[17] See Sherwin-White, *Roman Society*, 187–89.

among human beings is as much an expression of God's being as is any other natural process, and there is no reason to suppose that he would choose, or need, to circumvent this process to insure the historical reliability of the New Testament narratives. Nevertheless, I believe that his presence in the formation of the New Testament – and, more generally, scriptural – narratives was different from his presence in the formation of all other narratives, just as his presence in the formation of Israel and the church was different from his presence in the formation of all other nations and institutions.

I suppose that the New Testament writers and their communities were chosen by God and were rather special people. I suppose that if, say, St. Luke was told one of the bizarre stories about Jesus' boyhood that survive in the apocryphal infancy gospels, the Holy Spirit took care that his critical faculties – and, indeed, his sense of humor – were not asleep at the time. I suppose that if an elder of the Christian community at Ephesus in AD 64 was tempted by want of funds to twist the story of the widow's mite into an injunction to the poor to buy their way into the kingdom of God, the Holy Spirit saw to it that his conscience was pricked, or that no one believed his version of the story, or that the changed story never got out of Ephesus and soon died out. I suppose that the Holy Spirit was engaged in work like this on many occasions in many places during the formation of the New Testament books. I suppose that the Holy Spirit was at work in the church in similar modes during the process of canonization and during the formation of the opinion that the canonical books were the inspired word of God. I suppose that (although no good book is written apart from the work of the Holy Spirit) the Holy Spirit is present in just *this* way only in the formation of Holy Scripture, and that this mode of presence is part of what we mean by inspiration. (I say 'part of' because we are touching here only on the narrative aspect of Scripture.)

If I am right, God has guided the formation of the New Testament historical narratives by acting on the memories and consciences and critical faculties of those involved in their formation. His employment of this 'method' is certainly consistent with there being historically false statements in the New Testament. A false saying of Jesus might have arisen and gained currency without dishonesty or conscious fabrication on anyone's part. (No doubt many did.) And if it were in his 'voice', and if its content were consistent with his teaching, then it would not be of a sort to be 'filtered out' by the critical faculties of those who transmitted and recorded it, however perfect the operation of those faculties might be. The inclusion in the New Testament of such a false saying would, as I have said, do no one any harm, for it would by definition be consistent with his teaching. (There are many other, if less important, ways in which historically false but harmless ascriptions of words to Jesus might arise: for example, the attribution to him of an apposite quotation of a well-known proverb in a situation in which he said something less memorable; the substitution of one arbitrary place name for another in a parable and so on.) But if this method is consistent with there being some inauthentic sayings of Jesus in the New Testament (the same point, of course, applies to actions), it does not seem to allow any real possibility of a very high proportion of inauthentic sayings. One's critical faculties need something to work on: one cannot judge that an alleged saying of Jesus is not the sort of thing he would have said unless one has at one's disposal a large body of sayings characteristic of Jesus. And the only real possibility of having at one's disposal a large body of sayings characteristic of Jesus is this: having at one's disposal a large body of actual sayings of Jesus.

If the Holy Spirit has indeed been at work in the formation of the New Testament narratives in the way I have described, what would the results be? I think we could expect two results. First, we could expect the narratives to be historically reliable in the formal sense. Secondly, I think we could expect them to look pretty much the way they do – or at least we can say that the way they look is consistent with their formation having been guided by the Holy Spirit in the way I have described. In one sense, the New Testament narratives are far from coherent. That is, while 'harmonization' of the narratives is no doubt logically possible, any attempt at harmonization is going to look rather contrived. (The same could be said of the Tiberius sources.) But these incoherencies are of little consequence to the people I have called users of the New Testament, however important they may be to those engaged in critical studies. Let us grant for the sake of argument – I am in fact very doubtful about this – that it is impossible to reconcile Jesus' representation of himself in John with his representation of himself in, say, Mark. How Jesus represented himself to his audiences and to the authorities and to his disciples at various points in his ministry is no doubt of great interest to certain scholars, but what has it got to do with the Christian life, or with Christian ministry, or even with Christian theology? Or does this incoherency (supposing always that it exists) show that the Holy Spirit cannot have guided the formation of the New Testament narratives in the way I have supposed? How, exactly, would an argument for this conclusion go?

This completes my tripartite explanation of the meaning of 'historically reliable'. I now turn to my promised defense of Premises 4 and 5. This was Premise 4:

> There are grounds, grounds independent of critical studies, for believing that what-ever the church has presupposed is true.

I am a convert.[18] For the first forty years of my life I was outside the church. For much of my life, what I believed about the church was a mixture of fact and

---

[18] The ideas contained in the defense of Premise 4 that follows in the text are presented in a very sketchy and, I now think, not entirely satisfactory way. Soon after writing

hostile invention, some of it asinine and some of it quite clever. Eventually, I entered the church – an act that involved assenting to certain propositions. I believe that I had, and still have, good reasons for assenting to those propositions, although I am not sure what those reasons are. Does that sound odd? It should not. I mean this. I am inclined to think that my reasons for assenting to those propositions could be written down in a few pages – that I could actually do this. But I know that if I did, there would be many non-Christians, people just as intelligent as I am, who would be willing to accept without reservation everything I had written down, and who would yet remain what they had been: untroubled agnostics, aggressive atheists, pious Muslims or whatever. And there are many who would say that this shows that what I had written down could not really constitute good reasons for assenting to those propositions. If it did (so the objection would run), reading what I had written on those pages would convert intelligent agnostics, atheists and Muslims to Christianity – or would at least force them into a state of doublethink or intellectual crisis or cognitive dissonance. Perhaps that's right. If it is, then among my reasons there must be some that can't be communicated – or *I* lack the skill to communicate them – like my reasons for believing that Jane is angry: something about the corners of her mouth and the pitch of her voice, which I can't put into words.

Philosophers are coming to realize that the fact that one cannot articulate a set of reasons that support one's assent to a certain proposition, reasons felt as having great power to compel assent to that proposition by everyone who grasps them, does not mean one does not have good reasons for assenting to that proposition. And they are coming to realize that being in this sort of epistemic situation is not the peculiar affliction of the religious believer. Let me give an example of this – a rather less abstract example than most of the examples philosophers use to illustrate points in epistemology. When I was a graduate student, in the Vietnam era, it was widely believed among my friends and acquaintances that there was something called 'the socialist world', which was soon (within ten or fifteen years) to extend over the entire surface of the globe through the agency of something called 'the Revolution'. Now I believed at the time that all this was sheer illusion. In fact, I didn't just believe it was sheer illusion, I *knew* it was sheer illusion. Nevertheless, although I knew this, if you had asked me why I thought it was an illusion, I could not have cited anything that was not well known to, and which would not have been cheerfully conceded by, any reasonably alert campus Maoist: that such-and-such a story had appeared in the *New York Times*, that George Orwell had once said this, or that Leopold Tyman was currently saying that.

'Critical Studies', I gave what I believe is a more satisfactory presentation of those ideas (it is certainly a longer presentation) in 'Quam Dilecta', see esp. 41–59.

A second illustration of this philosophical point is provided by philosophy itself. A philosopher I deeply respect once told me that he could not accept any religion because there were many religions and they disagreed about important matters. I pointed out to him that he himself accepted many philosophical positions that other, equally able, philosophers rejected – philosophers who knew all the arguments *he* knew. (He resisted the parallel, but on grounds that are still opaque to me.) And his situation is not unique. Every philosopher, or so it seems to me, accepts at least some philosophical theses that are rejected by some equally able and equally well-informed philosopher. But I am not willing to say that no philosopher knows anything philosophical.

Such examples can be multiplied indefinitely. What do you think of psychoanalysis, the theory of evolution by natural selection or the Documentary Hypothesis? Someone as intelligent and as knowledgeable as you are rejects your position. Are you willing to say that this shows you lack reasons that support your opinions on these matters? If so, why do you continue to hold them? (Why, in fact, did you hold them in the first place, since you were perfectly well aware of the disagreements I have alluded to?) If not, then it would seem to follow that you should agree that it is possible for one to have reasons that support a belief, even if one is unable to give an account of those reasons that has the power to compel belief in others.

In my view, I have such reasons with respect to the propositions assent to which is essential to membership in the church – although, as is typical in such cases, many will dispute this claim. One of these propositions is the proposition that Jesus Christ (who, in addition to being the Way and the Life, is also the Truth) is the head and cornerstone of the church. I cannot reconcile assent to this proposition with assent to the proposition that falsehoods are presupposed in the essential operations of the church. I have contended that the historical reliability of the New Testament is presupposed in the essential operations of the church. I therefore claim to have good reasons for regarding the New Testament as historically reliable: they are my reasons for accepting the whole set of propositions essential to membership in the church. And those reasons are independent of the findings of critical studies.

Or so I say. But are they really, *can* they really be, independent of the findings of critical studies? Some would perhaps argue as follows. Among the propositions essential to Christianity are certain historical propositions – for example, that Jesus was at one time dead and was later alive. Therefore (the argument proceeds), if the believer has reasons for accepting the propositions essential to Christianity, reasons that actually warrant assent to those propositions, they must be partly historical reasons, reasons of the kind historians recognize as supporting a thesis about the past. (And it is in critical studies that we see the methods of objective historical inquiry applied to the task of sifting historical fact from myth, legend and fancy in the New Testament narratives.) I have said 'some would perhaps argue …'; I concede, however, that the only people I can remember actually arguing this way are avowed enemies of Christianity like Antony Flew. And they of course believe that it is impossible to demonstrate, on historical grounds, certain of the historical propositions essential to Christianity. While I would agree with them that it is impossible to demonstrate on historical grounds that, for example, Jesus was at one time dead and was later alive, I see no merit in the thesis that the only grounds that could warrant assent to that proposition are grounds of the kinds historians recognize. If I have, as I believe I have, good grounds for accepting what the church teaches, and if the church teaches certain things about the past, and if some of those things cannot be established by the methods recognized by historians, why should I cut myself off from those truths about the past by believing only those statements about the past that are endorsed by the methods recognized by historians?

I think it is worth noting that, whether the thesis that propositions about the past should be accepted only if they can be established by the methods recognized by historians is true or false, it is certainly incompatible with Christianity. A more careful statement of the thesis would be this: a proposition about the past should be accepted *by a given person* only if *that person knows* (or at least *has good reason to believe*) *that* it can be established by the methods employed by historians. Now it is obvious that many of the historical propositions essential to Christianity are rejected by large numbers of historians. I don't know whether it is possible for there to be a historical proposition that is (1) rejected by large numbers of historians, and (2) such that some people know, or have good reason to believe, that its truth can be established by the methods recognized by historians. But if this is possible, it can hardly be doubted that only a very well-educated person could know, with respect to a proposition rejected by large numbers of historians, that its truth could be established by the methods recognized by historians. It follows that some of the propositions essential to Christianity have the following feature: only a very well-educated person – if anyone – should accept them. This conclusion is, of course, radically inconsistent with the gospel. It is, in fact, very close to Gnosticism, for it entails that a form of knowledge accessible only to an elite is necessary for salvation.

I conclude that I do have grounds for accepting the historical reliability of the New Testament – grounds independent of critical studies.

As we have seen, however, it is still possible that my grounds may be *undermined* by critical studies. Let us therefore see what can be said in defense of Premise 5:

> Critical studies do not undermine these grounds, and there are good reasons for believing that they do not – reasons whose discovery requires no immersion in the minutiae of critical studies, but which can be grasped by anyone who attends to the most obvious features of critical studies.

That discoveries by those engaged in critical studies have undermined whatever grounds anyone may ever have had for accepting the historical reliability of the New Testament is not an unknown opinion. The late Norman Perrin, for example, says:

> In revealing the extent to which the theological viewpoint of the evangelist or transmitter of the tradition has played a part in the formation of the Gospel material, [redaction criticism] is forcing us to recognize that a Gospel does not portray the history of the ministry of Jesus from AD 27–30, or whatever the dates may actually have been, but the history of Christian experience in any and every age. At the same time this history of Christian experience is cast in the form of a chronicle of the ministry of Jesus, and some parts of it – whether large or small is irrelevant at this point – are actually based on reminiscence of that ministry. The Gospel of Mark is the prototype which the others follow and it is a mixture of historical reminiscence, interpreted tradition, and the free creativity of prophets and the evangelist. It is, in other words, a strange mixture of history, legend, and myth. It is this fact which redaction criticism makes unmistakably clear …[19]

It is obviously a consequence of the point of view expressed in this quotation that whatever grounds I may have for believing in the historical reliability of the New Testament have been undermined by critical studies – just as F.C. Baur's grounds for believing that the Fourth Gospel was a product of the late second century (whatever they may have been) have been undermined by the discovery of the Rylands Papyrus.

How shall I, who possess none of the tools of the New Testament critic, decide whether this evaluation (or other less extreme but still highly skeptical evaluations) of the historical reliability of the New Testament are to be believed? Someone might well ask why reasoning parallel to my earlier reasoning does not show that I need not raise this question. Why not argue that if one needed to decide whether the findings of critical studies undermined one's grounds for believing in the historical reliability of the New Testament before accepting the historical reliability of the New Testament, this would entail the false conclusion that only highly educated people – if anyone – could accept the historical reliability of the New Testament? The answer is that there are good reasons for thinking that critical studies do not cast any doubt on the historical reliability of the New Testament, and that one does not have to be a highly educated person to understand these reasons.[20]

---

[19] Perrin, *Redaction Criticism*, 75.

[20] At any rate, one does not have to have the tools of a trained NT scholar at one's disposal. It is certainly true that the reasons I shall give for believing that critical studies do not cast any doubt on the historical reliability of the NT could be understood only by someone who had enjoyed educational opportunities that have not

This is not surprising. In general, it is much harder to find reasonable grounds for deciding whether a certain proposition is true than it is to find reasonable grounds for deciding whether so-and-so's arguments for the truth (or for the falsity) of that proposition are cogent. If the proposition under consideration is one whose subject matter is the 'property' of some special field of study (like 'The continents are in motion' and unlike 'Mario Cuomo is the governor of New York'), and if the 'reasonable grounds' are those that can properly be appealed to by specialists in that field of study, then it is almost certain that only those specialists can find reasonable grounds for deciding whether it is true. (I suppose it is reasonable for me to believe that the continents are in motion on the basis of the fact that all the geology textbooks say they are. But this is not the sort of fact *geologists* can properly appeal to when they are asked to explain why they believe that the continents are in motion.) But if the 'reasonable grounds' are ones it is appropriate for the laity to appeal to, then it is almost always possible for the laity to find reasonable grounds for deciding whether the arguments employed by some group of specialists are cogent.

Suppose, for example, that the director of the Six Mile Island Nuclear Facility delivers to Governor Cuomo a long, highly technical case for the conclusion that the facility's reactor could never possibly present a radiation hazard. The governor, of course, doesn't understand a word of it. So he selects ten professors of nuclear engineering at what he recognizes as leading universities to evaluate the case with which he has been presented. Eight of the professors say that the reasoning on which the case is based is pretty shaky, one says it's abominable, and one – who turns out to be married to the director of Six Mile Island – says it's irrefutable. It seems to me that the governor has found reasonable grounds on which to decide whether the director's arguments in support of the proposition *Six Mile Island is safe* are cogent. And this is true despite the fact that he is absolutely unable to judge the case 'on its merits' – that is, unable to judge it using the criteria employed by nuclear engineers.

It is not impossible, therefore, that it turn out to be a comparatively easy matter for me to decide whether the findings of critical studies undermine my grounds for believing in the historical reliability of the New Testament. I say this in full knowledge of the fact that the field of New Testament scholarship is as opaque to me as nuclear engineering is (I suppose) to Governor Cuomo. I am aware that an academic field is an enormously complex thing, and that it takes years of formal study and independent research to be in a position to find one's way about in one of them. (Independent research in a field is absolutely essential for understanding it. This fact leads me to take with a grain of salt what

---

been available to everyone to whom the gospel has been preached. I would say, however, that these reasons could be understood by anyone who could understand the passage I have quoted from Perrin's book.

some of my fellow philosophers who have had some seminary or university training in New Testament studies tell me about the field. I think of new Ph.D.s in philosophy from Berkeley or Harvard or Pittsburgh, whose mental maps of academic philosophy are like the famous Steinberg *New Yorker* cover – the world as two-thirds midtown Manhattan – the philosophical world as two-thirds Berkeley or two-thirds Harvard or two-thirds Pittsburgh.)

Nevertheless, some facts about New Testament studies are accessible even to me. One of them is that many specialists in the field think – in fact, hold it to have been demonstrated – that the New Testament narratives are, in large part, narratives of events that never happened. I have quoted Perrin to this effect. On the other hand, one can easily find respectable workers in the field who take precisely the opposite view. In this camp I would place F.F. Bruce, John Drane and (to my astonishment, given *Honest to God*) John A.T. Robinson. Could it be that these people are *not* respectable? Well, their paper or '*Who's Who*' qualifications are excellent, and how else shall *I* judge them? That, after all, was how I judged Perrin: if he had not had impressive paper qualifications, I should have picked someone else to quote.

How can one expert in a field say what I have quoted Perrin as saying, when two other experts – as nearly simultaneously as makes no matter – write books called *The New Testament Documents: Are They Reliable?*[21] and *Can We Trust the New Testament?*[22] and answer their title questions 'yes'? (Drane's *Introducing the New Testament*[23] is, if anything, more trusting of the New Testament than the writings of Bruce and Robinson are.) A philosopher, at any rate, will not be at a loss for a possible answer to this question. A philosopher will suspect that such radical disagreement means that New Testament scholarship is a lot like philosophy. Either there is little *knowledge* available in the field, or, if there is, a significant proportion of the experts in the field perversely resist acquiring it.[24]

---

[21] Bruce, *New Testament Documents*. Bruce was Rylands Professor of Biblical Criticism and Exegesis in the University of Manchester.

[22] Robinson, *Can We Trust?*. Robinson was the Bishop of Woolwich and the Dean of Trinity College, Cambridge.

[23] Drane is Senior Lecturer in the School of Divinity and Religious Studies at Aberdeen.

[24] In the case of philosophy, my own view is that, while certain people know certain philosophical propositions to be true, it would be very misleading to say that philosophy, the academic subject, has any knowledge to offer. I consider cases of philosophical knowledge – a particular person's knowledge that human beings have free will, say – to be something on the order of individual attainments. A philosopher who knows that human beings have free will is not able to pass the grounds of his or her knowledge on to other persons in the reliable way in which a geologist who knows that the continents are in motion is able to pass the grounds of his or her knowledge on to other persons.

Is New Testament scholarship a source of knowledge? Or, more exactly, is what I have been calling critical studies a source of knowledge? Well, of course, the *data* of critical studies constitute knowledge: we know, thanks to the labors of those engaged in critical studies, that about ninety per cent of Mark appears in closely parallel form in Matthew, and that the phrase *en tois epouraniois* appears several times in Ephesians but in none of the other letters that purport to be by Paul, and many things of a like nature. But such facts are only as interesting as the conclusions that can be drawn from them. Do any of the conclusions that have been reached on the basis of these data constitute knowledge? Or, if you don't like the word *knowledge*, can any of these conclusions be described, in Perrin's words, as a 'fact' that critical studies 'make unmistakably clear'? (We know, thanks to the geologists, that the continents are in motion. This is a fact, which their investigations make unmistakably clear. Is there any thesis that we know in this sense that we can credit to the practitioners of critical studies?) I suppose that if any of the conclusions of critical studies is known to be true, or even known to be highly probable, it is this: Mark's Gospel was composed before Luke's or Matthew's, and both Luke and Matthew used Mark as a source. But this thesis, while it is almost universally accepted (at least everyone I have read says it is), has periodically been controverted by competent scholars, most recently by C.S. Mann in his commentary on Mark.[25] One might well wonder whether this thesis is indeed known to be true. If it is, how can it be that Mann, who is perfectly familiar with all of the arguments, denies it? If it is unmistakably clear, why isn't it unmistakably clear to *him?* And if the *priority* of Mark has not been made unmistakably clear, can it really be plausible to suppose that the much more controversial thesis that Mark is 'a strange mixture of history, legend, and myth' has been made unmistakably clear?

My suspicion that critical studies have made nothing of any great importance unmistakably clear, or even very clear at all, is reinforced when I examine the methods of some of the acknowledged experts in that field. Here I will mention only the methods of Perrin and his fellow redaction critics, for it is they and their predecessors, the form critics, who are the source of the most widely accepted arguments for the conclusion that the New Testament is historically unreliable. If someone supposes that critical studies undermine my supposed grounds for believing in the historical reliability of the New Testament, he will most likely refer me to the redaction critics for my refutation. (No doubt there are highly skeptical New Testament critics who reject the methods of redaction criticism. I can only say that I am very ignorant and do not know about them. I suppose them to exist only because it has been

---

[25] Mann, *Mark.*

my experience that, in the world of scholarship, every possible position is occupied. I shall have to cross their bridge when I come to it.)

I have few of the skills and little of the knowledge New Testament criticism requires. I know only enough Greek to be able on a given day to work my way painfully through one or two sentences that interest me on that day, using an interlinear crib, a dictionary and the paradigms at the back of the grammar book. I have more than once wasted time looking for a famous passage of Paul's in the wrong letter. But I do know something about reasoning, and I have been simply amazed by some of the arguments employed by redaction critics. My first reaction to these arguments, written up a bit, could be put in these words: 'I'm missing something here. These *appear* to be glaringly invalid arguments, employing methods transparently engineered to produce negative judgements of authenticity. But no one, however badly he might want to produce a given set of conclusions, would "cook" his methods to produce the desired results quite so transparently. These arguments must depend on tacit premises, premises the redaction critics regard as so obvious they don't bother to mention them.' But this now seems to me to have been the wrong reaction, for when I turn to commentaries on the methods of the redaction critics by New Testament scholars, I often find more or less my own criticisms of them – although, naturally enough, unmixed with my naïve incredulity.

I could cite more than one such commentary. The one I like best is an article by Morna Hooker,[26] and it articulates perfectly the criticisms I would have made of the methods of redaction criticism if I had been as knowledgeable as she and had not been hamstrung by my outsider's fear that there had to be something I was missing. If the author is right, I have certainly not missed anything: All the premises of the redaction critics are right out in the open. If she is wrong – well, how can *I*, an outsider, be expected to pay any attention to redaction criticism? If its methods are so unclear that a future Lady Margaret Professor of Divinity couldn't find out what they were, what hope is there for me? I might add that Professor Hooker's witness is especially impressive to an outsider like me because she does not criticize the methods of the redaction critics in order to advance the case of a rival method of her own; rather, their methods are the very methods she herself accepts. She differs from a committed and confident redaction critic like Perrin mainly in her belief that these methods can't establish very much – perhaps that certain logia are a bit more likely on historical grounds to be authentic than certain others – and she adheres to these methods only because (in her view) these methods are the only methods there are. (But if she accepts Perrin's methods, she would appear to dissent from one of his premises: that, owing to the pervasive influence in the

---

[26] 'On Using the Wrong Tool'.

formation of the Gospels of the theological viewpoints of the transmitters and evangelists, the gospel narratives are intrinsically so unreliable as historical sources that, in the absence of a very strong argument for the authenticity of a given saying, one should conclude that that saying is not authentic. If I understand Hooker, however, she would say in such a case that nothing can be said about its authenticity; she would conclude that a saying was inauthentic only if there were good arguments – arguments relating to the content and gospel setting of the particular saying – for its inauthenticity.)

I conclude that there is no reason for me to think that critical studies have established that the New Testament narratives are historically unreliable. In fact, there is no reason for me to think that they have established *any* important thesis about the New Testament. I might, of course change my mind if I knew more. But how much time shall I devote to coming to know more? My own theological writings, insofar as they draw on contemporary knowledge, draw on formal logic, cosmology and evolutionary biology. I need to know a great deal more about these subjects than I do. How much time shall I take away from my study of them to devote to New Testament studies (as opposed to the study of the New Testament)? The answer seems to me to be: very little. I would suggest that various seminaries and divinity schools might consider devoting a portion of their curricula to these subjects (not to mention the systematic study of the Fathers!), even if this had to be done at the expense of some of the time currently devoted to critical studies.

Let me close by considering a *tu quoque*. Is not philosophy open to many of the charges I have brought against critical studies? Is not philosophy argument without end? Is not what philosophers agree about just precisely nothing? Are not the methods and arguments of many philosophers (especially those who reach extreme conclusions) so bad that an outsider encountering them for the first time might well charitably conclude that he must be missing something? Must one not devote years of systematic study to philosophy before one is competent to think philosophically about whether we have free will or whether there is an objective morality or whether knowledge is possible? And yet, is one not entitled to believe in free will and knowledge and morality even if one has never read a single page of philosophy?

Ego quoque. If you are not a philosopher, you would be crazy to go to the philosophers to find anything out – other than what it is the philosophers say. If a philosopher tells you that you must, on methodological grounds, since he is the expert, take his word for something – that there is free will, say, or that morality is only convention – you should tell him that philosophy has not earned the right to make such demands. Philosophy is, I think, valuable. It is a good thing for the study of philosophy to be pursued, both by experts and by amateurs. But if it is a good thing for a certain field of study to be pursued by experts, it does not follow that that field of study comprises experts who can tell you things you need to attend to before you can practice a religion or join a political party or become a conscientious objector. And if it is a good thing for a certain field of study to be pursued by amateurs, it does not follow that anyone is under an obligation to *become* an amateur in that field.

This is very close to some of the depreciatory statements I have made about the authority of critical studies. Since I regard philosophy as a 'Good Thing', it should be clear that I do not suppose my arguments lend any support to the conclusion that the critical study of the New Testament is not a 'Good Thing'. Whether it is, I have no idea. I don't know enough about it to know whether it is. I have said only this: the very little I do know about critical studies is sufficient to establish that users of the New Testament need not – but I have said nothing against their doing so – attend very carefully to it.[27]

---

[27] I am grateful to Ronald Feenstra for his generous and careful comments on this essay in *Hermes and Athena*. The fact that I do not take this opportunity – the opportunity afforded by the re-publication of the essay – to discuss Professor Feenstra's criticisms of my argument does not mean that I think they are without merit. It rather reflects my judgement that even if all his criticisms were valid, this would not affect the argument in any essential way. I am also grateful to Harold W. Attridge, who sent me a long and thoughtful letter about various of the points raised in this chapter. I have tried to address one of his concerns in note 13. I should like, finally, to express my indebtedness to the writings of Professor E.L. Mascall, particularly his *Theology and the Gospel of Christ*, which directed me to many of the authors I have cited.

Bibliography

Adams, M.M., 'The Role of Miracles in the Structure of Luke-Acts', in *Hermes and Athena: Biblical Exegesis and Philosophical Theology* (ed. E. Stump and T. Flint; Notre Dame: University of Notre Dame Press, 1993), 235–73

Augustine, *The Literal Meaning of Genesis* (trans. J.H. Taylor; New York: Newman, 1982)

✓ Bruce, F.F., *The New Testament Documents: Are They Reliable?* (Leicester: Inter-Varsity Press, 6th rev. edn, 2000)

Cullmann, O., *Immortality of the Soul or Resurrection of the Body?* (London: Epworth Press, 1958)

Feenstra, R.J., 'Critical Studies of the New Testament: Comments on the Paper of Peter van Inwagen', in *Hermes and Athena: Biblical Exegesis and Philosophical Theology* (ed. E. Stump and T. Flint; Notre Dame: University of Notre Dame Press, 1993), 191–97

✓ Drane, J., *Introducing the New Testament* (New York: Harper & Row, 1986)

Harvey, V.A., 'New Testament Scholarship and Christian Belief', in *Jesus in History and Myth* (ed. R.J. Hoffman and G.A. Larue; Buffalo, NY: Prometheus Books, 1986), 194

Hooker, M., 'On Using the Wrong Tool', *Theology* 75 (1972), 570–81

——, and C. Hickling (eds.), *What about the New Testament? Essays in Honour of Christopher Evans* (London: SCM Press, 1975)

Mann, C.S., *Mark: A New Translation with Introduction and Commentary* (AB; Garden City, NJ: Doubleday, 1986)

✓ Mascall, E.L., *Theology and the Gospel of Christ: An Essay in Reorientation* (London: SPCK, 1977)

Perrin, N., *What is Redaction Criticism?* (Philadelphia: Fortress Press, 1969)

✓ Robinson, J.A.T., *Can We Trust the New Testament?* (London: Mowbray, 1977)

Sherwin-White, A.N., *Roman Society and Roman Law in the New Testament* (Oxford: Clarendon Press, 1963)

Stump, E., and T. Flint (eds.), *Hermes and Athena: Biblical Exegesis and Philosophical Theology* (Notre Dame: University of Notre Dame Press, 1993)

Van Inwagen, P., *God, Knowledge, and Mystery: Essays in Philosophical Theology* (Ithaca, NY: Cornell University Press, 1995)

——, 'Critical Studies of the New Testament and the User of the New Testament', in *Hermes and Athena: Biblical Exegesis and Philosophical Theology* (ed. E. Stump and T. Flint; Notre Dame: University of Notre Dame Press, 1993), 159–90

——, 'Genesis and Evolution', in *Reasoned Faith* (ed. E. Stump; Ithaca, NY: Cornell University Press, 1993), 93–127

✓ ——, 'Quam Dilecta', in *God and the Philosophers* (ed. T.V. Morris; New York: OUP, 1994), 31–60

6

Taking Soundings

History and the Authority of Scripture:
A Response to Peter van Inwagen

Colin J.D. Greene

Introduction

As a respondent to Peter Van Inwagen's chapter 'Do You Want Us to Listen to You?', I want to assure him that I *am* listening, and I am doing so with much sympathy toward the basic orientation of his argument. In case anyone is in doubt, Van Inwagen has a dispute with the fraternity of biblical scholarship – at least that part of the guild engaged in what he somewhat euphemistically refers to as 'critical studies'. He uses this phrase to refer to those biblical scholars who appear to refute the historical reliability of the Gospels as a reasonably accurate record of the sorts of things Jesus would have said and done, thereby by implication also denying that the New Testament possesses any inherent authority either for the church or the believing Christian. So, like Stephen Evans, who has taken issue with biblical scholars over the same matters, Van Inwagen wants a second airing of this dispute in the context of the debate generated by the Scripture and Hermeneutics Seminar.[1] In this context, the conversation is an interdisciplinary one affording philosophers like Van Inwagen and Evans the opportunity to participate in the discussion on their own terms.

In what follows I want to look carefully at the nature of Van Inwagen's dispute with critical studies, particularly as that relates to the central issue of what is meant by the notion of historical reliability. Secondly, I want to examine the

---

[1] See Evans's contribution to this volume, 'Tradition, Biblical Interpretation and Historical Truth', Ch. 14. See also Evans, *Historical Christ*.

arguments Van Inwagen utilizes to circumvent the difficulties presented to the ordinary believer by those scholars whose work appears to undermine the historical reliability of the gospel accounts of Jesus' messianic significance and status. And, thirdly, I want to advance some arguments of my own that would question the viability of the link Van Inwagen constructs between the criterion of historical reliability and the notion of the New Testament's authoritative claim upon the believing Christian.

Historical Reliability: What Does It Mean and How Should It Be Assessed?

The implications of Van Inwagen's disagreement are propounded in the familiar style of a philosophical argument. Consequently, if you cannot deny the logical cogency of the premises, you are invited to accept the plausibility of the conclusion. And what is the nature of this conclusion? Simply this: that those engaged in 'critical studies' have achieved nothing either to undermine the historical veracity of the gospel record to Jesus as the Christ, or indeed, to convince intelligent believers like himself, not well versed in the minutiae of such scholarly debates, that there is any warranty for taking the often sceptical nature of their conclusions seriously. Instead, claims Van Inwagen, warranted Christian belief can be established on other grounds – grounds that are in all probability more philosophically secure and existentially convincing than those offered by the critical scholars. All this, so to speak, is fighting talk – and all the more so because it emanates from a philosopher who is in fact sympathetic to much that goes on under the general term of biblical theology. The logical consistency of Van Inwagen's premises does in fact rest on particular propositions concerning the epistemological and veridical nature of what is meant by the notion of historical reliability, so it is here where the argument invites careful scrutiny.[2]

Van Inwagen restricts his investigation of the nature of historical reliability to the narrative structure of the gospel record; nevertheless he provides us with a succinct definition of what he means by historical reliability, which I will attempt to summarize. We can accept the Gospels as historically reliable, which is not the same as historically accurate, on the supposition that Jesus actually said and did most of what is ascribed to him by the gospel writers. On the rare occasions that such descriptions of the intentional acts and sayings of Jesus contain actual historical infelicities, we can safely conclude that this will do no harm to those who accept and believe such things at face value, as it were.

---

[2] For an interesting and informative discussion of the issues surrounding historical reliability and similar concerns, see Harvey, *Historian*.

Van Inwagen accepts that his phrase 'will do no harm' in regard to the unsuspecting believer requires further explanation. Unfortunately, the analogy he uses of a general involved in a military campaign is not as pertinently illustrative or convincingly illuminating as he might have hoped. Indeed, as I shall point out shortly, it fails to connect with his central point. Nevertheless, his argument relies on the supposition that there is within the Gospels a consensus of evidential material that functions as a legitimator in terms of providing us with an accurate picture of the type of person Jesus was, the sort of actions ascribed to him, and the likelihood of what he might have said. I suggest that this presupposition of a consensus *literalis* can only achieve that which Van Inwagen requires on the basis of the acceptance of the canonical veracity of the New Testament, and not merely in terms of what the Gospels tell us about Jesus.

It was, after all, the actual process of the church coming to some sort of general agreement about the canon of the New Testament that depended upon an equally general consensus in regard to the material that could be relied upon to provide an accurate portrayal of the person, ministry and messianic status of Jesus.[3] Furthermore, it is not clear that the phrase 'doing no harm' actually means that the hypothetically false statements we may encounter in the Gospels are actually irrelevant to the authentic portrayal of Jesus that the gospel writers apparently offer us. Nor is it clear that they are irrelevant to the practice of authentic Christian discipleship, which is what the analogy of the military general would suggest. Van Inwagen does admit, however, that historical reliability does not require us to accept that everything the gospel writers tell us about what Jesus said and did were recorded for us literally in the historical order these events occurred. Here the witness of the early church fathers is clearly on his side.[4] Having provided us with a fairly minimalist formal definition of historical reliability, Van Inwagen offers us a functional equivalent.

> My functional explanation of what is meant by the historical reliability of the New Testament narratives is this: the narratives are historically reliable if they are historically accurate to a degree consonant with the use the church has made of them.[5]

Throughout the long history of the church's homiletical and liturgical use of the Scriptures very few theologians or church leaders were prepared to suggest, until the advent of historical-critical scholarship in the eighteenth century, that the Gospels could be largely the result of the creative imagination of the early

---

[3] In this regard see von Campenhausen, *Formation*.
[4] See note 4 in Ch. 5, Van Inwagen, 'Do You Want Us to Listen to You?'.
[5] Van Inwagen, 'Do You Want Us to Listen to You?', Ch. 5.

Christian communities.[6] If this were in fact the case then the church is guilty, albeit unwittingly, of perpetrating a vast intellectual and spiritual fraud which would indeed fall under the rubric of doing ordinary believers a huge amount of wrong. At this juncture, the example Van Inwagen offers us in terms of John 3 is more helpful. Apparently all that the church's functional use of the story of Jesus' encounter with Nicodemus requires us to accept in terms of the historical reliability of this narrative is that there was a Pharisee called Nicodemus and that Jesus did on some occasion talk to someone, who may or may not have been Nicodemus, about the spiritual significance of being born again.[7] One cannot help wondering at this point if such a functional definition of historical reliability is in fact worth defending.

Arguments Used to Circumvent the Difficulties Surrounding the Notion of Historical Reliability

It is clear that, at this stage in the argument, we are dealing with what the distinguished Old Testament scholar Gerhard von Rad referred to as the history of the transmission of religious tradition.[8] In other words, as Van Inwagen recognizes, the gospel traditions witness to a process of oral and written storytelling. This process is inevitably influenced by a number of decisive factors such as the evangelists' point of view, the selection and editing of material and the spiritual needs of the various communities for which these accounts of Jesus' life and significance were written. It is precisely in all three respects, as biblical scholars have recognized, that the notion of historical reliability comes under threat.[9] In order to safeguard the basic integrity of the history of the transmission of the gospel traditions, Van Inwagen has recourse to the familiar notion of divine superintendence. In other words, he believes that it is not an unwarranted superstition to suggest that part of what we mean by the notion of the divine inspiration of the Scriptures was that God, through the agency of the Holy Spirit, ensured that the necessary degree of historical reliability was preserved.[10]

---

[6] See Bartholomew, 'Uncharted Waters'; also Greene, 'Arms'. Both chapters seek to chart the progress whereby such sentiments became typical of the fraternity of European biblical scholarship.

[7] Van Inwagen, 'Do You Want Us to Listen to You?', Ch. 5.

[8] Von Rad, *Old Testament Theology*.

[9] For a useful and lively discussion of how such issues are handled by those involved in the latest attempt to locate the historical Jesus see Powell, *Jesus;* also Witherington, *Jesus Quest*.

[10] This is a familiar hermeneutical move for those scholars who are committed to an evangelical defence of Scripture as the living word of God. See, e.g., Bloesch, *Holy Scripture*.

To make such claims allows room for the inevitable differences of viewpoint and emphases reflected in the various gospel accounts, as well as for the preservation of authentic core material concerning the true significance of Jesus, throughout the historical process – from the genesis of the original sources to the closing of the canon.[11]

The rest of Van Inwagen's arguments relate to more philosophical issues concerning the nature of warranted Christian belief as opposed to explicit claims for knowledge. Van Inwagen notes that many of our most cherished beliefs, for instance the theory of evolution or the belief in creation *ex nihilo*, are not accompanied by compelling arguments for their veracity that would entice others to accept them as irrefutable. Rather, they are often founded on another set of beliefs that are justified by other means – for instance, the appeal to scientific consensus or church tradition. Consequently, by implication, if church tradition accepts the resurrection of Jesus as the central christological event for establishing the belief in the divinity of Christ, then it is perfectly reasonable for the ordinary believer, through their membership of the church, to believe in the resurrection without requiring additional historical proof. Furthermore, when one looks at the arguments put forward by biblical scholars either to deny or establish the historicity of the resurrection, or indeed for that matter the arguments for something less contentious, such as the belief in Markan priority, there is so much dispute and disagreement that, in any other discipline, this would not amount to claims for genuine knowledge. In that regard, claims Van Inwagen, 'critical studies' is rather like philosophy, the practitioners of which clearly disagree on most of the main axioms of philosophical argument. Philosophy and critical studies may be good things, but no one should be expected to suspend membership of a particular religious community on the basis of the disputations and disagreements that clearly engage the scholars in both fields but which do not provide sufficient epistemological clarity to warrant an unprejudiced claim to knowledge.

So, in response to those who deny the historical veracity of the New Testament, Van Inwagen puts forward four central arguments. The first assertion is that there is within the New Testament a broad consensus of agreement concerning the nature of the Christ-event, against which the notion of historical reliability should be tested – rather than against the precise details of individual narratives and pericopes. Secondly, he points to the use that church tradition has made of these documents throughout the long history of Christian formation, discipleship and ministry. Third is the belief in the superintendence of the Holy Spirit throughout the process of the history of the transmission of

---

[11] It is clear that here we have moved beyond notions solely pertaining to the historical reliability of the NT to the integration of exegetical and theological issues, which is a real concern of much contemporary biblical scholarship. See, e.g., Green and Turner (eds.), *Between Two Horizons.*

the Christian tradition. Fourth is the recognition of the difference between establishing warranted grounds for Christian belief as opposed to apparent assent to contentious claims to knowledge.[12]

Does the Authority of the New Testament Depend upon the Notion of Historical Reliability?

There is, of course, a long tradition of biblical scholars, and indeed philosophers, who have sought to rigorously defend the historical reliability of the gospel record to Jesus utilizing similar arguments. In my own case, I have sought to demonstrate how biblical scholarship since the early eighteenth century has traded on quite different, and at times competing, philosophies of history in order to advance their various theories concerning the origins of Christianity. In the process, I suggest, three philosophies of history appear to have predominated: critical realist, idealist and now, of course, postmodern. Only in the latter case is the search for historical reliability given up altogether, with the frank admission that history is a text constantly under reconstruction and therefore immune to the kind of interrogation that would seek to find such grounds of justification.[13] In the second volume in this series I sought to advance my philosophy of history based on a particular understanding of the nature of apocalyptic that could, I suggested, tread a middle ground between both the positivism and pragmatism that have dogged the respective accounts of the nature of history from the proponents of modernity and postmodernity respectively.[14] In what follows I will pursue some of this thinking further. I will use as my conversation partner another account of the nature of apocalyptic first put forward by Martin Heidegger.

Heidegger's fundamental task as a philosopher was to chart the meaning of Being.[15] To do so he had to attend to those disclosures of Being located in the history of metaphysics.[16] This was by no means an unbroken line of communication; rather, the disclosure of Being that begins with Anaximander and ends with Nietzsche, the last great metaphysician, takes us on a journey beyond ontology into eschatology.[17] As is always the case with apocalyptic, it all turns on

---

[12] See the contributions to this volume by Bartholomew, '*Warranted* Biblical Interpretation', Ch. 2; Gordon, 'A Warranted Version of Historical Biblical Criticism?', Ch. 3; and Plantinga, 'Two (or More) Kinds of Scripture Scholarship', Ch. 1.

[13] Greene, 'Arms'; see also Harrisville and Sundberg, *Bible*.

[14] Greene, 'Rockslide'.

[15] Cf. Heidegger, *Basic Writings*.

[16] See particularly Heidegger, 'End of Philosophy'.

[17] See Heidegger, *Early Greek;* and *Gesamtausgabe*, V (particularly the fragment on Anaximander).

the power of a particular metaphor. In Heidegger's case, he deploys the epistolary postal principle.[18] Like some giant supernova explosion, Being first disclosed itself in a flash that irradiated the Greek countryside and just as swiftly faded from view. All that remained were the traces of the original explosion that come to us as a series of dispatches which must be deciphered and understood. Derrida would have us recognize that all postal services are inherently corrigible – letters get lost, dispatches are misdirected and we no longer know who the original sender was or indeed for whom the message was intended[19] – but that was not Heidegger's concern. With Heidegger, the traces of the original disclosure of Being are now so faint that we await a new eschaton. That can be the only reason for constructing a hermeneutical trajectory from Anaximander to ourselves at the end of the communication system. It is not the compressing of the vast historical or chronological distance that matters, but attending to the urgency of the message. The trace alerts us not just to the primordial disclosure of Being, but also to its eventual fading from view, to the *telos* of the event.[20] This is the urgency of the call that we receive from such disclosures – not that we can master the message, but that it interrupts and illuminates our own existence in the light of the end. Just as quickly as the pulse fades, so we know how precarious is our own time as we await a new eschaton.[21]

For Heidegger, this is how we distinguish teleology from eschatology. Teleology is the rule book of metaphysics. 'In teleology the beginning is small, progress is steady, and the end is a great fulfilment and parousia, an *Aufhebung*'.[22] Eschatology, on the other hand, is the playground of the gods. The beginning is a massive disclosure, the unconcealment of Being, which then vanishes like lightning – leaving only faint pulses of energy, disrupted traces of meaning which eventually disappear altogether into the darkness until the dawn breaks forth once again. This was Heidegger's understanding of the significance of our own time. We are at the end of the sterile efficiency of historical consciousness. Our age is the age of historicism, when all that matters is that we master the right historical technique and so connect the past with the present, message to the interpreter, sonar to the faint noises of the past that still echo across the ages. In the process we corrupt our relationship with the future. Our time is an essentially backward looking gesture of contempt for the true meaning of Being.[23] We no longer recognize the authority of the original message, now a mere blip on the sonar screen which, because of its very vacuity, alerts us that the past is gone and the end is nigh.

---

[18] In what follows I am indebted to Caputo's fine study *Radical Hermeneutics*.
[19] Derrida, *Margins*, 24–29.
[20] See Caputo, *Radical Hermeneutics*, 160.
[21] Caputo, *Radical Hermeneutics*, 161.
[22] Caputo, *Radical Hermeneutics*, 161.
[23] See Heidegger, *Early Greek*, 17; and *Gesamtausgabe*, V, 325–26.

In eschatology the earliest is not a seed which slowly ripens into the last but a flash which, having been all but extinguished by the last, is capable of flashing again and turning darkness into light, the evening into a new dawn. In teleology the last always comes after the first, after a long period of maturation; but in eschatology the first can overtake (*überholen*) the last, and with a suddenness that could not be anticipated.[24]

Clearly there are many resonances in Heidegger's eschatological hermeneutic with what I would term the corruptibility of historical consciousness. The latter makes great play with notions of historical reliability or the historicity of original events and commits the fallacy of teleology. The great purveyor of this kind of historicism was Ernst Troeltsch, with his notion of the homogeneity of all events that somehow allows us to correlate the past with the present.[25] As Heidegger reminds us, we become so technologically proficient in our mastery of historical science that we miss the real authority of the original message that resides not in the notion of historical reliability, but in the eschatological orientation of the Christ-event.

To transcribe Heidegger's metaphysics back into the biblical theology from whence it originated,[26] the resurrection of Jesus is the great disclosure of the meaning of Being because it connects us with the *telos*. It is the eschaton proleptically in advance. It is a warning that the kingdom is near, too near to ignore the urgency of the salvation procured on our behalf. This is surely the source of the authority that the New Testament witness to Christ possesses. It is the faintest trace of the originating unconcealment of Being, the meaning of which is contained in the summons to repent because the kingdom is at hand. Those various forms of historicism that endeavour to locate the authority of the New Testament in the contingency of historical events are a singular witness to the wrong kind of enquiry. They are a privileging of teleology over eschatology, a manifestation of the hubris of historical science that relies on technology rather than hermeneutics. Deep hermeneutics explores the power of metaphor in an effort to jolt us out of our historicist slumbers – as Heidegger, with his acknowledgement of the postal principle that dispatches the meaning of Being long after the original disclosure of its presence in our midst. Or, as in my own case, the expropriation of the meaning of apocalyptic, not fundamentally as a disclosure event, but a cataclysmic event that tears the fabric of history apart[27] – that fabric that purports to seamlessly connect the past with the future via the present. In reality, of course, a fiction that is by no means unintentional because it allows the historian to walk effortlessly down the corridors of history

---

[24] Caputo, *Radical Hermeneutics*, 163.

[25] See Greene, 'Arms', 215–16.

[26] In this regard see Ingraffia, *Postmodern Theory*, 110–23.

[27] See Greene, 'Rockslide', 199–209.

hearing only the sound of his own boots.[28] Van Inwagen concedes far too much to this kind of historicism when he binds the authority of the New Testament too closely to the notion of historical reliability and so makes himself a hostage to the fortunes of those who would seek to undermine the authority of Scripture via the same route. If the New Testament were essentially a gnostic tract, the essence of which was to initiate us into the secrets of salvation, it would be vulnerable to this kind of attack. In reality the New Testament is a public proclamation of the *kyrios*, who was raised from the dead. Its authority is not located in the historicity of the events it describes but in the eschaton that has already been thrust upon us.

Heidegger alerts us to the primacy of eschatological hermeneutics as a way of understanding the authoritative claim upon our lives connected with the primordial disclosure of Being. For too long, historical-critical investigation of the traditions and hermeneutical trajectories associated with the Christ-event has been overly enamoured with the lure of scientific teleology. The result is a form of positivistic historicism that reduces the authority of the canon of Scripture to the historical reliability of the originating events. When such a notion of historical reliability proves too brittle to bear the weight of authority imposed upon it, the text of Scripture suffers accordingly. Not surprisingly, then, other doctrinal or philosophical arguments are brought in to shore up the already hard-pressed notion of historical reliability by other means. It would be more honest to the intention of the New Testament witness to Christ to give the notion of historical reliability some respite from such an onerous task and attend instead to the eschatological disclosure of meaning present in the Christ-event. The early apostolic proclamation of the kerygma was almost solely orientated to the eschatological significance of the death and resurrection of Jesus, and with good reason. The canonical authority of the New Testament rests on the fact that these documents introduce us to Jesus, the eschatological prophet of the kingdom who is also the *kyrios* – the manifestation of the kingdom in our midst.

---

[28] Greene, 'Rockslide', 209–15.

Bibliography

Bartholomew, C., 'Uncharted Waters: Philosophy, Theology and the Crisis in Biblical Interpretation', in *Renewing Biblical Interpretation* (ed. C. Bartholomew, C. Greene and K. Möller; SHS 1; Carlisle: Paternoster; Grand Rapids: Zondervan, 2000), 1–39

Bloesch, D.G., *Holy Scripture: Revelation, Inspiration and Interpretation* (Carlisle: Paternoster, 1994)

Caputo, J.D., *Radical Hermeneutics: Repetition, Deconstruction, and the Hermeneutic Project* (Indianapolis: Indiana University Press, 1987)

Derrida, J., *Margins of Philosophy* (trans. A. Bass; Chicago: University of Chicago Press, 1982)

Evans, C.S., *The Historical Christ and the Jesus of Faith* (New York: OUP, 1996)

Green, J.B., and M. Turner (eds.), *Between Two Horizons: Spanning New Testament Studies and Systematic Theology* (Grand Rapids: Eerdmans, 2000)

Greene, C.J.D., 'In the Arms of the Angels: Biblical Interpretation, Christology and the Philosophy of History', in *Renewing Biblical Interpretation* (ed. C. Bartholomew, C. Greene and K. Möller; SHS 1; Carlisle: Paternoster; Grand Rapids: Zondervan 2000), 198–239

——, '"Starting a Rockslide" – Deconstructing History and Language via Christological Detonators', in *After Pentecost: Language and Biblical Interpretation* (ed. C. Bartholomew, C. Greene and K. Möller; SHS 2; Carlisle: Paternoster; Grand Rapids: Zondervan, 2001), 195–223

Harrisville, R.A., and W. Sundberg, *The Bible in Modern Culture* (Grand Rapids: Eerdmans, 1995)

Harvey, V.A., *The Historian and the Believer* (London: SCM Press, 1967)

Heidegger, M., *Basic Writings: Revised and Expanded Version* (ed. D.F. Krell; London: Routledge & Kegan Paul, 1993)

——, 'The End of Philosophy and the Task of Thinking', in *Basic Writings: Revised and Expanded Version* (ed. D.F. Krell; London: Routledge & Kegan Paul, 1993), 427–49

——, *Early Greek Thinking* (trans. F. Capuzzi and D. Krell; New York: Harper & Row, 1975)

——, *Gesamtausgabe*, V: *Holzwege* (Frankfurt: Klostermann, 1976)

Ingraffia, B.D., *Postmodern Theory and Biblical Theology: Vanquishing God's Shadow* (Cambridge: CUP, 1995)

Powell, M.A., *Jesus as a Figure in History: How Modern Historians View the Man from Galilee* (Louisville, KY: Westminster / John Knox Press, 1998)

von Campenhausen, H., *The Formation of the Christian Bible* (London: Adam & Charles Black, 1972)

von Rad, G., *Old Testament Theology* (2 vols.; Edinburgh: Oliver & Boyd, 1962)

Witherington, B., *The Jesus Quest: The Third Search for the Jew of Nazareth* (Carlisle: Paternoster, 1995)

7

Which Conversation Shall We Have?

*History, Historicism and Historical Narrative in Theological Interpretation:
A Response to Peter van Inwagen*

Joel B. Green

'For what you see and hear depends a good deal on where you are standing: it also depends on what sort of person you are.'[1] So observes the narrator of the creation of the world – and with it, talking beasts of all kinds – in book six of C.S. Lewis's *Chronicles of Narnia*. Foolish man that he was, Uncle Andrew heard only roaring when Aslan sang the melody of genesis, only snarling when Aslan spoke the words of first commissioning. Apparently, when it comes to powers of observation and meaning-making, we see what we allow ourselves to see and find the categories of evidence for which we had gone looking. This is certainly the case when it comes to the problem of 'meaning' in biblical interpretation.

Prior to the Reformation and its sequelae, biblical interpretation moved forward under the working assumption that text and history were coterminous, or at least that the history behind the text was not the sole or determinative factor in meaning-making. Modernity, however, posited a purposeful segregation of 'history' and 'text'. Consequently, the events to which the biblical text allegedly gives witness and the biblical text that provides such a witness were no longer presumed to be coterminous. Since interpretive privilege is accorded to 'history' in this perspective, biblical interpretation was construed as a discipline of 'validation' (when the biblical text is judged to represent historical events with accuracy) or of 'reconstruction' (when it is not). And this interpretive agenda would eventuate in the state of affairs that generally characterizes our

---

[1] Lewis, *Magician's Nephew*, 125.

current situation. Thus, Robert Miller can complain of Justo González' commentary on Acts that, though 'intended to relate Scripture specifically to the
lives of Latin-American Protestants', it is 'seriously flawed' for its failure critically to address the question, 'Are the accounts narrated in Acts based on actual
events?'.[2] As Robert Morgan notes, 'on the surface the aims of biblical historians seem quite remote from those of Jews and Christians who interpret the
Bible in the expectation of religious insight'.[3] For Morgan and, I take it, for
Professor Van Inwagen, noting that biblical historians (or, as Van Inwagen has
it, those engaged in 'critical studies') have one interpretive agenda, religious
communities another, is not so much a condemnation of either; rather, recognition of different interpretive aims serves to relativize the historical-critical
paradigm, and particularly the hegemony it has enjoyed up through the
closing decades of the twentieth century.

By way of response to Professor Van Inwagen's comments, I want, first, to
work from within this perspective. That is, I want to presume that the conversation he has framed around issues of historical veracity is a fruitful one, and
suggest areas where his approach seems less helpful and is unlikely to convince.
During the twentieth century, scholars became increasingly polarized in their
assessment of the historical veracity of the Gospels and Acts. While some took a
more positive view, others were less hopeful about the value of these New
Testament books as historical sources and preferred to examine these narratives
for their theological and/or ideological content. Unfortunately, the terms of
the debate have often been cast in such a manner that the whole discussion has
deteriorated into little more than a shouting match across the chasm separating
the two positions, and I fear that, overall, Van Inwagen's contribution is
unlikely to alter the status quo in this respect. This will lead to a second set of
comments – having queried whether Professor Van Inwagen has cast the
conversation in the most helpful way, I will suggest that, for theological interpretation of Scripture, or for ecclesially located interpretation of Scripture, our
discourse may require a different beginning point.

'Users', 'Critical Studies' and 'History'

Since Professor Van Inwagen first drafted his essay in 1993, 'critical studies' has
moved forward in perhaps predictable ways. Clifton Black had already undermined the work of redaction criticism, demonstrating in his study of *The
Disciples According to Mark* that the results of such efforts were governed less by

---

[2] Miller, 'Review', 759–60.
[3] Morgan with Barton, *Biblical Interpretation*, 15.

the method itself and more by the presumptions of the critic.[4] Form criticism in New Testament studies had already begun to be eclipsed by rhetorical criticism,[5] thus moving away from the sorts of historical-critical questions at which Van Inwagen took aim. As a consequence, the two methodological approaches that attracted Van Inwagen's attention deserve little comment. Moreover, that Van Inwagen's questions have been largely supplanted in many circles by other sorts of critical approaches that one might regard as equally challenging to 'ordinary churchgoers who read the New Testament and hear it read in church and hear it preached on' seems not to have caught his peripheral vision. I am thinking of new historicism, postcolonial theory and a host of other so-called postmodern approaches with presumptions about and orientations toward history and historicism that do not fit easily into Van Inwagen's analysis.[6] At the same time, the Jesus Seminar has now completed its work[7] and given birth, in 1999, to an Acts Seminar, the task of which is to 'evaluate and report on the historical authenticity of the Acts of the Apostles, in much the same way as the Jesus Seminar reviewed the sayings and events in the gospels'.[8] And in other ways, what Van Inwagen labels 'critical studies', what New Testament scholars typically call 'questions of introduction', continue to occupy a sizable segment of the guild. This leads me to consider briefly three questions concerning Van Inwagen's argument.

My first two questions may be taken together. Even though they relate to different aspects of Van Inwagen's argument, they focus on the same issue – namely, the problem of 'history'. First, is it not overly simplistic to claim, as Premise 2 has it, that the church has presupposed the historical reliability of the New Testament? Second, what utility resides in continuing to claim for the New Testament 'historical reliability', when the notion of historical accuracy requires such extensive qualification? That is, at what point has 'historical accuracy' become a slogan held tightly but vacated of recognizable meaning? Or, perhaps better, to what degree is the concept of 'historicity' so tainted by historical positivism, so static in its referential scope, that we are better served by moving on to other constructive claims regarding the nature of Scripture?

On the one hand, then, it is easy enough to say that, in the first centuries of the Christian movement, no contrast was drawn in biblical exegesis between the historical and the theological meaning of New Testament texts. *Historia* resided at the surface of narrative texts. But this is not 'history' in the later sense of 'historical evidence' or of 'what really happened', and it is worth

---

[4] Black, *Disciples*.

[5] E.g., Berger, *Formgeschichte*.

[6] Cf., e.g., Adam (ed.), *Handbook*; *Postmodern Interpretations*.

[7] See Funk, et al., *Five Gospels*.

[8] <www.westarinstitute.org/Westar/westar.html>; accessed 2 Jan. 2003.

remembering that, in part, interest in the fourfold meaning of Scripture developed as a result of the need to address those points at which historical data appeared to stand in opposition. How to reconcile the testimony of John's Gospel with that of the Synoptics? How to reconcile competing details among the Synoptics? The answer was not to deny historicity (as Van Inwagen might remind us), but a response was no less necessary. It might be urged that Van Inwagen's proposal for a more generous definition of 'historicity' thus returns us to a perspective more at home in the early church. If this is so, then we might query whether it is prudent and useful to deploy language and categories from the post-Enlightenment period to describe premodern perspectives, especially in order to shore up claims about the New Testament – themselves cast in modern(ist) categories – against indictments of a modern(ist) sort.

A different way of getting at these issues would be to worry over the way Van Inwagen has defined historical accuracy – namely, 'that (1) Jesus said and did at least most of the things ascribed to him in those narratives, and (2) any false statements the narratives may contain about what Jesus said and did will do no harm to those users of the New Testament who accept them as true because they occur in the New Testament'. Although I as a New Testament scholar and Christian believer might be willing to grant this as a working definition of historical accuracy, it cannot escape notice that this definition departs significantly from the way historical accuracy is typically understood, whether among those engaged in 'critical studies' or in the general population. Indeed, I wonder whether the vast majority of those of the class of people in which Van Inwagen claims membership ('those who regard the New Testament as historically reliable and who are not trained New Testament scholars') would not fault him for engaging in sleight of hand.

I also wonder how the claim embodied in this definition of historical accuracy could be falsified. I wonder by what criteria Van Inwagen would want to demonstrate that 'Jesus said and did at least most of the things ascribed to him'. And I wonder if Van Inwagen would be satisfied if it could be proven that only 51 per cent ('at least most') of the words and deeds ascribed to Jesus were found to be historically accurate. If, with this last question, my readers might fault me for grasping at absurdity, I would urge that this is because Van Inwagen wants me to work with categories of measure and canons of certainty that are alien to the purposes at hand.

My third question is this: Is the church well served by lining up 'respectable workers in the field' of New Testament studies (Van Inwagen mentions F.F. Bruce, for example, and John Drane) over against others, presumably equally respectable, in order to demonstrate, as Premise 5 has it, that 'critical studies' has not undermined the historical reliability of the New Testament materials? Certainly, Bruce was, and Drane is, 'respectable' as New Testament scholars, but neither could be counted as specialists in Gospels-study and/or in the quest of the historical Jesus. Even if they could, it is worth recalling that the Jesus Seminar, widely known as a group for its extreme skepticism concerning the historical veracity of the New Testament Gospels, supported their conclusions in precisely this way. That is, they drew attention to themselves as respectable scholars, leaders in the field, with impressive credentials and the like. One side has its scholars and the other side theirs; is Van Inwagen's proposal likely to serve as more than a rearguard action?

In other words, has Van Inwagen framed the discourse about history and New Testament interpretation in the best terms?

Reframing History

Let me now urge what I have already suggested – namely, that at issue here are two related problems: (1) problematic assumptions about the nature of 'history' and (2) the sort of truth-claims we might associate with biblical narrative. Proceeding as Van Inwagen does, by allowing the terrain to be mapped by a problematic historicism, is unlikely to produce the results needed for theological interpretation of Scripture.[9]

In spite of the progress made in the philosophy of history in the last third of the twentieth century, and the concomitant innovations in the academic field of historiography, biblical studies in the historical mode has generally continued on the basis of an 'old historicism' (i.e., a mode of critical study that tied meaning to historical reconstruction, behind the text) not identical with but with close ties to the historical positivism of the nineteenth century. Perhaps this is not surprising, given Stephen Neill's assessment of the need in New Testament research for a nuanced theology of history, taken up again and lamented by Tom Wright: 'But where are the scholars sufficiently familiar with actual history-writing, sufficiently at home in philosophy and the history of ideas, and sufficiently committed to the study of the New Testament, to undertake the task?'[10] Put with only a modicum of hyperbole, in the twentieth century biblical scholars of all theological stripes have cut deep ruts in the ground, tracing one after the other in the same tracks, turning to the New Testament materials with the focused question, 'Is this a record of "what actually happened"?'. Depending largely on the theological outlook of the individual asking the question, the answer was rather predictably mostly positive or mostly negative.

Against this backdrop, then, I want briefly to suggest how recent work in the philosophy of history might help us better to understand the nature of biblical narratives as history, mediate between competing views of the historical

---

[9] What follows is adapted from my essay, 'Book of Acts'.
[10] Neill and Wright, *Interpretation of the New Testament*, 366.

and theological agenda of the narrative, and breathe fresh life into theological and religiously significant readings of biblical narrative. In taking this route, I do not mean to undermine the importance of ongoing historical investigation of the world within which these documents are set and the events to which they give witness, as though this were unimportant to our reading of these narratives. Rather, on the one hand, I want more simply to urge that such study will never be able to resolve the impasse in historical study of the Gospels and Acts. Thus, for example, Cilliers Breytenbach can demonstrate that Acts 13–14 displays a familiarity with the 'local color' of the venues to which Paul and Barnabas are said to have traversed, that the Lukan narrative is at this point consistent with the available archaeological evidence, and that the speech-material in these two chapters includes Pauline tradition.[11] Moreover, Breytenbach can thus militate against Conzelmann's confident assertion that these two chapters constitute a Lukan creation designed to provide an exemplar for future missionary activity and to posit a theological problem for which the apostolic council in Acts 15 becomes the necessary resolution.[12] Even if such historical investigation can serve to demonstrate the verisimilitude of the Lukan account, however, it cannot establish the historical veracity of that account. On the other hand, the sort of work represented in Breytenbach's study, and perhaps even more so in the sort of archaeological attention devoted in the past decade to Philippi,[13] provides us with more contoured sociocultural horizons within which to grasp the interpretive significance of Luke's narrative. In electing an alternative route, then, I am proposing that the inability of the Gospels and Acts to divulge satisfying and conclusive answers to the historical questions posed them in the last century is a consequence of badly framed questions. Recent work on the nature of the narrative representation of historical events has drawn attention to other interests – for example, the tension in the writing of history between the general and the particular, the importance of teleology and causation and the inevitability of selectivity and partiality in historiography.[14]

Confronted with such emphases, some biblical scholars might immediately imagine a retreat into a-historicism or unfettered historical relativism, as if the only choices before the historian were scientific neutrality on the one hand, ideological imposition on the other. If these are the only choices, then there is good reason for anxiety. We would not want to give up burning incense at the altar of dispassionate empiricism, à la Leopold von Ranke ('*wie es eigentlich gewesen*', history 'as it actually was'), only to find ourselves enrolled in the cult of perspectivalism, locating history in the service of tribalism (each group its own

---

[11] Breytenbach, *Paulus und Barnabas*.

[12] Conzelmann, *Acts*, 98.

[13] See, e.g., Pilhofer, *Philippi*.

[14] Cf., e.g., Cook, *History/Writing*; Lowenthal, *Past*.

history). Although we may have learned that what passes under the banner of scientific objectivity is often the unselfconscious legitimation of a scholar's own ideological commitments, for most of us at least, the self-conscious imposition of a self-sustaining metanarrative is not a welcome antidote. Projected onto the New Testament evangelists, the choices in this case would be writers who either: 1) gave us an objective reconstruction of the past without practical interests of any sort, whether entertainment or propaganda or pedagogical; or 2) constructed for us a narrative (more or less) without historical reminiscence in order to serve as an instrument of religio-political or socially entertaining power. In this case, our error is one of category. 'Objectivity is not neutrality'[15] – that is, a *via media* exists, which recognizes that fairness and honesty, truth-seeking, critical sifting of evidence and other allegiances and practices necessary for and appropriate to intellectual community are not of necessity competitive with or contradicted by such theological commitments as Luke might have exercised in his construction of the narrative of Acts.

This means, on the one hand, that the person (or community) responsible for the telling is forever engaged in making choices about what to exclude and include, and how to relate one event to another. Decisions are required, and not only for the obvious reason that, if everything 'were written down, I suppose that the world itself could not contain the books that would be written',[16] but also to escape the democratization of events whereby nothing has significance because everything is of equal consequence. And yet, decisions involving valuation are inescapably subjective, oriented as they are around a particular teleology and chain of cause-and-effect. Historians are concerned with what they and their communities deem to be significant among the many events that might have been recorded, and in the relationships among the events that are recounted. If this 'significance' is parsed theologically, this does not make the consequent narrative any less 'historical'. The paradox of history/writing, as Albert Cook labels it, is that verification and narrative come into focus in every single sentence. Historiographical accounts cannot be peeled, layer after layer, as if the interpretive husk could be separated from the historical kernel, since each sentence (each 'layer', so to speak) has both an interpretive and a documentary force. This means that history/writing must be experienced and judged globally and cannot be disconfirmed event-by-event.[17]

Manifestly, this perspective on history/writing requires transformed perspectives on historiography as 'mimesis'. This is true, first, because it takes seriously that 'memory' is being formed long before the historian appears on

---

[15] Haskell, 'Objectivity'; also 'History'.

[16] Jn. 21:25.

[17] Cook, *History/Writing*, 55–72.

the scene with the twin tasks of research and narration before her. Oral history represents and shapes the community of memory. History/telling precedes and constrains history/writing. It is true, second, because memories are in a perpetual state of flux, being surfaced or suppressed, held or lost, in relation to their perceived importance. Interpretive commitments, rooted in and expressed by communities of memory, are already in play. As a result, the pressing questions become, on the micro-level, 'How is this event related causally to that one?' and, on the macro-level, 'What end is served by narrating the story in this way (rather than some other)?'. The task of reading Acts locates itself less in relation to concerns with *validation*, therefore, and more in terms of *signification*.

To push one step further, it is worth asking where this interpretive approach leaves us with regard to engaging the Gospels and Acts more specifically as Christian Scripture. First, a focus on the question of these narratives within the Christian Scriptures does not turn attention away from the need for historical investigation. If Scripture purports to narrate human–divine relations, then Scripture itself invites historical questions. Having said this, it is important to realize that historical study cannot accomplish what has often been desired of it, at least generally – namely, that these narratives might be proven to be true. Historical study alone cannot speak to such questions as whether Jesus of Nazareth is both Lord and Christ, whether Jesus' resurrection signaled the restoration of God's people and the ushering in of the new era, or any of a number of other claims that are central to the witness of the Gospels and Acts. And, in the end, this means that the meaning, truth and authority of the narrative of Acts cannot be tethered to or made dependent on modernist notions of history or historical veracity. Instead, as with other biblical narratives, the essential truth-claim with which we are concerned in our reading of the Gospels and Acts lies above all in the claim of these narratives to speak, as it were, on God's behalf – that is, to interpret reality in light of God's self-disclosure of God's own character and purpose working itself out in the cosmos and on the plain of human events. In this sense, the authority of these New Testament documents, read as Scripture, rests in their status as revealed history.

To focus on one of these documents, this perspective is already self-evident within the pages of Acts, where a particular reading of the narrative of Israel is promoted over against other possible readings. The choice centers on a singular question, 'What to make of Jesus?'. To be more specific, the pivot-point is a particular teleology. Does the history of Israel and the consummation of God's purpose bypass or pass through the death and exaltation of Jesus of Nazareth? According to the witnesses in Acts, and the witness of Acts itself, a 'true' history of Israel would be one whose plot-line includes Abraham, David, the crucified-and-resurrected Jesus, the restoration of Israel signaled in Jesus' exaltation and the outpouring of the Spirit, and proceeds on to the Spirit-empowered mission to 'the end of the earth' and end-time restoration and judgment. 'Truth', then, is a function of significance within the framework of God's restorative project as this comes to expression in the message and career of Jesus and is worked out in the common life and mission of those who have identified themselves with the Nazarene.

If we were to take seriously this perspective on history/writing, what sequelae would follow? First, the interests underwriting the historical-critical enterprise would be shifted away from the questions, 'Did this thing happen?' or 'Did it happen in just this way?'. Instead, we would see that the most important contribution of the quest of the historical Jesus would be our enhanced access to the Gospels *as cultural products*, as narratives that speak both out of and over against the world within which they were penned. This would allow us a sharper image of how Mark himself has pursued his task of shaping the identity of a people through shaping their history at the same time that it would mitigate our impulses toward domesticating his narrative by locating it within our own cultural commitments, as though it embodied and authorized our cherished dispositions. Second, we would attend more pointedly to the persuasive art of the narrator of each of these books, and particularly to what he has chosen to include, how he has ordered his material, and into what plot-line he has inscribed the whole. Like any historiographer or biographer, Matthew's work presumes not only the availability of 'facts' (i.e., 'low-level interpretive entities unlikely for the moment to be contested'),[18] but also a storyline into which his story is inscribed. This storyline includes a beginning and end, expectations and presumptions, which tacitly guide the actual narrativizing process. Readerly discernment around these issues would help to define the interpretive task for those of us who want to engage Luke-Acts as history/writing. Third, these narratives would materialize again as subjects in the work of interpretation, as narratives in general are wont to do. That is, they would be heard again to extend their invitation for people to embrace this story as their own, to indwell it, to be transformed in living it. Not inconsequently, this perspective would find support from within the pages of Luke-Acts itself, concerned as this narrative is with assigning meaning to 'the events that have been fulfilled among us'.[19]

---

[18] Haskell, 'Objectivity', 157.
[19] Lk. 1:1.

Bibliography

Adam, A.K.M. (ed.), *Handbook of Postmodern Biblical Interpretation* (St. Louis, MO: Chalice, 2000)
——, (ed.), *Postmodern Interpretations of the Bible: A Reader* (St. Louis, MO: Chalice, 2001)
Berger, K., *Formgeschichte des Neuen Testaments* (Heidelberg: Meyer, 1984)
Black, C.C., *The Disciples According to Mark: Markan Redaction in Current Debate* (JSNTSup 27; Sheffield: JSOT Press, 1989)
Breytenbach, C., *Paulus und Barnabas in der Provinz Galatien: Studien zu Apostelgeschichte 13f.; 16,6; 18,23 und den Adressaten des Galaterbriefes* (AGJU 38; Leiden: E.J. Brill, 1996)
Conzelmann, H., *Acts of the Apostles* (Hermeneia; Philadelphia: Fortress Press, 1987)
Cook, A., *History/Writing: The Theory and Practice of History in Antiquity and in Modern Times* (Cambridge: CUP, 1988)
Funk, R.W., R.W. Hoover and the Jesus Seminar, *The Five Gospels: The Search for the Authentic Words of Jesus* (San Francisco: HarperSanFrancisco, 1993)
Green, J.B., 'The Book of Acts as History/Writing', *LTQ* 37 (2002), 119–27
Haskell, T.L., 'History, Explanatory Schemes, and Other Wonders of Common Sense', in *Objectivity Is Not Neutrality: Explanatory Schemes in History* (Baltimore: The Johns Hopkins University Press, 1998), 1–24
——, 'Objectivity Is Not Neutrality: Rhetoric versus Practice in Peter Novick's *That Noble Dream*', in *Objectivity Is Not Neutrality: Explanatory Schemes in History* (Baltimore: The Johns Hopkins University Press, 1998), 145–73
Lewis, C.S., *The Magician's Nephew* (New York: Macmillan, 1970)
Lowenthal, D., *The Past Is a Foreign Country* (Cambridge: CUP, 1985)
Miller, R.J., Review of *Acts: The Gospel of the Spirit*, by Justo L. González, *CBQ* 64 (2002), 759–60
Morgan, R., with J. Barton, *Biblical Interpretation* (Oxford Bible Series; Oxford: OUP, 1988)
Neill, S., and T. Wright, *The Interpretation of the New Testament 1861–1986* (Oxford: OUP, 2nd edn, 1988)
Pilhofer, P., *Philippi*, I: *Die erste christliche Gemeinde Europas* (WUNT 87; Tübingen: J.C.B. Mohr [Paul Siebeck], 1995)

8

Historical Criticism of the Synoptic Gospels
William P. Alston

Introduction

This chapter is devoted to a critical analysis of certain lines of argument used by many New Testament scholars to support a negative conclusion on the historical value of reports of dominical sayings and of events in the Synoptic Gospels. It is therefore fairly restricted in scope, being limited to asserting that the lines of argument discussed fail to give adequate support to the negative conclusions that allegedly issue from them. What follows contains no attempt to muster positive reasons for the historical value of the Gospels. Although I do think they have such value, only some incidental remarks here will contain hints as to how I think of the matter. Moreover, even my negative thesis is limited to the lines of argument discussed. For all that is shown, or even claimed, in this chapter, there are other reasons, even conclusive reasons, for denying the historical value of the Gospels, although I do not believe this to be the case.

I should tighten up the loose references in the above to 'the historical value of the Gospels'. There is no sufficient reason to think that everything in the Gospels that is put forward as a historical account has the same degree of claim to historical accuracy. Except for a few complete skeptics on the fringes of New Testament scholarship, everyone recognizes some historical accuracy in the Gospel accounts. The question is only where to draw the lines.

I have already indicated that my discussion is restricted to the Synoptic Gospels. The reason for this is that the modes of argument I will be discussing have been much more extensively employed in that area than with respect to the Fourth Gospel. Battles over the historical reliability of the latter are mostly fought on other terrain, and even if I were equipped to enter into that I could not deal with all of the Gospels in one chapter. But within the Synoptics there are further restrictions – restrictions of a more general sort. For one thing I will be concentrating, though not exclusively, on reported utterances of Jesus rather than on his deeds and other happenings. I will also exclude the parables from discussion – not because I regard them as unimportant; quite the contrary. It is because the parables are, at least in what is regarded as their earliest form, more widely accepted as stemming from the historical Jesus than the sayings I will be discussing.

Much of the criticism of denials of the historical reliability of the Gospels has focused on substantive assumptions that undergird that denial. Although my primary concern is with types of argument I cannot wholly ignore background assumptions, since their status is often crucial for the force of the argument. In 'A Critique of the Criterion of Dissimilarity', below, I will criticize several such assumptions. But I will not be concerned in this chapter with one common assumption, namely naturalistic determinism – the view that all the causal influences on what happens in the physical universe are themselves within that universe.[1] This assumption often plays a determinative role in the rejection of reports of miracles wrought by Jesus. I will steer clear of alleged miracles not because I do not think the issue is important but because it, and the pros and cons of naturalism, have already been extensively explored. I will concentrate here on types of argument that have received less attention.

There are background assumptions commonly made by the scholars I will be criticizing that I will not contest, granting them for the sake of argument. These include such matters as (a) the dating of the Gospels; (b) features of the early church; and (c) what is characteristic of first-century Judaism. Doubts can be, and have been, raised about all of these. But for the purposes of the criticisms I launch here I will give my opponents their assumptions on these points.

Since my perspective on the Gospels differs significantly from that of a number of thinkers who are also critical of denials of the historical value of the Gospels, I need to say something about that perspective. First, I do not deny the value of 'secular' historical research into features of the gospel record – either for the Christian faith or for religiously neutral historical interests. By 'secular' historical research I understand research that in no way depends on religious commitments for its results or for the validity of those results. To be sure, secular history in this sense is not the only kind that is legitimate and valuable. A Christian may quite properly rely on his faith in, for example, making judgements as to which historical hypotheses are worthy of serious consideration. Proceeding in this way, a Christian may well dismiss without a hearing any historical hypothesis that implies that the historical person Jesus of Nazareth is not alive today and in vital connection with the Christian church. But secular history is also of vital concern to the Christian as well as to the religiously indifferent historian. For if, to take an extreme case, by the usual canons of

---

[1] See, e.g., Griffin, *Religion;* and Wagner and Warner, *Naturalism.*

historical evidence it is very probable that Jesus' body underwent the usual fate of deceased human beings, or that none of the teachings ascribed to Jesus of Nazareth in the Gospels stemmed from the Jesus of Nazareth crucified by the Romans, then the Christian would be faced with a crisis of faith. Hence it is by no means irrelevant for the Christian faith to determine whether ordinary historical research produces such results. I am not saying that secular historical research would necessarily have the last word in such a conflict. There are sources and supports of Christian faith other than secular history. But at least it is intellectually incumbent on the Christian to take account of the results of secular historical research when they impinge on articles of Christian faith in the way just indicated.

Second, I have no tendency to regard the Gospels or any of the rest of the Christian Bible as 'inerrant'. Sticking to the Gospels, I recognize that there are factual mistakes. For example, there are different days given for the Last Supper. I don't find incompatibilities wherever certain critics do. I don't see why the risen Jesus could not have appeared to his disciples both in Jerusalem and in Galilee. But there are discrepancies that cannot reasonably be harmonized. Third, I have no tendency to suppose that in the Gospels we have the exact words of Jesus, or exact translations thereof. Oral transmission of speeches and conversations even at its best cannot be expected to issue in a verbatim report. And various influences can prevent it from always being at its best. My assumption, for what it's worth, is that the early church's interest in preserving the memory of Jesus' utterances and actions was sufficiently stronger than any countervailing influences to give us a record that, by and large, preserves the gist of many of Jesus' most important utterances and most important actions.[2]

As further evidence of my partial (scholarly) orthodoxy, I accept the most common views on the 'synoptic problem' (the priority of Mark, etc., though not the more extravagant claims for successive strata of Q). I also find it indisputable that the Synoptics are (mostly) constructed from more or less independent pericopes that are ordered differently in different Gospels. And I fully recognize the point that different Gospel writers organize and emphasize material in accordance with their theological commitments, though not to such an extent as to massively affect the historical accuracy of their accounts.

Finally, although my concern here is with the historical accuracy of Gospel passages that on any natural reading are intended to be historically accurate (albeit, as I've already made explicit, just a tiny corner of that concern), it may be relevant, in view of the chaotic situation in biblical studies, that I recognize

---

[2] As with other positive claims, I will do nothing in this chapter to establish this claim. I mention it only as a part of my perspective on the Gospels.

the value of a variety of approaches to the Gospels. I am far from thinking that attempting to determine the accuracy of historical reports is the only important task of Gospel scholarship. There are also a variety of important issues concerning interpretation – one of which is the attempt within a Christian context to determine what God is trying to tell us in the Gospels and elsewhere in the Scriptures, and another of which applies work in the philosophy of language to the biblical record.[3] There is also the study of the theologies of the biblical writers. There are the literary analyses of biblical writings that have been proliferating recently – and so on and so forth. Let a thousand flowers bloom. We need all the light we can get on the subject, from all different quarters.

The Criterion of Dissimilarity

I now turn to the main business at hand – a critical analysis of certain ways of arguing for negative conclusions about the historical veracity of reports in the Synoptic Gospels. The first type of argument I will consider, and the one that will occupy the greatest part of this chapter, involves the application of what is called the 'criterion of dissimilarity' to reported words and actions of Jesus. Norman Perrin's *Rediscovering the Teaching of Jesus* offers the following statement of the criterion:

> the earliest form of a saying we can reach may be regarded as authentic if it can be shown to be dissimilar to characteristic emphases both of ancient Judaism and of the early Church.[4]

Like criteria can be found among many others.[5] But by no means do all scholars who use a criterion something like the above make the same claims for it as Perrin, and the criticisms launched here against Perrin's use of the criterion should not be assumed to be directed against anyone using a criterion so named.

The above formulation represents dissimilarity as a sufficient condition of authenticity, but not a necessary condition. It would leave open the possibility that there are other sufficient conditions of authenticity. But later Perrin goes on to make a claim to its necessity also.

---

[3] See, e.g., a previous volume in this series – Bartholomew, Greene and Möller, *After Pentecost*.

[4] Perrin, *Rediscovering*, 39.

[5] E.g., Meier, *Marginal Jew*; Funk, Hoover and The Jesus Seminar, *Five Gospels*; Sanders and Davies, *Studying*.

... if we are to ascribe a saying to Jesus ... we must be able to show that the saying comes neither from the Church nor from ancient Judaism ... there is no other way to reasonable certainty that we have reached the historical Jesus.[6]

Perrin makes it quite explicit that this criterion is needed because of the burden of proof borne by any claim that a saying can be validly attributed to the historical Jesus rather than to the early church. He says, after having made this assignment of the burden of proof:

> This means in effect that we must look for indications that the saying does not come from the Church, but from the historical Jesus. Actually, our task is even more complex than this, because the early Church and the New Testament are indebted at very many points to ancient Judaism. Therefore, if we are to ascribe a saying to Jesus, and accept the burden of proof laid upon us, we must be able to show that the saying comes neither from the Church nor from ancient Judaism. This seems to many to be too much to ask, but nothing less will do justice to the challenge of the burden of the proof.[7]

When all the dust has settled, Perrin isn't quite as severe as this passage would suggest. For, like Bultmann, he adds a criterion of *coherence:*

> ... material from the earliest strata of the tradition may be accepted as authentic if it can be shown to cohere with materials established as authentic by means of the criterion of dissimilarity.[8]

Note that Perrin speaks of applying both criteria only to items from the 'earliest strata of tradition'. An item is not even a candidate for authenticity until it qualifies as belonging to the 'earliest stratum'. That presupposes that we are able to carry out the Bultmann program of 'writing a history of the tradition' (or rather of each component of the tradition) and thereby determining what is the earliest form of each saying. But even where we have more than one form to work from, as is not always the case, there are many reasons to doubt the objectivity of these results. But I cannot enter into those issues here. Suffice it to say that in my discussion of the criterion of dissimilarity, said by Perrin to be 'the basis for all contemporary attempts to reconstruct the teaching of Jesus', I will ignore this restriction to the earliest stratum of tradition.

If this chapter were primarily concerned with criteria of authenticity I would have to bring into the picture other criteria, and other ways of under-standing and using criteria by other scholars. John P. Meier, for example, offers

---

[6] Perrin, *Rediscovering,* 39.
[7] Perrin, *Rediscovering,* 39.
[8] Perrin, *Rediscovering,* 43.

five criteria: *embarrassment, multiple attestation* (also mentioned but not stressed by Perrin), and *rejection and execution*, in addition to the two above.[9] 'Rejection and execution' has to do with whether a given saying or deed attributed to Jesus helps to explain his trial and execution. Meier is also careful not to use any criterion as a necessary condition of valid attribution to Jesus. Rather, he cautions us to use any one of them in concert with the others. J.D. Crossan puts the most weight on date of source (arrived at in highly controversial ways) and multiple attestation.[10] Funk and Hoover put forward a bewildering cornucopia of 'rules of evidence'.[11] A sizable book could be devoted to this topic alone. But here we are concerned with criteria only as an important influence on the modes of argument we will be examining.

The criterion of dissimilarity can be applied in more or less stringent ways. We have already noted a difference between taking it as a sufficient condition (leaving open the possibility of other sufficient conditions) and as a necessary condition. But there is also the question of what it is that it is a condition for. Perrin, in the second of the above quotes, speaks of it as a necessary condition of 'reasonable certainty' that a reported utterance stems from the historical Jesus. That would leave open the possibility of a lesser degree of certainty where the criterion is not satisfied, as well as the possibility of leaving the question open. A more stringent interpretation would assert that, where a saying fails to satisfy the criterion, it is to be rejected as a saying of Jesus. I will be concerned here with the most stringent use, in which whatever fails to satisfy it is thereby branded as inauthentic.

Clearly this is to put a heavy weight on the criterion. It amounts to privileging the alternative of inauthenticity, making that the default position – the one we are left with in case the criterion is not satisfied. Eventually I will subject this criterion, and the correlated burden of proof thesis, to critical examination. But first I want to exhibit and discuss a number of examples of application of the criterion (often without any explicit mention of it).

Bultmann and the Jesus Seminar

We begin with arguments that seek to discredit reports of words and actions of Jesus by claiming that they stem rather from the early church – its interests, concerns, needs and modes of thinking. Interpreters rarely explicitly mention the criterion in their treatments of individual pericopes. However, when the mere fact that the passage is in line with concerns of the early church is taken as

---

[9] Meier, *Marginal Jew,* ch. 6.
[10] Crossan, *Historical Jesus.*
[11] Funk, Hoover and The Jesus Seminar, *Five Gospels,* 16–34.

evidence that it originated with the early church rather than with Jesus himself, it is clear that this criterion is indeed calling the shots. In other words, by showing that it *could* come from the early church we show that it must be rejected as stemming from the pre-resurrection Jesus. No comparative evaluation of alternative hypotheses is required. This line of argument could be summarized as 'It *could* be this way, therefore it *is* this way'.

I begin with Bultmann's treatment of some pericopes. These treatments involve a variety of considerations in addition to the conclusions about provenance. In particular, he dissects the pericope into segments that he often takes to have different histories, offers judgements as to what was taken from the tradition and what was added by the author, makes allegations concerning the shaping of the material in accordance with the authors' theological perspective, and so on. However interesting and important all of that is, we focus solely here on negative judgements of the authenticity of attributions to the historical Jesus and such reasons as are given for that. These comments apply equally to other examples of this type of argument I will be discussing.

(1) Mark 2:1–12 (Mt. 9:1–8; Lk. 5:17–26) presents a memorable scene of the healing of a paralytic in connection with Jesus forgiving his sins. Bultmann, like a number of other scholars, takes the forgiveness theme to have been inserted into the middle of the healing story. Be that as it may, Bultmann says of this alleged 'insertion':

> There is no other reference in the tradition (apart from Lk. 7:47) to Jesus' pronouncing forgiveness of sins. Mk. 2:5b–10 has manifestly been given its place because the Church wanted to trace back to Jesus *its* own right to forgive sins. And indeed the language shows ... that the Palestinian Church demonstrates by her possession of healing power that she has the right to forgive sins. In this way she traced her authority back to an original action of Jesus.[12]

This passage is typical of Bultmann and of those who follow him closely. It clearly displays the hand of the criterion of dissimilarity, in simply asserting that the origin from the early church is 'manifest', without giving any argument at all for the superiority of this hypothesis to live alternatives. In this case, the livest alternative is that Jesus did in fact implicitly claim through actions such as this one an authority to forgive sins, perhaps as an aspect of an at least implicit messianic claim, and that the memory of this has been preserved by the tradition. Bultmann is right that a paucity of other references in the Synoptic Gospels to Jesus forgiving sins casts some doubt on his having done so, but, of course, there are other possible explanations for that. The Gospels are obviously highly selective in what they report of Jesus' ministry. As Bultmann

---

[12] Bultmann, *Synoptic Tradition*, 15–16.

and other like critics are constantly pointing out, what was preserved from the tradition in the Gospels was what was of special interest to the authors and of particular relevance to their milieu. Perhaps, for whatever reason, forgiveness of sins was not salient enough to receive frequent mention – as, for example, healing and exorcism were. Interestingly enough, the paucity of references to Jesus forgiving sins tells at least as strongly against Bultmann's provenance thesis as it does against an authenticity judgement. If the church was so anxious to support its claim to forgive sins by attributing this to Jesus, why does it not appear more frequently in the Gospels? But my most fundamental point here, as elsewhere in this section, is that a particular explanation is offered without any attempt at critical comparison with alternatives.

(2) In Mark 2:23–28 (Mt. 12:1–8; Lk. 6:1–5) we hear of the disciples picking corn on the Sabbath to satisfy their hunger. The Pharisees criticize them for this and Jesus defends them, saying that the Sabbath was made for man, not man for the Sabbath. Bultmann defends his judgement that 'the composition is the work of the church' as follows. 'Jesus is questioned about the disciples' behaviour; why not about his own? I.e., the Church ascribes the justification of her Sabbath customs to Jesus'.[13] But surely the fact that it is the disciples' behavior that is criticized, not that of Jesus, is at best a weak reason for the conclusion. Why shouldn't it have been only the disciples who were doing this, so that anyone who took exception to such behavior on the Sabbath would naturally be speaking of the disciples? Bultmann gives as a further reason the fact that Jesus is reported as giving a scriptural justification for the behavior, pointing out that scriptural proof was used in this way in the early church. No doubt it was, but why is this a reason for denying that Jesus did so as well? It certainly fits with the general synoptic picture of Jesus that he was well versed in the Scriptures. Is this another example of divorcing Jesus from his Jewish environment? Thus an explanation of the passage in terms of 'the church' justifying its attitude to the Sabbath has nothing substantial to recommend it, in comparison to a straightforward reading of the passage as a simple factual report – except for whatever support it gets from the criterion of dissimilarity.

(3) Here is a Bultmannian treatment of a bit of the Gospels (Mk. 8:27–33; Mt. 16:13–23; Lk. 9:18–22) that involves something more central to Christianity than Jewish Sabbath observance – Peter's recognition of Jesus as Messiah.

> The fact that Jesus takes the initiative with his question ['Who do you say I am?'] itself suggests that this narrative is secondary [i.e., not stemming from the historical Jesus], as does the content of the question altogether. Why does Jesus ask about

---

[13] Bultmann, *Synoptic Tradition,* 16.

something on which he is bound to be every bit as well informed as were the disciples? The question is intended simply to provoke the answer; in other words, it is a literary device. Once more the disciples appear here as a medium between Jesus and the people ... i.e, the disciples represent the Church, and the passages give expression to the specific judgement which the Church had about Jesus, in distinction from that of those outside. This then is a legend of faith: faith in the Messiahship of Jesus is traced back to a story of the first messianic confession which Peter made before Jesus.[14]

But why shouldn't Jesus be interested in the disciple's beliefs about his identity? It would be natural for him to be so. Of course the church confessed Jesus as Messiah. But the reasons given here provide little support for preferring the early church as the source over an interchange between the historical Jesus and Peter. Again we have an automatic, uncritical application of the criterion of dissimilarity. If it *could* have come from the early church, that is enough to discredit it as of historical value for the ministry of the historical Jesus.

Bultmann's approach to the Gospels has had a tremendous influence on twentieth-century gospel scholarship, although in British and American circles it is not easy to find distinguished scholars who follow him closely. But one hotbed of Bultmannian influence is the Jesus Seminar. In the summary of the Seminar's reaction to reports of Jesus' words we find many examples of the uncritical attribution of reported words of Jesus to the early church – the mark of a blanket application of the criterion of dissimilarity.[15] Here are two.

(4) 'Remember, those who try to save their own life are going to lose it, but those who lose their life for my sake and the sake of the good news are going to save it' (Mk. 8:35). Funk and Hoover treat six versions of this saying – the above in Mark, with somewhat changed derivatives in Matthew and Luke, two in Matthew and Luke from Q, and one from John. The fellows do not deny that something of this sort issued from the historical Jesus, but they take the above passage, as well as its parallels in Matthew and Luke, to be the result of 'Christianizing' the original saying, which they take to be most closely approximated in Luke 17:33, 'Whoever tries to hang on to life will forfeit it, but whosoever forfeits life will preserve it', which they regard as coming from Q. Their reason for rejecting the authenticity of the Markan version and its derivatives comes from what they call its 'Christian coloration', found in 'for my sake and for the sake of the good news'. This is undoubtedly a reason for losing one's life that is congenial to Christianity, but it is only by a blanket application of the criterion of dissimilarity that one can, without more ado, take this as a reason

---

[14] Bultmann, *Synoptic Tradition*, 257–58.
[15] Funk, Hoover and The Jesus Seminar, *Five Gospels*.

for rejecting an attribution to the historical Jesus. The treatment becomes even more tenuous when they give as a further reason for rejecting the Markan version that it employs 'the verb "save", which is a term used for Christian salvation'![16] Come now. Even an uncritical use of dissimilarity will not support this. The Christian church had no monopoly on that verb. Presumably people without any Christian involvement can, and do, speak of *saving* one's life. And even if 'save' is to be given some religious significance, we do not need a developed Christian doctrine of salvation to view Jesus as supposing that his mission would result in saving people from something.

(5) Next let's look at something of central importance to Christianity – the utterances, reported in all three Synoptics, one or another version of which became the 'words of institution' at the Eucharist. I only need mention their connection with the Eucharist to remove any suspense as to the attitude of the Jesus Seminar to this attribution.

> … most Fellows were convinced that the supper tradition has been so overlaid with Christianizing elements and interpretation that it is impossible to recover anything of an original event, much less any of the original words spoken by Jesus. Nevertheless, the Seminar readily conceded the possibility that Jesus may have performed some symbolic acts during table fellowship with his followers. And those symbolic acts may have involved bread and wine or perhaps fish.[17]

Quite a concession! I suggest that there is nothing of any significance to be said against the view that one such symbolic act performed by Jesus at his final table fellowship with his followers before his arrest and crucifixion was to symbolically identify the bread with his body and the wine with his blood, both of which he took to be on the verge of being sacrificed for something or other, the exact nature of which, in Jesus' conception of the matter at that moment, is a matter for further determination. But, apart from an uncritical employment of the criterion of dissimilarity, there is nothing to be said against the supposition that Jesus did say such things at this juncture.

(6) My next example involves a combination of an application of the criterion of dissimilarity with another favorite weapon of the Jesus Seminar, namely defining what kinds of utterances are 'distinctive of Jesus'. This, too, is used as a way of cutting down the list of authentic utterances by rejecting those that do not fall within the privileged categories. Here is the example.

In Mark 7:1–13 and Matthew 15:1–20, the Pharisees criticize the disciples for eating with unwashed hands. Jesus retorts by accusing them of departing

---

[16] Funk, Hoover and The Jesus Seminar, *Five Gospels,* 79.
[17] Funk, Hoover and The Jesus Seminar, *Five Gospels,* 118.

from God's commandments and holding fast to human traditions, citing Moses
and Isaiah in the process.

> There is abundant evidence in early Christian literature that Christian literature
> searched the scriptures ... for proof that the new movement had been anticipated.
> It is also clear that Jesus characteristically made his point by parables and apho-
> risms. In other words, Jesus taught on his own authority and seems not to have
> invoked scripture to justify his pronouncements. Consequently, most, perhaps all,
> quotations from the Greek version of the Hebrew Bible put on the lips of Jesus are
> secondary in the judgment of many fellows ... In the last analysis, the Fellows
> decided that the attempt to discredit Pharisaic tradition in principle fits better
> into the competitive environment of the later community [i.e., competition with
> Judaism], after the destruction of the temple and after Jesus had become the
> supreme teaching authority in the church.[18]

The criterion of dissimilarity comes into the above at the beginning and the
end, where features of the utterances that are characteristic of the early church
are taken as a (strong) reason for denying that they stem from Jesus. But there is
also an appeal to the alleged fact that invoking Scripture was uncharacteristic of
Jesus, in contrast to ' parables and aphorisms'. What are we to say of this latter
way of supporting a negative judgement.

First, as the above suggestion that quotations from the Hebrew Bible are
'put on the lips of Jesus' implies, the claim that speech of this sort is unch_arac-
teristic of Jesus *presupposes* rather than supports the inauthenticity of attributions of such speech to Jesus. Except for a prior decision to treat 'parables and
aphorisms' (and other utterances that do not involve biblical quotations) as the
only ways in which Jesus 'characteristically made his points', there is no basis
for treating the many scriptural invocations by Jesus reported in the Gospels as
'uncharacteristic'. Within the limits of this chapter I cannot explore the
question of whether Funk *et alii* have any sufficient reason for their selection of
the kinds of speech that are characteristic of Jesus. I will simply say that, as far as
anything I have seen from them is concerned, the selection is made in a way
designed to support the view of Jesus that is congenial to them, rather than
enjoying any significant support independent of that. With reference to the
particular application of this criterion under scrutiny, there is no reason to
suppose that participants in the early church, including the Gospel writers,
were in any better position, or were any more likely, to support judgements by
scriptural references than was Jesus himself.

But let's suppose, for the sake of argument, that we have identified what is
characteristic of Jesus' speech in some defensible way. There is still the question
of why we should suppose that this is a necessary condition of justifiable

---

[18] Funk, Hoover and The Jesus Seminar, *Five Gospels,* 68–69.

attribution. No human being is confined to what is *distinctive* of him or her. Everyone thinks, says and does things that are much like what countless other people do. Hence, if we are trying to determine whether X did or said what X was reported as doing or saying, it would be self-defeating to require for a positive answer that the deed or saying is something that is distinctive of X. In carrying that out we would lose many correct attributions. Funk and Hoover try to evade this point by saying the following.

> Jesus undoubtedly said a great many very ordinary things, such as 'hello' and 'good-bye' and whatever he hollered when he hit his thumb in the carpenter's shop or stubbed his toe on a rocky road. But if we are to identify the voice of Jesus that makes him the precipitator of the Christian tradition, we have to look for sayings and stories that distinguish his voice from other ordinary speakers and even sages in his day and time. We have to be able to pick out a distinctive voice in a Galilean crowd.[19]

No doubt, what is distinctive in Jesus' discourse played a role in making 'him the precipitator of the Christian tradition'. But it is gratuitous to suppose that only the ordinary utterances typified in the above quotation are non-distinctive things Jesus did or said. Our authors simply assume, without supporting argument, that none of the things Jesus said or did that did not distinguish him from all his contemporaries also played a role in 'precipitating the Christian tradition'.

A Critique of the Criterion of Dissimilarity

We have thus far been (mostly) pointing out that a common line of support for rejecting alleged utterances and acts of Jesus involves applying a stringent form of the criterion of dissimilarity. But we have not yet subjected the criterion, and in particular the satisfaction of it as a necessary condition of authenticity, to critical analysis. Without this, my suggestion – that similarity of a purported utterance of Jesus to what might well be said in the early church does not count as a good reason for rejecting that attribution – lacks substance. I now proceed to fill in this lacuna.

The first point is that the criterion lacks initial plausibility. It is plausible only if it is unlikely that the historical Jesus would say something that is similar to what would be said in his Jewish environment or in the church that sprang from his ministry, death and resurrection. For it is only if that is unlikely that such similarity counts decisively against an attribution of the saying to Jesus. But it seems clear that the prior probability runs in the other direction. It is very likely that he would say things that exhibit such similarities.

---

[19] Funk, Hoover and The Jesus Seminar, *Five Gospels,* 30.

First consider the Jewish similarities. In recent decades the literature on the historical Jesus has increasingly emphasized his continuity with, as well as his differences from, the Jewish society and traditions in which he was raised and within which his ministry was conducted. There is increasing recognition that he stood, and was perceived by his contemporaries as standing, in the line of the great Hebrew prophets. It is also reasonable to think that he was very familiar with and shared in (some of) the messianic expectations and hopes that were prominent in first-century Judaism – regardless of the verdict on the question of whether he took himself to have a messianic status. What could be more likely than that Jesus would, at least some of the time, sound and act like a first-century Jew who was very much involved in (some of) the Jewish movements of his time. There is no reasonable basis for taking *any* 'similarity to Judaism' as a reason for rejecting an attribution to Jesus. This would be to attempt to divorce Jesus from the context in which he lived and moved and had his being.

As for the early Christian church side of the criterion, we are faced with a similar question in, so to speak, an opposite direction. To be sure, the church developed in various ways that could not reasonably be supposed to be based on features of the life and work of the historical Jesus. The injunction at the end of the Gospel of Matthew to baptize with the Trinitarian formula is a plausible example of something that is likely to stem from the early church rather than from the earthly Jesus, and there are others. But, again, we must discriminate between 'Christian' features that would be unlikely to be found in Jesus' words and deeds and those that would not be unlikely, including those that would be likely. As for the latter, we must not forget that the Christian church stemmed, and self-consciously so, from the life, ministry, death and resurrection of Jesus of Nazareth. Hence it would be unreasonable in the extreme to suppose that no emphases, attitudes, beliefs and so on of the early church are to be found in the earthly ministry of Jesus. Indeed, a picture of the historical Jesus from which all such features are excised would, just by that fact, be under suspicion. So here, too, a blanket, undiscriminating use of the criterion of dissimilarity has nothing to recommend it. We must consider each case on its own merits, doing our best to decide whether the Christian feature in question could plausibly be supposed to be part of the activity of the historical Jesus.

The unfortunate effects of a blanket application of the criterion of dissimilarity can be dramatized by the following fable. Suppose that at some time far into the future, none of the writings of Martin Luther King, Jr. have been preserved, but there are attributions to him of written and spoken material in writings that date from several generations after his death. A scholar of this future period formulates and applies a criterion of dissimilarity according to which no such attributions can be accepted except what is sufficiently dissimilar both to what was being said and written by people in the civil rights movement of his time and to features of the civil rights movement after his death. It is obvious that the application of such a criterion would leave little or nothing of what King did in fact write and speak. Such are the wages of excessive scholarly caution.

So if we are to judge the criterion of dissimilarity simply by its prima facie plausibility, there is nothing to be said in its favor. But we can't consider the case closed until we consider what its advocates urge in its favor. For that purpose, let us return to Perrin's *Rediscovering the Teaching of Jesus*. Let me acknowledge first of all that Perrin does not explicitly present the material cited below as a series of arguments for the criterion. If I misinterpret him in so construing it, I offer a sincere apology. My interest is not in Perrin exegesis, but rather in examining certain lines of argument that I take to be widely influential.

> The fundamental problem in connection with knowledge of the teaching of Jesus is the problem of reconstructing that teaching from the sources available to us, and the truth of the matter is that the more we learn about those sources the more difficult our task seems to become. The major source, the synoptic gospels … contains a great deal of teaching *ascribed* to Jesus and yet, in fact, stemming from the early Church.[20]

The end of the above paragraph seems to be taking 'stemming from the early church' and being (validly, accurately) 'ascribed to Jesus' as mutually exclusive. But how are we to understand 'stems from the early church'? In the sense in which it is obviously true that the Gospels 'stem from the early church', it simply means that they were written by people involved in the early church – that they were written in that context. But the fact that they stemmed from the early church in that sense has no tendency to show that they are not correctly attributed to Jesus. It is a truism that, in a certain historical situation, one can be making true reports about what happened in an earlier historical situation. History would be in as bad a way as some 'postmodernists' suppose it to be if this were not the case. We get Perrin's negative conclusion only if 'stems from the early Church' means 'created by the early Church' or 'originates in the early Church'. If that is what is meant, then it does obviously follow that (much of) what is attributed to the earthly Jesus has its source in the post-resurrection church. But to claim *in that sense* that the Gospels stem from the early church simply begs the question, for that claim *presupposes* that much of what is attributed to Jesus in the Gospels did not originate with him. Hence it cannot support that negative conclusion. I suspect that Perrin and other people who think this way have confused these two senses of 'stems from the early church', taking the independent obviousness of the application of the first sense to the Gospels to rub off on the second sense.

The above passage continues as follows.

---

[20] Perrin, *Rediscovering,* 15.

The early Church made no attempt to distinguish between the words the earthly Jesus had spoken and those spoken by the risen Lord through a prophet in the community ... The early Church absolutely and completely identified the risen Lord of her experience with the earthly Jesus of Nazareth and created for her purposes, which she conceived to be his, the literary form of the gospel, in which words and deeds ascribed in her consciousness to both the earthly Jesus and the risen Lord were set down in terms of the former.[21]

Here we can discern a possible second reason for the likelihood of an early church origin of much that is attributed to Jesus. Since the 'early church' made no distinction between utterances of the earthly Jesus and of the risen Lord present to the church, they felt free to ascribe to the former what they received from the latter. What shall we say of this as a reason for the criterion, for taking attributions that could have an origin in the early church to have done so?

First, even if we accept the 'no distinction' premise, it fails to support the criterion of dissimilarity and its associated claim that 'the burden of proof will be on the claim to authenticity'.[22] The 'no distinction' thesis leaves wide open the possibility that any given proportion of alleged sayings of Jesus, however large, stem from the earthly Jesus rather than from the early church. If, indeed, the early church made no distinction between these origins, that tells us nothing as to the proportion with one rather than the other provenance, and hence it tells us nothing about the initial presumption as to origin with which we should approach a given saying. When people make no distinction between two different origins of reports, those of one origin could be established in the tradition just as well as those of another. Does, then, the 'no distinction' thesis have no bearing at all on the problem of authenticity? Not quite. It at least has the function of answering an *objection* to the supposition that a large proportion of alleged utterances of the earthly Jesus originated in the early church – namely, that this supposition implies that the gospel writers and/or contributors to the traditions on which they drew were practicing deceit in making false attributions. For the 'no distinction' claim implies that the authors and the tradition were not being deceitful; instead they were 'telling it like it is' or at least 'telling it like they supposed it to be'. But though the claim does have this function, it is of no use whatsoever in supporting the thesis that the balance in reported sayings, deeds and events tips in the direction of an origin in the early church rather than an origin in the ministry of the earthly Jesus. Perrin, and virtually all responsible New Testament scholars, recognize that some of the reported utterances of Jesus derive from Jesus' earthly ministry. But if this is the case, then the 'no distinction' thesis leaves wide open the possibility that any

---

[21] Perrin, *Rediscovering,* 15.
[22] Perrin, *Rediscovering,* 39.

given proportion of those reports, however large, stem from the earthly Jesus rather than the early church.

Secondly, in any event, there are strong reasons for rejecting the 'no distinction' thesis. First, there is no real evidence for such a sweeping claim, and strong evidence would be needed for a thesis that is so implausible on the face of it. In the above passage Perrin says that 'the early Church absolutely and completely identified the risen Lord of her experience with the earthly Jesus of Nazareth'. Of course it did. But that does not imply that no distinction was made between utterances of the earthly Jesus and those of the exalted risen Lord. I 'absolutely and completely identify' the woman with whom I live with the woman I married many years ago. But I am not unable or unwilling to distinguish between something she said just after our marriage and something she said yesterday. Moreover, there are indications in the New Testament that such a distinction was made. Consider Peter's vision on the roof of Cornelius's house in Acts 10, in which a voice from heaven, addressed by Peter as Lord, tells Peter (in effect) that all foods are clean. There is no attempt here to attribute this ruling to the pre-resurrection Jesus. Again, in 1 Corinthians 7, where Paul is discussing celibacy, marriage and divorce, he distinguishes between 'a word of the Lord' and his own advice. I conclude that the 'no distinction' thesis should be rejected, and that even if it were acceptable it would not have the implications Perrin supposes it to have.

The final argument for the criterion of dissimilarity that I extract from Perrin is this. Since the Gospels were written in the context of the early church, it is reasonable to suppose that they give historically reliable accounts of the ministry of the earthly Jesus only if the early church had an interest in doing so. But Perrin, and many others, deny that there was any such interest.

> ... the gospel form was created to serve the purpose of the early Church, but historical reminiscence was not one of those purposes. So, for example, when we read an account of Jesus giving instruction to his disciples, we are not hearing the voice of the earthly Jesus addressing Galilean disciples in a Palestinian situation but that of the risen Lord addressing Christian missionaries in a Hellenistic world, and if the early Church had not needed instructions for those missionaries in that situation, there would have been no such pericope in our gospels ... So far as we can tell today, there is no single pericope anywhere in the gospels, the present purpose of which is to preserve a historical reminiscence of the earthly Jesus.[23]

There is much in this that I can accept. I agree that a) the Gospels were designed to serve the purposes of the church. I also agree that b) this acts to some extent

---

[23] Perrin, *Rediscovering*, 15–16.

as a filter for what gets into the Gospels.[24] Going beyond what Perrin says here, I also agree that c) the ultimate or primary aim of the Gospels is to induce faith in Jesus as Christ or Lord rather than to provide accurate history and d) that the Gospel writers and their immediate successors were not disturbed by minor differences in details within a single Gospel or between one Gospel and another. And, finally, e) I agree that each author was shaping his account in terms of his own theological perspective and/or that of his particular community. But none of this implies that the writers were not concerned to give a report of Jesus' ministry that was historically accurate. All five of these points are quite compatible with the supposition that the Gospels embody items from the tradition that stretches to them from Jesus himself during his life on earth, and in such a way that it is sufficiently free from distortion to present an account that is by and large accurate. This is obviously quite compatible with a) and b), the function of the needs of the church in determining what gets *selected* from the tradition. As for c), the only thing that needs to be said is that an ultimate or primary aim at evangelization is compatible with having other ancillary and/or instrumental aims. Consideration d) is obviously compatible with historical accuracy by and large, which is not canceled by minor inaccuracies in detail. As for e), the same reports can receive different theological spins and still be accurate reports of what happened.

But, of course, if the Gospel writers and contributors to the tradition had no interest whatsoever in providing an accurate account of Jesus' worldly ministry, we would have little reason for supposing that the Gospels contain any such account. It would still be possible that some of the features of that ministry are transmitted up to the writing of the Gospels in spite of the lack of interest in this, but it would be an accident if this were so, and not something to be expected. But why should we accept that lack of interest? Perrin gives no reason for the claim except to say: 'So far as we can tell today, there is no single pericope anywhere in the gospels, the present purpose of which is to preserve a historical reminiscence of the earthly Jesus'. But what is his basis for supposing that no single pericope has any such purpose? How does he discern that? I fear that he and others who take this line have simply confused some of the points I agreed to above with a lack of interest in accurate history, supposing such interest to be incompatible with having other primary aims, not being disturbed by minor discrepancies in the accounts, and so on.

---

[24] Only to some extent, for it is agreed on (almost) all hands that the Gospels contain some reports that are not at all suited to their purposes, reports that constitute an embarrassment – e.g., Jesus being baptized by John and the rejection of his ministry by his family. These show that the purposes of the church were not the sole determinant of what was selected from the tradition for inclusion in the Gospels – but it was, no doubt, one of the important determinants.

Not only is the 'lack of interest' thesis without serious support. It is highly implausible. How can we suppose that people seriously involved in a religious movement that consciously stems from the teaching, deeds, life, death and resurrection of a human being on earth a few decades ago would not be interested in facts about that teaching, those deeds, that life, death and resurrection – at least those facts that are relevant to the thrust he gave that movement? What kind of mind-set could possibly lead to such lack of interest? No doubt, the 'lack of historical interest' thesis is closely connected, for Perrin and like scholars, with the 'no distinction between the historical Jesus and the risen Lord in contact with the church' thesis. The thought would be that since the church has the risen Lord present to it, it has no need to concern itself with the pre-resurrection Jesus. But Perrin himself says, as we noted above, 'The early Church absolutely and completely identified the risen Lord of her experience with the earthly Jesus of Nazareth'. And if that is so, then one could not be concerned with the former without thereby being concerned with the latter.

Here is another way to see the groundlessness of the 'lack of interest' thesis. The line of Perrin and his counterparts is that the needs and interests of the church call the shots with respect to the Gospels and the traditions from which they spring, and therefore concern for historical accuracy takes a back seat, if any at all. But can we seriously think that people who have thoroughly internalized the needs, concerns and interests of the church are unaware of the ultimate source of all that and are uninterested in preserving and keeping alive the memory of that ultimate source? How can we suppose that these people called themselves Christians and took the church to be the continuation of Jesus' ministry on earth after his death and resurrection without being interested in the details of that ministry? For that matter, why should the Gospels and their sources be in the form of a narrative account of Jesus' ministry and its immediate outcome if they were not concerned to get it as straight as possible? Perrin and his like are given to pointing out that contemporary standards of historical method were foreign to the Gospel writers and, indeed, to ancient historians generally. This is, no doubt, true in large part. But one doesn't need sophisticated contemporary historical methodology to be concerned about factual accuracy. A husband doesn't need a Ph.D. in history to be vitally concerned to get the exact truth about whether his wife has been faithful to him. Without going any further into this matter, let me just say that the 'no historical interest' thesis seems to me to be one of the worst moves in twentieth-century New Testament scholarship, and the sooner it is buried the better.[25]

---

[25] In Wright, *Jesus,* ch. 13, we find a much more elaborate defense of the claim that the evangelists were concerned with facts about the historical Jesus. This is based on his thesis that the story of Jesus was told in the New Testament as the climax of the basic Jewish story. See esp. 377–403.

The above criticism of the criterion of dissimilarity and its alleged supports may be profitably compared with the following passages. First one from Taylor's *The Formation of the Gospel Tradition:*

> If the Form-Critics are right, the disciples must have been translated to heaven immediately after the Resurrection. As Bultmann sees it, the primitive community exists *in vacuo,* cut off from its founders by the walls of an inexplicable ignorance. Like Robinson Crusoe it must do the best it can. Unable to turn to anyone for information, it must invent situations for the words of Jesus, and put into His lips sayings which personal memory cannot check.[26]

And here is a later and carefully measured judgement in Brown's *The Origins of Christianity:*

> The minimalism and scepticism of the 'new quest' for the historical Jesus stems from the theological postulates of Bultmann's school ... Bultmann's fear that fallible judgments about history might be made the basis for faith has no legitimate bearing on the conduct of historical inquiry, and the criterion of dissimilarity does not assist the investigation of the Jesus tradition. Since the historian claims nothing beyond probability for his reconstruction, he will prefer to make use of all material which is probably authentic, rather than to exclude what is possibly inauthentic, particularly if the reasons advanced for the inauthenticity are themselves improbable.
>
> Since Jesus was a Jew, it is not surprising that some of his sayings and parables have Jewish parallels. Unless some plausible reason can be given why the Christian community should attribute such material to him, it seems reasonable to suppose that Jesus is drawing on Jewish tradition. The crucial question of the burden of proof – for or against authenticity – will be viewed differently by the historian and by the type of theologian who insists on absolute certitude.
>
> If a unit of Jesus tradition clearly presupposes the proclamation of Jesus' death and resurrection, or a situation which did not exist during Jesus' ministry, such as the Gentile mission, then it is clearly the creation of the Christian community. But when no such indications of ecclesiastical origin are present, and when the material in question is consistent with the historical situation of Jesus' ministry, then the burden of proof lies with those who question the authenticity of the Jesus tradition, not with those who affirm it.
>
> The 'criterion of dissimilarity' cuts Jesus off from Judaism and cuts Christianity off from Jesus the Jew.[27]

In summary, I feel that there is little or nothing of any value to be said in favor of using the criterion of dissimilarity for determining the authenticity of Gospel reports. Hence I take my criticism of arguments that depend on that criterion

---

[26] Taylor, *Formation,* 41.
[27] Brown, *Origins,* 49–50.

to stand. This is not to say that there can be no sound arguments for taking this or that alleged saying or deed of Jesus to have originated in the early church. What I oppose is only the privileging of the hypothesis of origin in the early church or contemporary Judaism in each case where the content of the pericope is such that it *could* have had that origin, and the associated claim that the burden of the proof is on the hypothesis of authenticity. 'Where it can have originated in the early church or contemporary Judaism, take it to have done so unless we have strong reasons to the contrary.' Once we see the groundlessness of this criterion, we can see that what is needed is a level playing field. The burden of proof is on anyone who puts forward a definite hypothesis, whether for or against the authenticity of an attribution. This approach requires us to examine the particular case for reasons either to accept the attribution to Jesus or to accept some other provenance and prevents us from automatically accepting the latter until there are strong reasons for not doing so.

To flesh out a bit the suggestion of a level playing field, here is some of the discussion in Sanders of a set of conflict passages in Mark 2–3:6.[28] Instead of following Bultmann in a blanket application of the criterion of dissimilarity, Sanders brings out particular features of these stories and relevant material on first-century Judaism to support the claim that it is more likely that they are retrojections from later conflict between the nascent Christian church and Judaism over the law than that they stem from such conflicts during Jesus' ministry. For example, Sanders points out that the alleged violations of the law, such as picking corn on the Sabbath or healing a man with a withered hand on the Sabbath, are not as serious as they are represented as being. The Pharisees who represent the Jewish side of the conflict had nothing to do with Jesus' arrest and execution, and there was considerable disagreement among Pharisees and other pious Jewish leaders about details of the law and its observance. And when Sanders points out with respect to various exhortations in the Sermon on the Mount that their content has parallels in contemporary Judaism, he does not take that as a reason for rejecting their attribution to Jesus, but rather as a reason for underlining Jesus' acceptance of Jewish tradition.[29] My taking these contentions by Sanders to compare favorably with the blanket application of the criterion of dissimilarity reinforces the point that in rejecting the latter I do not reject all considerations involving contemporary Judaism and the early church as having relevance to a decision on the authenticity of an attribution to Jesus. For example, if these attributions are based on mistaken assumptions about first-century Judaism or contain contents or features that it is implausible to suppose date from the pre-resurrection Jesus, then that does constitute a significant reason against the attribution.

[28] See Sanders, *Historical Figure*, 212–18.
[29] See Sanders, *Historical Figure*, ch. 13. For another example see Brown, *Origins*, ch. 3.

Other Uses of the Criterion

Most of the arguments I have criticized are taken from Bultmann's *The History of the Synoptic Tradition* and Funk and Hoover's *The Five Gospels*, since these books are prime sources of concise statements of such arguments. But it would be a great mistake to suppose that arguments of these types are confined to these scholars and those who follow them closely. On the contrary, the ways of thinking that lie behind the use of the criterion of dissimilarity have permeated much of twentieth-century scholarship on the Synoptic Gospels, even among scholars who are considerably less negative about the historical reliability of the Gospels than Bultmann and the Jesus Seminar. It has become commonplace in dealing with the Synoptics to point out that they were created by the church to serve the purposes of the church; that they were written at some considerable temporal distance from the events they purport to narrate; that the material has been considerably modified in the light of theological developments in the early church; and that as a result we are confronted with the task of 'retrieving', 'recovering', even 'reconstructing' the historical Jesus of the period of his ministry from church-impregnated documents. Though none of this logically entails a stringent use of the criterion of dissimilarity, it certainly strongly encourages it. And, more generally, the criterion encourages an attitude of initial skepticism toward the Gospel record that carries with it the burden of proof claim that we have seen to be associated with a stringent form of the criterion of dissimilarity. I only need mention such names as Crossan, Borg and Meier to give some indication of the extent of this way of thinking. For a brief example I turn to a scholar who presents a softer, less radical form of this approach than we find in, for example, Crossan and Borg – namely, Paula Fredriksen in her book *From Jesus to Christ*.

After sketching out an approach like the above, Fredriksen introduces several criteria: dissimilarity, coherence, multiple attestation and linguistic suitability. She then confesses that 'we still know too little both about early first-century Judaism and about the church in the period of the gospels' composition to apply these criteria rigorously'.[30] Later in the book she then gives a mixed verdict on the prospects for getting an accurate picture of the historical Jesus.

> The intuition of earlier scholars was sound: 'what really happened' during Jesus' ministry is not recoverable from the evangelical descriptions of what happened. But by examining these descriptions in light of our knowledge of Jesus' historical context, we can establish with reasonable security what *possibly* happened, what *probably* happened, and what *could not possibly* have happened.[31]

---

[30] Fredriksen, *Jesus*, 5–6. My thanks go to William L. Craig for steering me to Fredriksen's book.
[31] Fredriksen, *Jesus*, 97.

So far this sounds like a sensible program. But in carrying it out, Fredriksen is still driven by a general approach of the sort we found in Bultmann and Perrin. Thus, in speaking of Jesus' baptism by John she writes, 'Did a voice from heaven announce to bystanders, or to Jesus alone, or possibly only to John, that Jesus was the beloved divine Son? Of course we cannot know; and these stories as they now stand bear too clearly the stamp of later tradition'.[32] In dealing with the healing of the paralytic and other controversies with the Pharisees she follows Bultmann in rejecting them as anything that (even possibly?) happened in Jesus' ministry. '... post–70 Gentile Christianity accordingly faced an adversarial or indifferent Pharisaic Jewish audience; and this is the situation projected, through the gospel narratives, onto the ministry of Jesus as well'.[33] And so it goes. The 'if it could have stemmed from the early church, it did' principle is still thriving.

Arguments from Traditional Wisdom and Earlier Literature

That is, no doubt, more than enough on the criterion of dissimilarity. But I want to point out that there are other forms of the general category of 'it could be so, therefore it is so' type of argument that involve appeals to what could be so other than an origin in the early church or contemporary Judaism. I will confine myself to attempts to dismiss purported sayings of Jesus by finding parallels in traditional wisdom or in earlier sacred or secular literature.

Here we can profitably return to Bultmann, who devotes considerable attention to similarities of 'wisdom' sayings attributed to Jesus (which he designates as 'logia') both to traditional proverbs and to those found in written sources, especially Jewish ones. In discussing particular passages we find Bultmann flatly, and without any significant reason, taking it that where a reported saying of Jesus is similar to some common proverb, the tradition has turned it into a saying of Jesus. See, for example, the treatment of Luke 9:58, 'Foxes have their holes, the birds their roosts, but the Son of Man has nowhere to lay his head'. Of this Bultmann says, 'this is presumably an old proverb which the tradition has turned into a saying of Jesus'.[34] But later in the book he is more cautious.

> When we pass from general considerations to examine the logia concretely, it is frequently impossible to do more than pass a subjective judgement. It seems to me

---

[32] Fredriksen, *Jesus,* 98.
[33] Fredriksen, *Jesus,* 105.
[34] Bultmann, *Synoptic Tradition,* 28.

that the following belong to the secular meshalim which have been made into dominical sayings in the tradition.

(What follows is a selection from Bultmann's list.)

> Luke 12:2: 'There is nothing covered up that will not be uncovered, nothing hidden that will not be made known.'
>
> Mark 6:4: 'A prophet will always be held in honour except in his home town, and among his kinsmen and family.'
>
> Matthew 15:14: '... if one blind man guides another, they will both fall in the ditch.'
>
> Matthew 10:24: 'A pupil does not rank above his teacher, or a servant above his master.'
>
> Matthew 7:6: 'Do not give your dogs what is holy; do not throw your pearls to the pigs ...'[35]

A bit later in this section he supplies some parallels from Jewish and other literature. This brief selection is limited to the former:

> Matthew 5:42: 'Give when you are asked to give; and do not turn your back on a man who wants to borrow'. (Cf. the similar admonitions in Pr. 28:27; Sir. 4: 4f., 29; Tob. 4:7.)
>
> Matthew 6:21: 'For where your treasure is, there will your heart be also'. (Cf. Pr. 10:2; 11:4, 28.)
>
> Matthew 24:28: 'Wherever the corpse is, there the vultures will gather'. (Cf. Job 39:30.)
>
> Luke 14:7–11: At a banquet choose the lowest rather than the highest place. (Cf. Pr. 25:6f.)[36]

In discussing the bearing of all this on the authenticity of attributions to the historical Jesus, Bultmann speaks in measured terms.

> It is ... precarious to try to indicate which of the logia Jesus could have taken from secular wisdom and made his own. In itself it is obviously by no means impossible that he should have taken the widespread figure of the doctor who tends the sick and not the healthy (Mk. 2:17), and used it to defend his own way of going to work. It is equally possible that in a time of resignation he should have applied to himself the proverb about the prophet who is without honour in his native place. Or why could he not have used the saying about serving two masters (Mt. 6:24) in his sermon if he knew it already as a proverb? Why could he not have expressed his eschatological consciousness and justified his behaviour by the proverb about the senselessness of

---

[35] Bultmann, *Synoptic Tradition,* 102–103.
[36] Bultmann, *Synoptic Tradition,* 106–108.

fasting at a wedding feast (Mk. 2:19)? One can go on asking questions like this about one saying after another, without getting any further. It is necessary to see that the tradition has taken many logia from popular wisdom and piety into itself, and to reckon with the fact that it has done so now and then because Jesus has made use of or coined such a saying. But it must also be seen that many a saying owes its reception into the tradition only to its suitability for a specific sphere of the Church's interests. It will only be in very few cases that one of the logia can be ascribed to Jesus with any measure of confidence: such sayings as arise from the exaltation of an eschatological mood, like Mk. 3:27 (Satan is already overcome) ... further sayings which are the product of an energetic summons to repentance like Mk. 8:35 (losing life and finding it) ... To these we may add the sayings about the first and the last (Mk. 10:31) and about the many called and the few chosen (Mt. 22:14) ... And finally we may include sayings which demand a new disposition of mind, like the sayings about purity (Mk. 7:15), children (Mk. 10:15) ... loving enemies (Mt. 5: 44–48). All these sayings ... contain something characteristic, new, reaching out beyond popular wisdom and piety and yet are in no sense scribal or rabbinic nor yet Jewish apocalyptic. So here if anywhere we can find what is characteristic of the preaching of Jesus.[37]

So despite beginning by saying that only a 'subjective judgment' is possible, Bultmann winds up with a straightforward application of the criterion of dissimilarity. Only those sayings that are 'new', reaching out beyond both popular wisdom and Jewish religiosity, can be 'ascribed to Jesus with any measure of confidence'. But this is as arbitrary, though put forward with more caveats, as we have seen other applications of the criterion to be. He acknowledges that there are two possibilities with each of the logia for which there are parallels in popular wisdom or earlier literature – namely, that Jesus took it over and used it, or that the church adopted it for its own purposes and ascribed it to Jesus. He also admits that we cannot choose between the alternatives in any objective fashion by looking at logia one at a time. But then he surreptitiously accords the latter alternative a privileged position, treating it as the default position to be espoused unless there are specific reasons not to do so. But the only reasons for the procedure are ones that we saw earlier to be unsound.

I will give two final examples of the acceptance of a particular explanation of a passage without sufficient attention to live alternatives. Both concern the account of resurrection appearances in Luke. Here I will take a momentary break from Bultmann- and Jesus Seminar-bashing, and first consider a bit of the treatment in Reginald Fuller's *The Formation of the Resurrection Narratives*. Before the passage that we will be discussing, Fuller has argued[38] that these accounts are later additions to the original resurrection tradition, since our earliest source for that tradition, 1 Corinthians 15:3–8, says nothing of any such

---

[37] Bultmann, *Synoptic Tradition,* 104–105.

[38] In a way that I criticize in Alston, 'Biblical Criticism'.

appearances. I will not repeat my criticism of that argument but instead focus on Fuller's further reason for taking the appearance narratives to be late.

> The Christophany of Matthew 28:11–17 is the first instance we have of a materialization of the appearances. This materialization seems to originate here … from the exigencies of narrations. So long as the appearances were merely listed (1 Cor. 15:5f.; Mk. 16:7), their spiritual character could be preserved intact. But they could be narrated as external events only by modeling them on the stories of encounters with Jesus during his earthly ministry. It is particularly significant that it is precisely those later traits in the narrative tradition of the earthly Jesus' ministry that represent him as a 'divine man' (*theios anēr*) that are taken into the resurrection. Thus the women 'touch' his feet (cf. Mk. 5:22) and they 'worship' him (cf. Mk. 5:6). This is the strongest argument against the primitive character of the appearance *narratives.*[39]

To spell out a bit what Fuller is saying to be the 'strongest argument', it is the similarity of the appearance narratives to certain stories about Jesus' earthly ministry in the Gospels. But to accept this as an argument for the late development, and hence (as Fuller and others take this) as an argument against the historical reality of the appearances, without anything to go on other than this similarity, is to commit the same fallacy of accepting an account of provenance without any serious consideration of live alternatives that we have been tracing in other connections. Why shouldn't the risen Jesus act and speak in ways that bear some similarity to the way he acted and spoke in his pre-crucifixion ministry? After all, he is, *ex hypothesi*, the same person. Why shouldn't there be such similarities, however authentic the accounts of these appearances? Again, a particular account of provenance is arbitrarily privileged against other possibilities.

In Luedemann's *The Resurrection of Jesus* we get a more summary dismissal of the historical value of resurrection narratives. What follows is a bit of Luedemann's treatment of what ensues when the two travelers return from Emmaus and rejoin the other disciples, whereupon Jesus appears in their midst, calling attention to his bodily nature.

> The tradition underlying Luke 24:36–43 is the story of an appearance in which the risen Jesus appears to his anxious disciples in bodily form. The focus is the fleshly, physical form of Jesus after the resurrection. What is presupposed is a discussion in the community of the nature of the corporeality of the risen Christ … Accordingly this is a secondary formation – probably of the second generation, which no longer had any connection with the key witnesses to the 'resurrection of Jesus'.[40]

---

[39] Fuller, *Formation*, 79.
[40] Luedemann, *Resurrection*, 149.

Again, the possibility of a late provenance is simply asserted without any attempt to compare it with other alternatives.

Appeals to What Is Most Memorable

I will criticize just one other way of supporting negative conclusions about the authenticity of attribution of sayings to the historical Jesus. This one is based on a consideration of what kinds of sayings would be most likely to be remembered in the oral tradition. Participants in the Jesus Seminar put an emphasis on this. Here is a general statement in the 'Introduction' of Funk and Hoover's *The Five Gospels:*

> We know that the oral memory best retains sayings and anecdotes that are short, provocative, memorable – and oft-repeated. Indeed, the oral memory retains little else. This information squares with the fact that the most frequently recorded words of Jesus in the surviving gospels take the form of aphorisms and parables. It is highly probable that the earliest layer of the gospel tradition was made up almost entirely of single aphorisms and parables that circulated by word of mouth, without narrative context.[41]

They then use these considerations to exclude attributions to Jesus of utterances that are not of this sort. Here are some examples.

(7) Mark 1:15: (An initial summary of Jesus' version of the gospel.) The time has come; the kingdom of God is upon you; repent, and believe the gospel.

> Jesus' disciples remembered his public discourse as consisting primarily of aphorisms, parables, or a challenge followed by a verbal retort. Since Mark 1:15 does not fall into any of these categories, it drew mostly gray and black votes from the Fellows of the Jesus Seminar.[42]

Before criticizing this dismissal I must acknowledge that the negative judgement was also based on the claim that Jesus would not have claimed (what the Jesus Seminar supposed this saying to be implying) that the rule of God was 'to be the beginning of a new age, at the end of history, following a cosmic catastrophe'. But since, as N.T. Wright[43] has convincingly shown, it is implausible to hold that Jesus' references to the coming of the kingdom had any such implication, that contention is misguided. They also maintain that Jesus would

---

[41] Funk, Hoover and The Jesus Seminar, *Five Gospels,* 28.
[42] Funk, Hoover and The Jesus Seminar, *Five Gospels,* 40.
[43] See Wright, *Jesus.*

not have called on people to repent. I cannot enter into that issue here, but at any rate, my present concern is with the contention that the utterance in question does not fall within any of the types that are distinctive of Jesus, and that is at least part of their reason for the negative judgement as to its authenticity. And how about that?

First, a general point. The principle that short sayings are most likely to be remembered fits ill with the principle that parables are among the alleged sayings most likely to be remembered. For some of the parables are considerably longer than many alleged sayings rejected by the Seminar. And with respect to the present case, we have a very short saying indeed. To make its case the Seminar would have to defend a choice in many instances between the criterion of brevity and the criterion of paradoxicality and other criteria having to do with content.

In any event, and apart from the criteria laid down by the Seminar, there are strong reasons for thinking that the content of Mark 1:15 would be remembered. After all, it purports to be a terse summary of the core of Jesus' version of God's good news. Surely the members of a movement initiated by Jesus would place a high priority on remembering accurately what he said when he set out to communicate God's good news to his listeners. How much more memorable could something be to the early church?

(8) Mark 8:1–3: 'And once again during that same period, when there was a huge crowd without anything to eat, he calls the disciples aside and says to them, "I feel sorry for the crowd, because they have already spent three days with me and haven't had anything to eat. If I send these people home hungry they will collapse on the road – in fact some of them have come from quite a distance." ' Funk and Hoover report the consensus of the Jesus Seminar on this as follows:

> The words quoted from Jesus in the story of the feeding of the crowd are all the product of some later scriptwriter. Since they are neither aphorisms nor parables, they could not have circulated independently. There is no valid reason to suppose that the first Christian storytellers would have remembered precisely these words.[44]

I need not repeat the general points made in discussing the first example. As for this case, first it is not a question of remembering precisely what words Jesus uttered on this occasion, but rather of remembering the gist of what he said. And as for that, there is every reason to suppose that the episode would be strongly etched in the memories of the disciples who were involved. After all, feeding four thousand people with seven loaves of bread and a few small fish is a

---

[44] Funk, Hoover and The Jesus Seminar, *Five Gospels,* 71.

great big deal. It does not matter for this point whether this was a genuine miracle that involved supernatural influence or some clever sleight of hand. So long as the disciples took it to be a miracle, it would be something they would be strongly inclined to remember, including what Jesus said in initiating the feeding. It would be very unusual if it were not remembered and passed down in the oral tradition.

(9) Mark 8:22–26: 'They come to Bethsaida, and they bring him a blind person, and plead with him to touch him. He took the blind man by the hand and led him out of the village. And he spat into his eyes, and placed his hands on him, and started questioning him: "Do you see anything?"

When his sight began to come back, the first thing he said was: "I see human figures, as though they were trees walking around."

Then he put his hands over his eyes a second time. And he opened his eyes, and his sight was restored, and he saw everything clearly. And he sent him home, saying, "Don't bother to go back to the village!" '

The comment on this episode is as follows:

> The words ascribed to Jesus are the invention of the evangelist. Because they are incidental dialogue and not memorable pronouncements, they would not have been remembered as exact words of Jesus.[45]

Again we can ignore the red herring of 'exact words'. There are strong reasons for thinking that such an episode would be remembered, including the gist of what Jesus said. The apparently miraculous character of the healing would be enough for that. But, in addition, there are various unusual features of the report that would tend to make the episode stick in the minds of witnesses. Unlike most of the reported healings, Jesus' activities do not have the complete intended result at first, and he is required to make a second attempt. Then the visual experiences of the patient after Jesus' first manipulation are unusual enough to catch the attention of onlookers. Finally, Jesus' injunction not to go back to the village seems unmotivated by anything in the story, and, assuming that Jesus did not accompany it by any explanation, that would also be memorable. I would judge by these three examples that the Jesus Seminar were not doing very well with their criterion of memorability.

---

[45] Funk, Hoover and The Jesus Seminar, *Five Gospels,* 75.

Conclusion

As I said at the outset, my aims in this chapter are modest. I have set out only to give reasons for supposing that certain lines of argument, and the background assumptions that are crucial for them, fail to provide adequate support for negative conclusions about the authenticity of reported sayings of Jesus, and of reported events, in the Synoptic Gospels. I have concentrated on the 'it could be so, therefore it is so' line of argument that involves uncritical applications of the criterion of dissimilarity and analogous criteria. Though I have chosen this focus because such arguments seem to me to be both widespread and patently without sufficient force, there are other types of arguments for the same sort of conclusion that could and should be criticized. But perhaps my sample constitutes a start at a reaction to the frequent current skepticism about the historical value of the gospel record.

Bibliography

Alston, W.P., 'Biblical Criticism and the Resurrection', in *The Resurrection* (ed. S.T. Davis, D. Kendall and G. O'Collins; Oxford: OUP, 1997)

Bartholomew, C., C. Greene and K. Möller (eds.), *After Pentecost: Language and Biblical Interpretation* (Carlisle: Paternoster; Grand Rapids: Zondervan, 2001)

Borg, M.J., *Jesus: A New Vision* (San Francisco: Harper & Row, 1987)

Brown, S., *The Origins of Christianity* (Oxford: OUP, 1984)

Bultmann, R., *The History of the Synoptic Tradition* (trans. J. Marsh; Peabody, MA: Hendrickson, 5th edn, 1963)

Crossan, J.D., *The Historical Jesus: The Life of a Mediterranean Jewish Peasant* (San Francisco: HarperSanFrancisco, 1991)

Fredriksen, P., *From Jesus to Christ* (New Haven: Yale University Press, 1988)

Fuller, R., *The Formation of the Resurrection Narratives* (New York: Macmillan, 1971)

Funk, R.W., R.W. Hoover and The Jesus Seminar, *The Five Gospels: The Search for the Authentic Words of Jesus* (New York: Macmillan, 1993)

Griffin, D.R., *Religion and Scientific Naturalism* (Albany: State University of New York, 2000)

Luedemann, G., *The Resurrection of Jesus* (Minneapolis: Fortress Press, 1994)

Meier, J.P., *A Marginal Jew: Rethinking the Historical Jesus*, I (New York: Doubleday, 1991)

Perrin, N., *Rediscovering the Teaching of Jesus* (New York: Harper & Row, 1967)

Sanders, E.P., *The Historical Figure of Jesus* (London: Penguin, 1993)

——, and M. Davies, *Studying the Synoptic Gospels* (London: SCM Press, 1989)

Taylor, V., *The Formation of the Gospel Tradition* (London: Macmillan, 1933)

Wagner, S.J., and R. Warner (eds.), *Naturalism: A Critical Appraisal* (Notre Dame: University of Notre Dame Press, 1993)

Wright, N.T., *Jesus and the Victory of God* (Minneapolis: Fortress Press, 1996)

9

Behind, in Front of … or Through the Text?

The Christological Analogy and the Lost World of Biblical Truth

Mary E. Healy

The first postmodern generation has witnessed a rising tide of challenges to the historical-critical approach to biblical interpretation. Contemporary scholars have exposed the flawed logic and tendentious application of the criteria of historical veracity often used by historical critics. They have pointed out that the judgements brought to bear on historical questions are not as impartial as is often claimed, and are sometimes wedded to unexamined philosophical pre-suppositions. Proponents of new, literary methods of analysis have even questioned whether the primary access to meaning – or any valid meaning at all – is found in a diachronic study of the background and sources of the text.[1] But in critiquing the shortcomings of the historical-critical method, postmodern critics have perhaps overlooked some of its deepest philosophical underpinnings. While challenging the hermeneutics of suspicion – the idea that biblical narrative must be dismantled and reconstructed in order to arrive at actual history – they have left intact a set of questionable assumptions regarding the interrelation between event and word. They have thus, in some cases, even further undercut the ability of a text to serve as a means of access to historical truth. Much work remains to be done in launching a new era of more philo-sophically aware and self-critical exegesis, but one important step is to probe the hidden epistemological premises animating both historical criticism and some of its most strident critics.

---

[1] For a sampling of recent critiques of historical criticism, see Donfried, 'Alien Hermeneutics'; Harrisville, 'Critique'; Hays, 'Corrected Jesus'; Johnson, 'Crisis'; Levenson, 'Bible'; Plantinga, *Warranted Christian Belief*, ch. 12 (= Ch. 1 in the present volume); Provan, 'Ideologies'; Ratzinger, 'Biblical Interpretation'.

My aim in this chapter is to raise questions and indicate avenues for further reflection in the direction of a more epistemologically adequate hermeneutic. To that end, I will first briefly comment on the influence of Kantian philosophy on the historical-critical school, especially as typified by Bultmann, and its relevance for evaluating the claims of historical criticism to reconstruct the world 'behind' the text. Second, I will reflect on what some recent developments in hermeneutic philosophy can contribute to our understanding of the function of narrative in mediating historical reality. I will then consider how these reflections bear on the case of biblical narrative, which purports to truthfully convey not only history, but also God's mysterious action within history and, moreover, claims to do so in a way that is inspired by God himself. Finally, I will show how an ancient analogy for Scripture sheds light on the current crisis of interpretation by pointing the way toward a hermeneutical approach that is adequate to the communicative aims of biblical narrative.

Kant and the Failed Quest for Historical 'Being-in-Itself'

In discerning the philosophical roots of the historical-critical method, the most obvious place to turn is to the Enlightenment and its rejection of divine transcendence. From Enlightenment rationalism, nineteenth- and twentieth-century biblical exegetes imbibed the scientific world-view and its *a priori* denial of the possibility of miracles. The world and history were viewed as a closed system of natural causes, from which divine action was categorically excluded.[2] As contemporary scholars usually recognize, these assumptions already have a noxious effect on one's view of the historical authenticity of the Bible. They lead one to envisage the exegetical task as that of dissecting texts, in order that what never could have happened (in the exegete's view) may be separated out from what *might* have happened, and explained away by other means (i.e., demythologized). However, the ultimate sources of this skepticism lie further back, in the philosophic 'turn to the subject' initiated by Descartes and brought to a culmination by Kant. For Kant, the activity of the thinking subject so dominates the act of knowing that we can be said to *produce* the objects of our knowledge. The mind does not receive being-in-itself, but rather takes in an amorphous mass of sensations and imposes order on it according to pre-existing mental categories, resulting in what we think of as the outside world. In effect, Kant reduces reality to a construct of the mind. Since the productive activity of reason is an inescapable part of every act of knowledge,

---

[2] See Murray Rae, 'Creation and Promise: Towards a Theology of History', Ch. 12 in this volume, for a lucid account of this immanentizing trajectory of modern thought.

there is no possibility of ever discovering what really lies 'out there' beyond the prison of our minds. For Kant, 'the voice of being-in-itself cannot be heard by human beings'.[3]

It is difficult to overestimate the impact of Kantian epistemology on modern thought in general and on biblical studies in particular.[4] In his chapter in this volume, Iain Provan describes how the search for historical 'being-in-itself' (*wie es eigentlich gewesen ist*) propelled the development of the positivist-empiricist school of historiography, which eventually despaired of its misguided quest.[5] In biblical studies, the alienation of being-in-itself manifested itself as the gap between the 'Jesus of history', the irretrievable real Jesus ever-receding into the shadows of the past, and the 'Christ of faith' fashioned by hopelessly entangled layers of myth and tradition. The task of historical criticism came to be envisioned as that of sifting through the strands of tradition present in the biblical text to recover whatever vestiges of historical facticity might be discerned. From these, the exegete proceeds to reconstruct events 'as they actually happened'. This ambitious goal is realized as the exegete discovers the laws supposedly governing the development of faith traditions, then traces them backward from the text to determine the original historical kernel. The biblical text and the oral traditions behind it thus function in a way analogous to Kant's productive reason: they are a product of the mind, a filter or veil which only serves to obscure our view of reality in itself. Once the exegete has eradicated this filter, his reconstructed history becomes the norm by which the canonical version of history is judged.[6] The real value of the biblical text itself is then reduced to the moral 'message' that can be extracted from its narrative context.

As critics have pointed out, although historical-critical exegetes in the Bultmann tradition are eager to identify and expunge the mythical constructs of earlier, 'pre-critical' ages, they are inexplicably blind to their own. In the words of Peter Berger,

> The present … remains strangely immune from relativization. In other words, the New Testament writers are seen as afflicted with a false consciousness rooted in their time, but the contemporary analyst takes the consciousness of *his* time as an unmixed

---

[3] Ratzinger, 'Biblical Interpretation', 15.

[4] The decisive influence of Kant on Bultmann, via the Marburg neo-Kantians, has been well documented by Michael Waldstein and others. See Waldstein, 'Foundations'. The Marburg school actually took Kant a step further and eliminated 'being-in-itself' as a remnant of the old realist metaphysics (Waldstein, 'Foundations', 121).

[5] 'Knowing and Believing: Faith in the Past', Ch. 11.

[6] Historical criticism is perhaps more sanguine than Kantian epistemology in holding that we can have at least some access, however tentative, to historical reality-in-itself.

intellectual blessing. The electricity and radio users are placed intellectually above the Apostle Paul.[7]

One of the foremost of these modern myths is that of absolute objectivity, an offshoot of the Kantian subject–object split. According to this notion, the goal of historical criticism is to attain the kind of absolute empirical certitude regarding history that is claimed by the natural sciences regarding physical phenomena. But Cardinal Ratzinger has made the telling point that if the natural sciences are the model, then the Heisenberg principle ought to be included in their application.[8] This principle states that the result of a given experiment is unavoidably influenced by the position of the observer. For more than half a century, it has been recognized in the empirical sciences that pure objectivity is an impossible abstraction; how much more so should it be recognized in the human sciences, where the objects of study include the mysterious thoughts and motivations of the human heart. The idea of an absolutely neutral observer standing on some plane outside the repercussions of history, able to judge interpretations of the past with impartial certitude, is as mythical as the gnostic 'Primal Man'. Rather, all interpretations presuppose the standpoint of the interpreter, since everyone approaches reality from a particular point of view. One's viewpoint is not necessarily a bias, but a perspective from which investigation can fruitfully proceed. This point leads us to a consideration of narrative and its role in mediating historical truth.

The Mediating Function of Narrative

Narrative is the literary genre most apt to mediate history. It is the means by which event becomes word.[9] Through narrative, a historical event is brought into a new, verbal mode of existence that renders it communicable to those who were not physically present. Because of the concrete particularity of a historical event, it cannot be mediated through a series of abstract propositions, but only through a 'story' which gives it shape through plot and character. In that very process, the event is interpreted.

Narrative interprets an event not only by presenting its various features as a meaningful whole, but also by giving access to its interior significance. To give an illustration, one might view a scene of an adult picking up a young child by

---

[7] *Rumor of Angels*, 41, quoted in Ratzinger, 'Biblical Interpretation', 15.

[8] Ratzinger, 'Biblical Interpretation', 7.

[9] This concise definition is provided by Francis Martin, 'Spiritual Understanding', 166. Literarily, narrative could be defined as 'the literary presentation of a complete action' (Martin, 'Spiritual Understanding', 167).

the feet and violently slapping the child. The scene appears to be an instance of child abuse. But then a narrative is provided: the child is a victim of cystic fibrosis, and the anxious parent is following the doctor's instructions on how to expel phlegm from the lungs. The narrative (presuming it is accurate) does not merely offer one of any number of valid competing interpretations, but also discloses the true interiority of the event. It does not compromise knowledge of the event, but rather enhances it. It is a window opening onto unseen dimensions of the event which otherwise might remain concealed.

Thus *all* narrative is interpretation. The ancients were more aware of this than the moderns, and instinctively interpreted events by retelling them, rather than by converting them into discourse. For example, 1–2 Chronicles is a rewrite of 2 Samuel through 2 Kings, in order to highlight those aspects of the events deemed most important to the Chronicler's own purposes. Deuteronomy 1:18–36 renarrates the incident of Kadesh-Barnea recounted in Numbers 13–14 with a very divergent perspective. And the four Gospels narrate some of the same episodes differently, each unveiling distinctive aspects of the inner significance of these events simply by the way they tell the story. Thus the discrepancies among the accounts are not due to defects in memory or to a lack of interest in the facts, but to the authors' intentions to bring to light unique facets of the event, each in his own way.

Probably the philosopher who has reflected most on the communicative role of narrative is Paul Ricœur. In Ricœur's terminology, an author transposes an event into word by 'configuring' it – that is, by giving it a certain narrative structure.[10] This structure has its own validity and value: it creates a world 'in front of' the text, which interacts with the world of the reader and opens up new possibilities for self-realization. Ricœur is seeking to overcome the 'hermeneutics of suspicion', which distrusts the surface meaning of the text, and the related error of 'historicism', or the presupposition that the intelligibility of a text derives primarily from the theological and social preoccupations of the author or community which produced it. Ricœur therefore opposes any attempt at interpretation that involves getting 'behind' the text to determine the historical conditions that gave rise to it. Instead, he advocates paying attention to the symbolic world opened up by the text on its own terms. This is similar to the practice of more recent methods of literary, semiotic and rhetorical analysis that deliberately exclude any data extrinsic to the text (the synchronic methods).[11] But Ricœur himself falls under Kantian influence in that he tends

---

[10] See esp. Ricœur, *Time*, I.

[11] Cf. the Pontifical Biblical Commission document, *The Interpretation of the Bible in the Church*, I.B.2: 'While the historical-critical method considers the text as a "window" giving access to one or other period ... narrative analysis insists that the text also functions as a "mirror," in the sense that it projects a certain image – a "narrative

to undervalue the connection between a text and the subject matter to which it ostensibly refers (whether historical or ontological), and he thereby detracts from the role of a text as inter-subjective communication.[12] The relationship between the meaning found within or in front of a historical narrative and the actual events recounted therein seems at best ambiguous in Ricœur, if not considered irrelevant or denied in principle.

But if we are to take a narrative (particularly a biblical narrative) at face value as something more than edifying fiction, interpretation must consider not merely the meaning of the text or the world it creates, but also the *actual events and realities* mediated by it. We cannot do justice to biblical narratives without taking seriously the claim of some of these narratives to convey historical truth. (The fact that precisely *which* texts claim to mediate history is a matter for dispute does not nullify the fact that some do.)[13] In such cases, the act of interpretation does not terminate in the texts, but rather in that to which they refer.[14] At the same time, however, Ricœur's analysis helps us to recognize that the narrative is precisely that *by which* we have access to the realities; we cannot bypass the written word to attain a raw, 'objective' factuality. In regard to Scripture, these two interrelated factors have traditionally been expressed as the intrinsic unity of word and deed in divine revelation, as stated in the Second Vatican Council's document on divine revelation, *Dei Verbum:*

> the deeds wrought by God in the history of salvation manifest and confirm the teaching and realities signified by the words, while the words proclaim the deeds and clarify the mystery contained in them.[15]

Thus, rather than speaking of getting 'behind' the text or 'in front of the text', I suggest that a more adequate prepositional metaphor would be to speak of coming into contact with the referent *through* the text. This conveys the inseparable importance of both the reality itself and the text by which we have access to it through the author's configuration.

---

world" – which exercises an influence upon readers' perceptions'. Along the same lines, formalist and structuralist methods can be described as focusing on the world 'within' the text. For a comparison and assessment of 'behind', 'in front of' and 'within' as interpretive metaphors, see Thiselton, 'Behind'.

[12] Ricœur's stance toward historical referent is a matter of debate. Cf. Comstock, 'Truth'; Vanhoozer, *Biblical Narrative*, chs. 6–7; Martin, 'Literary Theory', 599.

[13] Sternberg, *Poetics*, 23–35, 99–101, provides a penetrating analysis of historical truth-claiming in Scripture and its distinction from both fiction on the one hand and truth value on the other.

[14] Paraphrasing a statement of Thomas Aquinas regarding the act of faith (*Summa Theologiae*, II–II, q. 1, a. 2 *ad* 2).

[15] Vatican II, *Dei Verbum*, I, 2.

With this interdependence of word and event in mind, it may be helpful to articulate a distinction between historical criticism and the historical-critical methods. Although the terms are often used interchangeably, historical criticism is more properly viewed as one stage or subset of the historical-critical methods.[16] *Historical criticism* in the strict sense is applied exclusively to those biblical texts purporting to record actual historical events and envisages its task as identifying the genuinely historical data that can be discerned beneath narratives which come to us through a long, complex process of development, and whose final form is shaped by the redactors' theological concerns. In the deficient form typified by the Jesus Seminar, historical criticism judges the historical value of a given text by breaking it down and reconstructing history according to a new standpoint deemed more valid (i.e., that of the interpreter). The *historical-critical methods*, on the other hand, seek to ascertain as accurately as possible that which the biblical authors intended to express by employing textual, philological, literary, archeological and other tools of analysis.[17] Although both may suffer from faulty philosophical assumptions, the former is more liable to the risk of subordinating the text to the interpreter's own pre-occupations, whereas the latter can help the text to speak more clearly with its own voice. Whereas the former lacerates the text in order to get *behind* it, the latter, when practiced soundly, respects the text in order to gain access *through* it to the reality being communicated.

The Vertical Dimension of Biblical Narrative and Its Implications for Exegesis

All that has been said above regarding narrative in general can be applied to biblical narrative, taking into consideration the added factor of the biblical view of history as radically open to God – as possessing what Jean Lacroix calls a 'vertical dimension'.[18] For the biblical authors, every event is a mystery whose inner depths reveal something of God and his gracious dealings with humanity. God's absolute transcendence ensures that his intervention in the affairs of history does not violate or compete with creaturely causality, but actually

---

[16] The plural is more appropriate than the singular because the term is used for a diverse range of methodologies.

[17] For a helpful articulation of this distinction see Prior, *Historical-Critical Method*, 39–40; 280–81. Compare similar statements (which, however, use the terminology differently) by Brown, 'Contribution', 27; and Fitzmyer, 'Historical Criticism', 251.

[18] Lacroix, *Histoire*, 7, quoted in Martin, 'Literary Theory', 596. For this paragraph and the following two I am indebted to this article and another by Martin, 'Spiritual Understanding'.

allows free will its fullest expression. In the words of Henri de Lubac, the conviction of Scripture and of Christian tradition is that

> God acts in history and reveals himself through history. Or rather, God inserts himself in history and so bestows on it a 'religious consecration' which compels us to treat it with due respect. As a consequence historical realities possess a depth and are to be understood in a spiritual manner: *historika pneumatikōs*; conversely, spiritual realities appear in a constant state of flux and are to be understood historically: *pneumatika historikōs*. The Bible, which contains the revelation of salvation, contains too, in its own way, the history of the world.[19]

As in the cystic fibrosis example given above, an adequate interpretation is one that *correctly* perceives the interior dimension of an event and thereby gives the reader access to that interiority. Thus if God is truly a protagonist in the drama of human events depicted by Scripture, then to interpret Scripture in a way that *a priori* excludes or denies his involvement is automatically to sabotage real understanding. At best it is to remain on a superficial level, which skims the surface of what is being conveyed; at worst it is to incur the risk of serious distortion. Rather, an adequate interpretation requires that we at least to some degree penetrate the interior depth of the mysteries disclosed in the text.[20]

This principle applies in a particular way to the Gospels as the summit of biblical revelation. As virtually all New Testament exegetes recognize, Jesus' resurrection is a hermeneutical key for understanding the Gospels. The evangelists write with the conviction that because Jesus has been raised from the dead, all that he lived and taught on earth has been transfigured into a new mode of existence which becomes a source of power for all who believe in him.[21] They thus narrate each event in the earthly life of Jesus in such a way as to proclaim that this historically contingent event is *still present* because its central character is alive, and that the reader can come into contact with him by accessing the unique grace and power revealed in this event.[22]

---

[19] de Lubac, *Catholicism*, 167.

[20] Interpreting in this manner is what has traditionally been known as 'spiritual understanding' of Scripture. It is summed up in a well-known phrase of the Second Vatican Council: 'sacred Scripture must be read and interpreted in the same Spirit by which it was written' (*Dei Verbum*, III, 12).

[21] Cf. the references to the risen Jesus still bearing the marks of his passion in Jn. 20:27; Rev. 5:6.

[22] This conviction is the basis for the traditional notion that each event in the life of Christ is a 'mystery' which reveals his divine identity and redemptive plan, and which imparts a particular grace to believers (cf. the *Catechism of the Catholic Church*, par. 512–521). After stating that 'Christ enables us *to live in him* all that he himself lived, and *he lives it in us*', the *Catechism* goes on to quote St. John Eudes: 'We must

To read the Gospels in the Spirit in which they were written means first and foremost that we must understand that the Gospels were not written to defend, promote or perpetuate the memory of a dead master, but to put us in touch with the living Lord. As such, they are a sacrament: they contain what they signify ... [The gospel] narrates for us the events of Christ's life in a manner which enables us to see these events as they now exist in their completed state in the glorified humanity of Jesus.[23]

How does all this relate to the contemporary challenges to historical criticism? On the one hand, historical critics seek to reconstruct the actual events supposedly distorted by the ancient authors in the interests of their own theological or social agendas. On the other hand, their postmodern challengers cut the link with the past entirely and locate meaning solely in the narrative world created by the text. Both approaches dissolve the unity of word and deed, and thereby lose sight of that truth which the complete act of communication aims to disclose. Neither approach addresses the presupposition that anything shaping the report of events in accord with faith compromises historical integrity. If we recognize the mediating function of historical narrative in giving access to an event's interior dimension, then the falsity of this presupposition is exposed. We might then describe the authors' procedure more accurately, in the case of the Gospels, as narrating in such a way that the open quality of the events of Jesus' life is revealed. That is, they relate the events in a manner that is 'transparent' to the post-resurrection church and the present activity of the living Jesus, yet without thereby disregarding historical accuracy. An example might be found in the story of the healing of the paralytic lowered through the roof (Mk. 2:1–12). All three Synoptics recount the declaration of Jesus' power to forgive in such a way that it may readily be interpreted as a parenthetical remark to the reader: 'But that *you* may know that the Son of man has authority on earth to forgive sins, he said to the paralytic ...' (see Mk. 7:19; 13:37 for other examples of such asides to the reader).[24] In a move typical of historical criticism, Bultmann asserts that the theme of forgiveness is a later invention, inserted because the church wanted to trace back to Jesus *its* own right to forgive sins. As William Alston shows in his chapter in this volume, such a claim is gratuitous and explains the data no better than alternate hypotheses.[25] Once this

---

continue to accomplish in ourselves the stages of Jesus' life and his mysteries and often to beg him to perfect and realize them in us and in his whole Church ... For it is the plan of the Son of God to make us and the whole Church partake in his mysteries and to extend them to and continue them in us and in his whole Church. This is his plan for fulfilling his mysteries in us' (par. 521).

[23] Martin, 'Spiritual Understanding', 162.

[24] This reading does not preclude others, and it may well be that the evangelists deliberately left the syntax ambiguous (there being no punctuation in the Greek).

[25] 'Historical Criticism of the Synoptic Gospels', Ch. 8.

point is recognized, would not the passage be better explained as portraying the interior experience of forgiveness in someone who was also physically healed by Jesus, in a manner which helps the reader recognize that such forgiveness is now available to all those who are led to him in faith (i.e., through the church)? Again, for the evangelists to narrate this way is not to disregard history but to consciously interpret it in a way that is faithful to the transcendent mystery revealed through the event.

Biblical Inspiration and the Christological Analogy

If biblical narrative is unique in its claim to mediate not only the interior but also the vertical or divine dimension of historical events, what constitutes an adequate hermeneutic for interpreting such narrative? I would like to consider this question in light of some implications of the notion of biblical inspiration. The doctrine of inspiration may be expressed as the conviction that God himself is the primary author of the sacred books. That is, not only is the content of Scripture the mystery of God in himself and in his dealings with humankind throughout the history of salvation, but it is *God* who is speaking through the human authors whom he inspires. If this is so, it follows that interpretation must take into account both the human and divine authorship of Scripture. In explaining this doctrine, Catholic magisterial teaching of the last century has used an analogy in which Scripture is compared with the hypostatic union of two natures in Christ. The analogy was adopted by the Second Vatican Council and reaffirmed by Pope John Paul II in his 1993 address to the Pontifical Biblical Commission (PBC).[26] Its ultimate sources are patristic, as expressed for

---

[26] Pope Pius XII, *Divino afflante Spirito*, §37; Vatican II, *Dei Verbum*, III, 13; Pope John Paul II, address to the PBC, 23 April, 1993, published as the preface to *Interpretation of the Bible in the Church*. The Pope writes, 'The Church of Christ takes the realism of the incarnation seriously, and this is why she attaches great importance to the "historico-critical" study of the Bible'. Further on he adds, 'Nevertheless, this study is not enough ... it is obviously necessary that the exegete himself perceive the divine word in the texts. He can do this only if his intellectual work is sustained by a vigorous spiritual life' (par. 7 and 9). The interpenetration of critical methods and faith in the divine word is an instance of the broader interrelationship of reason and faith, as articulated by the Pope in the encyclical *Fides et ratio:* '[In the biblical texts] Faith intervenes not to abolish reason's autonomy nor to reduce its scope for action, but solely to bring the human being to understand that in these events it is the God of Israel who acts. Thus the world and the events of history cannot be understood in depth without professing faith in the God who is at work in them ... There is thus no reason for competition of any kind between reason and faith: each contains the other, and each has its own scope for action' (par. 16–17).

instance in Origen's comparison of Scripture to the flesh of Christ.[27] The Second Vatican Council version states it thus: 'For the words of God, expressed in human language, have been made like human discourse, just as of old the Word of the eternal Father, when he took to himself the weak flesh of humanity, became like other men'. This analogy is not merely a felicitously apt comparison; it is rooted in the sacramental character of Scripture, which itself corresponds to the sacramentality of Christ's humanity. As the eternal Word has become fully human, like us in all things but sin, so Scripture is fully human, composed by human agents within the limitations of their historical, cultural and linguistic settings and exercising the full powers of their intelligence and freedom. At the same time, as Christ was fully divine, so Scripture is able to express the revelation of God in all its fullness. These two 'natures' of Scripture are not in tension or juxtaposition but in indissoluble unity; we cannot pick apart a sentence or a pericope and assign its divine and human components. However, there is an order to the two with regard to our knowing. Just as one cannot come to know the triune God except through the humanity of Christ, so one cannot approach the divine or revelatory meaning of the Bible except through its human meaning. The spiritual meaning shines precisely *through* the literal, as the divinity of Christ radiates through his humanity.

The parallel with the incarnation suggests that just as there are imbalanced Christologies, so there can be forms of scriptural interpretation that fail to hold the two dimensions of the biblical word in full integrity and unity. One of these might be called a Monophysite type of exegesis. Like the ancient heresy that denied Christ's human nature, this kind of approach downplays or ignores the human factors that went into the composition of the biblical text. It accords the biblical words an absolute value, independent of the conditions of human language and culture.[28] In its extreme form, it seems to envision the human authors as sacred secretaries who simply transcribed as the Holy Spirit dictated – in other words, not as *authors* in any authentic sense. In a more mild form, it blithely disregards the literal sense of the text and thus gives rise to spiritual interpretations which range from the subjective and arbitrary to the self-serving and even frivolous. As critics often point out, it is not hard to find examples of such fanciful exegesis among certain writings of the Fathers.

---

[27] 'Just as this spoken word cannot be seen or touched according to its own nature, but if it is written in a book and, so to speak, become bodily, then it is seen and touched; so too the fleshless and bodiless Word of God, though it cannot be seen or written according to its divinity, when it has become flesh is seen and written. Therefore, since it has become flesh, there is a book of its generation.' Origen, *In ev. Matt*, at 1:18 (*PG* 17, 289AB); see also John Chrysostom, *Homilies on John*, at 1:18.

[28] Cf. Pope John Paul II, address to the PBC, par. 8.

The other one-sided form of exegesis, more typical of modern scholarship, might be called Nestorian.[29] This approach, while not necessarily denying the divine aspect of Scripture, so isolates it from the human that it is reduced to an artificial addendum. Such an approach deliberately and methodologically considers the text as a purely human reality and superimposes the divine only as a second operation *after* the crucial exegetical judgements have already been made. Questions regarding the genesis of the text and the concerns of the authors or redactors are asked and answered within a purely human framework, ignoring or abstracting from the fact that God himself is speaking through the biblical word. The danger is that horizontal explanations are then constructed for what actually has only a vertical explanation. The result is often a reductive interpretation, which leaves ordinary believers uneasy and confused about the compatibility of the exegetical conclusions with Christian faith, and doubtful about the divine realities being conveyed in the text. At times, this kind of exegesis can tend toward a kind of fideism in which church doctrine is affirmed even while the supposedly objective exegetical results are tending in a completely opposite direction. In its extreme form (the Jesus Seminar), it results in a secular explanation of the events narrated, irreconcilable with other biblical assertions and with the unity of the biblical testimony as a whole. It is important to note that this kind of interpretation is not incapable of producing valid insights; but its failure to come to grips with the vertical dimension of Scripture leaves it vulnerable to the risk of error and distortion and renders it ultimately inadequate as a means of access to the mysteries being revealed.

How, then, is the humanness of Scripture to be granted its legitimate autonomy without draining the word of its divine power? A 'Chalcedonian' form of exegesis, which does full justice to the human and the divine aspects of Scripture in their integral unity, might be described as one which takes seriously the human authorial processes and rigorously investigates the relevant manuscripts, languages, literary genres, historical contexts, cultural settings and so on – but as open *from the beginning* to the interior and vertical dimension. The logical priority of the human dimension is at the service of the teleological priority of the divine: interpretation is for the sake of the knowledge of God in Christ.

In pursuing this kind of exegesis, are methods such as the historical-critical methods to be considered as tools that are in themselves neutral? As Al Wolters has demonstrated, even the most technical levels of interpretation, such as textual criticism and lexicography, depend on the judgement of the interpreter and are thus influenced by the presuppositions he brings to his study.[30] Since, as

---

[29] This use of the term Nestorian as applied to exegesis seems to have originated with Louis Bouyer, 'Mouvement Biblique', 18. The Nestorian heresy denied the unity of Christ's two natures in one person.

[30] Wolters, 'Confessional Criticism'.

noted above, all interpretation presupposes a perspective, one's perspective on whether or not God acts in history will inevitably impinge on one's interpretation (of course, in varying degrees, depending on the level of interpretation). The only perspective that is adequate to the realities mediated by Scripture is that which is open to the living God: that is, the perspective of faith. Faith is here understood not merely as assent to confessional doctrines but as a prophetic, that is, divinely bestowed, interpretation of all reality.[31] Its absence – whether real or by artificial abstraction – will close off the most significant dimensions of reality from the perception of the interpreter. To propose an analogy, one cannot transmit color on black-and-white film; it is simply incapable of registering and transmitting the colored aspect of light. Nor can color be perceived by someone who lacks the retinal cones needed to see it; even if colored light enters his eye, the colorblind person is able to distinguish only black and white images. Both the vehicle and the recipient must be adequate to the content transmitted. When faith is considered a bias (consisting of a set of doctrinal commitments) and artificially imported only after all the exegetical judgements have been made, the consequence is itself a bias. 'Excluding the experience of faith from the exegetical process … is like subjecting a musical piece to the judgment of a jury whose members must be deaf, so that their aesthetic experience would not interfere with the unbiased objectivity of their judgment'.[32] This is not to deny that faith is in constant need of purification and is capable of making mistaken assumptions that can distort interpretation. Disciplined, methodical and open-minded attention to the text helps to unearth these assumptions; for instance, earlier generations of Christians had to come to the realization that faith does not require us to assert that Moses wrote the Pentateuch, or that the report that the sun stopped for a day in Joshua 10:13 contradicts Copernicus. But faith in itself is not an obstacle to rigorously objective scholarship; rather, it is its necessary and fertile complement.

It is my hope that deeper reflection on the christological analogy and its hermeneutical implications will take us a step closer toward overcoming the false dichotomy between critical exegesis and Christian faith, so that the biblical text will once again be illumined as a means of access into the mystery of the God who revealed himself in time and space.

---

[31] I am borrowing from Walter Kasper's definition of revelation in *The God of Jesus Christ*, 68, quoted in Martin, 'Literary Theory', 577. In traditional Catholic terminology, faith has two nuances: *fides quae* (the doctrine or content of what is believed) and *fides qua* (the divine light which illuminates one's view of all reality).

[32] Farkasfalvy, '"Post-Critical" Method', 303.

Bibliography

Aquinas, T., *Summa Theologiae*, II (trans. Fathers of the English Dominican Province; New York: Benziger, 1947)

Berger, P., *A Rumor of Angels: Modern Society and the Rediscovery of the Supernatural* (Garden City, NY: Doubleday, 1969)

Bouyer, L., 'Où en est le mouvement biblique?', *BVC* 13 (1956), 7–21

Brown, R., 'The Contribution of Historical Biblical Criticism to Ecumenical Church Discussion', in *Biblical Interpretation in Crisis: The Ratzinger Conference on the Bible and the Church* (ed. R.J. Neuhaus; Grand Rapids: Eerdmans, 1989), 24–49

Catechism of the Catholic Church (Vatican City: Libreria Editrice Vaticana, 2nd edn, 1997)

Chrysostom, J., *Homilies on the Gospel of John* (*NPNF*[1] 14; Peabody, MA: Hendrickson, 1995)

Comstock, G., 'Truth or Meaning: Ricœur versus Frei on Biblical Narrative', *JR* 66 (1986), 109–25

de Lubac, H., *Catholicism: Christ and the Common Destiny of Man* (trans. L. Sheppard and E. Englund; San Francisco: Ignatius, 1988)

The Documents of Vatican II (ed. W.M. Abbott and J. Gallagher; Piscataway, NJ: New Century Publishers, 1966)

Donfried, K.P., 'Alien Hermeneutics and the Misappropriation of Scripture', in *Reclaiming the Bible for the Church* (ed. C.E. Braaten and R.W. Jenson; Grand Rapids: Eerdmans, 1995), 19–45

Farkasfalvy, D., 'In Search of a "Post-Critical" Method of Biblical Interpretation', *Comm* 13 (1986), 288–307

Fitzmyer, J., 'Historical Criticism: Its Role in Biblical Interpretation and Church Life', *TS* 50 (1989), 249–52

Harrisville, R.A., 'A Critique of Current Biblical Criticism', *WW* 15.2 (1995), 206–13

Hays, R.B., 'The Corrected Jesus', *First Things* 43 (1994), 43–48

Johnson, L.T., 'The Crisis in Biblical Scholarship', *Commonweal* 120.21 (1993), 18–21

Kasper, W., *The God of Jesus Christ* (New York: Crossroad, 1984)

Lacroix, J., *Histoire et mystère* (Tournai: Casterman, 1962)

Levenson, J.D., 'The Bible: Unexamined Commitments of Criticism', *First Things* 30 (1993), 24–33

Martin, F., 'Literary Theory, Philosophy of History and Exegesis', *Thomist* 52 (1988), 575–604

——, 'St. Matthew's Spiritual Understanding of the Healing of the Centurion's Boy', *Comm* 25 (1998), 160–77

Origen, *In evangelium secundum Matthaeum* (ed. J.P. Migne; Patrologia Graeca 17; Paris, 1857)

Plantinga, A., *Warranted Christian Belief* (New York: OUP, 2000)

Pontifical Biblical Commission, *The Interpretation of the Bible in the Church* (Boston: St Paul, 1993)

Prior, J.G., *The Historical-Critical Method in Catholic Exegesis* (Tesi Gregoriana, Teologia 50; Rome: Editrice Pontificia Università Gregoriana, 1999)

Provan, I.W., 'Ideologies, Literary and Critical: Reflections on Recent Writing on the History of Israel', *JBL* 114.4 (1995), 585–606

Ratzinger, J., 'Biblical Interpretation in Crisis: On the Question of the Foundations and Approaches of Exegesis Today', in *Biblical Interpretation in Crisis: The Ratzinger Conference on the Bible and the Church* (ed. R.J. Neuhaus; Grand Rapids: Eerdmans, 1989), 1–23

Ricœur, P., *Time and Narrative* (trans. K. McLaughlin and D. Pellauer, vols. 1–2; K. Blamey and D. Pellauer, vol. 3; Chicago: University of Chicago Press, 1984–88)

Sternberg, M., *The Poetics of Biblical Narrative: Ideological Literature and the Drama of Reading* (Bloomington: Indiana University Press, 1985)

Thiselton, A., ' "Behind" and "In Front Of " the Text: Language, Reference and Indeterminacy', in *After Pentecost: Language and Biblical Interpretation* (ed. C. Bartholomew, C. Greene and K. Möller; Carlisle: Paternoster; Grand Rapids: Zondervan, 2001), 97–120

Vanhoozer, K., 'From Speech Acts to Scripture Acts: The Covenant of Discourse and the Discourse of Covenant', in *After Pentecost: Language and Biblical Interpretation* (ed. C. Bartholomew, C. Greene and K. Möller; Carlisle: Paternoster; Grand Rapids: Zondervan, 2001), 1–49

——, *Biblical Narrative in the Philosophy of Paul Ricœur: A Study in Hermeneutics and Theology* (Cambridge: CUP, 1990)

Waldstein, M., 'The Foundations of Bultmann's Work', *Comm* 2 (1987), 115–45

Wolters, A., 'Confessional Criticism and the Night Visions of Zechariah', in *Renewing Biblical Interpretation* (ed. C. Bartholomew, C. Greene and K. Möller; Carlisle: Paternoster; Grand Rapids: Zondervan, 2000), 90–117

10

The Place of History in Catholic Exegesis

An Examination of the Pontifical Biblical Commission's The Interpretation of the Bible in the Church

Peter S. Williamson

Introduction

The relationship between history and biblical interpretation may be of interest to the academy, but it is of vital importance for the life of the Christian people. It is the church of Jesus Christ, after all, who receives Scripture as the word of God by which she lives (Mt. 4:4) and as a norm by which 'all the preaching of the Church must be nourished and ruled'.[1] Since the Renaissance, and especially since the Enlightenment, historical questions have dogged exegesis. It is not only, or even primarily, the academic community that must confront the questions that critical history poses to biblical faith, but the Christian churches themselves. Although various churches will answer the questions differently, the general issues they face are similar, and the progress made by one church can benefit the rest. It is with this hope that I offer the recent orientations toward history and exegesis of the church to which I belong, the Catholic Church, for the consideration of other Christians and of other Christian churches.

In this chapter I will examine the approach of the Pontifical Biblical Commission's *The Interpretation of the Bible in the Church* to the relation of exegesis and history, explain how it views the historical–critical method and offer a critical evaluation.[2] Before doing so, I will introduce the Pontifical

---

[1] Second Vatican Council, *Dogmatic Constitution on Divine Revelation* (*Dei Verbum*), §21.

[2] This paper contains material presented in greater depth in chs. 3 and 15 of my *Catholic Principles*. I want to express my gratitude to the Pontifical Biblical Institute for permission to include this material here.

Biblical Commission (PBC) and its document and explain what the PBC means when it speaks of 'exegesis'.

The Pontifical Biblical Commission and their document

According to its charter, the PBC is a consultative body of 'scholars in the biblical sciences from various schools and nations who excel in their learning, their prudence and their Catholic attitude regarding the Magisterium of the Church'.[3] Catholics use the term 'magisterium' to refer to the teaching authority of the Pope and bishops. The role of the PBC is to study various scriptural topics for the benefit of the Pope and the Congregation of the Doctrine of the Faith, the Catholic Church's administrative arm for overseeing doctrinal matters. One Catholic exegete has described the PBC as 'the [Catholic] Church's official "think tank" for matters dealing with the Bible'.[4]

In 1989, the PBC began a study of contemporary exegesis that was completed in 1993 with the publication of a one hundred-page document, *The Interpretation of the Bible in the Church (IBC)*.[5] According to the *IBC*, the purpose of this study was 'to attend to the criticism and complaints' that had been raised about the historical-critical method, 'to assess the possibilities opened up by the new methods and approaches' which have arisen in the last thirty or forty years, and 'to try to determine more precisely the direction which best corresponds to the mission of exegesis in the Catholic Church' (Intro. B.a).[6]

---

[3] The quotation is from the papal decree that reestablished the PBC in 1971: Pope Paul VI, Motu proprio, *Sedula cura*, available in Filippi and Lora, *Enchiridion Biblicum* (from here onwards *EB*), §727. Its members are appointed for renewable five-year terms by the Pope on the nomination of the Cardinal Prefect of the Congregation for the Doctrine of the Faith – presently Joseph Ratzinger – after he has consulted the bishops' conferences of the entire Catholic Church for recommendations. Originally (in 1902) the PBC was established by Pope Leo XIII as a Congregation of Cardinals with magisterial authority regarding biblical matters; Paul VI made its role consultative and its membership exegetes rather than cardinals.

[4] See Collins, 'Hearing,', 8.

[5] The *IBC* may be found in several print editions including Origins 23.29 (1994) and is easily available on the Internet. The *IBC*, along with most of the other Catholic Church documents on Scripture cited in this chapter, is now available in Béchard, *Scripture Documents*.

[6] Citations in parentheses, e.g. '(I.A.1.c)' refer to sections and paragraphs in the *IBC*. The sections are numbered in accord with the divisions in the document, and paragraphs within a section are enumerated by lower case letters. 'Intro.' refers to the document's introduction and 'Address' refers to the address given by Pope John Paul II on 23 April 1993 when he formally received the *IBC* from the PBC, which is published with the document.

Criticisms of the historical-critical method had arisen from a variety of quarters for a variety of reasons: some found the method lacking in its relation to Christian faith, leading people to reject essential beliefs such as the virginal conception, the miracles and the resurrection of Jesus; others complained the method was sterile for Christian life. Leading theologians and exegetes were among the critics, including Cardinal Ratzinger, who, in 1988, had criticized supposed common presuppositions of historical-critical exegesis in a highly publicized address in New York.[7] The PBC felt the need to address a situation in which some Catholics were rejecting the historical-critical method altogether and replacing it with subjective 'spiritual' readings, while other scholars chose synchronic methods or sought to interpret texts from within contemporary philosophical, psychological, sociological or political perspectives.

The PBC's document consists of four chapters. The first describes and evaluates contemporary methods and approaches[8] for interpreting Scripture. The second discusses developments in philosophical hermeneutics and what is meant by the literal, spiritual and 'fuller' senses of Scripture. The third chapter describes the characteristics of Catholic interpretation, the role of the exegete and the relation of exegesis to theology. The final chapter discusses actualization, inculturation and the use of the Bible in the life of the church.

When the document was completed, Pope John Paul II, who had followed the development of the document closely, took the unusual step of officially receiving it and delivering an address[9] at a special audience attended by the cardinals resident in Rome, the Diplomatic Corps accredited to the Holy See, the PBC and the professors of the Pontifical Biblical Institute. Although *The Interpretation of the Bible in the Church* is not the last word, and is not, technically speaking, a document of the Catholic Church's magisterium, it does represent better than any other document the current official position of the Catholic Church regarding exegesis and the interpretation of sacred Scripture.[10]

---

[7] See Ratzinger, *Schriftauslegung*; Neuhaus, *Biblical Interpretation*.

[8] In a footnote at the end of the *IBC*'s introduction, the PBC explains its distinction between 'method' and 'approach': 'By an exegetical "method" we understand a group of scientific procedures employed in order to explain texts. We speak of an "approach" when it is a question of an enquiry proceeding from a particular point of view.'

[9] The audience and address commemorated the centenary of the encyclical of Leo XIII, *Providentissimus Deus* (1893), and the fiftieth anniversary of the encyclical of Pius XII, *Divino afflante Spiritu* (1943), both of which addressed the role of historical criticism in the interpretation of Scripture.

[10] In his preface, Cardinal Ratzinger makes clear that the PBC 'is not an organ of the teaching office' and that the 'struggle over [the] scope and over [the] proper configuration [of the historical-critical method] is by no means finished as yet' (Preface, c, a). However, in an interview, he offered this evaluation: 'The Holy Father was in agreement about the importance of the subject [i.e., contemporary exegetical methods]

The Pontifical Biblical Commission's definition of 'exegesis'

Before examining what the PBC says about history, it is important to realize that the PBC's focus – as the title of its document suggests – is the interpretation of the Bible *in the church*. This is a more specific topic than the relationship of history to biblical studies or the role of history in exegesis as it is commonly practiced in the academy. When the *IBC* refers to *exegesis*, it refers to it as a '*theological discipline*' (Conclusion e, emphasis original), a study of the meaning of Scripture that is grounded in Christian faith. 'What characterizes Catholic exegesis is that it deliberately places itself within the living tradition of the Church, whose first concern is fidelity to the revelation attested by the Bible' (III.b).[11] The PBC insists on this presupposition of faith not merely because the *IBC* is an intra-Church document, but rather on the grounds of philosophical hermeneutics' recognition of the inevitability of 'pre-understanding' of one type or another (III.b.) and the importance of a fundamental affinity between the interpreter and his object (II.A.2.c). A 'pre-understanding' of faith, shared with those who wrote, collected and handed on the biblical writings, permits Catholic exegesis to stand 'in continuity with a dynamic pattern of interpretation that is found within the Bible itself and continues in the life of the Church' (III.b). Christian faith is an apt presupposition for the interpretation of the Christian Scriptures.

The unique character of inspired Scripture supplies even stronger reasons for a hermeneutic of faith than those offered by philosophical hermeneutics. The *IBC* affirms,

> Biblical hermeneutics ... constitutes ... a unique instance of general hermeneutics.... Reason alone cannot fully comprehend the account of these events given in the Bible. Particular presuppositions, such as the faith lived in ecclesial community and the light of the Spirit, control its interpretation. As the reader matures in the life of the

---

which needed a clear word to update the magisterial teaching. But all in all, it turned out that the voice of the experts – the theologians – confirmed by the Pope, was better suited to meet the current challenges and new questions. I believe this to be a very interesting model. Theologians [referring to the exegetes who comprise the PBC] speak in all their responsibility as believers and pastors of the church, composing a scientific and pastoral work. *Then the Holy Father with a carefully prepared address confirms the essential points, thus assuming the essence of this text (as opposed to its details) into magisterial teaching* [emphasis mine]' (Ratzinger, 'Modernità', 67–68, my translation).

[11] Although it is a common practice to use the term 'exegesis' to refer exclusively to historical and literary analysis of a text, and other terms – such as 'interpretation', 'theology', 'biblical theology' or 'theological exegesis' – for the study of a text's theological sense, the *IBC* never separates the explanation of a text's meaning from the presupposition of Christian faith that underlies it.

Spirit, so there grows also his or her capacity to understand the realities of which the Bible speaks. (II.A.2.f)

Furthermore, interpretation of the Bible *in the Church* has a particular end in view – an end that corresponds fully to the character of the Bible and the writings that comprise it. The primary aim of Catholic exegesis is to explain the religious message of the Bible – that is, its meaning as a word which God continues to address to the church and to the world (IV.a):

> In their work of interpretation, Catholic exegetes must never forget that what they are interpreting is the Word of God. Their common task is not finished when they have simply determined sources, defined forms or explained literary procedures. They arrive at the true goal of their work only when they have explained the meaning of the biblical text as God's word for today. (III.C.1.b–c)

There is a pastoral orientation to Catholic exegesis, which functions simultaneously as an ecclesial service and a scholarly enterprise (III.C.a). Its ultimate purpose is to nourish and build up the body of Christ with the word of God.[12]

Catholic Exegesis and History

The *IBC* rates history as extremely important to Catholic exegesis for three reasons. First, Scripture bears witness to a historical reality. Second, historical study places biblical texts in context, shedding light on the meaning of the biblical authors. Finally, contemporary interpretation of biblical texts must respect their historical meaning (the meanings expressed by the inspired human authors). At the same time, the *IBC* rejects several approaches to the relation of history to exegesis that it considers inadequate.

Historical reality

Although the Bible is not a history book in the modern sense, and although it includes literary genres that are poetic, symbolic and imaginative, Scripture bears witness to a historical reality. Christianity, as a historical religion, speaks of a God who has revealed himself in the course of human events. In this it resembles Judaism and Islam and differs from Buddhism and Hinduism. Christian faith, and therefore Catholic exegesis, recognizes the Bible as not just a philosophy, not just a myth, and not just a moral lesson, although all of these elements may be found in the Bible. Rather, Scripture recounts real events

---

[12] See, e.g., *IBC* Intro B.b, Conclusion e and Address 10.

beginning in the history of Israel and reaching their climax in the life, death and resurrection of Jesus Christ that have implications for human existence in the present.[13] Explaining the reason for the use of the historical-critical method, the PBC says: 'The Bible ... does not present itself as a direct revelation of timeless truths but as the written testimony to a series of interventions in which God reveals himself in human history' (Conclusion c).

This does not mean that the Bible is a history book, much less that every statement in the Bible written in the past tense is historical, as some fundamentalists may assume (I.F.e). Catholic exegesis is fully aware of the presence of non-historical genres and fictional stories in the Bible (II.B.1.b) and is also aware of the fact that ancient authors wrote history differently than modern historians do, often for the purpose of conveying moral or religious lessons and without the same concern for exactitude.[14] For this reason the preoccupation of some authors with the accuracy of historical details misses the point. Nevertheless, for Catholic interpretation, 'ostensive reference' (i.e., the relation between the narrated events and extra-textual reality) is important because human history is the stage on which the drama of salvation unfolds.[15] This perspective contrasts with that of some contemporary approaches that concern themselves exclusively with literary or theological meaning, with a seeming indifference to the historical reality to which the text refers.

---

[13] Martin points out that 'in Christian antiquity, the events of the life of Christ were considered as the primary locus of revelation without much consideration being given to the verbal process by which those events reached the audience.... We may also see this in the list of events found in the creeds, both in the NT (e.g., 1 Cor. 15:3–5) and in later texts' ('Theory,' 601–602).

[14] Montague says it well: 'Unlike modern scientific research into history, the purpose of studying history, even secular history, was not the determination of facts in their particularity, not even the interrelation of events. History was studied for the lessons it contained. If this was true of the study of secular history, it was all the more true of biblical history. The events of history were more for *formation* than for information. For this reason there was little interest in verifying historical details ... [emphasis original]' (*Understanding*, 53).

[15] According to the *IBC*, even the spiritual sense of Scripture has a realistic historical basis. 'The spiritual sense results from setting the text in relation to *real facts* which are not foreign to it: the paschal event, in all its inexhaustible richness ...[emphasis mine]' (II.B.2.f). Jesus' resurrection 'has established a radically new *historical* context, which sheds fresh light upon the ancient texts and causes them to undergo a change in meaning [emphasis mine]' (II.B.2.a). Nevertheless, christological interpretation of the Old Testament is not granted the right 'to empty out of the Old Testament its own proper meaning' lest it 'deprive the New of its roots in history' (I.C.1.i).

Historical context

The second reason for Catholic interpretation's concern for history is that historical study enables the interpreter to understand the text according to the culture and literary conventions of the period (II.B.1.b) and to understand the social conditions, the institutions and the cultural and religious practices to which the biblical authors refer. Historical study places biblical texts in their historical contexts, helping to clarify the meaning of the biblical authors' message for their original readers and for us. In Pope Pius XII's 1943 encyclical *Divino afflante Spiritu* (*DAS*), often regarded as the 'Magna Carta' of modern Catholic biblical scholarship, Pius devoted several paragraphs to the importance of historical study.[16] He acknowledged the availability of new information that was not available to commentators of past ages that can enhance interpretation. According to Pius XII, 'rules of grammar and philology alone' are insufficient to understand the biblical authors' meaning. Rather,

> the interpreter must, as it were, go back wholly in spirit to those remote centuries of the East and with the aid of history, archaeology, ethnology, and other sciences, accurately determine what modes of writing ... the authors of that ancient period would be likely to use, and in fact did use. (*DAS* §35)

The Second Vatican Council's Constitution on Divine Revelation, *Dei Verbum* (*DV*), also stressed that an understanding of history is vital to understanding Scripture:

> For the correct understanding of what the sacred author wanted to assert, due attention must be paid to the customary and characteristic styles of perceiving, speaking, and narrating which prevailed at the time of the sacred writer, and to the customs men normally followed at that period in their everyday dealings with one another. (*DV* 12)

For its part, the *IBC* specifically underscores the importance of understanding the Jewish background to the New Testament[17] and the relation between the New Testament texts and the communities that gave rise to them.[18]

---

[16] *DAS* §31–42, *EB* §555–561.

[17] The *IBC* specifically recommends the study of Jewish traditions of interpretation in order to shed light on the intertestamental period and first-century Judaism (I.C.2.c) and the study of ancient methods of exegesis to understand how biblical authors themselves interpreted prior biblical texts (III.A.2.f).

[18] 'The task incumbent upon the exegete, to gain a better understanding of the early Church's witness to faith, cannot be achieved in a fully rigorous way without the scientific research which studies the strict relationship that exists between the texts of the New Testament and life as actually lived by the early Church' (I.D.1.e).

Consistent meaning

The third reason why Catholic exegesis is concerned with history is its conviction that God inspired the words of the human authors and editors of the Bible, and that valid interpretation must respect the authors' historical communication. The PBC's definition of the literal sense expresses this link between the human language and the divine meaning: 'The literal sense of Scripture is that which has been expressed directly by the inspired human authors. Since it is the fruit of inspiration, this sense is also intended by God, as principal author' (II.B.1.c).[19] It follows that later interpretation must be consistent with what the inspired authors wrote:

> *One must reject as unauthentic every interpretation alien to the meaning expressed by the human authors in their written text.* To admit the possibility of such alien meanings would be equivalent to cutting off the biblical message from its root, which is the Word of God in its historical communication; it would also mean opening the door to interpretations of a wildly subjective nature. (II.B.1.g, emphasis mine)

Catholic exegesis' insistence on interpretation being consistent with the meaning expressed by the biblical authors is due, at least in part, to Christianity's fundamental value of faithfulness to the original message (see *DV* 8, 10).[20] Paul exhorts the Thessalonians to hold fast to the traditions they have received (2 Thes. 2:15) and warns the Galatians not to yield to another gospel even if he himself or an angel from heaven should proclaim it (Gal. 1:8). Likewise, Jude 3 exhorts readers to contend 'for the faith that was *once for all* entrusted to the saints', and the letters to Timothy urge him to guard what has been entrusted to him (1 Tim. 6:20; 2 Tim. 1:14).

However, the *IBC* qualifies its emphasis on consistency of meaning through time to make clear that a text's meaning is not imprisoned in a single historical context:

> One should be especially attentive to the *dynamic aspect* of many texts. The meaning of the royal psalms, for example, should not be limited strictly to the historical

---

[19] See Williamson, *Catholic Principles*, 165–67, for the *IBC*'s approach to the relation of the author's intention and the literal sense.

[20] Fitzmyer defends critical interpretation on this basis: 'What ultimately lies behind the critical approach to the study of the Bible in the Church is the conviction that God's revelation in Christ took place in the past, and the ancient record of that self-manifestation of God in him is disclosed to the Church above all in the Bible, in the Word of God couched in ancient human wording. ... Thus historical criticism assists the Church in its ongoing life by helping it to uncover the essence of the revelation once given to it – the meaning of the Word of God in ancient human words' (Fitzmyer, 'Historical Criticism', 257–58).

circumstances of their production. In speaking of the king, the psalmist evokes at one and the same time both the institution as it actually was and an idealized vision of kingship as God intended it to be; in this way the text carries the reader beyond the institution of kingship in its actual historical manifestation. (II.B.1.e, emphasis original)

There are reasons ... for not taking 'alien' in so strict a sense as to exclude all possibility of higher fulfillment. (II.B.2.a)

Besides the 'dynamic aspect' inscribed in many texts, the PBC cites the insight of Paul Ricœur and others that when a text is read in new circumstances which illuminate it in various ways, they add new meanings to the original sense. This is doubly true of the Scriptures, because they are the word of God and because they were preserved by a believing community convinced 'that they would continue to be bearers of light and life for generations of believers to come. The literal sense is, from the start, open to further developments, which are produced through the "re-reading" ("*relectures*") of texts in new contexts' (II.B.1.f). It is these factors that make room for the christological or spiritual sense of the Old Testament in light of the radically new historical context brought about by the death and resurrection of Jesus.[21]

Problematic tendencies of historical criticism

Despite its commitment to history, there are three tendencies of historical criticism that Catholic exegesis seeks to avoid: historicism, historical positivism and the reduction of exegesis to a historical enterprise.

The view that the meaning of a biblical text is precisely what it meant in its original setting and nothing more typifies historicism. Examples might include interpreting the story of Cain and Abel primarily as the memory of an ancient conflict between shepherds and farmers or viewing the Epistle to the Galatians primarily as a monument to conflict regarding the circumcision of Gentiles in the early church. The PBC rejects the 'historicizing tendency' of 'the older historical-critical exegesis' (I.A.4.f). In another place the PBC

---

[21] The PBC's definition of the spiritual sense, 'the meaning expressed by the biblical texts when read under the influence of the Holy Spirit in the context of the Paschal Mystery' (II.B.2.b), focuses on the new aspects of meaning present in OT texts when they are recontextualized by Jesus' death and resurrection. This definition looks at the spiritual sense primarily 'from below', validating the spiritual sense's relationship to the literal sense in the light of philosophical hermeneutics. It does not explicitly attempt to plumb the intention of the divine Author in the earlier texts or the ontological relation between OT and NT realities, as do some traditional approaches to the spiritual sense. For more on the spiritual sense in the *IBC*, see Williamson, *Catholic Principles*, 189–203, 211–12.

contrasts its christological interpretation of Nathan's prophecy to David (about God establishing his throne 'forever', 2 Sam. 7:12–13) to the views of 'exegetes who have a narrow "historicist" idea about the literal sense' (II.B.2.a). In a word, historicism is belief in the adequacy of historical explanation for interpreting Scripture.[22]

Catholic interpretation likewise rejects 'historical positivism'. In its classic form, historical positivism 'aims to produce [and thinks it can produce] an accurate and complete picture of the past on the basis of "historically pure" sources',[23] discounting or reinterpreting sources 'biased' by faith. The nineteenth-century attempts at reconstructing the life of Jesus (and some of the late twentieth-century attempts) adopted this attitude.[24] This is a subject the PBC treated in a previous document, *Scripture and Christology* (§1.1.3.2–3).[25] Briefly summarized, the PBC said that the objectivity of the historical method is not the same as that of the natural sciences since it concerns itself with human experience, which cannot be verified by experimentation that produces repeatable results. Experience, *qua* experience, can only be understood 'from within'. The historian investigating human experience is confronted not only with the subjectivity of the authors of the sources under consideration, but also with the researcher's own subjectivity as he or she inquires into the 'truth' of history and brings his or her own questions and interests. The historical study of Jesus is an obvious example: it is never neutral, because Jesus' life and message require a decision on the part of anyone who studies them. In their present document the PBC states, 'Contemporary hermeneutics is a healthy reaction to historical positivism and to the temptation to apply to the study of the Bible the purely objective criteria used in the natural sciences' (II.A.2.c). Historical positivism fails to see that history, exegesis and the biblical texts themselves are all works of interpretation, and that historical facts untainted by interpretation do not exist. Philosophical hermeneutics corrects this misperception.

---

[22] Ricœur defines historicism as 'the epistemological presupposition that the content of literary works and in general of cultural documents receives its intelligibility from its connection to the social conditions of the community that produced it or to which it was destined' (*Interpretation Theory*, 89–90). Mandelbaum defines historicism as 'the belief that an adequate understanding of the nature of anything and an adequate assessment of its value are to be gained by considering it in terms of the place it occupied and the role it played within a process of development' (from 'Historicism', in *Dictionary of Philosophy*, IV [1967], as quoted in Morgan, 'Historicism', 291).

[23] Latourelle, 'Positivism', 785. See Bartholomew, *Reading Ecclesiastes*, for a discussion of positivism in philosophy and literature (108–10).

[24] See Green, 'Quest', 550–53; Schneiders, *Revelatory Text*, xxiii.

[25] Fitzmyer, *Scripture and Christology*, 6–7.

Despite its concern for history, exegesis itself is not a historical discipline whose task is to give an account of the past. Rather, the task of exegesis is to explain the meaning of the text. In carrying out its work, Catholic exegesis *makes use of* history and historical methods to shed light on the biblical text. This is important to affirm, because many biblical scholars understand their primary role differently – for example, as studying the history of Israel or the early church using biblical texts as sources, or as ascertaining the historicity of events narrated in the Bible, or as explaining the text's redactional history.[26] While these historical efforts make a valuable contribution to exegesis, they are not its fundamental task, nor does historical information drawn from biblical texts constitute biblical meaning. This is not to deny the value of specialized studies that are strictly historical; historical research fulfills an indispensable role in exegesis – but as a means rather than an end.

Historical literalism and non-historical approaches

In its approach to history, the *IBC* also seeks to steer clear of two errors some-times found in theological and literary approaches to Scripture – the Scylla of historical literalism and the Charybdis of ahistorical approaches. On the one hand, it rejects fundamentalist interpretation. According to the PBC, funda-mentalism errs by employing a

> naively literalist interpretation, one, that is to say, which excludes every effort at under-standing the Bible that takes account of its historical origins and development ... (I.F.a). It fails to recognize that the Word of God has been formulated in language and expression conditioned by various periods ... (I.F.d). Fundamentalism also places undue stress upon the inerrancy of certain details in the biblical texts, especially in what concerns historical events or supposedly scientific truth. It often historicizes material which from the start never claimed to be historical. It considers historical everything that is reported or recounted with verbs in the past tense ... (I.F.e).[27]

---

[26] Fusco discusses the uses of history in biblical study in 'Un secolo', 83.

[27] The PBC makes a number of critical generalizations about fundamentalist interpre-tation. This pleased some reviewers (Bergant, 'Fundamentalism'; Collins, 'Hearing'; Larraín, 'El valor hermenéutico'), but seemed excessive to others (Ayres and Fowl, '(Mis)Reading', 517; Marshall, 'Review: "Interpretation"'; and esp. Shea, 'Catholic Reaction'). It is indicative of the lack of dialogue between Catholicism and Fundamentalism that no fundamentalist review of the *IBC* has appeared. It may be questioned whether there are many fundamentalists who would identify with the approach to Scripture attributed to them by this document. But even if the *IBC* does not accurately describe the beliefs of many fundamentalists, it does define tendencies and a point of view from which Catholic interpretation may legitimately distinguish itself.

Fundamentalism and Catholic interpretation agree that Scripture bears witness to a historical reality. But Catholic interpretation takes a more nuanced approach to history, distinguishes among literary forms, allows greater scope for historical knowledge to enlighten interpretation, acknowledges historical conditioning in the biblical word and is not preoccupied with the accuracy of narrative details. This summary, of course, paints a picture with broad strokes.[28]

The other extreme, however, is to stand apart from history as do some literary and theological approaches which ignore or deny the reference of biblical texts to historical reality. The PBC addresses this tendency in its evaluation of semiotics:

> Semiotics can be usefully employed … only in so far as the method is separated from certain assumptions developed in structuralist philosophy, namely the refusal to accept individual personal identity within the text and extra-textual reference beyond it. The Bible is a Word that bears upon reality, a Word which God has spoken in a historical context and which God addresses to us today through the mediation of human authors. The semiotic approach must be open to history: first of all to the history of those who play a part in the texts; then to that of the authors and readers. (I.B.3.l)

Similarly, Bultmann's demythologizing interpretation is rejected because it empties the Bible 'of its objective reality' and tends to reduce it 'to an anthropological message only' (II.A.2.d). Bultmann was content to embrace and proclaim a Christ of faith detached from the Jesus of history.

Faith and history

If Catholic interpretation must distinguish itself from both fundamentalist literalism as well as from an indifference to history on the part of some literary or theological approaches, it must also distinguish itself from a third error. Given Catholic exegesis' respect for historical research, there exists a danger of reducing 'history' – in the sense of what is credited to have really taken place in

---

[28] While the PBC does well to distinguish Catholic interpretation from the two extremes regarding historical reference, there remains a need for greater clarity. On what basis does one determine which narrative 'details' are unimportant and which are essential to the biblical message? Does the essential historicity of the exodus matter? A similar tension exists in *Dei Verbum* 19 (following the 1964 PBC Instruction, *Sancta Mater Ecclesia*), which simultaneously affirms the historicity of the four Gospels, saying that they 'faithfully hand on what Jesus … really did and taught for [our] eternal salvation', yet acknowledges the lack of historical exactitude by describing the retrospective, selective, kerygmatic, pastoral and synthetic manner in which the truth has been recorded for us.

the past – to what modern historiography can demonstrate, and to substitute historical reconstructions (whether of the life of Jesus or of the gospel message) for the depiction of these realities which the biblical texts themselves propose. This, in fact, is what some of the recent studies of the historical Jesus urge their readers to do. For example, B.L. Mack presents Jesus as a Cynic philosopher,[29] and M. Borg maintains that eschatology was not an important part of his message.[30] Rather than enrich the understanding of Jesus communicated by the Gospels through additional historical insight, these approaches claim to offer more historically reliable depictions of Jesus and his message on the basis of critical methods and evidence from the apocryphal gospels.

In addition to problems in the historical methodology employed to produce these alternative depictions of Jesus (apparent in the diversity of results obtained from applying the same scientific methods to the same data),[31] Catholic interpretation has its own methodological basis for rejecting such proposals – a basis which is, in fact, an important theological principle. While Christian faith is open to considering and learning from new historical data, faith is governed by the presentation of Jesus and his message expressed in the canonical texts. Catholic exegesis grounds its knowledge of God's action in human history in Jesus Christ on the testimony of Scripture and tradition, which it has accepted, rather than on historical research. This is because, in the last analysis, Christian exegesis is a theological rather than a historical discipline, whose ultimate foundation is revelation and faith rather than historical research.

Does this mean that historical research is unimportant for Catholic exegesis' understanding of the life of Jesus or of history? By no means. Historical research can purify the church's understanding of what the revealed content of Scripture really is. Just as the growth of scientific understanding about the cosmos led to the clear realization that Scripture does not claim to give a scientific account of the solar system, historical research has also shown that traditional understandings of Scripture's relation to history were mistaken in a variety of ways. Many biblical books are the fruit of a long editorial process, rather than the work of the famous individuals in Israel's history whose names they bear, as was commonly assumed. In general, the authorship of biblical books is far from certain. Historically sensitive research has discovered minor contradictions and factual errors. Historical study makes clear that, although the Bible contains extraordinarily valuable historical information, it is not to be taken as a divinely inspired and inerrant history text. According to the *IBC*, the historical research of exegetes provides a perspective

---

[29] See Mack, *Myth*.

[30] See Borg, 'Non-Eschatological Jesus'.

[31] See Evans, 'Third Quest', 540–42; Schneiders, *Revelatory Text*, xxiv, citing Powell, *Introduction*, 13–14.

which systematic theologians should take into account as they seek to explain more clearly the theology of scriptural inspiration. ... Exegesis creates, in particular, a more lively and precise awareness of the historical character of biblical inspiration. It shows that the process of inspiration is historical, not only because it took place over the course of the history of Israel and of the early Church, but also because it came about through the agency of human beings. (III.D.1.b)

Like faith and reason, the testimony of Scripture and historical research are complementary sources of truth. Each has information the other lacks. From time to time, tensions may arise when scientific history appears to contradict the testimony of Scripture regarding its essential message. But Christian faith, holding to the unity of truth, expects to resolve such apparent contradictions eventually, either by a deeper understanding of the biblical witness or by a more exact historical judgement.

The Pontifical Biblical Commission and the Historical-Critical Method

A strong endorsement

Although it acknowledges the criticisms that had been brought to bear on historical-critical exegesis both by scholars and by lay readers of the Bible (Intro. A.d–f), the PBC wished to assert the importance of the historical-critical method. The very first sentence of the *IBC* after the introduction declares, 'The historical-critical method is *the* indispensable method for the scientific study of the meaning of ancient texts' (I.A.a, emphasis mine). The same paragraph concludes, '[Scripture's] proper understanding not only admits the use of this method but actually requires it'.

Some authors have questioned whether there is such a thing as a distinct historical-critical method, or whether it might not be more accurate to speak of a variety of critical procedures employed differently by various authors,[32] but the PBC does not nuance their identification of the method. Instead, the *IBC* simply identifies the historical-critical method with the set of historical and literary procedures that scholars use to study and to interpret ancient texts (Intro. d). The PBC characterizes the historical-critical method as a *diachronic* method, since it 'is particularly attentive to the historical development of texts or traditions across the passage of time' (Intro. d). It acknowledges that, more recently, the historical-critical method has found itself in competition with *synchronic* methods – which consider texts from the vantage point of 'language,

---

[32] See. e.g., Watson, 'Response', and Bartholomew, *Reading Ecclesiastes*, 66–67, 82–83.

composition, narrative structure and capacity for persuasion' (Intro. d) – and with approaches that view texts from contemporary philosophical, psycho-analytic, sociological or political perspectives.

When it comes time to describe the historical-critical method more specif-ically, the PBC begins historically, affirming that certain elements of the method 'were used in antiquity by Greek commentators of classical literature and ... by authors such as Origen, Jerome and Augustine' (I.A.1.a). The PBC identifies Renaissance humanists, early textual critics, Richard Simon and other early literary critics of the Pentateuch and the Gospels as contributors to the method, despite the inadequate attention some of them paid to the final form and message of the text. H. Gunkel, M. Dibelius, and R. Bultmann are viewed as making a positive contribution with their concern for the *Sitz im Leben* and literary forms of texts (even though problems in their exegesis – such as Bultmann's dependence on the existentialist philosophy of M. Heidegger – are acknowledged). The addition of *redaction criticism*, which examines the text in its final form for its theological *Tendenz*, permitting the exegete 'to gain a better grasp of the content of divine revelation' (I.A.2.d), is a necessary final step. The door is left open to further developments in the historical-critical method.

The PBC finishes its description of the historical-critical method with a summary of its procedures: 'at the present stage of its development' (I.A.3.a), the historical-critical method includes the following steps: textual criticism, linguistic and semantic analysis, literary criticism, genre criticism, tradition criticism and redaction criticism, which 'concludes with a study that is synchronic' (I.A.3.c).

According to the PBC,

> All this has made it possible to understand far more accurately the intention of the authors and editors of the Bible, as well as the message which they addressed to their first readers. The achievement of these results has lent the historical-critical method an importance of the highest order. (I.A.1.c)

This strong endorsement of the historical-critical method is one of the most obvious characteristics of the *IBC*, and most reviewers of the document have commented on it. Understood in the context of much recent criticism of the historical-critical method, the PBC's endorsement is correctly interpreted as a vigorous defense.[33] It is noteworthy that Pope John Paul II himself confirmed

---

[33] Vanhoye acknowledges that the document intends to defend the historical-critical method, but also, he adds, to defend the method against its own temptations – namely, historicism and getting lost 'in the sands of hypercritical analysis' (Vanhoye, 'L'interpretazione', 12–13, quoting Conclusion e; cf. Vanhoye, 'Catholicism', 38).

the value of the historical-critical method in his 'Address' officially receiving the *IBC*: 'The Church of Christ takes the realism of the incarnation seriously, and this is why she attaches great importance to the "historico-critical" study of the Bible' (Address 7).[34] Although previous magisterial documents had affirmed the value of critical procedures in the study of Scripture,[35] this is the first instance in which a Pope explicitly approved the historical-critical method by name.[36]

A 'properly-oriented' historical-critical method

At first sight it might appear that the PBC has given an unqualified endorsement to the historical-critical method as the means suited to ascertaining the literal sense of Scripture. Many reviewers, both sympathetic to and critical of the historical-critical method, interpreted the *IBC* this way. However, a more careful reading of the document reveals that the PBC criticizes and, in some important ways, redefines and 'redimensions' the historical-critical method it endorses. In a word, the PBC considered and accepted many of the criticisms that have been raised against the historical-critical method. The comments of two PBC members should be heard in support of this more nuanced interpretation of the document. Speaking of the *IBC*, Brendan Byrne states,

> The historical-critical method has indeed the leading place, but is placed in the context of all the other methods as just another method. This is one of the most significant features of the document: its relativization of the historical-critical method, while insisting upon its necessity and indeed according it a place of privilege.[37]

---

[34] The translator of the Pope's 'Address' uses the term 'historico-critical' while the translator of the *IBC* uses the expression 'historical-critical' to translate the identical French term, 'historico-critique'.

[35] In the same paragraph, Pope John Paul II goes on to cite Leo XIII's support of 'artis criticae disciplinam' and Pius XII's endorsement of textual criticism. For a brief summary of other precedents in official church documents see Fitzmyer, 'Historical Criticism', 255–57, or for a more detailed study, see Prior, *Historical Critical Method*, 89–159.

[36] The Pope offers some important qualifications, similar to those which the PBC itself proposes: 'Catholic exegesis does not have its own exclusive method of interpretation, but starting with the historico-critical basis *freed from its philosophical presuppositions or those contrary to the truth of our faith*, it makes the most of all the current methods …' (Address 13, emphasis mine). Also, 'Catholic exegesis *does not focus its attention on only the human aspects* of biblical Revelation, which is sometimes the mistake of the historico-critical method, or on only the divine aspects as fundamentalism would have it …' (Address 14, emphasis mine).

[37] Byrne, e-mail to Peter Williamson, 8 Dec. 1999.

Commission Secretary Vanhoye makes a similar comment: 'The document as a whole "redimensions" the position and function of the historical-critical method, affirming its value, but denying its sufficiency.'[38]

According to the PBC, not just any use of the historical-critical method will be fruitful for Catholic exegesis.[39] In various writings, PBC member Joseph Fitzmyer speaks of the need for a 'properly-oriented' use of the historical-critical method.[40] This study will adopt Fitzmyer's term, 'properly-oriented',

---

[38] Vanhoye, 'Catholicism', 38. Several reasons may explain why many readers failed to see the redimensioning aspect of the document's treatment of the historical-critical method. First, Chapter 1 of the *IBC*, which describes and evaluates the various methods and approaches, monopolized the attention of many readers on account of its novelty and length (39 per cent of the whole). It gave the impression that the document was mainly about methods, and that among these the historical-critical method had pride of place both by explicit entitlement and by the amount of text devoted to it (more than twice that given to any other method). Second, a consequent neglect of Ch. 3 on the characteristics of Catholic interpretation led some readers to overlook that all methods must make their contribution within the context of a Catholic hermeneutic. Third, the IBC *itself* sounds a note of ringing endorsement regarding the method, undoubtedly reflecting the polemical situation which preceded the document ('Too ringing!' said PBC member Byrne when commenting on the effects of the document [conversation with the author, 9 Aug. 1999]).

[39] Prior provides a useful summary of the *IBC*'s evaluation of the historical-critical method under three headings: Why is the historical-critical method necessary? Why is the historical-critical method limited? What are the ways in which the limitations of the method are rectified? (see *Historical Critical Method*, 248–62). According to Prior, the *IBC* recognizes the following limits in the historical-critical method (summarizing 253–59): 1) Its classical practice tended towards 'hyper-criticism', restricting attention to historical meaning and dismantling the text into sources while neglecting the final form. 2) Its usefulness depends on the presuppositions of the exegete. 3) It tends towards a narrow interpretation of the text, having difficulty recognizing plural meanings and lacking a methodological basis to move beyond the work or corpus of an author [to recognize canonical meaning?]. 4) It is not able to discover the spiritual sense of texts when that sense goes beyond the literal sense (e.g., in the OT). 5) It does not provide a methodology to determine the christological, canonical and ecclesial aspects of texts, which are basic to Catholic exegesis. 6) It provides no methodology for taking into account the interaction between reader and text that is necessary for understanding. 7) On account of its neutrality, the method is unable to recognize Scripture as the word of God. 8) It fails to consider the dynamic aspect of the text. 9) Its sociological studies lack sufficient data to provide a comprehensive picture of ancient society.

[40] Fitzmyer criticizes 'a kind of halfway use of the method' which has led to skepticism about it: 'Some of its practitioners think that their job is finished if they can sort out the sources of a certain text, tell you something about its prehistory, or about its

to refer to the distinctive approach to the historical-critical method endorsed by the PBC, without claiming to use the term in exactly the sense Fitzmyer intends it.

The PBC's 'properly-oriented' approach to the historical-critical method: 1) defines the object of historical-critical study in a particular manner; 2) excludes errors for which the method has been known; and 3) places the historical-critical method in a hermeneutical context. The following section will detail the PBC's qualifications of the historical-critical method that enable it to be 'properly-oriented' and indispensable for Catholic exegesis.

Defines the object of study in a particular manner

One of the characteristics of the PBC's approach to the historical-critical method that distinguishes it from the approach of many historical-critical scholars is the way the *IBC* defines biblical exegesis' object of study. This follows in part from the *IBC*'s understanding of the literal sense. Briefly stated, here are the elements that should command Catholic exegesis' attention:

(1) The text in its final stage, rather than its earlier editions, is the proper object of study, since it is the expression of the word of God (I.A.4.f). For this reason, a synchronic analysis of texts completes the historical-critical method and is an essential element of redaction criticism (I.A.4.f). Here the PBC parts ways with many scholars who would not agree that the final form deserves to be the privileged object of study, preferring the sources as they are able to reconstruct them – for example, the Yahwist, the prophet Jeremiah, or 'Q' – over the redactions which comprise the final form of the biblical writings. Likewise, not all practitioners of the historical-critical

---

synoptic relation ... or something about its form-critical character, without going the further step of accounting adequately for what the text means, what sort of theological or religious meaning is being conveyed or what sense the word of God has in that passage' (Fitzmyer and Stahel, 'Interview', 10). In *Scripture, the Soul*, 31, Fitzmyer says that it is 'faith presuppositions' which characterize a 'properly-oriented' use of the historical-critical method. In his commentary on the *IBC*, Fitzmyer states, 'Both faith and the guidance of the community by [the] Holy Spirit enrich the interpretation, and these are part of the presuppositions with which the historical-critical method becomes properly oriented' (Fitzmyer, *Biblical Commission's Document*, 69). In an article published just as the PBC was beginning its work, Fitzmyer writes, 'by reason of [faith presuppositions] it [the historical-critical method] becomes a *properly-oriented* method of interpretation, for none of the elements of the method is pursued in and for itself. They are used only to achieve the main goal of discerning what the biblical message was that the sacred writer sought to convey ...'('Historical Criticism', 255).

method concern themselves with a synchronic analysis of the final text, nor do they regard it as a defining characteristic of redaction criticism; instead, some redaction critics only take an interest in how the final redactor has modified his sources.

(2) The literal sense is the meaning that 'has been expressed directly by the inspired human authors' (II.B.1.c). This definition avoids explicit reference to the author's intention and confines itself to what is evidenced in the text. This contrasts with a common tendency among some historical-critical exegetes to explain a text's literal meaning as the author's intention, ascertained by a historical construction of circumstances or motives that lie behind the text. Thus, for example, for some interpreters the meaning of pentateuchal texts attributed to 'P' lies in the economic and political motives of a particular group.[41]

(3) The literal sense of some texts possesses a *dynamic aspect;* historical-critical exegesis should seek to determine the direction of thought expressed by the text, so as to recognize extensions of its meaning. The PBC acknowledges that this is not typical of historical-critical exegesis, which 'has too often tended to limit the meaning of texts by tying it too rigidly to precise historical circumstances' (II.B.1.e).

To summarize, a 'properly-oriented' historical-critical method seeks to explain the full content of what the human author has expressed in the final canonical text.

Excludes certain errors

The *IBC* introduces the historical-critical method by recounting its history before going on to describe it 'at the present stage of its development' (I.A.3.a). This enables the PBC to disassociate the use of the method it recommends from problematic tendencies attributed to earlier stages of the historical-critical method's development. In addition, the PBC criticizes some contemporary tendencies of the historical-critical method. By means of these criticisms, the *IBC* affirms that a sound use of the historical-critical method in Catholic exegesis will avoid the following errors:

(1) Dissecting and dismantling the text in order to identify sources while failing to pay sufficient attention to the final form of the text and its message (I.A.1.b). The *IBC* attributes this fault to source criticism that aims merely at establishing a chronology of biblical texts.

---

[41] For more on the shift in the PBC's definition of the literal sense away from narrowly-defined authorial intention, see my *Catholic Principles,* 165–67, 184–85.

(2) Combining the method with presuppositions hostile to or inadequate to Christian faith such as rationalism (IV.A.3.c), historical positivism (II.A.2.c), historicism (I.A.4.f), atheism (I.D.3.e) and materialism (I.E.1.l).

(3) Employing hermeneutical theories that are inadequate for interpreting Scripture by enclosing it within the constraints of a particular philosophy or by emptying it of its objective reality. The *IBC* cites the example of Bultmann's Heideggerian existentialist hermeneutic and his 'excessive demythologization' (II.A.2.d).

(4) Restricting the search for the meaning of a text to its historical circumstances and failing to attend to subsequent development of meaning (I.A.4.d; II.B.1.e; Conclusion d).

(5) Maintaining the view that a text can only have one single meaning (II.B.b–c; II.B.1.d).

(6) Paying excessive attention to the form of a text while paying too little attention to its content (I.A.4.e).

(7) Basing interpretation on hypothetical historical reconstructions of what the texts were allegedly designed to hide, rather than upon the content of the inspired text. This criticism is found in a discussion of feminist exegesis, but it applies to any historical-critical interpretations which employ a similar hermeneutic. According to the PBC, this form of argumentation is weak, since it is *ex silentio*. Also, 'this does not correspond at all to the work of exegesis properly so called. It entails rejecting the content of the inspired texts in preference for a hypothetical construction, quite different in nature' (I.E.2.l).[42]

Thus, according to the PBC, a 'properly-oriented' use of the historical-critical method avoids a number of errors that have at times characterized its use.

Places the historical-critical method in a hermeneutical context

Finally, in the *IBC* the PBC 'redimensions' the historical-critical method by placing it in the overall context of Catholic interpretation. Many of the criticisms that have been raised against the historical-critical method can be understood as criticisms of an allegedly neutral practice of the method (in reality, often influenced by hidden philosophical commitments), rather than of a method that consciously begins from a 'pre-understanding' of Christian faith. The PBC describes the presuppositions and the appropriate context for all the methods which Catholic exegesis employs in Chapter 3, 'Characteristics of

---

[42] Fitzmyer adds, 'it cannot be a substitute for the story told in the inspired text of the New Testament itself … [and therefore] can never be taken as a norm of Christian faith and praxis' (*Biblical Commission's Document*, 100–101).

Catholic Interpretation'. The following statement sums up this context and these presuppositions: 'What characterizes Catholic exegesis is that it deliberately places itself within the living tradition of the Church, whose first concern is fidelity to the revelation attested by the Bible' (III.b).

This fundamental hermeneutical choice shapes how the historical-critical method functions in Catholic exegesis in a number of important ways:

(1) A hermeneutic of faith recognizes that *God has spoken and is speaking* through the human language of Scripture. The historical-critical method can thus become 'an instrument for understanding the central object of all interpretation: the person of Jesus Christ and the saving events accomplished in human history' (II.A.d).[43]

(2) The interpretive context of 'the living tradition of the Church' provides the canon of Scripture and the basic doctrinal orientations of the church fathers. Tradition thus supplies Catholic historical-critical exegesis with its object of study and the faith affirmations that orient it.[44]

(3) The biblical tradition of interpretation demonstrates that biblical meaning develops over time as the Scriptures are actualized in new circumstances. The New Testament makes clear that the Old Testament takes on new meaning in the light of the paschal mystery of Christ. These precedents guide interpretation in the church and exclude an excessively narrow or historicist definition of biblical meaning.[45]

(4) The recognition that, in addition to the literal sense, Scripture bears canonical, christological and ecclesial meanings (III.C.1.c) and that some texts possess spiritual or fuller senses (II.B.2–3) – which the historical-critical method usually does not recognize – demonstrates that the historical-critical method does not provide a *sufficient* means of understanding Scripture.[46]

(5) The recognition that the texts of Scripture were composed, preserved and

---

[43] See my *Catholic Principles*, 95–108. In their context in the *IBC*, the words in quotation marks refer to what a hermeneutical theory ought to be, in contrast to Bultmann's hermeneutic, which failed due to inadequate presuppositions and the misuse of philosophy. But the potential of the historical-critical method as an instrument for grasping revelation is expressed elsewhere in the document (e.g., I.A.3.d, I.A.4.g).

[44] See my *Catholic Principles*, 137–44.

[45] E.g., IBC III.A.1.a: 'One thing that gives the Bible an inner unity, unique of its kind, is the fact that later biblical writings often depend upon earlier ones. These more recent writings allude to older ones, create "re-readings" (relectures) which develop new aspects of meaning, sometimes quite different from the original sense. A text may also make explicit reference to older passages, whether it is to deepen their meaning or to make known their fulfillment.' For more on this, see my *Catholic Principles*, 117–23, 128–32.

are read today for a religious purpose requires that an adequate interpretation explain what they *mean* and not exclusively what they *meant*. In other words, exegesis must explain the contemporary religious meaning of the text, or it has failed to complete its task.[47]

(6) The fact that historical-critical exegesis takes place in the church for the nourishment of the people of God means that it is oriented to the *use of the Bible* in the church (in preaching, teaching, catechetics, liturgy, *lectio divina*, theology and ecumenism).[48]

(7) The recognition that exegesis is above all a 'theological discipline' (III.D.a, Conclusion e–f) protects against reducing it to a purely historical or literary discipline.[49]

(8) The fact that Catholic exegesis does not claim any one scientific method as its own (III.a), as well as the fact that many other methods and approaches may make their contribution, denies any claim of sole validity to the historical-critical method (III.D.1.a).

A 'properly-oriented' use of the historical-critical method employs it in the service of Christian faith. The principles of Catholic interpretation implicit in the *IBC* provide a context for the historical-critical method, a context that permits the method to fulfill its noblest task – to help make clear the word of God.

Evaluation

Shortcomings of the **IBC***'s approach*

Two serious deficiencies in the *IBC*'s treatment of history and the historical-critical method may be noted. First, the PBC fails to distinguish the careful

---

[46] See my *Catholic Principles*, 189–211.

[47] In this regard, here are two strong statements of the PBC: 1) 'Exegesis is truly faithful to proper intention [sic] of biblical texts when it goes not only to the heart of their formulation to find the reality of faith there ... but also seeks to link this reality to ... faith in our present world' (II.A.2.b). 2) 'Their [Catholic exegetes'] common task is not finished when they have simply determined sources, defined forms or explained literary procedures. They arrive at the true goal of their work only when they have explained the meaning of the biblical text as God's word for today. To this end, they must take into consideration the various hermeneutical perspectives which help toward grasping the contemporary meaning of the biblical message and which make it responsive to the needs of those who read Scripture today' (III.C.1.b). See my *Catholic Principles*, 148–52, 289–302.

[48] See my *Catholic Principles*, 149–52, 312–13.

[49] See my *Catholic Principles*, 280–82, 284–88.

approach to the historical-critical method that they advocate (which this chapter describes as 'properly-oriented') from the presuppositions widely assumed in the practice of the historical-critical method in exegesis today. Second, the PBC fails to respond to the most common criticism of the historical-critical method by believers, namely its tendency to undermine faith in the reliability of Scripture by its excessive skepticism regarding the historicity of what is recorded in the Bible.

Problem of presuppositions

The PBC suggests that the inclusion of philosophical presuppositions contrary to Christian faith in the method was a problem in the past, but not the present:

> The early confrontation between traditional exegesis and the scientific approach, which initially consciously separated itself from faith and at times even opposed it, was assuredly painful; later however it proved to be salutary: once the method was freed from external prejudices, it led to a more precise understanding of the truth of Sacred Scripture (cf. *Dei Verbum*, 12). (I.A.4.c)
>
> For a long time now scholars have ceased combining the method with a philosophical system. (I.A.4.e)

However, there is considerable evidence of the continued use of the historical-critical method controlled by philosophical presuppositions contrary to Christian faith.[50] The most obvious example is the 'Third Quest' for the historical Jesus, which, along with some solid historical research about Jesus, has produced some very tendentious results in the name of the historical-critical method (e.g., the work of the Jesus Seminar).[51] Typically when scholars wish to define or describe the historical-critical method they refer to E. Krentz's *The Historical-Critical Method*, which presents the method as founded on E. Troeltsch's positivist principles, which are incompatible with historic Christian belief. Nevertheless, prominent Catholic exegete John J. Collins explicitly embraces these principles as the proper basis for biblical theology, urging the exclusion from biblical theology of 'the postulate of divine revelation'.[52] In the

---

[50]   See, for instance, the following treatments of the problem by exegetes of various confessions: Bartholomew, *Reading Ecclesiastes*, 53–97; Donfried, 'Alien Hermeneutics'; Harrisville, 'Critique' and 'Biblical Authority'; Harrisville and Sundberg, *Bible*; Johnson, 'Crisis' and 'State of Catholic Scholarship'; Levenson, *Hebrew Bible*; and Noble, *Canonical Approach*, 81–144.

[51]   See Evans, 'Third Quest', for a brief overview. For critical evaluation of the methodologies and biases of the leading works, see Green, 'Quest'; Johnson, *Real Jesus*; Witherington, *Jesus Quest*.

[52]   Collins, 'Biblical Theology', 9 and 'Review'.

conclusion of his article Collins makes clear that he understands the implications of his method: 'Historical criticism, consistently understood, is not compatible with a confessional theology that is committed to specific doctrines on the basis of faith.'[53]

The problem is complicated by the fact that followers of the rationalist Enlightenment tradition of historical-critical interpretation think they hold the high ground of scientific objectivity. However, the hidden bias and the inherent contradictions in their approach have been convincingly demonstrated.[54] The solution to the problem of conflicting presuppositions does not require either that believing exegetes renounce the historical-critical method or that exegetes of any stripe abandon their presuppositions. Rather, what is needed is an admission by all that neutral, objective, presuppositionless historical-critical exegesis has never existed – nor can it exist. When this is granted, scholars with diverse, publicly acknowledged presuppositions may engage in historical-critical study of the Bible that is properly grounded and genuinely pluralistic.

Because the PBC treats the problems of the historical-critical method as a phenomenon of the past, the nuances of the 'properly-oriented' historical-critical method that it advocates were lost on many readers. Most readers have understood the *IBC* to be endorsing the historical-critical method as it is commonly practiced. To put it in liturgical terms, the PBC confessed the true faith in relation to the historical-critical method, but failed to unambiguously renounce the devil and all his works. In consequence, the Catholic christening of the historical-critical method remains somehow incomplete.

Historicity and Christian interpretation

One of the common criticisms of the historical-critical method has been the way that critical history has served to undermine faith in traditional Christian doctrine and in the trustworthiness of the Bible.[55] Surprisingly, despite the

---

[53] Collins continues, 'It is, however, quite compatible with theology, understood as an open-ended and critical inquiry into the meaning and function of God-language' ('Biblical Theology', 14). Collins is aware that most theologies begin with the postulate of revelation ('Biblical Theology', 9; see also Collins, 'Review') and meet the classic definition of theology, *fides quaerens intellectum*. Essentially, Collins proposes a 'critical' theology based on reason alone, of which a 'critical' biblical theology would form a subdiscipline. In each instance, being 'critical' requires the systematic exclusion of assertions grounded on faith.

[54] See Noble, *Canonical Approach*, ch. 5; Levenson, *Hebrew Bible*, 109–26 and 'Bible; Bartholomew, *Reading Ecclesiastes*, 53–97; Plantinga, 'Two (or More)'; and Williamson, *Catholic Principles*, 236–48.

[55] A common way for the relation of history to biblical interpretation to present itself occurs in debunking exegesis which assumes a form roughly analogous to the

PBC's awareness of this criticism,[56] the *IBC* does not address this issue. Perhaps the PBC felt that problems of this kind are a holdover from the past and that they will be resolved as a more unbiased use of the historical-critical method takes hold. Yet some of the questions have pressing pastoral implications for preaching and teaching from the Bible. For many Christians, including clergy, real and specious historical problems have undermined confidence in Scripture as a reliable witness to God's saving action in the past and, therefore, as a reliable guide to Christian faith and practice in the present. The *IBC* makes only a few assertions about the relation between history and exegesis, and these do not resolve the more vexing questions.

Here are some of the important questions raised by historical-critical study of the Bible that require thoughtful answers by believing exegetes and theologians:

(1) How important is the veracity of the history recounted in the Bible? Can most of it (excluding the death and resurrection of Christ) be regarded as fiction without important theological loss? Some say that the biblical narrative, accepted on its own terms, is the proper basis for theology, and that questions about historicity are irrelevant.[57] Other scholars would say that the truth value of the Bible depends upon its being reliable in its fundamental historical affirmations (taking into account the difference in modern and ancient historical genres). Yet among those who hold this view, some do not consider historical issues relevant to the exegete's work.[58]

---

antitheses of Matthew 6: 'You have heard it said [in your church or synagogue] ....
But critical study of the Bible demonstrates ...' Debunking exegesis of this sort abounds in the Jesus Seminar writings and in introductory courses on Scripture in secular and religious university programs. Johnson and Levenson both describe this as a contemporary phenomenon (Johnson, 'State of Catholic Scholarship', 15; Levenson, 'Bible'; Blowers, Levenson and Wilken, 'Interpreting', 42).

[56] See, e.g., Intro A..e: '[Opponents of the historical-critical method] insist that the result of scientific exegesis is only to provoke perplexity and doubt upon numerous points which hitherto had been accepted without difficulty. They add that it impels some exegetes to adopt positions contrary to the faith of the Church on matters of great importance, such as the virginal conception of Jesus and his miracles, and even his resurrection and divinity.'

[57] Frei, *Eclipse*, rightly or wrongly, is commonly interpreted this way (see Comstock, 'Truth or Meaning'; Henry, 'Narrative Theology'; Olson, 'Back to the Bible'. According to Collins, 'the significance of the paradigm shift from history to story is that it abandons the last claim of biblical theology to certain knowledge of objective reality' ('Biblical Theology', 11).

[58] Noble says this is Childs's position (*Canonical Approach*, 84); see pp. 84–94 for an analysis of Childs's decoupling of historical reference and theological value.

Others, both on the theological left and right, are very concerned about historical facticity.

(2) How should the historical discipline be defined and what may reasonably be expected from it? Some define it in a way that necessarily excludes supernatural explanations of what it investigates. Thus, Robert Morgan and John Barton claim that it is an axiom of the historical discipline that 'acts of God cannot be spoken of, let alone established, by historical research', and that a historical explanation is 'a rational, … non-supernatural account'.[59] Still others, like Johnson, argue for a more modest reckoning of history's powers, seeing it as mode of knowing limited by the data available, the capabilities of historians and its object, namely a 'human event in time and space'.[60] Since the resurrection, defined as 'the passage of the human Jesus into the power of God' exceeds history's competence, Christ's resurrection is seen as real, but not historical.[61] On the other hand, some authors advocate a historical methodology broad enough to take into account natural and supernatural events.[62]

(3) What are the implications of the emerging consensus regarding the inescapably perspectival character of historical knowledge for historical-critical exegesis, 'historical Jesus' research and theology?[63] How *should* dialogue take place among scholars with radically different perspectives?

(4) In what biblical or theological specialty should foundational historical questions about Christianity be treated (e.g., the resurrection or the relationship of the Jesus of the Gospels to the 'historical' Jesus)? Should this be the domain of ordinary exegesis in the church, or should there be a specialization analogous to fundamental theology to evaluate such issues?

(5) How should exegetes respond to supposed findings of critical history which disagree with important biblical history, such as those that deny a historical basis to the biblical accounts of the exodus and conquest of Palestine? What principles should guide their response?

---

[59] Morgan and Barton, *Biblical Interpretation*, 70 and 68, as cited by Noble, *Canonical Approach*, 110–11.

[60] Johnson, *Real Jesus*, 136.

[61] Johnson, *Real Jesus*, 136. See pp. 81–140 for Johnson's views of history and its limits.

[62] Thus Pannenberg, for whom 'revelation occurs in the events of history, and must therefore be discovered through historical research' (Pannenberg, 'Redemptive Event'; Noble, *Canonical Approach*, 111). Noble evaluates and suggests improvements to Pannenberg's model (108–44).

[63] See Green, 'Quest', for a consideration of this issue in regard to 'historical' Jesus research; Green's notes refer to recent publications which reflect on the nature of the historical discipline.

(6) What is the historical value of the various historical genres in the Bible? What sort of factual accuracy is appropriate to expect from each?

(7) What value should historical reconstruction of circumstances behind the text have for interpretation in the church? For example, Raymond Brown and others have proposed elaborate hypotheses about the historical situation that lies behind the gospel and the Letters of John.[64] How much weight should be given to such hypotheses in determining biblical meaning?

(8) In terms of historical method, is it a valid use of sources to detach the accounts of events and sayings from their narrative contexts (in the Gospels or Acts) in order to construct an alternative historical portrait of Jesus or the early church?[65]

(9) How is historical development within the biblical tradition (and then within the tradition of the church) to be evaluated theologically? When is the earlier tradition more authoritative? When is the later?[66]

Contribution to exegesis

The Interpretation of the Bible in the Church's approach to history and the historical-critical method within a Christian hermeneutic makes a valuable contribution to the progress of exegesis in the Catholic Church and, one would hope, to biblical interpretation by other Christians as well. It spells out a

---

[64] It may be significant that, in his final work, Brown, *Introduction*, devotes only two pages to his reconstruction of the history of the Johannine community (originally set out in *Community of the Beloved Disciple*), and precedes that summary with the following warning: 'One should not confuse such reconstructive research with exegesis, which has to do with what the Gospel meant to convey to its readers. The evangelist tells us his purpose in 20:31, and it was not to recount background. ... I shall now present a reconstruction of the community history, warning that while it explains many factors in the Gospel, it remains a hypothesis and "perhaps" needs to be added to every sentence' (374). In his foreword, Brown makes clear that he intends to concentrate on the NT, not on 'early Christianity', and that he likewise focuses on the extant text of the NT and not its prehistory (viii–ix).

[65] Johnson succeeds in raising reasonable questions about this procedure (*Real Jesus*, 92–104, 124–26).

[66] Alternatively, does Christian interpretation in light of the canon have a counterpart to the 'Eighth Principle' of Judaism's 'literary simultaneity of Scripture'? See Levenson, 'Eighth Principle', and *Hebrew Bible*, 62–81. Levenson believes that the application of a diachronic perspective to Scripture seriously undermines the principle that the Bible is a unity (*Hebrew Bible*, 70–71). Can the diachronic principle, linked to the theological notion of progressive revelation within the Bible, be applied alongside the principle of the unity of Scripture?

role for history that is appropriate, as a means of ascertaining the meaning of the biblical text, rather than as an end itself. It upholds important theological principles – namely, the historical character of Christian revelation and the priority of the historical communication of the word of God. The *IBC*'s reaffirmation of the importance of history and of the historical-critical method is necessary in the face of postmodernist interpretation and other theological and literary approaches that discount the ostensive historical reference of the text or the notion of objective meaning rooted in a historical communication.

The PBC's decision to retain the historical-critical method while seeking to purify it of its problematic tendencies has the advantage of preserving the method's positive contributions. In the long run, this approach is more likely to prevail than would an outright rejection of the method, since the historical-critical method has shaped scholarly study of the Bible for nearly two centuries. Likewise, the orientations which the PBC gives for the proper use of the historical-critical method – attending to the proper object, rejecting certain errors that have characterized it, placing it in a hermeneutical context – are quite promising, *if they are implemented*. In the meantime, the tasks of criticizing the historical-critical method as it is commonly practiced and of freeing biblical exegesis from arbitrary presuppositions that are biased against Christian faith remain an important and unfinished work.

Bibliography

Ayres, L., and S.E. Fowl, '(Mis)Reading the Face of God: *The Interpretation of the Bible in the Church*', *TS* 60 (1999), 513–28

Bartholomew, C.G., *Reading Ecclesiastes: Old Testament Exegesis and Hermeneutical Theory* (AnBib 139; Rome: Pontificio Istituto Biblico, 1998)

Béchard, D.P., *The Scripture Documents: An Anthology of Official Catholic Teaching*, (Collegeville, MN: Liturgical Press, 2002)

Bergant, D., 'Fundamentalism and the Biblical Commission', *CS* 34.3 (1995), 95

Blowers, P., J.D. Levenson and R.L. Wilken, 'Interpreting the Bible: Three Views', *First Things* 45 (Aug./Sept. 1994), 40–46

Borg, M.J., 'A Temperate Case for a Non-Eschatological Jesus', *Forum* 2 (1986), 81–102

Brown, R.E., *The Community of the Beloved Disciple* (New York: Paulist Press, 1979)

——, *An Introduction to the New Testament* (ABRL; ed. D.N. Freedman; New York: Doubleday, 1997)

Collins, J.J., 'Is a Critical Biblical Theology Possible?', in *The Hebrew Bible and Its Interpreters* (ed. W.H. Propp, B. Halpern and D.N. Freedman; Winona Lake, IN: Eisenbrauns, 1990), 1–25

——, 'Review: *The Hebrew Bible, the Old Testament and Historical Criticism: Jews and Christians in Biblical Studies*', *ChrCent* (28 July 1993), 743–45

Collins, R.F., 'Hearing the Word: Methods of Biblical Interpretation', *Living Light* 31.1 (1994), 3–9

Comstock, G.L., 'Truth or Meaning: Ricœur versus Frei on Biblical Narrative', *HvTSt* 45.4 (1989), 741–66

Donfried, K.P., 'Alien Hermeneutics and the Misappropriation of Scripture', in *Reclaiming the Bible for the Church* (ed. C.E. Braaten and R.W. Jenson; Grand Rapids: Eerdmans, 1995), 19–45

Evans, C.A., 'The Third Quest of the Historical Jesus: A Bibliographical Essay', *Christian Scholar's Review* 28.4 (1999), 532–43

Filippi, A., and E. Lora (eds.), *Enchiridion Biblicum* (Bologna: Dehoniane Bologna, 1993)

Fitzmyer, J.A., *The Biblical Commission's Document 'The Interpretation of the Bible in the Church': Text and Commentary* (ed. J. Swetnam; SubBi 18; Rome: Pontifical Biblical Institute, 1995)

——, 'Historical Criticism: Its Role in Biblical Interpretation and Church Life', *TS* 50 (1989), 244–59

——, *Scripture and Christology: A Statement of the Biblical Commission with a Commentary* (New York: Paulist Press, 1986)

——, *Scripture, the Soul of Theology* (New York: Paulist Press, 1994)

———, and T.J. Stahel, '*Scripture, the Soul of Theology:* An Interview with Joseph A. Fitzmyer, S.J.', *America* 172.16 (1995), 8–12

Frei, H., *The Eclipse of Biblical Narrative* (New Haven: Yale University Press, 1974)

Fusco, V., 'Un secolo di metodo storico nell' esegesi cattolica', *StPat* 41.2 (1994), 37–94

Green, J.B., 'In Quest of the Historical Jesus, the Gospels, and Historicisms Old and New', *Christian Scholar's Review* 28.4 (1999), 544–60

Harrisville, R.A., 'A Critique of Current Biblical Criticism', *WW* 15.2 (1995), 206–13

———, 'The Loss of Biblical Authority and Its Recovery', in *Reclaiming the Bible for the Church* (ed. C.E. Braaten and R.W. Jenson; Grand Rapids: Eerdmans, 1995), 47–61

———, and W. Sundberg, *The Bible in Modern Culture: Theology and Historical-Critical Method from Spinoza to Käsemann* (Grand Rapids: Eerdmans, 1995)

Henry, C.F., 'Narrative Theology: An Evangelical Appraisal', *TJ* 8.1 (1987), 3–19

Johnson, L.T., 'The Crisis in Biblical Scholarship', *Commonweal* 120.21 (1993), 18–21

———, *The Real Jesus: The Misguided Quest for the Historical Jesus and the Truth of the Traditional Gospels* (New York: HarperCollins, 1995)

———, 'So What's Catholic About It? The State of Catholic Biblical Scholarship', *Commonweal* (16 Jan. 1998), 12–16

———, and W.S. Kurz, *The Future of Catholic Biblical Scholarship: A Constructive Conversation* (Grand Rapids: Eerdmans, 2002)

Krentz, E., *The Historical-Critical Method* (Philadelphia: Fortress Press, 1975)

Larraín, E.P.-C., 'El valor hermenéutico de la eclesialidad para la interpretación de la Sagrada Escritura', *TV* 36.3 (1996), 169–85

Latourelle, R., 'Positivism, Historical', in *Dictionary of Fundamental Theology* (ed. R. Latourelle and R. Fisichella; New York: Crossroad, 1995), 785–88

Levenson, J.D., 'The Bible: Unexamined Commitments of Criticism', *First Things* 30 (1993), 24–33

———, 'The Eighth Principle of Judaism and the Literary Simultaneity of Scripture', *JR* 68.2 (1988), 205–25

———, *The Hebrew Bible, the Old Testament, and Historical Criticism: Jews and Christians in Biblical Studies* (Louisville, KY: Westminster / John Knox Press, 1993)

Mack, B.L., *A Myth of Innocence: Mark and Christian Origins* (Minneapolis: Fortress Press, 1988)

Marshall, I.H., 'Review: "The Interpretation of the Bible in the Church"', *SBET* 13.1 (1995), 72–75

Martin, F., 'Literary Theory, Philosophy of History and Exegesis', *Thomist* 52.4 (1988), 575–604

Montague, G.T., *Understanding the Bible: A Basic Introduction to Biblical Interpretation* (New York: Paulist Press, 1997)

Morgan, R., and J. Barton, *Biblical Interpretation* (The Oxford Bible Series; Oxford: OUP, 1988)

Morgan, R.T., 'Historicism', in *A Dictionary of Biblical Interpretation* (ed. R.J. Coggins and J.L. Houlden; London: SCM Press, 1990), 290–91

Neuhaus, R.J. (ed.), *Biblical Interpretation in Crisis: The Ratzinger Conference on Bible and Church* (Encounter Series; Grand Rapids: Eerdmans and the Rockford Institute Center on Religion and Society, 1989)

Noble, P.R., *The Canonical Approach: A Critical Reconstruction of the Hermeneutics of Brevard S. Childs* (BIS 16; Leiden: E.J. Brill, 1995)

Olson, R.E., 'Back to the Bible (Almost)', *Christianity Today* 40.6 (1996), 31–34

Pannenberg, W., 'Redemptive Event and History', in *Basic Questions in Theology* (trans. G.H. Kehm; London: SCM Press, 1970), 15–80

Plantinga, A., 'Two (or More) Kinds of Scripture Scholarship', in *Warranted Christian Belief* (New York: OUP, 2000), 374–421

Powell, M.A., *Fortress Introduction to the Gospels* (Minneapolis: Fortress Press, 1998)

Prior, J.G., *The Historical Critical Method in Catholic Exegesis* (Tesi Gregoriana, Serie Teologia 50; Rome: Gregorian University, 1999)

Ratzinger, J., 'Modernità atea religiosità post-moderna', *Il Regno-Attualità* 1994, no. 4 (1994), 65–70

——, (ed.), *Schriftauslegung im Widerstreit* (Quaestiones Disputatae 117; Freiburg: Herder, 1989)

Ricœur, P., *Interpretation Theory: Discourse and the Surplus of Meaning* (Fort Worth, TX: Texas Christian University Press, 1976)

Schneiders, S.M., *The Revelatory Text: Interpreting the New Testament as Sacred Scripture* (Collegeville, MN: Liturgical Press, 2nd edn, 1999)

Shea, W.M., 'Catholic Reaction to Fundamentalism', *TS* 57.2 (1996), 264–85

Vanhoye, A., 'Catholicism and the Bible', *First Things* 74 (1997), 35–40

——, 'L'interpretazione della Bibbia nella Chiesa: Riflessione circa un documento della Commissione Biblica', *Civiltà Cattolica* 145.3457 (1994), 3–15

Watson, F., 'A Response to Professor Rowland', *SJT* 48.4 (1995), 518–22

Williamson, P.S., *Catholic Principles for Interpreting Scripture: A Study of the Pontifical Biblical Commission's 'The Interpretation of the Bible in the Church'* (ed. J. Swetnam; SubBi 22; Rome: Pontifical Biblical Institute, 2001)

Witherington, B., III, *The Jesus Quest: The Third Search for the Jew of Nazareth* (Downers Grove, IL: InterVarsity Press, 2nd edn, 1997)

Rethinking History

11

Knowing and Believing

Faith in the Past

Iain W. Provan

There is no more 'ancient Israel.' History no longer has room for it. This we do know. And now, as one of the first conclusions of this new knowledge, 'biblical Israel' was in its origin a Jewish concept.[1]

If we ask why it is that a conference on history and hermeneutics is important, as part of an ongoing consultation that is concerned with the impact of the Bible on society, then one answer is this: it is important because misconceptions about the nature of history abound, and these misconceptions inhibit many modern people from being able to take the Bible seriously in its claims to reveal truth. History is still widely perceived, in spite of the postmodern turn and the convictions of many historians themselves, as comprising 'facts' – facts that can be scientifically established and woven together to produce 'the past', which can then be used as a canonical rule against which to measure particular stories about the past and to pronounce them uncertain or false. It is not only the biblical story that has suffered in this way over the course of time; but the biblical story has certainly been among the more prominent victims in recent years, as myriad television documentaries, books and newspaper articles have revealed to the general public all the ways in which 'history has shown that' the Bible cannot be taken very seriously in historical terms. The patriarchs and the exodus are myths, David and Solomon figments of the romantic imagination,

---

[1] Thompson, 'Neo-Albrightean School', 697. The article is a response to Provan, 'Ideologies', and itself finds an answer throughout Provan, 'Stable'. Readers especially interested in the exchange are directed to this latter essay, upon which the present chapter is partially based.

and Jesus an interesting man now hopelessly obscured by later tradition that has invented a Messiah/Son of God and attributed to him sayings that he never said and actions that he never carried out. The intelligentsia whose scholarly contributions are ultimately responsible for such popularized understandings of history and Bible are well represented by T.L. Thompson, whose confident assertion of knowledge is cited above. His claim is that we 'know' a considerable amount about something rather solid called 'history', and that this knowledge of history means that we cannot any longer believe (in this case) in 'ancient Israel'. There are no 'gaps' left in the historical record into which we can fit the ancient Israel about which scholars (in considerable dependence on the Old Testament) have hitherto been writing. This is a fundamental claim of some recent historiography on Israel, which embraces the general tendency in modern times to downplay the importance of testimony about the past which has come down to us via a chain of human carriers of tradition. In contrast, this historiography emphasizes the importance of empirical research in leading us into knowledge.

On this kind of view we may still, in our private world of leisure or faith, enjoy our Bible stories, or even find some manner of truth in them – for which literature does not offer us truth? It is not the kind of truth that really counts, however – the hard-edged and empirically grounded truth, including historical truth, which provides the foundation upon which the modern world is built. In this world to raise questions about the Bible's historicity is, for many people, to raise questions about its truthfulness (in just the same way that to raise questions about its scientific accuracy is to raise questions about its truthfulness), and to invite them to turn elsewhere for the truth that fundamentally shapes their lives. That is why the matter of history is a crucial matter for those interested in presenting the Bible to the culture with a view to the culture taking seriously what it has to say about God and the world.

This chapter seeks to address some of the misconceptions about the nature of history that lie at the root of the problem. It will focus specifically on the history of Israel, since that is the area of the author's expertise; but its more general comment is intended to be of much wider application than simply to the history of Israel. For this is a chapter above all about epistemology: how do we 'know' about the past? In pursuit of a coherent answer to that question, we first review the development of the 'scientific model' of historiography that so dominates the modern imagination and offer a critique of this model, before moving on to suggest an alternative to it. The alternative, against the modern stream, is grounded in the assertion that we know about the past, to the extent that we know about it at all, *primarily* through the testimony of others and *not* through other avenues. I thus dispute the accuracy of the description of reality commonly advanced by modern historians of Israel when they claim to describe how we 'know' what we think we know about the past. The implications for our understanding and presentation of 'the Bible and history' of what I claim as my own more accurate description of reality, which asserts that we 'know' by listening to testimony and interpretation, and by making choices about whom to believe, shall in due course become clear.

The Scientific Model of Historiography

Background to the scientific model

The immediate background that needs to be sketched briefly here[2] is the overall shift in the modern age from philosophy to science as the foundational method for human endeavor: the institution under the influence of thinkers like Bacon and Descartes of an empirical and critical approach to all knowledge (not merely knowledge of the natural world), which tended to eschew prior authority in its pursuit of truth and to hold all tradition accountable to reason. The consequences for historiography of the popularity of this general approach to reality were ultimately profound. It was not that questions had never been asked in earlier times about the plausibility of tradition – whether individual traditions or parts of traditions could in fact be regarded as reflecting historical truth. In relation specifically to the history of Israel, for example, the early Jewish historian Josephus, although his work is heavily dependent upon biblical tradition as contained in the Hebrew Scriptures, nevertheless elucidated these Scriptures in relation to the science and philosophy of his day, harmonizing where necessary and sometimes rationalizing events which struck him as extraordinary. More generally, it was already a feature of the scholarship of the Renaissance that there was an acute awareness of the difference between past and present – a sense that the world described in tradition was not the same as the one inhabited by its receivers – and both a critical stance towards the literary evidence of the past and an openness to archaeological evidence as a way of reconstructing the past. Yet broadly speaking, tradition can be said to have provided the accepted framework within which discussion of the past took place, even where elements of tradition might be criticized or considered problematic. This situation generally obtained throughout the succeeding period until the late eighteenth century – a period during which history was not in any case widely regarded as a source of reliable truth, and the idea that a 'scientific method' could be developed to discover such truth in history had not yet arisen. History was the story of the merely contingent and particular – a view enunciated by Aristotle himself, and held by a great variety of thinkers

---

[2] For an excellent and full account of the history of historiography, see Breisach, *Historiography*, to which various sections of this essay are heavily indebted.

throughout the sixteenth to the eighteenth centuries. The Jesuits who produced the *Ratio Studiorum* (1559), for example, assigned no significant role in their curriculum to history (in contrast to logic and dialectic, which were regarded as approaches to truth). The seventeenth-century Descartes, who rooted his thinking in self-evident axioms, moving on to trustworthy knowledge and certainty by way of deductive reasoning and mathematical method, likewise did not think highly of history, since historians employed observation and interpretation rather than logic and mathematics. Writing in the eighteenth century, Lessing famously opined (succinctly summing up the general belief of the age): 'Accidental truths of history can never become the proof of necessary truths of reason.' Where history writing was valued in the rapidly emerging scientific age, it was in general so valued as an art with close links to the ancient art of rhetoric. Its purpose was to delight the reader and to teach morals through example. The ancient words of Dionysius of Halicarnassus encapsulate the position on history that was thus commonly adopted: 'History is philosophy teaching by examples.'

It is only in the late eighteenth and nineteenth centuries that we find a pronounced shift in how history and history-writing was conceived, as the idea emerged that the past itself might, if subject to the appropriate sort of inductive scientific analysis, reveal truths about human existence. The factors involved in this general change in perspective are many and complex. On the one hand tradition about the past, including tradition rooted in the Bible, had been progressively undermined for many people. It had been undermined by the work of humanist text-critics since the Renaissance, with all of that work's potential to destroy the claims to authority for a document that had been accepted for centuries; by geographical exploration, which subverted long-held perspectives on the nature of the world; by philosophical perspectives, which were either new or were new versions of older pre-Christian ideas with which scholars had become reacquainted during the Renaissance revival in classical learning; and by the Reformation assault on church authority and mediaeval faith. On the other hand, the scientific approach to reality was already beginning to enjoy prestige as a way in which certain and timeless truth might be appropriated and human existence understood. It remained only for the suggestion to be widely adopted that perhaps a scientific approach to *historical* reality might shed further light on this human existence – an idea already found in earlier thinkers like Machiavelli.

Development of the scientific model

The catalyst for this change of general viewpoint was undoubtedly some of the intellectual activity that preceded and surrounded the French Revolution, as represented by the thought of many of the French *philosophes*, who argued that history revealed the transformation of a *potentially* rational humanity into an *actually* rational humanity – it was a story of inevitable progress. Tradition should no longer guide actions in the present and hope for the future, especially as it was seen as deriving from earlier stages of human history characterized as periods of folly and superstition – with institutional religion itself embodying such superstition. Rather, expectations for the *future* should govern both the life of the present and the evaluation of the past. God had created the universe, setting an orderly system of causes and effects in motion, and from there it proceeded of itself (in the realm of human affairs as well as the realm of nature) in Newtonian orderliness. The increase in rationality that would inevitably occur over time would in due course lead to an increase in happiness, as every-one was drawn to live in accordance with the principles enshrined in nature. Newtonian science thus provided the model for understanding not only present and future human existence, but past human existence as well.

The particular viewpoint advanced by these French *philosophes* was by no means generally adopted elsewhere by those who were reflecting on the nature of history. The German historiography of the late eighteenth and early- to mid-nineteenth centuries which responded to this French world-view, for example, was far less inclined to see the past in terms of the simple cause-and-effect relationships envisaged in Newtonian physics. It was more inclined to believe that reason itself had to be seen within its total human context; that Nature did not encompass everything; and that religion was not just the convenient tool of a not-yet rational mankind – it was a basic element of human life. It preferred to view history not as the story of rationality ascending through time to ever-greater perfection, but as a series of discontinuities. The aim of the historian was the intuitive grasping of complex, intertwining forces inaccessible to simple explanations. German historiography in this mode is often referred to as 'historicism'. Yet, for all that, this response to French devel-opments was in many ways antagonistic. It was itself framed as a response that was scientific in nature, illustrating the way in which the scientific model had now come to dominate the discussion, at least in continental Europe. One of the main German criticisms of the *philosophes* was that they speculated about the past without proper consultation of the sources. The Germans, in turn, sought to ground their historiographical work in 'the facts', building on a long erudite tradition which itself inherited elements from Italian humanist histori-ography (in its critical attitude toward texts and undocumented traditions), from work on French legal history which stressed the importance of primary sources, and from antiquarianism (with its concern, for example, with the physical remains of the past). Vigorous study of the sources, utilizing proper empirical scientific method, would reveal, in Leopold von Ranke's famous words, *wie es eigentlich gewesen ist* – 'the way it really was'. For most of the nine-teenth century, Ranke himself presided over the vast scholarly enterprise of searching out the facts and presenting them in an objectively scientific form, allegedly free from bias and presupposition. The historian's task was conceived, indeed, precisely as that of the natural scientist – at least insofar as it was thought of as letting the facts (envisaged as simply 'out there') speak for themselves, and as allowing people to form judgements about them at a later stage. Historiography was now to be firmly understood, at least in the first instance, as an endeavor with the purely theoretical interest of reconstructing the past and without any practical interest in the purposes for which such a reconstruction might be used (whether in terms of moral instruction, religious devotion, entertainment or propaganda). By the end of the eighth decade of the nineteenth century, this history-as-science had replaced philosophy as the discipline to which many educated people in Europe and elsewhere in the Western world turned as the key that would unlock the mysteries of human life. The move away from the limits set by tradition, and towards an unlimited freedom of explanation after the model of the natural sciences, had become ever more decisive. The value and authority of all older historiographical models and all histories based on them had, indeed, come into serious question. Since histories written prior to the nineteenth century had not been produced by those who possessed proper scientific methods, everything now had to be done again in the proper manner by those who did now employ proper methods.

Ranke himself stopped well short of a full-blown scientific positivism in the narrower sense of the term, in that he did not believe that the finding of facts through critical research was to be followed by induction leading to more and more general and hence abstract concepts – scientific 'laws'. Ranke was a Christian and an idealist, believing that God with his plan and his will stood behind all the phenomena of the past. He also believed that the ideas that shape phenomena and events were not only the keys to understanding, but that they also provided an absolute moral structure and a yardstick for assessing the past. He did not, then, believe with Auguste Comte (the original proponent of positivism as a philosophical system) that science provides us with the only valid knowledge that we can possess, superseding theology and metaphysics – that only positive facts and observable phenomena count as knowledge. It was not long, however, before Ranke's manner of scientific approach to the past, which we may rightly refer to as a kind of 'quasi-positivism' (insofar as it at least advocates the establishment or verification of positive 'facts' through empirical inquiry and the construction thereby of an objective, scientific picture of 'the way things were'),[3] gave way to a more thoroughgoing version of it, in an era in

---

[3] It is the case that the term 'positivism' itself has recently come to be used somewhat loosely in discussion about the nature of science to refer simply to the modern critical/empirical scientific approach to reality in general, whether or not any allencompassing claims about the nature of valid knowledge are made. Barstad,

which many had long since ceased to share his Christian faith and now came to doubt also his idealism. Having used science so well to debunk the uncritically-presented past, nineteenth-century historiography in the German tradition in the end found that such science was a sharp and dangerous two-edged sword; for it could be brought to bear no less decisively on the broadly shared nine-teenth-century idealist philosophical framework that dominated much of the historiography of that century. Idealism itself could be seen only as a traditional view or prejudice – one of those philosophical explanations of the world's order that could not be inductively demonstrated and which, therefore, the truly scientific person should reject as a component of historiography. By the end of the nineteenth century, precisely this suggestion had been made and adopted, as many historians – in common with scholars in other fields who noted the immense prestige enjoyed by the sciences, and felt impelled to emulate their success by transferring its views and methods from the inquiry into nature to the inquiry into human phenomena – began to adopt a fully positivist stance on the past. Positivism thus strictly defined holds not only that all knowledge should be based on directly observed phenomena (i.e., it is not simply committed to empiricism and verification in the Rankean sense), but further that all scientific endeavors should aim at finding the general laws governing phenomena. Observing, searching for regularities, generalizing from research results and forming laws must be the task of all scientific disci-plines, and only this positivist approach can yield knowledge sufficiently reli-able to function as a guide for the reshaping of human life. Since on this view only sensory experience counts, the whole structure of idealist philosophy collapses (since gods, ideas and the like cannot be 'known' in this way), and so does the structure of idealist *historiography*, with its emphasis upon the unique individual or nation in their idiosyncratic context. Positivist historiography is, by contrast, resolutely deterministic, focusing on general (and hence predictable) phenomena or forces in history *rather than* on the unique and idiosyncratic.

With this kind of historiography, the marginalization of tradition in pursuit of the past becomes more complete. Tradition becomes, at best, only a mine out of which such 'facts' as can be ascertained empirically may be quarried, with a view to establishing the true, scientific relationship between the 'facts' and then moving on towards broad generalizations and laws arising from them (the approach, e.g., of Hippolyte Taine, who believed that the past could be wholly explained through this process). It was not even clear to some

---

'History', thus suggests (51, n. 35) that a useful definition of positivism in the context of a discussion about history would be 'belief in scientific history' – a suggestion with which we have considerable sympathy, in that it highlights the truth that all avowedly scientific history, whether fully positivistic or not, inevitably contains positivistic elements within it.

intellectuals at the turn of the twentieth century that it was any longer the *historian's* task to relate these 'facts' or to generalize from them. Emile Durkheim argued, on the contrary, that historians should only find, cleanse and present the 'facts' to the sociologist for generalization. In such a generalizing process, causal analysis was to be given priority over description and narration; the general over the unique and individual; and the directly observable present over the unobservable past.

Whether in Durkheim's precise formulation or not, it is clear that historiography on the positivist model ceases to be a story about the past in which human individuals and groups play the central and crucial roles. It becomes instead a narrative about the impersonal forces that shape both the past and the present. The early positivist history of H. Buckle foreshadowed many later works in the same spirit when it thus emphasized climate, food, soil and nature more generally – rather than *people* – as the shapers of civilization, and argued that historians must abandon the historiography of description and moral lessons for a historiography modelled on the successful natural sciences, if they did not wish to be ignored. In general, the twentieth century indeed saw an increasing preference for such social and economic interpretations of history, with their emphasis on collective forces, quantifiable aspects and repeatable developments, over against political, event-oriented interpretations which stress the unique and human (especially the individualistic) dimensions of history. Perhaps most influential among the more recent proponents of such interpretations are the French *Annales* group, with their interest in 'total history' and their emphasis on the larger structures which provide the context in which particular events take place and human beings think and act. Most important for understanding the past, on this view, are the relatively stable geographical and demographic forces of history. These are followed in order by economic and social developments involving the masses of the people; the culture of the common people; and lastly the political phenomena. Such an approach, in practice if not entirely in intention, has tended to neglect the importance of the individual, as well as radically diminishing the importance of the political, in the past.

The history of historiography since the Enlightenment can thus be seen to be, to this point, the story of a discipline progressively seeking to escape from a dependence upon tradition, under pressure as a result of the perceived success of the natural sciences to justify itself as a proper academic discipline by becoming more 'scientific' (whether this is interpreted in a Rankean-empirical or a positivist-empirical way). The new empirical and critical approach to knowledge in general was increasingly brought to bear in a thoroughgoing way on historical knowledge in particular, the aim of historians in general becoming, certainly by the end of the nineteenth century, to reconstruct past history 'as it had actually happened', over against traditional *claims* about what had happened.

History and tradition were no longer to be assumed to be generally in close relationship to each other. Rather, history was to be assumed to lie behind tradition and to be more or less distorted by it. The point, then, was not to listen to tradition and to be guided by it in what it said about the past but, if possible, rather to see *through* tradition to the history which might (or indeed might not) exist as a kernel within it. The onus now fell on tradition to verify itself, rather than on the historian to falsify it. The 'science' of historiography had been born. Its character is well exemplified in the following quotation from J. Huizinga:

> History adequate for our culture can only be scientific history. In the modern Western culture the form of knowledge about occurrences in this world is critical-scientific. We cannot surrender the demand for the scientifically certain without damaging the conscience of our culture.[4]

The Scientific Model of Historiography Reviewed

Science and the philosophy of science

It was Newtonian science that provided the model for understanding the past that we have just described; yet as time has passed and as scientific inquiry has progressed, this model has come to be questioned within the natural sciences themselves. The firm hope of previous generations of thinkers that science would soon reveal 'the true order of things' has been disappointed. As it turns out, reality has become *less and less* understandable, the deeper scientists have penetrated into it; and doubts have arisen about our ability ever to find out 'what exactly reality is like'. These doubts arise in part because of the inevitable involvement of the observer of the natural world, in the very act of observing. We understand more clearly than many of our predecessors how what is perceived in the so-called 'real' world is inevitably connected with the knowledge, the prejudices and the ideologies that the perceiving person brings with him or her. We understand also how the myth of 'the neutral, uninvolved observer' has functioned and continues to function as an ideological tool in the hands of those whose political and economic interests it has served. The 'objective' spectator of classical Newtonian physics has thus become the 'impossible' spectator of the newer physics; and scientists are becoming much more aware (as a result of the work of philosophers of science)[5] of the ways in which the great broad theories of science are underdetermined by the facts – and aware, too, of how experiments themselves are, from the moment of their

---

[4] Huizinga, *Geschichte*, 13, cited in translation from Smend, 'Tradition', 66.

[5] E.g., Habermas, *Knowledge*; Hesse, *Revolutions*.

conception, shaped by the theories of those conducting them. Scientific theories come and go, argue the philosophers and sociologists of knowledge – partly on the basis of their success in prediction and control of the environment, but partly also on the basis of the interests which they serve in a particular culture, whether theological and metaphysical, sociological or simply aesthetic. Scientists cannot, any more than other human beings, escape from this matter of 'interests'. There is no such thing as value-free academic endeavor.

It turns out, then, that the Newtonian scientific model is an inadequate account of reality even in terms of the natural world and of human inquiry into that world. As the science of the twentieth century itself suggested, we live in a much less rigid and more complex world than was previously suspected: multi-structured, far from any simple materialism, and mysterious. What the 'facts' are about this world, as a totality, it is impossible for science (as science) to say. Science can, at a practical level, tell us much about how things normally work in the natural world, insofar as the world does demonstrably possess predictable, mechanistic aspects that can be revealed through experimentation leading to reproducible results. Even insofar as it succeeds in this demonstration, however, it must of necessity operate within the larger context of what is taken to be valid human knowledge – albeit that this knowledge itself cannot be established 'scientifically'. The grounding belief of modern science itself falls into this category: for it is a presupposition, and not a scientific finding, that the universe as a whole is rational and intelligible. It is equally clear that science of itself cannot properly tell us what to do with its findings. The ends to which science provides the means must be (and always are) chosen according to what is believed and valued by those doing the choosing; and this is a matter of religion, ethics and politics – not a matter of science, as such. The realm of valid knowledge is not, and cannot, be filled by science. On the contrary, the very way in which people do science, and what they do with it, depends on ideas or beliefs derived from a larger reality than science embraces.

If the Newtonian scientific model is an inadequate account of reality even in terms of the *natural* world and human inquiry into it, however, then we must clearly ask whether this model can helpfully be applied to the world of the *human past* and inquiry into that. By no means did every historian in the nineteenth and twentieth centuries think that it could. Some of those in the past who thus resisted the temptation to embrace the scientific model will help us to gain clarity on the matter for ourselves as we ponder the present and the future.

History as science: A brief history of dissent

The period of the French Revolution was a decisive one for the development of modern historiography. This is the case not least because it can be argued that it was this particular period of radical social and political change in France, with its lasting repercussions throughout Europe, which was in some measure responsible for the triumph of historiography over philosophy in the nineteenth century as the crucial interpretative discipline in respect of human reality. Philosophy as it had been, with its emphasis on static and eternal essences, did not appear capable of the explanatory task in a period of notable change and development. It is important to note, however, that it was also the French Revolution itself, and its aftermath, which confirmed in some minds the folly of abandoning tradition entirely in favor of reason. In France, for example, F.R. de Chateaubriand argued that all attempts to change conditions radically and quickly, as in the French Revolution, must of necessity fail because they are based on the illusion of human control over unknown forces that are subject only to divine providence. 'The French past illustrated how the true, the gradually changing, and the lawful always prevailed over all sudden and violent changes ... the cultivation of rationality in isolation from emotion and imagination destroyed a civilization by eroding age-old tradition.'[6] In Britain, E. Burke argued similarly that a good society was shaped by tradition, and attempts to employ weak reason and will in place of this traditional wisdom could only result in anarchy, which could not be put right once tradition had been destroyed. These two thinkers represent a more positive view of tradition than some of the other thinkers we have encountered to this point in our discussion. They hold a less affirming view of a scientific approach to reality that remakes reality *de novo* by means of appropriate scientific method. They form a suitable starting point, therefore, for our analysis here, in that they remind us that, even in an age of science, there was nothing historically or intellectually inevitable about the adoption of an all-embracing scientific approach to human reality in general. It is important to be reminded of this, since the rhetoric of modern scientific historians is often designed to make us forget it.

However, we pick up the threads of our story at the turn, not of the eighteenth and nineteenth centuries, but of the nineteenth and twentieth centuries; and in particular with three German thinkers: J.G. Droysen, W. Dilthey and W. Windelband. Droysen, well aware of the increasing prestige of the natural sciences and of the challenge that positivism represented to the Rankean historiographical tradition, was driven as a result to fresh reflection on the methodology of the discipline of history. The result was not only a rejection of positivism, but also a critique of Ranke's historical school. He denied the Rankean idea of what historians do — that is, that they retrieve the remains of the past, mostly documents; critically assess them; and synthesize the parts through empathetic intuition into a whole that reflects a transcendent reality. On this view historians stood completely apart from ongoing life, recreating in methodological purity what was taken to be objective past reality. Droysen,

---

[6] Breisach, *Historiography*, 239.

conversely, understood all historical work as resulting from the encounters of the historian, whose own life was shaped by elements of the past, with that past. 'From such encounters came a creative and critically controlled recreation of the past, clearly from the standpoint of the present.'[7] A reconstruction that assumed a static past, testified to by its remains, was possible neither by Rankean nor positivistic method. Indeed, the positivists compounded the error of objectivism with the error of transforming all aspects of reality, including intellect and morality, into natural phenomena. Such things could not be submerged in nature, according to Droysen, as if all belonged in one sphere of life.

Dilthey also 'rejected the attempts to see the world of human phenomena as an analogue to the world of atoms and mechanical forces and to separate strictly the subject and object in all research'[8] along Cartesian lines. He found elements in the human realm – intentions, purposes and ends, and the actions guided by them – which were absent in nature and which rendered human reality too complex to grasp by a counting and measuring which resulted in finding regularities and formulating laws. Historians could only grasp this complexity through *Verstehen* (entering empathetically into the motives and intentions of actors in the past).

Windelband similarly distinguished between two kinds of analysis of reality: nomothetic analysis, which aims at general insights (and is typical for the natural sciences) and idiographic analysis, which attempts to understand the unique, individual event (typical for the humanities). He argued that the idiographic could make use of the nomothetic as a helpful tool without surrendering to its generalizing aim.

In these three thinkers we find, in different ways, an unhappiness with the notion of scientific history, connected in part with the false objectivism of such an approach to the past; and in part with the implausible reductionism which seeks to explain all reality in terms of a mechanistic model of the universe, and especially gives no place to the individual and the unique. They have not been lone voices as the decades of the twentieth century have passed. B. Croce saw human life as an ever-creative process in which the historian fully participates, striving for impartiality while never able to be objective. The historian's task is not the collection and critical assessment of sources, as facts on which to build an interpretation (as in Ranke) or general laws (as in positivism). It is to incorporate a living past into the present. C. Becker expressed skepticism about the possibility of capturing the real past, noting that historians can only deal with statements about events, not with the events themselves, which they do not observe. Early philosophical neo-positivists were themselves apt to draw attention to the pseudo-empiricism of scientific historians in these terms, since

---

[7] Breisach, *Historiography*, 279.
[8] Breisach, *Historiography*, 281.

these philosophers recognized only statements based upon direct observation as having the status of hypotheses. Statements that were not accessible to proper verification were declared meaningless, leading some to wonder 'whether we have sufficient ground for accepting any statement at all about the past, whether we are even justified in our belief that there has been a past'.[9] C. Beard affirmed more optimistically (having abandoned an earlier conviction that history should be a science in the positivist manner) that the past could be grasped as an external object, yet that the 'subject matter of history is so charged with values that historians themselves cannot avoid making judgments when they select and arrange facts for their accounts.'[10] He wrote of the historian's 'act of faith' in determining the meaning of history, since every historian has to choose non-objectively and non-scientifically whether history is simply chaotic, moves around in a cycle, or moves in some linear direction. Finally in this brief list of examples, the philosopher H.-G. Gadamer distinguished the conventional approach to the past through sources, with objective knowledge as its goal, from *Verstehen*, involving a sympathetic acceptance of tradition by the historian.

It would be quite easy to extend much further this list of thinkers who, while certainly not all agreeing with each other in their overall perspective, have at least qualified the idea that history is a science in the old Newtonian sense of the term – even if we were to grant that the Newtonian model is an adequate one for the study of the *natural* world. The fact is that there has been an ongoing debate among philosophers and historians since the turn of the twentieth century about the nature of history as a discipline. There has been widespread unease with regard to the positivist-empiricist model, and resistance, in particular, to the assimilation of history into the social sciences. The focus for the defense of history as an autonomous discipline has been a rejection of the generalizing tendencies of science and a historicist insistence upon the importance of grasping the separate eras and moments of the past in all their non-reducible uniqueness. At the same time there has also been an increasing awareness that even to think of history as a science in the more limited Rankean sense is far from unproblematic, precisely because of doubts about the historian's ability to see things 'as they really were'. It has been widely accepted that in history, if not in science, the subject does not observe a clearly defined object (i.e., historical reality), but rather an object that is at least partially constructed in the process of observing. As the preceding century moved on and came towards its end, indeed, and as we have moved into what many refer to as the 'postmodern' era, the emphasis upon the *construction* of the past by the

---

[9] Ayer, *Philosophical Essays*, 168. The discussion that follows this comment illustrates well the difficulties of responding to such philosophers if one grants their basic premises.

[10] Breisach, *Historiography*, 332.

historian has increased. Thus it is not difficult at the present time to find those who deny that there is one object, the past, which *exists to be discovered* by the historian. Historians (it is said) construct, rather than discover, the past. They narrate a story about it. Indeed, whereas older philosophers of history who favored the scientific model worried about the narrative form of much histori-ography because narrative statement remains art and not science, more recent contributors to the debate have moved in the opposite direction, questioning any strict distinction between history and story. We may with confidence say, then, that the whole movement of the last century was in general (at least at the scholarly level among historians) a movement away from the notion that history is a science and back towards the notion that history is an art. To be entirely accurate, in fact – and drawing in our comments above on science itself – we should put it in the following way. The idea that history is a science in the nineteenth-century sense – already questioned by some in the nineteenth and early twentieth centuries for reasons unrelated to what was happening in the philosophy of science – has come under increasing pressure as the nature of science itself has further been clarified. As one recent book puts the matter:

> In the nineteenth-century sense, there is no scientific history, nor is there even scientific science.[11]

An earlier author had already written:

> Even the most casual reader of the *American Historical Review* ... realizes that the scientific historian with his definitive picture of what really happened is an extinct breed.[12]

The hope of notable nineteenth-century historians and their successors that by embracing an empirical and critical approach to historical knowledge they might achieve a purely objective reconstruction of the past, whether in the Rankean or the positivist manner, has thus turned out to be an impossible dream. To the extent that historians have believed that this is what they have achieved, indeed, it is now clear with the benefit of hindsight that they have been sadly self-deluded. Even while embracing Newtonian science in place of philosophy as the foundational method for human endeavor, and setting their hearts on discovering 'the way it really was' rather than accepting traditional accounts of the way things were, they have been entirely unable to escape the influence of philosophy and tradition when articulating their own vision of the past. They have each possessed their own presuppositions about the nature of reality in general and of historical reality in particular – their own story about

---

[11] Appleby, Hunt and Jacob, *Telling the Truth*, 194.
[12] Watkins Smith, *Carl Becker*, 103.

the world of the past, present and future. Although not deriving this story from historical research itself, they have nevertheless brought it to bear on the 'facts' of the past in an attempt coherently to explain them. In establishing what these 'facts' are, moreover, they have been dependent to a greater or lesser extent upon the stories of other people about the past, since they have themselves lacked any independent access to the events of the past and have been unable to 'reproduce' them in experiments. That is, they have been unable to proceed as natural scientists are often able to do when attempting to verify for themselves that certain claims about reality are true. Philosophy and tradition in fact underlie all historiography of the nineteenth-century scientific kind, no matter what may be the rhetoric to the contrary. It is important to grasp that this is not simply because of some deficiency in practice rather than in theory. It is, rather, *inevitably* the case. Philosophy and tradition necessarily set the parameters for all thinking about the world with which human beings engage.

Testimony, Tradition and the Past

To this collapse of the nineteenth-century historiographical model there are three possible responses. The first is the response of the intellectual ostrich: to place one's head firmly in the sand and to deny reality. It is tempting to describe much recent writing on the history of Israel as ostrich-like in this way, in that it steadfastly continues, on the whole, to regard scientific history either in the Rankean manner, or more recently in the positivist manner, as the only proper kind of academic history. Ostriches are at least aware of the reality that they deny, however; and there is some evidence that many historians of Israel have simply been *unaware* of the wider developments in science and history that we have been describing to this point. These kinds of developments have not in fact impinged *generally* on the world that is inhabited intellectually by scholars in various disciplines, who continue to cling to the popular mechanistic and reductionist outlook on the world engendered by the successes of early modern science. Perhaps it is only when the blessings of modern science, and its offspring modern technology, are more widely perceived as mixed, that attachment to this world-view will diminish. Be that as it may, the ostrich approach is not one that will appeal to those genuinely interested in what is true.

The second response we may characterize as postmodern. Convinced that scientific history is impossible – and, further, that the great stories about reality which have been depended upon to make sense of historical reality[13] are

---

[13] These 'great stories' are commonly referred to as 'metanarratives' – overarching accounts of reality that claim to make sense of it and to allow coherent explanation of its various aspects (e.g., the idea of history as humankind's upward progress).

simply creations of the human mind – postmodernists are apt simply to deny
either the *existence* of a given past or at least any *access* on our part to the past.
History writing as such is, therefore, impossible. This postmodern response to
'modernist' scientific history represents an extreme reaction to it, over-
emphasizing the subjectivity of historiography just as much as modernism
overemphasized its objectivity.[14] It is a response that flies in the face of common
sense just as much as did the theses of those philosophers in the earlier part of the
twentieth century who adopted a skeptical stance in respect of external reality,
whether historical or present reality. We cannot but believe that there has
been a past, even if we cannot justify our belief and even if we now know that
speaking about it is a somewhat more complex business than hitherto suspected.
We know that we may partially *construct* reality that is external to us, whether
present or past; but we also know that reality is 'out there' and independent of
us. It is a human necessity, indeed, to speak about the past as a reality that is
external to us. A postmodernist view of history is thus a view that cannot
ultimately be held with intellectual and moral integrity. It is the last, desperate
refuge of those who have come to see the impossibility of modernist scientific
history, but who cannot bring themselves to accept the true implications of
their discovery.

The third possible response to the collapse of the nineteenth-century
scientific historiographical model, which is the response offered here,
embraces these same implications in preference to avoiding them. I interpret
the crisis with regard to the scientific model of historiography – and indeed the
self-defeating postmodernist response to this crisis – as an invitation to revisit
some fundamental questions about epistemology. I agree with postmodern
analyses that claim that the nineteenth-century perception of progress in historiography was, to a large extent, self-delusion. The modernist suggestion that
all previous historiography was fatally flawed because it had not been produced
by those who possessed proper scientific methods but was produced, rather, by
those in thrall to philosophy and tradition – a suggestion made by historians
who were and are themselves just as bound by philosophy and tradition –
cannot be taken seriously. It is merely rhetoric in pursuit of the validation of
one's own particular view of the past. Yet the proper response to this fact is not

---

[14] However, the postmodern response to modernity is in this respect, as in others, not a
new phenomenon. Skepticism about the acquisition of objective knowledge in the
modern world is as old as the Pyrrhonism of the seventeenth century, and is to be
found among thinkers throughout the succeeding centuries. Among those skeptical
of our human ability to gain objective *historical* knowledge per se may be numbered
T. Lessing, who opposed the idea that history was a science with the notion that it
was a creative act that gave meaning to meaningless life: all historiography is myth
created by those who wish to engender faith and hope in the future.

subjectivism. It is no rational rejoinder to the failure of modern historiography to construct a past that is independent of philosophy and tradition, that we should claim that *nothing that is not already in our heads can be known about the past*. A more coherent response – rather than offering facile statements that simplistically oppose philosophy and tradition to 'scientific method' as routes to historical knowledge – is to seek to articulate a view of the historiographical task that gives a proper place to philosophy and tradition. This inevitably involves questioning the rationality of the principled suspicion of tradition, and ultimately (if not initially) of philosophy, that lies at the heart of Enlightenment thought about the past. Thus it is that we return to our opening comments on the nature of our 'knowledge' of the past.

Testimony and knowledge

In seeking to capture more accurately than 'scientific historians' the reality of the process by which we gain knowledge of the past, I set testimony at the heart of the enterprise. There is the testimony of people(s) from the past about their own past, communicated in oral and written forms. There is the testimony of people(s) from the past about the past of other peoples, also communicated in oral and written forms. There is also the testimony of figures from the *present* about the past, whether the past of their own peoples or of others – contemporary figures like archaeologists, who make certain claims about what they have found and what it means in respect of what has previously taken place. It is *testimony* that gives us access to the past, to the extent that anything does. There is no way of writing historiography that does not involve such testimony. Even if I am the very person who digs up an artifact from the Palestinian soil, I am still entirely dependent upon the testimony of others who have gone before me when I try to make sense of its significance – when I try to decide how I shall add my testimony to theirs.

Testimony – we might also refer to it as 'storytelling' – is central to our quest to know the past; and therefore *interpretation* is unavoidable as well. All testimony about the past is also interpretation of the past. It has its ideology or theology; it has its presuppositions and its point of view; it has its narrative structure; and (if at all interesting to read or listen to) it has its narrative art, its rhetoric. We cannot avoid testimony, and we cannot avoid interpretation. We also cannot avoid faith. I employed the language of 'knowledge' towards the beginning of this chapter: how do we know what we claim to know about the past? In truth, however, this is a concession to the view of what historians are doing from which I wish to distance myself. What is commonly referred to as *knowledge of the past* is more accurately described as *faith in the testimony*, in the interpretations of the past, offered by others. We consider the gathered testimonies at our disposal; we reflect on the various interpretations offered;

and we decide in various ways and to various extents to invest faith in these – to make these testimonies and interpretations our own. If our faith is very strong, or we are simply not conscious of what we are in fact doing, then we tend to call our faith 'knowledge'; but this is a dangerous term to use, since it too easily leads us into self-delusion, or deludes others who listen to us or read what we write, as to the truth of the matter. It is this delusion that seems to lie at the heart of the problem with much of our modern writing on the history of Israel. In particular, it is this delusion (among other things) that has led many historians of Israel, in common with many of their colleagues elsewhere in the discipline of history, to make the false move of sharply differentiating in principle between dependence upon tradition and dependence upon 'scientifically established' facts.

In setting testimony at the heart of the epistemological enterprise, I consciously take my stand against an intellectual tradition, reaching at least as far back as Plato and certainly underlying the scientific view of the world that we have been discussing, which marginalizes testimony as a source of knowledge about reality in favor of such things as perception. I propose, rather, that reliance on testimony is fundamental to knowing about reality in general – *as fundamental* as perception, memory, inference and so on. We depend upon it extensively, not only in everyday life (e.g., when as tourists we rely on a map to guide us around a foreign city), but also in areas like legal process or scientific endeavor (as when psychologists rely on the testimony of subjects about their perception of reality; or scientists more generally rely on the testimony of colleagues about their research results). We are, in short, intellectually reliant upon what others tell us when it comes to what we call knowledge. This is simply the fact of the matter, whether we like it or not and however much we are aware that the testimony of others may sometimes be untrustworthy. It has admittedly not been readily *perceived* as the fact of the matter since the Enlightenment, which requires some explanation. An explanation lies readily at hand, however, in the dominance of individualist ideology in the modern period – an ideology articulated by Descartes himself, with his emphasis on the centrality of the individual as the knowing subject, dependent upon reason alone rather than upon the knowledge provided by such things as education. It is this individualist ideology that has so often prevented modern thinkers from describing accurately how it is that they acquire knowledge, even as they are plainly doing so in dependence upon others (including their educators).

In the same way that reliance on testimony is fundamental to knowing about reality in general, so it is also fundamental to knowing about historical reality in particular. We depend here primarily on the testimony of those who actually lived in the past. As R.G. Collingwood once put it (albeit only to take issue with the statement), 'history is … the believing of someone else when he says that he remembers something. The believer is the historian; the person believed is called his authority'.[15] Collingwood himself stands firmly in the tradition of scientific (though not positivist) history, setting his face against both ancient/mediaeval and seventeenth-/eighteenth-century historiography precisely because the earlier historians were so thoroughly dependent on testimony – even if they exercised some judgement in selecting, editing and sometimes rejecting material – and thus were not properly scientific historians. In this view, proper (i.e., scientific) history does not depend on testimony at all. In fact, to depend on testimony is to give up one's intellectual autonomy as a scientist – to give up 'the condition of being one's own authority, making statements or taking action on one's own initiative and not because those statements or actions are authorized or prescribed by anyone else'.[16]

One could hardly ask for a better example of self-deluding individualism than this. Collingwood clearly thinks, at least in one part of his mind, that history 'as a science' requires that the historian as an individual must somehow do everything for himself, including fashioning the 'data' to be incorporated into his historical account. The consequence of this must inevitably be (if his position is taken seriously) that the 'scientific' historian will not write history, but rather a fantasy spun out of his own theorizing imagination. Since Collingwood aspires to write history, however, he is constantly to be found retreating from his theoretical position on testimony and depending upon it to provide the basic material for his own imaginative reenactments of the past. It could not be otherwise, even in the case of a historian who seems to wish that it could be. History, it turns out, is indeed, *fundamentally*, 'the believing of someone else when that person says that he remembers something'; or to put it more accurately, it is the openness to acceptance of accounts from the past that enshrine such people's memories.

It is, of course, true that the past has left traces of itself besides such testimony, most notably those that can be examined by the archaeologist: coins, pots, the remains of dwellings and the like. In the modern period of historiography it has sometimes been assumed (by those bewitched by the prestige of the sciences and anxious to ground historical statements in something more solid than testimony) that such archaeological remains offer us the prospect of independent access to the past. Here, after all, are data that are directly observable and upon which scientific testing can be carried out, akin to the data available to the natural scientists.

Yet I maintain, in my description of the acquisition of historical knowledge, that the assumption is false. Archaeological remains (when this phrase is taken to exclude written testimony from the past) are of themselves mute. They do not speak for themselves: they have no story to tell, and no truth to

---

[15] Collingwood, *Idea*, 234–35.
[16] Collingwood, *Idea*, 234–35.

communicate. It is archaeologists who speak about them, testifying to what it is that they have found and placing the finds within an interpretive framework that bestows upon them meaning and significance. This interpretative frame-work is certainly not entirely, or even mainly, derived from the finds them-selves, which are mere fragments of the past that must somehow be organized into a coherent whole. The framework is, in fact, derived largely from testi-mony – whether it is the testimony of people from the distant past who have written about the past, or the testimony of other more recent inquirers into that past who have gone before and were themselves dependent upon testimony from the distant past. It is this testimony that enables the archaeologist even to begin to *think* about intelligent excavation. It is this testimony that helps him to choose where to survey or dig; that gives him his sense of the general shape of the history he might expect to find in any given place; that enables him tenta-tively to suggest the allocation of such destruction levels as he finds to specific events he already knows about; and that permits him to correlate material finds with certain named peoples of the past. The 'filling out' of the picture of the world that is thus produced is itself much more general than specific. For literary remains are much more useful where specific historical issues are to the fore; non-literary artifactual remains are most useful to the person interested in general material culture and everyday life.

The whole business of correlating archaeological finds with the specifics of the past as described by texts is, in fact, fraught with difficulty. Interpretation inevitably abounds as to what has been in fact found. Is this destruction layer to be associated with this or that military campaign? Is this site in fact the site of the city mentioned in that particular text?[17] Leaving aside specific sites, the data collected even in large-scale regional surveys represent a highly selective sampling at best, and they are open to a range of interpretations. Interpretation also abounds as to what has *not* been found. The absence of evidence on the ground for events described by a text cannot necessarily be interpreted as evi-dence of the absence of those events, even if a site has been correctly identified. The archaeologist interprets data in the context of testimony, adding his own suggestions about what he has discovered to the mix – his own nuance to the story of the past that is history. As one author has put this so well:

> Data derived from archaeological artifacts exist only in linguistic form. Being elements of a linguistic structure, however, they are subject to interpretation as well. The description of archaeological findings is already interpretation and it is subject, like any other literary form of expression, to the singular choice of the narrative

---

[17] The correlation of sites on the ground with places mentioned in texts is by no means as straightforward as it is sometimes made to appear by those who are keen to 'prove' or 'disprove' the truthfulness of texts.

procedure, to the concept of explanation, as well as to the value-orientation of the descriptive archaeologist.[18]

There is no 'objective knowledge' here, independent of testimony about the past. As one author has rightly said, 'archaeology, dealing with the wreckage of antiquity, proves nothing in itself'.[19] Making sense of the fragmentary traces of the past is only possible, rather, when testimony about the past has already been embraced; and in fact, suggestions about this 'sense' only confront the majority of us, who did not witness the archaeological discoveries and were not involved in the process of interpretation, as testimony. Whatever the value of archaeology, then, in filling out our picture of the past, we repeat: history is *fundamentally* openness to acceptance of accounts from the past that enshrine other people's memories.

It is naturally the case, as we have already noted, that as a matter of fact the testimony of others may sometimes be untrustworthy. Maps may mislead; subjects may fail to tell the truth to psychologists; scientists (including archaeologists) may fake their research results or simply produce poor interpretations of the data; witnesses at a trial may commit perjury; and the bearers of tradition may distort the past, whether by accident or design. It is clear, then, that among the tools that individuals bring to the task of comprehending reality, critical thinking must be among the foremost. I am by no means advocating, in insisting on the inevitability of our reliance on testimony, a *blind faith* in testimony, whether it concerns present or past reality. Given the mixed nature of testimony, this would be a far from rational approach to it. Some *kind* of autonomy in respect of testimony, of the sort after which Collingwood is grasping, is clearly necessary if the individual is to have any possibility of differentiating falsehood from truth. Yet just as autonomous agency in normal adult life does not necessitate the renunciation of dependence on others, so autonomous *thinking* is entirely compatible with fundamental reliance on the word of others as a path to knowledge. We need only conceive of critical thought, not as the enterprise of working everything out for ourselves from first principles, but as the open-minded but deliberate exercise of controlling intelligence over the testimony that we receive, so that such judgements as we feel able to make about its truth or falsehood are indeed made. Neither blind faith in testimony, nor radical suspicion in response to it, is necessary. We require merely what I would characterize as 'epistemological openness'.

It is this approach to testimony that is characteristically adopted by most of us in regard to everyday reality. We do not characteristically and as a matter of principle bring suspicion to bear on the testimony of others, demanding of

---

[18]   Schäfer-Lichtenberger, 'Sociological and Biblical Views', 79–80.
[19]   Wright, 'Archaeology', 76.

each and every person that they validate their testimony to us before we accept its veracity. In fact, we generally regard it as a sign of emotional or mental imbalance if people ordinarily inhabit a culture of distrust in testimony at the level of principle, and most of us outside mental institutions do not inhabit such a universe. Suspicion, we know, may sometimes be justified. Yet we recognize that healthy people generally place trust in the testimony of others, reserving suspicion for those who have given grounds for it. In everyday life, then, the exercise of a thoroughgoing 'hermeneutic of suspicion' with regard to testimony is considered no more sensible than the exercise of blind faith in terms of our apprehension of reality in general. Nor should either approach be considered sensible in terms of our apprehension of *past* reality in particular.

In making judgements about testimony in respect of present reality, moreover, we do not characteristically view the adoption of a 'method' as a rational course of action. For example, we do not always (as a matter of 'method') – if we are intelligent, critical people – invest faith in eyewitnesses as opposed to those people who testify to us secondarily, nor vice versa. More generally: if we characteristically believe the testimony of one sort of person rather than another – for example, if we are Caucasians and consistently accept 'insider' accounts of reality offered by Caucasians over against 'outsider' accounts such as those offered by Asians – then we are considered not intelligent, but prejudiced. Reality, we recognize, is more complex than is allowed for by method. We do not, therefore – if we are intelligent, critical people – allow method overly to influence us in seeking to apprehend reality.

It is strange, therefore, why it should be so commonly believed that 'scientific method' can in some way help us to distinguish between testimonies about the past in terms of their likely truthfulness. The idea goes at least as far back as Ranke himself, who proposed that texts produced in the course of events as they were happening are more worthy of the historian's attention than those texts which were produced afterwards. Priority is thus to be given in scientific historiography to what are called primary sources, over against secondary and later sources. There is, however, no good reason to assume in advance that so-called 'primary' sources are going to be more reliable than any others. The assumption has quite a bit to do with the naïve belief that eyewitnesses 'tell it like it is', while others inevitably filter reality through various distorting screens. As in art, however, so it is in history: close proximity to subject and canvas by no means guarantees a more 'accurate' portrait (since the painter sometimes gets lost among the proverbial trees, and loses sight of the overall shape of the forest). On the one hand eyewitnesses, like everyone else, have a point of view, and in the process of testifying they must inevitably simplify, select and interpret. On the other hand, those who secondarily pass testimony along, whether oral or written, may do this not only accurately but also intelligently and with a better sense than the eyewitness of the way in which a particular testimony fits the larger picture.[20] We must exercise our judgement on a case-by-case basis. Method will not help us, whether in the Rankean mold or – more absurdly – the mold of those who have brought mathematical probability theory to bear on testimony in an attempt to attain greater scientific certainty as to its truthfulness.[21]

The history of historiography reconsidered

Testimony ('storytelling') is central to our quest to know the past. In fact, all historiography is story – whether it is ancient, mediaeval or modern. It is ideological narrative about the past that involves, among other things, the selection of material and its interpretation by authors who are intent on persuading themselves or their readership of certain truths about the past. This selection and interpretation is always made by people with a particular perspective on the world – a particular set of presuppositions and beliefs which do not derive from the facts of history with which they are working, but are already in existence before the narration begins. All historiography is like this, whether we are thinking of the ancient Greek Thucydides or the mediaeval English Bede; or of the modern Gibbon, Macaulay, Michelet or Marx;[22] or indeed of T.L. Thompson, with whom we began this chapter. All knowledge of the past is in fact more accurately described as faith in the interpretations of the past offered by others, through which we make these interpretations (in part or as a whole) our own. 'Acts of faith' do not simply have to be made at the level of our presuppositions about history – whether history is chaotic, cyclical or moving in a linear way towards a designated end; whether or not history can be explained in terms of simple cause-and-effect relationships; and so on. They are intrinsic to the very process of coming to 'know' *particular* things about the past as well.

This is just the way things are, I claim, as a matter of fact and regardless of the attempts of rhetoricians to persuade us otherwise; and this claim brings us

---

[20] Ackroyd, 'Historians and Prophets', 21.

[21] The approach is discussed in Coady, *Testimony*, 199–223. This excellent philosophical study of the dependence of human knowledge on testimony undergirds the present chapter in numerous ways, and repays careful study. Shils, *Tradition*, is another general study worthy of note in this context.

[22] These and other historians are discussed entertainingly and illuminatingly by Clive, *Not By Fact Alone*. Clive is himself a historian who understands very clearly the extent to which written history is 'knowledge of the past filtered through mind and art' (cf. his Preface). Rigney, *Rhetoric*, further compares and contrasts Michelet with both Lamartine and Blanc. Each of these wrote histories some sixty years after the French Revolution which they describe; each of them deployed his own particular discursive and narrative strategies to represent and give meaning to events; and each of them revealed, in so doing, his particular ideology.

to the conclusion of this section and to the end of our review of the history of historiography in general. For the rhetoricians whom we mainly have in mind are those same scientific historians of the nineteenth and twentieth centuries with whom we are taking issue in this essay, and who have sought to persuade the rest of us to adopt a view of reality that is, upon inspection, deeply implausible. In their world, the history of historiography is one of progress from darkness into light. The Greeks laid the foundations of science and history and kindled the torch of intellectual freedom, but the on-ward march of humankind towards truth was halted in mediaeval times by barbarism and religion. The Renaissance rekindled the torch, which became a blazing beacon in the nineteenth century when scientific historiography was born, providing us with the method that for the first time enabled us to speak the truth about the past.

It is a stirring narrative, but it has little relationship to the truth. No gener-alized distinction of this kind between the historiography that precedes the nineteenth century and the historiography since that time can plausibly be defended. This is not just because modern historians, like their precursors, in fact depend on testimony, interpret the past and possess just as much faith as their precursors, whether religious or not. It is also because ancient, mediaeval and post-Reformation historians as a group were no less concerned than their modern counterparts with differentiating historical truth from falsehood, as even a passing acquaintance with their work demonstrates.[23] Critical thought did not begin in the nineteenth century, but was to be found throughout the preceding centuries happily coexisting with faith about the nature of the world (religious and otherwise) and in the midst of much that was truly barbaric. It has continued to coexist since the nineteenth century and down to the present with all kinds of faith about the nature of the world (religious and otherwise) and in the midst of even greater barbarism. Critical thought was not always found in the earlier periods of historiography, certainly; but then, it has not always been found in the modern period either, even (and perhaps especially) among many of those who have claimed to employ it. The claim to be a critical thinker is easy to make; but the reality that lurks beneath it has all too often proved to be only a mixture of blind faith in relation to the writer's own intellectual tradition and arbitrary, selective skepticism in relation to everything else.

---

[23] On the contrary, we encounter a real concern for accuracy and truthfulness, whether we read ancient authors like Tacitus (*Annals* 1.1), Cicero (*De Oratore*, 2.36, 62), or the biblical writer Luke (Lk. 1:1–4); early mediaeval authors like Wipo or John of Salisbury (see Breisach, *Historiography*, 124–125, 144), or any number of historians from the thirteenth century through to the eighteenth century. It is modern prejudice rather than acquaintance with the past that characterizes the past as otherwise.

Knowing about the History of Israel

It is, unsurprisingly, scientific history that has dominated the scene in the past two hundred years of the study of the history of Israel. Historians of Israel, no less than other historians, have felt the pressure to conform their work to the scientific model. They have progressively done so, abandoning biblical testimony in favor of the 'knowledge' that scientific inquiry produces, until we have arrived at claims like Thompson's: 'There is no more "ancient Israel" … This we do know.'[24] It is clear that many scholars who work with the Old Testament and are interested in the history of Israel are deeply uneasy about this kind of radical claim and would like to avoid having to agree with it. It is not so clear that they can do so with any logical consistency, however. For they have often and in large measure already embraced a Thompson-like approach to the relative worth of testimony and empirical inquiry in general. They therefore already feel the need to justify the acceptance, rather than justify the rejection, of biblical testimony in particular. Modern biblical study was indeed forged in the fires of the nineteenth-century scientific world-view. That is why the Enlightenment myth of progress – ever-onwards-and-upwards until truth and goodness are attained – so often finds expression in its writings. It is unsurprising, therefore, that we find among modern historians of Israel – just as much as in the case of modern historians generally – both the tendency to exalt the modern period as that blissful time in which we discovered, in Rankean terms, 'how it really was', and the concomitant disparagement of the 'pre-critical' era (i.e., the entirety of human history before the nineteenth century) as that benighted time in which the whole truth about the past could not be, and was not, laid bare.

What is perhaps at first sight a little more surprising, and requires some explanation, is the fact that such a nineteenth-century view of the historiographical task should still, at the beginning of the twenty-first century, be so widely held among biblical scholars in general and historians of Israel in particular. Indeed, we must face the remarkable fact that for most of the twentieth century, the discipline 'history of Israel' proceeded in apparent blithe ignorance of the furious debate about the nature of history that was raging among historians more generally, so that the nineteenth-century scientific model should still be widely seen at present as the only viable scholarly model that exists and, as such, to require no justification. It is only in such a closeted environment that most of the recent debate about the history of Israel could have taken the shape that it has, as a rerun of already decades-old disputes

---

[24] Theologians, at the same time, have conceded that 'real' history resides elsewhere than in biblical testimony, while basing their theology on the testimony (note, e.g., von Rad's concession to positivism in his *Old Testament Theology*, I, 105–128).

between Rankean and positivist empiricists in which the participants have appeared generally unaware both of these earlier disputes and of the wider issues raised by them. It is only in such an environment that T.L. Thompson, without any evident sense of embarrassment or compulsion to justify his position with respect to epistemology (among other things), could make claim to knowledge of the past such that we also 'know' that Israel's testimony about its own past is fiction.

Only a serious lack of interdisciplinary and integrative thinking could possibly have produced such a state of affairs. Since the origins of modern biblical studies lie not just in the nineteenth century generally, however, but specifically in a reaction against integrative thought of a philosophical or theological kind – in favor of attention to the biblical text in itself – it is perhaps not unexpected that this closeted environment should have arisen. Narrow specialist training, and the need to demonstrate specialism and love of detail in order to advance in the profession, leave many modern biblical scholars ill-prepared for anything other than occasional raids on the territory of other disciplines in order to find some new 'angle' on biblical studies that will enable them to make a distinctive contribution to their field. The intellectual booty that is brought back from such raids is all too often not well understood in relation to the intellectual context from which it was stolen. The consequence is a discipline that is highly, if inaccurately, derivative of other disciplines, and more often than not dependent on ideas taken from these other disciplines that are already at least several decades out of date in terms of their popularity and general plausibility. It is perhaps for these general reasons that the history of the history of Israel in the past twenty years has seen the widespread and enthusiastic adoption of a positivist approach to history without any great awareness of the problems to which this approach gives rise or of the debate that it has previously engendered among historians, philosophers and theologians alike. In the 'Lost Valley' of biblical studies, it seems, the scientific historian with his definitive picture of what really happened is far from an extinct breed.

Be that as it may, our philosophical and historical reflections to this point allow us to take a very different view from Thompson's as to what is 'known' about the history of Israel. The knowledge that he professes is readily seen, in fact, merely as faith in disguise. What Thompson 'knows', he 'knows' because he has decided to invest faith in certain testimonies about the past rather than others, the most notable of the 'others' being the testimony of the Old Testament. He has, in essence, privileged nonbiblical testimony epistemologically. He is open to receive testimony about Israel's past predominantly or entirely from nonbiblical sources, and he generally exercises a high level of trust in these sources. He is predominantly or entirely closed to testimony from the Bible itself about Israel's past, generally exercising a high level of distrust in these sources. The question arises as to which defensible grounds could possibly be advanced for such a stance.

This is a question to be answered by other historians of Israel than Thompson; for he only makes explicit statement of the kind of position that has commonly and implicitly been adopted by others. It has in fact been a *common* feature of the discourse of biblical studies that knowledge of Israel's past has been assumed to have been accumulated in various ways which can then be used as a yardstick against which to measure biblical testimony and come to some judgement upon it – or indeed as a basis upon which to build a 'scientific' history in complete *independence* of biblical testimony. Aside from archaeology, the most common source of such 'knowledge' has been extrabiblical texts. Egyptian, Assyrian and Babylonian texts, in particular, are often regarded as providing us with not only a reliable, overarching chronological framework for ancient Near Eastern history, but also with a basic narrative about that past in relation to which any testimony from the Old Testament must be assessed. These are some of the main resources to which we can turn if we wish to 'verify' particular Old Testament claims because (it is claimed or implied) they do not share the deficiencies of Old Testament narrative when it comes to the ideological, and particularly the religious, aspect. They grant us access to 'how it really was'.

Two examples of this kind of thinking will suffice. In the course of recent reflections on history writing, L.L. Grabbe compares the Old Testament and other ancient Near Eastern (largely Assyrian) texts with regard to their testimony about the later Israelite monarchy.[25] It is clear from the discussion that he assumes that the ancient Near Eastern texts simply describe for us the facts of the matter. He is therefore able to use these texts to assess the Old Testament material; and he proceeds to conclude that the Bible is 'reasonably accurate about the framework' of events, but that the details are at times 'demonstrably misleading or wholly inaccurate and perhaps even completely invented'. In the same volume, H. Niehr insists that a clear distinction between primary and secondary sources for the history of Israel must be upheld, on the ground that the primary sources 'did not undergo the censorship exercised by, for example, the Deuteronomistic theologians nor were they submitted to the process of canonization'. The Assyrian sources are among the primary sources. Their historical reliability, Niehr asserts, has recently been shown to be very high.[26]

It is entirely unclear, however, what are the truly defensible grounds for such an epistemological privileging of extrabiblical texts; for these texts certainly do *not* provide us with immediate access to 'the way it was' – not even to 'the way it was' for the peoples who produced them, much less for the

[25] Grabbe, 'Historians', 24–26.

[26] Niehr, 'Some Aspects', 157–58.

Israelites. The reality is that we possess only limited insight into the history of these other peoples, and not simply because of historical accident. It is well known, on the contrary, that their literature is no less selective and ideologically loaded than the Old Testament in the way that it presents the past. We may take the Assyrian texts as our primary example.[27]

It is undeniable that the various inscriptions and chronicles deriving from Assyria from the ninth century BC onwards – specifically from the reign of Shalmaneser III (858–824 BC) onwards – are important external sources for any history of Israel. Shalmaneser and many of his successors campaigned in, and eventually in the eighth century BC came to dominate, the entire region between the Euphrates and Egypt. Writings originating during their reigns are therefore often important in setting a broader context within which the biblical narratives can be read.[28]

The first thing to be noted about these records, however, is that they are uneven, particularly where they touch upon the activities of Assyrian kings on their western border – and Israel was situated, of course, to Assyria's west. The written sources for the reign of Shalmaneser III himself are abundant; but the same cannot be said for his successors Shamshi-Adad V (823–811 BC), Adad-nirari III (810–783 BC), Shalmaneser IV (782–773 BC), Ashur-dan III (772–755 BC) and Ashur-nirari V (754–745 BC). The situation markedly improves when we reach the reign of Tiglath-pileser III (744–727 BC) and on through the succeeding reigns down to Ashurbanipal (668– c. 630 BC). Here the sources are in general numerous and helpful, although there are notable exceptions: we know virtually nothing, for example, about the reign of Shalmaneser V (726–722 BC). Some of these sources, however – even where they are extant – are not in wonderful condition; substantial portions of the annals of Tiglath-pileser III, for example, have come down to us in poor condition, while for Esarhaddon (680–669 BC) we possess only fragments of the annals. All of this presents certain challenges even to those who are intent on writing a history of *Assyria*. What is quite clear is that, simply on the ground of *coverage*, the extent to which Assyrian sources can be of help in writing a history of *Israel* should not be overstated. As A. Kuhrt says of the whole Levant:

---

[27] A voluminous bibliography is available which addresses, in some way or another, the selective and highly ideological nature of Assyrian scribal compositions. A good place to begin is with the brief summary discussion in Brettler, *Creation*, 94–97, and the helpful footnote references there; or with Liverani, 'Deeds'. We may note here further only two of the many resources: Fales (ed.), *Assyrian Royal Inscriptions;* and Younger, *Ancient Conquest Accounts*, 61–124. It is the easy availability of such resources that makes so puzzling the manner in which Assyrian texts have been employed in some recent studies of the history of Israel.

[28] The point is well made in respect of ancient Near Eastern texts generally by Millard, 'Story', who proceeds himself to use mainly Assyrian examples.

It is the Assyrian royal sources which provide the richest and, chronologically and historically, most useful information for the states with which they came into contact. But, admittedly, it makes for a very partial picture only.[29]

However, the problem that exists in reconstructing the history of Assyria and adjacent territories, as it provides a context for Israelite history, lies not just in the unevenness of our sources as a matter of historical accident. It lies, secondly, in their very nature. The sources that provide the backbone for the reconstruction derive from the Assyrian royal court; and chief among them are the 'royal annals' just mentioned – personal memorials of individual kings that provide accounts of royal achievements, especially military campaigns. What is their character?[30]

They are, first of all, clearly selective in what they say – it could not be otherwise, since all history writing is selective.[31] For example, although the annals of Sargon II (721–705 BC) mention a campaign against Ashdod around 713 BC, they do not mention in this context the involvement (or possible involvement) of Judah, about which we know from a different source. In this case we are probably to explain the selectivity simply in terms of a lack of Assyrian interest in tiny Judah. More significantly, though, Sargon II's annals claim as his own the conquest of the Israelite capital of Samaria around 722 BC; yet both the Old Testament (2 Kgs. 17:1–6) and the Babylonian Chronicle[32]

---

[29] Kuhrt, *Ancient Near East*, II, 459.

[30] For a brief and good recent discussion of these and other sources for the neo-Assyrian empire, see Kuhrt, *Ancient Near East*, II, 473–478, 501–505, 540–543.

[31] It is not just the Assyrian *annals* that are selective. The same is true of the Assyrian King List, which is influenced by such things as which kings the authors of the list recognized or knew about, or wished to tell others about; as it is true of the *limmu*-chronicle, which lists Assyrian eponyms (officials who gave their names to successive years of the Assyrian calendar) from the middle of the ninth century BC to the end of the eighth, accompanied by a short notice of a particular event that happened in that year. A particular event is of necessity an event that has been selected from among many; and the chronicle does not in fact always identify the *same* significant event as the corresponding annals for a certain year. The brevity of the entries themselves produces certain challenges in interpreting them, not least in terms of deducing where the military campaigns that they often mention might actually have taken place. The correlation of Assyrian textual toponyms with ancient regions or cities is often fraught with difficulty. As Parpola, *Toponyms*, says: 'Especially the location of peoples and countries presents difficulties, for many peoples did not stay permanently in one place ... and the ancients themselves were apparently not always well informed about the exact borders of foreign countries' (xv). We are not dealing here, any more than in any other area of historical endeavor, with an exact science.

[32] The Babylonian Chronicle is an important source for ancient Near Eastern history from 744 BC to 668 BC: a year by year account of political events as they affected the

suggest that the conqueror was Shalmaneser V. This raises at least the possibility that Sargon's scribes were intent on embellishing Sargon's record by giving him a victory as king that was not strictly his. Likewise, Sennacherib's Que and Til-Garimmu campaigns of the first decade of the seventh century BC appear to have been edited out of later versions of that king's annals, perhaps because the king did not himself lead them or perhaps because their outcomes were less than fortunate (the former was a costly victory, and the latter a victory with no apparent long-term gains).[33]

These latter examples in fact fit a much larger pattern which helps us to see that the Assyrian royal annals are selective not merely because their authors were faced with too much material, but also because these authors had particular ends in view. That is, the annals are ideologically loaded. Perhaps the word 'annals' itself has helped to obscure this fact from some of the Old Testament scholars who have interacted with this material in recent years; for 'annals' carries with it the connotation (for the modern reader) of 'objective chronicle'. 'Objective chronicles' do not in reality exist, of course; but if they did, it would be impossible in any case to regard these so-called 'annals' as being of this nature.[34] They are in fact primarily commemorative texts, dedicatory building

---

region of Babylonia, which also provides useful cross-references for the claims of Assyrian texts.

[33] For the relevant texts and some comment, see Luckenbill, *Annals*, 14, 23–47 (esp. the transition from fifth to sixth campaigns on p. 38), 61–63.

[34] Even the *limmu*-chronicle, to which we refer as a *chronicle*, is far from 'objective' in this narrow sense. It presents a *particular* point of view. For example, the chronicle knows of a certain Shamshi-ilu as both eponym for 752 BC and also the holder of the important state and military office of *turtanu* (commander-in-chief). We do not know when he became *turtanu*, although he must have ceased holding this office before 742 BC, when another man is thus named. In any case, that is the chronicle's *perspective* on Shamshi-ilu. The reality was probably a good deal more complex. His own inscriptions from his provincial residence of Til-Barsip describe him as, among other things, 'governor of the land of Hatti' – effectively the Assyrian ruler of the west. His claimed victory over Argishti of Urartu is plausibly identified by many with the Urartian campaigns recorded in the chronicle for the period 781–774 BC, although the list itself would lead us to think of King Shalmaneser IV as the prime mover. The Pazarcik Stela suggests that it is in fact Shamshi-ilu's campaign against Damascus that appears in the chronicle for 773 BC. Here is an important 'semi-royal' figure, then; and the case of Shamshi-ilu is not the only example of apparently differing perspectives in our Assyrian records of this kind. We may note also, e.g., Nergal-erish (eponym for 803 and 775), who was governor of Rasappa according to the chronicle, but ruler of much else besides according to various inscriptions, and who took a prominent role in various western campaigns. Such examples raise interesting questions about the precise relationship between what is claimed in our various *texts* about the wielders of power in the Assyrian Empire at any given point and the

inscriptions, originally written as pious reports by the ruler to a god and with an eye to inspiring the admiration of the future peoples who would read them. This purpose must always be taken into account in assessing what they have to say. Assyrian kings regarded themselves as viceroys of the gods on earth. The tasks of the kings (i.e., those tasks which were worth recording) were to rule their subjects, extend their sway to the furthest ends of the earth and, in return for the power and victories given to them by the gods, to build temples and maintain their worship practices. Assyrians recorded such things on memorial tablets, prisms and cylinders of clay or alabaster, on obelisks and stelae, and on the walls of palaces and temples. The annals in particular were commonly reedited many times during a reign; most texts now extant are the products of considerable redaction, selecting and conflating of various sources by scribes intent on finding the best way to laud their ruler. Each fresh edition could involve not only the updating of the king's record, but also a significant re-shaping of the whole account. It cannot be assumed under these circumstances that an accurate portrayal of events was always the principal or guiding motive of the royal scribes. Moreover, we certainly cannot expect these inscriptions to be 'objective', even where we may be reasonably sure that they were intended to be accurate. On the contrary, they are works of literary art with a political and religious focus. As such, their detailed accounts of the conquests of states are stylized and repetitive and their claims about royal dominion are often hyperbolic and biased. It is not that they lack factual content, nor that they necessarily engage in outright falsehood as a matter of habit. Nevertheless, in pursuit of the glorification of the king, failures are omitted, successes empha-sized and the whole account artistically slanted to the point that a careless reader who did not understand their genre and style could be seriously misled about the historical reality to which they seek to refer.[35] As A. Kuhrt puts it:

---

realities of power on the ground. We are reminded of the inevitable reality that even 'chronicles' always describe the past selectively and from a particular point of view, with the intention to persuade the reader of some truth. As Kuhrt says of Shamshi-ilu in particular (*Ancient Near East*, II, 493): 'In the Assyrian perspective, he and his predecessors were provincial governors, servants of the Assyrian king; but within their area of authority and in relation to neighbours they could present themselves ... as local dynasts.'

[35] For example, the uninitiated reader of the version of Sennacherib's annals that appears on the Oriental Institute Prism Inscription might imagine that (s)he had found there a straightforward record of Sennacherib's eight military campaigns. Yet we know of other campaigns not recorded there, and it is questionable whether the 'eight' campaigns of which we read were in fact of similar nature and importance. In Luckenbill's view (*Annals*, 14; see further above) the Que campaign, which was omitted, was a far more serious military undertaking than the so-called 'fifth' cam-paign of 699 BC that preceded it and which was merely a raid carried out on some

considerations such as factual truthfulness, balanced assessments, historical precision and objectivity were bound to play a less important role in inscriptions of this nature than an emphasis on spectacular exploits, success rather than failure, and the king's personal role in these achievements: the king as centre of all action. What was presented was the truth according to Assyrian ideology ...[36]

Assyrian royal scribes were, in fact, more concerned about the *image* of the king and his activity as a warrior than they were about merely recording the facts of his reign. This was the case whether they were composing 'annals' or 'display inscriptions' for the palace walls. The artists who produced the narrative reliefs with which Assyrian kings decorated their royal palaces shared the same objectives. They too focused on war, victory and building, presenting their monarch as master of all aspects of life (albeit with direct help from the gods).

It can readily be seen, then, just how impossible it is to regard our Assyrian sources as granting us all but unmediated access to the naked facts of history, in the light of which we may then make judgements on the accuracy or otherwise of our 'selective and ideologically loaded' Old Testament texts. There are, in fact, no grounds for granting the Assyrian sources any epistemological primacy in principle in our striving for knowledge about Israel's past. The shaky ground upon which we stand when we do this is evidenced by well-known examples from the past, such as the case of Sargon II's claim to have conquered Samaria. It was commonly thought in earlier times, when scholars only possessed Sargon's annals and the Bible, that Sargon was simply 'telling us how it was', and that 2 Kings 17 was simply wrong. The Babylonian Chronicle has now provided further food for thought on this point. Ancient history is vast and complex, and all of our meager testimony about it is only capable of providing us with glimpses into this vastness and complexity. It makes no sense at all to absolutize *some* of this testimony as the standard against which *everything else* should be measured. It is particularly strange that such extrabiblical testimony is sometimes said to be preferable to biblical testimony on the grounds of the *religious* nature of the latter, when it is perfectly clear that religion permeates the former as well, not least in the common references within it to divine involvement or intervention in military affairs. Theological intent is just as clear in Sennacherib's inscriptions, for example, as it is in the literature of the Bible.

Having focused on the Assyrian texts, I should make it clear more briefly that the situation is no different with any other of our nonbiblical sources. Egyptian

---

villages because 'royal vanity demanded royal campaigns to be recorded in highsounding phrases on dedicatory cylinders and prisms or on the walls of the steadily growing palace at Nineveh'. For further commentary on Sennacherib's inscriptions, see Laato, 'Assyrian Propaganda'. The movement of the reader from text to historical event plainly requires some caution.

[36] Kuhrt, *Ancient Near East*, II, 475.

pharaohs, for example, also regarded themselves as viceroys of the gods on earth, and their texts unsurprisingly present precisely the same kinds of challenges that we find in the Assyrian texts. In addition, it may be noted in passing that the chronology of ancient history before the tenth century – the period in which historians of Israel are most interested in Egypt, given the centrality of Egypt in Israel's story before the settlement in the land – is far less secure than for the period that follows the tenth century. Chronological issues continue, therefore, to be debated and to cause difficulty in reading Israel's history against the background of the Egyptian texts that are thought relevant to this history.[37] The main point is this, however: that whether we are dealing with Mesopotamian, Egyptian or Hittite texts, or indeed with a more local inscription from one of Israel's near neighbors, such as the Moabite Stone – itself written in stereotypical language and with some degree of hyperbole, at least in its claim that 'Israel has perished forever' – we are only and ever dealing with selective and ideologically-focused texts. All historiography is, in fact, like this. It is written by people possessing both a general *world*-view and a particular *point* of view that they bring to bear on reality, seeking selectively to organize the facts of the past into some coherent pattern and in respect of some particular end.

   Is it at all sensible, in the light of these realities, to privilege nonbiblical over biblical testimony in reflecting on the history of Israel? For it is certainly clear that in the biblical literature we evidently have, among other sorts of texts, testimonies about (interpretations of) Israel's past in narrative form. Indeed, the literature is unique in the ancient world in its interest in the past:

---

[37] The fixed point from which Egyptian chronology is retrojected is the relatively late sacking of Thebes by the Assyrian emperor Ashurbanipal in 664 BC. Since this was also the last year of the rule of Pharaoh Taharka in Thebes, we can then work back from Taharka using Manetho's history of Egypt as it is partially preserved in Josephus, along with the accounts of Herodotus and Diodorus Siculus (a Greek historian living in Sicily who wrote a partial history of Egypt in the first century BC). Adjustments may then be made where possible in reference to archaeological finds (e.g., inscriptional evidence). It can readily be seen how heavily ancient Egyptian chronology, just as much as ancient Israelite history, depends upon testimony, interpretation and faith; and archaeological finds suggest, in fact, that Manetho's dates should not in any case be added together cumulatively to produce a history of Egypt, but that there must have been some coterminous dynasties in Egypt (as in Assyria). The number of such coterminous dynasties is still an uncertain matter. For a good brief discussion of Egyptian chronology, see Kuhrt, *Ancient Near East*, II, 623–26, whose comment on the period of interest to us here (the 'third intermediate period', 1069–664 BC) reminds us of how carefully we must tread as historians of Israel in using Egyptian sources: 'It is quite impossible to write a narrative history [of Egypt in this period], as there are so many gaps' (626).

Alone among Orientals and Greeks, it addresses a people defined in terms of their past and commanded to keep its memory alive ... [a people] more obsessed with history than any other nation that has ever existed ... [who] stand alone among the people of the ancient world in having the story of their beginnings and their primitive state as clear as this in their folk-memory ... Recall how often customs are elucidated, ancient names and current sayings traced back to their origins, monuments and fiats assigned a concrete reason as well as a slot in history, persons and places and pedigrees specified beyond immediate needs, written records like the Book of Yashar or the royal annals explicitly invoked.[38]

To tell us about Israel's past is certainly not the only purpose of these narratives; it is arguably not even their main purpose. Yet so far as can be deduced from the texts themselves, it is clearly one of their purposes. Whether it were one of their purposes or not, they might still succeed in doing it. What sense does it make in our pursuit of knowledge of Israel's past, therefore, to adopt the kind of principled distrust of major sections of, or even the totality of, the Old Testament that is so often evident in the histories of Israel of the past two hundred years? What defensible grounds exist for such a position?

I suggest that there are none; and I have sought elsewhere to demonstrate in more detail that this is so.[39] I shall not unduly extend the length of this discussion by rehearsing the detail here. I move instead towards my conclusion.

Conclusion

... history cannot base itself on predictability ... Lacking universal axioms and theorems, it can be based on testimony only.[40]

This is essentially the case that I have been arguing here – albeit that I disallow any such sharp distinction between inquiry into the *natural* world and inquiry into the world of the *past* as this statement may imply. Our knowledge of the past is dependent on testimony. This being the case, and biblical testimony being the major testimony about Israel's past that we possess, it must be folly to marginalize biblical testimony in any modern attempt to recount the history of Israel. It can be considered perfectly rational to consider that testimony along with other testimonies. It should be considered irrational, however, to give epistemological privilege to these other testimonies, even to the extent of ignoring biblical testimony altogether. It may be that we shall find good reason in considering what the Bible has to say – as in considering what other

---

[38] Sternberg, *Poetics*, 31, depending partially on Butterfield, *Origins*, 80–95.

[39] See esp. my 'Stable'.

[40] Halpern, *First Historians*, 28.

sources have to say – to question in one way or another the extent to which statements are reflective of history at any given point. We should make our judgements on a case-by-case basis, however, rather than prejudging the matter by utilizing faulty methodological criteria that allegedly lead us to 'firm ground' for historiography within or outside of biblical testimony. I juxtapose the above quotation, therefore, with the following, with which I profoundly disagree:

> If we have no positive grounds for thinking that a biblical account is historically useful, we cannot really adopt it as history. True, the result will be that we have less history than we might. But what little we have we can at least claim we know (in whatever sense we 'know' the distant past); this, in my opinion, is better than having more history than we might, much of which we do not know at all, since it consists merely of unverifiable stories.[41]

I disagree, because history *is* the telling and retelling of unverifiable stories. Knowing any history aside from the history in which we are personally involved requires trust in unverified and unverifiable testimony. The kind of historical knowledge beyond tradition and testimony that this author seeks is a mirage. We do not require 'positive grounds' for taking the biblical testimony about Israel's past seriously. We require positive grounds, rather, for *not* doing so. Only by embracing such epistemological openness to testimony, biblical and otherwise, can we avoid remaking the past entirely in our own image – can we avoid submitting to the delusion that we already 'know' about reality and to the consequent mistake of trying to impose that 'knowledge' on everything that questions it. Only thus can the history of the history of Israel hope in the future to be different from what it has been in the past – a slow capitulation to those who have asserted, without good grounds, that the principled suspicion of tradition should be considered the *sine qua non* of the intellectual life. 'Critical history' has all too often meant, in the debate that has surrounded this capitulation, 'history that does not criticize the tradition as much as I, a truly critical historian, would prefer it to'. It has not sufficiently often meant simply 'thoughtful, intelligent history' – history that involves the exercise of critical thought *both* about tradition *and* about modern presuppositions about reality. The fact is that we either respect and appropriate the testimony of the past, allowing it to challenge us even while thinking hard about it; or we are doomed – even while thinking that we alone have 'objectivity' and can start afresh on the historical quest – to create individualistic fantasies about the past out of the desperate poverty of our own very limited experience and imagination. To conclude:

---

[41] Davies, 'History', 105.

the objectivity of modern historiography consists precisely in one's openness for the encounter, one's willingness to place one's intentions and views of existence in question, i.e. to learn something basically new about existence and thus to have one's own existence modified or radically altered.[42]

---

[42] Robinson, *New Quest*, 77. The book provides numerous interesting reflections on historiography and historical method in relation to the New Testament.

Bibliography

Ackroyd, P.R., 'Historians and Prophets', *SEÅ* 33 (1968), 18–54

Appleby, J., L. Hunt and M. Jacob, *Telling the Truth about History* (New York: Norton, 1994)

Ayer, A.J., *Philosophical Essays* (Westport, CT: Greenwood Press, 1980)

Barstad, H.M., 'History and the Hebrew Bible', in *Can a 'History of Israel' Be Written?* (ed. L.L. Grabbe; JSOTSup 245; Sheffield Academic Press: Sheffield, 1997), 37–64

Breisach, E., *Historiography: Ancient, Medieval and Modern* (Chicago: University of Chicago Press, 1983)

Brettler, M.Z., *The Creation of History in Ancient Israel* (London: Routledge, 1995)

Butterfield, H., *The Origins of History* (New York: Basic Books, 1981)

Clive, J., *Not By Fact Alone: Essays on the Writing and Reading of History* (London: Collins Harvill, 1990)

Coady, C.A.J., *Testimony: A Philosophical Study* (Oxford: Clarendon, 1992)

Collingwood, R.G., *The Idea of History* (Oxford: OUP, 1970)

Davies, P.R., 'Whose History? Whose Israel? Whose Bible? Biblical Histories, Ancient and Modern', in *Can a 'History of Israel' Be Written?* (ed. L.L. Grabbe; JSOTSup 245; Sheffield Academic Press: Sheffield, 1997), 104–22

Fales, F.M. (ed.), *Assyrian Royal Inscriptions: New Horizons in Literary, Ideological and Historical Analysis* (Rome: Istituto per l'Oriente, 1981)

Grabbe, L.L., 'Are Historians of Ancient Palestine Fellow Creatures – or Different Animals?', in *Can a 'History of Israel' Be Written?* (ed. L.L. Grabbe; JSOTSup 245; Sheffield Academic Press: Sheffield, 1997), 19–36

Habermas, J., *Knowledge and Human Interests* (trans. J.J. Shapiro; London: Heinemann, 1972)

Halpern, B., *The First Historians: The Hebrew Bible and History* (San Francisco: Harper & Row, 1988)

Hesse, M., *Revolutions and Reconstructions in the Philosophy of Science* (Brighton: Harvester, 1980)

Huizinga, J., *Geschichte und Kultur* (Stuttgart: Kröner, 1954)

Kuhrt, A., *The Ancient Near East c. 3000–330 B.C.* (2 vols.; London: Routledge, 1995)

Laato, A., 'Assyrian Propaganda and the Falsification of History in the Royal Inscriptions of Sennacherib', *VT* 45 (1995), 198–226

Liverani, M., 'The Deeds of Ancient Mesopotamian Kings', in *Civilizations of the Ancient Near East*, IV (ed. J.M. Sasson; 4 vols.; Peabody, MA: Hendrickson, 1995), 2353–66

Luckenbill, D.D., *The Annals of Sennacherib* (The University of Chicago Oriental Institute Publications 2; Chicago: University of Chicago Press, 1924)

Millard, A.R., 'Story, History and Theology', in *Faith, Tradition and History: Old Testament Historiography in its Near Eastern Context* (ed. A.R. Millard, J.K. Hoffmeier and D.W. Baker; Winona Lake, IN: Eisenbrauns, 1994), 37–64

Niehr, H., 'Some Aspects of Working with the Textual Sources', in *Can a 'History of Israel' Be Written?* (ed. L.L. Grabbe; JSOTSup 245; Sheffield Academic Press: Sheffield, 1997), 156–65

Parpola, S., *Neo-Assyrian Toponyms* (AOAT 6; Neukirchen-Vluyn: Neukirchener Verlag, 1970)

Provan, I.W., 'Ideologies, Literary and Critical: Reflections on Recent Writing on the History of Israel', *JBL* 114 (1995), 585–606

——, 'In the Stable with the Dwarves: Testimony, Interpretation, Faith and the History of Israel', in *Congress Volume: Oslo 1998* (ed. A. Lemaire and M. Sæbø; Papers of the 16th Congress of the International Organization for the Study of the Old Testament; Leiden: Brill, 2000), 281–319

Rigney, A., *The Rhetoric of Historical Representation: Three Narrative Histories of the French Revolution* (Cambridge: CUP, 1990)

Robinson, J.M., *A New Quest of the Historical Jesus* (SBT 25; Chicago: Allenson, 1959)

Schäfer-Lichtenberger, C., 'Sociological and Biblical Views of the Early State', in *The Origins of the Ancient Israelite States* (ed. V. Fritz and P.R. Davies; JSOTSup 228; Sheffield: Sheffield Academic Press, 1996), 78–105

Shils, E., *Tradition* (Chicago: University of Chicago Press, 1981)

Smend, R., 'Tradition and History: A Complex Relation', in *Tradition and Theology in the Old Testament* (ed. D.A. Knight; Philadelphia: Fortress, 1977), 49–68

Sternberg, M., *The Poetics of Biblical Narrative: Ideological Literature and the Drama of Reading* (Bloomington: Indiana University Press, 1985)

Thompson, T.L., 'A Neo-Albrightean School in History and Biblical Scholarship?', *JBL* 114 (1995), 683–98

von Rad, G., *Old Testament Theology* (trans. D.M.G. Stalker; 2 vols.; Edinburgh and London: Oliver and Boyd, 1962)

Watkins Smith, C., *Carl Becker: On History and the Climate of Opinion* (Carbondale: Southern Illinois University Press, 1956)

Wright, G.E., 'What Archaeology Can and Cannot Do,' *BA* 34 (1971), 70–76

Younger, Jr., K.L., *Ancient Conquest Accounts: A Study in Ancient Near Eastern and Biblical History Writing* (JSOTSup 98; Sheffield: JSOT, 1990)

12

Creation and Promise

Towards a Theology of History

Murray A. Rae

Introduction

In his Bampton Lectures of 1992, subsequently published under the title *The One, the Three and the Many: God, Creation and the Culture of Modernity*, Colin Gunton contends that one of the characteristics of modernity is disengagement.[1] Disengagement describes the propensity of the modern mind to treat the world instrumentally, 'as a mere means of realising our will and not as in some way integral to our being'. 'Its other side', Gunton further explains, 'is that we do not seek in the world for what is true and good and beautiful, but create our truth and values for ourselves.'[2] Whereas in modernity it was expected that such creativity would, through the exercise of reason, produce consensus among all people,[3] those of postmodern persuasion insist that we accept the relativity of all value and truth. What interests me here, however, is the assumption common to both that truth and value are of our own making and depend not at all on what is given in the world. Whether the appeal is to reason (as in modernity) or to personal experience and intuition (as in postmodernity), the quest for truth and value repudiates tradition[4] and refuses to accord authority to that which has taken place in the past. The

---

[1] Gunton, *The One*, 13–16. Gunton is following here the analysis of Charles Taylor.

[2] Gunton, *The One*, 14.

[3] Witness, for example, Ernst Troeltsch's supposition that 'the essential uniformity of human nature provides a foundation for consensus in recognising supreme standards of value' ('Method', 25).

[4] Gunton, *The One*, 75.

disengagement of which Gunton speaks includes a disengagement from history and, in the realm of theology, means that the modern, as also the postmodern, mind typically resists the Christian proclamation that it is through the particular history of Jesus of Nazareth, and not otherwise, that the Truth[5] is established and made known.

It is the purpose of this chapter first to examine that resistance, second to trace its implications for the way in which we read the Bible and third to offer an alternative account of history in which history is viewed as the space and time given to humankind to be truly itself as the covenant partner of God. Such an account will seek to give due recognition not only to the transcendence of God, but also to his immanence in the history of Jesus of Nazareth and through the work of his Spirit. It will be argued, further, that the very idea of history requires both the biblical doctrine of creation and a teleology – a conviction that life itself is directed towards some purpose. It is only within this framework of creation and divine promise that human action can properly be said to be historic. We begin, however, with a brief account of how, within the Western intellectual tradition,[6] the disengagement from history has been apparent.

Disengagement from History in Western Thought

The disengagement from history in Western thought has two forms, both of which are premised on the conviction that history and divine action are mutually exclusive categories. Both forms involve the belief that it is improper to speak of God's participation in the unfolding nexus of historical life. The first form supposes, therefore, that attention to the contingent realm of history is of little or no value in humanity's quest for truth. Truth, it is thought, belongs to the eternal realm of the divine and is not amenable, therefore, to historical mediation. History, on this view, is not a proper object of knowledge. The second form of incredulity concerning divine action in history is the more typically 'modern' form, and it proceeds under the assumption that both the integrity of historical inquiry and the legitimacy of our claims to historical knowledge must be safeguarded by resisting the utilization of theological categories in our accounts of what has taken place. Both forms of this

---

[5] Following the prologue to John's Gospel, I write Truth with upper-case 'T' here to designate that Truth which concerns us ultimately and which provides the decisive clue to our understanding of the world as a whole. In Christian faith, of course, the Truth is identified with the One who proclaims himself to be the Truth.

[6] I do not mean to suggest that disengagement from history is unique to the Western intellectual tradition; indeed it is also evident in all other Indo-European cultures, and most clearly so where it has not been tempered through an encounter with the contrasting Semitic view of history.

hermeneutical suspicion, as it is applied to the reading of Scripture, will be encountered in the following survey of Western historiography.

The first form noted above has its roots, as is well known, in the metaphysics of classical Greek philosophy. Illustrated by Plato's model of the cave, the life of human beings lived in the realm of space and time is recognized as a life of change and impermanence and is, on this account, presumed to be alien to the truth which is, by definition, eternal and unchanging. The material imperfections of the spatio-temporal world offer only a shadowy reflection of the unchanging perfection of the eternal. To consider that one might have knowledge of this ephemeral realm of human action was thought to be a contradiction in terms, 'an attempt to know what, being transitory, is unknowable'.[7] In the view of Plato, for instance, the world of change and decay was perceptible but not intelligible, and claims about what went on in history were matters of opinion (*doxa*), but not of knowledge (*episteme*). This dualism between the temporal and the eternal, between the *cosmos aisthetos* and the *cosmos noetos*,

---

[7] Collingwood, *Idea*, 28. Despite the metaphysical bias against the study of history in the classical world, historical reconstruction as such was not completely unknown. Herodotus, the first advocate of historical reconstruction, opposed the dominant stream of Greek thought by setting out to develop a science of history. Herodotus proposed to preserve for future generations an account of what had taken place and, more importantly still, to discern within the particulars of human action a rationally intelligible pattern of cause and effect. History became, under Herodotus, a proper object of human inquiry and knowledge, not because contingency and change were denied – these are the stuff of history – but because arbitrariness was. The variable particularities of history were thought by Herodotus to succeed each other according to intelligible relationships of cause and effect. In the historiography of Thucydides, however, who followed Herodotus in thinking history to be a worthy sphere of investigation, there is a retreat from this interest in particulars. Despite writing an account of history, most famously in his 'History of the Peloponnesian War', Thucydides was interested less in the events themselves and the causal connections between them than in the universal laws allegedly determining the events. His inquiry, anticipating Plato's theory of Forms, concerns the nature of the eternal and unchanging principles by which historical life is thought to be determined. Truth and meaning, for Thucydides, are vested not in the particulars but in the universal laws beyond the events themselves. In his conception, therefore, history takes on a deterministic character as events are understood to succeed each other in necessary conformity to those eternal laws. The freedom of the creation to be itself is thus brought under threat and the historic potential of all human action is undermined. For all his interest in history, Thucydides' recourse to the concept of universal and eternal law meant that he did not finally break free from the ahistorical conception of truth and meaning which we have seen in Greek thought. For Thucydides too, in the end, it was not in the immanent sphere of contingency and change but in the transcendent and unchanging realm of eternal forms that the truth of things was to be discovered.

yielded, as R.G. Collingwood has put it,[8] an anti-historical tendency in Greek thought, and an account of truth from which all historical reference is excluded. It is for this reason that the Greek mind was not well disposed to the New Testament proclamation that the eternal Word of God had become flesh. The gospel of the incarnation – the supreme instance of God's involvement in history – appears, within this context, to be a form of intellectual foolishness, a kind of naïve category mistake that, if not simply false, must be consigned to the realm of the mythological. The first four centuries of the church's life are thus marked by a titanic struggle to counter the Greek incredulity, even as it sometimes occurred within the church itself.

For a time it seemed that the Christian (and Jewish) view that God is indeed active in history would win out against the philosophical scepticism of the Greeks. Alan Richardson, for instance, claims that by the time of Augustine, the Hebraic-Christian view of history had triumphed over the classical.[9] If it really was a triumph it was not to be an enduring one, for with the rise of modernity the Western philosophical tradition began again to question whether truth and history could be regarded as coalescent terms.

It is with Descartes (1596–1650) that the problematic character of history begins to re-emerge. Echoing the scepticism of the Greek mind, Descartes asserted the impossibility of any knowledge being produced by historical inquiry. Descartes contends,

> Even the most accurate historical accounts, while neither changing nor amplifying the value of things in order to make them more worth reading, at least almost always leave out the basest and least illustrious circumstances, with the result that *what remains does not appear as it really is.*[10]

In history we are dealing with the contingent and the uncertain, whereas knowledge and truth, according to Descartes, are characterized by necessity and indubitability. The Cartesian quest for truth eschewed the contingent realm of history and sought satisfaction in the deliverances of human reason.

Descartes' view was soon to secure the support of Baruch Spinoza (1632–77), who argued that the study of history was not a science but a form of practical surmisal useful (as opposed to veridical) for political ends.[11] Truth, along with divine purpose and will, were thus rejected as categories that could be employed in the study of history. Abandoning his Jewish heritage, Spinoza's

---

[8] Collingwood, *Idea*, 29.

[9] Richardson, *History*, 59. The residual Platonic dualism in Augustine's thought, along with the occasional tendency to disparage material reality, qualifies Richardson's judgement a little.

[10] Descartes, *Discourse*, 31 (emphasis mine).

[11] The point is taken from Novak, *Election*, 26.

logic follows that of the Greeks: purpose, he argued, entails development and change through time, but what is eternal cannot change. To speak of divine purpose, therefore, is a compromise of God's eternal perfection. Truth, accordingly, is not to be found in claims of a historically mediated revelation but rather through the 'natural light' of reason that is common to all. Spinoza explains that knowledge of the divine law

> does not demand belief in historical narratives of any kind whatsoever. For since it is merely a consideration of human nature that leads us to this natural Divine Law, evidently it applies equally to Adam as to any other man ... Nor can the belief in historical narratives, however certain, give us knowledge of God, nor, consequently, of the love of God. For the love of God arises from the knowledge of God, a knowledge deriving from general axioms that are certain and self-evident, and so belief in historical narratives is by no means essential to the attainment of our supreme good.[12]

Spinoza, even more than Descartes, represents a fateful turn for Christian theology. For it is under his influence that there arose in biblical interpretation a separation between history and faith. 'The point at issue [in the study of Scripture]', Spinoza explains, 'is merely the meaning of the texts, not their truth'.[13] Historical study of the texts seeks to uncover what the authors intended, to ascertain thus 'the meaning' of the texts, but discovery of this meaning has no bearing upon the truth. Truth is not mediated through the historical narratives of the Bible, but only through the natural light of reason. It is quite possible under Spinoza's scheme that the historical narratives be judged false, but this is no threat to faith which is concerned principally with right conduct. Spinoza explains that 'the divinity of Scripture must be established solely from the fact that it teaches true virtue'.[14] The historical narratives – and all that about miracles – serve only a pedagogical purpose and bear no essential relation to the content of Christian (or Jewish) faith. The Jewish and Christian faiths are thus dehistoricized. It is the abstract and universal *ideas* of the Bible that are to be reckoned with, and not the history to which its narratives bear witness. The implication eventually to be drawn – not by Spinoza himself but by those who followed him – was that the historical narratives of the Bible should properly be regarded as mythical. To employ the terminology to be used later by Søren Kierkegaard in critique of this position, the 'Moment' of divine action in history is reduced to a vanishing point. History is no longer decisive.[15]

---

[12] Spinoza, *Tractatus*, iv, 104–5.
[13] Spinoza, *Tractatus*, vii, 143.
[14] Spinoza, *Tractatus*, vii, 142.
[15] See Kierkegaard, *Fragments*.

The distinction apparent in Spinoza between the realm of history and the concerns of faith was encouraged by the concurrent emergence of modern science. The spectacular success of scientific explanation, though arguably having its foundation in a Judaeo-Christian world-view,[16] was accomplished with less and less reference to God. While many scientists retained allegiance to Christian faith, their theology was very often deistic in character. The world was conceived as a closed causal nexus, intelligible without reference to God. Historical explanation increasingly followed the natural sciences in seeking to account for things in these immanentist terms. This allowed to historical inquiry a measure of epistemic legitimacy that had been denied to it in the first flowerings of the rationalistic spirit. If history too could be conceived as conforming to a pattern explicable according to a set of natural laws, then it would regain credibility as a mode of scientific inquiry.

Contending thus against Descartes' rejection of historical inquiry as an avenue to truth, Giovanni Battista Vico (1668–1744), the Italian philosopher of history, developed a periodic view of history in which the essential characteristics of a period recur in cyclical succession. The task of the historian, therefore, was to identify the essential characteristics and to plot their rise and fall as well as their inevitable recurrence. Vico conforms to the spirit of the age by recommending the exclusion of all transcendent reference in accounting for the events of history.[17] While in Vico's view history has its own inner necessity bestowed upon it by God, this inner necessity, like the laws of nature discovered by science, was presumed to preclude any need for God to 'interfere'. The gain in respectability afforded to the study of history by Vico's proposals came, however, at a great cost, which only now in the postmodern era is becoming apparent – namely the loss of history itself. Vico's project struck a fateful blow to the idea that history has a purpose. Vico's understanding eliminates the idea of eschatology, of a goal and consummation of history, and replaces it with a circular, though spiral, view of history.[18] Divine purpose, one of the critical conditions for the very idea of history, as I shall argue below, is thus abandoned as an explanatory category. Things are no longer conceived in terms of their movement towards a goal. Instead they are understood, once more in Greek fashion, as the spiralling reconfiguration of the same old things in new patterns. It is to be noted here that the spiral character of the historical process does not imply for Vico that there is a mounting progression towards some goal. It simply reflects his view that while the essential characteristics of a period will recur, the particular conditions in which they are manifest will be different.

---

[16] For a proffering of that argument see, for example, Jaki, *Saviour*; Kaiser, *Creation*; and Turner, *Roots*.

[17] Vico's historiography is developed in *Principles*.

[18] For further discussion of Vico's historiography, see Bultmann, *History*.

Divine promise and the providential direction of history towards its goal have no place in Vico's account.

It was inevitable that the deistic conception of the world and the thirst for immanentist explanation would eventually be brought to bear upon the account of history that is set forth in the Bible. It was the biblical critic Hermann Reimarus (1694–1768) who took up the task of applying the new wisdom of immanentist explanation to the biblical material, thus dealing a blow to the confidence that Christian truth was founded upon the solid rock of historical occurrence. The Gospels, alleged Reimarus, precisely because of their transcendent reference, cannot be considered as reliable historical testimony but represent a falsification of who Jesus really was. The explanatory power of the new historical science allegedly reveals that Jesus was no divine saviour but preached a simple message of repentance and the immanence of the 'kingdom of heaven'. Such a kingdom was conceived of as a temporal kingdom presided over by a messiah chosen, it was believed at the time, by God. Though Jesus himself expected to take on that role, he was frustrated in his plan. Sharing his frustration, the disciples fabricated stories of a resurrection in order to keep the dream alive. Strangely, Reimarus thought it possible to salvage from the rubble of his immanentist explanations a form of Christian faith still worthy of our allegiance. His messianic delusions notwithstanding, Jesus' ethical teaching provided worthy guidance, it was supposed, for a life well pleasing to God. The echo of Spinoza resounds clearly here; what Christian faith is finally concerned with in the biblical material is not the dubious historical claims but the teaching about virtue.

Although he had published the work of Reimarus and shared Reimarus's scepticism about basing one's Christian faith upon the historical testimony of the Bible, G.E. Lessing (1729–81) introduces a rather different anxiety to the task of reading the biblical narratives. Whereas Reimarus was sure that the Gospels' depictions of the life of Jesus were wilful fabrications, Lessing professed agnosticism about that and contended instead that the increasing temporal distance between the events to which the Bible bears witness and those who read the Bible now undermines, for those readers, any epistemic confidence in the historical claims found there. Historical inquiry, in Lessing's view, can neither confirm nor deny the truth of the biblical witness. We are separated from the events of the past by 'a broad ugly ditch', the bridging of which is thought to be impossible, and we are left, therefore, unable to assess the veracity of the Bible's historical claims.[19] Christian faith, in Lessing's view, must find its sure point of reference elsewhere. Linking his concern to the

---

[19] It may well be the case that Lessing did disbelieve many of the claims of the biblical narratives, but in public debate he claimed to be merely agnostic. This more moderate position was sufficient for the prosecution of his case.

dualistic metaphysics of Greek philosophy, mediated to him through Spinoza and Leibniz, Lessing famously remarked that 'accidental truths of history can never become the proof of necessary truths of reason'.[20] Just because the past is 'lost' and inaccessible, it cannot be the bearer of eternal truth.

It is true, as Lessing alleges, that the past is no longer the content of immediate experience, but it is by no means clear that it cannot therefore be the object of knowledge. The study of history may not yield absolute certainty, but perhaps the demand for such certainty derives from a wrong idea of what constitutes knowledge. We cannot here offer a philosophical defence of this suggestion,[21] but for the sake of our present argument the appeal to common sense will suffice. In the course of our daily lives we claim knowledge of all sorts of things about which we cannot be absolutely certain. Even if only some of those claims are warranted, then knowledge is not what Lessing thinks it is. Knowledge is not something from which every possible cause of doubt has been eliminated. Rather, it applies to those things that we have 'good enough' reasons to believe. The question then arises: what might constitute good enough reasons to believe the narratives of history? May it not be that the contingent truths of history are reliably mediated to us through the faithful testimony of tradition? Hans-Georg Gadamer writes,

> The important thing is to recognise the distance in time as a positive and productive possibility of understanding. It is not a yawning abyss but is filled with the continuity of custom and tradition, in the light of which all that is handed down presents itself to us.[22]

Lessing need not be as sceptical as he is about the reliability of historical testimony. While it may not yield the absolute certainty he craves, historical testimony, where it is offered by trustworthy witnesses, might well give us good reasons to believe. It remains true, however, that the witness cannot remove from the believer the onus of personal judgement. The epistemic importance of testimony applies, as Iain Provan explains in this volume,[23] not just to our reading of the biblical texts but equally to the vast proportion of what each of us claims to know about the world. Lessing, however, thinks that belief in the gospel narratives is a special case. He thinks so because what is required in Christian faith is the total commitment of one's life. Where

---

[20] Lessing, 'Proof', 53.

[21] Though see, for example, the essays in Evans and Westphal, *Christian Perspectives*. Evans and Westphal suggest in their 'Introduction' to that volume that Enlightenment critiques of religious belief have been operating with 'the wrong idea of what it is to know something and how we know what we know', 2.

[22] Gadamer, *Truth*, 265.

[23] Provan, 'Knowing and Believing: Faith in the Past', Ch. 11.

absolute commitment is required, this must be founded, Lessing thinks, upon absolute certainty about the truths that Christianity proclaims. To make an absolute commitment on the basis of an uncertain knowledge would involve us, in Lessing's view, in an abdication of our responsibility as rational beings to seek the most stringent rational warrant for all our truth claims, thereby dispelling all doubt. Short of attaining such certainty, we must maintain a studied agnosticism. Because such warrant can never be offered in respect of the truths of history, Lessing, like so many before him and since, dismisses the notion that God's claim upon our lives is historically mediated. It must be rationally mediated instead. But again, it is not at all clear why absolute certainty should be required as a basis for Christian faith. The very fact that Christian discipleship has been regarded from the beginning as a matter of faith – even for those who were eyewitnesses of Jesus' life – suggests a lack of embarrassment about the fact that Christianity is concerned with a truth that is contingent and thus always open to doubt. It is concerned with a Truth, in other words, that does not permit of the kind of certainty that Lessing craves. Why should this be a problem? It did not trouble Jesus, who appears consistently to suggest that the commitment of Christian discipleship has the character of interpersonal trust rather than rational certainty.

Because it is an oft-repeated pattern, it is worth noting before we leave Lessing how his disparagement of historical testimony effects his soteriology. If, so as to maintain our integrity as rational beings, the Christian life is to involve one's assent to rationally indubitable truth, salvation will likewise be conceived in terms of the autonomous exercise of our rational capacities. The truth to which Lessing turns is the truth of the law – the truths evident in the ethical teaching of Jesus. These truths are reducible in Lessing's scheme to one (only) of the great commandments: love one another. This is a good in which the rational person can believe, and, when the will is disciplined by one's reason, it is also a good that the rational person can accomplish. This, then, is what Christian faith amounts to – or reduces to, perhaps – love one another. Lessing's tract 'On the Proof of Spirit and of Power' closes with the words, 'I conclude, and my wish is: May all who are divided by the gospel of John be reunited by the Testament of John. Admittedly it is apocryphal this testament. But it is not on that account any less divine'.[24] The testament referred to here is, 'Little children, love one another'. This is the sum of Lessing's soteriological proposal. Jesus, and John too, are approved as good teachers of this wisdom, but – and here is the crucial point – the truth affirmed in this proposal bears no essential relation to Jesus himself. It matters not whether the narrative is apocryphal. Its meaning has saving power irrespective of whether it was taught by Jesus or not, and so, to employ Kierkegaard's terminology once more, the

---

[24] Lessing, 'Proof', 56.

teacher and all the historical particulars of Jesus' life become a vanishing point. They have no soteriological significance. The person seeking the truth of Christian faith, therefore, has only to contemplate the truths of practical reason, as Kant would later call them, and has no need to venture to the far side of that ugly ditch on which is found an uncertain testimony to the historical particularities of Jesus of Nazareth. Aside from finding in that testimony a happy agreement with what we have established ourselves through the power of reason, Christian faith, in Lessing's scheme, need take no account of such reports. The abandonment of history is complete.

Lessing's reduction of Christianity to a wisdom that has no essential connection to Jesus himself sets a pattern that is replicated many times over among those who reject the decisive soteriological significance of Jesus' history – from Lessing himself, through Kant and Hegel and right up to the Jesus Seminar of our own day, whose members typically consider Jesus' 'theological' significance to consist in the wisdom of his teaching. Jesus is styled as a mere teacher, and perhaps exemplar, of a salvation that we are now responsible to attain for ourselves. That is also the pattern apparent in postmodernism; Jesus is again styled as a good teacher, or perhaps, with even more appeal to the extreme individualism of postmodernity, as some kind of personal guru – fashioned, however, to suit one's own particular spirituality.[25] Modernity and postmodernity converge upon the notion of a true humanity which is realized by every individual who works out her own salvation without necessary recourse to anything other than her own best insights.

The result of Reimarus's scepticism about the reliability of the Gospels as historical witness, combined with Lessing's conviction that the passing of time is corrosive of any certainty we may aspire to concerning the events of history, has convinced many people that the truth of Christian faith ought to be established on grounds other than that of historical testimony. The scepticism is played out in the religious philosophies of Kant, Hegel and Schleiermacher – who, for all their differences, share the conviction that while the essence of Christian faith can be distilled from the reports of Jesus' life, that essence has no necessary connection to that historical life itself. What one finds in Jesus is the confirmation of a truth that can be established independently of him. For Kant the truth is ethical; for Hegel it is the pantheistic unity of Spirit; and for Schleiermacher it is the general anthropological truth of the religious consciousness of human beings. In each case, the supposed essential truth of Christianity depends not at all upon the fact and form of Jesus' historical existence. It merely finds confirmation there, albeit, in Kant's case, with rather

---

[25] William Hamilton's *Quest* provides an example of a postmodern 'Christology' that has no qualms about the fictional character of its portrayals of Jesus. The point of Christology is merely to fashion symbols of our current concerns.

grudging acknowledgement.[26] Faith has become dehistoricized. Its truth no longer depends on anything that has happened in history. Johann Gottlieb Fichte gives precise expression to this modern spirit: 'Only the metaphysical but not the historical contributes to our salvation', he writes, 'the latter only makes it intelligible'.[27]

It might be thought that Hegel does not belong with these other two. It is his philosophy of history, after all, that has impacted most forcefully upon modern thought, and it is through history itself, Hegel contends, that the truth of things is unfolded. And yet, despite his laying claim to the category of history, his account of things does not allow to the created order of space and time the freedom to be itself.[28] The truth may be worked out through the dialectical process of history, but its working out is shaped by the prior necessity of rational law. There is, Hegel argues, 'an *a priori* structure of history to which empirical reality must correspond'.[29] For Hegel, echoing Thucydides,[30] such *a priori* structures or laws may be identified as a matter of rational necessity in advance of historical inquiry itself. It is thus not surprising to find also in Karl Marx, Hegel's intellectual heir, the conviction that history conforms to a pattern determined in advance of any particular actions or events. The moment in time, accordingly, can only instantiate the preordained truth. It can never be the means of its establishment. In principle, therefore, the truth may be learned without reference to history. In Hegel and Marx, the great modern interpreters of history, we find the modern rejection of the decisiveness of the moment in full cry.

That is also the position of D.F. Strauss (1808–74), who applies Hegel's philosophy of history to the interpretation of the New Testament. With Strauss, the immanentist bias of modernity finds expression in the quest for the historical Jesus – a Jesus stripped bare of the accretions of theological dogma. In his *Life of Jesus Critically Examined*, Strauss argues that much of the testimony of the New Testament is not history but myth, the clothing of timeless religious truth in the dress of historical narrative. Thus, according to Strauss, it is not history but timeless truth that is to be reckoned with. The particular truth with which the Bible is concerned is the synthetic unity of the divine and the human – that same truth that is given mature expression in the philosophy of Hegel. Jesus of Nazareth merely instantiates the ideal of humanity as it is present to

---

[26] Witness Kant's refusal to speak of Jesus by name. He refers instead to the mere possibility that the 'archetype' of the truly moral life has appeared among us. See *Religion*.

[27] Fichte, *Anweisung*, 97.

[28] We shall argue below that precisely such freedom is required in order for human action to be considered historic.

[29] Hegel, *World History*, 131.

[30] See note 7, above.

human reason, so that his life has exemplary but not effectual soteriological significance. We see in him what we can just as well see without him.

It was suggested at the beginning of this section that the disjunction between history and faith has taken two forms in the Western intellectual tradition. In the first form the disjunction has required that Christian faith be set free from the historical narratives of the New Testament. Its essence has been defined in such a way that it depends not at all on the truth or falsity of the New Testament's historical claims. In the alternative form of this disjunction, however, it has been supposed that history must be set free from faith. The historical narratives of the Gospels must be purged of their dogmatic content in order to lay bare the truth of who Jesus really was. We have seen that form anticipated in the work of Reimarus, and, as Iain Provan explains,[31] it is evident in the nineteenth century in the historiography developed by Leopold von Ranke (1795–1886), who famously seeks to recover the past *wie es eigentlich gewesen ist* ('as it really was'). In the twentieth century, that approach was taken further by the work of Ernst Troeltsch (1865–1923) who, in a famous essay written in 1898, distinguished between 'historical' and 'dogmatic' method in theology.[32] The historical method, which Troeltsch considered to be the only intellectually respectable option, treats the rise of Christianity merely as a cultural phenomenon. Just because it is a cultural phenomenon and is open, therefore, to historical investigation, Troeltsch supposes that God cannot be involved. But why is this so? The reason has been charted in all that we have said so far. Whether because of particular presuppositions about the eternal and unchanging nature of truth, or, in this case, because of the conviction that the world is a closed causal nexus explicable entirely within categories of immanence, divine action and human history are thought to be mutually exclusive categories. To be sure, Troeltsch does claim that something called the 'divine reason' is disclosed through history,[33] but it turns out that this divine reason is identical with the 'divine' depth of the human spirit. There is a resemblance here to Spinoza, who similarly thought that divine reason was a phenomenon of the natural order. The adjective 'divine' in Troeltsch looks rather like simply a means of absolutizing the claim and power of reason as such.

With Troeltsch however, as with almost all thinkers who advocate the separation of historical and dogmatic method, the separation cannot finally be

---

[31] Provan, 'Knowing and Believing: Faith in the Past', Ch. 11.

[32] Key aspects of Troeltsch's separation between 'dogmatic' and 'historical' method are echoed in the proposals for biblical studies in the academy set forth by Philip Davies. For an account of Davies' proposals see Craig Bartholomew's Ch. 2 in this volume, '*Warranted* Biblical Interpretation: Alvin Plantinga's "Two (or More) Types of Scripture Scholarship"'.

[33] Troeltsch, 'Method', 27.

sustained. The method does not proceed in the absence of dogma, but rather in the service of a dogma other than that of orthodox Christian faith. In seeking thus to defend the 'absoluteness of Christianity', Troeltsch fails to conform to his own methodological proposals. He insists, towards the beginning of the essay to which we have referred, that the Judeo-Christian tradition must be 'resolutely subjected to all the consequences of a purely historical method' – a central tenet of which, according to Troeltsch, is the principle of analogy. The principle of analogy requires us to assess the probability of an event actually having happened by its agreement with 'normal, customary, or at least frequently attested happenings and conditions as we have experienced them';[34] ergo, nothing happens that is unique. And yet, later in the same essay, Troeltsch asks us to believe that '*at one point*' the usual limitations of the human spirit are broken through, namely in the person of Jesus. 'Here', Troeltsch explains, 'a God distinct from nature produced a personality superior to nature with eternally transcendent goals and the willpower to change the world'.[35] Troeltsch's own criteria, however, make it impossible to believe in such a unique manifestation of divine action. It was Troeltsch himself who laid upon us the obligation to do theology within the limits of historical reason alone, but these limits turn out to be so restrictive that they are violated as soon as Troeltsch begins to speak of God.

History and Hermeneutics

While we have given indication at various points above of the impact upon biblical hermeneutics of the prevailing Western scepticism about the epistemic value of the historical narratives of Scripture, we turn now to give more explicit attention to that impact. The suspicion of history began, we noted, with classical Greek philosophy, and the roots of modern hermeneutics are also to be found there. Werner Jeanrond explains that in reading the Homeric epics, the *Iliad* and the *Odyssey*, two methods of critical reading developed – the grammatical and the allegorical. The first method seeks 'to reach the text's sense by studying the linguistic devices and connections within it', and the second 'looks for the hidden sense of a text with the aid of an interpretative key from outside it'.[36] 'This [allegorical] approach to the "sacred" texts', Jeanrond further explains, 'allowed the reader to search for ways of understanding the meaning of these without being forced to dwell on their literal message'.[37]

---

[34] Troeltsch, 'Method', 13–14.
[35] Troeltsch, 'Method', 27.
[36] Jeanrond, *Theological Hermeneutics*, 14.
[37] Jeanrond, *Theological Hermeneutics*, 15.

While we do not wish to set a literal hermeneutic in opposition to an allegorical one as the simple alternatives in biblical interpretation, the preference in classical Greek thought for an allegorical approach diminishes or even precludes interest in the question of historical truth. It counts questions of historical fact as unimportant to the meaning of the text. That is surely appropriate in respect of *some* of the biblical material – not all forms of biblical writing belong to the genre of historical narrative – but the imposition of an exclusively allegorical approach upon texts that do intend a historical reference does violence to the integrity of the texts themselves.

Out of deference to the Greek view, and perhaps with the best of apologetic intentions, the allegorical approach to Scripture as a whole was promoted within Judaism by Philo and gave rise to strident debate within Christian faith between the Alexandrian and the Antiochene schools. Theodore of Mopsuestia was among those in the Antiochene School who alleged that the allegorical readings of the Alexandrians amounted to a denial of the biblical stories' actual historical reality.[38] The Antiochenes sought, in opposition, to preserve the reference of Scripture to God's action in the actual world of historical truths rather than merely to an ideal world of symbolic truths. While not entirely accurate in their assessment of Alexandrian hermeneutics,[39] the Antiochene critique could well be applied to the hermeneutics of Spinoza, Lessing, Hegel,[40] Strauss and so on – the roll-call of modern, essentially docetic, interpreters could continue at length. Where such biblical interpreters proceed to offer an account of why the Jesus stripped of the falsifying dogma of the New Testament witness should be regarded still as worthy of our allegiance, what is retained – as the essence of Christian faith – is typically reducible to a set of ideas: the wisdom of the wandering cynic, the insight of the great moral teacher, the revolutionary ethic of the inspired prophet. There is no necessary connection between this essence of faith and the person of Jesus himself.

It might be thought that the work of some contemporary scholars, and especially perhaps the members of the 'Jesus Seminar', redresses the neglect of history. It is they, after all, who insist that the dogmatic content of the New Testament must be abandoned in favour of a truth discoverable by historical inquiry alone. The methodological weaknesses of the Jesus Seminar's

---

[38] On which, see Jeanrond, *Theological Hermeneutics*, 21; and Vanhoozer, *Is There a Meaning?*, 115.

[39] Although the Antiochenes charged Origen with neglecting the historical reference of Scripture, Henri de Lubac has shown that the allegation against Origen himself is misplaced. See de Lubac, *Histoire*, and his four-volume *Medieval Exegesis*. I am grateful to Mary Healy for pointing out to me the common misrepresentation of Origen's position.

[40] This attitude is especially evident in the early work of Hegel. See, for example, 'Positivity'.

deliberations have been well documented[41] and need not be repeated here, but it is of interest to highlight the conception of history that is operative in its work. For again it is supposed that God is not involved in human history. Like Troeltsch before them, the members of the Jesus Seminar apparently conceive the rise of Christianity as merely a cultural phenomenon, so that talk of God has no place in the retelling of that history except when referencing what some people apparently believed. The only 'defense' of this presupposition to be found in the Jesus Seminar's flagship publication, *The Five Gospels*, is that 'the Christ of creed and dogma ... can no longer command the assent of those who have seen the heavens through Galileo's telescope'.[42] Quite apart from the fact that countless scientists well acquainted with Galileo's telescope do still believe in the Christ of creed and dogma, this explanation gives us no reason whatsoever to suppose that the truth about Jesus is discoverable through historical inquiry alone.[43] It is simply a statement of the dubious contention that we of the modern world are not as naïve as our forebears were.

A second feature of the method adopted by the Jesus Seminar is its devotion to a reductionistic account of history. It is supposed that the truth is arrived at by breaking the biblical texts into fragments and assessing the authenticity or otherwise of each fragment. This has resulted in the practice of dealing with individual sayings of Jesus in units not only of sentence length, but even of part sentences. The process further fragments the biblical witness by separating the sayings from the actions of Jesus and by considering their authenticity as historical data in isolation from one another. What remains after this process is complete is a collection of fragments of evidence isolated from the theological narrative of the Bible from which the evidence was plundered. It is important to be clear on two assumptions underlying this procedure. The first is that the New Testament evangelists are untrustworthy witnesses. Their interpretation of what has taken place is treated for the most part as false. It is important only to note here that, contrary to the Seminar's own claims, this assessment is not a *conclusion* of scholarly inquiry but is, rather, a dogmatic presupposition.[44] I do

---

[41] See, for example, Wright, *Victory* and 'Five Gospels'; and Hays, 'Corrected Jesus'.

[42] See the 'Introduction' to Funk, Hoover and The Jesus Seminar, *Five Gospels*, 2.

[43] The claims of the Seminar about what the 'modern' mind can and cannot believe are just one more instance of the extraordinarily weak '*force majeure*' argument that is critiqued by Alvin Plantinga in his *Warranted Christian Belief*, 403ff.

[44] Witness, for example, the following 'criteria' employed by the Seminar to determine the authentic words of Jesus. All are quoted directly from *Five Gospels*.
- Sayings and parables expressed in 'Christian' language are the creation of the evangelists or their Christian predecessors (24).
- Jesus' characteristic talk was distinctive – it can usually be distinguished from common lore. Otherwise it is futile to search for the authentic words of Jesus (30).

not for this reason demean the judgement; my point merely is that it should be called by its proper name. It can then be evaluated on appropriate terms. A second assumption is that only that which we deem to be absolutely certain counts as evidence. Here there is an echo of Lessing, and more broadly of the epistemic predilections of modernity to which we have already referred. A striking parallel is also to be found in Fundamentalism. Both the Jesus Seminar and Fundamentalism share a view of knowledge in general and historical knowledge in particular, in which only absolute certainty will do. Fundamentalists secure certainty by their doctrines of biblical inerrancy and infallibility; the Jesus Seminar does so by stripping from their Jesus database anything deemed by them to be the least bit doubtful. Both, however, do violence to the Scriptures themselves and fail to recognize, in contrast with Gadamer and Provan above, that the testimony of fallible human witnesses might also contribute to an epistemic warrant.[45]

It will be obvious that the story we have told here is one-sided. It does not chart the significant strands of Christian tradition that have been developed under the conviction that it is through the historic incarnation of the Word of God and Second Person of the Trinity that the Truth is given to be known. It is the side of the story upon which we have concentrated thus far, however, that has dominated biblical hermeneutics in the recent past and that has generated the artificial distinction and uneasy relation between biblical studies and theology. It has been the contention of this chapter so far that the heart of the problem is a faulty view of history – a view that supposes, for varying reasons, that history cannot be the medium of divine self-disclosure. God is not known, it is thought, through the concrete and the particular but only, if at all, through the abstract and the universal. The time has now come to consider an alternative account of history – an account that is not offended at the fact of God's involvement in history and which seeks, by virtue of its derivation from

---

Footnote 44 (*continued*):

- Jesus' sayings and parables cut against the social and religious grain (31).
- Jesus does not as a rule initiate dialogue or debate, nor does he offer to cure people (32).
- Jesus rarely makes pronouncements or speaks about himself in the first person (32).
- Jesus makes no claim to be the Anointed, the messiah (32).

These criteria clearly fly in the face of the evangelists' testimony and might appear to have the form of conclusions arrived at after extensive research. They are all described, however, as 'rules of evidence'. They are the premises with which the Jesus Seminar sets to work. Clearly these 'rules' are nothing more than a means of ensuring that the Seminar will find what it is looking for.

[45] I use the word 'contribute' deliberately here. The testimony of human witnesses constitutes only a part of the case for an assent to the witness of Scripture. The testimony of the Spirit is indispensable.

Scripture itself, to enable a hermeneutical approach to that same Scripture that does not begin by impugning the truthfulness of its witness.

Towards a Theology of History

While the books of the Bible are clearly comprised of a great variety of literary genres – poetry, myth, prophecy, proverb, prayers, hymns and so on – much of the Bible also takes the form of historical narrative. The Bible tells the story of the history of Israel, a history set within the context of God's purpose for all nations. The telling of that story, furthermore, arises from the conviction that a true account of history will relate the involvement of God in the successive unfolding of events. Thus can Gerhard von Rad declare that 'any study of the Old Testament that does not begin with its character as a witness to God's action in history is condemned to sterility because it does not take account of the facts'.[46] It is a mistake, therefore, to presume that the biblical writers, in the New Testament as well as in the Old Testament, were not concerned with history and that they set out instead to construct a religious mythology, or that they chose, as a communicative strategy, to couch essentially spiritual or rational truths in the form of a fictional historical narrative. There can be no doubt that the writers of the historical narratives in the Bible intend to refer to the prior historical reality and, as Francis Watson has put it, whatever fictionalizing tendency may be present is always subordinate to the backward historical reference.[47]

We may say, therefore, that the Bible is a theological account of history. It is an account that is shaped by the conviction that all that takes place does so within the context of God's providential care for the created order. That it is a theological account, employing categories peculiar to its own concerns, does not render it illegitimate as history – any more than a political history or an economic history should be called into question just because it is shaped by and seeks to explain the course of history according to a strictly defined interest. A distinction made by Hegel between history and chronicle is important at this point.[48] While chronicle is the mere recording of events without any attempt to discern or chart any relation between them, the writing of history is an undertaking that seeks and offers an explanation for the unfolding of events. As such, every telling of the story of history involves the selection and interpretation of evidence according to the historian's convictions about the meaning and purpose of the whole. There is no good reason to suppose that a purely secular

---

[46] Von Rad, *God at Work*, 154–55.
[47] Watson, *Text and Truth*, 33.
[48] See Hegel, *World History*, 12.

account of history, in which divine action is dispensed with as an explanatory category, brings the historian closer to the truth. Western historiography, however, in most of its variant forms, has typically been founded upon just this assumption. In quest of a status and supposed legitimacy comparable to that of the natural sciences, historical inquiry in the modern era has been undertaken, as we have seen, without recourse to the 'God hypothesis'. For all the epistemological challenges involved in discerning the work of God in history, however, the truth or falsity in principle of theological versus secular accounts of history depends not at all on such difficulties as may be involved in a theological account, much less upon the agnostic or atheistic predilections of the age, but solely on whether God has or has not acted. There is no *a priori* basis upon which that matter can be determined. The conviction of Israel, therefore, that its own history as a people is inaugurated by God and is shaped throughout by God's action, is an account that needs to be reckoned with. It cannot be dismissed in advance.

There are two conditions, I think, that give shape to the Hebraic understanding of history. First is the creation of the world by God *ex nihilo*, and second is God's direction of history towards its goal. We will discuss this second aspect below, under the rubric of divine promise. It is within this framework of creation and promise that human action can properly be conceived as historic.

The Doctrine of Creation

The disparagement of history described above is a symptom of the malaise identified by Colin Gunton as the neglect of the doctrine of creation.[49] In his book *The Triune Creator*, Gunton outlines three aspects of the Christian doctrine of creation that are unique among the range of philosophic and religious accounts about how things came to be.[50] First is the notion of creation 'out of nothing'. The import of this, Gunton argues, is that 'the creation is an act of divine sovereignty and freedom, an exercise of God's will that there be something other than himself. It further implies that the universe had a beginning in time; it is neither eternal nor infinite.'[51] Two things follow from this for our concern with history. Because, in contrast with the doctrine of *creatio ex nihilo*, the Greeks believed that the matter of the universe had always existed,

---

[49] This is especially true of Spinoza, who denies that God can be the creator of anything outside of himself. The extended and thinking things of this world are simply attributes of God or affections of God's attributes. See *Ethics*, Pt. I, Proposition XIV, Corollary 2.

[50] I am following the discussion in ch. 1 of Gunton, *Triune Creator*.

[51] Gunton, *Triune Creator*, 9.

that it 'just is', they presumed that it had no particular meaning, nor any purpose. That the world should be brought forth by God 'out of nothing', however, implies that God creates with some purpose in mind. The principle of *creatio ex nihilo* implies that the world is invested with a *telos*. There is a reason for its being; and history, in consequence, is to be understood as the space and time opened up for the world to become what it is intended to be.

Second, the idea of creation out of nothing means that the world is fully God's world. Unlike the demiurge in Plato's *Timaeus* who simply gives order to the matter that already is, the God testified to in the Christian doctrine of creation is not constrained in his creative work by some pre-existent matter. The world in both its form and in its matter is the outcome of the Creator's will. That means, for our understanding of history, that history cannot be conceived along Manichean lines as a struggle between opposing forces. Everything is held in God's hands so that, even in the face of evil and sinfulness, it is possible to affirm, along with the biblical writers, that all things happen under the will and purpose of God. History may be confessed to have an overall coherence under the creative, providential and redemptive care of God.

This introduces us to the second unique aspect of the Christian doctrine of creation identified by Gunton. Taking his point of departure from the creedal confession – 'I believe in God the Father, Maker of heaven and earth' – Gunton points out that the doctrine is a matter of belief. It is to be distinguished, therefore, from something that is known intuitively, from something that reason shows us, or from something that is self-evident.[52] The corollary of this for our understanding of history is that the purpose of history is not given up to rational inquiry without recourse to revelation; nor is that purpose reducible to a set of laws so that everything must fall into analogous conformity with what has gone before. It is neither within the limits of reason alone, therefore, nor within the limits of historical inquiry alone, that the purpose of history is disclosed. This has a decisive implication for all our efforts to investigate the historical reality of Jesus Christ. The reality of his person cannot be treated as merely an object for human interpretation, a brute fact which it is our task now to interpret. The study of Christ cannot begin, as Kierkegaard nicely puts it, by letting him be dead. The fact of Christ is rather an event – and here I am in agreement with Wolfhart Pannenberg – which, in its pneumatological extension through time, itself gives rise to a community of interpretation, a body of faith and witness constituted by the headship of the risen Christ.[53] God himself, that is to say, is involved in our understanding of who Christ is. It is through the action of God in the community of faith that the true reality of Christ comes to light. The decisive mistake of those engaged

---

[52] See Gunton, *Triune Creator*, 8.
[53] See Pannenberg, *Systematic Theology*, II, 437ff.

in the nineteenth-century quest of the historical Jesus was to presume that the truth of the history of Jesus would yield itself up by means of a deliberate isolation of the inquirer from the pneumatological extension of this event in time through the faith and witness of the church. That error is replicated on every occasion that biblical interpretation is thought to be the task of the academy in isolation from the community of faith.

The third aspect identified by Gunton as uniquely characterizing the Christian doctrine of creation is the creation of the world as the act of the triune God – Father, Son and Holy Spirit. Here again, there are important implications for our understanding of history. Gunton explains that

> because [the doctrine of the Trinity] holds that God is already, 'in advance' of creation, a communion of persons existing in loving relations, it becomes possible to say that he does not need the world, and so is able to will the existence of something else simply for its own sake. Creation is the outcome of God's love indeed, but of his unconstrained love. It is therefore not a necessary outcome of what God is, but is contingent. This is important because it enables us to say that the world is given value in its own right.[54]

So, too, is human action given value in its own right. It is not simply the necessary unfolding of God's own being, as is seen both in Hegel and in various forms of process theology. Hegel's scheme renders the particulars of history of no account, for they are but the inevitable outworking of a process that is determined apart from them. In contrast with such views, God entrusts to the precarious stewardship of human beings a measure of responsibility for the way that history takes shape. Things are not simply the inevitable outcome of all that has gone before. Human response matters. It is in this way that human action can be genuinely historic – shaping the course of things in obedience to, or sometimes in defiance of, the guiding hand of God. History and human responsibility go hand in hand. One finds recognition of this point even in a writer like Jacques Derrida whose work is, in other respects, corrosive of the idea of history. Drawing upon the thought of Jan Patočka, Derrida observes that the reluctance of historical man to admit to the historicity of our existence is a reluctance to accept responsibility. Responsibility is only accepted by the one who has faith that history matters.[55] The same point is apparent in Lucien Goldmann's claim that one can only answer the question 'How ought I to live?' 'by situating one's life inside an eschatological or historical whole in which it inserts itself by faith'.[56] Human action, to make any sense and to be evaluated ethically, requires some notion of the purpose of history as a whole.

---

[54] Gunton, *Triune Creator*, 9–10.

[55] See Derrida, *Gift*, 4–6.

[56] Goldmann, *Hidden God*, 264. Cited by Nicholas Wolterstorff in *Until Justice*, vii.

Christian faith holds that it is within the framework of divine creation and promise, and particularly within its christological articulation, that the true *telos* of history is disclosed.

The second crucial implication of a Trinitarian account of God's creative action is that it defeats Deism. That the world is the creation not of the Father alone but also of the Son and the Spirit enables us to speak of God's continuing action in the world. Becoming incarnate in the midst of history, and pouring out his Spirit on all flesh, God confirms creation as his own project. It is not left to its own devices but is redemptively refashioned after the tragedy of human sin and is set again on its trajectory to fulfilment in reconciled relation with God. This action of the triune God enables us also to conceive how, under both christological and pneumatological description, the human agency in history upon which we have insisted can be directed toward the fulfilment of the divine purpose. We have observed above the biblical conviction that God enlists human participation in the working out of his purpose. Again, it is in Jesus Christ that such participation reaches its fulfilment – his human life of obedience to God, his death, his resurrection and his ascension are the events that truly make history. It is through Christ that God restores the world to its true purpose. By sending then his Holy Spirit, who bestows gifts and fruits for truly human life, Christ ensures that our own human action may become, under the impact and empowerment of that Spirit, a like participation in God's purpose.

Summarizing my argument, then, we have seen that the idea of *creatio ex nihilo* identifies the creation as a contingent act of divine will, gives to the created order its own being and integrity in distinction from God, and thus accords to human action a meaning and a value within the purpose of God. The Trinitarian description of divine creativity adds to our conception of history the further insight that God does not abandon the world to its own devices, nor does he withdraw his promise, but instead he involves himself in bringing creation to its goal.

God at Work in Israel: Promise and Fulfilment

The biblical account of Israel's history as a nation distinct from other nations begins with the story of Abraham and Sarah and, as von Rad again points out, it is a measure of Israel's historical consciousness that Abraham does not descend directly from the heavens like so many mythical founders of cities or peoples. Instead, he emerges from the diverse array of nations described in Genesis 10, all of which are equally the creation of God. The readiness of Israel to see herself, 'quite unmythically, as belonging to the world of nations',[57] implies that

---

[57] See von Rad, *God at Work*, 139.

God's purpose of salvation, as it is related in the biblical story, takes place *within* history – not apart from it. What follows, then, is that historical events are themselves decisive for the working out of God's purpose. So we read in Genesis 12:

> Now the LORD said to Abram, 'Go from your country and your kindred and your father's house to the land that I will show you. I will make of you a great nation, and I will bless you, and make your name great, so that you will be a blessing. I will bless those who bless you, and the one who curses you I will curse; and in you all the families of the earth shall be blessed.' (Gen. 12:1–3)

Whatever the provenance of this story may be, by recounting it as they do, the people of Israel seek a historical grounding for their present experience of God's blessing and guidance. They offer thereby a radically different conception of history than those adhered to by the surrounding cultures. In the words of Walter Eichrodt,

> The Old Testament writers find in the self-disclosure of God the factor in world events by which individual events are placed in a spiritual connection, and which makes events meaningful; i.e. only through it can a chaos of changing and hurrying events become comprehensible as *real history*. Under the impression of this divine experience they cannot describe world events in any other way than as historical succession in which everything is united under God's leading, and moves to a definite objective.[58]

History is affirmed by the biblical writers as the *locus* of God's action ('I will show you a land, and make of you a great nation') and the terrain upon which his *purpose* is worked out ('and in you all the families of the earth shall be blessed'). It is the action of God, therefore, that is understood to give history its purpose and that directs it towards its goal. Only thus is the succession of events conceivable as 'real history'. Furthermore, it is God's enlisting of human participation – the address of his Word to humankind and the call for a response – that gives to human action its meaningful[59] and teleological character. Human action becomes 'historic'[60] in a way not thought of by surrounding peoples, who typically saw history in cyclical terms and thus robbed it of its directedness

---

[58] Eichrodt, 'Offenbarung', 321–22 (emphasis mine).

[59] There is no space here to engage in philosophical debates about the meaning of meaning. My own view, stated briefly for the purposes of this chapter, is that the meaning of a thing refers to its place and role in a wider context, whether that be a word in a sentence, a sentence in a wider story or an event in the course of history. Meaning refers to the way in which that thing, as part of something larger, contributes to and shapes the whole.

[60] The term 'historic' is used here to speak of those actions and events which contribute to the making of a new future, being as such neither an endless cycle of recurring

towards a goal and divested human action of its capacity to contribute to a future that is new.

The importance of teleology for the idea of history is acknowledged in the theory recently espoused by Francis Fukuyama that, with the arrival of modernity and particularly of liberal democracy, history has come to an end; there is nothing else towards which we might be expected to evolve. Contestable though Fukuyama's judgement is that we have now reached the end, the point is right that, without any further purpose, without something new to be striven for or waited upon, there is no history. Western intellectual discourse about history is thoroughly permeated with teleology – as it must be if the idea of history is to be coherent – and yet it determinedly eschews reference to God, who alone can credibly be thought of as bestowing a purpose upon history as a whole. That error is part of humanity's efforts to foist upon history a purpose of its own – and that, in turn, is what the Bible calls sin.

Without teleology, without the conviction that history has some purpose that can be either hindered or advanced by all that happens, history itself is rendered meaningless. It is simply 'one damn thing after another' as Henry Ford once remarked of life in general, and all change is simply the same old thing in new constellations. The soteriological consequence of this cyclical and non-purposive view of 'history' found in the non-Semitic religions is that humanity's ultimate fulfilment or salvation is conceived in terms of an escape from the endless round of events, an escape from this historical life which can only frustrate our search for fulfilment and can never be the means through which our salvation is worked out.

In contrast with cyclical views of history in which the future is essentially no different from the past, the biblical narrative emphasizes that Abraham sets out in obedience to the divine command 'without knowing where he is going'. His lack of foreknowledge renders his action historic in the sense I have outlined above. What is yet to come is not simply the inevitable and necessary outworking of what has already come to be, nor is it the cyclical return of that which has already appeared before. Under the guidance and promise of God, Abraham is setting out on a new course, the outcome of which is unknown. Although he is motivated by the promise of God, God does not determine Abraham's particular actions. Determinism, too, would rob human action of its historic character; Abraham's own action would no longer matter. But Abraham's action does matter. It is under the condition of his obedience that God chooses to see his promise through.[61]

---

events, nor the necessary unfolding of an idea or principle that is transcendent of history and essentially unaffected by it.

[61] It is important to head off the suspicion of Pelagianism here. Two things need to be said, more extensively no doubt than is attempted here. First, that God enlists

A further feature of the biblical story of Abraham is that the *particular* events of Abraham's life are thought to be of *universal* significance. Under the condition of his obedience to God's promise, '*all* the families of the earth shall be blessed'. In the Hebrew view of things, historical events are not robbed of a wider significance simply by virtue of their particularity. It is rather the case that God invests the whole of history with its meaning and purpose precisely through the particularities of time and place. It was not because of their particularity as such, therefore, that the events of Jesus' life, death and resurrection were said by Paul to be a stumbling block to the Jews. It is rather the Greek mind that balks at the suggestion that through the particularities of Jesus' history the eternal truth of God is mediated once and for all time. In like manner, the discounting of particularity evident in both the modernist tendency 'to suppress the particular through the universal and in postmodernism's homogenizing tendency to attribute to all particulars essentially the same value', as Colin Gunton has put it,[62] undermines the proclamation of God's self-disclosure in a particular time and place, and is nothing less than the abolishing of history itself. It is on these grounds that D.F. Strauss rejects the incarnational narrative of the New Testament. He writes,

> If reality is ascribed to the idea of the unity of the divine and human natures, is this equivalent to the admission that this unity must actually have been once manifested, as it never had been, and never more will be, in one individual? This is indeed not the mode in which Idea realizes itself; it is not wont to lavish all its fulness on one exemplar, and be niggardly towards all others – to express itself perfectly in that one individual and imperfectly in all the rest. … Is not the idea of the unity of the divine and human natures a real one in a far higher sense, when I regard the whole race of mankind as its realization, than when I single out one man as such a realization? Is not an incarnation of God from eternity, a truer one than an incarnation limited to a particular point in time?[63]

Abraham's obedience to the working out of his promise is essential to the content of the promise itself, i.e., that there shall be a covenant between God and his people. The promise is of a two-sided relationship. While it is true that the covenant is a unilateral covenant, initiated by God and sustained by God, its fulfilment requires human response. Unlike Pelagius, however, we shall not suppose that such response can have anything other than a christological ground. Jesus Christ, a 'son of Abraham', is the one through whom the human response is eventually brought to fulfilment. Second, we must speak of the Holy Spirit. For just as a theological account of human response requires Christology, so also it requires pneumatology. It is under the impact of God's Spirit that we are made one with Christ and share thus in his human response to the divine promise.

[62] Gunton, *The One*, 70.

[63] Strauss, *Life of Jesus*, §151.

As Søren Kierkegaard would make clear very soon after the first publication of Strauss's 'examination of the life of Jesus', this dehistoricizing inclination of the Western mind is opposed by the incarnational narrative of the New Testament.[64] That narrative has its place within Israel's doctrine of election. By this doctrine, found at the very heart of Jewish faith, it is confessed that, beginning with Abraham, God works out his purpose for the world through the election of a particular people and through the actions of particular individuals. For the Christian mind, this election is finally brought to fruition in Jesus of Nazareth, called a son of Abraham by both Matthew and Luke, and so implying both that God is at work again here, and further, that through *this* offspring of Abraham the promise of blessing to all the families of the earth is finally being fulfilled.[65] It is for this reason that Karl Barth makes the doctrine of election central to his theology and places it within his discussion of the doctrine of God. The electing grace of God, fulfilled in Christ, reveals at once both who God is: the one who determines to be none other than God for us; and what history is: the medium through which God works out his promise.[66]

The christological focus of the doctrine of election in Christian thought brings us to the heart of the Christian concern with history – namely, to the story told in the Gospels of God's redemptive participation in history by which history itself, turned away from God through human sin, is reoriented to its proper goal in the kingdom of God. Robert Jenson explains, however, that the incarnation is to be seen 'not merely as remedy, but as the provision of the very conditions for participation in the divine community, according to God's intention'.[67] The point is being made that redemption, reconciliation, the fulfilment of the divine purpose – all of these – take place not without but precisely through this set of historical particularities. I side here with the view of Duns Scotus that the incarnation is not a mere expedient consequent on the fall, but the outworking of God's purpose to enter into communion with his people. In the event of incarnation, God's purpose in creation is realized; the goodness of the created order is confirmed and its suitability as the medium for the working out of God's purpose is made clear. It is for this reason that the gospel writers take care to locate historically their accounts of the things that have taken place concerning Jesus – including, quite crucially, the resurrection.[68] If the

---

[64] See Kierkegaard's *Fragments*, published in 1844 – 9 years after the first appearance of Strauss's Hegelian treatise on the life of Jesus.

[65] See also Paul's discussion of the same theme in Gal. 3:15ff.

[66] See Barth, *Church Dogmatics*, II/2, 3–506.

[67] I am indebted here to Jeremy Ive for his explanation of Jenson's theology. See Ive, 'Jenson's Theology', 147.

[68] Luke's resurrection narrative in particular offers a sustained polemic against those who might have argued that the resurrection of Christ was an event in the minds of believers.

resurrection of Jesus is not an event located in (while not confined by) time and space, then we revert once more to the non-Christian idea that the fulfilment of human life and victory over death occurs 'outside' of the created order, thus casting aspersions on the goodness of creation itself. The Christian hope, rather, is for the resurrection of the body, the salvific transformation of *all* that makes us who we are.

The course of our lives, therefore, the historicity of our existence, is not to be disparaged. It is not to be left behind when the *dis*embodied soul returns or progresses to some spiritual realm after death. This is the gnostic error that has been repeated all too frequently in the Christian tradition. The biblical view, in contrast, consistently held throughout the Old and New Testaments, is that not merely the human soul but also the material creation, along with the whole course of history, has a future. The vision of the book of Revelation of a new heaven and a new earth summarizes the hope articulated throughout the Bible that, far from treating the material world and its history as a cast-off in the process of the human soul's redemption, God's purpose is to redeem the world as a whole, to gather the whole of our history into reconciled relationship with himself and thus to see to it that every tear will be wiped from our eyes.

This is the point of the incarnational narrative. In the incarnate life of Jesus Christ, the Word of God and Second Person of the Trinity graces our history with his own presence. He thus confirms history's goodness and shows it to be the medium through which God's loving purpose is worked out. In Jesus Christ, God's relation to the world takes the form of his becoming a subject within it. The one through whom and for whom all things were created and hold together (Col. 1:17) renews through his presence that which human sinfulness had subjected to disorder and decay and 'reconstitutes it in its relation to God'.[69]

It is through Holy Week and Easter most especially that God's love for his creation is made apparent. Through the trials of Gethsemane and his death on the cross at Calvary, the Son of God, through whom all things were created and hold together, exposes himself to the reality of this world's dissolution, drains once and for all time the cup of bitterness that has been filled to overflowing with human treachery to God, and thus ensures that not even the worst that humanity does can thwart God's purpose of communion with all that he has made. If death means the same thing as a life alienated from God, then in submitting himself to that death the Son of God, by virtue of the fact that it is he who suffers these things, robs humanity of its power to render the world godless and saves us thus from the dread consequence of our sin. Or, to put it in

---

[69] Gunton, *Christ and Creation*, 33.

the language of John's prologue, the term '*logos*', used there of Christ, signifies the reason and order of the universe. He is the world's reason for being and the one who gives it its order and purpose. That this Logos, therefore, should confront on the cross humanity's tragic efforts to foist upon the world an order and purpose of its own making and to wrest from God, by crucifying his Son, the prerogative to preserve the world and guide it to its fulfilment – that Christ should confront this evil at the greatest depths to which it may sink, establishes and confirms his sovereignty at the point of humanity's most profound rebellion against it. What this means is that the world and its history is not finally in our hands but in God's. This does not mean that we have been absolved of that responsibility for history about which we have spoken above. But it is precisely 'response-ability', a responsive sharing in the purposes of God. The fact is, we remain capable of abusing that trust. We remain capable of making a hell out of that which has been created for good. But we are not capable of defeating the steadfastness of God's love for the world. For even where we do our worst, God is to be found there, in the crucified figure of Jesus, gathering together in himself all things in heaven and on earth and preparing them for that day when all things will be completed and presented to the Father.

The distinctiveness of the Christian understanding of things is readily apparent here. The kingdom of God is not yet, and disbelief has evidence upon which it can base its claims. So the faith of which we have been speaking, as also the act of redemption itself, is yet an anticipation of things hoped for. The work of Christ does restore God's project, but it requires us still to wait for and work towards something that is not yet. Such hope and work is founded, however, upon that further aspect of Christ's encounter with evil – namely his resurrection and ascension. The victory over the disorder that humanity has wrought in history is not accomplished solely through the presence within it of the Logos himself, but also through God's raising to new life the one whose faithfulness to the world had taken the form of suffering love within it. The chaotic human arraying of things is robbed thus, not only of its godlessness, but also, and concomitantly so, of its bondage to death. The resurrection of Christ, the *first born* of a new creation, is the beginning and condition of the transformation towards fulfilment of the whole of God's creation. And Christ's ascension to sit at the right hand of the Father in glory confirms, once and for all, this Logos and not our own as the Word by which the world will be upheld.

We referred above to the claim of Alan Richardson that, by the time of Augustine, the Hebraic-Christian view of history had triumphed over the classical. That triumph comes about most especially, Augustine argues, because of the resurrection of Jesus Christ. Here, in the midst of history itself, the *telos* of history is decisively revealed and creation's bondage to decay, or otherwise to endless repetition, is defeated once and for all. 'Christ, being raised from

the dead, will never die again; death no longer has dominion over him'
(Rom. 6:9).[70] Richardson comments,

> The Christian experience of the conquest of death through Christ's resurrection
> brought to an end the classical view of history. The European mind was freed by the
> proclamation of God's saving act in history from the fatalistic theory of cyclical
> recurrence which had condemned Greek historiography to sterility.[71]

The resurrection of Jesus is the refutation not only of the cyclical view of
history, but also of the many ways in which history itself is devalued. The
resurrection of Jesus from the dead is God's vindication of this man and his
history as the means through which participation in his coming kingdom is
opened up. We may say, therefore, that through the death and resurrection
of Christ God's action makes history. It is through the series of events that
make up the life of Jesus of Nazareth that creation's destiny is secured and
its meaning revealed. Here the Truth is made known. This moment – of
incarnation and death, resurrection and ascension – is decisive. It is not lost.
It is not a vanishing point of no eternal significance. It is the event in the midst
of history that secures the fulfilment of God's promise and brings creation
to its goal.

Without any such *telos* it is difficult to imagine what sense there could be in
the unfolding of historical life. It could be, presumably, only a sense of our own
making and not one that inheres in the events themselves. It is the theological
framework of creation and promise, then, that provides a conceptual grounding for the meaningfulness of human life. Apart from these conditions the idea
of a purpose in history, and thus of the historic character of human action, must
be either abandoned or contrived.

This, it seems to me, reveals the plight of that form of biblical scholarship
that we have seen represented in the Jesus Seminar. Rejecting the New Testament proclamation that God is working his purpose out in Christ, and rejecting
thus the incarnational narrative that is intelligible only within such a view of
history, the scholars have only a few scraps of data left. The task of understanding 'who Jesus really was' then becomes, very nearly, a feat of *creatio ex nihilo* – a
kind of miracle, one might suggest, in which the power in which we are
invited to trust is not that of the Holy Spirit, as the narrative itself commends,
but of the biblical scholars themselves.

---

[70] See Augustine, *City of God*, XII.13.
[71] Richardson, *History*, 60.

History and Hermeneutics Revisited

We have attempted to trace in this chapter the reasons for and the character of a fundamental resistance in the Western intellectual heritage to the historical mediation of truth and salvation. Identified by Christian theology as the scandal of particularity, this resistance takes offence at the proclamation of Christ crucified and raised from the dead as the decisive action of God in bringing about the reconciliation of the world with himself. The rejection of this historical mediation of truth and salvation has its roots, we have argued, in the devaluation of the realm of space and time in Greek thought, and has been allowed to flourish in the Christian theological tradition because of a neglect of the doctrine of creation. The soteriological consequence of this rejection of history is that, forsaking dependence upon what has taken place in Jesus, the individual finds within himself the resources of wisdom and insight to work out his own salvation. Our project has been to offer an alternative conception of what history is – a conception drawn from the Bible itself. I offer now, by way of conclusion, an indication of how this biblical conception of history might make an impact upon the task of biblical hermeneutics.

(1) The first point is straightforward. There is no good reason to decide as a presupposition of biblical hermeneutics that God is not involved in history. To do so is to set the biblical writings in a conceptual framework that is alien to them and will, very likely, preclude our understanding them aright.

(2) Just because the books of the Bible are theological documents does not mean that they are not also history. The only justification for such a claim would rest on God's certainly not being involved in history. If, on the other hand, God is involved in history, that would mean that there cannot be history without theology. History and theology, therefore, are not mutually exclusive by definition.

(3) If God is active in history, guiding his people and bringing about his purpose of reconciliation with him, then it is reasonable to suppose that God is also involved in our apprehension of the events through which this purpose is worked out. Primarily, this means that God is involved in our understanding of Scripture. It is at the very least, therefore, a regrettable impoverishment of that understanding, if not a falsification of Scripture itself, if we undertake to read while trusting in our own resources alone. We ought instead to claim the promise that Christ will send the Holy Spirit to bear witness to himself and to guide us into all Truth.

(4) Because the Spirit is a gift, not to individuals but to a people gathered by God into the community of faith, the interpretation of Scripture under the guidance of God's Spirit is not primarily the task of individual scholars undertaken in the privacy of their own studies. First and foremost, it is the

task of the church in public acts of witness and worship. Biblical scholarship is done properly when it is put in service of that task.

(5) The church is a body extended through space and time. Every local gathering of the church is bound in fellowship with the communion of saints. The apostolic witness, therefore, for all that it has been shaped by the cultural conditions of the first century, is not something from which we are separated by a 'broad ugly ditch'. The apostles are not citizens of a world that we moderns no longer inhabit. They are part of the one community that is called into being and continues to be shaped by God to bear witness to the working out of his purpose. That christocentric and pneumatological reality overrides what differences there certainly are between Jew and Greek, male and female, ancient and modern, and thus enables the Spirit-inspired speech of the apostles to be heard 'in our own language'.

(6) Because the central theme of the Bible is the action of God through history culminating in the life, death, resurrection and ascension of Jesus, then Jesus himself must be understood as the hermeneutical key to the biblical canon as a whole. The Bible is not to be treated as a disparate collection of texts with no intrinsic unity, but it constitutes rather a consistent and coherent witness to Christ. To be sure, Christ is not explicitly known to the writers of the Hebrew Scriptures, but neither is he unknown. He is present, rather, as the Word of God throughout Israel's history, and he shines his light backwards, as it were, when in incarnate form he makes himself known as the One to whom those Scriptures point.

(7) Because Christian faith depends for its very essence and truth upon certain things that have taken place in history, that faith is not reducible to a set of abstract propositions recognized as necessarily true by the power of human reason. The truth with which we are concerned in Christianity, and which is proclaimed in the biblical writings, is contingent truth. It is simply not amenable, therefore, to the kinds of epistemic procedure that require an indubitable warrant for all truth claims. But then, very little of the truth we are most concerned with as human beings does fit that particular straightjacket. It is not for that reason untrue. This means for biblical hermeneutics that we should not be constrained by the demand for absolute certainty. Some things may be taken on trust – not because we have proven them beyond all doubt, but because they fit with what else we have learned of God's gracious accommodation to our human incapacity. That does not mean that we cannot know what took place in and through Jesus. It means, rather, that we know in part. That is a suitable kind of knowledge for human life, and it is enough to be going on with until that day when we shall see face to face.

It is probable that these hermeneutical considerations will not satisfy those who are determined to read Scripture within the limits of historical-critical method alone. Be that as it may. I have tried to show what is involved in reading Scripture on its own terms, while at the same time arguing that there is no good reason why those terms should not also be our own.

Bibliography

Augustine, *The City of God* (trans. J. Healey; London: J.M. Dent, 1945)

Barth, K., *Church Dogmatics*, II (trans. ed. G.W. Bromiley and T.F. Torrance; Edinburgh: T. & T. Clark, 1957)

Bultmann, R., *History and Eschatology* (Edinburgh: Edinburgh University Press, 1957)

Collingwood, R.G., *The Idea of History* (ed. T.M. Knox; London: OUP, 1946)

de Lubac, H., *Histoire et Esprit: L'Intelligence de l'Écriture d'après Origène* (Paris: Aubier, 1950)

——, *Medieval Exegesis*, I: *The Four Senses of Scripture* (trans. M. Sebanc; Grand Rapids: Eerdmans, 1998)

Derrida, J., *The Gift of Death* (trans. D. Wills; Chicago: University of Chicago Press, 1995)

Descartes, R., *Discourse on Method and the Meditations* (trans. F.E. Sutcliffe; Harmondsworth: Penguin Books, 1968)

Eichrodt, W., 'Offenbarung und Geschichte im Alten Testament', *TZ* IV (1948), 321ff.

Evans, C.S., and M. Westphal, *Christian Perspectives on Religious Knowledge* (Grand Rapids: Eerdmans, 1993)

Fichte, J.G., *Die Anweisung zum seligen Leben* (ed. F. Medicus; Hamburg: Felix Meiner, 1954)

Funk, R.W., R.W. Hoover and The Jesus Seminar, *The Five Gospels: The Search for the Authentic Words of Jesus* (New York: Macmillan, 1993)

Gadamer, H., *Truth and Method* (London: Sheed & Ward, 2nd edn, 1975)

Goldmann, L., *The Hidden God: A Study of Tragic Vision in the 'Pensées' of Pascal and the Tragedies of Racine* (London: Routledge & Kegan Paul, 1964)

Gunton, C.E., *The One, the Three and the Many: God, Creation and the Culture of Modernity* (Cambridge: CUP, 1993)

——, *The Triune Creator: A Historical and Systematic Study* (Edinburgh: Edinburgh University Press, 1998)

——, *Christ and Creation* (Carlisle: Paternoster Press, 1992)

Hamilton, W., *A Quest for the Post-Historical Jesus* (London: SCM Press, 1993)

Hays, R.B., 'The Corrected Jesus', *First Things* 43 (May 1994), 43–48

Hegel, G.W.F., *Lectures on the Philosophy of World History* (trans. H.B. Nisbet; intro. D. Forbes; Cambridge: CUP, 1975)

——, 'The Positivity of the Christian Religion', in *Friedrich Hegel on Christianity: Early Theological Writings* (trans. T.M. Knox; New York: Harper Torchbooks, 1961), 67–81

Ive, J., 'Robert W. Jenson's Theology of History', in *Trinity, Time and Church: A Response to the Theology of Robert W. Jenson* (ed. C.E. Gunton; Grand Rapids: Eerdmans, 2000), 146–57

Jaki, S.L., *The Saviour of Science* (Edinburgh: Scottish Academic Press, 1990)

Jeanrond, W., *Theological Hermeneutics: Development and Significance* (London: SCM Press, 1994)

Kaiser, C.B., *Creation and the History of Science* (Grand Rapids: Eerdmans, 1991)

Kant, I., *Religion Within the Limits of Reason Alone* (trans., intro. and notes by T.M. Greene and H.H. Hudson; New York: Harper & Row, 1960)

Kierkegaard, S., *Philosophical Fragments* (ed. and trans. H.V. Hong and E.H. Hong; Princeton: Princeton University Press, 1985)

Lessing, G.E., 'On the Proof of Spirit and of Power', in *Lessing's Theological Writings* (ed. H. Chadwick; London: Adam and Charles Black, 1956), 51–56

Novak, D., *The Election of Israel: The Idea of the Chosen People* (Cambridge: CUP, 1995)

Pannenberg, W., *Systematic Theology*, II (trans. G.W. Bromiley; Edinburgh: T. & T. Clark, 1994)

Plantinga, A., *Warranted Christian Belief* (New York: OUP, 2000)

Richardson, A., *History Sacred and Profane* (London: SCM Press, 1964)

Spinoza, B., *Tractatus Theologico-Politicus* (trans. S. Shirley; Leiden: E.J. Brill, 1991)

——, *Ethics* (trans. A. Boyle; London: J.M. Dent, 1959)

Strauss, D.F., *The Life of Jesus Critically Examined* (trans. G. Eliot; Philadelphia: Fortress Press, 1972)

Troeltsch, E., 'Historical and Dogmatic Method in Theology', in *Religion in History: Ernst Troeltsch* (Edinburgh: T. & T. Clark, 1991), 11–32

Turner, H.W., *The Roots of Science: An Investigative Journey Through the World's Religions* (Auckland: DeepSight Trust, 1998)

Vanhoozer, K.J., *Is There a Meaning in this Text?* (Grand Rapids: Zondervan, 1998)

Vico, G.B., *Principles of a New Science about the Common Nature of Nations* (trans. T.G. Bergin and M.H. Fisch; Ithaca, NY: Cornell University Press, 1948)

von Rad, G., *God at Work in Israel* (trans. J.H. Marks; Nashville: Abingdon Press, 1980)

Watson, F., *Text and Truth: Redefining Biblical Theology* (Edinburgh: T. & T. Clark, 1997)

Wolterstorff, N., *Until Justice and Peace Embrace* (Grand Rapids: Eerdmans, 1983)

Wright, N.T., 'Five Gospels but No Gospel: Jesus and the Seminar', in *Crisis in Christology: Essays in Quest of Resolution* (ed. W.R. Farmer; Livonia, MI: Dove Booksellers, 1995), 115–17

——, *Jesus and the Victory of God* (London: SPCK, 1996)

Tradition and History

13

The Conflict of Tradition and History
Walter Sundberg

Goethe's Observation

In a letter to the composer Carl Friedrich Zelter (1758–1832), dated 18
March 1811, Johann Wolfgang von Goethe (1749–1832) makes the following
observation about the vocation of the artist:

> Every true artist is to be regarded as a person who seeks to preserve something
> acknowledged to be holy and serious and deliberately to transmit it to others. But
> every century has its specific tendency to secularism and endeavors to make profane
> what is holy, easy what is difficult, and ludicrous what is serious, to which there would
> be no objection, if only it did not result in the destruction of seriousness and mirth.[1]

It would appear that what Goethe says of the artist could be said of the
Christian theologian. The theologian is the preserver of a specific past that is
acknowledged to be holy. This means that the theologian understands this past
not as a relic, but as an active force that he or she feels responsible to transmit as
a witness to the present. The vocation of theology is one of high seriousness.
The theologian serves the sacred by confronting the profane in order to judge
it, enrich it, give it hope and, perhaps, even make it laugh (not an easy thing,
especially when the profane is defended by other theologians). In short, the
business of the theologian is to bear the Christian tradition.

   Bearing the Christian tradition often means fierce opposition. 'If they persecuted me', says Jesus, 'they will persecute you' (Jn. 15:20). To defend tradition
may require extraordinary faithfulness and fortitude. There are occasions, however, when church traditions deserve to be challenged. Then tradition must
undergo revision and change – always an arduous task. Other times, the situation is ambiguous. At the time Goethe wrote his letter, the Christian tradition
faced sustained assault by the powerful, and decidedly ambiguous, enemy of

---

[1] Quoted in Pieper, 'Tradition', 489.

historical criticism. History was the 'specific tendency toward secularism' of the age that promised true knowledge of religion. Many notable bearers of the Christian tradition attempted to accommodate the claims of history. Others rejected these claims altogether. The conflict between tradition and history emerged in the early nineteenth century as the defining mark of serious theology.

The purpose of this chapter is twofold. The first is to provide a brief historical overview of the conflict between tradition and history leading up to the nineteenth century. This account will be necessarily sketchy and quite conventional. But it is important to set the context for the second and main purpose of the chapter, which is to examine a theologian who, writing at a time when the conflict was in full force, did not forget – and does not let the reader forget – what is at stake: Søren Kierkegaard (1813–55). Kierkegaard's criticism of the academic and ecclesiastical establishment of his day, his creative employment of the idea of tradition and his willingness to accept the secular challenge that history poses to the theological enterprise are relevant to the contemporary scene.

The Conflict of Tradition and History

'Tradition', says G.L. Prestige, 'means delivery'.[2] This delivery begins in the Bible itself, where numerous *tradita* operate as fundamental building blocks of the faith (e.g., Rom. 1:3–4; 1 Cor. 11:23–26; 15:3–7; Phil. 2:6–11). These served the early church as explicit declarations for interpreting the gospel by the community as a whole. They formed a network of beliefs, enabling the Christian proclamation to be perceived not only as kerygma – that is, the missionary message announcing Christ 'where he is not yet known'[3] – but also as creedal statements of an established community. In late New Testament letters especially, these creedal statements are understood to pass on the knowledge of Christ in the form of a deposit of faith (2 Tim. 1:12, 14). Tradition (*paradosis*) is the authentic articulation of revelation by means of recollection. It requires protection from falsifiers (1 Tim. 6:20) and is itself a judgement upon such falsifiers (2 Pet. 2:21). It is based on the fundamental realization that the decisive events of redemption that encompass the life of Jesus are concluded. What the church passes on is 'the faith once for all delivered to the saints' (Jude 3).

Beginning with the Apostolic Fathers, this 'faith once delivered' becomes, in the words of Gerhard Ebeling, 'a *primum movens*' that has 'abiding, normative, absolute significance' and is 'withdrawn from the relativity and transience

---

[2] Prestige, *Fathers*, 6.
[3] Dahl, *Jesus*, 19.

of all historic events'.[4] Tradition witnesses to the true church that is at one with the pure teaching of its Lord, passed on to humanity by the authority of the apostles. Under the aegis of tradition, the Bible is seen to be, especially after the fixing of the canon in the fourth century, 'a literary genius of a wholly peculiar kind'. 'Since [the Bible] is the sole way of approach to the revelation, it even comes to take the place of revelation. As communication of revelation it must be ontologically the same in kind as the event of revelation itself'.[5]

To pass from one generation to the next, this ontology of Scripture-as-revelation requires a disciplined process of transmission in the church. This process is based on at least four assumptions.[6] The first is that the relationship of the present generation to the past is conceived in terms of the latter's absolute superiority in knowledge. In tradition, there is no two-sided conversation taking place. The past alone does the teaching – or so it must appear. This assumption is deeply embedded in ancient culture. 'The ancients are better than we', says Plato (427–347 BC), 'for they dwell nearer the gods'.[7] Eusebius (c. 260 – c. 340), the first church historian, asserts that Christ's teaching is not 'new and strange', but goes back to the sacred origin: 'the very first and most ancient and antique discovery of true religion by Abraham and those lovers of God who followed him.[8] For Eusebius, it is not the newness of the covenant in Christ that attracts. What ultimately counts is that Christ embodies a teaching that predates the foundations of Greece and Rome. Second is the belief that an enduring social structure transmits that truth faithfully from generation to generation as 'a timeless continuum where cause and effect, antecedent and consequence play no part'.[9] So Vincent of Lérins (d. c. 450) speaks of the *traditio ecclesiae Catholicae* that has been believed *ubique, semper, omnibus* – 'everywhere, always, and by all'.[10] The third operating assumption is that no premium is to be placed on creative or revolutionary thought. On the contrary, all originality is distrusted. The truth given in tradition is to be passed on and must be passed on exactly as received. So Christian theologians condemn heretics as 'innovators', declaring that the content of faith is 'the same for all time' and the church lives according to the axiom: 'In every age ... the same things should be believed'.[11] Crucial in this connection is finally the act of receiving tradition.

---

[4] Ebeling, *Word*, 29.
[5] Ebeling, *Word*, 31.
[6] On the following see especially Pieper, 'Tradition', 475–80; Wilken, *Myth*, 77–118; Sundberg, 'Luther'.
[7] Plato, *Philebus*, 16c, quoted in Wilken, *Myth*, 50.
[8] Eusebius, *History*, I, 39, 42.
[9] Headley, *History*, 57f.
[10] McCracken and Cabaniss, *Early*, 38.
[11] Aquinas, *Summa*, XXXI, 33 (2a2ae 1, 7).

Each generation is called to fideistic obedience. An objective or neutral stance cannot be taken. What is called for, rather, is loyalty in the form of sheer allegiance. According to I Clement, writing at the very beginning of theology and drawing on a typical sentiment of Roman thought, the duty of the Christian, especially in times of conflict, is to 'turn to': 'the glorious and holy rule of our tradition'.[12]

The power and authority of this traditioning process cannot be underestimated. It animated the theology and cultic practice of the church without a serious rival for 1,500 years. The allure of tradition centers around its ability to satisfy the deep-seated religious need that human beings have for security and familiarity in their relations with the divine. In the view of Martin Buber (1878–1965),

> man desires to have God ... he desires to have God continually in space and time. He is loath to be satisfied with the inexpressible confirmation of the meaning; he wants to see it opened out as something that we can take out and handle again and again – a continuum unbroken in space and time.[13]

Tradition provides exactly this continuum in space and time. It asserts direct communication with the divine through the church as the organ of redemption. Tradition is believed to be able to solve any conflict, repel any challenge. It demands loyalty and receives it. 'People will die for a dogma', says Robert Nisbet, 'who will not even stir for a conclusion'.[14]

The rise of historical scholarship places this ancient hermeneutic of tradition in doubt. The earliest historians, at least the ones we honor as progenitors of the modern practice of history, exercised their craft by assaulting traditions. So Laurentius Valla (1407–57) proved convincingly in *Declamatio* (1440) that the so-called Donation of Constantine was a fraud. Valla argued from common sense that an emperor would not disinherit his children from the full possessions to which they were entitled and that the Roman senate would never have agreed to the loss of land. He examined the text for anachronistic phrasing and false references. While Valla did not take on the Bible, he demonstrated that scholarship, motivated by suspicion, is a powerful force against the church. Valla served at the time as royal secretary to Alfonso of Aragon, King of Naples, who was at war with the pope. 'There is nothing like violent partisanship', observes Herbert Butterfield, 'for setting criticism alight and driving its ingenuity'.[15]

---

[12] Richardson, *Fathers*, 47.
[13] Buber, *I and Thou*, 161f.
[14] Nisbet, *Prejudices*, 91.
[15] Butterfield, 'Historiography', 485.

The exercise of critical judgement, provoked by violent partisanship, is characteristic of the Reformation's assault on tradition. Martin Luther's (1483–1546) commitment to the gospel of justification is the partisan principle by which he asserts that much of church practice and teaching is without biblical sanction.[16] The Roman Church, in his view, collapses tradition into the jurisdictional authority of the magisterium, justifying this move on the spurious notion that revelation is integrated sacramentally into the hierarchy of the priesthood and takes legal form. The resulting illusion – that somehow this priestly hierarchy, and especially the papacy, guarantees revelation across time and represents Christ in a direct way – means in reality that the church has no independent critical measure by which to test the spirits and judge its life. To accept 'tradition' is to accept the legal power of the priesthood, to the gospel to be overshadowed by ecclesiastical authority; in short, it is to make the community of faith hermeneutically impenetrable, hidden behind the gilded curtain of canon law. It is against this that the revolutionary power of the gospel asserts itself. 'What is not Christ is not light. As often as I hear "the fathers, Augustine, Jerome, the councils," I ask: "Is there also a proclamation?" If not, I say: "Be off!" '[17] Adolf von Harnack (1851–1930) said,

> The Reformation obtained a new point of departure for the framing of Christian faith in the Word of God, and it discarded all forms of infallibility which could offer an external security for faith, the infallible organization of the Church, the infallible doctrinal tradition of the Church, and the infallible Scriptural codex.[18]

If the continuity of revelation is not guaranteed by infallible agencies, then how is it passed on? In Luther's view, the authentic form of the gospel is Jesus Christ reaching believers across time through oral proclamation. Jesus and the apostles were preachers of the word. Certainly they drew upon the Scriptures; but they did so in living speech. It was only because there 'was a serious decline and lack of Spirit' in the church, allowing 'heretics' and 'false teachers' to gain a foothold, that God's word was necessarily set to writing.[19] The written text of the New Testament, at least when considered in the specific terms of its origin (a crucial question for tradition), is a tragic necessity of Christian experience that functions to stabilize the oral proclamation and protect the fidelity of Christians against heretical challenge. While *sola scriptura* is the watchword of the Reformation, the *verbum Dei non scriptum* is prior. This makes the oral word the critical principle of interpretation. When it comes to the test, the preaching of Christ stands against church tradition and even Scripture: 'The Scriptures must

---

[16] On the following, see Sundberg, 'Luther', 115–16.
[17] Luther, *Works*, XXX, 226–27.
[18] Harnack, *History*, VII, 24.
[19] Luther, *Works*, LII, 205–206.

be understood in favor of Christ, not against him. For that reason, they must either refer to him or must not be held to be true Scriptures'.[20] While Luther may not practice historical criticism in the modern sense, he helps to prepare the ground for its appearance.

Even more radical is Desiderius Erasmus (1466?–1536). The impetus for his attack on tradition is the debate over predestination. In *De libero arbitrio* (1524), Erasmus declares predestination to be an 'exaggerated view' of theology for which there is no clear warrant. His argument rests on skepticism that tradition, as the original reception of revelation by the apostles, can be accurately delivered from past to present. Erasmus does not doubt (or so he claims) that the apostles had 'the gift of the Spirit'. The apostles could interpret Scripture confidently just as they 'shook off vipers, raised the dead, and by the laying on of hands bestowed the gift of tongues'. 'But I have the suspicion', Erasmus argues, 'that just as the charismata of healings and tongues ceased, this charisma [of interpretation] ceased also'. The present age is far removed from the ancient past and tradition cannot overcome the distance. To the question: 'what ought to be done in this carnal age?' Erasmus offers no firm answer.[21]

Baruch Spinoza (1632–77) does have an answer that goes directly to the authority of Scripture itself. The Bible should be read like any other book, subject to critical research.[22] In the *Theological-Political Treatise* (1670), Spinoza proposes rational biblical criticism to separate acceptable religious truth from the 'superstition' of exaggerated views. It does this by interpreting the Bible apart from ecclesiastical and political bias. The key to rational interpretation is the distinction between truth and meaning. 'Truth' refers to matters of universal significance that reason is able to discover regardless of time and place. 'Meaning' refers to the cultural expressions of particular peoples bound to time and place. Meaning is the preeminent historical category in Spinoza's philosophy that allows the biblical critic to explain epiphanies of the divine, prophecies, miracles and especially barbarous prescriptions as transient, cultural phenomena. Truth appears in the Bible whenever there are clear and distinct commands to love God and neighbor. Such commands have timeless import. They exemplify the true virtue that reason seeks: that is, the universal moral characteristics of 'love, joy, peace, temperance, and honest dealing with men'.[23] No one less than Christ himself summarizes the truth of the Scriptures as the teaching to love God and neighbor (Mt. 22:37–40).

Erasmus and Spinoza (unlike Luther) operate with what Peter Burke calls 'a sense of anachronism' which is crucial to the emergence of genuine historical

---

[20] Luther, *Works*, XXXIV, 112.

[21] Rupp and Watson, *Luther*, 44–45.

[22] On the following, see Harrisville and Sundberg, *Bible*, 30–45; Sundberg, 'Spinoza'.

[23] Spinoza, *Tractatus*, 52.

sensibility. This is the understanding that the past is different from the present; that it is subject to causes and beliefs that no longer hold.[24] In order to know the past, one must go behind tradition, examining its texts as source material. The historian must take details, random facts and separate pieces of information and see them precisely in their separateness, variety and conflict. The past must be dismantled and then reconstructed to make it understandable to the present. The past is therefore not automatically superior to the present. To be alienated from the past in this way – a way that tradition cannot resolve – is but a step from asserting that tradition is false altogether.

One who comes close to taking this step is Gotthold Ephraim Lessing (1729–81). Lessing carries over from Spinoza the distinction of truth and meaning as it applies to biblical interpretation. Lessing identifies this distinction, using common terminology of the Enlightenment, as the difference between absolute and contingent truth. Absolute truth is the product of reason; contingent truth is the information provided by sense experience and history. Absolute truth is reliable because it is grounded in reason. Contingent truth is unreliable because it is 'accidental', the particular stuff of mundane events that display no pattern or universal necessity. Absolute truth thus cannot depend on history.[25] Lessing is willing to concede that in biblical times, and in the early church, prophecies may indeed have been fulfilled and miracles may have taken place. 'But I live in the eighteenth century, in which miracles no longer happen'. Thus 'the problem is that this proof of the spirit and of power no longer has any spirit or power, but has sunk to the level of human testimonies of spirit and power'.[26] Critical investigation of these testimonies, the attempt to go behind them to uncover their human motivation, is not encouraging. The history of Christianity – because it is the story of confusion and vulgar human striving – illustrates the unreliability of contingent truth. This is the lesson of the 'Fragments' by Hermann Samuel Reimarus (1694–1768) that Lessing published to great scandal between 1774 and 1778. For Lessing, history 'is the ugly broad ditch which I cannot get across, however often and however earnestly I have tried to make the leap'.[27]

Despite this skepticism, Lessing offers a constructive proposal in his famous essay, 'The Education of the Human Race' (1780), in which he attempts to show how the truth of Christianity may be understood to survive its historicity. History, says Lessing, displays a teleological rationale in which the Bible and tradition, despite their historical contingency, may have a legitimate place in the search for absolute truth. In principle, the Bible provides nothing to

---

[24] Burke, *Renaissance*, 1.
[25] Chadwick, *Lessing's Theological Writings*, 53.
[26] Chadwick, *Lessing's Theological Writings*, 52.
[27] Chadwick, *Lessing's Theological Writings*, 55.

humanity that it cannot get on its own by reason. But humanity must be educated over time in the ways of God. This educational process is necessary
because human potential cannot be fulfilled all at once. Historical revelation is
thus appropriate for the human race in its childhood. In this regard, the Old
Testament accommodates the truth to 'the Israelitish people, unpractised in
thought as they are'.[28] The New Testament is 'the second, better primer for the
race of man'[29] because Christ taught 'an inward purity of heart'.[30] That the New
Testament succeeds the Old shows that truth is a developmental force that
employs changing external means for its realization. Together, the Old and
New Testaments 'have occupied human reason more than all other books'.[31]
This influence points to the superiority of Christianity – that is, to its cultural
and intellectual dominance. But reason moves on and the human race grows
up in 'the development of revealed truths into truths of reason', a process that
'is absolutely necessary, if the human race is to be assisted by them'.[32] Maturity
in interpretation means treating the Bible as a step on the way to truth. Not the
origin, but the end, is the measure of things. The contingent Christian tradition
is absorbed into a rational idea of history conceived as a metanarrative
grounded in the principle of progress.

'The Education of the Human Race' was enormously influential and adapt-
able. Among liberal Protestants, like Friedrich Schleiermacher (1768–1834)
and G.W.F. Hegel (1770–1831), it encouraged a 'new historico-critical and yet
religion affirming theology' in which the Christian tradition was reinterpreted
according to cultural imperatives such as the psychological integration of
personhood (Schleiermacher) or the transformation of myth into philosophy
(Hegel).[33] Lessing also influenced, at least indirectly, religious conservatives who
sought a historical apologetic to justify the institutional church and its doctrines.
For example, Johann Sebastian Drey (1777–1853), founder of the Catholic
Tübingen School, speaks of Christ as a 'seed' (*Keim*) in the arena of history from
which emerges 'the idea of the church' as the center of continuing revelation
in history.[34] Likewise, John Henry Newman (1801–90) defines Christ as a
'legislature in germ' and asserts that the fullness of faith in the unfolding history
of the church transcends the 'fabulous primitive simplicity' of biblical origins.[35]

---

[28] Chadwick, *Lessing's Theological Writings*, 87.
[29] Chadwick, *Lessing's Theological Writings*, 93.
[30] Chadwick, *Lessing's Theological Writings*, 92.
[31] Chadwick, *Lessing's Theological Writings*, 93.
[32] Chadwick, *Lessing's Theological Writings*, 95.
[33] Troeltsch, *Absoluteness*, 50.
[34] Geiselmann, *Geist*, 263, 302; on the influence of Lessing, see Drey, *Einleitung*, vi.
[35] Newman, *Essay*, 67, 382; on the influence of Lessing, see Chadwick, *Lessing's Theological Writings*, 48.

These proposals, both liberal and conservative, attempt to resolve the conflict of tradition and history in favor of history. But the idea of history that is operating in these theologies is one that is imbued with philosophical necessity and divine purpose. Is this true to the nature of history? One for whom this remained a nagging question was Lessing. While Lessing's 'Education of the Human Race' influenced many, it apparently did not convince its author. In the same year that he wrote the essay, which was also the year before his death, Lessing confided to Friedrich Heinrich Jacobi (1743–1819): 'The orthodox ideas of the Deity are no longer possible for me ... There is no philosophy except the philosophy of Spinoza'.[36] Lessing could not or would not leap across the 'ugly broad ditch'.

Søren Kierkegaard

Søren Kierkegaard enters the conflict of tradition and history fully conversant with the range of academic debate in his day.[37] In his mind, the problem is not the need for an apologetic theology that reinterprets the meaning of Christianity according to modern historical consciousness. The real problem is moral. Contemporary apologetics serves a false purpose. Academic professors and ecclesiastical leaders employ apologetics to protect themselves, and the constituencies they represent, from the rigorous claims of the Bible. 'We have invented scholarship', says Kierkegaard, 'in order to evade doing God's will'.[38] As Kierkegaard argues in *Concluding Unscientific Postscript* (1846), this evasion is accomplished in two ways – both of which exploit historical consciousness to distort tradition.

The first way is academic. Kierkegaard calls it 'speculative thought'.[39] Here 'Christianity is viewed as a historical document', the understanding of which at any given time can only be 'an approximation'.[40] If one can know an object of belief only at an intellectual distance, then one is relieved of the burden of making a passionate commitment that involves personal risk, sacrifice and the censure of academic colleagues. Speculative thought produces spectators: detached observers adept at schematizing and criticizing reality, but little affected in their actual behavior by the object of their attention. At most, speculative thought engenders a mild allegiance to Christianity that finds pleasure in intellectual curiosity. This is an agreeable stance for the professorate, for whom intellectual curiosity is a familiar and comfortable vocation.

---

[36] Chadwick, *Lessing's Theological Writings*, 46.
[37] On the following see Harrisville and Sundberg, *Bible*, 169–74.
[38] Kierkegaard, *Journals*, III, 657.
[39] Kierkegaard, *Postscript*, I, 31.
[40] Kierkegaard, *Postscript*, I, 23.

The second way to evade God's will is what Kierkegaard calls 'the Church theory'.[41] Here ecclesiastical authorities keep the object of faith at a safe distance by absolving church members of all responsibility to make a decision for faith. The church theory assumes that everyone is a Christian already, membership being guaranteed by the prestige of a historic institution, enduring across time, that possesses orthodox creeds and confessions, divinely mandated liturgy and, above all, the sacrament of infant baptism conceived 'as something magical to hold on to' that replaces the responsibility of personal faith.[42] Kierkegaard satirizes this as 'a Danish idea'. His specific object of derision is Nikolai Grundtvig (1783–1872).[43] But what he is after generally is the conventionality of nominal faith that characterizes the European territorial church and is defended by High Church romanticism that traffics in sentimentality and nostalgia. The church theory is an ideology of 'sheer estheticism'.[44] It is 'a Christianity from which the terror has been removed'.[45] No doubt it offers an appealing cultural vision of religion as a blend of sacramental theology, piety and patriotism. But its driving force is to reduce Christianity to the lowest common denominator of the immature. This may be Christendom, but it is not Christianity.

True Christianity involves what Kierkegaard calls 'the Socratic secret', that is, the decision of faith that entails a painful examination of the self and a 'subjective transformation' of one's entire way of being in the world.[46] Only by making this decision can one realize personal existence and become what God intended: an individual self. The vast majority does not reach individual personhood. Most people spend their lives avoiding serious decisions. Instead of seeking commitments, they drift along on the surface of life seeking momentary pleasure and diversions, conforming to the wishes of others, refusing to take responsibility, living as anonymous members of the crowd. In the end, such a life becomes an increasingly panicky flight from boredom and is bound to end in despair. In order to become a true self, one must face the predicament of one's existence. This is a risky and unattractive business. It is the polar opposite of academic curiosity or nominal church membership: 'remember that the higher the religious is taken, the more rigorous it becomes, but it does not necessarily follow that you are able to bear it'.[47] True faith entails taking on an alien consciousness, becoming a stranger in the world, embracing

---

[41] Kierkegaard, *Postscript*, I, 40, 43, 608.

[42] Kierkegaard, *Postscript*, I, 44.

[43] Kierkegaard, *Postscript*, I, 36.

[44] Kierkegaard, *Postscript*, I, 608.

[45] Kierkegaard, *Postscript*, I, 122.

[46] Kierkegaard, *Postscript*, I, 38; *Self-Examination*, 10–11. On what follows, see also Kierkegaard, *Stages*.

[47] Kierkegaard, *Self-Examination*, 11.

a life of striving that is the essence of the human: 'continued striving is the consciousness of being an existing individual'.[48]

This is not easy to do – especially in a secular age. 'There is always a secular mentality', writes Kierkegaard, that 'wants to become Christian as cheaply as possible'.[49] This mentality rejects the strenuous imposition of commands. It refuses to acknowledge that one's life, in order to belong to God, must change. It desires faith to be a passive assurance, the simple possession of a comforting, non-threatening truth. True faith can be no such thing. Rather, it is like 'a true love affair': a 'restless thing' that grips one's very being and constantly tosses one about.[50] True faith demands examination of the self – an examination that begins with the hearing and reading of Scripture.

In a celebrated passage in *For Self-Examination* (1851), Kierkegaard offers a basic account of his biblical hermeneutic as he exposits James 1:22–24:

> But be doers of the word, and not hearers only, deceiving yourselves. For if any one is a hearer of the word and not a doer, he is like a man who observes his natural face in a mirror; for he observes himself and goes away and at once forgets what he was like.

To avoid deceiving oneself, one must be mindful of three dangers. The first danger is spending one's time looking at the mirror and not looking at the self in the mirror. This happens when the reader hides behind the necessary but essentially busy work of attending to the text, its setting and proper translation. Certainly one wants to know exactly what Scripture says. But to read Scripture is like reading a letter from a lover. The point is to find out what the lover is saying: 'all these scholarly preliminaries [are] as a necessary evil so that he can come to the point – of reading the letter from his beloved'.[51] The second danger is forgetting that Scripture is addressing the self directly and personally: '*It is I to whom it is speaking; it is I about whom it is speaking*'.[52] The word of God is misconstrued if it is defined as an objective text, impersonal and historically bound. To make this mistake is to allow the speculative mind-set of the academic class to remove Scripture and keep it at a distance so that it cannot become for the reader looking in the mirror of its words that which it truly is, 'an extremely dangerous book for me' that is out 'to change my whole life on a prodigious scale'.[53] The reader must be earnest – even if he risks being ridiculed as naïve, even if he is admonished for being immoderate and uncultured. The reader must eschew the modern penchant for seeking protection in ironic

---

[48] Kierkegaard, *Postscript*, I, 122.
[49] Kierkegaard, *Self-Examination*, 16.
[50] Kierkegaard, *Self-Examination*, 21.
[51] Kierkegaard, *Self-Examination*, 27.
[52] Kierkegaard, *Self-Examination*, 35 (emphasis original).
[53] Kierkegaard, *Self-Examination*, 31.

distance and see himself in the mirror: 'Then when the parable ends and Christ says to the Pharisee, "Go and do likewise," you shall say to yourself, "It is I to whom this is addressed – away at once!" '[54] Finally, to hear and read Scripture properly, one must never forget how one looks in the mirror of the word after one turns away. This requires an 'honest distrust of oneself'; one must readily treat oneself 'as a suspicious character', an 'unreliable client' always ready to look for a loophole in harsh commands, to justify oneself by rational excuse, to distract oneself by 'the hullabaloo' of the world.[55] One must hear the word and be silent before it; listen and take it in to the deepest recesses of the self.

If these dangers of the false reading of Scripture are avoided and examination of the self begins, then a crucial step will be taken on the path to the true self. This step in this striving to be a true self is the fear of God: 'The fear of the LORD is the beginning of wisdom' (Prov. 9:10). There is nothing in life more serious than taking this first step. Only by fearing God, by being anxious and feeling dread about ultimate fate, can a person turn away from who he or she is and seek what he or she can become. To understand this crucial first step, Kierkegaard calls upon both tradition and history to be his witnesses; but he calls upon them in his unique way.

Kierkegaard's witness from tradition is Abraham: that figure whom Eusebius – captive to the principle that the ancients are closest to the gods – saw as the origin of true religion and the equivalent of Christ. Kierkegaard agrees: Abraham is the origin of true religion and the equivalent to Christ. Thus in *Fear and Trembling* (1843), Kierkegaard refuses to consign Abraham to academics who distance themselves from the patriarch by explaining his predicament to be the result of primitive and barbaric religious practices; nor will he allow Abraham to serve the church theory as an illustration, however bizarre, of a pallid doctrine of churchly grace. Instead, Kierkegaard argues that Abraham's readiness to sacrifice his son is the preeminent disclosure of God's will. If one is willing to pursue true faith, to face the dread of personal existence that demands that a decision be made, then Abraham may engage one's imagination as guide and pioneer. He is the ancient hero, the chosen one, embodying and intensifying the possibilities of human existence. As long as one has the courage to face God, one may compare one's private experience to the example of this hero, and do so honestly and forthrightly. 'I require every person', says Kierkegaard:

> not to think so inhumanely of himself that he does not dare to enter those palaces where the memory of the chosen ones lives or even those where they themselves live. He is not to enter rudely and foist his affinity upon them. He is to be happy for every time he bows before them, but he is to be confident, free of spirit, and always

---

[54] Kierkegaard, *Self-Examination*, 41.
[55] Kierkegaard, *Self-Examination*, 47.

more than a charwoman, for if he wants to be no more than that, he will never get in. And the very thing that is going to help him is the anxiety and distress of which the great were tried, for otherwise, if he has any backbone, they will only arouse his righteous envy.[56]

Abraham teaches that the religious level of existence is the level demanded by one's private and unique relationship to God: the relationship of personal faith. It demands that we have an absolute relation to the Absolute and a relative relationship to all things relative in this life – even one's own family. This is the teaching of Abraham. This is also the teaching of Christ: 'Whoever loves father or mother more than me is not worthy of me; and whoever loves son or daughter more than me is not worthy of me; and whoever does not take up his cross and follow me is not worthy of me. Those who find their life will lose it, and those who lose their life for my sake will find it' (Mt. 10:37–39). Christ's teaching is indeed, as Eusebius observed, not 'new and strange', but goes back to the 'antique discovery' of Abraham.

Kierkegaard's witness from history – and one should credit him for the irony and mirth of his choice – is none other than Gotthold Ephraim Lessing, that unrepentant secularist who, more often than not, plays with his reader and refuses to make his own position known. Kierkegaard is perfectly willing to play with Lessing. Therefore, instead of turning to 'The Education of the Human Race' as his guide to the meaning of Christianity in history – the conventional choice of professors and bishops – Kierkegaard draws upon Lessing's more mercurial and ambiguous theses about belief being based on 'accidental events' and the unattractiveness of 'the leap of faith'. The style of these theses is fitting for the subject of history. If one considers the matter aright, one must acknowledge that history is, if anything, a mercurial and ambiguous reality.

According to Kierkegaard, Lessing knows – or at least seems to know – what is at stake in Christian claims: that the individual is being presented with the prospect of eternal happiness in the miracle of Christ's resurrection. To obtain this happiness, however, the individual must first prove his or her allegiance to God by accepting the historical witness that reports this miracle. Historical witnesses by themselves prove nothing. They do not mediate anything. Only the belief in God makes them reliable. Faith is the decision to accept these historical claims as having eternal validity. This is the leap of faith. Lessing, it appears, cannot make the leap. But at least he knows that a leap is required and that this leap must be taken by each individual because the 'religious' has 'infinitely to do with God' and not with human mediators of God.[57] Lessing thus knows better than professors and bishops that historical

---

[56] Kierkegaard, *Fear*, 64. See Halkin, 'Genesis', 47.
[57] Kierkegaard, *Postscript*, I, 65.

truths are irreducibly contingent and cannot be made to serve a philosophical or theological principle claiming divine necessity:

> Everything that becomes historical is contingent, inasmuch as precisely by coming into existence, by becoming historical, it has its element of contingency, inasmuch as contingency is precisely the one factor in all coming into existence. And therein lies again the incommensurability between a historical truth and an eternal decision.[58]

Lessing the unbeliever teaches professors, bishops and believers the hard lesson about history. The individual cannot escape the difficulty and insecurity of contingency. No theological explanation can get around this problem. Theology can only face up to the problem and confess that contingency cannot be escaped. The believer (who must never be automatically equated with the theologian) proclaims that the real reason contingency cannot be escaped is because God simply will not allow it. God refuses to be an approximate object of speculation by the academic in some sort of philosophy of history. Nor will he make himself directly recognizable in a tradition that asserts the pure church of priests, dogma and ritual: Indeed, such direct recognizability is simply 'paganism'.[59] Even Scripture cannot be relied on as an external guarantee. Let the canon be proved authentic beyond a shadow of a doubt, says Kierkegaard, let biblical authors be trusted by all so that one may say that it is 'as if every letter was inspired'. This still will not protect the individual. 'Faith does not result from straightforward scholarly deliberation, nor does it come directly; on the contrary, in this objectivity one loses that infinite, personal, impassioned interestedness, which is the condition of faith, the *ubique et nusquam* [everywhere and nowhere] in which faith can come into existence'.[60] The individual must accept contingency in fact; he or she must rely on God to accept historical revelation in faith, no matter how hard it is to do: 'In a human being there is always a desire to have something really firm and fixed that can exclude the dialectical, but this is cowardliness and fraudulence toward the divine'.[61] To believe, one must leap across the ugly broad ditch.

Like Goethe's artist, Kierkegaard refuses to accept anything that profanes the holy and makes hard things easy. The true measure of a Christian theologian is a theology that uncovers the 'radical and decisive choice' that is the heart of authentic faith. To be serious, the theologian must deliberately transmit the urgency of this decisive choice to others: 'unless we have seen the challenge of Christianity and stood before it in fear and trembling, we have not understood Christianity. Once we have seen what Christianity is, we can never

---

[58] Kierkegaard, *Postscript*, I, 98.

[59] Kierkegaard, *Postscript*, I, 600.

[60] Kierkegaard, *Postscript*, I, 28, 29.

[61] Kierkegaard, *Postscript*, I, 35.

think it ordinary nor ever again go about our business as before'.[62] The conflict is not between tradition and history. The real conflict is with both tradition and history made easy.

[62] Allen, *Outsiders*, 53.

Bibliography

Allen, D., *Three Outsiders* (Cambridge: Cowledy, 1983)

Aquinas, T., *Summa Theologiae* (61 vols.; London: Blackfriars; New York: McGraw Hill, 1964)

Buber, M., *I and Thou* (trans. W. Kaufmann; New York: Macmillan, 1970)

Burke, P., *The Renaissance Sense of the Past* (New York: St. Martin's, 1969)

Butterfield, H., 'Historiography', in *Dictionary of the History of Ideas*, II (New York: Charles Scribner's Sons, 1973), 464–98

Chadwick, H. (ed.), *Lessing's Theological Writings* (Stanford: Stanford University Press, 1957)

Dahl, N.A., *Jesus in the Memory of the Early Church* (Minneapolis: Augsburg, 1976)

Drey, J.S., *Kurze Einleitung in das Studium der Theologie* (1819) (ed. with intro. by F. Schupp; Darmstadt: Wissenschaftliche Buchgesellschaft, 1971)

Ebeling, G., *Word and Faith* (trans. J.W. Leitch; Philadelphia: Fortress Press, 1963)

Eusebius, *The Ecclesiastical History* (trans. and ed. K. Lake; 2 vols.; London and Cambridge: W. Heinemann, 1926)

Geiselmann, J.R. (ed.), *Geist des Christentums und des Katholicimus* (Mainz: Matthias Grünewald, 1940)

Halkin, H., 'Genesis and Talking Heads', *Commentary* 103 (Feb. 1997), 44–50

Harnack, A. von, *History of Dogma* (trans. N. Buchanan; 7 vols.; New York: Dover, 1961)

Harrisville, R.A., and W. Sundberg, *The Bible in Modern Culture: Baruch Spinoza to Brevard Childs* (Grand Rapids: Eerdmans, 2nd edn, 2002)

Headley, J.M., *Luther's View of Church History* (New Haven: Yale University Press, 1963)

Kierkegaard, S., *Concluding Unscientific Postscript to Philosophical Fragments* (ed. and trans. H.V. Hong and E.H. Hong; 2 vols.; Princeton: Princeton University Press, 1982)

——, *Fear and Trembling/Repetition* (ed. and trans. H.V. Hong and E.H. Hong; Princeton: Princeton University Press, 1983)

——, *For Self-Examination/Judge for Yourself!* (ed. and trans. H.V. Hong and E.H. Hong; Princeton: Princeton University Press, 1990)

——, *Journals and Papers*, III (ed. and trans. H.V. Hong and E.H. Hong; Bloomington and London: Indiana University Press, 1975)

——, *Stages on Life's Way* (ed. and trans. H.V. Hong and E.H. Hong; Princeton: Princeton University Press, 1988)

Luther, M., *Luther's Works* (ed. J. Pelikan and H. Lehmann; 55 vols.; St. Louis: Concordia; Philadelphia: Fortress Press, 1955–86)

McCracken, G.E., and A. Cabaniss, *Early Medieval Theology* (Philadelphia: Westminster Press, 1957)

Newman, J.H., *An Essay on the Development of Christian Doctrine* (1878 edn) (Westminster: Christian Classics, 1968)

Nisbet, R., *Prejudices: A Philosophical Dictionary* (Cambridge, MA: Harvard University Press, 1982)

Pieper, J., 'The Concept of Tradition', *The Review of Politics* 20 (1958), 465–91

Prestige, G.L., *Fathers and Heretics* (London: SPCK, 1940)

Richardson, C.C. (ed.), *Early Christian Fathers* (New York: Macmillan, 1970)

Rupp, G., and P. Watson (eds.), *Luther and Erasmus: Free Will and Salvation* (Philadelphia: Westminster Press, 1959)

Spinoza, B., *Tractatus Theologico-Politicus* (trans. S. Shirley; Leiden: E.J. Brill, 1989)

Sundberg, W., 'Luther on Tradition', *Dialog* 25 (1986), 114–18

——, 'Spinoza, Baruch', in *The Dictionary of Historical Theology* (ed. T.A. Hart; Carlisle: Paternoster; Grand Rapids: Eerdmans, 2000), 526–27

Troeltsch, E., *The Absoluteness of Christianity and the History of Religions* (trans. D. Read; intro. J.L. Adams; Richmond: John Knox Press, 1971)

Wilken, R.L., *The Myth of Christian Beginnings* (Garden City, NJ: Doubleday, 1971)

14

Tradition, Biblical Interpretation and Historical Truth

C. Stephen Evans

What role should tradition play in biblical interpretation? This is a question that is much more closely related to questions about the historical truth of biblical narratives than might first appear to be the case. In 1996, I published *The Historical Christ and the Jesus of Faith*, a book that defends the claim that it is reasonable to take the picture of Jesus provided in the New Testament as basically reliable as history in its main outlines. In making this case I developed a concept – that of the 'incarnational narrative' – that made explicit use of the church as a community that has passed down a living tradition. I originally defined this 'incarnational narrative' in the following way: 'the story of Jesus of Nazareth, taken from the New Testament as a whole, as that story has traditionally been told by the Christian Church'.[1] Though I acknowledged the possibility of interpreting the New Testament in other ways, it seemed obvious to me that the church's reading was at least one possible reading, since it embodies an interpretation that has endured for many centuries. Rather than debate the merits of this interpretation relative to others, a task I was not suited to undertake since I am not trained as a biblical scholar, I wanted to look at the question of whether the story thus interpreted was historically *true*.

I thought that this feature of the book would probably call forth some sharp critical reactions, for a variety of reasons. First of all I anticipated, and tried in the book to defend myself against, the claim that there is no such thing as '*the* church's story', since the New Testament has been read in many ways by different branches of Christendom. Secondly, I feared that some Protestants would see my hermeneutical strategy as too 'Catholic', since it seems to give the church a privileged position with respect to the interpretation of the Bible. Finally, I feared that those who are critical of the historical reliability of the Bible would see my interpretive strategy as viciously circular, since many think

---

[1] Evans, *Historical Christ*, 2. I should add that, just prior to giving this definition, I stressed that the narrative of Jesus must be read as part of a larger biblical story that encompasses the OT as well.

that it is precisely the church's traditional teachings that are in need of critical historical foundations. No interpretation of the Bible could hope to provide an evidential foundation for the church's faith in a non-circular way if that interpretation is governed by the faith it is attempting to support. To my surprise, however, my strategy in simply beginning with the story of Jesus as it has been traditionally interpreted by the church has not called forth critical notice of any kind; it has simply been ignored.[2]

An optimistic interpretation of this fact is that my practice in this case is unremarkable. I thought of myself (and still do) as following the 'rule of faith' in my interpretive practice, and perhaps this ancient way of looking at Scripture is too commonplace to call for critical comment.[3] I fear, however, that this is not the case, and that the interpretive practice may have been ignored because it seems so idiosyncratic and bizarre that many readers simply did not understand it. Or perhaps some considered it charitable simply to ignore such a benighted move.

In this chapter I want to raise the question explicitly of the legitimacy and value of interpreting the Bible in accordance with the rule of faith. I shall raise the three types of problems I anticipated my book would engender and try to respond to each in turn. Thus, I will first briefly discuss whether the rule of faith provides a unified basis for interpretation. Is there really *a* rule of faith, or are there many rules of faith that are in conflict with each other? This question requires discussion of whether or not 'the church' really refers to some identifiable reality. Secondly, I will discuss the related questions of whether such a practice is compatible with the Protestant principle of *sola scriptura* and whether it requires some kind of ecclesiastical *magisterium* to be implemented. Finally, I will consider the question of whether the Bible is likely to be a source of historical truth when it is interpreted according to the rule of faith. What kind of epistemological theory best fits the practice of interpreting the Bible according to the rule of faith? Is there a plausible epistemological account on which such a practice seems likely to lead to historically reliable results?

Is There Such a Thing as the Rule of Faith?

I turn first to the question of whether there really is such a thing as the rule of faith that can govern the church's interpretation of the Bible. This question must not be confused with others in the neighborhood. It should not, for

---

[2]   Perhaps this fact is not really so surprising, since the book has been largely ignored by NT scholarship in its entirety, and the few NT scholars who have reviewed it seem to have largely misunderstood it.

[3]   A hopeful sign supporting this view is a recent book edited by Radner and Sumner, *The Rule of Faith*. This book looks at biblical interpretation as an authoritative source for theology when it is guided by the creeds of the church.

example, be confused with the question of whether there is a substantial amount of agreement in the church concerning conclusions of biblical inter-pretation. It is certainly a commonplace that different Christian traditions, and even Christians within the same tradition, disagree over many points of biblical interpretation. Notoriously, for example, Christians disagree as to whether the 'words of institution' spoken by Jesus at the Last Supper ('This is my body') are to be interpreted literally or symbolically. I take it that such disagreements are not total and complete, at least with respect to the biblical message as a whole, and are compatible with a substantial body of agreement among the majority of Christians about how the Bible should be interpreted.

However, I do not need to determine how much Christians actually agree with respect to their *conclusions* in biblical interpretation, because the question about whether there is such a thing as a rule of faith is not a question about the results of biblical interpretation, but rather about the principles that should guide such interpretation. It seems quite possible that Christians could agree that the Bible should be interpreted according to the rule of faith, and even agree as to what that rule of faith means, and still reach different conclusions about the meanings of particular passages. Of course this implies that the practice of interpreting according to the rule of faith does not completely determine the results of interpretation, but it seems highly likely that this will be true of any plausible principles of interpretation. It is certainly true for those who follow the interpretive principle of interpreting according to the 'original intent' of the human authors, on the assumption that this intent is to be discerned through ordinary historical investigation.

My concept of the rule of faith essentially follows a definition given in a standard reference work: '… certain brief summaries of Christian faith, already current in the Church in the apostolic age, which were gradually expanded and fixed in the form of the creeds still used today, especially as designed to guard against heretical notions'.[4] By 'the creeds' I assume the authors of this reference work meant to refer to the early, ecumenical creeds of the church accepted by Catholic, Orthodox and Protestant churches; at least that is how I understand the definition. To interpret the Bible according to the rule of faith is, then, to interpret in accordance with these early creeds.

These creeds represent, at least to a substantial degree, 'that which has been believed everywhere, always, and by all', to use the classic criterion of catho-licity invoked by Vincent of Lerins.[5] One might think that in fact nothing passes Vincent's test, and that is doubtless true if we include in the scope of the term 'all' everyone who thinks of himself or herself as a Christian. There is

---

[4] Rahner and Vorgrimler, *Dictionary*, 451.

[5] Vincent of Lerins, *The Commonitories*, 270.

probably no Christian doctrine at all, including those contained in the classical creeds, that has not in the last century been denied by some Christians, even by some Christian theologians. However, I believe that this criticism can be deflected if we think of those creeds as definitive of Christianity, or at least of Christian orthodoxy. Those ecclesiastical traditions, such as Unitarianism, that explicitly deny central items in the creeds can be seen as self-consciously choosing not to be part of the catholic and apostolic tradition. Obviously they reject the claim that in the formation of the early creeds the church was guided by God so as to get the message of the gospel essentially right. We can then apply Vincent's test to all those Christians who accept the teachings of the early church as summarized in the creeds. The creeds themselves will, tautologically, pass the test. Other beliefs will also pass the test in a non-tautological manner, namely the intersection of all those beliefs consistent with each other that are held by all of the Christian traditions that accept the ecumenical creeds.[6]

It is worth reminding ourselves of what is fixed by these creeds and what is left open. They clearly affirm that God is the 'Creator of heaven and earth, of all things visible and invisible'. However, they do not include any theory as to *how* God creates and sustains the universe. They clearly affirm that Jesus of Nazareth is both fully human and fully divine, and yet a unified person. However, they do not adopt any particular theory as to how the incarnation occurred, and it is hardly surprising that Christian theologians and philosophers disagree as to how to make metaphysical sense of the incarnation, or even whether we can make such sense of it. They affirm that human salvation is made possible by Jesus, who, though a real historical figure who 'suffered under Pontius Pilate', nevertheless 'came down from heaven for us and for our salvation'. However, no particular theory of atonement is affirmed, and it is not surprising that various theories have been affirmed over the life of the church. The lesson I draw from this is that the creeds have enough content to give definition to Christian faith; not just any set of beliefs will count as Christian, particularly if by 'Christian' we mean 'orthodox Christian'. They nevertheless leave many areas open and subject to disagreement.

If we define the church by Vincent of Lerins' formula, I believe that it is a recognizable reality, despite the organizational disunity that characterizes the Christian churches today. Nor is the church in this sense simply an abstraction. Rather, the church on this view corresponds roughly with what C.S. Lewis termed 'mere Christianity'.[7] Of course Lewis is careful to explain that 'mere

---

[6] I am assuming here that the creeds themselves are logically consistent, though this is certainly not granted by everyone. I recently was e-mailed an unpublished paper by Evan Fales, a philosopher of religion at the University of Iowa, in which he claims that the intersection of the classical creeds is 'the null set'.

[7] See Lewis, *Mere Christianity*, especially the 'Preface'.

Christianity' is not itself a church that one could belong to in competition with such bodies as the Roman Catholic Church or the United Methodist Church.[8] Rather, Lewis says that 'mere Christianity' is more like a hallway or common room that various churches share. The actual churches are the rooms in which people live their lives, and no one should think that one can be a 'mere Christian' without eventually being part of some more robust church community as well. Nevertheless, those who live in those various rooms can pass back and forth and, when they meet those who live in other rooms, they can recognize that they have something in common. One might say that they are all part of a common house.

I think that Lewis's metaphor here corresponds to my own experience, in which I have with gratitude recognized and learned much from my fellow Christians in other traditions. The church universal is to me an experienced reality. I do not, by the way, believe that this implies that all disagreements among orthodox believers are trivial. Where there are significant disagreements, truth matters. However, love and a recognition of what Christians share in Christ matter even more. There is, I believe, in the contemporary Christian world, a grass-roots ecumenism that is more valuable than denominational mergers. I therefore dare to affirm that we can speak meaningfully of 'the church', and therefore of the Bible as 'the church's book', and try to follow interpretive practices in which we seek to be guided by the central beliefs of the church.

Is Interpreting by the Rule of Faith Consistent with *Sola Scriptura*?

One might think that interpretation that is guided by the rule of faith is an abandonment of the Protestant principle of *sola scriptura*. After all, at the heart of this Protestant principle lies an understanding that even popes and councils can err. In theory at least, the creeds could be in error and are subject to correction by scriptural teachings. The Bible must in some way be a more fundamental source of religious authority than the creeds, since the creeds themselves are ultimately grounded in the Scriptures.

To this Protestant line of thought, Catholics have often responded that the Bible can be interpreted in many different ways, as is evidenced especially by the history of Protestantism. Catholics agree that the Bible is a fundamental religious authority, even the fundamental authority for Christians, but they argue that the Bible has this authority only when properly interpreted. Proper interpretation can only be assured if there is a magisterium, a teaching office

---

[8] Lewis, *Mere Christianity*, 11.

of the Church, which can serve as a check against individual, eccentric interpretations.

Protestants can certainly agree on the need for proper interpretation. I will not argue against claims that the Catholic Church possesses a magisterium; I am not interested in contributing to Catholic–Protestant polemics. I want to focus on the narrower question as to whether interpretation that is governed by the ecumenical creeds is consistent with Protestant views of the authority of the Bible. I believe that when interpretation is governed in this way it at least reduces the need for an authoritative teaching office, leaving open the question of whether there is such a need and, if so, how great the need is.

Recently, Stephen Davis has written a helpful article on 'Tradition, Scripture, and Religious Authority'.[9] In this article he canvasses the possible meanings that might be given to the phrase 'Scripture alone' to find a defensible thesis. After examining and discarding several candidates, Davis concludes that something like the following principle is essentially correct: Scripture, once it is canonically and textually established and interpreted correctly, is '*our source of religious truth above all other sources, our norm or guide to religious truth above all other norms or guides*'.[10] The qualifications in this formula are important, for, as Davis says, 'Christians notoriously disagree in interpreting Scripture'. This implies that 'there must be religious norms or criteria other than Scripture, viz. those that establish how Scripture is to be interpreted'.[11] We cannot, then, simply hand out Bibles to people and expect that they will necessarily arrive at orthodox Christian beliefs if they accept what they read. This is cheerfully conceded by such a staunch Protestant as Reformed theologian Hendrikus Berkhof: 'The Bible is … a library full of heights, depths, and plains, with central and marginal sections. To gain entrance and to find its central perspective the reader needs help. The community of believers must offer an introduction, a guide, a summary'.[12]

Davis's point here (and Berkhof's) is quite similar to a claim I made in *The Historical Christ and the Jesus of Faith*:

> The history of New Testament interpretation strongly suggests that the New Testament under-determines its own interpretation; it seems foolish even for a Christian believer to claim that an honest, reasonable interpreter of the New Testament would necessarily arrive at readings consistent with Christian orthodoxy, *if the interpretative process proceeded independently of the guidance of the Church and the Holy Spirit.*[13]

---

[9] Davis, 'Tradition'.
[10] Davis, 'Tradition', 55 (emphasis original).
[11] Davis, 'Tradition', 55.
[12] Berkhof, *Christian Faith*, 93; as quoted in Davis, 'Tradition', 54.
[13] Evans, *Historical Christ*, 4 (emphasis original).

Whatever we take 'Scripture alone' to mean, it cannot imply that the Bible is always easy to interpret, or that it will necessarily be a sure religious guide if it is wrongly interpreted.

Nor is this claim inconsistent with the Protestant doctrine of the 'perspicuity' or 'perspicacity' of Scripture. It seems to me that the most reasonable understanding of this claim is that the Scriptures are clear enough so that an ordinary person, without special training or learning, can read them and understand them well enough to know what is necessary for salvation. Even here, however, we surely must admit that such an ordinary reader must interpret the Scriptures properly. The claim that the Scriptures are perspicuous cannot imply that it is impossible to misunderstand them in basic and grievous ways, or else the doctrine can easily be shown to be false. Still it is possible, I think, to hold that the honest seeker who is guided by the Spirit of God can understand what he or she needs to understand in the Bible to be saved. However, we must distinguish between having a basic understanding that is sufficient for salvation and having an understanding of the Bible that is sufficient to guide the church in the development of its doctrine.

Can we not hold, however, that the necessary hermeneutical guidance can be provided by the Spirit of God, thus eliminating any need for a normative role for tradition? In theory this seems possible. However, to raise an important epistemological question, how can an individual be sure that his or her interpretive stance is Spirit-guided? It is clear that wildly divergent and incompatible readings of Scripture can be, and have been claimed to be, guided by the Spirit. At this point, an appeal to tradition as a criterion for genuine guidance by the Spirit seems eminently reasonable. An individual who puts forward an interpretation of the Bible that is inconsistent with 'what has been believed everywhere, always, and by all' would surely carry a heavy burden of proof. For such an individual would be claiming that all the followers of Jesus who claim to have been guided by the Spirit over the centuries would be wrong; he and he alone has the truth. It is hard not to see such a claim as arrogant and suspect.

Davis argues that an interpretive practice that assigns normative weight to tradition is entirely compatible with a defensible version of 'Scripture alone'. For the creeds that have this normative weight do not have to be seen as a source of religious truth in addition to Scripture. They themselves grew out of Scripture, or the apostolic teachings that are embedded in Scripture, and are distillations of scriptural teaching. Interpretation cannot proceed at all without coming to the text with what Gadamer has called 'prejudices' or 'pre-judgments'.[14] We cannot understand the Bible if we are blank tablets. It seems eminently reasonable to approach the Scriptures from the perspective of those who have, as committed followers of Jesus, wrestled with their meaning over the centuries.

---

[14] Gadamer, *Truth and Method*, 277–99.

This does not mean that the creeds themselves cannot be criticized in light of Scripture. One might, for example, come to believe that the creeds contain internal tensions, and that these tensions must be resolved by going back to the Scriptures and testing the creeds against them. It is possible to read a text from an interpretive stance and still find that the text resists that stance, and ultimately requires revision of that stance. If that were not the case, texts could not really speak to us at all. Interpretation that is guided by the rule of faith can still submit to scriptural authority.

Nevertheless, in practice the central claims of Christian faith as embodied in the ecumenical creeds have a much higher status than would, say, traditional theological teachings not included in the creeds. For example, one might cite the current debate about God's relation to time. Many contemporary philosophers and theologians have questioned the view of most traditional theologians that God is a timelessly eternal being, and those critical questions of the tradition are often grounded in readings of the Bible. Even here I think the tradition carries some weight; one would not lightly go against the judgements of Augustine and Aquinas. However, the authority of a theological tradition not embedded in the creeds of the church is much weaker than the authority of the creeds themselves.

Another way of putting my point is to say, as Davis does, that the church as the whole people of God can function as a magisterium, at least with respect to basic interpretive principles. Whether or not there is a teaching authority that is located in specific church offices, the church's interpretive practice can be guided by the consensus of the church through the centuries.

Is Interpretation by the Rule of Faith Viciously Circular?

The last question I want to discuss in this chapter is whether or not interpreting the Bible in accord with tradition as embodied in the rule of faith introduces some kind of objectionable epistemological circularity, especially if we are concerned with the historical truth of the biblical narratives. If one is concerned with whether Christian doctrines are epistemologically justified or warranted, then one might think that the basic doctrines of the church cannot be justified by the Bible if some of those doctrines in turn serve as a regulative principle in biblical interpretation. Surely, one might think, the biblical texts that are supposed to support the Christian doctrines have in that case been approached in such a way that the truth of those doctrines is presupposed. How, then, can the texts offer independent support for the doctrines?

This question is particularly acute for Christian doctrines that have historical content. The early creeds include such claims as that Jesus was born of the virgin Mary, suffered under Pontius Pilate and was raised from the dead on the third day after crucifixion and burial. They thus seem to affirm the historical truth of the major outlines of the New Testament narrative about Jesus. Can the New Testament provide evidence for such truths if our interpretive practice presupposes them?

I believe that the reply to this objection must assume some basic epistemological stance, and that different epistemological stances allow for different answers. How are basic Christian doctrines known? There are, I believe, at least two different types of answers to this question currently on offer, each presupposing a different epistemological standpoint. In *The Historical Christ and the Jesus of Faith* I labeled the two different types of answers the 'evidentialist' and 'non-evidentialist' strategies. I shall briefly explain each type of strategy and discuss how it can respond to the charge of circularity if it endorses interpreting the Bible by the rule of faith. As we shall see, the problem of circularity is greater for the evidentialist, but even in this case the problem is not fatal.

The evidentialist perspective typically thinks of knowledge as 'justified, true belief' and thinks of justification as a matter of having evidence for the belief in question. An excellent contemporary example of evidentialist apologetics can be found in the work of Richard Swinburne.[15] Swinburne first offers evidence for belief in God from natural theology. He then inquires as to whether it is reasonable to believe that we have a revelation from God, and he offers evidence that Christianity does indeed offer such an authentic revelation – a revelation that is manifested mainly through the Bible. Although philosophical arguments can be given on behalf of some Christian doctrines, the bulk of the evidence consists in the fact that these doctrines are taught in the Scriptures. So far as I can tell, Swinburne follows the practice of interpreting those Scriptures by the rule of faith, *once it has been established to his satisfaction that the Scriptures are an authentic revelation from God.* He certainly holds that if a revelation from God is to be transmitted successfully, then God must provide a community, a church, to ensure that the revelation is interpreted properly, though he does not say whether that function of the church must be exercised through some particular office or through the consensus of the church as a whole.[16]

To avoid the problem of vicious circularity, however, Swinburne holds that the Scriptures must initially be treated differently. In developing his case that Jesus provides the supreme revelation of God to humans, Swinburne treats the Scriptures differently than he does after that case has been made. They are not to be regarded in this initial context as a divinely inspired infallible

---

[15] Swinburne's massive body of work includes such books as *The Coherence of Theism; The Existence of God; Faith and Reason; Revelation: From Metaphor to Analogy* and *The Christian God.*

[16] See, e.g., Swinburne, *Revelation*, chs. 5, 7 and 8.

revelation, but as a source for 'historical investigation of just the same kind as that which would be pursued by historians investigating the teaching of any other teacher'.[17] When investigated in this way, Swinburne claims that it is possible to find enough evidence (particularly in the resurrection) to conclude that Jesus was a true prophet and that the community he founded (the church) is authorized to interpret the revelation he brought. Once this is achieved, biblical interpretation can take on a different character and can follow the rule of faith.

The example of Swinburne shows, then, that one way for an evidentialist to avoid the problem of circularity is to distinguish between different contexts for the interpretation of the Bible. When one is determining such foundational questions as whether Jesus is a supreme prophet and whether he originated an authoritative church, one must look at the Bible as an 'ordinary historical document' in a way that seems incompatible with reading according to the rule of faith. However, once it is established that the Bible is indeed a true revelation certified by the church, then the rule of faith seems appropriate.

I would like to suggest that an evidentialist can go beyond Swinburne's strategy here. Swinburne seems to assume that the interpreter who is an 'ordinary historical investigator' comes to the text with no interpretive assumptions at all, at least ideally. If, however, we agree with Gadamer (and many other hermeneutical theorists) that some kind of 'pre-understanding' is a necessary prerequisite to interpretation, then I think that a version of interpreting according to the rule of faith can still be defended even within the initial apologetic context. One can approach the Scriptures and examine them through the lens of the creeds without necessarily assuming the truth of the creeds. Rather, the rule of faith could be adopted as a heuristic device, a hermeneutical strategy. A reading of the Scriptures could be developed in this way and offered in the marketplace, to be defended against competing interpretations on the grounds that it makes better sense of the text as a whole than any of those competitors. This reading, it might be argued, helps us see coherent themes that might otherwise be missed. It illuminates more of the text and seems to face fewer problems with awkward passages than its competitors. Such an evidential procedure is not viciously circular, because the creeds that govern the interpretation of Scripture are not in this case being dogmatically asserted to be true, but provisionally and heuristically assumed. Since there is no circularity, there is no reason the Scriptures cannot here serve as an evidential base for the establishment of historical claims as well. Rather, the procedure recognizes the 'holistic' character of interpretation and offers the church's interpretive stance as a viable competitor in the marketplace of ideas. I conclude that even the evidentialist can employ the rule of faith in biblical interpretation.

---

[17] Swinburne, *Revelation*, 103.

However, in *The Historical Christ and the Jesus of Faith* I defend a non-evidentialist account of how Christians come to know basic Christian truths, including historical truths. This is the kind of account more recently developed in what I take to be a somewhat purer version by Alvin Plantinga in *Warranted Christian Belief* (*WCB*).[18] The non-evidentialist rejects the claim that the justification or warrant for belief in the central Christian doctrines must come through evidence. Most evidentialists (though not all) about Christian doctrines, have assumed some form of philosophical internalism, which claims that what justifies our beliefs must be something, such as evidence, that is internal to consciousness in the sense of being accessible to it. The non-evidentialist, however, typically assumes an externalist epistemological perspective.[19] There are many versions of externalism, but all in some way affirm that what converts a true belief to knowledge is not solely something internal to consciousness, but rather something about the relation of the knower to the external reality that his or her knowledge is about. The key insight is that a true belief cannot 'accidentally' amount to knowledge. If we have knowledge, it is because the belief has been formed in a manner that allows us to 'track' reality accurately. On Plantinga's view a belief has warrant (roughly) if it is the product of a faculty that is designed to obtain truth, and which is functioning properly and in the kind of environment in which it was designed to operate.[20] If we switch to the language of William Alston's epistemology, a belief is justified if it is based on a truth-conducive ground.[21] Alston's view is at least partly externalist because what is important to him is that the ground is, as a matter of fact, objectively truth-conducive; it is not essential for the knower to be able to establish this.

This is not the place to try to argue the dispute between externalism and internalism. It is important to note, however, that the development of externalist epistemology was not motivated primarily by religious concerns. Rather, this kind of epistemology was originally developed by naturalistic philosophers who wished to see knowledge as a natural phenomenon. Externalism,

---

[18] I say that Plantinga's version is purer because in my own book, while I basically defend a non-evidentialist perspective, I qualify that claim in several ways that allow evidentialist strategies to serve complementary functions. For example, I hold that one of the ways God could reliably produce true beliefs would be by way of giving evidence, and by making it possible to see the force of evidence and properly to interpret it. In addition, I hold that in some cases evidence might be necessary for 'second-level knowledge'. One might know without evidence, but to know that one knows evidence might be necessary. Plantinga and I both agree that evidence can play a valuable role in defusing potential 'defeaters' for Christian belief.

[19] For a somewhat expanded, though still brief account of these matters, see ch. 9 of Evans, *Historical Christ*.

[20] For a full account see Plantinga, *Warrant and Proper Function*.

[21] See Alston, 'Internalist Externalism'.

as I understand it, lowers the ambitions of epistemology. The internalist, at least as classically developed by such modern philosophers as Descartes and Locke, seeks a guarantee for knowledge. Classical foundationalism, understood as a species of internalism, attempts to ground knowledge in beliefs that are self-evident, or at least evident to the senses. The ideal seems to be to give some kind of guarantee or certification to our knowledge claims – a refutation of skepticism. This becomes explicit in the writings of such contemporary thinkers as Keith Lehrer, who describes the successful epistemologist as being able to vanquish the skeptic in a kind of dialectical game.[22]

Externalist epistemology has more modest aims. This kind of epistemology assumes that knowledge is possible and that we can identify some of the things we know. The goal of the externalist is not to refute the skeptic; he or she assumes that the skeptic is wrong. He or she agrees with Hume, Kierkegaard and Thomas Reid that complete skepticism is impossible, but that if such a state could be realized, it would be incurable by reason.[23] Thus the skeptic cannot be refuted but does not have to be. The goal of epistemology is simply to become clearer about what knowledge is and how we get it. It stands to reason that the modest epistemologist will be open to the possibility that knowledge does not require absolutely certain foundations. The basic beliefs in our noetic structure do not have to be absolutely certain.

Obviously, the externalist gives up any pretensions that he or she can supply some kind of universal guarantee or certification for knowledge claims, since the enterprise depends on accepting some knowledge claims at the outset – at least provisionally. The philosopher on this view may give us insight into what we know and how we know it. However, it is not the case that until the philosopher comes to the rescue by providing his or her certificate of authenticity, the scientist or theologian or moral agent is necessarily in some kind of crisis, bereft of either knowledge or rationality or both. A certain degree of circularity is inherent in knowing, at least for the justification of what we might call basic kinds of knowledge.[24] The quest of modern philosophy for some kind of

---

[22] See Keith Lehrer's account of what he calls the 'justification game' in his *Theory of Knowledge*, 119ff. Lehrer thinks that to gain this kind of justification, one must move to a version of a coherence theory of knowledge and reject classical foundationalism.

[23] See Thomas Reid's own memorable words: 'A man that disbelieves his own existence is surely as unfit to be reasoned with, as a man that believes he is made of glass. There may be disorders in the human frame that may produce such extravagancies, but they will never be cured by reasoning' (*Inquiry*, 16). Compare Reid here with the similarly sarcastic words of Kierkegaard's pseudonym Johannes de Silentio in *Fear and Trembling*, 5–7, who pokes fun at modern philosophers who have supposedly doubted everything.

[24] For a good account of this circularity, see Alston, 'Epistemic Circularity', and for an application to religious knowledge see Alston, 'On Knowing'.

'method' that would guarantee our knowledge claims by showing that they rest on absolutely certain foundations is an impossible one.

I would argue that one of the main lessons of the history of modern philosophy is that no such method is available to us human beings, finite and historically situated as we are. Whatever knowledge we have is fallible, and the desire to overcome disagreements by embarking on what John Dewey termed 'the quest for certainty' is a quixotic one. Ambitious epistemology has had a good run, and there is little agreement as to how to solve its problems. Great efforts have been devoted to refuting skepticism: attempting to prove that we are not deceived by all-powerful demons, or to show that we are not brains in vats being electrically stimulated by a race of super-scientists. Even such apparently modest tasks as proving that other people have minds or that the universe is more than five minutes old have proved elusive. Perhaps Thomas Reid is right when he claims, alluding to Descartes' mention of people who believe their heads are made of glass, that such maladies cannot be healed by philosophy. It seems reasonable, then, for theology at least to explore the possibility that religious knowledge, like other forms of knowledge, should be understood in externalist terms.

There are many different desirable epistemic qualities. We want beliefs that are justified, rational, warranted and true, to name just a few. These qualities have often been confusedly run together, but Alvin Plantinga's recent work in epistemology has usefully tried to distinguish them.[25] Plantinga considers justification to be mainly a deontological concept. To be justified is to have fulfilled one's epistemic duties, to be within one's epistemic rights in one's beliefs and belief-forming practices. Rationality comes in many forms, but it primarily has to do with the coherence of our beliefs as a system, 'downstream from experience', as is sometimes said. Plantinga argues at some length that these epistemic qualities, valuable as they may be, are not the crucial qualities that turn true beliefs into knowledge. A person can be well justified in holding a belief and eminently rational, and yet that belief, even if true, may not amount to knowledge. For that quality, whatever it may be, that is sufficient to make true belief knowledge Plantinga uses the term 'warrant'. For him, the most crucial questions in epistemology concern the nature of warrant and how our beliefs get that quality.

Plantinga's own account of warrant clearly aligns him on the externalist side of the contemporary epistemological debate between internalism and externalism. On Plantinga's view, knowledge requires a true belief that is the result of 'cognitive faculties functioning properly in a congenial epistemic

---

[25] See *WCB*, 67–134, where Plantinga discusses different forms of justification and rationality.

environment according to a design plan successfully aimed at the production of true belief '.[26] From the perspective of externalism, it is clear that whether the warrant necessary for knowledge is present is not always something that can be determined by the knower simply by 'reflecting on his state of mind', to use Roderick Chisholm's phrase.[27] Whether a belief-forming process is reliable, or whether a belief's 'ground' is objectively truth-conducive, or whether my faculties are functioning properly in a congenial epistemic environment are things that a person cannot immediately know simply by reflecting on her own consciousness.

When this kind of epistemological perspective is applied to the question of how Christians know what Plantinga terms 'the great things of the gospel', it is clear that it is not necessary to think that such knowledge is grounded in evidence. Plantinga himself develops what he calls the 'Aquinas–Calvin' model, in which Christian knowledge is seen as a product of God's revelation in Scripture and the work of the Holy Spirit in shaping the beliefs and affections of human beings so that they can respond properly to that revelation in faith.[28]

On this kind of account, the Scriptures play a key role in the formation of Christian belief, but that role is not that they furnish us with evidence. Rather, the Scriptures are part of the means whereby God creates faith in those who come to know the 'great things of the gospel'. In saying that such beliefs are not based on evidence, Plantinga does not mean to imply that they are groundless or arbitrary. In earlier work Plantinga distinguishes between a ground for a belief and evidence. If we accept Calvin's idea of a *sensus divinitatis*, then it is possible for humans to have a belief in God that is not based on evidence. Rather, we may think that God has created us so that in certain circumstances, such as when we see a stunning mountain or a new baby, or when we feel guilty because of some sin, as humans we naturally form a belief in God. Humans naturally come to affirm such things as 'a glorious God made this' or 'God disapproves of what I have done'. We can say in such cases that the circumstances in which the beliefs are formed constitute a ground for the beliefs, even though they do not function as propositional evidence. No

---

[26] Plantinga, *WCB*, 498.

[27] Chisholm, *Theory*, 17.

[28] In calling this account a 'model', Plantinga affirms several things: that it is possible (epistemically) that this is the means whereby God makes it possible to know Christian truths, and that there are no cogent objections, philosophical or otherwise, to the model that do not presuppose the falsity of Christianity. If Christianity is true, then the model, or something similar to the model, is very likely true as well, and thus the model provides Christians with a good way of thinking about their faith. If the model is indeed true, then Christians who believe the great things of the gospel are warranted in doing so, and if their degree of confidence is high enough, the warrant is sufficient for knowledge.

process of inference is involved. Rather, God has created us in such a way that we spontaneously form the relevant beliefs in the appropriate circumstances.

In a similar way, Plantinga holds that specifically Christian beliefs have a ground, even though they are not based on evidence. And part of that ground will be the Scriptures, which serve as a means whereby God communicates what humans need to believe. What role might interpretation of the Scriptures according to the rule of faith play in such a process? Plantinga does not seem to give the church and its traditions a prominent role to play in this process. However, in an important footnote he concedes that the church does in fact play an important role in the process: 'It is the church or community that proclaims the gospel, guides the neophyte into it, and supports, instructs, encourages, and edifies believers of all sorts and conditions'.[29] This note seems consistent with understanding the church in the 'mere Christianity' way I have urged, and with thinking of this process of guiding and instructing as one that is conducted in accord with the rule of faith. Whether Plantinga would include this interpretive practice as part of his 'model' or not, it is fully consistent with it. If it is not part of his model, then it will be part of an alternative model that lies in the near neighborhood of his.

In such a case, the practice of interpreting Scripture according to the rule of faith is not viciously circular. There is no 'begging the question' by presupposing what one is trying to support, because the Scriptures are not being viewed as evidence at all, but rather as part of the non-evidential ground for Christian beliefs, part of the process God has designed to make salvation possible. Since the beliefs that are acquired as part of the process of acquiring faith include historical beliefs, such beliefs are part of what interpreting according to the rule of faith can help us come to know.

How is it possible for faith (using the term to refer to the outcome of the whole process by which Christian beliefs are formed) to have warrant? The answer for Plantinga is simply that, according to the model, the standard conditions for warrant are met. The beliefs in question come into existence 'by a belief-producing process that is functioning properly in an appropriate cognitive environment (the one for which they were designed), according to a design plan successfully aimed at the production of true beliefs'.[30]

Plantinga does recognize one significant difference between his extended model and other cases of warranted belief. The extended model does not view the beliefs in question as produced by a natural human faculty alone, but by a cognitive process 'that involves a special, supernatural activity on the part of the Holy Spirit'.[31] However, Plantinga claims that this makes no difference. The

---

[29] Plantinga, *WCB*, 244n.
[30] Plantinga, *WCB*, 246.
[31] Plantinga, *WCB*, 246n.

'deliverances' of this process can enjoy warrant, even 'warrant sufficient for knowledge'.[32]

As apologetics, such a move might appear very weak. However, it is important to see that Plantinga is not here doing apologetics. The basic insight underlying this strategy is that being justified or warranted should not be confused with being able to justify a belief to someone else. William Alston has taught us to make this distinction.[33] A person may well be justified, in Alston's sense of having a truth-conducive ground for a belief, or warranted, in Plantinga's sense, even if the person cannot show to someone else that this is the case. It follows from this that an account of how Christians know what they know does not have to consist in an apologetic argument. That does not mean that apologetic arguments cannot be given, or that they are not valuable. It just means that the task of apologetics and the task of giving an account of Christian knowledge are not the same tasks.

There is, then, no necessary circularity involved in reading the Bible according to the rule of faith if we accept an externalist account of Christian knowledge. On such a view the Bible, as well as the creedal summaries that function as interpretive guide to reading the Bible, are not functioning as evidence at all, and therefore cannot be evidence that begs the question. I conclude that the practice of reading the Scriptures in accord with the ecumenical creeds is one that is neither viciously circular nor inconsistent with Protestant views about the priority of Scripture. These creeds not only themselves contain basic historical landmarks that anchor the Christian gospel in history. They also provide an interpretive framework that precludes any reading of the Bible that takes away the significance of that historical narrative. All Christians – Protestant, Catholic or Orthodox – can agree that the Bible is the church's book and should be read in accordance with the church's basic teachings. Part of that teaching is that history matters. Of course history is not all that matters, and it is perfectly obvious that the writers of the Gospels felt free to rearrange incidents and modify speeches. But it seems obvious as well that the writers who did this saw themselves as communicating a portrait of Jesus that is fundamentally reliable. The reader who believes these reports will have a good understanding of the kind of person Jesus was, the kinds of things he did and the kinds of things he said. Most importantly, such a reader will understand the passion, death and resurrection of Jesus and something about the meaning of these events. The individual who is worshipped as the Christ of faith is the same person as the historical figure, Jesus of Nazareth.

---

[32] Plantinga, *WCB*, 246n.

[33] See Alston, 'Foundationalism', 43–47.

Bibliography

Alston, W.P., 'An Internalist Externalism', in *Epistemic Justification: Essays in the Theory of Knowledge* (ed. W.P. Alston; Ithaca, NY: Cornell University Press, 1989), 185–226

——, 'Epistemic Circularity', in *Epistemic Justification: Essays in the Theory of Knowledge* (ed. W.P. Alston; Ithaca, NY: Cornell University Press, 1989), 319–49

——, 'Has Foundationalism Been Refuted?', in *Epistemic Justification: Essays in the Theory of Knowledge* (ed. W.P. Alston; Ithaca, NY: Cornell University Press, 1989), 39–58

——, 'On Knowing that We Know', in *Christian Perspectives on Religious Knowledge* (ed. C.S. Evans and M. Westphal; Grand Rapids: Eerdmans, 1993), 15–39

Berkhof, H., *Christian Faith: An Introduction to the Study of the Faith* (trans. S. Woustra; Grand Rapids: Eerdmans, 1979)

Chisholm, R., *Theory of Knowledge* (Englewood Cliff, NJ: Prentice-Hall, 1977)

Davis, S.T., 'Tradition, Scripture, and Religious Authority', in *Philosophy and Theological Discourse* (ed. S.T. Davis; New York: St. Martin's Press, 1997), 47–68

Evans, C.S., *The Historical Christ and the Jesus of Faith* (New York: OUP, 1996)

Gadamer, H.-G., *Truth and Method* (ed. and trans. J.C. Weinsheimer and D.G. Marshall; New York: Continuum, 1993), 277–99

Kierkegaard, S., *Fear and Trembling* (trans. and ed. H.V. Hong and E.H. Hong; Princeton: Princeton University Press, 1983)

Lehrer, K., *Theory of Knowledge* (Boulder, CO: Westview Press, 1990)

Lewis, C.S., *Mere Christianity* (New York: Simon and Schuster, 1996)

Plantinga, A., *Warrant and Proper Function* (New York and Oxford: OUP, 1993)

——, *Warranted Christian Belief* (New York and Oxford: OUP, 2000)

Radner, E., and G. Sumner (eds.), *The Rule of Faith: Scripture, Canon, and Creed in a Critical Age* (Harrisburg, PA: Morehouse Publishing, 1998)

Rahner, K., and H. Vorgrimler, *Dictionary of Theology* (New York: Crossroad, 2nd edn, 1981)

Reid, T., *An Inquiry into the Human Mind on the Principles of Common Sense* (ed. D.R. Brookes; Edinburgh: Edinburgh University Press, 1997)

Swinburne, R., *Revelation: From Metaphor to Analogy* (Oxford: OUP, 1992)

—— , *The Coherence of Theism* (Oxford: OUP, 1977)

——, *The Existence of God* (Oxford: OUP, 1979)

——, *Faith and Reason* (Oxford: OUP, 1981)

——, *The Christian God* (Oxford: OUP, 1994)

Vincent of Lerins, *The Commonitories*, in *The Fathers of the Church*, VII (Washington, DC: The Catholic University of America Press, 1970)

History and Narrative

15

Ricœur on History, Fiction, and Biblical Hermeneutics

Gregory J. Laughery

Introduction

Jean-François Lyotard's volume *The Postmodern Condition*, and its 'incredulity toward metanarratives',[1] broke open a large fissure of uncertainty in many disciplines. The rising force of such postmodern ideas is having a profound impact on the discipline of history. In recent years, debate among historians has taken new directions. At present, serious challenges pertaining to the truth of written history and the knowledge of the historian are in evidence.[2] While controversy concerning the truth-value of history has a long tradition, postmodern theories argue for new ways of viewing and doing history. Historical truth, objectivity, facts, events and knowledge are all targets for revision.[3] Marc Trachtenberg expresses his concern in the following manner:

> Increasingly the old ideal of historical objectivity is dismissed out of hand. The very notion of 'historical truth' is now often considered hopelessly naïve.[4]

For Trachtenberg, and others, postmodern proposals represent a contemporary crisis in the discipline of history.[5] What is viewed as a radical scepticism and

---

[1] Lyotard, *Postmodern*, xxiv.

[2] See Jenkins, *Re-Thinking*, 12–32: 'We know that such truths are really "useful fictions" that are in discourse by virtue of power (somebody has to put and keep them there) and power uses the term "truth" to exercise control' (parenthesis his). See also Jenkins, *Postmodern*, 1–30, and the discussion of historiographic metafiction in Hutcheon, *Poetics*, 87–120, where it is argued that the problematic we face today is not so much that of a historiographical external reality, but of a loss of faith in our capacity to know that reality.

[3] Appleby, Hunt and Jacob, *Telling*; and Southgate, *History*, have excellent discussions of these matters.

[4] Trachtenberg, 'Past'.

[5] Zagorin, 'History', includes this in a list of several responses by historians to postmodern ideas.

a virulent relativism are considered to be an assault on traditional forms of all that history stands for, including objectivity, knowledge, clarity and evidence.[6] Facts and truths that are objectively discovered and conveyed were assumed to be the emblem of historical accounts, but this view of history is changing.[7]

The postmodern reply to these assumptions is that new ways of thinking about history are essential. The old Enlightenment fantasies of certainty and objectivity that were thought to be at the centre of a writing of history are no longer taken into account. Keith Jenkins states:

> the attempt to pass off the study of history in the form of the ostensibly disinterested scholarship of academics studying the past objectively and 'for its own sake' as 'proper' history, is now unsustainable. … In fact history appears to be just one more foundationless, positioned expression in a world of foundationless, positioned expressions.[8]

Writing history, for Jenkins and others, is merely a subjective enterprise, exclusively based on literary construction without objective grounding.[9] As such, getting the story straight has little to do with the events of the past.[10] Under the template of postmodern theory, 'new wave'[11] historians argue that a discovery of an accurate recounting of historical events in time is an impossible task.[12] In this scenario, writing history has more to do with inventing meaning than with finding facts. Any pursuit of the truth of historical occurrence in the past becomes highly dubious. How, then, are we to understand written accounts of past events as 'new wave' historians influence and reshape the discipline of history? Does the discipline face a growing crisis?

The contemporary debates over history writing and historians also have enormous repercussions for biblical truth, which in some sense claims to be

---

[6] Zagorin, 'History', 2. See also, Southgate, *History*, 1–11.

[7] Zagorin, 'History', 5: 'In place of grand narratives of this kind, so it is held, have come a multiplicity of discourses and language games, a questioning of the nature of knowledge together with a dissolution of the idea of truth, and problems of legitimacy in many fields'.

[8] Jenkins, *Postmodern*, 6.

[9] Jenkins, *Re-Thinking*, 12–32.

[10] Kellner, *Language*, xi, 3–25, 273–93, argues that as a result of the blurring of distinctions between historiography and literature, we find ourselves needing to get the story crooked. 'To get the story crooked is to understand that the straightness of any story is a rhetorical invention and that the invention of stories is the most important part of human self-understanding and self-creation' (xi).

[11] Munslow, *Deconstructing*, 19, refers to 'new wave' historians, such as Hayden White and Keith Jenkins, who emphasize the form–content relation and the inescapable relativism of historical understanding.

[12] Carr, 'Life', refers to this pejoratively as the 'standard' view today.

connected to real events in history. In addition to historical questions, there is another related dimension to our present context that merits consideration. Biblical interpretation is much influenced by the contemporary interest in literary criticism and narrative.[13] The narrative turn has drawn the attention of literary theorists, philosophers, biblical exegetes, theologians and historians, and it has become the object of intense debate.[14] What is the relation, or lack thereof, between history and historical accounts of the past? How might narratives recount something about the real world? In the light of contemporary literary theories promoted by 'new wave' historians, how are we to view the biblical narratives?

This chapter will reflect on and evaluate recent proposals that are at the heart of these questions. We will focus on three major issues: history and historical discourse; historical discourse and fictional literature; historical discourse, fictional literature and the Bible. My purpose in what follows is to interpret and apply the reflections of the French philosopher Paul Ricœur to these issues and to draw out several implications for biblical hermeneutics.[15]

History and Historical Discourse

One response to postmodernism and its influence on historical questions has been for some scholars to claim that the text *is* history. Daniel Marguerat, in a discussion of postmodernism and historiography, argues that there is no history without the written plots and interpretations of the historian. He maintains that any distinction between history and written accounts of history has now been destroyed.[16] A somewhat similar view is advanced by Paul Veyne, who proposes

---

[13] Alter in *Art*, 15, remarks that a more marked interest in a literary perspective of the Bible begins to arise in the 1970s. See also Blocher, 'Biblical Narrative'.

[14] See, e.g., Kermode, *Sense*; Ankersmit and Kellner (eds.), *New History*; White, *Metahistory*, and *Content*; Chatman, *Story and Discourse*; Ricœur, *Temps*, I–III; Carr, *Time*; Mitchell (ed.), *On Narrative*; Bühler and Habermacher (eds.), *La Narration*; Marguerat and Bourquin, *How to Read*; Stenger, *Narrative Theology*; Lanser, *Narrative Act*; Harris, *Literary Meaning*, and *Interpretive Acts*; Frei, *Eclipse*; Hauerwas and Jones (eds.), *Why Narrative?*; Ellingsen, *Integrity*; Sternberg, *Poetics*; Long, *Art*; Longman, *Literary Approaches*; Vanhoozer, *Biblical Narrative*, and *Meaning*; Stiver, *Philosophy*, and *Theology*; Laughery, *Living Hermeneutics*; Bartholomew, Greene and Möller (eds.), *Renewing*, and *After Pentecost*; Jeffrey, *People*; offer a variety of different perspectives and orientations.

[15] Ricœur's work is one of the most prominent enterprises to peruse for an investigation into the questions of history, narrative and biblical hermeneutics, as his writings for the last two decades clearly evidence. Ricœur, *Temps*, I–III; 'Philosophies', *La Mémoire*; *Essays*; *Figuring the Sacred*; *From Text to Action*; Ricœur and LaCocque, *Penser*.

[16] Marguerat, *First Christian*, 5–7.

a narrativist model of history that is plot-centred; there is no history without the writing of a plot.[17] History, Veyne contends, is made by the written construction of plots.[18]

Such notions of history and history writing are useful in pointing out the role of the historian as interpreter and the importance of narrative configurations, but they have the severe disadvantage of reducing history to interpretation and emplotment, hence devaluing any distinction between historical discourse and history.[19] How do we arrive at historical discourse, a selectively written account of history? There has been much discussion on this issue, and it is impossible to cover the wide diversity of views here.[20] I shall closely follow Paul Ricœur's work and commentary on this controversial aporia.[21] Ricœur suggests a critical threefold historiographic operation that comprises, at each level, enrichment and problematization.[22]

First, Ricœur argues, we begin with an investigation of what we find in sources and documentation. These *detail* sources – for example, traces, testimony and chronicles – can be evaluated and to some degree verified as to their reliability. Sources are not, at this stage, what Ricœur refers to as 'la connaissance historique' (historical knowledge). According to Ricœur, on this level, historical occurrence has a twofold epistemological status: it brings about statements of details that can be affirmed or negated by testimony, trace or documentation, and it plays a role in the overall explanation and narrative configuration, where it passes from the status of a verifiable occurrence to an interpreted occurrence. In spite of the instability of the relation between the occurrence and its documentation, there is no reason to assume that the occurrence was not an *actual* event in the world prior to its documentation.

---

[17] Veyne, *Comment*. Kellner, *Language*, 305–07, esp. 306, has a brief discussion of Veyne's work. He is appreciative of Veyne's position as 'it is couched in terms that are *moral* and *aesthetic*' (emphasis original).

[18] See Ricœur, *Temps*, I, 239–46 (*Time*, I, 169–74) for a critical interaction with this perspective.

[19] I will be using the term 'historical discourse' to refer to written accounts of the past. My hope is that the different terminology used by myself and others will be clear enough for the reader to discern the meaning of the terms 'history', 'historiography' and 'historical discourse', which all may refer to written accounts.

[20] For further discussion see Evans, *In Defence*; Appleby, Hunt and Jacob, *Telling*; Jenkins, *Re-Thinking*; McCullagh, *Truth*; and Southgate, *History*.

[21] Especially, but not exclusively, Ricœur, 'Philosophies'; and *La Mémoire*.

[22] Ricœur, 'Philosophies', 140, views this enriching as the capacity of one level to bring greater clarity and precision to the other, while at the same time there remain epistemological problems that pertain to each level. Ricœur, *La Mémoire*, 170, also stresses that the threefold operation is not to be understood as a chronological succession.

Second, there is an explicative/comprehension level, which concerns not just 'who', 'where' and 'when', but 'why', 'to what effects' or 'results'.[23] This level comprises such elements as social, political or economic considerations that ripple out from an occurrence in the past. On this level, as Ricœur points out, there are conflicting models of the *Erklären* (explanation) and *Verstehen* (understanding) of past occurrences as historical knowledge: some *explain* by subjecting the past to laws or regulations, others *understand* by connecting the past to a teleology. The notions of epistemological value are attached to one or the other of these models of cultivating and articulating the past. In effect both attempt, albeit in different ways, to establish something of a scientific dimension of historical discourse through centring on understanding (Dilthey) or explanation (Hempel). However, in Ricœur's view, the problematic is that explanation without understanding or understanding without explanation results in a truncated epistemology. In the debate between these models, Ricœur highlights the work of G.H. von Wright in *Explanation and Understanding*[24] (who situates the conflict in Plato and Aristotle). Wright attempts to synthesize the regulatory and the causal or teleological in connection with human action. In finding such a point of view promising, Ricœur ponders the following question: does a narrative ordering assure the unity of a mixed model?[25] This question leads us to the next stage of the historiographic operation.

Third, the interpreted sources and the explanations and understandings are configured in (re)writing a grand historiographical narrative,[26] which aims to be a representation of the past. This (re)written representation is connected to memory, to the intentionality of the historiographer, and to the target of recounting truth about the past in dependence on the previous levels. At this point, the historiographical operation is brought to closure.[27] Ricœur employs the term *représentance*[28] for the combined three-level operation in order to emphasize that historical representation is working towards bringing to light the targeted reference. These three distinct, yet related, levels of operation offer a critical knowledge of the past.[29]

Ricœur's threefold notion of the historiographical operation shows that history and historical discourse are not to be equated. For Ricœur, there is a

---

[23] Ricœur, *La Mémoire*, 169.

[24] von Wright, *Explanation*.

[25] Ricœur, 'Philosophies', 154.

[26] While it is true that there is also non-narrative historiography, it is narrative historiography that has recently created the greater amount of discussion.

[27] Ricœur, *La Mémoire*, 169–70, 303–304.

[28] Ricœur, *La Mémoire*, 304, 340–69.

[29] Ricœur, *La Mémoire*, 168–69, 323.

reality behind or outside the text that merits consideration in historical inquiry. Trace, testimony and *représentance* stand for something that took place outside the text.[30] While the events behind or outside the text are not the only concerns in the interpretation of historical discourse, they nevertheless remain valid interests.[31] Historical occurrences only become historical discourse when they are written, while history remains history even though it is not written down.[32] Thus, we are not merely interested in texts, but in a reliable interpretation of the historical character of the events which the texts represent.

Historical Discourse and Fictional Literature: The Turn to Literature

The disciplines of literature and modern literary criticism are having a marked impact on the discipline of history.[33] One important reason for this is the contemporary emphasis on literature inaugurated by both French and Anglo-Saxon theorists.[34] The main goals of this section will be first to examine Ricœur's response to recent perspectives that attempt to transform historical discourse into fictional literature and, second, to map out his own proposals for preserving a distinction.

Louis Mink, frequently understood as a pivotal figure in this discussion, was one of the first in recent times to pose the problematic of the relation between historical discourse and fiction. Mink noted that both types of narrative literature 'recount'.[35] His point is well taken; however, it brings with it the following query: if both types of narrative recount, is there any difference between a historical and a fictional recounting? Mink warns of an impending disaster if the distinction between historical discourse and fiction disappears, although he remains somewhat perplexed as to how one might preserve the

---

[30] It is true that what interpreters have is the text, but the text has the capacity to point, beyond itself, to who and what are behind it.

[31] Ricœur has stressed that the interpretation of a text is concerned with the world that unfolds in 'front' of the text, but this does not mean that he refuses an appropriate emphasis on a historical referent behind the text. See his discussions in *From Text to Action*, 75–88; *Interpretation Theory*; 'Du Conflit'; and 'Esquisse de Conclusion'.

[32] Bebbington, *Patterns*, 1–2, points out that 'in the English language the word "history" can mean either what people write about time gone by, that is historiography; or else it can mean what people have done and suffered, that is the historical process'.

[33] See Long, 'Historiography', 161–65, for an explanation of the difference between modern and older styles of literary criticism.

[34] Ricœur, 'Philosophies', 159, 168–77. Ricœur discusses these schools of thought, drawing out both the convergences and divergences in a useful manner.

[35] Mink, *Historical Understanding*.

contrast.[36] How have postmodern theories in the discipline of history attempted to respond to this problem? This vexing question merits further investigation.

We will now sketch out an analysis of the literary turn in the discipline of history, following Ricœur's work on two postmodern 'new wave' scholars: Hayden White and Hans Kellner. White's enterprise has had a profound impact on this discussion, and thus is important to peruse.[37] He states:

> there has been a reluctance to consider historical narratives as what they most manifestly are: verbal fictions, the contents of which are as much *invented* as *found* and the forms of which have more in common with their counterparts in literature than they have with those in the sciences.[38]

And further:

> It is sometimes said that the aim of the historian is to explain the past by 'finding', 'identifying', or 'uncovering', the 'stories' that lie buried in chronicles; and that the difference between 'history' and 'fiction' resides in the fact that the historian 'finds' his stories, whereas the fiction writer 'invents' his. This conception of the historian's task, however, obscures the extent to which 'invention' also plays a part in the historian's operations.[39]

White's complex taxonomy cannot be fully developed here. My purpose in what follows is to present briefly something of its trajectory.[40] Two of White's major presuppositions are that the historian invents as much as finds, and that narratives are a mode of recounting, not a mode of discovery.[41] He views the historian as working with disordered and unrelated chronicle-type data. The writer then imposes a sequential order – beginning, middle, end – and an emplotment strategy, which may take the form of a romance, tragedy,

---

[36] Mink, 'Narrative Form', 211–20. For a fecund discussion of this issue see, Sternberg, *Poetics*, 1–57, and Long, *Art*, esp. 54–87.

[37] H. White has sent shock waves through, and had a tremendous influence on, the discipline of history. See Jacoby, 'New Intellectual History'; Munslow, *Deconstructing*, 140–62.

[38] White, 'Historical Text', 16 (emphasis original).

[39] White, *Metahistory*, 6–7. For White, in a 'chronicle' an event is merely 'there', whereas, in history writing, events are assigned different functions in the story.

[40] See Munslow, *Deconstructing*, 140–62, for a fuller introduction to White's views.

[41] White, 'Afterword', argues that it is an illusion that 'facts' are discovered, not constructed. Carroll, 'Interpretation', esp. 251, usefully points out in respect to White's view that 'the notion of *invention* here is a bit tricky and open to equivocation. In one sense, historical narratives are inventions, viz. in the sense they are made by historians; but it is not clear that it follows from this that they are *made-up* (and are, therefore, fictional)' (emphasis original).

comedy or satire. By virtue of this imposition of a form, which is the mode of explanation, moral meaning or content is attached to the narrative.[42] In White's point of view, a plot form or structure functions as a control model, a sort of pre-encoding, a metahistory.[43] This is because emploting presides over, and is that through which the historian is obliged to recount, the story. White observes:

> History-writing thrives on the discovery of all the possible plot structures that might be invoked to endow sets of events with different meanings. And our understanding of the past increases precisely in the degree to which we succeed in determining how far that past conforms to the strategies of sense-making that are contained in their purest forms in literary art.[44]

On the narrative level, the historian constructs narrative meaning through the chosen plot form or typology as a literary endeavour. This literary configuring gives the narrative a fictional content, while a reliable representation of events in the world pales into relative obscurity on the referent register of the grand narrative.[45]

The fact that narratives are constructed is not in dispute, yet there are questions concerning White's views. Why should narrative construction, which many scholars acknowledge, banish historical occurrence, sense and reference? Does narrative construction exclude a credible representation of the past?[46] Furthermore, why should one presuppose that there is no narrative structure (beginning, middle and end), which a narrative may reflect, prior to

---

[42] White, 'Narrativization', esp. 253. Narrativization teaches about 'moral wisdom, or rather about the irreducible moralism of a life lived under the conditions of culture rather than nature ... narrative has the power to teach what it means to be *moral* beings (rather than machines endowed with consciousness)' (emphasis original).

[43] White, *Metahistory*. See Kellner, *Language*, 193–227, esp. 197, for a discussion of *Metahistory*. Kellner reads White's world-view as centred on humanism. Historiography is about human choice and a fortification of human mastery, connected to rhetorical language power. See also Dray, 'Narrative', for an insightful discussion of White's views.

[44] White, 'Historical Text', 15–33, esp. 24.

[45] White is correct to reject a naïve realism found in a positivist notion of historical discourse, but his reclassification seems to do away with the problematic of the referential dimension of such a literature. See Ricœur, *La Mémoire*, 324–33.

[46] See Norman, 'Telling', esp. 191, where he argues that 'a good historian will interact dialogically with the historical record, recognizing the limits it places on possible construals of the past. Of course historians select their facts, and obviously the stories they tell are incomplete. But by itself this does not mean that the result is distorted or false'.

its literary construction?[47] While appreciative of White's emphasis on the structured imagination and its correlation to creativity and form, Ricœur remarks:

> On the other hand, I deplore the impasse in which H. White encloses himself in treating the operations of emplotment as explicative modes, at best indifferent to the scientific procedures of historical knowledge, at worst a substitute for these. There is a real *category mistake* here which engenders a legitimate suspicion concerning the capacity of this rhetorical theory to draw a strong line between historical narrative and fictional narrative [*récit historique et récit de fiction*].[48]

White's theory includes further drawbacks. He both neglects the realist dimension of fiction and stresses an almost exclusive focus on the choice of pre-narrative strategies and emplotment, to the detriment of a concern for the fidelity of a representation of the past.[49] One of the marked results of this strategy is that it becomes necessary to view historical discourse as constitutive of, rather than connected to, historical occurrence and life.[50]

Historical investigation and the view of historical discourse today have been strongly influenced by White's work. He has made a forceful contribution towards moving historical discourse from the domains of history, literature, science and epistemology, and locating it exclusively in the realm of literature. White relegates or reduces historical inquiry to a third-level (in Ricœur's operation) literary quest.[51] In so doing, White's views render it extremely difficult to draw distinctions between historical discourse and fiction.[52] The major aporia that such an incapacity creates is that it puts in question the reality of the past. Ricœur states:

---

[47] White, *Content*, 192–93, strongly argues that there is no narrative structure in life, prior to a literary construction. Carr, *Time*, 49–50, 59–60, esp. 49, maintains that White and other theorists treat structures, 'as if they were imposed on meaningless data by the act of narration itself, as if the events of life, experiences and actions, had no structure in themselves and achieved it only at the hand of a literary invention'. Carr challenges White's perspective, contending that life itself has inherent structures that are reflected in narrative.

[48] Ricœur, *La Mémoire*, 327–28 (emphasis original). *La Mémoire* has not, to my knowledge, appeared in English. The English translations for this work are my own.

[49] White, *Content*, 192–196; and 'Historical Text'.

[50] Harris, *Literary Meaning*, esp. 157–74, argues that if historical discourse is merely a narrative construction, fictionality reigns.

[51] See the development of Ricœur's notion of historical discourse, above. For Ricœur, the third level is the last in a sequence which depends on sources (trace, testimony, documents) and explanation and understanding.

[52] Ricœur, *La Mémoire*, 328, notes that it is urgent to 'specify' the referential moment which distinguishes historical discourse and fiction.

it is the relation between the organizing paradigms of the discipline of history and those which control the composition of literary fictions which has provoked a declassification of history as knowledge with a scientific pretension and its reclassification as literary artifice, and in relation to this caused a weakening of epistemological criteria of differentiation between history proper and the philosophy of history.[53]

Another contemporary scholar who has had a marked influence on the field of history is Hans Kellner. In his work on language and historical representation,[54] Kellner points out that he does not believe there are 'stories' of the past out there waiting to be told, or that there is any 'straight' way to write a history.[55] No historical discourse is straight, regardless of the methodological rigour or honesty of the historian. Any historical text, in spite of its straight appearance, is to be understood as rhetorical invention: crooked. Historical epochs or events represented in the text are literary creations that have more to do with self-understanding than with something that happened in the past. Recounting invented stories, according to Kellner, is how humans understand themselves. There is always a human language story outside the narrative that demands our attention. Getting the story crooked, for Kellner, equally amounts to something of a reading strategy. This means reading a historical text for the areas of concern and decision, no matter to what degree concealed, that have forged particular tactical writing schemes. On his account, underlying rhetorical constructs tell the real story – hence the need to read stories crooked.

In Kellner's view, a rhetorical interest drives historical investigation. Rhetoric and discourse are the other (real) sources of history, not found in past occurrences or archives.[56] Kellner's presupposition is that historians lack knowledge of the past, and that this lack perpetuates anxiety. Historians, as a result, turn from inadequate historical evidence and endeavour to construct the past through language and rhetorical conventions which attempt to bring order to the potentially terrifying and disordered chaos. Narratives and narrative organization are oppressive weapons used by historians in the attempt to mask anxiety and the fear of anarchy concerning the past. On this understanding, rhetoric and language constructions are the construction of reality itself. In challenging what he terms the 'ideology of truth' (that reality and history are

---

[53] Ricœur, 'Philosophies', 171–72. 'Philosophies' has not, to my knowledge, appeared in English. The English translations for this work are my own.

[54] Kellner, *Language*. See also, Kellner, 'As Real as it Gets', on Ricœur and narrative.

[55] Kellner, *Language*, 24: 'Historians do not "find" the truths of past events; they create events from a seamless flow, and invent meanings that produce patterns within that flow'.

[56] Kellner, *Language*, vii and 1–25, esp. 7: 'Crooked readings of historical writings are beginning to abound'.

more than human construction), Kellner asserts that we are obliged to face the constructed nature of the human world and to accept that meaning is always reducible to human purpose. To acknowledge that reality is the product of language and rhetoric amounts to the 'deepest respect for reality'[57] – as reality, in truth, is no more than a human construction.

Historical investigation, for Kellner, is not interested in sources, explanations and understandings of historical occurrences in time, but rather in rhetoric. According to Ricœur, when the search for rhetoric becomes the sole driving force of the discipline of history, other legitimate historical interests are ignored. If one accepts Kellner's view, truth disappears – and with it, historical reality.[58]

This brief examination of Ricœur's interaction with two contemporary scholars should not be read as merely a critique of their thought, but also as a means of conveying his own positive proposals. Clearly, in Ricœur's opinion, an overdetermined literary focus has the tendency to reduce historical discourse to fictional literature and rhetorical strategies. Ricœur strongly argues for maintaining the distinction between historical discourse and fictional literature in that historical discourse has different concerns, referents and targets. The reductionism of White and Kellner brings with it an epistemological dilemma with respect to the fidelity of a *representation* of the past.[59] We have underscored Ricœur's conflict with such scholarship by showing that the literary-narrative turn, in this school of thought, is now more often concerned with literature and literary criticism than it is with epistemology and scientific inquiry.[60] Ricœur has forcefully contributed to the move towards narrative as a literary vehicle for recounting events of the past,[61] but he also aims to alert

---

[57] Ricœur, 'Philosophies', 178–79. Kellner, *Language*, 25. In my view, Kellner's work clearly represents a postmodern shift of emphasis in the discipline of history. Historical inquiry into what happened in the past recedes in importance, while literary or ontological concerns (the nature of the historian) flourish. I believe the latter may be the allure of Heidegger's philosophy influencing Kellner. Heidegger's move from epistemology to ontology is having a noticeable impact upon the disciplines of literature and history. There is no doubt that this change of direction was necessary. In contrast to Heidegger, however, Ricœur attempts to acknowledge the significant import of the turn to ontology, without undermining epistemology. The latter remains a crucial and critical aspect of the interpretation of the self, world and texts. See also Kellner, 'As Real as it Gets'; Ricœur, 'Existence'; Laughery, *Living Hermeneutics*, 28–42; and Zagorin, 'History', for fuller discussion.

[58] Ricœur, 'Philosophies', 179.

[59] Ricœur, *La Mémoire*, 170, argues that in the domain of history as a human science, the intentional direction of the historian is credibly, but not completely, to represent the past.

[60] Ricœur, 'Philosophies', 163–68.

[61] Ricœur's work in *Temps* is one major example of this contribution.

interpreters to the perils of a declassification of historical discourse into fictional literature and appeals, therefore, for a vigilant epistemology.[62] Historical discourse is indeed literature yet, in Ricœur's view, it is essential that we do not abandon scientific investigation or critical analysis with respect to sources, explanations and understandings that pertain to questions of the past.[63]

In addition to the value of Ricœur's proposals and his critique of White and Kellner, it is important to elucidate further something of his response to the aporetic character of *representation* of the past and then to reflect on his views regarding the problem of distinguishing historical discourse and fictional literature. Ricœur affirms the spontaneous realism[64] of the historian, implicated by what he refers to as 'l'intentionnalité de la conscience historique' (the intentionality of the historical conscience). Ricœur's presupposition here is that

> the historian has for an ultimate object people like us, acting and suffering in circumstances that they have not produced, and with desired and non-desired results. This presupposition links the theory of history and the theory of action.[65]

People of the past are different, yet this difference is not so great that people of the present have no capacity to understand them. The creative connection model here is language, combined with the presupposition that all languages can be translated into our own.

Furthermore, a historian is linked, in a practical, spatio-temporal manner, to the object of study. This schema, chronological in focus though it may be, provides the essential condition of *dating* a historical occurrence.[66] In Ricœur's perspective, the value of this linking goes beyond merely formal chronology. In dating an occurrence the historian is able to connect past actions to calendar time, a mixed time between lived present time and cosmological time.[67] Ricœur aims to show that historians are indebted to those who came before them and that they receive an inheritance from those of another time. There are others, from the past, who contribute to making us who we are.

---

[62] Ricœur, *La Mémoire*, 223–26, views a vigilant epistemology as also guarding against a naïve realism – the notion that historical occurrence and historical discourse amount to the same thing.

[63] Ricœur, 'Philosophies', 167–68; Evans, *In Defence*, 73. See also Bebbington, *Patterns*, 5, who writes that history is a science in that it is comparable to '*Wissenschaft*: the systematic quest for ordered knowledge'.

[64] Ricœur, 'Philosophies', 190. See below. This is critical as opposed to naïve realism.

[65] Ricœur, 'Philosophies', 191.

[66] Ricœur, 'Philosophies', 192.

[67] See Ricœur's extensive discussion of this in *Temps*.

A concluding reflection on the aporia of representation of the past is an appeal to trace. Trace is something that someone has left in passing through a place in time. Ricœur points out:

> Two ideas are involved here: on one hand, the idea that a mark has been left by the passage of some being, on the other, the idea that this mark is the sign 'standing for' ['*valant pour*'] the passage. The significance of the trace combines a relation of causality between the thing marking and the thing marked, and a relation of signification between the mark left and the passage. The trace has the value of effect–sign.[68]

The representation of the past, Ricœur argues, is not a copy or projection, a correspondence of mental image and something absent, but rather a something represented *standing in place of* that which once was and no longer is. In this sense, the trace does not belong to some form or expression of a naïve realism or idealism, but to what Ricœur refers to as a 'critical realism' based in a 'profound analysis of what constitutes the intentionality of historical discourse'.[69]

At this juncture, we return to the vexing question that Mink was so instrumental in raising: as historiographical and fictional narratives both recount, is it possible to maintain any distinction between them? In response to this question, Ricœur has forcefully argued against White and Kellner for this distinction. He appeals to the truth of 'représentance', in that it comprises the expectations, requirements and problems of historical intentionality. A *représentance* of the past is expected to be connected to reconstructions of actual occurrences, real people and factual circumstances.[70] This historical narrative articulation can be said to constitute a 'pact' between author and reader.[71] Historians, on this view, are not mere narrators but argue a case for the actual occurrences and real people they attempt to represent. Historical discourse has a target – a reliable representation of the past. Ricœur states:

> It is in no way my intention to cancel or to obscure the differences between history and the whole set of fictional narratives in terms of their truth-claims. Documents and archives are the 'sources' of evidence for historical inquiry. Fictional narratives, on the other hand, ignore the burden of providing evidences of that kind.

---

[68] Ricœur, 'Philosophies', 196.

[69] Ricœur, 'Philosophies', 196. See also Lemon, *Discipline*, 4–41, for a fecund discussion of history.

[70] Ricœur, *Time*, III, 142, points out: 'Unlike novels, historians' constructions do aim at being *re*constructions of the past … historians are subject to what once was'.

[71] Ricœur, *La Mémoire*, 359–69. See also Steiner, *Real Presences*, 89–97, who writes of a 'semantic trust' without which there would be no history as we know it – a trust between word and world – a necessary covenant between word and object that calls us to respond. He argues for 'real presence' versus 'real absence'.

I should want to stress that as 'fictive' as the historical text may be, its claim is to be a representation of reality. And its way of asserting its claim is to support it by the verificationist procedures proper to history as a science. In other words, history is both a literary artifact and a representation of reality. It is a literary artifact to the extent that, like all literary texts, it tends to assume the status of a self-contained system of symbols. It is a representation of reality to the extent that the world it depicts – which is the 'works world' – is assumed to stand for some actual occurrences in the 'real' world.[72]

In fictional literature, there is equally a 'pact' between author and reader, but there is no expectation, nor demand, for the same level of extralinguistic *referent* on the narrative register. While historical discourse and fiction are story, in that both are configured through the imagination and emplotment, historical discourse cannot be reduced to fictional literature. The field of operation for historical discourse is obliged to include other considerations than merely the imagination, plot and a literary form.

As Ricœur has pointed out, there are major distinctions between historical discourse and fictional literature. First, the goals and expectations of the author and reader are different. Second, historical discourse aims to represent past occurrences in the real world. Furthermore, in historical discourse as opposed to fiction, every effort must be made to work back from the third-level grand narrative[73] to explanation and understanding, to documentation in traces and testimony, in order to evaluate critically the third-level narrative claim.[74] Historical discourse claims to represent an actuality behind or outside the text.

Historical Discourse, Fictional Literature and the Bible

Postmodern theories have not only had an impact on the disciplines of history and literature, but they are funding much of the discussion in biblical studies, biblical hermeneutics and theology.[75] It has been suggested that theological modernists may be left longing for the nostalgia of presence, while theological postmodernists play with juxtaposition in the absence of sense and referent.[76] George Aichele states:

---

[72] Ricœur, 'Fictional Narratives', 3–19, esp. 4–7.
[73] See 'History and Historical Discourse', above.
[74] Ricœur, *La Mémoire*, 363; Chartier, *On the Edge*, 26–30.
[75] Moore, ' "Post-" Age Stamp'. Heelas (ed.), *Religion*; Ward (ed.), *Postmodern God*; and Vanhoozer, *Meaning*, are all examples of an awareness of the influence of postmodernism on these fields.
[76] Aichele, 'Postmodern Theology'.

Postmodern thought centers upon a fantastic, generic indeterminacy, the non-identity and self-referentiality inherent in language, which makes decisive truth claims impossible. Insofar as one can continue to speak of reality at all, it is generically indeterminate, fantastic. We never escape from the literal alphabetic surface and its endless dissemination to an ideal, conceptual realm; the fantastic fictionality of language undercuts every attempt to refer to an extratextual reality.[77]

In addition to this form of postmodern scepticism towards a reality outside ourselves and to textual reference, the recent flourishing of narrative criticism in literature has contributed to raising a number of questions for the interpretation of the Bible. Does the biblical text have the capacity to have extralinguistic referents? Is there anything 'behind' the text? Do we interpret the Bible as 'historicized fiction' or 'fictionalized history'?[78] Some claim that the Bible is fictional in character, while others argue that biblical history and any notion of fiction are in total conflict.[79] My interest in this section is to explore how Ricœur's views might provide a response to these questions and forms of postmodern incredulity.

Ricœur has given us helpful insights in the discussion above concerning history and historical discourse and historical discourse and literature, but precisely how these would now apply to his thinking in the context of biblical hermeneutics must remain somewhat tentative. To my knowledge, Ricœur has not published on this subject post *La Mémoire, l'Histoire, l'Oubli* (2000).[80] There are, however, a number of significant earlier works that Ricœur has written which pertain to this, and we will sketch out several trajectories in dialogue with these texts.

---

[77] Aichele, 'Postmodern Theology', esp. 328.

[78] Alter, *Art*, 34, 41, uses these terms without a great deal of clarity as to whether they are the same or different modes of narrating. See Long, *Art*, 59–62, for an insightful perspective and clarification of such terminology. Also, Sternberg, *Poetics*, 1–57.

[79] See Long's excellent discussion of these two views in *Art*, 58–87. Long's own position can be summarized in the following manner. The word 'fiction' may be understood in two senses. Fiction is a literary genre and fiction is artistry, creativity, skill. The former may be in conflict with historiography, while the latter need not be. If these two senses are kept in mind, it may be possible to continue to speak of fiction and history as opposites, while at the same time acknowledging that all historiography is fictionalized and recognizing nevertheless that this does not negate the intent to recount historical occurrences in the real world.

[80] Ricœur, post-1994 (when 'Philosophies' was published), has co-written with LaCocque *Penser la Bible*, which appeared in 1998, but this work deals with other relevant matters. To be more precise, a philosopher (Ricœur) reads the work of an exegete (LaCocque) and comments on it. Ricœur does not often, in this volume, deal with the matters before us.

While Ricœur is frequently understood to be affirming different things on the subject of the Bible and biblical interpretation,[81] his general hermeneutical discussion of historical discourse and literature is of value for maintaining that historical accounts have referents outside the text.[82] Working from a general hermeneutical perspective, one must not automatically reduce the biblical text to simply fictional literature. Does this equally hold true for Ricœur's biblical hermeneutics?

Ricœur strongly argues for an intertextual approach to the biblical text.[83] This means that biblical narrative must be interpreted in relation to other biblical genres such as wisdom, hymn, prophecy and so on.[84] Whether it be Exodus, Psalms, Isaiah, a gospel or letter, each text has a temporal dimension and message that needs to be put into a historical, literary and theological dialogue with the other. This hermeneutical perspective orients the interpreter towards an investigation and evaluation of each text on a case by case basis in order to determine the author's literary act as expressed in the genre of the text.[85]

Several biblical texts, including Exodus and the Gospels, vehemently announce that there is a theological dimension to history. As a listener to that which is recorded in the Scripture,[86] Ricœur may be open to a view that the God who is named by the text does something outside the text, which is now a *représentance* in the text. Ricœur states:

> the naming of God in the resurrection narratives of the New Testament is in accord with the naming of God in the deliverance narratives of the Old Testament: God called Christ from the dead. Here, too, God is designated by the transcendence of the founding events in relation to the ordinary course of history.
>
> In this sense, we must say the naming of God is first of all a moment of narrative confession. God is named in 'the thing' recounted. This is counter to a certain emphasis among theologies of the word that only note word events. To the extent that the narrative genre is primary, God's imprint is in history before being in speech. Speech comes second as it confesses the trace of God in the event.[87]

---

[81] See Vanhoozer, *Biblical Narrative*; Fodor, *Christian Hermeneutics*; Stiver, *Theology*; and Laughery, *Living Hermeneutics*, for recent evaluations of Ricœur's work.

[82] Ricœur, 'Philosophical and Biblical Hermeneutics'. Stiver, *Theology*, 123–36, esp. 124; and 'Ricœur', argues that Ricœur's position is 'much more historical than some believe', while including the caveat that he is emphasizing that Ricœur's philosophical views allow for diverse theological appropriations.

[83] Ricœur and LaCocque, *Penser*.

[84] Ricœur, 'Naming' and 'Herméneutique', esp. 35.

[85] See Long, *Art*, and 'Historiography', who has insightful suggestions on the importance of genre and the various methods of investigating the Old Testament.

[86] Ricœur, 'Naming', esp. 224.

[87] Ricœur, 'Naming', 225.

Ricœur does not abandon the historical character of the Gospels. The testimony to the resurrection,[88] for example, requires the historical status: *something happened*, which left a trace and was recorded in the narratives as an event in time. The gospel writers' interpretations concern that *which actually happened*.[89]

> The witness is a witness to things that have happened. We can think of the case of recording Christian preaching in the categories of the story, as narration about things said and done by Jesus of Nazareth, as proceeding from this intention of binding confession-testimony to narration-testimony.[90]

Numerous testimonies in the biblical text are not merely text, but they represent, stand for and are a trace of God's activity in time in the real world.[91] Ricœur has argued that the mark or trace of God in history is prior to it being recounted in a narrative.[92] Biblical historical narrative aims to be a representation of what is behind the text. Ricœur draws from both the prophetic tradition and the gospel narratives for a notion of testimony. Historical occurrences of God's action have taken place and are witnessed to by the prophets. Prophetic moments are connected to historical moments – testimony is bound to confession and narration – in a motion from Old Testament prophecy to New Testament gospel and letter.[93]

---

[88] Ricœur, *La Mémoire*, 457–80, shows that the devastating result of the death of metanarratives is the metanarrative of death. He argues that for Heidegger the future is under the sign of *being towards death*, and as such the indefinite time of nature and history is subsumed to mortal finitude. In contrast, Ricœur contends that death is an interruption and proposes *being towards life* as the desire to be (to live) and the power to act, which gives the historian a remembering voice in time. See also 604–56, where Ricœur discusses in detail the notions of love, pardon, memory and gift frequently connected to the two Testaments.

[89] Ricœur, *Essays*, 43–44. At this juncture, 1979–80, Ricœur is wrestling with the question of whether testimony can preserve the connection between sense and referent. It would appear, from his more recent work in *La Mémoire* and 'Philosophies', that the response would be 'yes'. See also Vanhoozer, *Biblical Narrative*, 140–41 and 275–89; Fodor, *Christian Hermeneutics*, 226–89; Stiver, *Theology*, 123–24 and 188–250; Laughery, *Living Hermeneutics*, 105–48 and 151–62, for more extensive development of this question.

[90] Ricœur, 'Hermeneutics of Testimony', 134–35. Confession is central to testimony, but this is not merely a confession of faith, but also of meaning. For Ricœur, there is the dialectic of meaning and fact and confession and narration.

[91] Ricœur, *La Mémoire*, 366–67. See also Ricœur, *From Text to Action*, 89–101. There is a coherence here on the level of general and biblical hermeneutics in that both affirm there is a behind or outside the text that must be taken into consideration in its interpretation. For a discussion of Ricœur's views of the relation between a philosophical (general) and biblical hermeneutics, see Laughery, *Living Hermeneutics*, 43–55, and 'Language'.

[92] Ricœur, 'Toward a Hermeneutic', 73–118, esp. 79.

[93] Ricœur, 'Hermeneutics of Testimony', 135–39.

Ricœur points out, for example, that the christological kerygma is some-thing 'which demands narrative'. In other words, there is something preceding that which is narrativized, something 'behind' or outside the text. Ricœur appeals to 1 Corinthians 15:3–8, 'that Christ died for our sins according to the Scriptures, that he was buried, that he was raised on the third day according to the Scriptures, and that he appeared to Peter and then to the Twelve', arguing that the four aorist verbs show a provocation to narration.[94]

As I have mentioned above, Ricœur is often interpreted in a variety of ways on the question of biblical interpretation. He has explored the aesthetic narrative interests of the fictional dimension of the biblical text; however, he has also maintained an emphasis on the realism of its historical event character.[95] One finds in his work an ongoing challenge to a non-referential literary focus on biblical narrative combined with an illuminating historical interest in a representation of times past in the text.

Conclusion

We are now in a position to conclude our reflections. Ricœur's work on general and biblical hermeneutics gives useful insights for the issues addressed in this essay. First, in contrast to a postmodern uncertainty pertaining to histori-cal discourse and history, Ricœur affirms there is a real history outside the text and a scientific and epistemological pretension in writing history. His notion of a critical threefold historiographic operation – a diversity of sources, explana-tion and understanding, and a grand narrative – avoids the reductionism so prevalent in the discipline of history today. Historians create and construct historical discourse as a *représentance* of something that was there in the world. The distinction between a text and a world outside the text is crucial if the discipline of history is to remain concerned with the way it once was.

Second, while Ricœur has emphasized the literary aspect of historical discourse, he forcefully critiques a postmodern declassification of historical discourse into fictional literature. He maintains a distinction between the two on the grounds of a historical intentionality of representation that targets real people, events and situations. Historical discourse is marked by the truth of

---

[94] Ricœur, 'Récit Interprétative', esp. 20–21; 'Herméneutique'; and 'From Proclamation'.

[95] Stiver, *Theology*, 196–219. See also Vanhoozer, *Biblical Narrative*, 282, who while not always sharing the view that Ricœur does enough to distinguish history and fiction, states: 'Indeed, I have already suggested that Ricœur's own prescriptions for mediating history and fiction and preserving the realism of the event are a sufficient cure for the occasional lapses in hermeneutic equilibrium'.

'représentance', which author and reader expect to be reconstructions of the past. Literary strategies and rhetorical constructs however, which attempt to function as modes of explanation, divert an interest in a knowledge of the truth of the past and are a deficient substitute for critical investigation. Furthermore, Ricœur underscores the importance of epistemology for historical inquiry. This means that historical discourse does not create the meaning of a past occurrence through a literary endeavour, but is rather concerned with explanation and understanding based on the traces (the marks left in passing), the testimonies and the documents – all of which are connected to a real world outside the discourse. Fictional literature bears no such burden. The discipline of history must remain attuned to the risks of a declassification of its subject matter.

Third, there is a rapport between Ricœur's general and biblical hermeneutics, in that both argue for a real world outside the text and a distinction between historical discourse and fictional literature. Ricœur's biblical hermeneutics affirm that the Bible is concerned with historical discourse, which aims at recounting events that actually took place. This orientation points to the credibility of a biblical world-view and a theology of history: God is the Creator and Redeemer, the Great Actor of salvation in history. The drama of creation and God's saving action make a real world and a real history possible.[96] Traces and testimonies of God's activity in the real world filter into the text as a 'représentance', a targeted *standing for*, which militates against postmodern theories and their tendencies to reduce the Bible to a text making history or to fictional literature lacking an extralinguistic referent behind the text. Moreover, an intertextual approach to the Bible may open the way towards the historical, theological and literary features of the message of each text in time. The different genres in the biblical text have the capacity to point to the living God behind the text. History, as a discipline with scientific, epistemological and literary pretensions, must be aware of the problems of reductionism and be open to a consideration of theological insights that offer explanations and new understandings of the real world.

---

[96] See Naugle, *Worldview*, for a thorough investigation into the subject. A biblical world-view affirms that there is a real world that is related to and distinct from the human constructions and productions of historical discourse, fiction or language. How could there be fiction if there was no real world from which to measure and evaluate? In other words, the genre of fiction necessarily presupposes the real. On this register, the literary genre of fiction is parasitic in that it must borrow from what is not its own in order to exist.

Bibliography

Aichele, G., Jr., 'Literary Fantasy and Postmodern Theology', *JAAR* LIX/1 (1991), 323–37

Alter, R., *The Art of Biblical Narrative* (New York: Basic Books, 1981)

——, and F. Kermode (eds.), *The Literary Guide to the Bible* (London: Collins, 1987)

Ankersmit, F.R., *Narrative Logic: A Semantic Analysis of the Historian's Language* (The Hague: Nijhoff, 1983)

——, and H. Kellner (eds.), *A New Philosophy of History* (London: Reaktion Books, 1995)

Appleby, J., L. Hunt and M. Jacob, *Telling the Truth About History* (New York: W.W. Norton, 1994)

Barthes, R., 'Introduction à l'Analyse Structurale des Récits', *Communications* 8 (1966), 1–27

Bartholomew, C., C. Greene and K. Möller (eds.), *Renewing Biblical Interpretation* (SHS 1; Carlisle: Paternoster; Grand Rapids: Zondervan, 2000)

——, *After Pentecost: Language and Biblical Interpretation* (SHS 2; Carlisle: Paternoster; Grand Rapids: Zondervan, 2001)

Bebbington, D.W., *Patterns in History: A Christian View* (Downers Grove, IL: InterVarsity Press, 1979)

Blocher, H., 'Biblical Narrative and Historical Reference', in *SBET* 3 (1989), 102–22

Bühler, P., and J.F. Habermacher (eds.), *La Narration: Quand le Récit Devient Communication* (Lieux théologiques 12; Genève: Labor et Fides, 1988)

Carr, D., 'Life and the Narrator's Art', in *Hermeneutics and Deconstruction* (ed. H.J. Silverman and D. Ihde; New York: State University Press of New York, 1985), 108–21

——, *Time, Narrative, and History* (Bloomington: Indiana University Press, 1986)

Carroll, N., 'Interpretation, History and Narrative', in *The History and Narrative Reader* (ed. G. Roberts; London: Routledge, 2001), 246–65

Chartier, R., *On the Edge of the Cliff: History, Language and Practices* (Baltimore: The Johns Hopkins University Press, 1997)

Chatman, S., *Story and Discourse: Narrative Structure in Fiction and Film* (Ithaca, NY: Cornell University Press, 1978)

Cockburn, D., *Other Times: Philosophical Perspectives on Past, Present and Future* (Cambridge: CUP, 1997)

Culler, J., *Structuralist Poetics: Structuralism, Linguistics, and the Study of Literature* (Ithaca, NY: Cornell University Press, 1975)

Dray, W.H., 'Narrative and Historical Realism', in *The History and Narrative Reader* (ed. G. Roberts; London: Routledge, 2001), 157–80

Ellingsen, M., *The Integrity of Biblical Narrative: Story in Theology and Proclamation* (Minneapolis: Fortress Press, 1990)

Evans, R.J., *In Defence of History* (London: Granta, 1997)

Fodor, J., *Christian Hermeneutics: Paul Ricœur and the Refiguring of Theology* (Oxford: OUP, 1995)

Frei, H., *The Eclipse of Biblical Narrative* (New Haven: Yale University Press, 1974)

Frye, N., *The Great Code: The Bible and Literature* (London: Routledge, 1982)

Harris, W.V., *Interpretive Acts: In Search of Meaning* (Oxford: Clarendon Press, 1988)

——, *Literary Meaning: Reclaiming the Study of Literature* (London: Macmillan, 1996)

Hauerwas, S., and G.L. Jones (eds.), *Why Narrative? Readings in Narrative Theology* (Grand Rapids: Eerdmans, 1989)

Heelas, P. (ed.), *Religion, Modernity and Postmodernity* (Oxford: Basil Blackwell, 1998)

Hutcheon, L., *A Poetics of Postmodernism: History, Theory, Fiction* (London: Routledge, 1988)

Jacoby, R., 'A New Intellectual History?', in *Reconstructing History* (ed. E. Fox-Genovese and E. Lasch-Quinn; New York: Routledge, 1999), 94–118

Jeffrey, D.L., *People of the Book: Christian Identity and Literary Culture* (Grand Rapids: Eerdmans, 1996)

Jenkins, K., *Re-Thinking History* (London: Routledge, 1991)

——, (ed.), *The Postmodern History Reader* (London: Routledge, 1997)

——, 'A Postmodern Reply to Perez Zagorin', *History and Theory* 39 (2000), 181–200

Kellner, H., *Language and Historical Representation: Getting the Story Crooked* (Madison: University of Wisconsin Press, 1989)

——, 'As Real as it Gets: Ricœur on Narrativity', in *Meanings in Texts and Actions: Questioning Paul Ricœur* (ed. D.E. Klemm and W. Schweiker; Charlottes-ville:University Press of Virgina, 1993), 49–66

Kermode, F., *A Sense of Ending: Studies in the Theory of Fiction* (London: OUP, 1966)

Lanser, S.S., *The Narrative Act: Point of View in Prose Fiction* (Princeton: Princeton University Press, 1981)

Laughery, G.J., *Living Hermeneutics in Motion: An Analysis and Evaluation of Paul Ricœur's Contribution to Biblical Hermeneutics* (Lanham, MD: University Press of America, 2002)

——, 'Language at the Frontiers of Language', in *After Pentecost: Language and Biblical Interpretation* (ed. C. Bartholomew, C. Greene and K. Möller; SHS 2; Carlisle: Paternoster; Grand Rapids: Zondervan, 2001), 171–94

——, 'Evangelicalism and Philosophy', in *The Futures of Evangelicalism* (ed. C.G. Bartholomew, R. Parry and A. West; Downers Grove, IL: InterVarsity Press, 2003)

Lemon, M.C., *The Discipline of History and the History of Thought* (London: Routledge, 1995)

Long, V.P., *The Art of Biblical History* (Grand Rapids: Zondervan, 1994)

——, 'Historiography of the Old Testament', in *The Face of Old Testament Studies: A Survey of Contemporary Approaches* (ed. D.W. Baker and B.T. Arnold; Leicester: Inter-Varsity Press, 1999), 145–75

——, D.W. Baker and G.J. Wenham (eds.), *Windows into Old Testament History: Evidence, Argument, and the Crisis of 'Biblical Israel'* (Grand Rapids: Eerdmans, 2002)

Longman, T., *Literary Approaches to Biblical Interpretation* (Grand Rapids: Zondervan, 1987)

——, 'Storytellers, Poets and the Bible: Can Literary Artifice be True?', in *Inerrancy and Hermeneutic* (ed. H. Conn; Grand Rapids: Baker, 1988), 137–50

——, and L. Ryken (eds.), *The Complete Literary Guide to the Bible* (Grand Rapids: Zondervan, 1993)

Lyotard, J-F., *The Postmodern Condition: A Report on Knowledge* (trans. G. Bennington and B. Massumi; Minneapolis: University of Minnesota Press, 1984)

Marguerat, D., *The First Christian Historian: Writing the 'Acts of the Apostles'* (trans. G.J. Laughery, K. McKinney and R. Bauckham; Cambridge: CUP, 2002)

——, and Y. Bourquin, *How to Read Bible Stories: An Introduction to Narrative Criticism* (trans. J. Bowden; London: SCM Press, 1999)

Marrou, H-I., *Théologie de l'Histoire* (Paris: Seuil, 1968)

McCullagh, C.B., *The Truth of History* (London: Routledge, 1998)

Mink, L.O., *Historical Understanding* (ed. B. Fay, E. Golob and R. Vann; Ithaca, NY: Cornell University Press, 1987)

——, 'Narrative Form as a Cognitive Instrument', in *The History and Narrative Reader* (ed. G. Roberts; London: Routledge, 2001), 211–22

Mitchell, W.J.T. (ed.), *On Narrative* (Chicago: University of Chicago Press, 1981)

Moore, S.D., 'The "Post-" Age Stamp: Does it Stick?', *JAAR* LVII/3 (1989), 543–59

Mullen, S.A., 'Between "Romance" and "True History"', in *History and the Christian Historian* (ed. R.A. Wells; Grand Rapids: Eerdmans, 1998), 23–40

Munslow, A., *Deconstructing History* (London: Routledge, 1997)

Naugle, D.K., *Worldview: The History of a Concept* (Grand Rapids: Eerdmans, 2002)

Norman, A.P., 'Telling it Like it Was: Historical Narratives on their own Terms', in *The History and Narrative Reader* (ed. G. Roberts; London: Routledge, 2001), 181–96

Ricœur, P., 'Existence et Herméneutique', in *Le Conflit des Interprétations* (Paris: Seuil, 1969), 7–28 (ET 'Existence and Hermeneutics', in *The Conflict of Interpretations* [trans. K. McLaughlin; Evanston, IL: Northwestern University Press, 1974], 3–26)

——, 'Du Conflit à la Convergence des Méthodes en Exégèse Biblique', in *Exégèse et Herméneutique* (ed. X. Léon-Dufour; Paris: Seuil, 1971), 35–53

——, 'Esquisse de Conclusion', in *Exégèse et Herméneutique* (ed. X. Léon-Dufour; Paris: Seuil, 1971), 285–95

——, *The Conflict of Interpretations* (ed. D. Ihde; Evanston, IL: Northwestern University Press, 1974)

——, 'Biblical Hermeneutics', *Semeia* 4 (1975), 29–148

——, *Interpretation Theory: Discourse and the Surplus of Meaning* (Fort Worth: Texas Christian University Press, 1976)

——, *Essays on Biblical Interpretation* (ed. L. Mudge; Philadelphia: Fortress Press, 1980)

——, 'Toward a Hermeneutic of the Idea of Revelation', in *Essays on Biblical Interpretation* (ed. L. Mudge; Philadelphia: Fortress Press, 1980), 73–118

——, 'The Hermeneutics of Testimony', in *Essays on Biblical Interpretation* (ed. L. Mudge; Philadelphia: Fortress Press, 1980), 119–54

——, 'Can Fictional Narratives Be True?', *Analecta Husserliana* XIV (1983), 3–19

——, 'Le Récit Interprétative: Exégèse et Théologie dans les Récits de la Passion', *RSR* 73 (1985), 17–38

——, *Temps et Récit* (3 vols.; Paris: Seuil, 1983–1985) (ET *Time and Narrative* [trans. K. McLaughlin and D. Pellauer, vols. 1–2; K. Blamey and D. Pellauer, vol. 3; Chicago: University of Chicago Press, 1984–1988])

——, 'From Proclamation to Narrative', *JR* LXIV (1984), 501–12

——, *From Text to Action* (Evanston, IL: Northwestern University Press, 1991)

——, 'Philosophical and Biblical Hermeneutics', in *From Text to Action* (Evanston, IL: Northwestern University Press, 1991), 89–101

——, 'Herméneutique: Les Finalités de l'Exégèse Biblique', in *La Bible en Philosophie: Approches Contemporaines* (ed. D. Bourg and A. Lion; Paris: Cerf, 1993), 27–51

——, 'Philosophies Critiques de l'Histoire: Recherche, Explication, Écriture', in *Philosophical Problems Today*, I (ed. G. Fløistad; Dordrecht: Kluwer Academic Publishers, 1994), 139–201

——, 'Naming God', in *Figuring the Sacred: Religion, Narrative, and Imagination* (ed. M.I. Wallace; Minneapolis: Fortress Press, 1995), 217–35

——, *La Mémoire, l'Histoire, l'Oubli* (Paris: Seuil, 2000)

——, and A. LaCocque, *Penser la Bible* (Paris: Seuil, 1998) (ET *Thinking Biblically: Exegetical and Hermeneutical Studies* [trans. D. Pellauer; Chicago: University of Chicago Press, 1998])

Roberts, G. (ed.), *The History and Narrative Reader* (London: Routledge, 2001)

Southgate, B., *History: What and Why? Ancient, Modern and Postmodern Perspectives* (London: Routledge, 1996)

Steiner, G., *Real Presences* (London: Faber & Faber, 1989)

Stenger, W.R., *Narrative Theology in Early Jewish Christianity* (Louisville, KY: Westminster / John Knox Press, 1989)

Sternberg, M., *The Poetics of Biblical Narrative: Ideological Literature and the Drama of Reading* (Bloomington: Indiana University Press, 1985)

Stiver, D.R., *The Philosophy of Religious Language: Sign, Symbol and Story* (Oxford: Basil Blackwell, 1996)

——, *Theology After Ricœur: New Directions in Hermeneutical Theology* (Louisville, KY: Westminster / John Knox Press, 2001)

——, 'Ricœur, Speech-act Theory, and the Gospels as History', in *After Pentecost: Language and Biblical Interpretation* (ed. C. Bartholomew, C. Greene and K. Möller; SHS 2; Carlisle: Paternoster; Grand Rapids: Zondervan, 2001), 50–72

Trachtenberg, M., 'The Past Under Seige: A Historian Ponders the State of his Profession – and What to Do about It', in *Reconstructing History* (ed. E. Fox-Genovese and E. Lasch-Quinn; London: Routledge, 1999), 9–11

Vanhoozer, K.J., *Biblical Narrative in the Philosophy of Paul Ricœur* (Cambridge: CUP, 1990)

——, *Is There A Meaning in This Text? The Bible, the Reader and the Morality of Literary Knowledge* (Grand Rapids: Zondervan, 1998)

——, 'From Speech Acts to Scripture Acts: The Covenant of Discourse and the Discourse of Covenant', in *After Pentecost: Language and Biblical Interpretation* (ed. C. Bartholomew, C. Greene and K. Möller; SHS 2; Carlisle: Paternoster; Grand Rapids: Zondervan, 2001), 1–49

Veyne, P., *Comment on Écrit l'Histoire* (Paris: Seuil, 1971)

Ward, G. (ed.), *The Postmodern God: A Theological Reader* (Oxford: Basil Blackwell, 1998)

White, H., *Metahistory: The Historical Imagination in Nineteenth-Century Europe* (Baltimore: The Johns Hopkins University Press, 1973)

——, 'Narrativization', in *On Narrative* (ed. W.J.T. Mitchell; Chicago: University of Chicago Press, 1981), 249–54

——, *The Content of the Form: Narrative Discourse and Historical Representation* (Baltimore: The Johns Hopkins University Press, 1987)

——, 'The Historical Text as a Literary Artifact', in *History and Theory: Contemporary Readings* (ed. B. Fay, P. Pomper and R.T. Vann; Oxford: Basil Blackwell, 1998), 15–33

——, 'Afterword', in *Beyond the Cultural Turn: New Directions in the Study of Society and Culture* (ed. V. Bonnell and L. Hunt; Berkeley: University of California Press, 1999), 315–24

Wright, G.H. von, *Explanation and Understanding* (Ithaca, NY: Cornell University Press, 1971)

Zagorin, P., 'History, the Referent, and Narrative Reflections on Postmodernism Now', *History and Theory* 38 (1999), 1–24

——, 'Rejoinder to a Postmodernist', *History and Theory* 39 (2000), 201–209

16

(Pre) Figuration[1]

Masterplot and Meaning in Biblical History

David Lyle Jeffrey

Now all these things happened unto them for examples: and they are written for our admonition, upon whom the ends of the world are come

(1 Cor. 10:11 KJV)

This history not only declares that which appears on the face of it, but announces something more far-reaching, whence it is called an allegory. And what has it announced? Nothing less than all things now present.

(St. John Chrysostom, *Commentary on Galatians* 4:24)

Grand narrative, it seems, has proven more resilient than its recent detractors imagined. When, in 1979, Jean François Lyotard announced the birth of postmodern consciousness as the coming of an age in which there no longer could be any culturally sustaining masterplot,[2] many of those most distressed to think he might be right had a vested interest of some sort in the grand narrative of classical and biblical literary tradition. Their favorite works of literature lived and moved and had their intellectual being within the ethos circumscribed by a masterplot. Superficially, such folk had less to fear than they thought. Lyotard's anomie was occasioned not by the reflective anxieties of a post-Christian age, but rather of a post-Marxist age. For Marxism, true to its Hegelian under-pinnings, is itself a metanarrative; the goal of its dialectical development through history, the heavenly kingdom on earth of the classless utopia, is a secularized and materialized revision of the dominant Christian grand narra-tive. Unfortunately, by the late 1970s and 1980s, it was all too apparent to most

---

[1] Scripture quotations in this chapter are taken from the Authorised Version and the New International Version.

[2] Lyotard, *La Condition*.

Marxist intellectuals that the classless society had become just as illusory as the Christian heaven or kingdom of God that they had rejected before it. Stung and embittered, they turned inward in paroxysms of alienation, narcissism and the pursuit of privatized fantasy or narrow political advantage.

The institutional power of the French intellectuals of the poste-garde in particular, and their American and European imitators secondarily, has been such that, in the last two or three decades, more effort has been spent on semiotics and revisionary gender politics than on the reading of traditional and culturally foundational works themselves. Few would want to argue that all of this has been wasted time. Still fewer, however, will be likely to spend more time chronicling it a decade hence.

Here then, as scholars lodged 'between past and future', we are at a moment from which a kind of stocktaking prospect seems both possible and propitious. Inevitably, of course, such reflection takes us back to basics, to questions about structure as well as style, about projected world-view, as well as *Rezeptionsgeschichte* (the history of interpretation and criticism).[3] The excursus I propose here is preliminary. Nevertheless, I hope you will come to agree with me that a basic literary reflection is not, in our present historical context, without its merits. At the very least it will help us further our appreciation of why it is that, postmodernists of Lyotard's persuasion notwithstanding, ethnic and religious groups in a multicultural context insist upon the maintenance of their own culture's grand stories, even seeing them as essential to cultural survival.

Further, it may help us intuit why it is that those cultures with a firm grip on their own native grand narratives have often the clearest appreciation of the signal differences in world-view signified by the structure and resulting historiography of others. Islamic historiography affords one pertinent example. In Islam, history has unfolded as a series of incomplete realizations of an ideal kingdom in the past: the Medinan reign of the Prophet is the Golden Age to which the aspirant desires to return, so far as this may be possible. The goal of Islamic historiography is to teach the individual that his duty 'is to transcend himself and his natural condition in order to become akin to the ideal man whose perfect example is the Prophet Muhammad'.[4] The Islamic myth, even in its typical modern guise, is one of incorporation and symbolic return.[5] That which resists incorporation and return is intractably alien and infidel; among purists, to the

---

[3] This is the territory into which N.T. Wright has taken us so magisterially in his *New Testament*, and if what follows here entails something of a qualifier to his superb discussion of grand story and world-view, my interlocution is one prejudiced by largely unadulterated admiration for what he has accomplished in that volume and its sequel.

[4] Azmeh, *Islam*, 134.

[5] Azmeh, *Islam*, 134–37; 163.

degree that the impurity of others threatens to pollute or structurally challenge the ideal, it may – even must – be opposed with holy warfare.

Narrative Structure, Historiography and World-View

To state the obvious in a more literary way: the structure of formative narratives, as much as their style, bespeaks a *Weltanschauung*, or world-view.[6] This elementary insight tends to escape us when we are dealing with a familiar or representative grand story from our own linguistic culture. Even in cases where (as in biblical studies in the West) the grand story is formatively naturalized, though not native, the putatively obvious can go so long unremarked that at last no one conjures with its decisive importance for *meaning in history* – either in the then-and-there of the original work or in the here-and-now of its culturally contextualized interpretation. But when we come to epic or otherwise foundational literature in a truly alien culture, we are much more likely to notice immediately how not style alone but, still more deeply, structure itself expresses a world-view.

China affords another example – pertinent because its grand narrative patterns are ancient yet persist in modern literature as well as in historiography. *Journey to the West*, a sixteenth-century epic (c. 1570) by Wu Cheng'en, has until recently been best known to Westerners (if they know it at all) through the Peking Opera redaction, 'The Monkey King'. An earlier and mostly unavailable translation by Jenner has been superseded by the translation of Anthony Yu (sometime New Testament scholar) and has now begun to attract a much wider literary audience.[7] In this pilgrimage epic of one hundred chapters, the pilgrim protagonist Tang Seng is modeled on an actual Buddhist priest and translator, Xuanzang, also known as the Dharma Master, who had died a millennium earlier. Tang Seng is aided by an acrobatic trickster, Sun Wukong (the Monkey King), and other disciples as he makes his quest to find the True Scriptures. The little band of pilgrims journeys through episode after episode, conquering bandito *arhats*, symbolic of vices that would beset the pilgrim, and make their way to the 'West' – India or Nepal – where Tang is successful in acquiring the True Scriptures. This takes ninety-seven chapters. Possessed at last of this foundation-building text, Tang and his sidekicks return

---

[6] Erich Auerbach perhaps most famously demonstrated that style bespeaks a world-view. His examples of world-view starkly contrasted by narrative style were Homeric epic and the biblical story of Abraham, notably in his opening chapter of *Mimesis*.

[7] Wu Cheng'en, *Journey* (trans. Jenner) is the text used here. The translation by Yu is slightly more recent.

in only three chapters to the East (China), 'where the nine nines are complete, the demons are all destroyed', and, 'after the triple threes are fulfilled the Way returns to its roots'. Summarily, in Chapter 100, 'the journey back to the East is complete and the five immortals achieve nirvana'.[8]

As in all epic and romance, the structure here is key to meaning.[9] The point in *Journey to the West* is that one travels outward in search of that which will enrich or add value to what always remains the only possible home. The myth here is even more strongly one of return, and enrichment – not so much of the individual as of one's national home and its people – is the realized goal of a successful journey. Journeys to the West in search of wisdom are a cultural and literary motif in the Orient; they recur again and again. When wise men came from the East, following a star and seeking a Wisdom more luminous than their own to worship, they seem to have been living out a characteristic oriental impulse. Having seen the Wisdom they sought, they presented gifts and 'departed for their own country another way' (Mt. 2:12) – that is, they returned home, bearing their knowledge with them.

In Chinese culture, the paradigm for such narratives and the sense of obligation they confer is called *luoye guigen* – and implies the inevitability of return to China: 'you must go home again'. To fail to return to one's source prompts great community anxiety and loss of honor. Fear of assimilation (*zancao-cugen*), or *tong hua*, the elimination of racial and cultural heritage, firmly identify sources of the deepest shame. Accordingly, resistance to 'homecoming' remains a dark shadow force in the Chinese world-view – even, to some degree, among diaspora Chinese Christians.[10]

If we are struck by this grand narrative structure – or repetitions of the masterplot in modern Chinese, Korean or Japanese literature[11] – it is likely because it seems to Westerners somewhat counterintuitive. The characteristic form of such narrative in Western Christian cultures involves a journey out from and beyond one notion of civilization almost entirely in order to found another. It is a voyage in which, in certain crucial respects, the initial civilization is left behind, emigrated from, in pursuit of a certain emancipation of the

---

[8] These chapter titles quite accurately reflect the swift recension and sense of religious closure effected by 'return' in this text.

[9] This is a point much stressed, of course, by structuralists. N.T. Wright cites Vladimir Propp, but Roland Barthes and Northrop Frye are perhaps more accessible proponents of such structural analysis, Frye most notably in his *Anatomy* and *Secular Scripture*, but also in his *Great Code*.

[10] It is of some interest that the greater willingness of Chinese to settle now in other parts of the world – in effect to become permanent emigrants – is related to the (cultural) Christianization of many of them. See Wang Ling-chi, 'On Luodi-shenggen'; cf. Horn, *Chinese Women*.

[11] See my study, 'Journey to the West'.

spirit that becomes possible only when that which is 'old' is transcended or transformed in the light of a 'new' vision. There is at least the suggestion that to return to the precise beginning, even if enriched by foreign treasure, is not possible without losing precisely what in the new understanding was most valuable. Or to put in Tom Wolfe's way, for such folk, 'You can't go home again'. In Western cultures after the incorporation of Christianity, it is an additional feature that reaching the new land, the better city, is dependent not merely on the acquisition and mastery of certain kinds of knowledge (*gnōsis*), but also upon a fundamental change of heart, a turning of the will in conscious preference for a new good (*metanoia*), hence choosing a new identity.[12] But it is instructive, I think, to consider the way in which Western epic narrative – pilgrimage story – has developed through and away from narrative forms that were originally much more like the circular Chinese pattern. *The Iliad* and *Odyssey* of Homer are, taken together, the prominent example. Together, these epics comprise a journey out from the Greek homeland and, after suitable conquest and discovery, an emphatic return home. In the battle at Troy, the Greeks are represented as in various ways achieving a conquest of the vices attached to wrath; manly *aretē* (honor) is accumulated through a lifetime of deeds of bravery coupled with actions of self-restraint. Yet the overall metanarrative does not conclude, as we might at first expect, with the cremation and burial of the heroic Hector at the end of the *Iliad*. Rather, for full closure to occur there must be added a vicarious return journey. In Homer it produces fully as long a narrative as the first; *The Odyssey* also is twenty-four books, the return home is symmetrical with the journey out in its scope, the ardors of *eros* are weighted equally in importance with the *agōn* of conquest and, in their challenges, they prove equally essential for the acquisition of *aretē*.[13]

In the episodes of *The Odyssey*, the now mostly female antagonists are in their own way symbolic of the lure to settle elsewhere, a lust for evading all the responsibilities that home entails. Shacked up with Calypso, the goddess who promises him immortality in exchange for sexual servitude, Odysseus can only bring shame upon himself. When he responds to the invitation of Wisdom

---

[12] This is a point considered thoughtfully by Wright, *New Testament*, 67–69; 135–39, etc. With respect to biblical and post-biblical Christian literature in the West, it is a theme also in my *People of the Book*.

[13] In addition to Auerbach, *Mimesis* (see n. 4, above), the classic source for *aretē* is Jaeger's *Paideia*, though a concise and reliable synopsis occurs in Bowra, *Greek Experience*, 206–15. MacDonald, in *Homeric Epics*, has made the case that parallels between Mark's Gospel and Homeric epic are persistent enough that a conscious or unconscious dependence must be assumed to exist. I think this is to argue too much, but there is enough evidence to suggest that Mark's Greek audience could be expected to see the narrative of Jesus' *aretē* against Homeric epic as a familiar (yet contrastive) background.

(Athena) to leave her and set out for Ithaca, his becomes a pilgrimage in search of renewed *aretē*. His voyage is instructive, pedagogical and finally exemplary – a trope of the progress from unwisdom to wisdom. *Nostos* (nostalgia) – longing for one's tribal home – is of the essence of the protagonist's motivation. Despite myriad sexual misadventures, the journey is circular; it culminates in confirmation of the old, original marriage and thus a reaffirmed identity in the city from which the pilgrim has set out (Ithaca). In Homer also, then, the greatest liability for the pilgrim is temptation to settle down along the way (e.g., Nausica and the Phaikians), to fall into complacency or anesthetic evasion (Kirke; *ek de Kalypsemenos*). In short, the world-view projected from Homer's double epic is not entirely unlike that which we find in *Journey to the West*.

With Virgil, we enter into new territory and stay there. His pilgrim protagonist, Aeneas, journeys out from a Troy that can no longer be home; his is the exile of 'losers', of the defeated, and his pilgrimage is true wandering. In the deepest possible sense it is a journey out of the past, away from a history that is bankrupt, toward a future history yet unwritten. What Leonardo da Vinci captures so memorably in his drawing of Aeneas with his old father Anchises on his back is a universal, yet revolutionary, truth. The pilgrim unable to return bears his past with him, but not all the way. With the death of Anchises the past recedes irrevocably, and with it Aeneas's yearning for rootedness in history deepens; there is pathos in his joyful discovery of those wall paintings in Dido's temple in which the terrible destruction of Troy is revisited as he remembers that there was some honor for the Trojans too.[14]

The journey of Aeneas has all the standard features of Greek epic narrative, including the destructive second-order affections so familiar to readers of *The Odyssey*. Here too such lesser affections, no matter how appealing (e.g., Dido), must also be overcome in order for the journey to continue. But this is not a 'journey home'. The arc is broken off. As such, the *Bildungsroman* (novel of education) moral shifts away from the older focus, having less to do with self-restraint and self-knowledge. Rather, a much stronger sense of manifest destiny is the moral here. The journey culminates in a *new* marriage, rather than reaffirmation of an old marriage, and announcement of imperial civic purpose: 'Romans, remember! Govern; rule the world!'[15] In *The Aeneid* there is considerable strengthening of the idea that the end justifies the means. A New City is founded – a civilization now of winners. The poem exudes a tone of triumphalism as well as a strongly historicist world-view – a strong theory of

---

[14] Virgil, *The Aeneid*: 'it was only a picture on a wall, but the sight afforded food for the spirit's need. He saw the Greeks, hard pressed, in flight, and Trojans coming after ...'

[15] It is of more than passing significance that a poem meant to apostrophize Roman *pietas* should quite literally end with a briefly premeditated revengeful death – as Aeneas slays Turnus.

historical progress. The honor of a complete life is expressed not precisely as *aretē*, or even *fama* (though that is desirable), but as the achievement of that civic virtue the Romans called *pietas*, with its close proximity to patriotism and nationalistic pride. The most exalted love is love of country: *amor/ Roma/ amor*.

Roman epic narrative, though heavily dependent upon Homeric epic narrative and even to some degree upon the expectations a reader's familiarity with that narrative creates, thus also fundamentally challenges it at the most basic level. One is almost tempted to say that *The Aeneid* is the first 'tale of two cities'. 'Almost', because of course that very phrase calls up a biblical historiography and with it, especially in the Roman context, Augustine's later riposte to the Roman grand narrative in which he superimposes upon it another masterplot – one drawn from his biblical sources.[16] But let us not hasten too quickly into the rhetorical and historiographical *tour de force* of the brilliant North African theologian. For our purpose at hand it is the canonical New Testament Scriptures themselves with which we have principally to reckon, and that in respect of the structure they imply or project into Hellenic and Mediterranean expectations, shaped as they were in part by the Hebrew Scriptures – and in part, I think we should acknowledge, by Greek and Roman epic narrative.[17] All of this, I want to suggest, still bears upon the question of 'history' in relation to biblical interpretation.

Meaning and History

It is possible (as Iain Provan and Murray Rae have reminded us) to employ the word 'history' in several senses. Among these we may include: a) what happened; b) what is alleged to have happened (reportage, witness); c) the

---

[16] Augustine, *City of God*. A comment by Walzer in his *Exodus* is relevant here. Walzer writes: 'In the literature of the ancient world only *The Aeneid* resembles the Exodus in its narrative structure, describing a divinely guided and world-historical journey to something like a promised land. That is why *The Aeneid* was the only rival of the Exodus in the arguments over the American Great Seal.' Walzer thinks that 'Rome, though it represents for Virgil a "new order of the ages" is not, after all, significantly different from Troy; it is only more powerful; while Canaan is the very opposite of Egypt' (11–12). I am inclined to think the comparison more fraught with complexity than Walzer suggests, as the following pages may indicate.

[17] Cf. Richardson, *History*. That the Old Testament stories are deliberately rooted in history and lived out as a reiteration of an ancestral history is of the essence of the literary forms that predominate in biblical narrative. As Alter and others have observed, only Israel among the ancient peoples chose to cast its ancestral history in prose – to eschew poetry and the epic genre which they would have known to be normative to other cultures for 'grand narrative' purposes.

narrative memory (usually trans-generational) of what happened; d) attempts at
historical or scientific retrieval of documentary evidence; e) academic speculation concerning what 'might' or 'most probably' did or did not happen; and
even f) *ex post facto* revision of received witness for some pressing political or
personal purpose (e.g., new historicism). There is thus an intractable sense (as
Provan suggests) in which everything of received history is received by faith.

Intellectuals and laypeople alike must reckon with yet another and super-
vening dimension, and we recognize it in the form of the tacit (less often
explicit) question already alluded to: 'what is the meaning in history?' In
modernity in the West, this last and richer question had yielded to a subsequent
and purely rhetorical interrogation borne out of a neo-positivist skepticism
concerning in part the possibility of reliable (i.e., verifiable) answers to the
others: 'Can anything of the past be an authority for us today?' As the world
becomes secularized or modernized (perhaps 'Americanized'), there has grown
up a general popular perception that to this question the pragmatic answer
must be 'no'. (There are, accordingly, strong reasons, powerfully expressed in
the American grand narrative itself, for the abysmal failure of repeated attempts
by educators to overcome the comparatively dismal historical knowledge
possessed by American high school and university students. In a context of
such overwhelming commitment to 'now' and the 'new', there is simply not
sufficient public will to have it otherwise.) But this deeply reflexive negative
answer about the authority of the past is certainly not one concerning which
the Christian church could hope to remain neutral: the Scriptures upon which
we ground our faith are undeniably 'of the past'. Thus, with respect to the
textual sources of authority in the church, preeminently Scripture, a general
cultural indifference to history weighs heavily against the typical preoccupations of biblical scholars concerning historicity. This indifference also pre-
disposes – though that is a subject for another occasion – to an ethically
counterproductive obsession with future speculation.

Authority in the forms of remembering, I think we can say, is something
with which the church as a community ought still most properly to be concerned. In the adage sometimes attributed to Augustine, 'we are what we
remember'. If God's emancipatory action in delivering Israel from bondage is
what at its core defines orthodox Judaism, so God's central redemptive action
in Christ Jesus is the common memory which defines the church. This is not to
say that there are no other parts of the biblical story important to memory in
both traditions. Rather, it is to say that the central memory, narratively articulated, of an emancipatory experience of God in history – transforming history –
is the matrix in which these other stories are embedded and in terms of
which they make sense of a diversity of possible particular readings and parallel
experiences. Secondary stories acquire additional profundity when seen in the
light of the central undergirding narrative or masterplot from which derives

their (and our) common identity. (I say 'common', and stress it, because any authentically biblical identity must be communal – all the anarchic individualism of modernity/postmodernity notwithstanding.)

Now it is generally to be observed, I think, that the centering memory of a community's past (roots) – that is, the general consensus of a given people concerning what their shared history *means* – is typically found as a literary construct rather than as a laundry list of evidentially corroborated facts.[18] Thus, for the Roman sense of meaning in their early post-Etruscan history one sensibly gives more weight to *The Aeneid* than, say, to a catalogue of archaeological findings, however valuable in their own right the latter may be for certain narrower kinds of possible discovery. A shard of pottery or even a strand of hair may tell us something we could not otherwise know. But for an intelligible witness to questions of meaning and religious substance (truth, value, authority), one turns elsewhere. It is in such texts as Virgil's narrative of exile, pilgrimage, new immigrant foundations and subsequent cultural conquest that we get at the really formative truths about early Roman history; this, hardly anyone doubts. That such a commonsensical trust in the purport of the literary texts does not now pertain when we turn from the criticism of classical texts to biblical criticism is obvious. Presumably, questions about the authority projected by the Roman past are far less troubling to us than questions about the authority projected by the narratives of biblical history.

From a purely literary (but also, I think, anthropological) point of view, it is possible to say that a fervent preoccupation with listings of documentary evidence, a 'scientific' retrieval of facts, is a pretty certain sign that what was once a living tradition is running out of gas. For many, to study the Bible 'scientifically' – either to subvert or to uphold its veridical relation to history – can be to engage *ipso facto* in a rejection of the meaning of history as the Bible's authors themselves understood it. This does not mean that the activity is worthless; it may mean that the scholarship is worth much less either for or against the historical truth upon which the church depends than its practitioners on either side imagine.

British sociologist Anthony Giddens has reasonably contended that what we call postmodernism is really just a working out of the consequences of modernity. We can surely confirm this in the history of biblical scholarship over the last couple of centuries.[19] Moreover, it may be confirmed on both sides of the debate about the Bible's authority. C.S. Lewis, for example,

---

[18] Alter, observing differences in the Bible's notion of sacred history from modern historiography, writes: 'There is, to begin with, a whole spectrum of relations to history in the sundry biblical narratives but none of these involves the sense of being bound to documentable facts … that characterizes history in its modern acceptation' (*Art*, 24).

[19] Giddens, *Consequences*.

lamented both the literalism of fundamentalists in America and the literarily obtuse grunt work of Bultmannians in the United Kingdom almost in the same breath.[20] Quite reasonably, it seems to me, Lewis regarded the antagonists on both sides as bad readers of the basic narratives. On both sides, he might have added, the obsession with evidentialism is an attempt to substitute facticity for faith. By contrast, what the vast majority of intelligent readers of the Bible have always assumed about grand narrative texts such as Deuteronomy 6, Psalm 78 and Hebrews 11, is that they reflect little or no concern with the establishment of data or, in any modern empiricist sense, 'historical certitude'. They simply – and reasonably – have assumed reliability in the witness to history, received this witness as 'parable' (*mashal* – Ps. 78:2) or prefiguration (*typos* – 1 Cor. 10:11) and moved on to the question 'what shall we then do?' That is, for them, as evidently for the biblical writers themselves, the question which most matters concerns the *authority* of the past. To refer to received history as a metaphor – a *mashal* – or as an 'example for us today' – is not in any sense to diminish or call into question matters of fact; it is (in fact) to reveal more confidence in the essential truth of biblical history than could ever be warranted by archaeo-logical evidence or a documentary hypothesis.

The passages to which I have just alluded are pivotal remembrances of history-as-to-meaning both for other biblical narratives and for other narra-tives where the Bible is a foundational text. They remind us that the herme-neutic underpinnings of specific acts of interpretation are not often reducible to matters of method, or even of ideology more or less philosophically conceived. There is a deeper structure to world-views, almost invariably referred to as 'history' as the ancients rather than we moderns might define it, and it is invari-ably narratively encoded in forms or genres that are conventionally regarded as literary rather than historical. The power of shared memory, so constituted, is such that it has consequences for many things that might at first seem unrelated to the core narrative – theories of education, for example. As both the *Bildungs-roman* and the Christian dream-vision pilgrimage texts it supplants make clear, Western literature and, I would say, historiography, has been an ongoing tussle between classical Roman and biblical notions of what it is, and of what value it is, to 're-member' the past.[21]

It will be further apparent that core narratives – those commonly held to characterize community identity, imply definite attitudes toward the past. Typically (as, for example, in biblical and other oriental core narratives), this attitude will be one of profound respect. But this norm is not without exceptions. What we call modernity, with all of its consequences, implies a categorical contrary to this traditional regard for the past. This is apparent in

---

[20] Jeffrey, 'C.S. Lewis'. This is substantially the argument of Hauerwas in *Unleashing*.

[21] One might consider here, for example Ross, *Making*; Brenneman, *Canons*.

modernity's defining moments. The French Revolution is nothing if not a dismissal of the reigning grand narrative. The American Revolution affords another example of an emphatic rejection of the past.

What ensues in these events, undeniably, is a powerful myth of new beginnings. Old things have passed away, all things become new. Yet even in the comparatively recently formed secular 'grand narrative' we can see looming certain consequences for traditional approaches to biblical history. A sharply accentuated disdain for prior history, almost Virgilian in its firmness, and, in America especially, determination to make the frontier and future history supplant it, goes hand in hand with an inherent distrust of the authority of the more distant past – eventually perhaps a disregard for any authority that is not both contemporary and 'popular'. It is small wonder that, to the chagrin of their grandparents, North American evangelical congregations of this generation possess little more of biblical knowledge – that is, biblical history in the plainest sense – than they do of the secular history which, more notoriously, they have also forgotten. But is the biblical scholarship of today, for all of our preoccupation with the questions of biblical history, doing very much to offset this nearly incalculable loss of biblical history in the shared memory of the church? Or is it the case that both in the guild and in the church biblical scholarship is serving merely to abet the fading from memory and imagination alike of the actual content of biblical narrative? For the erasure or fading away from present Christian consciousness of centering memory – in all its richness of texture and narrative detail – constitutes a loss of authority for the biblical past far more devastating in its implications than the obscure dubieties of academics about this or that textual correspondence or correlation.

Biblical Metanarrative and Historiography

The readers of this essay are quite unlikely to need a review of Old Testament narrative. Permit me therefore to recall again something elementary: the narrative motif of exile and pilgrimage. Throughout the Hebrew Bible it recurs as a concomitant of the persistent dialectic of bondage and freedom. Strangers and sojourners are aliens, whether in captivity or on the road. Their exodus is above all emancipatory narrative, their famous names (*shemōt*) are all associated with an outward bound journey, and it is no accident that their supreme deity is identified directly with emancipation: 'I am the LORD your God, who brought you out of the land of Egypt, out of the house of slavery. You shall have no other gods before me' (Ex. 20:2 ESV). This foundational passage suggests a deep connection of law and liberty in the Jewish biblical imagination. But careful reading of the biblical texts shows that this view of civic order is typically more effective when culture and identity are obliged to be a moveable feast. The tabernacle, not the temple, is thus the perdurable symbol of sanctuary for the writer of Hebrews (chs. 9–10), even as it was in the book of Exodus and continues to be in Revelation (21:1–3; 22). *Wayikra el-mosheh ... ohel mō'ed* (Lev. 1:1): one worships; one moves on; and the symbols of communion and community move along with the faithful travelers.

Storytelling along the way is mandatory because of the covenant obligation to pass on the grand narrative's enduringly pertinent emancipatory message (Deut. 6:4–9; Ps. 78). Postponement and frustration of progress toward the promised land are a result of disobedience and a neglect of holiness as well as worship. Sin skews the itinerary; forgetfulness of the emancipatory metanarrative leads to cul-de-sacs and to bondage all over again. Reiteration of the narrative is thus a necessity – especially where there are few fixed land-marks. Master-narrative becomes a kind of spiritual map; the 'story line' anchors thought when thought is most prone to drift; it encourages thought to press forward to better prospects. Mount Zion, the City of David, Jerusalem the Golden seem so credibly to be the goal and journey's end. There will be a promised land, a place of Sabbath rest and closure: one may say, one *must* say: '*Lashanah haba'ah bi Yerushalayim!*'

In the New Testament, *Yeru-shalem* remains the vision – the '*visio pacis*' as Augustine would later call it. Yet the literal historical Jerusalem under the Romans becomes soon enough its own kind of captivity. By the first century, not the Roman occupation only but also the ossification of Jewish *halakah* and, in some quarters, a resulting spiritual bondage to a petrified notion both of spiritual culture and of Law, has robbed Jerusalem of its *shalom*.[22] As we can see so readily in Jesus' interlocutions with the Pharisees and scribes, for them the Law is no longer about liberty. And this, for our purposes here centrally, is substantially the charge Paul brings against the diaspora Galatians. A problem with some of the Galatians, it seems, is that in their diaspora struggle to maintain Jewish identity they have become fixated on the Jerusalem they thought was their journey's end and whose golden era they think their eventual just reward. They too are filled with *nostos*-longing, nostalgia for Jerusalem, and Paul's tactic in addressing their spiritual misprision is to begin by showing them that he himself has made no fetish of return to the holy city but has consistently, constantly journeyed out in obedience to his calling, and that even when, so to speak, business drew him back (to confirm the gospel), he stayed only fleetingly (long enough to admonish Peter's Judaizing tendencies) and then took to the road again (Gal. 1:17–2:2).

In calling the Galatians to account, Paul draws heavily upon the meta-narrative that the Judaizers most cherish – to make the point that the end of the journey through history set out in Torah (Gal. 3:11ff.) is not a place but

---

[22] See, e.g., Schiffman, *From Text*.

a person, and that person the seed of Abraham, the true Son to whom the promise was made. Torah has acted as a pedagogue or tutor to bring us not to Jerusalem, but to Christ (Gal. 3:24–25), a destiny in which all who belong to Christ are now not slaves but adopted heirs. Indeed, this new state is a condition of spiritual life; the norms of political and social distinction vanish (Gal. 3:28). There is no property or geography associated with this inheritance, no distribution of acreage from Dan to Beersheba, no condominium waiting in Jerusalem. It is of the essence of Paul's overall argument in Galatians that the allegorical passage in 4:22–31 delegitimates the diaspora-longing for a return to Jerusalem even as it rejects the traditional Jewish reading of Torah-covenant – a reading in which Jerusalem certainly had been both symbolic and political home. The promise, on the other hand, fulfilled at last to Abraham's seed, Christ and all those adopted in him, points now to quite another destination: Christ and his kingdom are the new journey's end (3:24).[23] But they are the very condition of the journey as well. Here, too, we have a moveable feast – for the liberty to which we have been called is inseparable from a new law, the law of love (5:13–14); the pilgrim code for those who continue to 'walk in the Spirit' (5:16) includes love of the neighbors through whose turf we make our way.

In this context the counterintuitive reversals of expected significance in the Abraham–Hagar–Sarah story make perfect sense. To the faithful Jew, Paul's identification of Hagar with 'that Jerusalem which now is and is in bondage with her children' (4:25) must have seemed perilously close to blasphemy. It constitutes a revision of Jewish metanarrative and historiography as decisive as that which Virgil's *Aeneid* achieves in relation to the epics of Homer. Paul is not, I think, simply undermining what N.T. Wright, in his *The New Testament and the People of God*, describes as the old Jewish conviction that 'the biblical period ... runs out without a sense of an ending'.[24] Rather, he is preempting world-view assumptions about historical closure that people like the Hasmoneans, as well as other Zionists before and since, were so ardently to pursue, 'the full liberation and redemption of Israel'.[25] Wright is surely right to think that the apologia of Josephus in the *Antiquities* is inadequate as a means of obtaining closure on any account[26] – except, perhaps, a Virgilian one. By having 'Israel's god [go] over to the Romans', so that Rome may legitimately decimate Jerusalem and scatter its survivors, Josephus simply exchanges a politicized version of Old Testament metanarrative for the Gentile metanarrative that looks most like it. But does Paul endorse in any way what

---

[23] Wright, *New Testament*, 79.
[24] Wright, *New Testament*, 216.
[25] Wright, *New Testament*, 217.
[26] Wright, *New Testament*, 117.

Wright describes as the first-century hope for a restoration of Jerusalem? Not, as far as I can see, in this text. He is as far from that particular aspiration as he is from the secularizing justification and implied politic of Josephus.

When Paul writes that since Christ it is 'the Jerusalem above' which is 'free and the mother of us all' (4:26), he makes diaspora unsettledness the normative Christian condition. This is the way that Origen, Augustine, Jerome, Gregory the Great, Luther, Bunyan and a host of interpreters since have understood him: he was speaking about temporal Christian experience.[27] To be a stranger in the world is normative; to be a wayfarer en route between the city of this world and the celestial city, 'that Jerusalem which is above', is to participate in a new grand narrative. This new grand narrative differs both from the Old Testament Jewish metanarrative and the official Roman mythos: history's destination is no longer the Jerusalem in Palestine. Nor, on the other hand, do all roads lead to Rome. To be a stranger and a sojourner is still, as it was for pre-Christian Jews, to be a creature wandering through space and time. Now, however, the pilgrim heads toward no literal land of milk and honey, nor does she return to a capital city once thought of as home. Resist it how we will, there is a deep and abiding sense in which the African-American spiritual expresses the new grand narrative accurately:

> This world is not our home,
> we're just a-passing through.
> Our treasures are laid up
> somewhere beyond the blue ...

If centuries of hymns and, as we shall shortly remind ourselves, Christian era literary texts, have since construed the Christian metanarrative in this way, Paul's letter to the Galatians surely bears a considerable share of the blame.[28]

---

[27] Augustine, for example, ties into this understanding also Heb. 11; 13; 1 Pet. 2:11; Ps. 28:13 (*City of God*, 1; cf. *Sermo*, 14.4.6; 70.7; *Joannes*, 40.10). Gregory the Great, in his *Moralia on Job*, remarks that 'temporal comfort on earth is to the just man what a bed in an inn is to the traveler (*viator*): he will rest in it for awhile bodily, but mentally he is already somewhere else' (*Moralia*, 8.54.92; cf. *Epistolae*, 2.204). But these concepts are already highly visible in the early church, where Peregrinus and Viator became common baptismal names. *The Epistle to Diognetus* says of the earthly lot of Christians that 'they reside in their own fatherlands, but as if they were non-citizens; they partake in all things as if they were citizens and suffer all things as if they were strangers. Every foreign country is thus a fatherland to them, and every fatherland a foreign country ..... They sojourn on earth, but they are citizens in heaven' (5:5, 9).

[28] In the interpretative history reflected in n. 16 above, Galatians 4 plays a crucial role, even as it does in Origen, *Contra Celsum* (8.75). It is invoked by Augustine, e.g., in *City of God*, 15.2; likewise by Aquinas, to turn the 'inherent gospel principle' of

The kingdom order – if we are to use such a phrase of this particular Pauline letter – is one in which the old itinerant relationship between law and liberty has been brought to its fulfillment in Christ in such a way as to make absolutely clear that this relationship flourishes at its redemptive best when least locked down to a fixed political agenda. In the new world-view, as we have seen, political and legal status, gender and ethnicity are all transcended. The new order of culture is fluid, dynamic and, more than ever, portable. Pentecost and missionary pilgrimage are key elements in the new master story. As old law/covenant gives way to new law/promise, much in the definition of familiar historical objectives that has been outward and of Palestinian geography is now spoken of as inward and of the Spirit. Thus, though externally bound, one may be internally free. We lose our life to find it; grace makes paradox of much that under the old law had been simply contradiction – discursively imperative and performatively impossible. Thus, too, not only is the old Jerusalem and its law a locus of our captivity, there is in some deep spiritual sense transience at best, captivity at worst, in any worldly city and its culture. This world is not our home: we are now again to be like Abraham – strangers, sojourners, pilgrims.

As I turn now to Hebrews, I want to affirm my strong agreement with N.T. Wright's observation that 'all world-views, the Christian one included, are in principle public statements', 'stories which attempt to challenge and perhaps to subvert other world-view-stories'.[29] That might seem, indeed, almost precisely the point of this essay. But to any who have read him carefully, it should by now be apparent that on my view Bishop Wright has gone somewhat further than either the texts or the preponderant traditions of interpretation warrant in insisting – in the way he does – on the 'irreducible publicness', as he calls it, or politically immanent dimension, of the Christian world-view. Here is an example of what he says:

> It [the Christian metanarrative] claims to be telling a story about the creator and his world. If it allows this to collapse for a moment into a story about a god who is rescuing people *out* of the world, then it has abandoned something extremely fundamental in the world-view.[30]

What I want to offer here is a modest caveat, or at least a *sic et non*. One cannot help but be sympathetic with Wright's preemptive parry of gnostic readings of

---

spiritual interpretation, and by Wyclif (*Sermons*, 2.33–36). Later Protestant commentators such as Matthew Poole, in his *Annotations* (1635), emphasize that the spiritual children of Sarah, being obedient through faith, will be true pilgrims – even as Hagar's offspring, carnal by nature, wish to return to a condition of exile.

[29] Wright, *New Testament*, 135.

[30] Wright, *New Testament*, 135.

the gospel both of the second and the twenty-first centuries.[31] But while it may be entirely sufficient to say, even of hellenized Jews, that 'as good creational monotheists ... [they] were not hoping ... to "go to heaven", or at least not permanently, but to be raised to new bodies when the new kingdom came',[32] I am less sure than he that the pilgrim journey to which Galatians and Hebrews invites its Christian readers is not, after all, toward a celestial rather than a restored earthly Jerusalem.[33] There are political as well as theological consequences for each view.

There is a strong hermeneutical sense in which Hebrews is a recapitulation of Galatians. This begins with its theme, but it works itself through the textual exposition, phrase by phrase, of the tabernacle. The apparent shift to grand narrative at chapter 11 presumably accounts for traditional discussions of the structure of the letter. From patristic times and the Middle Ages to the eighteenth century, most saw the epistle as having two movements. Aquinas is representative in describing chapters 1–10 as about the *excellentiam Christi* (the perfection in excellence of Christ) and chapters 11–13 as an exhortation that we should follow him in the pilgrimage of life.[34] The writer sees himself as writing in succession with the narrative of the Old Testament, but so as to stress its messianic portent, its signs and wonders (Heb. 2:2–4), and thus his participation in the tradition of emancipatory grand narrative to which he is heir.

But the bondage from which one journeys out is now spiritual; even the fear of death is bondage (Heb. 2:15). The deliverer is not Moses, but Christ – true Son rather than servant of God (Heb. 3:5–15). All who were on the original pilgrimage out of captivity rebelled and so did not have any closure of that voyage (Heb. 3:16–19). The promise (not the covenant) 'remains of entering his rest' (Heb. 4:1). Indeed, 'there remains a rest for the people of God, for He

---

[31] A list here would be long, especially if it were to include not only direct biblical commentary but also the sermons of televangelists and 'Christian fiction'.

[32] Wright, *New Testament*, 286.

[33] Cf. Wright, *New Testament*, 307, who says, much as might E.P. Sanders and others, 'This Kingdom was not a timeless truth, nor an abstract ethical ideal, nor the coming end of the space-time universe. Nor did the phrase itself *denote* a community, though it would *connote* the birth of a new covenant community. It would denote, rather, the action of the covenant god, within Israel's history, to restore her fortunes, to bring to an end the bitter period of exile, and to defeat through her, the evil that ruled the whole world' (307). The idea of either Israel (or New Israel) as 'chosen arm of God' for the destruction of evil is the volatile element. Here, then, is an implication of real concern: apocalypticists both Christian and Jewish focus obsessively on the historical Jerusalem in some considerable measure because of their identification with this traditional Jewish eschatological grand narrative expectation.

[34] Aquinas, *Omnes S. Pauli*, 228. For a fresh and systematic contemporary study of the structure of Hebrews see Guthrie, *Structure*.

who has entered his rest has himself also ceased from his works as God did from his' (Heb. 4:9–10). We too are to 'be diligent to enter that rest' (Heb. 4:11 NKJV).

The eschatological overtones here are evident; in several Jewish and Christian apocalyptic writings, as well as in talmudic sources, the age to come is described as a perpetual Sabbath.[35] In Hebrews 4 the temporal Sabbath observed by physical rest is transformed into an eschatological rest, entered into by faith. Augustine allegorizes at this point: it is 'the peace of rest, the peace of the Sabbath, which has no evening'[36] and therefore figuratively an 'eternal life'[37] which is anticipated here on earth in those 'reasonable creatures' who try to orient their life's journey toward 'the perfectly ordered and harmonious enjoyment of God, and of one another in God'[38]. As is well known, Augustine was on this model led to see world history as divided into six ages, of which the last would be followed by the millennial reign of the faithful with Christ (cf. his commentary on Rev. 20:1–7; 2 Pet. 3:8, etc.). But he was also led to see the foretold descent of the tabernacle of God and the eschatological making of all things new (Rev. 21:2–5) as the ultimate pilgrim's reward – which, on the warrant of Hebrews as well, he is as inclined as ordinary Christians of all centuries to call 'heaven'. In his *City of God*, to which he claims as epigraph Hebrews 11:13–16 and in which he famously expounds upon Revelation 21, Augustine declares the basic understanding of the church as he knows it. This vision concerns not the historical 'city set on a hill', but the future dwelling of the 'immortality and eternity of the saints'. The celestial Jerusalem he calls the *visio pacis* of the Christian pilgrim, glimpsed only from afar in this life but at last 'to come down out of heaven, because the grace with which God formed it is of heaven'.[38] Principal commentators after him (e.g. Aquinas, Nicholas Lyra, Wyclif) continued to regard the New Jerusalem as the eternal and celestial city of the faithful, and the culmination of history in which history as we know it ceases to be (Is. 34:4; Rev. 6:14). Were all of these commentators improperly representing in their grand narrative the metanarrative of the New Testament?

Reading Hebrews, one would seem to find little to contradict this traditional version of the Christian grand story. According to the writer of the letter, a fundamental difference between the Old Testament metanarrative and his own reconstruction is that now the 'true tabernacle [is that] which the Lord erected, and not man' (Heb. 8:2), and it is not present on earth any more than is Christ – who, in effect, is himself that tabernacle now (Heb. 8:4; cf. Rev. 21:3). When Christ was on earth he came as the 'high priest of the good things to

---

[35] See, e.g., Andreason, *Rest*, and Greenberg, 'Sabbath'.
[36] *Confessions*, 13.35.50.
[37] *Confessions*, 13.36.51.
[38] *City of God*, 19.17; cf. *De Genesi*, 4.9.
[39] *City of God*, 20.19.17.

come, with the greater and more perfect tabernacle not made with hands, that is, not of this creation' (Heb. 9:11), 'for Christ has not entered the holy places made with hands, which are copies of the true, but into heaven itself' (9:24). Whatever we make of the possible Alexandrian context of this letter, it seems to me inescapably the case that a literate first- or second-century reader of this letter would be invited to contrast its implied metanarrative, a revision of the preexisting Jewish grand story, with the most famous Hellenic grand story and its celebrated Roman revision.

Let us come now to the second 'movement' in the structure of Hebrews, divided as it is neatly from the first in the headings of all extant early manuscripts, and in such a way, happily for these purposes, that 11:1 to the end and 12:1–11 form discrete but evidently connected pericopes.[40] What is emphasized here above all is that the heritage of faith is a multigenerational, transhistorical pilgrimage *through* history, and not to 'Canaan land' but rather toward a destination undisclosed. Thus, Abraham journeyed out 'not knowing where he was going' (Heb. 11:8), and en route he 'dwelt in the land of promise as in a foreign country, dwelling in tents' (Heb. 11:9). As he journeyed, he lived in anticipation of an unseen destination: 'he waited for the city which has foundation, whose builder and maker is God' (Heb. 11:10). That this is not the journey of a single protagonist (like Odysseus or Aeneas), but rather of a 'people of God' who make their way by stages through history, is in continuity with the Jewish grand story that the chapter recalls. Their journey cannot be complete or 'made perfect', the writer insists, 'apart from us' (Heb. 11:40). But the striking revision we saw in Galatians now appears again directly:

> These all died in faith, not having received the promises, but having seen them afar off, and were persuaded of them, and embraced them, and confessed that they were strangers and pilgrims on the earth. For they that say such things declare plainly that they seek a country. And truly, if they had been mindful of that country from whence they came out, they might have had opportunity to have returned. But now they desire a better country, that is, an heavenly: wherefore God is not ashamed to be called their God: for he hath prepared for them a city. (Heb. 11:13–16)

On earth these folk were but strangers and pilgrims. The home for which they were seeking was not, as a Greek might have it, 'that country from which they had come out' (Heb. 11:15) any more than it is the kingdom from which they became refugees and which is now 'being shaken' (Heb. 12:27; cf. Gal. 4:22–27). As Galatians has it from the outset, there is a normative Christian sense (or senses) in which Christ 'gave himself for our sins, that He might deliver us from this present evil age' (Gal. 4:1) – not a gnostic deliverance, but emancipation from this world surely, and there is a normative Christian sense

---

[40] See here Guthrie, *Structure*, 3.

(or senses) in which we pilgrims are to 'know that if our earthly house, this tent, is destroyed, we have a building from God, a house not made with hands, eternal in the heavens' (2 Cor. 5:1). The apparent echo of Jesus' words of assurance to his disciples in John's Gospel may be evidence of Paul's careful attention to the disciples' report of Jesus' teaching: 'In my father's house are many mansions. I go to prepare a place for you. And if I go and prepare a place for you, I will come again and receive you unto myself, that where I am, there you may be also' (Jn. 14:2–3). As we read on in this earlier gospel passage, we see that Jesus invokes the language of the Abrahamic pilgrimage, or grand narrative, to disciples who are not sure they really do 'know the way' (Jn. 14:4–5) to make this unprecedented voyage. In the Johannine report, of course, Jesus himself is the Way (Jn. 14:6) – a presuppositional assurance also apparent in the writer to the Hebrews.

Accordingly, the writer to the Hebrews is now able to return via Moses to the distinction between sons and slaves so familiar to us from Galatians (Heb. 12:6–9), and to demonstrate the continuity of the journey through history, cheered on by the 'great cloud of witnesses' (Heb. 12:1), always 'looking unto Jesus, the author and finisher of our faith, who for the joy that was set before him endured the cross, despising the shame and has sat down at the right hand of the throne of God' (Heb. 12:2). In Hellenic terms, it is not for us but for Christ to overcome shame, acquire unsurpassable *aretē* and return to his home. But his eternal abode is not our home yet – we simply journey toward it, in holy anticipation, by a radical *mimesis* coming to obedience through suffering as he did and as he has called us to do (Heb. 5:8–9; Lk. 9:23). That is, to invoke the metonym of another hymn, for the Christian pilgrim, 'the way of the Cross leads home'. In an extension of the pilgrim imagery, we are to make 'straight paths' and 'strengthen the lame' (Heb. 12:12–13), and to 'pursue peace with all people' among whom we sojourn. Finally, in a last allusion to the mistaken impulse to return to the historical Jerusalem, the writer to the Hebrews invokes the same contrast Paul uses in Galatians 4 – that between Sinai (Hagar and the Law) and the celestial Jerusalem:

> You have not come to a mountain that can be touched and that is burning with fire; to darkness, gloom and storm; to a trumpet blast or to such a voice speaking words that those who heard it begged that no further word be spoken to them …
>
> But you have come to Mount Zion, to the heavenly Jerusalem, the city of the living God. You have come to thousands upon thousands of angels in joyful assembly, to the church of the firstborn, whose names are written in heaven. You have come to God, the judge of all men, to the spirits of righteous men made perfect, to Jesus the mediator of a new covenant, and to the sprinkled blood that speaks a better word than the blood of Abel. (Heb. 12:18–19; 22–24 [NIV])

And the coda to this excursus is surely, for this apostle at least, definitive: 'for here we have no continuing city, but we seek the one to come' (Heb. 13:14). That coda has been largely definitive for Christian literary tradition also, and it is to that, finally, and in what I hope will be indicative brevity, that I turn by way of conclusion.

Vernacular Literary Understanding as Interpretation

Augustine is, of course, both famously and infamously associated with turning the implied historiography of the New Testament as he understood it into a form of historiographical apologia for Christianity in his *City of God*. In this he may be said to be, formally speaking, the first Christian philosopher of history. The alternative grand narrative with which he had to deal was not the narrative cherished by Old Testament Judaism or its Hellenic revision as a myth of return. It was rather a thoroughly entrenched Virgilian two cities model – the profound historicism by which Roman citizens and much of the empire clung to a world-view in which the triumph of Rome was still the only acceptable *telos* for history. When that *telos* was threatened again and again by political forces within and military incursions from without, Romans looked for a scapegoat and found Christianity ready to hand and obviously suspect. They knew, however dimly, that Christian praxis did in some way subvert their own world-view. Nor was it lost on them that in some of the regions and cultures in which Christianity had most flourished there was evident political threat to Roman imperial supremacy. For them, the prospect of an end to 'Roman rule' would be as unthinkable as would the end of American supremacy be for many Americans today. Even Christian Romans, we know, found this prospect unthinkable – and Augustine himself was sympathetic to them. But he saw, as did few others, the idolatry in the Romanized manifest-destiny co-opting of the New Testament world-view, and in *The City of God* he did his best to set it to rights.

To do this, as is well known, he had to subvert the Roman metanarrative, in part by an extended deconstruction both of *The Aeneid* and of Homer.[41] He begins by showing that the gods credited with establishing and maintaining Roman supremacy were unable to prevent the sack of Troy (1.3), and that the morality of the Roman gods, even in the literature which mythologizes them, is so capricious as to be risible (3.1–7). Throughout *The City of God* his purpose, announced in his preface, is to show that the Virgilian *pietas*, that high courtesy and patriotism which was Rome's answer to Greek *aretē*, has given way in practice to overweening imperial pride.[42] Thus, 'the earthly city [Rome] ...

---

[41] Richardson, *History*.

[42] Cf. Augustine, *City of God*, 10.1.

though it be mistress of the nations, is itself ruled by the lust of rule' (1.pr).[43]
The Virgilian transformation of Greek metanarrative is carefully built into
Augustine's contextualization of his theme, largely with numerous and skill-
fully deployed citations from the *Aeneid*. Augustine refers to Juno (goddess of
marriage) and her hostility to the exiled Trojans, for example, as a means
of establishing that the Roman story is effectively about the reestablishment of
losers as perpetual victors. He also refers to the elevation of the more frankly
sensual Venus, rather than Juno, as mother of the new civic culture.

> A race I hate now ploughs the sea,
> Transporting Troy to Italy,
> and home gods conquered ...[44]

Augustine quotes Virgil's Juno saying these words, subverting further the
Roman claim to superior civic morality (cf. 2.22). Similarly, the Roman claim
to patriotic and militaristic imperial destiny is likewise undermined:

> Why allege to me the mere names and words of 'glory' and 'victory'? Tear off the
> disguise of wild delusion, and look at the naked deeds: weigh them naked, judge
> them naked. Let the charge be brought against Alba, as Troy was charged with
> adultery. There is no such charge, none like it found: the war was kindled only in
> order that there
> > 'might sound in languid ears the cry
> > Of Tullus and of victory'.
> This vice of restless ambition was the sole motive to that social and parricidal war.[45]

Augustine does not deny the pagan virtues entirely; he concedes that in some
respects the Rome Virgil celebrates began well, yet he insists that its progress
has bankrupted by investing so heavily in temporal power:

> At that time it was their greatest ambition either to die bravely or to live free; but
> when liberty was obtained, so great a desire of glory took possession of them, that
> liberty alone was not enough unless domination also should be sought, their great
> ambition being that which the same poet [Virgil] puts into the mouth of Jupiter.[46]

The 'city' Augustine will celebrate seeks other virtues than earthly power.

Later Augustine moves on to describe the progress of the 'two cities, the
earthly and the heavenly', through history, though he will settle at last on

---

[43] *Confessions*, 13.36.51.

[44] Augustine, *City of God*, 1.2; q. *The Aeneid*, 1.71–3. It is not without continuing reso-
nance for Augustine, one suspects, that Juno was the civic goddess of Carthage.

[45] Augustine, *City of God*, 3.14; q. *The Aeneid*, 6.813.

[46] Augustine, *City of God*, 5.12; q. *The Aeneid*, 1.279ff.

the progress of the heavenly city alone. The earthly city – whether historical Jerusalem or Rome – is indeed a city of captivity, figuratively Babylon: 'the city which was called confusion' and which he associates with Babel and the project of self-made men to ascend to heaven by their own devices (16.4–5). By contrast, the celestial Jerusalem toward which the faithful travel through history cannot be reached or conquered by human effort. One must set out in faith, joining the vulnerable company of the blessed en route, but in the end the New Jerusalem is not so much to be attained (by works) as granted (by grace), as it descends. Citizenship in this city is nonetheless proleptic, participated in already by the faithful as they journey. (In the Johannine paraphrase of St. Catherine of Siena, 'There is a heaven all the way to heaven; for He said, "I am the Way."'[47]) But this prolepsis is experienced now through a vale of tears; it is not an earthly political realization of the kingdom of God. The 'city of God', Augustine says, 'lives by faith in this fleshly course of time, and sojourns as a stranger in the midst of the ungodly'. One day, however, 'it shall dwell in the fixed stability of its eternal seat'.[48]

Augustine, it seems to me, has read the New Testament grand narrative of Galatians and Hebrews against the grand narrative of the Roman epics in a manner quite consistent with the way in which the two canonical letters themselves subvert the grand narrative of Old Testament Judaism. In so doing he has assisted rather than supplanted their projection of the idea of a heavenly home, a celestial city and a 'tabernacling journey' toward it, onto the Christian literary imagination. He has thus provided a constructive constraint upon 'Constantinian' co-optings of the Virgilian master narrative, with its culture-specific and aggrandizing assertion of manifest destiny. That this constraint has been better appreciated in some contexts (notably those of political adversity) than in others (notably those of political supremacy) will be apparent to the most modest reflection on ecclesial and political history.

To put this in another way: when Christians have been in largely unchallenged political power (e.g., Rome, Holy Roman Empire, British Empire, America) there has tended to emerge a neo-Constantinian reassertion of what amounts to Virgilian rather than New Testament symbolism of the 'city set on a hill'. The earthly city, or in the case of Puritan America the 'New Canaan', tends to be apostrophized as a kind of heavenly kingdom in the here and now.

That was the force also of the mediaeval Arthuriad, or 'romances' (Old French *romans*, 'of the Romans'), which in their metanarrative matrix recapitulate (as did the first Old French text in the genre, *Le Roman de Troie* by Benoit de St. Maur) the basic features either of the Homeric or Virgilian epic.[49] Later,

---

[47] Catherine of Siena, *Dialogues*.
[48] Augustine, *City of God*, 10.1.
[49] See Gibbs, *Middle English Romances*, 4–7; also Jeffrey, 'Literature'.

the Arthurian Round Table is symbolic of the earthly city become in itself a vision of peace; the grail or chalice, were it to be recovered, anticipates in a realized temporal eschaton the dream of restored and unbroken communion. But the countervailing Augustinian redaction of New Testament grand narrative has tended to win out, if only by virtue of the persistent apprehension, even in such narratives, that heavenly kingdoms in the here and now are not realizable by human effort, not even by Galahads in a state of grace. In a final gesture toward the New Testament rather than the Roman imperial story, even the grand Arthurian romance must wistfully look to a once and future king and kingdom.

This, I think, is why Milton, fresh from the defeat of the Puritan Commonwealth and politically at risk, rejected his first choice for an epic, the Arthuriad, and wrote instead *Paradise Lost*. In abandoning a classical structure with evident political and nationalistic potential for the 'end is not yet' New Testament structure, he in effect also reverses *The Aeneid*, otherwise his most important epic source. Adam and Eve start in communion, but end in alienation and brokenness, exiled from Eden. Even as they journey toward their hope of redemption it is 'with wandering steps and slow'; in *Paradise Regained* it is Christ who wins the way for them, and the heavenly city, as in Revelation, may by God's power alone come down.

Much that is too obvious to dwell on must accordingly be passed over here in silence. But just a few examples to confirm: the fact that Dante's pilgrim persona, having wandered off track in the middle of the city of this world, should be guided only part of the way en route to *Paradiso* by a chastened Virgil is a reflection of the influence of Augustine's kind of New Testament historiography. Chaucer's *Canterbury Tales* is another 'tale of two cities', in which the city of this world (not here Rome or Babylon but London) must be left behind in a communal penitential voyage toward Canterbury, figuratively a 'city of God'. At the end of this great work and before his 'knitting up' sermon on repentance, Chaucer's Parson makes explicit the connection between the two journeys by specifically invoking the New Testament grand narrative according to Galatians, Hebrews and, one assumes, Augustine. Immediately following a series of quotations from Paul's letters he says:

And Jesu for his grace wit me sende
to shewen you the way in this viage
of thilke parfit glorious pilgrimage,
that highte Jerusalem celestial.[50]

The imperfect earthly journey is trope, a metonym; the Canterbury trail is merely indicative of a deeper pilgrimage of faith. But Bunyan's Christian

---

[50] Chaucer, *The Canterbury Tales*, 10.48–51.

pilgrim will also leave an English worldly city for the celestial city, here yet more clearly heaven. Examples abound.

But the Virgilian narrative of manifest destiny and the Jewish myth of return also have their voices both in later literature and in politics: there are mediaeval reiterations such as Tasso's *Gerusalemme liberata* (1580) and, of course, the Crusades. In our time we have Zionism, Christian Zionism and the neo-dispensationalism now made sensational by Jenkins and LeHaye.[51] What may receive less attention than it ought is the degree to which in American political and literary culture the Virgilian metanarrative has, since the founding fathers, appropriated to itself a largely Calvinist and hence typologized Old Testament version of the Christian grand story. When in *Magnalia Christi Americana* (1698; published 1702) Cotton Mather advertised himself as 'Herald of the Lord's Kingdome now approaching', he set to interpreting the Bible's 'Prophetical as well as … Historical Calendar' in such a way as to constitute a westward expanding New England as the New Jerusalem.[52] His was far from a singular American historicism;[53] Yale President Timothy Dwight's *Conquest of Canaan* (1775) and James Russell Lowell's Harvard 'oration Ode' (1865) are only two among many such Americanized or neo-Constantinian – even neo-Zionist – versions of Christian history. Melville's *White Jacket* contains a narrative passage on national destiny that captures some of the most deeply troubling aspects of the New World conflation of what, for Augustine's philosophy of history, were two antithetical metanarratives:

> The Future [is] the Bible of the Free. … We Americans are driven to a rejection of the maxims of the Past, seeing that, ere long, the van of the nations must, of right, belong to ourselves. … Escaped from the house of bondage, Israel of old did not follow after the ways of the Egyptians. To her was given an express dispensation; to her were given new things under the sun. And we Americans are the peculiar, chosen people – the Israel of our time; we bear the ark of the liberties of the world. God has given us, for a future inheritance, the broad domains of the political pagan, that shall yet come and lie down under the shade of our ark, without bloody hands being lifted. God has predestinated, mankind expects, great things from our race; and great things we feel in our souls. The rest of the nations must soon be in our rear. We are the pioneers of the world. … the political Messiah has come. But he has come in us, if we would but give utterance to his promptings.[54]

---

[51] The *Left Behind* series, now eleven novels and still counting, though subliterary and almost tabloid in its style and character, affords a kind of gnostic myth of return. See my '*Left Behind* and Getting Ahead' for comment on the series' historicism and neo-dispensationalism.

[52] Mather, *Magnalia*, 1.44, 46; 2.579.

[53] See Jeffrey, *People of the Book*, 320–24, for a fuller account.

[54] Melville, *White Jacket*, 152–53.

It would be hard to imagine a Virgilian perversion of the New Testament grand narrative of Galatians and Hebrews more troubling than this. Yet in countless and various ways, it has become institutionalized as the *de facto* civic religion of America.

Does it matter that Galatians and Hebrews make the New Testament grand narrative a journey *through* history, but with a celestial or heavenly rather than earthly home as the journey's end? I suspect it matters a great deal for faithfulness to the teachings of Jesus. These two New Testament letters get only slight treatment, I realize, in Wright's *The New Testament and the People of God*, and in stressing them so forcefully here I fear that I may seem to be merely evading the main arguments of his eloquent and provocative book, with much of which I find myself in fact to be in most hearty agreement. But my point here is admonition concerning canonical balance: that Galatians, the most authenticated letter of Paul, and Hebrews, in many ways almost as influential as Romans in the literary history of Christendom, are very important constraints upon any disposition to make too much of history in the way the Enlightenment did.

This is a point of consequence, necessarily, for scriptural hermeneutics, since it touches upon the context of interpretation at every point on which eschatology matters in the way we understand a text. If, for example, some form of temporal restoration of Zion is a firm postulate in our sense of the projected meaning of biblical grand narrative, then the way is opened for political readings of many passages that might not otherwise invite it. That a commitment to millennialism can tend to gather up *historia humanae salvationis* (salvation history) into a species of historicism is but one among several points that might be considered here: liberationist, reformed and dispensationalist applications of the idea of a restored Zion may vary significantly in the world-view projected, but each has consequences for the use of ascendant political power. The history of hermeneutics shows that when strong views of this type are articulated (as, e.g., in Mather's *Magnalia Christi Americana*), nationalism and even imperialism may seem to be justified. In such a context heaven is less likely to be anticipated as a place of which 'eye hath not seen or ear heard, nor hath it entered into the heart of man what God has prepared for those who love him' (1 Cor. 2:9; cf. Is. 64:4; 65:17), than it is assumed to be a lot like present politic and material culture, so becoming in effect a projected heavenly kingdom in the here and now.

By the same token, insufficient attention to the role in biblical consciousness of a book of the canonical importance of Hebrews may tend to result in narrower views of the atonement, the operation of grace and divine intervention in history. In this way, too, it plays a role in our interpretation of other biblical passages subtending doctrines of the resurrection and the afterlife: is heaven to be imagined as a 'return home' to the Eden from which, genetically, we have been exiled? Or is it best thought of as a new creation, entirely surpassing the one we know in its reflected glory – in effect a future for which we have no earthly categories? It is difficult to dismiss nearly two millennia of biblical interpreters, both professional and lay, who have construed the relation of biblical grand narrative to history as overlapping, but not coeval, narratives. Nor, I think, should we be condescending toward that habit of prayerful mind we call liturgy. Traditional Christian liturgy, in its cyclical reiteration of the biblical *historia humanae salvationis* through the Christian year, maps the Christian mind *through* the history we ourselves traverse, urging us to live simultaneously according to two calendars, so to speak, all the while foretelling a point of closure in which heavenly realities shall eclipse earthly realities altogether (cf. Mt. 24–25; 1 Cor. 15; Revelation, etc.). But this liturgy is heavily indebted to the book of Hebrews, and to its discourse about salvation history and the sanctification wrought by our 'great high priest'.

To summarize: in literary terms, there is a significant hermeneutic divergence between a narratology in which the normative aspiration for full closure requires a return home, and one in which the category of future hope requires pressing forward to a closure still to be revealed. One of these seeks its meaning, as its sense of comfort, within history more or less as we know it. The other seeks to understand God's actions in history as prolegomena to a closure that transcends history as we know it. If we are able to read Scripture as 'strangers and pilgrims on the earth' (Heb. 11; 1 Pet. 2:11), temporal constraint and material comfort will alike be provisional, 'for here we have no continuing city, but we seek the one to come' (Heb. 12:14). In this case, the interpretation of eschatological and apocalyptic passages will likewise tend to be less compulsively determined on present political judgements; figurative eschatological passages whose primary purpose, after all, would seem to have been to inculcate interpretative restraint (e.g., Dan. 12:4, 9), might be less likely to abet *either* a morbidly voyeuristic anti–politic or a triumphalist geopolitical program. If it is really to be the case that 'the just shall live by faith … [and not] … draw back' (Heb. 10:38), living thus by faith in God's faithfulness, then all judgements about future history, it seems to me, must necessarily be extraordinarily tentative.

All that matters to us as Christians is certainly of history; God's providence in history, the *historia humanae salvationis*, the resurrection of Christ on the third day – *all* of these are indispensable as historical events in the plain sense, and without them, as indeed the Apostle warns, we are of all creatures most to be pitied (1 Cor. 15:19).[55] On my view, both as a student of literary interpretations

---

[55] Wright, *New Testament*, 136, cites G.B. Caird (1980) to stress his view, shared here, that 'the Christian is committed to the belief that certain things are true about the past'. It is interesting to see how strongly, in a historical review of the importance to Christian biblical interpretation of allegory, Henri de Lubac, S.J., makes the same

of biblical narrative and as a common Christian in the world, we nevertheless must pay attention also to the degree to which the New Testament grand narrative is about a journey through history to the fulfillment of a promise that transcends history. Ours, in the end, is not a view of history that can comfortably integrate with that of the Enlightenment.[56] Hegel's contention that 'the God of the Jewish people is the God only of Abraham and of his seed', and that 'national individuality and a special local worship are involved in such a conception of deity' is only true insofar as we do not push it to the point at which Hegel's *Philosophy of History* sets the terms for our own conception of the Christian hope.[57] Germinal as it is for the Marxist historicism, which in its own drab way also for a time subverted or secularized the New Testament metanarrative, Hegel's view can occlude for us the profound respect in which Christian history becomes, by lived faith in a living church, history considered in the light of eternity. To say this is to say firmly that ours is not a history that 'marches on' to a historical destiny or utopia, but that, like the pages of a book written by Another, it is a narrative of time which unfolds meaningfully until the book is complete, when the heavens shall be 'rolled up like a scroll' (Is. 34:4; Rev. 6:14). It is to say that the community of faith, generation upon generation, moves through history to a destination which is finally beyond history. History, or *Weltgeschichte*, is not the protagonist here; nor is *Heilsgeschichte* (salvation history). The protagonist is Christ, in whom the community of faith lives and moves and has its being.

---

point, citing literally dozens of early and mediaeval commentators to support their insistence that allegory is not, in faithful Christian exegesis, a rejection of history (*Medieval Exegesis*, II). His seventh chapter, 'The Foundation of History' (2.41–82), is a particularly helpful contextualization of the way in which Christian allegory arises from history, both in the biblical text and in more than a millennium of commentary. For de Lubac and the tradition he represents, 'allegory is in truth *the truth* of history' (2.201).

[56] *Pace* Wright, *New Testament*, 136.

[57] By contrast, Hegel's *Philosophy of World History* (here cited from Pt. 1, 3.3) has had a pervasive influence since its early reception, even upon biblical criticism. But this is an influence that can distort our understanding not only of the New Testament, but also of its early church, mediaeval and Reformation commentators. De Lubac's monumental *Ressourcement* study (which includes *Medieval Exegesis*) is a welcome caution on this point. It is surely true that for Christians at least (though not for Virgilians), historicism of any kind is alien: 'Our ancient exegetes', writes de Lubac, 'did not have any idea, thanks be to God, of that "absolutized History" which is one of the principal idols invented by our age. On the other hand, they did have a sense of biblical history, or even of universal history, because they held on to its principle of discernment in the mystery of Christ' (2.72).

History considered in the light of eternity, not in Aristotle's or Matthew Arnold's sense but in the sense of St. John the Divine, is history as poetry conceives of it, a trope. Or, as Paul puts it in Galatians 4, an allegory. Nothing in this Pauline view denies the factuality of history. It does invite us to believe that some historical events have become grand narrative for us, upon whom these latter ages have come, that we might be instructed concerning what in our faith is of bondage and what of the freedom wherewith Christ has made us free.

Bibliography

Alter, R., *The Art of Biblical Narrative* (New York: Basic Books, 1981)

Andreason, N.A., *Rest and Redemption: A Study of the Biblical Sabbath* (Fife: St. Andrews University Press, 1978)

Aquinas, T., *In Omnes S. Pauli Apostoli Epistolas Commentaria*, II (Taurini: Petri Marietti, 1924)

Auerbach, E., *Mimesis: The Representation of Reality in Western Literature* (trans. W.R. Trask; Princeton: Princeton University Press, 1953)

Augustine, *The City of God*, in *A Select Library of Nicene and Post-Nicene Fathers of the Christian Church*, II (ed. Philip Schaff; trans. M. Dods; Grand Rapids: Eerdmans, 1973)

——, *Sermo* 14.4.6; 70.7; *Sermones de Vetere Testamento* (Turnholti: Typographi Brepols, 1961)

——, *In Joannes Evangelium*, 40.10, *In Evangelium Iohannis tractatus* (trans. J. Rettig; Washington, DC: Catholic University Press, 1988)

——, *Confessions* (Oxford: Clarendon Press, 1992)

——, *De Genesi ad litteram* (trans. J.H. Taylor; New York: Newman Press, 1982)

Azmeh, Aziz al, *Islam and Modernities* (London and New York: Verso, 2nd edn, 1996)

Bowra, C.M., *The Greek Experience* (Oxford: OUP, 1957; New York: Mentor, 1959)

Brenneman, J.E., *Canons in Conflict: Negotiating Texts in True and False Prophecy* (Oxford: OUP, 1997)

Catherine of Siena, *Dialogues* (trans. S. Nofke; New York: Paulist Press, 1980)

Chaucer, *The Canterbury Tales* (ed. L. Benson; The Riverside Chaucer; New York: Houghton-Mifflin, 1987)

de Lubac, H., *Medieval Exegesis*, II (trans. E.M. Macierowski; Grand Rapids: Eerdmans, 2000)

Frye, N., *Anatomy of Criticism* (Princeton: Princeton University Press, 1957)

——, *Secular Scripture: A Study of the Structure of Romance* (Cambridge, MA: Harvard University Press, 1976)

——, *The Great Code: The Bible and Literature* (London: Routledge, 1982)

Gibbs, E.A. (ed.), *Middle English Romances* (Evanston: Northwestern University Press, 1966)

Giddens, A., *The Consequences of Modernity* (Stanford: Stanford University Press, 1990)

Greenberg, M., 'Sabbath', in *Encyclopedia Judaica* 14 (Jerusalem: Encyclopedia Judaica, 1971)

Gregory the Great, *S. Gregorii Magni Moralia in Iob* (Turnholt: Brepols, 1979)

——, *Epistolae*, in *Registrum epistularum* (Turnholt: Brepols, 1982)

——, *The Epistle to Diognetus*, in *Registrum epistularum* (Turnholt: Brepols, 1982)

Guthrie, G., *The Structure of Hebrews: A Text-Linguistic Analysis* (Leiden and New York: E.J. Brill, 1994)

Hauerwas, S., *Unleashing the Scripture: Freeing the Bible from Captivity to America* (Nashville: Abingdon, 1993)

Hegel, G.W.F., *Lectures on the Philosophy of World History* (trans. H.B. Nisbet; intro. D. Forbes; Cambridge: CUP, 1975)

Homer, *The Iliad* (trans. R. Lattimore; Chicago: University of Chicago Press, 1951)

——, *The Odyssey* (trans. R. Lattimore; Chicago: University of Chicago Press, 1991)

Horn, S.K. (ed.), *Chinese Women Traversing Diaspora: Memoirs, Essays and Poetry* (New York: Garland, 1999)

Jaeger, W.W., *Paideia: The Ideals of Greek Culture* (3 vols.; New York: OUP, 1943)

Jeffrey, D.L., 'Literature in an Apocalyptic Age', *Dalhousie Review* 61.3 (1981), 426–46

——, *People of the Book: Christian Identity and Literary Culture* (Grand Rapids: Eerdmans, 1996)

——, 'C.S. Lewis, the Bible, and its Literary Critics', *ChrLit* 50.1 (2000), 95–110

——, 'Journey to the West/Journey to the East: Globalization and the Fate of Masterplots', in K. Yan, *European Literature in the Chinese Context* (Beijing: Peking University Press, 2002), ch. 1

——, '*Left Behind* and Getting Ahead', *Christian Reflection* 2.2 (2002), 70–78

Jenkins, T.F., and J.B. LeHaye, *Left Behind* series (Carol Stream, IL: Tyndale House, 1996–)

Lyotard, J.F., *La Condition Postmoderne: Rapport sur le Savoir* (Paris: Les Editions de Minuit, 1979); ET: *The Postmodern Condition* (trans. G. Bennington and B. Massumi; Minneapolis: University of Minnesota Press, 1984)

MacDonald, D.R., *The Homeric Epics and the Gospel of Mark* (New Haven: Yale University Press, 2000)

Mather, C., *Magnalia Christi Americana* (ed. T. Robbins; Hereford: S. Andrus and Son, 1853–55)

Melville, H., *White Jacket: Or, the World in a Man-of-War* (Oxford and New York: OUP, 1967)

Origen, *Contra Celsum* (trans. H. Chadwick; Cambridge: CUP, 1953)

Poole, M., *Annotations upon the Holy Bible* (London, 1688)

Richardson, A., *History Sacred and Profane* (London: SCM Press, 1964)

Ross, T., *The Making of the English Literary Canon: From the Middle Ages to the Eighteenth Century* (Montreal: McGill-Queens, 1998)

Schiffman, L.H., *From Text to Tradition: A History of Second Temple and Rabbinic Judaism* (Hoboken, NJ: Ktav, 1991)

Virgil, *The Aeneid, Book 1* (trans. R. Humphries; New York: Scribners, 1951)

Walzer, M., *Exodus and Revolution* (San Francisco: HarperCollins, 1985)

Wang Ling-chi, 'On Luodi-shenggen', in *The Chinese Diaspora: Selected Essays*, I (Singapore: Federal Publications, 1998)

Wright, N.T., *The New Testament and the People of God* (Christian Origins and the Question of God, I; Minneapolis: Fortress Press, 1992)

Wu Cheng'en, *Journey to the West* (trans. W.J.F. Jenner; 3 vols.; Beijing: Foreign Languages Press, 1982, 1993, 1997); (trans. A. Yu; 4 vols.; Chicago: University of Chicago Press, 1980, 1983, 1984)

Wyclif, J., *Sermons*, in *Iohannis Wyclif Sermones* (ed. I. Loserth; London: Trubner, 1897–1890)

History and Biblical Interpretation

17

Reconstructing and Interpreting Amos's Literary Prehistory

A Dialogue with Redaction Criticism

Karl Möller

In a recent study entitled *Religion and the Rise of Historicism*, Howard has noted that 'the category "history" was experienced as a theological and biblical-exegetical problem long before the popularization of the nineteenth century's "historical method"'.[1] Yet he claims that the historicization of human thought, which has its roots in the nineteenth century, has had an enormous influence on all humanistic discourse throughout the Western world,[2] providing us 'with a world view of the same universality as that of the religious world view of the past'.[3]

In biblical studies, one of the main effects of this historicization has been the rise of historical criticism. And while recent years have witnessed much talk of the 'collapse of history'[4] and of a paradigm shift away from historical methods, historical-critical approaches are still exerting a major influence on the discipline of biblical studies. In prophetic research, this is most evident in the plethora of redaction-critical studies on the books' literary prehistories. This chapter surveys and responds to some of the key trends in current redaction-critical practice, focusing on the investigation of Amos's literary prehistory and pointing to some of redaction criticism's limitations and deficiencies.

---

[1] Howard, *Religion*, 14.
[2] Howard, *Religion*, 12.
[3] Mannheim, *Essays*, 85, as quoted in Howard, *Religion*, 12.
[4] See, e.g., Perdue, *Collapse*.

From Amos's *Ipsissima Verba* to the Book's Literary Prehistory

However, before we turn to the current interest in Amos's redaction history, some comments on the older literary-critical quest for the prophet's *ipsissima verba* are pertinent. For both Barton and Kratz have rightly stressed that redaction criticism can be understood as an outgrowth of the literary-critical paradigm in that it employs many of the latter's findings, even if these are now being interpreted differently.[5] Redaction criticism has also inherited the historical outlook of its predecessor, which expressed itself not only in its ambition to retrieve the unadulterated, inspired words of the religious geniuses, but also in many of the criteria employed to decide issues of authenticity. Yet, as the following survey of late nineteenth- and early twentieth-century attempts to reconstruct Amos's *ipsissima verba* illustrates, this by no means exhausts the correspondences between the two approaches.

From Wellhausen to Wolff – and back to Duhm, Ewald and Hitzig: Reconstructing the ipsissima verba *of the 'historical Amos'*

The beginning of the 'search for the historical Amos and the *ipsissima verba*, the "very words," of the real Amos of the eighth century' is commonly traced back to Wellhausen,[6] who in his short but influential 1892 commentary suggested the deletion of various supposedly inauthentic passages. He adduced a variety of reasons for his decisions but historical considerations, which particularly affected his views on 1:9–10, 11–12; 2:4–5; 6:2 and 9:8–15, clearly played a major role.[7] Four years later, G.A. Smith, who together with Harper introduced the new developments in the critical exegesis of the Minor Prophets to the English-speaking world,[8] asserted that 'hardly one book has escaped later additions – *additions of an entirely justifiable nature*, which supplement the point of view of a single prophet with the richer experience or the richer hopes of a later day'.[9]

Smith's affirmative evaluation of textual additions deserves particular attention because it contrasts starkly with the predominantly negative perception of secondary material at that stage in the history of interpretation.[10] This

---

[5] See Barton, 'Redaction Criticism', 644; and Kratz, 'Redaktionsgeschichte', 371.

[6] See, e.g., Hasel, *Understanding*, 20–21.

[7] See Wellhausen, *Propheten*, passim.

[8] Cf. Hasel, *Understanding*, 21. On the significance of Smith's 'eloquent Victorian commentary', see Childs, *Introduction*, 397.

[9] Smith, *Twelve Prophets*, ix (emphasis mine).

[10] Of course, more than half a century later, a more positive view of editorial or redactional additions was to become one of the key features of redaction criticism.

is evident, for instance, in Wolfe's talk of the 'formidable challenge ... of restoring [the prophetic] writings to something approaching the original forcefulness and beauty they possessed as they left the lips of those prophets'. According to Wolfe,

> marvelous restorations are carried out these days in all branches of art. Why cannot the same be done with these masterpieces of literary and religious art? ... As with the art critics and their restored paintings, it has been a thrilling adventure to remove the secondary accretions here and there ... and see these writings re-emerge, after all the centuries, to display once more their original grandeur and again speak their powerful messages.[11]

However, Smith did not maintain his positive outlook throughout. Suspecting the authenticity of the Judah oracle (2:4–5), he for instance concluded that 'we ought to pass, then, straight from the third to the sixth verse of this chapter'.[12] Such a move, while characteristic for that period of scholarship,[13] does not sit well with his verdict that the additions are 'of an entirely justifiable nature'.

Smith acknowledged that 'in the beginnings of such analysis as we are engaged on, we must be prepared for not a little arbitrariness and want of proportion', only to claim that 'they are as easily eliminated by the progress of discussion'.[14] Although Smith did not accept Wellhausen's judgements uncritically, his views on 9:7–15 are strongly indebted to Duhm and Wellhausen's reconstruction of the historical development of Israelite religion and their conception of the prophets' ethical monotheism, which elicit his historical judgement that the salvation oracle could not derive from Amos, the ethical monotheist.[15]

Wellhausen's views are embraced even more strongly in Nowack's 1897 commentary, which follows the great master closely, indeed too closely for his liking,[16] but which offers unprecedentedly detailed discussions of the critical issues. Driver's commentary of the same year also features an extensive discussion of the issue of authenticity.[17] Beginning with Duhm and ending with G.A. Smith, Driver lists all contested passages but rejects the arguments adduced in support of their inauthenticity. Thus, although he gradually came to accept

---

[11] Wolfe, *Meet Amos and Hosea*, xx–xxi.

[12] Smith, *Twelve Prophets*, 136.

[13] See Wellhausen's translation of Amos, where all supposedly inauthentic passages have been relegated to the footnotes (Wellhausen, *Propheten*, 1–10).

[14] Smith, *Twelve Prophets*, x–xi.

[15] See Smith, *Twelve Prophets*, 194–95.

[16] Cf. Wellhausen, *Propheten*, 89, 215, and see also Nowack's resentful ripostes in *Propheten*, 97, 160–61.

[17] Driver, *Joel and Amos*, 119–26.

Wellhausen's views on the history of Israelite religion,[18] he considered the salvation oracle in 9:8–15 an authentic part of Amos's message.

Marti, whose 1904 commentary on the Minor Prophets lists a sizeable number of (mostly postexilic) additions,[19] was known as a staunch supporter of Wellhausen.[20] His view, that without the additions Amos's monumental words might not have been preserved,[21] foreshadows the current redaction-critical notion that adaptations of the prophetic message were necessary to ensure its continuing significance. Harper's 1905 commentary also acknowledges several secondary passages, which are classified as Judaistic/deuteronomic, historical, theological, technical or archaeological and messianic.[22] Of these, the deuteronomic additions are the most significant for our purposes, as redaction-critical studies still frequently posit a deuteronomistic redaction. Sellin, on the other hand, gradually came to reject many of the critical conclusions advanced by Wellhausen, Duhm, Nowack and Marti.[23] And though he considered the Judah oracle (2:4–5) a later addition, he denied that its language is deuteronomic,[24] thus anticipating some recent criticisms of Schmidt's proposed deuteronomistic redaction in Amos.[25]

As noted above, Wellhausen is often thought to have initiated the quest for the *ipsissima verba* of the 'historical Amos'. Yet while his views tended to be more radical than those of his predecessors, he had not been the first to address questions of authenticity. Wellhausen readily acknowledged this, referring to Bickell and Schrader, who had cast doubt on 6:2,[26] to Oort, who deleted 8:11–12,[27] and most importantly to Duhm.[28] Duhm's comments on Amos, which partly pre- and partly postdate Wellhausen's 1892 commentary, illustrate how the two scholars influenced each other.

As early as 1875, Duhm had argued that the hymn fragments (4:13; 5:8–9; 9:5–6) and the Judah oracle (2:4–5), with its supposedly deuteronomistic style, stem from a later hand.[29] But contrary to Kraus's claim that his view

---

[18] Cf. Bray, *Biblical Interpretation*, 295.

[19] Marti, *Dodekapropheton*, 151–53 and *passim*.

[20] See Smend, *Deutsche Alttestamentler*, 143.

[21] Cf. Marti, *Dodekapropheton*, 227.

[22] Harper, *Amos and Hosea*, cxxx–cxxxiv.

[23] See Sellin, *Zwölfprophetenbuch*, vii–viii, cf. also 193.

[24] Sellin, *Zwölfprophetenbuch*, 202.

[25] Cf. Lohfink, 'Deuteronomistische Bewegung'; Bons 'Denotat'; and see Schmidt, 'Deuteronomistische Redaktion'.

[26] Wellhausen, *Propheten*, 85.

[27] Wellhausen, *Propheten*, 93.

[28] Wellhausen, *Propheten*, 72.

[29] Duhm, *Theologie der Propheten*, 119.

of the prophets as harbingers of doom led Duhm to deny the authenticity of 9:8–15,[30] in his early work on the prophets' developing theology and the general development of Israelite religion,[31] he still considered the salvation oracle integral to the book.[32] Thirty-five years on, however, Duhm had followed Wellhausen in attributing not only 9:8–15,[33] but also several other passages, to later editors.[34]

'Pre-Duhm', however, the question of authenticity had not yet become an issue. Keil does not address it in his 1866 commentary.[35] Even Ewald still regarded the book as an accomplished whole, which, exactly as we have it today, came from Amos's hand.[36] And Hitzig, who has become known for his then radical claim that Zechariah 9–11 and 12–14 did not derive from the same author,[37] also did not doubt that the material in Amos was genuine.

From Schmidt and Wolff to the present day – and back to Budde and Wolfe: Charting the literary prehistory of the book of Amos

Beginning in the 1960s and following Schmidt's influential article on the deuteronomistic redaction of the book of Amos, interest shifted from the prophet's authentic words to the reconstruction of the book's redactional history.[38] This changing perspective has had significant consequences. First, redaction criticism has clearly advanced the study of the Old Testament by offering a more positive outlook on the redactors' work.[39] For instance, Steck

---

[30] Kraus, *Geschichte*, 282.

[31] See the subtitle of Duhm's *Theologie der Propheten: Als Grundlage für die innere Entwicklungsgeschichte der israelitischen Religion*.

[32] Cf. Duhm, *Theologie der Propheten*, 117, 122, 124–25.

[33] Duhm, *Anmerkungen*, 17; *Israels Propheten*, 97; and *Zwölf Propheten*, xxxvi–xxxvii.

[34] Duhm, *Zwölf Propheten*, xxxvi.

[35] ET: 1878.

[36] Ewald, *Propheten*, 121. In his own words, he concludes 'daß dieses kleine buch ein in sich vollendetes Ganzes bildet und gerade so wie wir es jetzt haben aus 'Amôs' hand hervorgegangen ist'.

[37] Hitzig, *Propheten*, vii. The first edition was published in 1838; the second came out in 1852.

[38] Marxsen, *Evangelist*, appears to have been the first to use the term 'redaction criticism'. Yet the references by those working on the redaction history of the Twelve to Budde and Wolfe (see below) illustrate that some pre-1960s works already displayed interests similar to those at the fore in today's redaction criticism.

[39] Introductions to the approach can be found in Perrin, *Redaction Criticism*; Koch, *Formgeschichte*, §5; Steck, *Old Testament Exegesis*, §6; Fohrer, 'Überlieferungskritik', 119–50 (Fohrer differentiates between redaction criticism and composition criticism); and Barton, *Reading*, ch. 4; and 'Redaction Criticism'.

and Fohrer insist that the negative classification of redactional editing as 'secondary' or 'inauthentic' ought to be abandoned.[40] Secondly, redaction-critical theories have become ever more complex, as scholars have concluded that many Old Testament books underwent a series of redactions at the hands of redactors with different theological and political agendas.[41]

Mention of these changes should not obscure the continuities with the older paradigm, however. For, as Kratz has noted, by isolating 'inauthentic' passages, the literary-critical approach has provided redaction criticism with its working material.[42] Or, as Barton puts it, 'the discovery of "redactors" in the OT belongs to classical source criticism, as a side effect of the analysis'.[43] In what follows, I will focus on major redaction-critical trends in Amos research, seeking to sketch the main developments and highlight some of the key issues.

Werner H. Schmidt (b. 1935)

Schmidt's 1965 article, in which he attributed 'a decisive editorial activity to the work of a Deuteronomistic editor',[44] has had a major impact on Amos studies, affecting not least Wolff's presentation of the book's redactional growth. Arguing mainly from philological observations (i.e., from comparisons of certain phrases in Amos with the language and style of the deuteronomists), Schmidt claimed that a number of passages could clearly be attributed to a deuteronomistic redaction. These include parts of the heading in 1:1; the transitional formula in 3:1; the oracles against Tyre (1:9–10), Edom (1:11–12) and Judah (2:4–5); the references to the exodus and the raising up of prophets and Nazirites in 2:10–12; the statement in 3:7 and the reference to the cultic veneration of foreign deities in 5:26.

In one sense, Schmidt's article was not revolutionary at all, because almost all the passages ascribed by him to the deuteronomists had been denied to Amos long ago. Duhm's *Die Zwölf Propheten in den Versmaßen der Urschrift übersetzt* (1910) displays almost all of them, as well as some additional verses, in a smaller print to indicate their inauthenticity. And yet, Schmidt did explore new territory by analysing the redactors' theological motivations for expanding the text. In the wake of Schmidt, more analyses of that sort were undertaken, and his essay also paved the way for more detailed investigations into the text's redactional history, which is still an ongoing scholarly concern.

---

[40] Steck, *Old Testament Exegesis*, 80; and Fohrer, 'Überlieferungskritik', 141.
[41] Cf. Carroll R., *Amos*, 19, 32, 49.
[42] Kratz, 'Redaktionsgeschichte', 371.
[43] Barton, 'Redaction Criticism', 644.
[44] Thus Childs, *Introduction*, 398; see Schmidt, 'Deuteronomistische Redaktion'.

Hans Walter Wolff (1911–93)

Wolff opens his discussion of Amos's formation with the claim that 'even a cursory examination … forces one to posit behind it a long history of literary growth', stretching from the eighth century down to postexilic times.[45] Outlining this history, Wolff distinguishes:

(1) 'the words of Amos from Tekoa', which comprise most of Amos 3–6 and which may go back to Amos himself;

(2) 'the literary fixation of the cycles' (i.e., the visions in 7:1–8; 8:1–2 and 9:1–4 and [most of] the oracles against the nations in 1:3–2:16), which could have occurred in connection with Amos's banishment from Bethel and the end of his activity in the northern kingdom;

(3) 'the old Amos school', which sometime between 760–730 BCE added parts of the superscription (1:1), the Amaziah narrative (7:9–17) and some further material in 5:5a, 13–15; 6:2, 6b; 8:3–14; 9:7–8a, 9–10;

(4) 'the Bethel-exposition of the Josianic age', which contributed the 'altars of Bethel' in 3:14b, the hymnic pieces in 4:13; 5:8–9 and 9:5–6, the 'homilies' in 4:6–12 and 5:6 and possibly the motto in 1:2;

(5) 'the deuteronomistic redaction', which added the synchronizing dating in 1:1, the oracles against Tyre (1:9–10), Edom (1:11–12) and Judah (2:4–5), the allusion to God's past acts in 2:10–12, the references to the 'whole family' in 3:1b and Zion in 6:1, the statement on prophecy in 3:7, the cult-critical comments in 5:25–26 and possibly the threats in 8:11–12; and

(6) 'the postexilic eschatology of salvation', which contributed the promise of a future hope in 9:11–15, the reference to burnt offerings in 5:22a, the words 'like David' in 6:5 and the assurance that the coming destruction will not be total in 9:8b.[46]

In distinguishing six redactional layers, Wolff surpassed his predecessors (including Schmidt). Of course, as stages 1 to 3 all date roughly to Amos's own time, most of the book is still understood in close connection with the prophet himself. Wolff accepts Schmidt's proposals concerning a deuteronomistic redaction but also assigns 5:25 and 8:11–12 to that redactional layer. He does not regard the motto (1:2) as deuteronomistic, however, allocating it to the Bethel-exposition instead. This proposed Bethel-exposition is perhaps Wolff's most significant redaction-critical contribution, but it is also the most contested one. For instance, Willi-Plein has voiced her concern about attributing 4:6–12 and 5:6, the key examples of Wolff's Bethel-exposition, to a later time.

---

[45] Wolff, *Joel and Amos*, 106–107.

[46] See Wolff, *Joel and Amos*, 107–13.

She is also adamant that the hymnic pieces (4:13; 5:8–9; 9:5–6) cannot possibly be dated to the time of Josiah.[47]

Ina Willi-Plein

Childs correctly notes that Willi-Plein seeks 'to interpret the redactional role of the alleged glosses in Amos rather than simply deleting them as "non-genuine" '.[48] Yet she herself described her primary aim as the discovery of the prophet's *ipsissima vox*,[49] claiming that

> the thicket of the reworking by later [redactors] will have to be thinned out before one can have a look at the more or less original word. However, that this thicket cannot simply be rooted up and thrown away has its reason in a phenomenon, whose significance can be expounded along dogmatic as well as historical lines, i.e. the [phenomenon] of the canon.[50]

Having investigated all passages that could conceivably be secondary,[51] Willi-Plein posits four principal stages of literary growth:

(1) the creation of the vision-cum-narrative cycle, possibly during Amos's life-time but certainly not long after his death;

(2) the *dibrê ʿāmôs* collection, which ends at 4:12 and which also came into being not long after Amos's ministry;

(3) the 'ring-forming' collection, redaction and actualizing shaping of Amosian words or fragments around the vision-cum-narrative cycle after the collapse of the northern kingdom, perhaps at the time of Manasseh; and

(4) the combination of Amos 1–4 and 5–9 by an exilic redactor, who also up-dated the text with further additions, not least the expectation of the re-building of the state.[52]

In addition to these stages, Willi-Plein posits yet further addenda, some of which cannot be dated, while others originated in the second half of the exilic period or in postexilic times.[53] She also identifies 520 BCE as a *terminus a quo* and Alexander's conquest of Palestine in 333–32 BCE as a *terminus ad quem* for the book as it has come down to us.

---

[47] Willi-Plein, *Vorformen*, 59 n. 5.

[48] Childs, *Introduction*, 398.

[49] Willi-Plein, *Vorformen*, 1.

[50] Willi-Plein, *Vorformen*, 1 (my translation).

[51] Cf. Willi-Plein, *Vorformen*, 13.

[52] Willi-Plein, *Vorformen*, 62–63.

[53] Willi-Plein, *Vorformen*, 64–66.

Jörg Jeremias
The most prolific of contemporary Amos scholars, Jeremias has published a series of redaction-critical studies as well as a commentary, which summarizes his views on the book's literary prehistory. Noting that it was 'continually updated on the basis of its meaning for an ever new and changing present', Jeremias claims that 'Amos's message ... can be recovered only through complicated, and in many instances only hypothetical, reconstruction'.[54] The book, as we know it, comes from the (late) postexilic period and underwent a long redactional process spanning several centuries:[55]

(1) 'The oldest book of Amos was framed by two compositions – oracles against the nations (Amos 1–2*) and visions (Amos 7–9*)'.[56] 'The sayings against Israel in chaps. 3–6 are to be read within the horizon of this framework'.[57] The three parts, which contain sayings by the prophet Amos himself, probably began as separate collections.

(2) Early tradents 'formulated sayings strongly influenced by the language and conceptual world of Hosea' in order 'to prompt the readers of the book ... to associate Amos' own accusations with Hosea and thereby to relate the sayings of the two prophets'.[58]

(3) In the seventh century BCE, 'certain theological tendencies that became powerful in Judah were combined with older Amos texts ... filling out in detail the portrayal of the death of all Israel'.[59]

(4) But the most significant alterations in the form of a deuteronomistic redaction and the addition of various liturgical texts, such as the worship liturgy in 4:6–13 and the doxologies of judgement in 1:2; 4:13; 5:8–9 and 9:5–6 were not made until after the fall of Jerusalem.[60]

(5) Postexilic additions that reconcile Amos's message of judgement with the old traditions of salvation now conclude the book (9:7–15).[61]

Jeremias concludes his account of the book's growth by claiming that 'the modern exegete must deal first of all with the exilic/postexilic history of transmission of Amos' message. Any attempt to get back to earlier strata of the book,

---

[54] Jeremias, *Amos*, 5; cf. also 'Beobachtungen', 124; and 'Oral Word', 217.
[55] See the summary of Jeremias's position in Melugin, 'Amos', 78–81.
[56] Jeremias, *Amos*, 6; see also 'Völkersprüche' and 'Zwei Jahre'.
[57] Jeremias, *Amos*, 6.
[58] Jeremias, *Amos*, 7; see also 'Anfänge' and 'Interrelationship'.
[59] Thus Melugin's summary in 'Amos', 81.
[60] Jeremias, *Amos*, 7–8.
[61] Jeremias, *Amos*, 9.

not to speak of Amos' actual words themselves, is necessarily burdened by a
(variously differing) degree of uncertainty'.[62]

Dirk U. Rottzoll

Rottzoll's redaction-critical analysis builds on studies by de Waard, Lust and
Bergler, who proposed a concentric arrangement for Amos's middle section.
While earlier scholars often complained about the apparent disorderliness of
Amos 5,[63] de Waard demonstrated that 5:1–17 is arranged chiastically.[64] Some
years later, Lust extended the boundaries of the chiasm to 4:1 and 6:7[65] and,
independently from both de Waard and Lust, Bergler suggested that the chiasm
includes all of Amos 3–6.[66] Building on these findings, Rottzoll now argues
that this 'ring composition' comprises all of Amos 1:2–9:6.[67] He also presents an
extraordinarily sophisticated redaction-critical analysis, isolating the following
redactional layers:

(1) the core material,
(2) the school of Amos,
(3) a Judaic redaction of 722/1,
(4) a Judaic redaction of 711,
(5) a first deuteronomistic revision of the exilic period,
(6) further (early) postexilic additions,
(7) the creation of a ring composition by R^{RK},[68]
(8) a priestly-deuteronomistic redaction,
(9) two unknown redactional layers in 5:11, 13 and 6:9–10,
(10) a second addendum to the vision cycle and the book's ending,
(11) the addition of the oracles against Tyre and Edom,
(12) additions of a chronicling kind.[69]

Rottzoll's outline of the core material of 1:3–2:16, which he summarizes as
1:3–8, 13–15; 2:1–3, 6, 7aα[x], b, 8aα, 7bα, 8bα, 12a, 13a, bα, gives a good idea

---

[62] Jeremias, *Amos*, 9. In addition to the works referred to above, see also 'Tod und
     Leben', 'Heiligtum', 'Mitte', 'Prophetenwort' and 'Rezeptionsprozesse'.

[63] See, for instance, Budde, 'Text', *JBL* 43, 105–106; Fey, *Amos und Jesaja*, 25 n. 3; and
     Rudolph, *Joel, Amos, Obadja, Jona*, 184.

[64] De Waard, 'Chiastic Structure'.

[65] Lust, 'Remarks'.

[66] Bergler, 'Passagen'.

[67] See Rottzoll, *Studien*, 1–5. There is a sense in which de Waard's and Lust's findings
     have led to some kind of 'chiasm mania' in Amos studies (see Möller, *Prophet*, ch.
     1.1, for further discussion).

[68] The acronym refers to the redactor of the ring composition.

[69] Rottzoll, *Studien*, 285–90; see also the summary in Melugin, 'Amos', 81–83.

of his minute and almost mathematically-inspired analysis. However, this list of verses and verse-fragments appears in an almost ironic light given Conroy's plea not to satirize redaction criticism as being concerned with half-verses, the halves of half-verses or indeed parts of the halves of half-verses.[70] To be sure, this is not what redaction criticism is all about, and yet this kind of approach is by no means *passé*.

Rottzoll's work on Amos exemplifies historical criticism in overdrive. To my knowledge, no one before or since has ever linked the textual material to as many as twelve historical settings. Where Schmidt, for instance, found one deuteronomistic redaction, Rottzoll now detects two, adding that some of the supposedly deuteronomistic passages are either not deuteronomistic at all or at best only feature what he calls a 'deuteronomism *sui generis*', thus requiring yet another redactional strata.[71]

In addition to the studies discussed above, there has been a flood of articles offering redaction-critical readings of (parts of) Amos. Many commentaries, too, have employed the approach, thus confirming Melugin's comment, made in a review of recent Amos research, that 'redaction history still lives'.[72] This judgement is borne out also by the current interest in the redaction history of the Book of the Twelve, to which we now turn.

The quest for the redaction of the Twelve[73]

In recent years, beginning in the mid-1980s and gathering momentum in the 1990s, scholars have increasingly moved beyond the boundaries of the individual prophetic books and have attempted to trace the redaction history of the Twelve as a whole.[74]

---

[70] Conroy, 'Disappearing Redactor'.

[71] Cf. Rottzoll, *Studien*, 6.

[72] Melugin, 'Amos', 78.

[73] In addition to the works mentioned below, see also the studies in Watts and House (eds.), *Forming Prophetic Literature*; and Nogalski and Sweeney (eds.), *Reading*.

[74] The subsequent review excludes studies that conceptualize the unity of the Twelve in synchronic terms and/or regard it as a compilation of previously existing books into one collection. These include Ewald, *Propheten*, 73–81; Steuernagel, *Lehrbuch*, 669–72; Schneider, 'Unity'; Lee, 'Canonical Unity'; Marks, 'Twelve Prophets'; House, *Unity*; Coggins, 'Minor Prophets'; Barton, 'Canonical Meaning'; Sweeney, *Twelve Prophets*; Conrad, 'Forming'; Everson, 'Canonical Location'; and House, 'Endings'. However, it is not always possible to make a clear-cut distinction between redaction-critical approaches and those that assume an editorial compilation and/or synchronic unity. As Jones, *Formation*, 14, has noted, 'most scholars recognize that the Book of the Twelve is the result of some degree of both compilation and redactional composition'.

Weimar's 1985 study, which argues that Obadiah's redactors linked the Book to the Twelve as a whole through cross-references with other redactional passages, marks the beginning of the modern quest.[75] Two years later, Bosshard pointed to structural similarities between Isaiah and the Twelve, suggesting that these reflect deliberate redactional efforts by the same tradents.[76] In a subsequent article, published in 1990, Bosshard and Kratz investigated the incorporation of Malachi into the Twelve, which they took to be the final level of redactional activity.[77] Mention must also be made of Bosshard-Nepustil's 1997 monograph on the interrelationship between Isaiah 1–39 and the Twelve, which is said to consist of two major redactional layers (an 'Assyrian-Babylonian layer' and a 'Babylonian layer') that are common to both corpora.[78]

Steck's monograph *Der Abschluss der Prophetie im Alten Testament* (1991) also focused on the latest redactional strata in Isaiah and the Twelve, proposing multiple textual layers and suggesting that the redactional processes in the two works had been interdependent. Collins, in turn, has argued for four stages of growth in the Book of the Twelve (1993).[79] These include (1) an exilic layer (i.e., Hosea, Amos, Micah, Nahum, Zephaniah and Obadiah); (2) a 'revised edition' (Haggai, Zech. 1–8, Jonah, probably Joel as well as 'optimistic' insertions such as Zeph. 3:9–20), dating to a time before the completion of the second temple; (3) Habakkuk and Malachi together with further eschatological additions; and (4) Zechariah 9–14 and Malachi 3:22–24.

In an article from the same year, van Leeuwen focuses on the intentions and the tradition-historical location of the book's final redactors.[80] Nogalski's massive two-volume work,[81] also published in 1993, investigates (redactional) catchword links and proposes that two multi-volume collections – a 'deuteronomic corpus' consisting of early versions of Hosea, Amos, Micah and Zephaniah[82] and a Haggai–Zechariah 1–8 corpus – have been combined into a 'Joel layer'. This layer, dated to the fourth century BCE, also included Nahum, Habakkuk, Joel, Obadiah and Malachi. Subsequent additions of Zechariah 9–14 and Jonah finally completed the Twelve's redaction history.

---

[75] Weimar, 'Obadja'.

[76] Bosshard, 'Beobachtungen'.

[77] Bosshard-Nepustil and Kratz, 'Maleachi'.

[78] Bosshard-Nepustil, *Rezeptionen*.

[79] Collins, *Mantle*, 59–87.

[80] Van Leeuwen, 'Scribal Wisdom'.

[81] Nogalski, *Literary Precursors* and *Redactional Processes*. For different appraisals of Nogalski's work, see Jones, *Formation*, 32–40; and Wolters, 'Review of *Literary Precursors*', 493–96.

[82] For a refinement of Nogalski's proposals concerning the so-called 'Book of the Four', see now Albertz, 'Exile'.

In a study on *The Formation of the Book of the Twelve* (1995), Jones investigated the different orders of the Twelve presented by MT, LXX and 4QXII[a]. He surmised that Jonah, Joel and Obadiah, whose places in the collection varied, had been the last to be added. Jones also argued that the ordering of the LXX, which features Joel and Obadiah after Micah, is the original one. Jeremias's articles from 1995 and 1996 focus on the redactional links between Hosea and Amos, which are alleged to have been inserted in order to relate the messages of the two prophets to each other.[83] In 1997, Zapff sought to relate the redactional formation of the book of Micah to the models put forward by Steck, Bosshard-Nepustil and Nogalski.[84]

Schart's 1998 monograph similarly builds upon these earlier works, claiming that tradents combined a collection of Amos's words with Hosea into a 'Book of the Two'. This gave way to a deuteronomistic corpus, which also included Micah and Zephaniah. Next to be added were Nahum and Habakkuk, together with passages such as Hosea 4:3; Amos 4:13; 5:8–9; 9:5–6; Micah 1:3–4 and Zephaniah 1:2–3, followed by a salvific redaction (Amos 9:11–15; Haggai; Zechariah 1–8), an eschatological layer (Joel, Obadiah and Zechariah 14) and, finally, Malachi and Jonah.[85] Curtis, in turn, suggests two initial collections – that is, Hosea–Amos–Micah from Hezekiah's time, and Nahum–Habakkuk–Zephaniah from the time of Josiah, with Obadiah having been inserted shortly after the fall of Jerusalem. Haggai and Zechariah 1–8 also circulated together before the addition of Zechariah 9–14 and Malachi created another precursor to the Twelve as a whole.[86]

The story of this quest for the redaction of the Twelve has been told repeatedly in recent years,[87] and it is interesting to note that the narrators tend to begin long before the mid-1980s, indeed long before the self-conscious emergence of redaction criticism. It is common for surveys to start with a 1921 article by Budde. He argued that the aphoristic and often enigmatic form of the Twelve, which, he claims, has been purged of almost all narrative material relating to the prophets' backgrounds (the so-called 'human' material), is the result of a redaction that sought to produce a collection of prophetic materials holy enough for inclusion in the emerging canon.[88]

---

[83] Jeremias, 'Anfänge'; 'Interrelationship'.

[84] Zapff, *Redaktionsgeschichtliche Studien*; see also 'Perspective'.

[85] Schart, *Entstehung*; cf. Möller, 'Review of *Entstehung*'.

[86] Curtis, 'Zion-Daughter Oracles'.

[87] Cf. Nogalski, *Literary Precursors*, 3–12; Jones, *Formation*, 13–40; Schart, *Entstehung*, 6–21; 'Reconstructing', 41–45; Sweeney, *Twelve Prophets*, xix–xxvii; Redditt, 'Formation'; 'Recent Research'; and Carroll R., *Amos*, 36–39.

[88] Budde, 'Redaktion'. His arguments did not win the day, however; for criticisms, see, e.g., Willi-Plein, *Vorformen*, 3, 62 n. 21; Rudolph, *Haggai, Sacharja 1–8, Sacharja*

Another early precursor is Wolfe's 1935 study, which posits a lengthy process of successive editions, 'beginning with a Judaistic editor of the Book of Hosea and ending with the thirteenth and final editorial layer produced by the scribes who made the minor changes reflected in the differences between the MT and the LXX texts'.[89] The whole process, in Wolfe's opinion, began in the mid-seventh century and was completed by 225 BCE.[90]

Sherlock Holmes or Dr Watson? Some Reflections on the Quest for Amos's Literary Prehistory

Following the review of older attempts to unearth the 'original' words of the 'historical' Amos and the ongoing quest for the book's literary prehistory, it is time to draw conclusions and point to some achievements as well as the pitfalls and potential impasses of these reconstructions. Most of my criticisms relate especially to redaction criticism, which at present is arguably the dominant historical-critical methodology and as such deserves special attention.

In the introduction above I quoted Howard's comments on the 'historicization' of human thought – a term that carries the negative connotation of historical study having been taken too far, which is what I believe has happened in some redaction-critical work. Yet before developing that charge, I must repeat my 'plea for an historical approach', made in an earlier article on 'Renewing Historical Criticism'.[91] As Dobbs-Allsopp has argued, there are pragmatic, ethical and salvific reasons for reaffirming the importance of historical inquiry.[92] Pragmatic, because texts (as well as other objects) have a reality independent of the reader; ethical, because scholarship needs to respect 'the otherness of the Other as Other';[93] and salvific, because knowledge of the past can transform us and enable us to criticize present ideologies.

Turning from historical study to historical-critical scholarship, it first bears emphasizing that the latter has clearly advanced our understanding of the

---

9–14, *Maleachi*, 298; Schneider, 'Unity', 11; and Jones, *Formation*, 15 (according to Jones, though, 'Budde's observations have been too hastily dismissed').

[89] Thus Jones, *Formation*, 16–17; cf. Wolfe, 'Editing'.

[90] Wolfe, too, has been criticized for the subjectivity of his proposals and the simplistic, unilateral nature of his conclusions (all similarities in the materials are explained in terms of common authorship). See, for instance, Fohrer, 'Glossen', 46 n. 34; Willi-Plein, *Vorformen*, 3; and Jones, *Formation*, 17–18 (who is, however, appreciative of Wolfe's contribution).

[91] Möller, 'Renewing', 163–65.

[92] Dobbs-Allsopp, 'Rethinking'.

[93] The phrase is from Thiselton, *Interpreting*, 51.

biblical literature. In his contribution to the present volume, Gordon has out-lined some of the benefits of 'historical biblical criticism', as he prefers to call it.[94] Barr, who favours the term 'biblical criticism', has also recently reaffirmed the value of, for instance, providing linguistic information as well as informa-tion relating to 'other *realia*, such as geographical facts, knowledge about animals, and so on'.[95] And, in connection with Dobbs-Allsopp's points mentioned above, Barton's insistence on the value of historical criticism is also worth noting in this context. Barton stresses that

> so-called 'historical criticism' has the task of telling the reader what biblical texts can or cannot mean ... to say of this or that interpretation, 'No, the text cannot possibly mean that, because the words it uses will not bear that meaning.' This is potentially an enormous iconoclastic movement, because it refuses to allow people to mean anything they like by their sacred texts. So far from this movement having had its day in the churches, it has scarcely even arrived there.[96]

Gordon, Barr, Barton and others are right to highlight the value and the achievements of historical-critical scholarship. More specifically, redac-tion criticism too has made a positive contribution to the study of the Old Tes-tament. In addition to its positive outlook on the redactors' work, which is no longer regarded as inauthentic and thus inferior, Barton rightly lauds redac-tion criticism's 'minute attention to details of the text ... and its success ... in explaining puzzling features, such as the sequence in which incidents are related'.[97]

However, as we move on to some critical reflections, it should be noted first that, contrary to my claim that there may be a general tendency to 'over-historicise',[98] Barr is insistent that much of 'historical-critical' scholarship is concerned not so much with historical issues but with 'literary criticism'.[99] In his view, the 'identification of strata is essentially a literary and theological operation, working from vocabulary, style, cohesion, and theological com-monage', and 'not necessarily a historical one'.[100] Barton similarly notes that 'it is in the sophistication of their literary analysis that most so-called "historical"

---

[94] See Gordon, 'A Warranted Version of Historical Biblical Criticism?', Ch. 3, esp. the section entitled 'The Value of HBC'.

[95] Barr, *History and Ideology*, 42; he expresses his preference for the term 'biblical criticism' on p. 40.

[96] Barton, 'Historical-critical Approaches', 17–18.

[97] Barton, 'Redaction Criticism', 645.

[98] Seitz, *Word*, 10, 33, 107, similarly complains that historical questions often virtually run on autopilot.

[99] Barr, *History and Ideology*, 40; cf. Barton, 'Historical-critical Approaches', 16–19.

[100] Barr, *History and Ideology*, 41.

critics excelled. When they turned to write history in the normal sense of the term their efforts were usually far less sophisticated'.[101]

Barr concedes, however, that 'the quite different operation of deciding the date and the circumstance of origins of texts' is 'one of the main fashions in which biblical criticism can fairly be considered as "historical"'.[102] This, together with the fact that the 'literary-critical' step of identifying textual strata is not devoid of historical considerations either,[103] prohibits reducing the emphasis on the historical. Indeed, scholarly objectives have often been primarily of a historical nature. In the older paradigm, they included uncovering the prophet's original words, which had to be separated from the secondary material. Yet redaction criticism is no less historically focused. According to Steck, who actually prefers the term 'redaction *history*',[104] it

> traces the *text's history* from its first written form through its expansion, or relatedly commentary, by means of additions. It also traces a *text's history* through its incorporation into larger complexes all the way up to its final version in the current literary context. This approach thereby determines the *operative historical factors* and the intentions of the statements.[105]

Jeremias similarly emphasizes historical considerations, referring to the scholarly interest in the adaptations of the prophetic word, which are assumed to have taken place in order to apply it to changing historical circumstances.[106] Thus, according to Coote, 'each stage of recomposition represents an interpretation of Amos's words, and thus an actualization of them, a reading and understanding of them that makes them real and important in a new and different present'.[107] Statements like this could be multiplied, but the historical drive behind redaction criticism is too obvious to require further elaboration.

The main reason for discussing the approach's pitfalls and potential impasses in connection with the historicization of human thought noted by Howard

---

[101] Barton, 'Historical-critical Approaches', 14.

[102] Barr, *History and Ideology*, 41, 42.

[103] After all, historical assumptions about the age of certain phrases or stylistic features have influenced textual stratification in no small degree.

[104] Strictly speaking, 'redaction criticism' denotes the effort of distinguishing between *Vorlagen* and redactions, whereas 'redaction history' represents the investigation of the text's genesis (see Kratz, 'Redaktionsgeschichte', 367). The terms are not always used with this analytical precision, however; and in this chapter 'redaction criticism' refers to both processes.

[105] Steck, *Old Testament Exegesis*, 80 (emphasis mine); cf. also Kratz, 'Redaktionsgeschichte', 369 and 'Redaktion', 24–25, who stresses redaction criticism's contribution to the study of Israel's *history* of literature and theology.

[106] Jeremias, 'Proprium', 31.

[107] Coote, *Amos*, 3.

lies in the fact that in historical-critical scholarship – redaction criticism is no exception here – the presence of 'textual problems', such as perceived inconsistencies or discrepancies, has almost always led to the proposal of diachronic or historical solutions. This illustrates the enormous influence that the category 'history' has had on biblical studies. To be sure, diachronic solutions are sometimes called for – but they can be, and perhaps often have been, taken too far.

However, the following investigation is not restricted to quintessentially historical issues such as the dating of textual strata or the concept of *Fortschreibung*, which captures the idea of a text growing slowly over time (often over centuries). For while these are no doubt key aspects of the redaction-critical enterprise, an assessment of the approach's validity also has to consider the viability of its literary-critical manoeuvres and address the consequences of redaction-critical conclusions and presuppositions – theological, practical or otherwise.

The rationale for redaction-critical study[108]

Textual inconsistencies: Verbal, historical and theological

According to Barton, historical-critical readings are often *demanded* by textual inconsistencies and dislocations.[109] While Barton was thinking primarily of verbal inconsistencies, historical and theological considerations have also often provided a rationale for diachronic solutions. This is true both for the older historical-critical approaches as well as for redaction-critical study,[110] although the latter increasingly relies on intertextuality as well (see below). At this point though, to avoid duplicating discussions, I will concentrate on verbal inconsistencies.[111]

To be sure, perceived verbal inconsistencies may provide a potentially legitimate point of departure for redaction-critical analysis. Yet they are far from reliable, because one interpreter's inconsistencies sometimes are another reader's 'deliberate components of the literary artwork'.[112] Willi-Plein saw

---

[108] The following headings (referring to redaction criticism's rationale, criteria, assumptions, consequences and practice) serve a mere heuristic purpose and should not be taken as absolute. The boundaries are often blurred, for what provides the rationale for redaction-critical study can also serve as a criterion in its pursuit and what counts as a criterion may turn out to be an assumption of redaction-critical work.

[109] Barton, *Reading*, 20–29.

[110] Cf. Kratz, 'Redaktionsgeschichte', 368; 'Redaktion', 13.

[111] For a discussion of perceived theological and historical irregularities, see 'Criteria for textual stratification' and 'Problems relating to redaction-critical practice', below.

[112] Thus Alter, 'Introduction', 27.

this clearly, stressing that our ideas of what counts as a redaction are all too often determined by what one regards as superfluous in a text or by what one would have expected to find in it.[113] However, the issue here is not the interpreter's subjectivity per se, for it has become a commonplace in recent years to insist that subjectivity cannot be avoided. After all, we have no unmediated access to reality;[114] there is, to employ Nagel's apt *bon mot*, no 'view from nowhere'.[115]

What I am objecting to is the literalism, coupled with a preference for simplistic readings,[116] that has often marked and marred biblical interpretation. As I have argued elsewhere, historical-critical scholarship, including recent redaction-critical work, has all but ignored insights offered by the philosophy of language, which could have helped exegetes overcome the literalism responsible for many perceived inconsistencies.[117] Avis rightly put his finger on a lack of 'imagistic thinking', arguing that we need 'an integrated ... model in which reason and imagination could be seen as two interrelated aspects of the mind working as a whole, analytically and synthetically'.[118] This is needed 'in order to counterbalance the traditional historical-critical preference for analytical and vivisective thinking'.[119]

Interestingly, in his eloquent rebuttal of the charges brought against historical criticism by Gunn and Fewell, Barr fails to respond to precisely this one: that 'the analysis of sources was "basically dependent on *aesthetic premises* which were often arbitrary and rarely acknowledged". Underlying most source criticism has been an "*aesthetic preference for rationalistic, literal reading of literature*".'[120] To be sure, Barr does respond to the charge of arbitrariness, and he does so with his usual aplomb. Unfortunately, however, he does not discuss the issue of literalism, which would have been both interesting and desirable.

---

[113] Willi-Plein, *Vorformen*, 3.

[114] Cf. Sternberg, *Poetics*, 16; Dobbs-Allsopp, 'Rethinking'; Eagleton, *Literary Theory*, 60; and see Möller, 'Renewing', 150–53, for further discussion.

[115] Nagel, *View*. See, however, Kratz, 'Redaktion', 11–12, who somewhat idealistically contrasts the canonical approach's subjectivity with Steck's (apparently objective) historical approach.

[116] Ben Zvi, 'Studying', 133, has also noted this tendency towards simplistic readings, which in his view has arisen from the mistaken assumption that the prophetic texts reflect public speech.

[117] See the introduction to Möller, *Prophet*; 'Renewing', 153–56; 'Words'; and 'Rehabilitation', 45–48, for further discussion.

[118] See Avis, *God*, 18–22; the quote is from p. 20.

[119] Thus Möller, 'Words', 379.

[120] Barr, *History and Ideology*, 34 (emphasis mine). The quotes are from Gunn and Fewell, *Narrative*, 8.

Intertextuality

In recent years, however, the rationale for redaction-critical work has come not so much from textual inconsistencies as from 'various types of intertextuality'.[121] These include superscriptions, catchwords and catchphrases, allusions, shared themes and so on. A look at the relevant literature, especially on the quest for the redaction of the Twelve, confirms that there has been no lack of suggested intertextual links, which have supplied the rationale for redaction-critical work but which have also been adduced as criteria for the identification of redactional layers. It is to these that we now turn.

Criteria for textual stratification

Verbal clues (intertextuality)

Concerning these clues, two questions suggest themselves: First, which clues are significant and why? And secondly, do they always necessarily point to or demand a history of redactions? In his review of redaction-critical works on the Twelve, Redditt admits that adduced clues such as catchwords are sometimes debatable.[122] Indeed, it would be wrong to suggest that redaction critics have been unaware of this problem, and yet a case for more rigour can and must be made. More than that, it is important to reconsider whether, and to what degree, verbal clues can ever provide a viable criterion for the identification and dating of redactional layers. Some examples may serve to illustrate the problems that beset this practice.

Melugin has aptly noted that even 'some exceptionally sophisticated literary-historical analyses have failed to attract a large following ... because of insufficient evidence'.[123] For instance, Wolff's reconstruction of Amos's redaction history, 'despite its *brilliant use of stylistic differences* for the purpose of distinguishing layers of redaction', is not widely accepted.[124] Noting, for example, that 'the credibility of Wolff's reconstruction of an "Old School of Amos" depends upon an ability to show that differences in speech can most probably be accounted for as indicators of different authors or schools', Melugin concludes that 'the evidence is not strong enough to create a scholarly consensus in favor of the *probability* of his proposal'.[125]

---

[121] See Redditt, 'Recent Research', 54.

[122] Redditt, 'Recent Research', 56.

[123] Melugin, 'Prophetic Books', 65.

[124] Melugin, 'Prophetic Books', 65 (emphasis mine).

[125] Melugin, 'Prophetic Books', 68, 69 (emphasis original). Melugin expresses similar concerns regarding Wolff's 'Bethel-Exposition of the Josianic Age' but is more positive about the assumed deuteronomistic redaction.

Secondly, in a review of Nogalski's *Literary Precursors to the Book of the Twelve*, Wolters has argued that the author's proposal of a 'catchword phenomenon' (i.e., that adjacent writings in the Twelve are linked by catchwords at the ends and beginnings of the individual books) has 'serious methodological and philological flaws'. He comments that

> methodologically, Nogalski never actually defines what can legitimately count as a 'catchword', nor what can reasonably be considered the 'end' of one writing and the 'beginning' of the next, which together constitute what he calls the 'seam' connecting them. Clearly, if these terms are sufficiently generously defined, it is possible to establish a literary link between almost any two adjacent blocks of canonical material.[126]

Wolters specifically notes that Nogalski adduces some common Hebrew terms as 'catchwords' and that the 'ends' and 'beginnings' of adjacent writings tend to become rather sizeable on occasion. And he charges that Nogalski has expanded his definition of catchwords to include 'lexemes which resemble each other only in his English translation, not in the Hebrew original' and 'when there is more shared vocabulary in a given "seam" than he needs to make his point, [he has] ignore[d] some of the repeated lexemes which he is otherwise at such pains to point out'. Given this lack of methodological rigour, Wolters contends that 'it would be possible to find "catchwords" linking almost any sizable pericope of the Hebrew Bible with almost any other'.[127]

Sometimes counter-arguments to redaction-critical conclusions are quite ingeniously circumnavigated rather than being faced head on. In recent years, the supposed deuteronomistic redaction of Amos (or the Twelve) has come under attack by scholars such as Lohfink, Bons and Ben Zvi, who are not convinced that the textual evidence warrants the assumption of a deuteronomistic redaction.[128] Schart, however, evades the problem by speaking of a 'D redaction'. He thus avoids using the term 'deuteronomistic' but maintains that this 'D redaction' is linguistically and thematically close to the deuteronomists.[129] What he fails to appreciate is that the studies by Lohfink

---

[126] Wolters, 'Review of *Literary Precursors*', 494.

[127] Wolters, 'Review of *Literary Precursors*', 495; see Jones, *Formation*, 37–39, for similar comments; and also Barton, 'Redaction Criticism', 645, who complains about 'a tendency to exaggerate the importance of small details and to foreclose the possibility that some features of the biblical text may be the result of accident or inadvertence'.

[128] See Lohfink, 'Deuteronomistische Bewegung'; Bons, 'Denotat'; and Ben Zvi, 'Deuteronomistic Redaction'.

[129] See Schart, *Entstehung*, 46, 156 n. 2.

and Bons make the assumption of a redactional layer per se (whether 'deuteronomistic' or simply 'D') unwarranted.

These examples, which could be multiplied, confirm that more methodological rigour is required in this chase for catchwords and other verbal clues.[130] One should even be open to the possibility that the whole endeavour might turn out not to be a viable avenue for future research. Perhaps Melugin is right to suggest that 'the evidence needed for convincing historical reconstruction can actually be obtained only in a limited number of instances'.[131] In suggesting as much, I happily risk being compared to Sir Arthur Conan Doyle's somewhat obtuse Dr Watson. That honour has already been bestowed on Ben Zvi, who criticized the current quest for the redaction history of the Twelve. For instance, Ben Zvi questioned the value of clues such as intertextual allusions, which, he concurs with Wolters, can be found across 'a wide range of texts and types of texts'.[132] To this Redditt responded, declaring that

> one might do well to remember the fictional detective Sherlock Holmes, who saw things his companion Watson never saw, precisely because Holmes was looking for them. Watson, by contrast, either did not see the clues at all, or drew wrong inferences from them, because he did not have the proper theory or frame of reference.[133]

Indeed, but one should also be aware that

> a solved mystery is ultimately reassuring to readers, asserting the triumph of … order over anarchy, whether in the tales of Sherlock Holmes or in the case histories of Sigmund Freud which bear such a striking and suspicious resemblance to them. That is why mystery is an invariable ingredient of popular narrative, whatever its form – prose fiction or movies or television soaps. Modern literary novelists, in contrast, wary of neat solutions and happy endings, have tended to invest their mysteries with an aura of ambiguity and to leave them unresolved.[134]

Since in the real world clues are often confusing and not necessarily significant and mysteries often unpredictable and not always solvable, one hopes that redaction critics are not driven to such desperate actions as Bernhard Schlink's private detective Gerhard Selb in *Selbs Justiz*. In the desire for an acceptable conclusion to his case, he eventually takes justice into his own hands, pushing the culprit/victim over the edge of a steep sea cliff. Dr Matthäi's end in

---

[130] Schultz's *Search for Quotation*, which assesses various attempts to establish verbal parallels in the prophets, is a step in the right direction. See now also Schultz, 'Ties'.

[131] Melugin, 'Prophetic Books', 70.

[132] See esp. Ben Zvi, 'Twelve Prophetic Books'. The quote is from p. 136.

[133] Redditt, 'Recent Research', 63.

[134] Lodge, *Art*, 31.

Friedrich Dürrenmatt's *Das Versprechen: Requiem auf den Kriminalroman* presents another warning. For when higher forces prevent a successful solution of the case, the detective turns, slowly but unstoppably, into an obsessed lunatic.

Thus far, the focus has been on the search for significant clues. Even assuming that such can be found, it then still needs to be established whether these clues always necessarily point to or demand redaction-critical explanations. Redaction criticism has too quickly arrived at this unilateral conclusion, without giving alternative options due consideration. Yet,

> the conclusion that ... complex [verbal and literary] relationships are uniformly the results of common redactional shaping is only one possible explanation of these phenomena. Literary dependency, shared traditions,[135] the often limited vocabulary of classical Hebrew, and even coincidence are some of the alternative explanations.[136]

Ideological or theological clues

Sometimes passages are assigned to subsequent textual layers because of their ideological stance, which is thought to be different from that of the text in which they occur.[137] Wellhausen's comments on the salvation oracle in Amos 9, which he regarded as a 'triumph of illusion' and 'a falling back into the mania' Amos had fought, are an apt example of this type of judgement. Smend, too, does not think highly of the passage and blames the book's redactors for diluting Amos's message and, by doing so, effectively betraying the prophet.[138]

Others have come to different conclusions, however. For instance, Duhm claims that the editors would not have regarded their work as a forgery of Amos's message.[139] Williamson, following Clements,[140] has similarly argued that the expressions of hope in Isaiah, Amos and Hosea are not arbitrary additions but 'draw out the implications of taking the word of judgement seriously'.[141] Wolff does find some 'mitigations' but insists that 'on the whole ... the uniquely sombre message of Amos concerning the end of Israel remains unmistakably audible through all layers of tradition'.[142] And, turning to the

---

[135] In prophetic research, tradition history in particular seems to have fallen victim to the preference for redaction-critical solutions. Yet the fact that some textual allusions elude tradition-historical explanations hardly warrants putting all of one's eggs in the basket of redaction criticism.

[136] Jones, *Formation*, 22–23.

[137] Kraus, *Geschichte*, 282, in this context speaks of 'ideenkritische Maßnahmen'.

[138] Smend, 'Nein', esp. 422.

[139] Duhm, *Zwölf Propheten*, xxxvii.

[140] See Clements, 'Patterns'.

[141] Williamson, 'Hope', 306.

[142] Wolff, *Joel and Amos*, 113.

proposed deuteronomistic redaction, Schmidt considers the deuteronomists' contribution a largely appropriate extension of Amos's message but maintains that it has shifted the emphasis from the announcement of judgement to accusations and indictments.[143]

These opinions, chosen more or less at random, raise at least two questions, which both have far-reaching consequences. Thus, one might ask, rather naively perhaps, who then is right and, less naïvely, what does that mean? Of course, the first question can only be decided by going back to the texts, and I do not intend to abuse scholarly disagreement to rule redaction criticism as such out of court. What I want to draw attention to, however, is the phenomenon that revisions of earlier assumptions or perceptions often fail to lead to apposite conclusions.

If, for instance, Wellhausen and Smend were wrong to regard the salvation oracle in Amos 9 as out of sync with the rest of the book, may they not also have been wrong in assigning it to later editors or redactors? Not one of the aforementioned scholars, to the best of my knowledge, has given this serious consideration. And maybe they have had no reason to do so based on this question alone, for the dating of the passage depends on a variety of factors (such as vocabulary, one's understanding of Israel's history of religion, etc.).

The issue at stake, though, is that new perspectives on old questions and, even more critically, the deployment of fresh approaches, far too often do not lead to a questioning of the results yielded by the older approaches.[144] This is often true even when, for instance, the philosophical presuppositions of the older approaches have been undermined.[145] Barr essentially confirms this in speaking of a convergence between traditional criticism and the newer approaches,[146] noting that

> things like the adoption of a late date for biblical sources in recent scholarship arise from the convergence of two quite different traditions: on the one hand the continuance of Pentateuchal criticism … and on the other hand the influence of literary reading practices, revisionist historical approaches, and ideological critical aims.[147]

Regrettably, this easy convergence can become problematic when all kinds of momentous hypotheses are built on rather fragile foundations.

---

[143] Schmidt, 'Deuteronomistische Redaktion', 192.

[144] See in this context Kratz's admission, already referred to above, that the older literary-critical isolation of 'inauthentic' passages provided redaction criticism with its initial working material ('Redaktionsgeschichte', 371).

[145] See Möller, 'Words', for further discussion.

[146] Barr, *History and Ideology*, 55.

[147] Barr, *History and Ideology*, 57.

The second issue raised by divergent opinions on textual additions, such as Amos 9:11–15, concerns the reading process, which will be discussed below in connection with 'The consequences of redaction-critical study'. First, though, we need to look at a common and surprisingly uncontroversial assumption of biblical criticism – namely, that most Old Testament books underwent a long process of redactional work, a process that has come to be known as *Fortschreibung*.[148]

A redaction-critical assumption and its implications

Fortschreibung

This is a sacred cow one dare not touch for fear of coming to grief in the process. It is commonly assumed that the prophetic books underwent numerous redactions, as the prophetic message was adapted to changing historical circumstances. I have already quoted Steck, Jeremias and Coote to that effect, but it might be worth pointing out that this assumption did not originate with redaction criticism. It is much older and, in the words of a past commentator on Amos, has been expressed as follows:

> Men in later days of prophecy seem to have regarded it as a pious duty to illustrate older utterances by making application to their own times.... The intention was not to preserve and transmit what the prophet had actually said, but rather to indicate what, in the opinion of the later editor, he would have had to say in order to 'fulfil the religious purpose which he once meant to serve'.[149]

Willi-Plein, herself the author of a redaction-critical study on Amos, Hosea and Micah, once noted that the process of adapting the prophetic message might be explained in three ways: (1) as the interpretation of prophecy by means of further prophecy, (2) as the attribution of foreign material to a respected authority, or (3) as a literary forgery. The third case would be given if the glossators or interpolators (or redactors) deliberately sought to endow their words with an aura of authenticity, thus misleading their readers.[150] Notably, Willi-Plein does not invalidate this option with the oft-repeated claim that such a notion would be anachronistic. Referencing some ancient Greek authors, she maintains rather that in antiquity, literary forgeries could be thought of and exposed as forgeries.[151]

---

[148] The development of the concept of *Fortschreibung* is usually credited to Zimmerli, who deployed it in his commentary on Ezekiel (cf. Zimmerli, *Ezechiel*, I:106–10).

[149] Harper, *Amos and Hosea*, cxxxi.

[150] Willi-Plein, *Vorformen*, 9.

[151] See Willi-Plein, *Vorformen*, 9–10 (esp. n. 33).

However, vis-à-vis the prophetic literature, she rejects this explanation, claiming that it is *Offenbarungsliteratur* (literature that claims to be a divine revelation), which obeys a different set of principles. 'If it is the word of Yahweh that came to the prophet, it can at any time be modified or its true meaning be illuminated by a new word from Yahweh. As long as prophecy as such is alive, the past prophetic word can be supplemented by new prophecies'.[152] Maybe that is so, or maybe one just has to conclude this if one accepts that biblical criticism has sufficiently proven that the prophetic books did evolve over a long period of time. In that case, the sacred cow would turn out to be a red herring after all. But I am hesitant to move in that direction too quickly. As Willi-Plein herself notes, if in Old Testament times there had been no interest in distinguishing different authors,[153] there would have been no need for the superscriptions with their details about the prophetic personae.[154]

Kratz's views on the issue may help to put all of this into sharper focus. According to Kratz, the term 'redaction' refers to a process of reception that allows an older, *authoritative* text to speak into a new situation. In this process, the text is adapted to the new situation (it may also be rearranged, supplemented or even corrected), but it is not displaced or distorted, for the new text is meant to be identical with the old in terms of its wording, subject and authoritative claim.[155]

This conception of *Fortschreibung* raises some important issues. First, in the light of the earlier discussion of Wellhausen's and Smend's views on Amos 9:11–15, it is clear that the claim for the authoritative text not to have been distorted in the redactional process is no more than one assumption among others. This becomes even clearer in connection with Carroll's views on Jeremiah 1:1–3, which will be addressed in the following section. Secondly, how the new text can be identical with the old in terms of its wording ('dem Wortlaut nach') simply escapes me. Thirdly, and most importantly, Kratz too quickly assumes that an *authoritative* text could easily and repeatedly be supplemented and even corrected. To be sure, I am not denying that this could have happened, but this issue would at least seem to require some further reflection.

In connection with Willi-Plein's three options, one should also note that, in Kratz's model, the messages of the prophetic personae mentioned in the superscriptions are irretrievably lost.[156] For in the process of turning into

---

[152] Willi-Plein, *Vorformen*, 10.

[153] I myself would avoid the term 'author' in this context, for the attribution of the prophetic material to the personae mentioned in the superscriptions does not necessarily have to be construed in terms of authorship.

[154] Willi-Plein, *Vorformen*, 10 n. 33.

[155] Thus Kratz, 'Redaktionsgeschichte', 370; cf. also *Kyros*, 218–19.

[156] For the issues discussed in this paragraph, see Kratz, 'Redaktionsgeschichte', 375–76; and 'Redaktion'.

writing (the *Verschriftung*), prophecy completely changed its face. It thus is not the inauthenticity of a prophetic oracle, but rather its authenticity, which needs to be proved. More importantly, prophecy as prophecy of judgement only came into being in connection with the *Verschriftung* of the prophetic word.[157] Originally, neither Amos nor Hosea was a prophet of judgement. Indeed, Isaiah too was a prophet of salvation, who was turned into a prophet of judgement only retrospectively.[158] Prophecy of judgement, as we know it from the Old Testament, in fact originated with the theological reflection of circles of scribes.[159]

Given these notions, I profess not to understand what Kratz means when he insists that the original authoritative text has not been displaced or distorted in the redaction-historical process and that the adapted text is meant to be identical with the old in terms of its wording, subject and authoritative claim. Was it only at the transition from the oral to the literary stage (the *Erstverschriftung*) that these drastic changes took place, so that subsequent redactions did not distort the original *text*? If so, what does Kratz gain in making a claim for continuity, given that extensive changes clearly did take place in connection with the *Erstverschriftung*? And, if such changes have taken place, how can he be sure that later redactors handled their material less heavy-handedly? Or, to return to Willi-Plein's options, what prevents us from concluding that the process of *Fortschreibung* did not result in forgery?

According to Kratz's model, the authority of the prophet lending his name to the developing collection does not count for much, for it did not prevent redactors from turning Isaiah, the prophet of salvation, into Isaiah, the prophet of judgement. Yet at some stage the prophetic books became 'sacrosanct' and canonical.[160] Why, one wonders, did that happen? If the words of the 'original' prophet were not sacrosanct, why should those of later scribes enjoy such a status? Kratz attributes this to, among other things, a 'peculiar understanding of the time' at work in the redactional process. Again, I am not sure what that means. If it means that it was only later generations of readers, who began to regard the message of the by then dim and distant prophetic figure as sacrosanct, would one not have to conclude that they had been thoroughly misguided, given that the message had not much to do with that prophetic figure? Or, if the authority was that of the redactors, understood as prophets in their own right along the lines suggested by Willi-Plein, why appeal to Amos or Isaiah at all? Is this not misleading, a distortion, a forgery?

---

[157] 'Die unbedingte Gerichtsprophetie ist … ein Produkt der Überlieferungsbildung' (Kratz, 'Redaktion', 20).
[158] Kratz, 'Redaktion', 20.
[159] Kratz, 'Redaktion', 21.
[160] See Kratz, 'Redaktionsgeschichte', 376.

One might object that Kratz's model presents an extreme case and thus is not representative of redaction-critical views on *Fortschreibung* generally. But the same ambiguities pertain to the more balanced and restrained account offered by Barton. He also notes the redactors' 'great respect for the material', commenting that this accounts for the inconsistencies in the first place, without which the redaction-critical enterprise would never have got off the ground.[161] Yet Barton at the same time holds that the redactors 'made substantial alterations to the documents'; that 'redactional additions, even of a few words, can have a profound effect' on a passage's meaning; and that 'some of the biblical editors have reshaped the material at their proposal so freely that we might call *them* "authors" rather than mere redactors'.[162] Barton concludes that 'the mixture of an *extreme respect* for an old text and a great freedom in reshaping it to contemporary needs and ideas is one of the most puzzling features of the growth of the Bible for a modern reader'.[163]

In the light of the above, it seems fair to conclude that the concept of *Fortschreibung* is not unproblematic. I have discussed it here as a redaction-critical assumption, though some would probably consider it an assured result of biblical criticism. Either way, given the problems it raises, more consideration of the issues raised here would seem desirable. After all, it befits a critical discipline, such as redaction criticism, to constantly re-examine its own assumptions — and even its 'assured results' — critically. Yet, all too often, redaction-critical study appears to proceed on autopilot, without so much as reflecting on its presuppositions.[164]

To be sure, the problem with *Fortschreibung* may turn out to be one of degree rather than kind. For even if the assumed wearing of the prophetic mantle by subsequent redactors were to be less unproblematic than is often thought, it would not necessarily follow that the assumption of redactional work as such is mistaken. Some of the more complex scenarios of multiple redactions, which almost give the impression that anyone could have a go at 'updating' the prophetic message,[165] might well be aversely affected by such a conclusion, however.

---

[161] Barton, 'Redaction Criticism', 646. See also the discussion of Barton's 'disappearing redactor' below.

[162] Barton, 'Redaction Criticism'; the quotes are from pp. 645–46.

[163] Barton, 'Redaction Criticism', 647 (emphasis mine).

[164] Barr, *History and Ideology, passim*, has criticized the postmodern penchant for 'presuppositionalism'. Of course, bringing one's presuppositions out in the open will not solve everything. But a critical discipline surely ought to be prepared to reconsider and, if appropriate, re-conceptualize, its presuppositions.

[165] See Kratz, 'Redaktion', 13: 'Ist erst einmal eine literarische Vorlage vorhanden, wird sie fortlaufend mit Material aus der mündlichen Überlieferung und spontanen Neuformulierungen ergänzt.'

The consequences of redaction-critical study

The reading process

Redaction-critical work supposedly must make a difference to the way we read the prophetic literature – otherwise, what would be the point? Yet the reconstruction of multiple textual layers with either conflicting or complementary ideas leads to at least two serious challenges in relation to the reading process. And although these challenges do not necessarily rule out redaction-critical suggestions, they nevertheless need to be addressed.

The first challenge concerns the ability of readers to differentiate between layers – which, one assumes, redaction critics would have to claim to be necessary for an informed and appropriate reading. The second issue relates to the divergent evaluations of redactional additions noted above. Supposing that readers are aware of the texts' composite nature and capable of distinguishing between textual layers, there would still remain the not insignificant matter of evaluating redactional supplements and adopting suitable reading strategies. What is at stake here will become clearer when we compare Carroll's comments on Jeremiah 1:1–3 with some opinions voiced by Darr, Rendtorff, Childs and Ben Zvi.

Concerning the first question, one might say that the texts are, for the most part, not conducive to the redaction-critical exercise. Except for those cases where, for instance, historical allusions clearly point to a later time, subsequent additions are difficult, if not impossible, for readers to identify. Detailed stratification is completely out of the question, and reading a layered document poses its own problems. One might of course conclude, as Ben Zvi has done, that these documents were composed and redacted by an educated elite for use by an educated elite.[166] If so, does that mean that they can only be read by today's educated elite? Or that maybe today's elite will have to help the uninitiated?

To be sure, most scholars would consider it desirable for 'ordinary readers' to develop informed reading strategies. So do I. Yet it is one thing to tell readers that there might be more to a certain term than is apparent from the translations, or that some background information might shed further light on a passage. Having to hold readers' hands, reminding them at every second step that, excuse me, this would now be the Judaic redaction of 711 BCE and that, if I may just interrupt again, this is a supplement made by R^{RK}, you know, the redactor responsible for the creation of the ring composition, is quite another thing. If biblical criticism owes so much to Reformation principles such as *sola scriptura* and the 'plain sense', which emphasize biblical consultation apart from 'any official church *magisterium* and ... any overriding authority of the later

---

[166] Ben Zvi, *Obadiah*, 5; 'Studying', 133–34.

interpretation of the biblical documents', as Barton and Barr hold,[167] it might not be advisable to insist on too much hand-holding. Yet precisely this would have to be done if, for instance, 'the Twelve is to be read diachronically ... *in full cognizance of its history*'.[168]

Considering redaction-critical work useful if often highly speculative, Melugin has recently made the opposite claim, arguing that 'if one's primary concerns were ... with the use of Scripture for the shaping of life in today's communities of faith, I doubt whether [such an] approach would be useful as the *primary* paradigm for interpretation'.[169] By implication, it might be useful as a secondary, or maybe tertiary, paradigm – but Melugin fails to tell us how and why. In fact, the general thrust of his comments suggests that he has serious doubts about the usefulness of what he deems to be 'highly speculative redaction-historical proposals'.

This brings us to the conflicting opinions about redactional additions and the question of how these additions influence or ought to influence (or ought *not* to influence) the reading process. Carroll once lamented that Jeremiah 1:1–3 'is an inflection of the tradition which has given rise to so many *misreadings* of the book', having 'misdirected generations of readers into reading the book as if its utterances and events actually took place during' the seventh and early sixth century BCE.[170] Darr, by contrast, commenting on Isaiah, has emphasized that 'text's invitation to read Isaiah as what it purports to be – the vision that the eighth-century prophet saw'.[171] Rendtorff similarly notes that 'the books themselves always give the historical framework in which they are to be read and understood'.[172] And Childs has criticized Wolff because his 'historical interpretation of the redactional layers of Amos has the effect of reading the biblical text from a perspective which often runs counter to that demanded by the literature itself'.[173]

Ben Zvi has specifically stressed the interpretative value of prophetic superscriptions, arguing that they represent the author's point of view and should, therefore, be taken into account.[174] Of course, this does not cause the

---

[167] Barr, *History and Ideology*, 53–55 (the quote is from p. 53); cf. also Barton, 'Historical-critical Approaches', 16–17, who incidentally admits that, while the underlying motivation of biblical criticism was 'to free the text to speak', 'the proliferation of historical-critical writings' has in itself become 'a fresh set of' 'stifling wrappings of interpretation' (p. 17).

[168] Redditt, 'Recent Research', 72, summarizing Nogalski's position (emphasis mine).

[169] Melugin, 'Prophetic Books', 77 (emphasis original).

[170] Carroll, 'Arguing About Jeremiah', 230 (emphasis mine).

[171] Darr, 'Literary Perspectives', 141.

[172] Rendtorff, 'Old Testament Theology', 11.

[173] Childs, *Introduction*, 408.

[174] Ben Zvi, *Zephaniah*, 11.

diachronic questions to disappear, as Rendtorff has rightly noted.[175] For, as Ben
Zvi illustrates, the superscriptions could still be understood in various ways –
for example, as indicating that the book contains the prophet's *ipsissima verba*,[176]
as presenting the oracles as the prophet's message *in essentia*, or as providing
'the literary hero who holds together otherwise diverse traditions'.[177] In each
of these cases, though, the superscriptions are acceded interpretative significance, rather than being understood as an impediment to a proper reading of
the book.

Yet, from a redaction-critical point of view, Carroll's misgivings are legitimate. If a prophetic book contains multiple redactional layers so that significant
parts post-date the historical framework supplied in the superscription, then
how are we to read the text and what, specifically, are we to make of the superscription? Redaction criticism and the canonical approach, one suspects, can
never become friends. For while the latter urges us to respect the books'
canonical shape, redaction critics may have cause to insist that texts such as
Jeremiah 1:1–3 might actually lead us astray. At some point in Jeremiah's literary prehistory the superscription may have provided an appropriate *entrée*
into the book, but subsequent additions have since rendered it anachronistic
and misleading.

Of disappearing and fecund redactors

Barton's well-known notion of the disappearing redactor highlights another
consequence of redaction-critical study. Noting the tendency, observable not
only in synchronic studies but also in redaction-critical works, to stress the artistry of the biblical documents and to credit redactors for the production of
readable and coherent texts,[178] Barton worries that this might lead to what he
calls the 'biblical critic's conjuring trick'. He describes this as follows:

> The more impressive the critic makes the redactor's work appear, the more he
> succeeds in showing that the redactor has, by subtle and delicate artistry, produced
> a simple and coherent text out of the diverse materials before him; the more also he
> reduces the evidence on which the existence of those sources was established in
> the first place. No conjuror is required for this trick: the redaction critic himself
> causes his protégé to disappear. ... Thus, if redaction criticism plays its hand too
> confidently, we end up with a piece of writing so coherent that no division into

---

[175] Rendtorff, 'Historical Criticism', 28.
[176] Ben Zvi strongly rejects the view that the superscriptions point to the text's authorship by the named individual; see Ben Zvi, 'Studying'.
[177] For these options, see Ben Zvi, *Zephaniah*, 11.
[178] Of course, as has been noted above, redactors are also still frequently identified on
the basis of assumed textual inconsistencies.

sources is warranted any longer; and the sources and the redactor vanish together in a puff of smoke, leaving a single, freely composed narrative with, no doubt, a single author.[179]

Two comments should be in order at this point. First, worrying though it may be (for whatever reasons), one does at least have to allow for the *possibility* that texts that have been considered incoherent and of a composite nature are in fact much more coherent than some of the older commentators believed. Our increasing knowledge of the Hebrew *ars poetica* and closer attention to the texts' socio-linguistic dimension highlighted by some philosophies of language appear to point in that direction.[180]

Secondly, I am not sure that Barton needs to worry about the future of redaction criticism and its protégés. While one might think that 'it is in the nature of the case impossible to identify a *perfect* redactor, since *ex hypothesi* his perfection would consist in having removed all the inconsistencies which enable us to know that he exists at all',[181] this in fact depends on one's definition of 'perfect'. It would be conceivable to think of 'perfect' redactors, who produce coherent texts and yet betray themselves, for instance, by historical allusions to later situations. Of course, a truly perfect redactor might be said not even to commit that 'blunder' (which has indeed been argued, as we shall see below). Yet, if there is anything at all in the quest for shared keywords or themes, redactors could still be identified on that basis. But Barton does have a point in that a complete lack of inconsistencies would surely undermine the redaction-critical quest.

Jones, on the other hand, has drawn attention not to the disappearance of redactors but to what one might call their fecundity. As we have seen, not only do these redactors have a tendency in some cases to multiply like rabbits, but the amount of material attributed to their efforts is also constantly increasing. Thinking especially of the work of Weimar, Bosshard, Kratz and Steck, Jones notes that 'the sheer volume of secondary materials that they isolate makes a reconstruction of the redactional history extremely complex'.

> The increased amount of redactional material in the book also decreases dramatically the possibility that the redactional reconstructions of these scholars are correct. The redactional reconstructions of Weimar, Bosshard, Kratz, and Steck therefore *suffer from their own success* at identifying proposed redactional materials within the text of the Book of the Twelve.[182]

---

[179] Barton, *Reading*, 57.
[180] See Möller, 'Renewing', esp. 153–56; and 'Words'.
[181] Thus Barton, *Reading*, 58.
[182] Jones, *Formation*, 21 (emphasis mine).

As with Barton's disappearing redactor, redaction criticism's success is once again deemed problematic. Only in this instance, successful redaction-critical work is not thought to do itself out of a job but rather to jeopardize the credibility of its arduous labours.

Problems relating to redaction-critical practice

Historical classification of textual strata

This need not necessarily be a problem, for unambiguous historical allusions may, in some cases, turn this into a straightforward task for the critic. Sometimes, though, the historical referents prove to be elusive, as in Amos's oracles against the nations. Melugin has noted this, commenting that scholars tend to 'draw conclusions far beyond what the text will support'.[183] The problem of historical classification is aggravated when textual layers begin to mushroom, as in Rottzoll's redaction-critical analysis of Amos. Just how confident can or should we be in distinguishing the Judaic redaction of 722/1 BCE from the one of 711, not to mention the other ten strata with their specific historical backgrounds?

Yet another problem arises when redactors are said not to have betrayed their time and place. Some commentators have argued that an early eighth-century perspective has been maintained throughout the book of Amos in that, for instance, Assyria is never referred to by name, or that the chaotic situation in Israel following the death of Jeroboam II is nowhere reflected.[184] Rofé, however, rejects this, calling it an *argumentum e silentio*. Yet, quite apart from the fact that his own conclusion – that 'the interpolators and editors ... took care not to betray their time or place'[185] – would seem not to fare much better in that respect, one wonders whose argument is the more convoluted one.

The tendency of uncritical self-perpetuation

Finally, I submit that the redaction-critical enterprise is marked, and marred, by a distinct lack of critical self-reflection. To be sure, scholars are aware that the approach has generated a host of at times conflicting scenarios for the development of the biblical books.[186] And, for instance, those interested in the redaction history of the Twelve generally acknowledge that many scholars remain unconvinced that the whole was ever meant to be read as one book.

Still, all too often, the value, aims and methodological procedures of redaction criticism, as it is currently practised, are simply taken for granted. Neither

---

[183] Melugin, 'Prophetic Books', 73.

[184] Thus Blenkinsopp, *History*, 93; and Andersen and Freedman, *Amos*, 192.

[185] Rofé, *Introduction*, 34.

[186] See, for instance, Redditt, 'Recent Research', 56.

Steck, whose approach has been particularly influential,[187] nor Fohrer seem to suspect any problems or potential pitfalls.[188] Streete's essay, by contrast, does include a brief discussion of possible limitations and drawbacks, although it is oddly restricted to the single problem of committing the 'intentional fallacy'.[189] Apart from being strangely restrictive, the criticism is largely off-target for, while redaction critics may sometimes have fallen into this trap, by and large the approach is not characterized by the kind of psychologizing reading so strenuously rejected by Wimsatt and Beardsley in their seminal article 'The Intentional Fallacy'.

Even Melugin's account of the problem of historical reconstruction, which only in part concerns redaction-critical issues, is rather tame. Noting that historical reconstructions too often leave the available evidence far behind, and that 'the epistemic foundations of any claim to be able actually to recover the past' have been challenged,[190] he eventually comes to far-reaching conclusions, suggesting an 'increasing reliance on synchronic over diachronic analysis'[191] and calling for historical criticism generally to 'play a more modest role'.[192] His analysis of the methodological problems, not to mention the presuppositions, of redaction criticism could have been more penetrating, however.

Jones goes further in that respect, pointing not only to alternative explanations for verbal and literary relationships (see above), but suggesting also that 'contemporary redaction critics ... appear to be far less analytical regarding the literary unity of their reconstructed redactional layers than toward the literary unity of the text in its final form'.[193] Even more importantly, Jones criticizes that 'Steck, Bosshard, Weimar and others do not offer a range of probability, from very likely to less likely, for their suggested redactional stages' and that 'often, a subjective judgment about a text's redactional origins becomes an accepted fact upon which further judgments are made'.[194]

---

[187] See Jones, *Formation*, 19.

[188] See Steck, *Old Testament Exegesis*, 75–93; Fohrer, 'Überlieferungskritik', 139–50 (who at least cautions that the approach's reach should not be overestimated); and Kratz, 'Redaktionsgeschichte'. More balanced accounts have been offered by Barton, *Reading*, 45–60; 'Redaction Criticism', esp. 645; and Osborne, 'Redaction Criticism', esp. 213–18.

[189] Streete, 'Redaction Criticism', 116–17. His only other reservation is that redaction criticism has most often been applied only to the New Testament ('Redaction Criticism', 117). Not only is this not much of a criticism, it is also an extraordinary statement to make in a 1999 publication.

[190] Melugin, 'Prophetic Books', 64.

[191] Melugin, 'Prophetic Books', 70.

[192] Melugin, 'Prophetic Books', 78.

[193] Jones, *Formation*, 22.

[194] Jones, *Formation*, 23.

This is aggravated by the fact that subsequent generations of scholars all too often take the results produced and the presuppositions held by their predecessors for granted, thus adding to what is becoming an increasingly unstable stack of hypotheses and assumptions. Lohfink once put his finger on this problem, criticizing 'pandeuteronomistic tendencies' in Old Testament studies and complaining that 'a proper doctoral student today has to find a deuteronomistic hand somewhere in the Bible. Only then is he part of the guild.'[195] This, while surely not always the case, aptly illustrates what I have called a tendency of uncritical self-perpetuation.

Has the Handmaiden Overreached Herself ?

Melugin notes, using language that Barr would probably consider quintessentially postmodern,[196] that 'any proposed historical reconstruction is in no small degree the *historian's* story'.[197] Of course, statements like this can be, and in recent years often have been, used to promote an unashamedly subjective (or ideological) approach to historical issues, but this does not affect the basic truth of Melugin's statement. What redaction criticism does is to tell a story about the development of the prophetic books. And it does that by asking certain questions (and failing to ask others), by according importance to certain factors (but not to others), by deciding which 'facts' to connect with other 'facts' (and also which to ignore) and by assessing questions of probability and improbability from the vantage point of a certain world-view (or set of beliefs).[198]

To be sure, these decisions are not entirely arbitrary in that they conform to 'rules' shared by a certain interpretative community.[199] Yet, as Melugin notes, 'rules change as communities of interpretation evolve over time; future generations will undoubtedly consider our methods and conclusions quaint'.[200] Whether this will *undoubtedly* be the case remains to be seen, but Melugin's allusion to history's own historical relativity is helpful. As Howard notes, this relativity 'should raise a significant hesitation concerning the universality and long-term relevance of the modern historicist attitude'.[201] Furthermore, taking up Jarausch's claim that history, the former 'handmaiden of theology', has

---

[195] Lohfink, 'Deuteronomistische Bewegung', 316.

[196] See Barr, *History and Ideology, passim*.

[197] Melugin, 'Prophetic Books', 76 (emphasis original).

[198] I am paraphrasing Melugin, 'Prophetic Books', 76, applying his points to redaction criticism in particular. Melugin in turn refers to Fish, *Text*, 1–17 (esp. p. 13).

[199] This, of course, is again the language of Fish.

[200] Melugin, 'Prophetic Books', 76.

[201] Howard, *Religion*, 16.

become the 'dominant form of humanistic scholarship',[202] one might ask whether, in the redaction-critical penchant for complex diachronic solutions for perceived textual problems, the handmaiden has overreached herself.

However, before developing this notion, let me repeat that the redaction-critical approach is beset with a variety of problems, historical and otherwise. As we have seen, it is often marred by a literalism that is responsible for many perceived inconsistencies. These, in turn, are typically seen to demand diachronic solutions, just as 'significant intertextual clues', whose identification is often tenuous due to a lack of methodological rigour, are almost unilaterally explained by means of theories of redaction. I have also noted the problems surrounding the concept of *Fortschreibung*, the difficulty of identifying 'disappearing' and 'fecund' redactors and of assigning textual strata to specific historical settings. I have asked whether readers can be expected to interpret the books in full cognizance of their literary prehistories and how redaction-critical results relate to the books' canonical forms (including the prophetic superscriptions). And I have also suggested that redaction critics may have been too uncritical in inheriting source-critical findings and in perpetuating redaction-critical presuppositions.

Of course, Barr and Barton are right to stress the literary-critical dimension of biblical criticism, but problems encountered on the literary, textual level have, for some time, almost by default led to historical (or synchronic) solutions. So, has the handmaiden overreached herself? Has the historical consciousness taken on too dominant a role? This is an important question given McIntyre's argument that history is, or ought to be, only one of many fields in the discipline of theology. Starting with Harvey's observation that history comprises a great variety of fields (such as geography, genealogy, archaeology, etc.),[203] McIntyre argues

> that theology is also a field-encompassing field and that in fact the historical field is one of the fields which theology encompasses. It is the presence in the theological field of the non-historical fields, and the field-dependent criteria which they employ, which creates the problem for the theologian.[204]

Could it be, then, that historical considerations have assumed too important a role to the detriment of the other fields encompassed by theology or, as in our case, the study of the prophetic literature? All the talk of the 'collapse of history' notwithstanding, this is a question that redaction critics would do well to ponder. And, rather than multiplying redaction-critical studies, those engaged

---

[202] Jarausch, 'Institutionalization', 46–48.
[203] See Harvey, *Historian*.
[204] McIntyre, 'Historical Criticism', 378.

in the quest for the texts' literary prehistories could do worse than to rethink their presuppositions, aims and methodological procedures.

Bibliography

Albertz, R., 'Exile as Purification: Reconstructing the Book of the Four (Hosea, Amos, Micah, Zephaniah)', *SBLSP* 41 (2002), 213–33

Alter, R., 'Introduction to the Old Testament', in *The Literary Guide to the Bible* (ed. R. Alter and F. Kermode; London: Fontana Press, 1989), 11–35

Andersen, F.I., and D.N. Freedman, *Amos: A New Translation with Introduction and Commentary* (AB 24a; New York: Doubleday, 1989)

Avis, P., *God and the Creative Imagination: Metaphor, Symbol and Myth in Religion and Theology* (London: Routledge, 1999)

Barr, J., *History and Ideology in the Old Testament: Biblical Studies at the End of a Millennium* (Oxford: OUP, 2000)

Barton, J., 'Redaction Criticism: Old Testament', in *ABD* V (ed. D.N. Freedman, et al.; New York: Doubleday, 1992), 644–47

——, *Reading the Old Testament: Method in Biblical Study* (London: Darton, Longman & Todd, 2nd edn, 1996)

——, 'The Canonical Meaning of the Book of the Twelve', in *After the Exile: Essays in Honour of Rex Mason* (ed. J. Barton and D.J. Reimer; Macon, GA: Mercer University Press, 1996), 59–73

——, 'Historical-critical Approaches', in *The Cambridge Companion to Biblical Interpretation* (ed. J. Barton; Cambridge: CUP, 1998), 9–20

Ben Zvi, E., *A Historical-Critical Study of the Book of Zephaniah* (BZAW 198; Berlin: W. de Gruyter, 1991)

——, *A Historical-Critical Study of the Book of Obadiah* (BZAW 242; Berlin: W. de Gruyter, 1996)

——, 'Studying Prophetic Texts against Their Original Backgrounds: Pre-Ordained Scripts and Alternative Horizons of Research', in *Prophets and Paradigms: Essays in Honor of Gene M. Tucker* (ed. S.B. Reid; JSOTSup 229; Sheffield: Sheffield Academic Press, 1996), 125–35

——, 'Twelve Prophetic Books or "The Twelve": A Few Preliminary Considerations', in *Forming Prophetic Literature* (ed. J.W. Watts and P.R. House; JSOTSup 235; Sheffield: Sheffield Academic Press, 1996), 125–56

——, 'A Deuteronomistic Redaction in/among "The Twelve"? A Contribution from the Standpoint of the Books of Micah, Zephaniah, and Obadiah', *SBLSP* 36 (1997), 433–59

Bergler, S., 'Die hymnischen Passagen und die Mitte des Amosbuches: Ein Forschungsbericht' (unpublished dissertation; Tübingen, 1978)

Blenkinsopp, J., *A History of Prophecy in Israel* (Philadelphia: Westminster Press, 1983)

Bons, E., 'Das Denotat von כזביהם "ihre Lügen" im Judaspruch Am 2,4–5', *ZAW* 108 (1996), 201–13

Bosshard, E., 'Beobachtungen zum Zwölfprophetenbuch', *BN* 40 (1987), 30–62

Bosshard-Nepustil, E., *Rezeptionen von Jesaja 1–39 im Zwölfprophetenbuch* (OBO 154; Freiburg: Universitätsverlag, 1997)

———, and R.G. Kratz, 'Maleachi im Zwölfprophetenbuch', *BN* 52 (1990), 27–46

Bray, G., *Biblical Interpretation: Past and Present* (Downers Grove, IL: InterVarsity Press, 1996)

Budde, K., 'Eine folgenschwere Redaktion des Zwölfprophetenbuchs', *ZAW* 39 (1921), 218–29

———, 'Zu Text und Auslegung des Buches Amos', *JBL* 43 (1924), 46–131; and *JBL* 44 (1925), 63–122

Carroll, R.P., 'Arguing About Jeremiah: Recent Studies and the Nature of a Prophetic Book', in *Congress Volume, Leuven 1989* (ed. J.A. Emerton; VTSup 43; Leiden: E.J. Brill, 1991), 222–35

Carroll R., M.D., *Amos – The Prophet and His Oracles: Research on the Book of Amos* (Louisville, KY: Westminster / John Knox Press, 2002)

Childs, B.S., *Introduction to the Old Testament as Scripture* (Philadelphia: Fortress Press, 1979)

Clements, R.E., 'Patterns in the Prophetic Canon', in *Canon and Authority: Essays in Old Testament Religion and Theology* (ed. G.W. Coats and B.O. Long; Philadelphia: Fortress Press, 1977), 42–55

Coggins, R.J., 'The Minor Prophets – One Book or Twelve?', in *Crossing the Boundaries: Essays in Biblical Interpretation in Honour of Michael D. Goulder* (ed. S.E. Porter, P. Joyce and D.E. Orton; BIS 8; Leiden: E.J. Brill, 1994), 57–68

Collins, T., *The Mantle of Elijah: The Redaction Criticism of the Prophetical Books* (BibSem 20; Sheffield: JSOT Press, 1993)

Conrad, E.W., 'Forming the Twelve and Forming Canon', *SBLSP* 41 (2002), 234–47

Conroy, C., 'The Case of the Disappearing Redactor in Second Isaiah' (unpublished paper given at the Summer Meeting of The Society for Old Testament Study, Dublin 2002)

Coote, R.B., *Amos among the Prophets: Composition and Theology* (Philadelphia: Fortress Press, 1981)

Curtis, B.G., 'The Zion-Daughter Oracles: Evidence on the Identity and Ideology of the Late Redactors of the Book of the Twelve', in *Reading and Hearing the Book of the Twelve* (ed. J.D. Nogalski and M.A. Sweeney; SBLSS 15; Atlanta: SBL, 2000), 166–84

Darr, K.P., 'Literary Perspectives on Prophetic Literature', in *Old Testament Interpretation: Past, Present, and Future. Essays in Honour of Gene M. Tucker* (ed. J.L. Mays, D.L. Petersen, et al.; Edinburgh: T. & T. Clark, 1995), 127–43

Dobbs-Allsopp, F.W., 'Rethinking Historical Criticism', *BibInt* 7 (1999), 235–71

Driver, S.R., *The Books of Joel and Amos* ([1897] adapted and supplemented by H.C.O. Lanchester; Cambridge: CUP, 1915)

Duhm, B., *Die Theologie der Propheten als Grundlage für die innere Entwicklungs- geschichte der israelitischen Religion* (Bonn: Adolph Marcus, 1875)

——, *Die Zwölf Propheten in den Versmaßen der Urschrift übersetzt* (Die poetischen und prophetischen Bücher des Alten Testaments. Übersetzungen in den Versmaßen der Urschrift, 4; Tübingen: J.C.B. Mohr [Paul Siebeck], 1910)

——, *Anmerkungen zu den zwölf Propheten* (Giessen: Alfred Töpelmann, 1911)

——, *Israels Propheten* ([1916] Tübingen: J.C.B. Mohr [Paul Siebeck], 2nd edn, 1922)

Eagleton, T., *Literary Theory: An Introduction* (Oxford: Basil Blackwell, 2nd edn, 1996)

Everson, A.J., 'The Canonical Location of Habakkuk', *SBLSP* 41 (2002), 248–57

Ewald, H., *Die Propheten des alten Bundes, I: Jesaja mit den übrigen älteren Propheten* ([1840] Göttingen: Vandenhoeck & Ruprecht, 2nd edn, 1867)

Fey, R., *Amos und Jesaja: Abhängigkeit und Eigenständigkeit des Jesaja* (WMANT 12; Neukirchen-Vluyn: Neukirchener Verlag, 1963)

Fish, S., *Is There a Text in This Class? The Authority of Interpretive Communities* (Cambridge, MA: Harvard University Press, 1980)

Fohrer, G., 'Die Glossen im Buche Ezechiel', *ZAW* 63 (1951), 33–53

——, 'Überlieferungskritik, Kompositions- und Redaktionskritik, Zeit- und Verfasserfrage', in G. Fohrer, H.W. Hoffmann, et al., *Exegese des Alten Testaments: Einführung in die Methodik* (UTB 267; Heidelberg: Quelle & Meyer, 5th rev. edn, 1989), 119–50

Gordon, R.P., 'A Warranted Version of Historical Biblical Criticism?', Ch. 3 in the present volume

Gunn, D.M., and D.N. Fewell, *Narrative in the Hebrew Bible* (OBS; Oxford: OUP, 1993)

Harper, W.R., *A Critical and Exegetical Commentary on Amos and Hosea* (ICC; Edin- burgh: T. & T. Clark, 1905)

Harvey, V.A., *The Historian and the Believer: The Morality of Historical Knowledge and Christian Belief* (New York: Macmillan, 1966)

Hasel, G.F., *Understanding the Book of Amos: Basic Issues in Current Interpretations* (Grand Rapids: Baker Book House, 1991)

Hitzig, F., *Die zwölf kleinen Propheten* ([1838] Kurzgefasstes exegetisches Handbuch zum Alten Testament, 1; Leipzig: Weidmann, 2nd edn, 1852)

House, P.R., *The Unity of the Twelve* (JSOTSup 97; Sheffield: Almond Press, 1990)

——, 'Endings as New Beginnings: Returning to the Lord, the Day of the Lord, and Renewal in the Book of the Twelve', *SBLSP* 41 (2002), 258–84

Howard, T.A., *Religion and the Rise of Historicism: W.M.L. de Wette, Jacob Burckhardt, and the Theological Origins of Nineteenth-Century Historical Conscious- ness* (Cambridge: CUP, 2000)

Jarausch, K.H., 'The Institutionalization of History in 18th-Century Germany', in *Aufklärung und Geschichte: Studien zur deutschen Geschichtswissenschaft im 18. Jahrhundert* (ed. H.E. Bödeker, G. Iggers, et al.; Göttingen: Vandenhoeck & Ruprecht, 1986), 25–48

Jeremias, J., 'Amos 3–6: Beobachtungen zur Entstehungsgeschichte eines Prophetenbuches', *ZAW* 100, Sup. (1988), 123–38

——, 'Amos 3–6: From the Oral Word to the Text', in *Canon, Theology, and Old Testament Interpretation: Essays in Honor of Brevard S. Childs* (ed. G.M. Tucker, D.L. Peterson, et al.; Philadelphia: Fortress Press, 1988), 217–29

——, 'Völkersprüche und Visionsberichte im Amosbuch', in *Prophet und Prophetenbuch: Festschrift für Otto Kaiser zum 65. Geburtstag* (ed. V. Fritz, K.-F. Pohlmann, et al.; BZAW 185; Berlin: W. de Gruyter, 1989), 82–97

——, 'Tod und Leben in Amos 5,1–17', in *Der Weg zum Menschen: Zur philosophischen und theologischen Anthropologie. Für Alfons Deissler* (ed. R. Mosis and L. Ruppert; Freiburg: Herder, 1989), 134–52

——, 'Das unzugängliche Heiligtum: Zur letzten Vision des Amos (Am 9,1–4)', in *Konsequente Traditionsgeschichte: Festschrift für Klaus Baltzer zum 65. Geburtstag* (ed. R. Bartelmus, T. Krüger and H. Utzschneider; OBO 126; Freiburg: Universitätsverlag, 1993), 155–67

——, ' "Zwei Jahre vor dem Erdbeben" (Am 1,1)', in *Altes Testament – Forschung und Wirkung: Festschrift für Henning Graf Reventlow* (ed. P. Mommer and W. Thiel; Frankfurt: Peter Lang, 1994), 15–31

——, 'Die Anfänge des Dodekapropheton: Hosea und Amos', in *Congress Volume: Paris, 1992* (ed. J.A. Emerton; VTSup 61; Leiden: E.J. Brill, 1995), 87–106

——, 'The Interrelationship Between Amos and Hosea', in *Forming Prophetic Literature: Essays on Isaiah and the Twelve in Honor of John D.W. Watts* (ed. J.W. Watts and P.R. House; JSOTSup 235; Sheffield: Sheffield Academic Press, 1996), 171–86

——, 'Das Proprium der alttestamentlichen Prophetie', in J. Jeremias, *Hosea und Amos: Studien zu den Anfängen des Dodekapropheton* (FAT 13; Tübingen: J.C.B. Mohr [Paul Siebeck], 1996), 20–33

——, 'Zur Entstehung der Völkersprüche im Amosbuch', in J. Jeremias, *Hosea und Amos: Studien zu den Anfängen des Dodekapropheton* (FAT 13; Tübingen: J.C.B. Mohr [Paul Siebeck], 1996), 172–82

——, 'Die Mitte des Amosbuches (Am 4,4–13; 5,1–17)', in J. Jeremias, *Hosea und Amos: Studien zu den Anfängen des Dodekapropheton* (FAT 13; Tübingen: J.C.B. Mohr [Paul Siebeck], 1996), 198–213

——, 'Rezeptionsprozesse in der prophetischen Überlieferung am Beispiel der Visionsberichte des Amos', in *Rezeption und Auslegung im Alten Testament und in seinem Umfeld: Ein Symposion aus Anlass des 60. Geburtstags von Odil Hannes Steck* (ed. R.G. Kratz and T. Krüger; OBO 153; Freiburg: Universitätsverlag, 1997), 29–44

——, *The Book of Amos* (trans. D.W. Stott; OTL; Louisville, KY: Westminster/ John Knox Press, 1998 [trans. of *Der Prophet Amos* (ATD 24.2; Göttingen: Vandenhoeck & Ruprecht, 1995)])

——, 'Prophetenwort und Prophetenbuch: Zur Rekonstruktion mündlicher Verkündigung der Propheten', in *Jahrbuch für Biblische Theologie*, XIV: *Prophetie und Charisma* (ed. E. Dassmann, W.H. Schmidt, et al.; Neukirchen-Vluyn: Neukirchener Verlag, 1999), 19–35

Jones, B.A., *The Formation of the Book of the Twelve: A Study in Text and Canon* (SBLDS 149; Atlanta: Scholars Press, 1995)

Keil, C.F., *The Minor Prophets* (trans. J. Martin; Commentary on the Old Testament 10; orig. publ. as *The Twelve Minor Prophets*, 2 vols.; Biblical Commentary on the Old Testament; Edinburgh: T. & T. Clark, 1878 [trans. of *Biblischer Commentar über die zwölf kleinen Propheten* (Biblischer Commentar über das Alte Testament 3.4; Leipzig: Dörffling und Franke, 1866)]; repr., Peabody, MA: Hendrickson, 1996)

Koch, K., *Was ist Formgeschichte? Methoden der Bibelexegese* (Neukirchen-Vluyn: Neukirchener Verlag, 3rd edn, 1974)

Kratz, R.G., *Kyros im Deuterojesaja-Buch: Redaktionsgeschichtliche Untersuchungen zu Entstehung und Theologie von Jes 40–55* (FAT 1; Tübingen: J.C.B. Mohr [Paul Siebeck], 1991)

——, 'Die Redaktion der Prophetenbücher', in *Rezeption und Auslegung im Alten Testament und in seinem Umfeld: Ein Symposion aus Anlass des 60. Geburtstags von Odil Hannes Steck* (ed. R.G. Kratz and T. Krüger; OBO 153; Freiburg: Universitätsverlag, 1997), 9–27

——, 'Redaktionsgeschichte/Redaktionskritik', *TRE* 28 (ed. G. Müller, et al.; Berlin: W. de Gruyter, 1997), 367–78

Kraus, H.-J., *Geschichte der historisch-kritischen Erforschung des Alten Testaments* (Neukirchen-Vluyn: Neukirchener Verlag, 4th edn, 1988)

Lee, A.Y., 'The Canonical Unity of the Scroll of the Minor Prophets' (unpublished PhD thesis, Baylor University, 1985)

Lodge, D., *The Art of Fiction Illustrated from Classic and Modern Texts* (London: Penguin Books, 1992)

Lohfink, N., 'Gab es eine deuteronomistische Bewegung?', in *Jeremia und die 'deuteronomistische Bewegung'* (ed. W. Gross; BBB 98; Weinheim: Beltz Athenäum, 1995), 313–82

Lust, J., 'Remarks on the Redaction of Amos V 4–6, 14–15', in *Remembering All the Way: A Collection of Old Testament Studies Published on the Occasion of the Fortieth Anniversary of the Oudtestamentisch Werkgezelschap in Nederland* (ed. B. Albrektson, et al.; OTS 21; Leiden: E.J. Brill, 1981), 129–54

Mannheim, K., *Essays on the Sociology of Knowledge* (ed. P. Kecskemeti; New York: OUP, 1952)

Marks, H., 'The Twelve Prophets', in *The Literary Guide to the Bible* (ed. R. Alter and F. Kermode; London: Fontana Press, 1987), 207–33

Marti, K., *Das Dodekapropheton* (KHAT 13; Tübingen: J.C.B. Mohr [Paul Siebeck], 1904)

Marxsen, W., *Der Evangelist Markus: Studien zur Redaktionsgeschichte des Evangeliums* (FRLANT 67; Göttingen: Vandenhoeck & Ruprecht, 1956)

McIntyre, J., 'Historical Criticism in a "History-Centred Value-System" ', in *Language, Theology and the Bible: Essays in Honour of James Barr* (ed. S.E. Balentine and J. Barton; Oxford: Clarendon Press, 1994), 370–84

Melugin, R.F., 'Prophetic Books and the Problem of Historical Reconstruction', in *Prophets and Paradigms: Essays in Honor of Gene M. Tucker* (ed. S.B. Reid; JSOTSup 229; Sheffield: Sheffield Academic Press, 1996), 63–78

——, 'Amos in Recent Research', *CRBS* 6 (1998), 65–101

Möller, K., 'Rehabilitation eines Propheten: Die Botschaft des Amos aus rhetorischer Perspektive unter besonderer Berücksichtigung von Am. 9,7–15', *EuroJTh* 6 (1997), 41–55

——, 'Review of *Die Entstehung des Zwölfprophetenbuchs: Neubearbeitungen von Amos im Rahmen schriftenübergreifender Redaktionsprozesse*, by A. Schart', *JETh* 13 (1999), 105–108

——, 'Renewing Historical Criticism', in *Renewing Biblical Interpretation* (ed. C. Bartholomew, C. Greene and K. Möller; SHS 1; Carlisle: Paternoster Press; Grand Rapids: Zondervan, 2000), 145–71

——, 'Words of (In-)evitable Certitude? Reflections on the Interpretation of Prophetic Oracles of Judgement', in *After Pentecost: Language and Biblical Interpretation* (ed. C. Bartholomew, C. Greene and K. Möller; SHS 2; Carlisle: Paternoster Press; Grand Rapids: Zondervan, 2001), 352–86

——, *A Prophet in Debate: The Rhetoric of Persuasion in the Book of Amos* (JSOTSup 372; London: Sheffield Academic Press, 2003)

Nagel, T., *The View from Nowhere* (New York: OUP, 1986)

Nogalski, J.D., *Literary Precursors to the Book of the Twelve* (BZAW 217; Berlin: W. de Gruyter, 1993)

——, *Redactional Processes in the Book of the Twelve* (BZAW 218; Berlin: W. de Gruyter, 1993)

——, and M.A. Sweeney (eds.), *Reading and Hearing the Book of the Twelve* (SBLSS 15; Atlanta: SBL, 2000)

Nowack, W., *Die kleinen Propheten übersetzt und erklärt* ([1897] HKAT 3.4; Göttingen: Vandenhoeck & Ruprecht, 2nd edn, 1903)

Osborne, G.R., 'Redaction Criticism', in *New Testament Criticism and Interpretation: Essays on Methods and Issues* (ed. D.A. Black and D.S. Dockery; Grand Rapids: Zondervan, 1991), 199–224

Perdue, L.G., *The Collapse of History: Reconstructing Old Testament Theology* (OBT; Minneapolis: Fortress Press, 1994)

Perrin, N., *What is Redaction Criticism?* (GBS; Philadelphia: Fortress Press, 1970)

Redditt, P.L., 'The Formation of the Book of the Twelve: A Review of Research', *SBLSP* 40 (2001), 58–80

——, 'Recent Research on the Book of the Twelve as One Book', *CRBS* 9 (2001), 47–80

Rendtorff, R., 'Between Historical Criticism and Holistic Interpretation: New Trends in Old Testament Exegesis', in R. Rendtorff, *Canon and Theology* (trans. and ed. M. Kohl; Edinburgh: T. & T. Clark, 1994), 25–30

——, 'Old Testament Theology: Some Ideas for a New Approach', in R. Rendtorff, *Canon and Theology* (trans. and ed. M. Kohl; Edinburgh: T. & T. Clark, 1994), 1–16

Rofé, A., *Introduction to the Prophetic Literature* (trans. J.H. Seeligmann; BibSem 21; Sheffield: Sheffield Academic Press, 1997 [trans. of *mabo' l'siprut hann'bu'ah* (Jerusalem: Academon, 1992)])

Rottzoll, D.U., *Studien zur Redaktion und Komposition des Amosbuchs* (BZAW 243; Berlin: W. de Gruyter, 1996)

Rudolph, W., *Joel, Amos, Obadja, Jona* (KAT 13.2; Gütersloh: Gütersloher Verlagshaus, 1971)

——, *Haggai, Sacharja 1–8, Sacharja 9–14, Maleachi* (KAT 13.4; Gütersloh: Gütersloher Verlagshaus, 1976)

Schart, A., *Die Entstehung des Zwölfprophetenbuchs: Neubearbeitungen von Amos im Rahmen schriftenübergreifender Redaktionsprozesse* (BZAW 260; Berlin: W. de Gruyter, 1998)

——, 'Reconstructing the Redaction History of the Twelve Prophets: Problems and Models', in *Reading and Hearing the Book of the Twelve* (ed. J.D. Nogalski and M.A. Sweeney; SBLSS 15; Atlanta: SBL, 2000), 34–48

Schmidt, W.H., 'Die deuteronomistische Redaktion des Amosbuches: Zu den theologischen Unterschieden zwischen dem Prophetenwort und seinem Sammler', *ZAW* 77 (1965), 168–93

Schneider, D.A., 'The Unity of the Book of the Twelve' (unpublished PhD thesis, Yale University, 1979)

Schultz, R.L., *The Search for Quotation: Verbal Parallels in the Prophets* (JSOTSup 180; Sheffield: Sheffield Academic Press, 1999)

——, 'The Ties that Bind: Intertextuality, the Identification of Verbal Parallels, and Reading Strategies in the Book of the Twelve', *SBLSP* 40 (2001), 39–57

Seitz, C.R., *Word without End: The Old Testament as Abiding Theological Witness* (Grand Rapids: Eerdmans, 1998)

Sellin, E., *Das Zwölfprophetenbuch übersetzt und erklärt*, I: *Hosea–Micha* ([1922] KAT 12; Leipzig: Deichert, 2nd and 3rd edn, 1929)

Smend, R., 'Das Nein des Amos', *EvT* 23 (1963), 404–23

——, *Deutsche Alttestamentler in drei Jahrhunderten* (Göttingen: Vandenhoeck & Ruprecht, 1989)

Smith, G.A., *The Book of the Twelve Prophets Commonly Called the Minor*, I: *Amos, Hosea and Micah. With an Introduction and a Sketch of Prophecy in Early Israel* ([1896] The Expositor's Bible; London: Hodder & Stoughton, 13th edn, 1908)

Steck, O.H., *Der Abschluß der Prophetie im Alten Testament: Ein Versuch zur Frage der Vorgeschichte des Kanons* (Biblisch-theologische Studien 17; Neukirchen-Vluyn: Neukirchener Verlag, 1991)

——, *Old Testament Exegesis: A Guide to the Methodology* (trans. J.D. Nogalski; SBLRBS 39; Atlanta: Scholars Press, 2nd edn, 1998 [trans. of *Exegese des Alten Testaments: Leitfaden der Methodik. Ein Arbeitsbuch für Proseminare, Seminare und Vorlesungen* (Neukirchen-Vluyn: Neukirchener Verlag, 13th edn, 1993)])

——, *The Prophetic Books and Their Theological Witness* (trans. J.D. Nogalski; St. Louis, MO: Chalice Press, 2000 [trans. of *Die Prophetenbücher und ihr theologisches Zeugnis: Wege der Nachfrage und Fährten zur Antwort* (Tübingen: J.C.B. Mohr [Paul Siebeck], 1996)])

Sternberg, M., *The Poetics of Biblical Narrative: Ideological Literature and the Drama of Reading* (Bloomington: Indiana University Press, 1987)

Steuernagel, C., *Lehrbuch der Einleitung in das Alte Testament* (Tübingen: J.C.B. Mohr, 1912)

Streete, G.P.C., 'Redaction Criticism', in *To Each Its Own Meaning: An Introduction to Biblical Criticisms and Their Application* (ed. S.L. McKenzie and S.R. Haynes; Louisville, KY: Westminster / John Knox Press, rev. and expanded edn, 1999), 105–21

Sweeney, M.A., *The Twelve Prophets* (Berit Olam; 2 vols.; Collegeville, MN: Michael Glazier, 2000)

Thiselton, A.C., *Interpreting God and the Postmodern Self: On Meaning, Manipulation and Promise* (Edinburgh: T. & T. Clark, 1995)

Van Leeuwen, R.C., 'Scribal Wisdom and Theodicy in the Book of the Twelve', in *In Search of Wisdom: Essays in Memory of John G. Gammie* (ed. L.G. Perdue, B.B. Scott and W.J. Wiseman; Louisville, KY: Westminster / John Knox Press, 1993), 31–49

Waard, J. de, 'The Chiastic Structure of Amos v 1–17', *VT* 27 (1977), 170–77

Watts, J.W., and P.R. House (eds.), *Forming Prophetic Literature: Essays on Isaiah and the Twelve in Honor of John D.W. Watts* (JSOTSup 235; Sheffield: Sheffield Academic Press, 1996)

Weimar, P., 'Obadja: Eine redaktionskritische Analyse', *BN* 27 (1985), 35–99

Wellhausen, J., *Die kleinen Propheten übersetzt und erklärt* ([1892] Berlin: W. de Gruyter, 4th edn, 1963)

Williamson, H.G.M., 'Hope under Judgement: The Prophets of the Eighth Century BCE', *EvQ* 72 (2000), 291–306

Willi-Plein, I., *Vorformen der Schriftexegese innerhalb des Alten Testaments: Untersuchungen zum literarischen Werden der auf Amos, Hosea und Micha zurückgehenden Bücher im hebräischen Zwölfprophetenbuch* (BZAW 123; Berlin: W. de Gruyter, 1971)

Wimsatt, W.K., and M.C. Beardsley, 'The Intentional Fallacy', *Sewanee Review* 54 (1946), 468–88

Wolfe, R.E., 'The Editing of the Book of the Twelve', *ZAW* 53 (1935), 90–129

——, *Meet Amos and Hosea, the Prophets of Israel* (New York: Harper & Brothers, 1945)

Wolff, H.W., *Joel and Amos: A Commentary on the Books of the Prophets Joel and Amos* (trans. W. Janzen, S.D. McBride, Jr. and C.A. Muenchow; Hermeneia; Philadelphia: Fortress Press, 1977 [trans. of *Dodekapropheten*, II: *Joel und Amos* (BKAT 14.2; Neukirchen-Vluyn: Neukirchener Verlag, 1969)])

Wolters, A., 'Review of *Literary Precursors to the Book of the Twelve*, by J.D. Nogalski', *BO* 53 (1996), 493–96

Zapff, B.M., *Redaktionsgeschichtliche Studien zum Michabuch im Kontext des Dodekapropheton* (BZAW 256; Berlin: W. de Gruyter, 1997)

——, 'The Perspective of the Nations in the Book of Micah as a "Systematization" of the Nations' Role in Joel, Jonah, and Nahum? Reflections on a Context-Oriented Exegesis in the Book of the Twelve', *SBLSP* 38 (1999), 598–605

Zimmerli, W., *Ezechiel* (BKAT 13; 2 vols.; Neukirchen-Vluyn: Neukirchener Verlag, 2nd edn, 1979)

18

What Lesson Will History Teach?

The Book of the Twelve as History

Christopher R. Seitz

The appeal to the significance of the canon for Biblical Theology is not to defend an ecclesiastical harmonization of scripture into a monolithic block, but rather to retain the full range of prophetic and apostolic witnesses, *even when large areas of the biblical text appear to lie dormant for the moment in anticipation of some unexpected new and surprisingly fresh role for a future moment.*[1]

Context

Appropriate to our topic, let me begin on a historical note. Twenty years ago, I started researching a specific historical problem. What happened on the date 597/596 – a date we can only assign retrospectively, and inexactly, with reference to another set of historical events, and then gloss with BC or BCE?

The facts are reasonably clear. The Babylonians overran Jerusalem, exiled her young king, deported a large number of her citizens, including the prophet Ezekiel, placed their own king (Jehoiachin's uncle Zedekiah) in charge, and essentially brought an end to her nationhood.

For at least a decade prior to this, the prophet Jeremiah had announced that the God of Israel had lost patience with his people, due to their apostasy, and would therefore be the agent of their judgement, executed at the hands of the Babylonians. Prophets before Jeremiah had announced this judgement, and God's patience was finally tested beyond the limit. He would come as judge.

---

[1] Childs, *Biblical Theology*, 522–23 (emphasis mine).

These facts of historical reference and prophetic word are reasonably clear. They are not under dispute. But what have we got when we call this history? For we are still left with the question of how to assign significance to these events and these words in the context of God's providence. How do these historical events fit into a larger history of God's ways with his people?

For one prophetic figure of the day, the events marked the true judgement of God and the final judgement of God. God had come as judge in the events of 597, had exiled a people in his wrath and had brought Jerusalem and Judah under a punishing display of submission. Now it was time to break the yoke, for those in the land, and return to a state of peace and calm (Jer. 28:10–11).

For another prophet, judgement was a true state of affairs, but it was as true of the citizens in Judah as of the exiled Israel, and therefore the judgement of God had yet to be finalized. There was persistent apostasy in Jerusalem, even after 597, and the prophet saw it and condemned it and announced that the God of Israel was effectively exiling himself and withdrawing into a punishing absence of glory (Ezek. 11:22–25).

For another prophet, the prophet Jeremiah in Jerusalem, the situation was closer and more personal – and yet proximity to the historical events did not lessen the need for historical assessment and interpretation; it heightened the burden upon him. He stood face to face with the first prophet mentioned above, the prophet Hananiah, and he was confronted with the twin burden of assessing his word and office and offering his own endangering, truthful word. We cannot know whether Jeremiah was familiar in any direct sense with the second prophet's (Ezekiel's) word. We do know that he wrote a letter to the exiles in Babylon and did not, like Hananiah, set his eyes on the people of Judah as a kind of 'good figs' over against 'bad figs' (to use the image later adopted by the prophet; Jer. 24:1–10). Indeed, according to Jeremiah 24, the exiles were those who could expect, as a consequence of receiving God's judgement, favourable assessment; they were the 'good figs'. And Jeremiah accepted the yoke of wood for a season, but then he called for a yoke of iron, stating in no uncertain terms to Hananiah that the period of submission to Babylon was not over, but would continue (Jer. 28:12–15).

What I tried to show in my research was the (somewhat messy and erratic) way the Jeremiah traditions passed on to us found their way to a coherent (if rough-edged) historical portrayal of what happened between 597 and the fall of Jerusalem in 587, and thereafter.[2] It would take time before one could speak of what was happening in an organic and integrated way. Even as Ezekiel and Jeremiah offered distinctive geographical, temporal and tradition-historical perspectives, in the end they were prophets speaking a consistent word and

---

[2] Seitz, *Theology.*

offering complementary portrayals of what happened historically in the last years of Judah's existence.

So it is indeed meaningful to speak of history as something out in front of us as well as something behind us, capable of being given words and a narrative description. History writing is reporting past events, to be sure – but from a perspective the future alone can grant. This is especially true of Israel's history, which over time sought an organic comprehensiveness that could not be gained until the future had given a proper sense of organization and sequence. As a question posed to the future, 'What lesson will history teach?' is a fully rational way to describe something of the burden of waiting and humbly standing before God's judgements in time, in order to say what they mean as historical facts. In the end, 'when all was said and done', the disaster of 597 was not the judgement of God but a type or figure of it, one which anticipated a later type in the Babylonian defeat of 587/6 – full-orbed though it decidedly was for a people who lived at the time and who indeed found themselves exiled away to Babylon.

The final form of Jeremiah, with its array of traditions on this matter, presented in the end a coherent historical word about 'what really happened' in the events of 597 and 587/6.

Gerhard von Rad

I was recently asked to evaluate the contribution of Gerhard von Rad for an event in Heidelberg honouring the hundredth anniversary of his work. The following brief reference to that essay explains the historical context in which my present reflections have occurred.[3] What follows focuses solely on the matter of history in von Rad's tradition-historical method.

Von Rad was able to move beyond a nineteenth-century concern with factuality and diachronic reference (especially focused on an original author and secondary tradents, usually regarded as successive waves of distortion) by granting a positive theological value to the entire history of tradition. The original historical event, shorn of interpretation, was a deeply ambiguous thing. In a brilliant turn of phrase, said to be aimed at W.F. Albright, von Rad said he (Albright) and his school had been seeking to penetrate to a place that was 'theologically speechless'. Gilkey made something of the same criticism of 'Mighty Acts of God' imaginatively given concrete historical dress by the so-called Biblical Theology Movement.[4]

---

[3] Seitz, 'Prophecy'.
[4] Gilkey, 'Cosmology'.

But did von Rad go far enough in giving room for a theologically rich tradition-history, even one that reached into and included New Testament credenda?

My view, which I had begun to develop in other places, was that von Rad saw the potential in crediting the final form of the text with a certain sort of historical reporting, but then he worried about it. In his latest work, the commentary on Genesis, the high value he placed on the Yahwist is evident.[5] What a brilliant treatment he gave us! The Yahwist emerges as something like the inventor of history writing. Still, we learn as well of the enormous theological insight of the Priestly writer, even though von Rad never gives him the same sort of 'historical' high praise.

But to assert that von Rad, given his dynamic view of tradition-history, regarded the Priestly writer as producing something avowedly non-historical, would be to say too much. Once the clutch on the mechanism of tradition-history is released, new insights emerge through subsequent reflection on the original credenda, and these retain positive interpretative value for von Rad. Indeed they are the ways by which von Rad sees positive theological and historical linkage from one covenantal witness to a second, culminating one.[6]

What I endeavoured to discover in research for this recent essay was the precise reason for the uneasiness von Rad reported when it came to an assessment of the final form of the text. What prevented von Rad from taking, not just the Yahwist or the Priestly writer or any other tradent as essential to Israel's witness to YHWH, but also the combination of them in the final form of the text? I pointed to two examples in his introduction to Genesis where von Rad saw quite clearly that it was in *the combination of the sources* that real theological interpretation of history came into sharpest profile.[7] I therefore needed to find the reasons for von Rad's hesitancy in letting his commentary focus here. And von Rad obliged.

Oddly, to my mind, he credited an interest in this dimension of Old Testament theological history to an alien, non-Christian, stance. According to von Rad it is Christ who provides 'collation' of the witness, or an explicit key to its significance theologically understood, as this is received from Israel in the church. It was the insight of Rosenzweig that brought to von Rad's attention a focus on the witness itself as collated, as historically and theologically formed into just that witness and none other. The final form of the text had a specific theological voice. Rosenzweig called the 'redactor' (R) of the sources and traditions 'our teacher' (R for 'Rabbenu'), since 'we receive the rich

---

[5] The English-language version is *Genesis: A Commentary*.
[6] See Seitz, 'Historical-Critical Endeavor'.
[7] Von Rad, *Genesis*, 42.

diachronic legacy at all only from his hand' (my paraphrase).[8] And that von Rad took Rosenzweig in Childs's sense of final form, and not that of tradition-history, is evident in the way he spoke specifically about the combination of the sources producing a different, final, privileged theological presentation of Israel's prior witness. The final form is 'the lesson that history teaches us', when 'it has had its say' and 'when all is said and done'. We only know the extent of the fall for the Yahwist when we hear the 'very good' of P's creation account.[9] So it was my conclusion that von Rad was wrong when he stopped short of crediting theological significance to the final form of the text. Rosenzweig's concern was not in conflict with von Rad's 'christological' appeal and indeed could be meaningfully coordinated with it. The final form of Genesis was its own special kind of 'history writing'.[10]

The Twelve

In what follows I apply this general heuristic notion – that is, involving the possible integrity of the final form of the presentation as a piece of history writing – to a specific instance of interpretation: the prophets. I can only do this in a suggestive way, given the constraints of our format; to establish the thesis in detail would require an in-depth investigation of the redaction history of the Book of the Twelve.[11] A certain sort of historical sense has demanded, for more than 150 years now, that we establish the proper chronological sequentiality of the prophets in order to do justice to their teaching and ongoing witness (and not only their sequentiality as individual books, but also in respect of parts and

---

[8] Von Rad states, 'Franz Rosenzweig once remarked wittily that the sign "R" (for the redactor of the Hexateuch documents, so lowly esteemed in our Protestant research) should be interpreted as Rabbenu, "our master", because basically we are dependent only on him, on his great work of compilation and his theology, and we receive the Hexateuch at all only from his hands' (*Genesis*, 42).

[9] Von Rad, *Genesis*, 42.

[10] 'If God is thought of as revealing himself to his people in increasing measure over time, in the course of a teleological process of salvation worked out within history, then there is a prima facie case for privileging the witness of the later communities who were witnesses to the greatest extent of that revelation. ... A reading of the Old Testament which assumes this view of revelation will naturally give theological privilege to the later compilers of the final form of the canonical texts. *It is their historical location*, rather than some special moral quality of trustworthiness which they supposedly lacked, that gives their text theological priority' (Ward, *Word*, 249; emphasis mine).

[11] For a good recent survey of the issues affecting reading the Book of the Twelve as a unity, see Nogalski and Sweeney (eds.), *Reading and Hearing*.

sub-parts of books and later editorializing and so forth). It is important that we keep in mind that, whatever theological justification for this procedure once existed, it is now the case that the primary justification is that to do otherwise would not be 'historical'.

No one will contest that, in terms of simple intelligibility, the prophets' message and the form of that message will be misunderstood without a sense of historical referentiality. No one will contest that the material itself assumes knowledge on the part of readers of events and figures to which it refers (e.g., Babylon, wilderness, the fall of Samaria, the year that King Uzziah died, Edom, Tyre, Rechabites, the former prophets, Zedekiah, Cyrus, Sennacherib, Nisroch, etc. – these historical details need explanation).

But what has counted for history, generally speaking, is an etic description[12] of how these various referential indicators cohere in a universe of sequentiality and cross reference and tradition-history, the construction of which is the task – the true theological task as well as the historical challenge – of biblical interpretation for our day. Almost without considering it, or indeed in an effort to correct and displace it, the material form of the witness recedes in importance as the quest for historical reference or religion or tradition history or an interpreter's presentation of 'the intentions of Isaiah or Jesus or redactor X' become the critical projects of academic biblical interpretation.

What I try to show below is that a balancing act is now required. The interpreter must indeed do justice to historical reference and must inquire about the individual prophetic witnesses of the Twelve, their possible historical sequence, their reporting of historical events, and so forth. At the same time, building on the work of Jeremias[13] and others, it is clear that a larger historical project must also be respected in the Twelve. It appears that the earliest tradents were themselves concerned, not with individual historical prophets and their message in this or that period, but with the correlation of these prophets and these messages, in the name of a large-scale account of YHWH's dispensation of history, under his providential care and sovereignty. Already in Amos and Hosea, the concern of the prophet's tradents or pupils is with relating the work of these two very different prophets (see the discussion of Jeremias, below).

---

[12] 'Etic' and 'emic' are anthropological terms, widely used in critical analysis. The first is sometimes called 'talk about natives' as opposed to 'native talk'. An etic description of Israel's history judges the self-presentation of Israel's literary witness to be confused, neutral, biased, in need of sorting out according to a theory of development, and so forth. Classically, histories of Israel have judged the literary presentation as either reliable but in need of a properly described chronology, or as unreliable and incapable of use for wide-scale historiographic purposes. Either judgement is largely an etic judgement.

[13] Jeremias, 'Interrelationship', 171–86.

Whatever else may be said of the success of this approach, it is clear that its historical assumptions are quite different from what has held sway. Tradition-history saw relatedness as something the interpreter would have to construct and supply by means of an external scaffolding: namely, the way these (twelve) individual prophets (as well as the Three, or 'major prophets', further broken down in the case of Isaiah) used traditions available to them all, in response to historical events unfolding before them, and on occasion (though actually quite rarely) with explicit reference to one another (e.g., Jeremiah mentioning Micah; Jer. 26:18). This construction project worked completely oblivious to the final material arrangement of the Twelve and the Three, as itself a potential framework within which to comprehend a 'history' stretching from Hosea's message of election and grace in the days of the early Assyrian period right down to the eschatological finale of Malachi. The older method was content to date, on internal and external grounds, books like Jonah and Obadiah and Joel quite late in Israel's religious history. But it never inquired whether these books were situated where they were so as to offer a mature, seasoned perspective on Israel's history that only time could teach, and that the earlier witnesses could only adumbrate – an achievement that is by no means called into question but rather endorsed and seconded in the final arrangement of the Twelve.

Apart from the specific details of the presentation of the Book of the Twelve to follow, I am interested more generally in what view of history and historiography we have been working with in recent biblical interpretation. Specifically, I have a question about whether the material form of the canon has often been ignored as a broker of history. I raised a very modest question about this in *Figured Out* in respect of John and the fourfold gospel witness.[14] I am persuaded that similar sorts of questions reside within the composition of the Twelve. My modest plea is that, for purposes of introduction and interpretation, we do not simply assume that inherited views of sequentiality (and this includes the thorny problem of Q) control the field, in the name of 'history'.

I think we can all credit historical-critical method for much hard work in constructing a plausible, if tortuously complicated, grid of development and progression when it comes to the biblical witness – whether from Amos to Jonah or from Paul's earliest letters and Q to John. Can we now return to the final form of the witness and see if an interpretation of that history is being offered as well, one that should at least be included in our introductions and interpretations? My own view is that such a move is mandated, because of the canonical process itself.[15] But even where disagreement over this issue exists,

---

[14] Seitz, *Figured Out*. Other studies on the final form of the gospel witness have been done by B.S. Childs, R. Bauckham and D. Trobisch. See Bauckham (ed.), *Gospels*, and Trobisch, *First Edition*.

[15] On this see note 10, above.

there ought to at least be an openness to considering whether more thinly referential views of history have not driven out a perspective the canon seeks to describe as well. Whether this involves the 'intrusion' of Joel between Hosea and Amos or John between Luke and Acts, can our view of 'history' learn anything of importance from the material form of the presentation?[16]

Transition

I began with a quote from Childs about the way each generation must learn again to heed aspects of the canon's full presentation that have dropped out, given this or that blindness, preference, abiding concern or amnesia. There may be a kindred concern in the canonical process itself, wherein earlier prophetic words require the march of time to display their full authority under God's inspiring and providential governance.

In his prefatory remarks for Volume 1 of this series, Childs spoke of the hope that the Scripture and Hermeneutics Seminar would not become adrift in methodological struggles over the philosophy of language.[17] I suspect the same concern applies to a preoccupation with historiography and biblical interpretation. In what follows, therefore, I try to remain engaged with biblical texts (if only in an introductory way) and let that engagement generate methodological reflection.

Childs made another observation in that foreword which his critics often miss. Childs saw much positive contribution in the rise of historical criticism.

---

[16] I would be inclined to put Schart's diachronic work on the Twelve, which K. Möller discusses in Vol. 1 of this series ('Renewing'), under the constraints here commended, and in that sense his view of historical-critical analysis as 'preface' and mine are actually not too far apart (see esp. Schart, 'Reconstructing'; his indebtedness to Jeremias is quite clear there). Moreover, when I spoke of 'spotting repugnance' as analogous to historical criticism, it was in the strict context of the language of the Thirty-nine Articles. I was trading on a certain conceptuality I believed the authors had in mind there. In a development of that conceptuality at a later period, historical analysis seeks to locate difference (contradiction or 'repugnance') and then develop a history-of-religions or tradition-history grid that ultimately absorbs the material form of the witness. Apart from that context, I would not use the language of 'repugnance', but I would press further to discover what conceptuality was at work in historical-critical labour. In this essay I am setting forth a different conceptuality, built on the general historiographic assumptions inherited from the historical-critical method, and moving beyond them in a way I believe von Rad saw, but hesitated to follow. Newer studies in the unity of the Twelve have pressed ahead.

[17] Childs, 'Foreword', xv–xvii.

He regarded debates that degenerated into inerrancy squabbles or preoccupation with dogmatic frameworks and propositions as unfortunate – every bit as unfortunate as present methodology debates which simply never get around to reading texts closely. The beauty of the historical-critical method was that it opened up the text in an imaginative way and read the text with care and close attention. Childs saw this in nineteenth-century biblical studies, and he regarded it as the recovery or discovery of some essential element in the canon's witness.

My plea here for a different model of history and historiographical concern is not a repudiation of 150 years of work in academic contexts, but a request that we examine texts mindful that other views of history and reading have animated previous generations of Jewish and Christian readers. While we value historical approaches, might we do well to let a past before the rise of the historical-critical method also teach us a lesson about how to read? I confess I learn quite a lot about history hearing Diodore and Theodore spar with the school of Alexandria over literal sense, history, *theoria, allegoria* and the material form of the witness. I am not interested in imitating their methods or their debates. But the sorts of problems that beset biblical interpretation in our crisis period are not resolvable with reference only to Ricœur, Kant, Gadamer and other leading figures in the history of ideas from our most recent period of hermeneutical *Auseinandersetzung*. Debates from a prior period most frequently emerge over a specific exegetical problem (one thinks immediately of Prov. 8:22–23 in the writings of Athanasius). The exegesis urges and gives rise to the discussion of method. Multiple examples from Origen and others would confirm this.[18]

So the problem is this: how do we read the prophetic collection of the Twelve? From the context of this practical problem a whole range of hermeneutical and historiographical issues follow.

How to Introduce the Prophets?

The standard modern procedure for interpreting the prophets is familiar.[19] On the basis of a close reading of the material, with attention to the ancient Near Eastern context, the prophets are lined up in historical order. Amos is operating in the early eighth century and Hosea a bit later. We then move to those parts of Isaiah from a slightly later period, then to Micah and Zephaniah and Jeremiah. The rise and fall of the northern and southern kingdoms, through the

---

[18] See the insightful essay by M. Ludlow, 'Theology and Allegory'.

[19] For one example among many, see Blenkinsopp, *History*. Theologically 'conservative' and 'liberal' interpreters both adopt this approach.

Assyrian, neo-Babylonian and Persian periods, is the backdrop against which the prophets' message, as this can be extracted from the canonical books, comes to expression. Of course the linkages are imperfect, because Israel's prophets do not simply pick up where the last one left off. We only know about their relationship to one another on the basis of scholarly speculation. Indeed, there is surprisingly little information in the plain sense record of Kings, Chronicles and the prophets themselves where the prophets – in the manner of something like Elijah and Elisha – are shown in explicit connection to one another. We know more about Jeremiah and Hananiah than Jeremiah and a supposed contemporary Zephaniah or Habakkuk. Indeed, this distinguishing characteristic – the isolation of the prophetic office – has been given theological significance, alongside efforts to spot tradition-historical affiliations.[20]

This depiction should be familiar to New Testament interpreters as well. How one tracks Paul's views on justification may require a meandering trail from Galatians to 1 and 2 Corinthians before halting at Romans – no matter that Romans is placed canonically at the beginning of the epistles associated with the apostle. In order rightly to comprehend the message of Paul, it is argued, we must have as clear a picture as we can of how his thought emerged, changed and reached final expression – an accounting derived by putting the varieties of his views as they appear in the New Testament in their proper chronological order. The final arrangement of the letters is not thought to be a commentary on how to interpret different nuances in Paul's thinking on this or other matters. Comparisons from Q, to Mark, to special Luke, to special Matthew, to John are ready to hand.[21]

Now in the case of the prophetic books, the rough chronological development of prophecy against its historical backdrop is not entirely lost in the canonical arrangement (and indeed here comparison with Paul's epistles would require adjustment). One can see a rough movement from Syro-Ephraimitic to Assyrian to Babylonian to Persian periods of international upheaval reflected in the final form of the prophetic collection. Stated negatively, the prophets are not random sections of an otherwise synchronic single statement about God and Israel (whatever such a thing might look like literarily). Prophecy exists in time and space and reports God's sovereignty precisely over time and space.

The canon allows this dimension to come to the fore by presenting fifteen individual books, with a temporal range far outstripping anything in the New Testament and marked explicitly (with superscriptions) in the case of a majority of the witnesses.

---

[20] Von Rad's portrayal of Jeremiah and Isaiah registers this dimension; see my discussion in 'Prophecy', 30–31.

[21] Though compare now the intriguing work in Bauckham, *Gospels*.

Three things must, however, be noted. First, in no collection of the Book of the Twelve known to us does Amos (argued to be the first prophet using a diachronic approach) take the signal position. Instead Hosea, if not also Joel, precede Amos. The superscription to the book of Hosea closely resembles that of Isaiah, and its signal position may owe something to that, alongside the fact that the book of Hosea is a longer and more comprehensive treatment than Amos.[22] So the earliest prophet, Amos, is not first, but third; or, in the case of the LXX, second.[23]

Secondly, we do not have a single linear collection with fifteen books. Isaiah, Jeremiah and Ezekiel do not find their place after Micah, Habakkuk or Zephaniah, respectively (if that is where, according to the modern approach, they belong). These three large collections exist independently of the Twelve, and Isaiah is an anthology whose chronological scope mirrors that of the Twelve itself: all the way from eighth-century reflections of the Syro-Ephraimitic war (Isa. 7–8), through the Assyrian, to Babylonian, to Persian periods, with references to Cyrus (Isa. 40–48) and conflicts over temple and nations in the final chapters (Isa. 56–66). In most orders that have come down to us, Isaiah is first, Jeremiah second and Ezekiel third. A talmudic citation (*Baba Bathra* 14b) knows of an order in which prophecies of all judgement, half-judgement and half-promise, and all salvation are the explanation given for an order it knows as Jeremiah, Ezekiel and Isaiah. But this is an isolated finding.[24] It should also be said that the Three usually precede the Twelve, but not always.

Finally, while clearly dated books in the Twelve (that is, those with chrono-logical superscriptions) are in proper order (so Hosea/Amos, Micah, Zephaniah, Haggai, Zechariah), and while some which are undated are argu-ably in proper order on internal grounds (Nahum, Habakkuk, Malachi), the location of other books (both in the LXX and MT) cannot be explained with such a criterion. These books are frequently dated to the latest period of Israel's history, on grounds of language, theology and other history-of-religions considerations (so Joel, Obadiah and Jonah). Jonah's position in the MT (in proximity to Amos) may be due to knowledge of him from 2 Kings

---

[22] See the intriguing remarks of J. Trebolle Barrera, 'Qumran Evidence'.

[23] 'Why does Hosea precede Amos? Perhaps length and unwillingness to interrupt the clear connections of Joel, Amos, and Obadiah explain the priority of Hosea' (Crenshaw, *Joel*, 22). 'The writing of Hosea was deliberately placed in the first position, although the historical prophet Amos probably delivered his oracles earlier than Hosea. The redactors wanted the reader to perceive the warning of Amos in the light of Hosea' (Schart, 'Reconstructing', 43).

[24] See, however, Trebolle Barrera, 'Qumran Evidence', 95. Isaiah and the Twelve seem to be paired in some lists, following the pairing Jeremiah–Ezekiel.

14:25–27, where he is a prophet of salvation just prior to the fall of the northern kingdom; but this cannot be the whole explanation. Obadiah's oracle against Edom, most believe, fits the context of the fall of Jerusalem in 587/6 BC, and Joel is frequently dated to the exilic period because it appears to be replete with citations from a known prophetic corpus including much of the Twelve, as well as Isaiah and Ezekiel.[25] Why Joel is located where it is – if not completely accidental – requires some sort of explanation. Because certain principles of arrangement (chronological sequence) are in evidence, it would be strange to find superimposed on that a completely random splicing-in of additional prophetic witnesses, bringing thereby the total number to twelve, on analogy with the twelve patriarchs.

In this context it should be mentioned that reference to a twelve-book collection, and not twelve or fifteen discrete messages, is ancient and well attested. The second century BC Sirach speaks of such a twelve-book collection (Sir. 49:10: 'May the bones of the twelve prophets send forth new life from where they lie ...'). Ancient Hebrew (*Wadi Murabba'at*) and Greek (*Nahal Hever*) texts have been discovered in which many, if not all, of the Twelve appear together on one scroll. Rabbinic tradition indicates that twelve books were written on one scroll so that smaller books should not get lost (*Baba Bathra* 13b). The Babylonian Talmud mentions a scribal requirement that four lines of text be left between biblical books but, in the case of the Twelve, three lines sufficed. As to size and comparability, 'when written together the Twelve filled a scroll of a length similar to the major prophets' (Isaiah, Jeremiah, Ezekiel).[26]

The Shape of the Twelve

Our goal here is to offer an interpretation of the shape of the Twelve that seeks to explain the positioning of the books. Our attention will be to the order found in the MT precursors and in other ancient witnesses, to which an alternative can be seen in later LXX orders. Once this is in place, it is easier to see which is the proper direction of change, as we assume that the rule of *lectio difficilior* applies roughly to the logic of arrangements of books as well. That is, it is our view that the LXX is best seen as an effort to recast a strange MT order, along the lines of its classification intuitions known elsewhere. A movement from LXX to MT admits of no obvious explanation.[27]

---

[25] See, among others, Barton, *Joel and Obadiah*.

[26] Peterson, 'Book of the Twelve', 5.

[27] 'The main problem with [an original LXX order] is that it does not explain how the Masoretic order came into being. Much more convincing is that the Septuagint placed Amos and Micah immediately after Hosea and left all other writings in the

In tackling a question like this it is easiest to work with clusters of books. While containing its own internal complexities, the final three-book collection of Haggai, Zechariah and Malachi seems relatively straightforward. Haggai and Zechariah (especially chapters 1–8) are frequently read together (compare their superscriptions), and Malachi forms the final 'massa' for a series with this heading beginning in Zechariah 9 and 12.[28] As we shall see, moreover, Malachi is a logical conclusion to the twelve-book collection, on internal and external grounds, by virtue of its epilogue and the issues that it raises in chapter 3.[29] These three books all come from the Persian period and later. Chronologically, they belong at the end.

As we shall see, the placements of Joel, Obadiah and Jonah represent the biggest challenge to final-form reading. It is not hard to understand Obadiah as a 'virtual commentary on Amos 9:12', as Allen and many others have seen, and so its position after Amos makes sense.[30] Amos calls for the house of David in latter days to possess the remnant of Edom. Obadiah recounts the destruction of Edom. At its end, we hear of rule over Zion and Edom 'and the kingdom will be the LORD's' (v. 21). What is less than clear is what sort of chronological perspective the transition from Amos to Obadiah intends to inculcate. Is Obadiah meant to be a prediction of events associated with 587 BC and thereafter? While the linkage of Amos and Obadiah finds explanation in the key word 'Edom', we must still inquire about matters of proper interpretation of this linkage in the overall temporal depiction of the Twelve.[31]

The question of the placement of Joel belongs together with larger considerations of the placement of Hosea in first position, and especially its

---

Masoretic order. The reason probably was the historical setting given by the superscriptions; since Hosea, Amos, and Micah prophesied partly under the same kings, they form a closed group to which Joel, Obadiah, and Jonah do not belong' (Schart, 'Reconstructing', 37–38).

[28] For a discussion of the hermeneutical issues at stake in Malachi vis-à-vis Zech. 9–14, see Childs's discussion in *Introduction*, 480ff.

[29] Watts, 'Frame'.

[30] '… the book [Obadiah] may be viewed as a virtual commentary on Amos 9:12' (Allen, *Books*, 129).

[31] Concerning 'the Day of the LORD': 'This topic is mentioned once in Amos (5:18–20), where the reader gets the impression that such a day *is* well-known to Amos's audience. But from what source do they know? The present reader of the Book of the Twelve knows from the writing that precedes Amos, from Joel, where the Day of the LORD is the central topic. It is again the central topic in the writing that follows Amos: Obadiah. That means that these three, Joel, Amos, and Obadiah form a group … Joel and Obadiah are undated; they could have been placed for other than chronological reasons' (Rendtorff, 'How to Read', 77).

relationship to its chronological counterpart Amos.[32] If we can understand the logic of the order Hosea, Joel and Amos, we might find clues for other confusing stretches in the Book of the Twelve, including those that include Obadiah, Jonah and Micah.

Here the groundbreaking work has been undertaken by Jeremias, Utzschneider, Schart and others. Although Amos would appear to be the younger prophet, it is argued that his book was never without a distinct influence from Hosea. So Hosea belongs in first position by virtue of its strong influence on the formation of Amos. But Hosea, too, has been edited in such a way that its specific address to the cultic abuses of the northern kingdom is not capable of simple historicizing. As we will see later, specifically in the early chapters of Jeremiah, the northern kingdom is to be a severe example for Judah.

Many have noted a Judah redaction in Hosea, but Jeremias has gone further in describing the exegetical and theological issues at stake in this redaction. He provides two examples. First, a typical condemnation of the northern cultic harlotry (4:11–14) concludes with reference to Judah in 4:15. This verse draws on language familiar from Amos (4:4), flattening its irony through direct imperative prohibitions (and see also Amos 5:5). The point is that Judah, too, might be tempted to participate in such pilgrimages: 'the intention of verses like Hos. 4.15 was to actualize the prophetic words for a people living later than the prophet and under new circumstances'.[33] The second example Jeremias gives is Hosea 8:14; here again it is a matter of drawing on language from the book of Amos in order to make a point concerning Judah in the book of Hosea. The oracle of judgement against Ephraim in 8:11–13 clearly culminates in the punishment of return to Egypt (for Deuteronomy, this brings down the curses of the covenant). 'No further intensification of Hosea's accusation is possible.'[34] Drawing upon the familiar language of Amos ('fire upon' in 1:4, 7, 10, 12, 14; 2:2, 5) in 8:14, 'a typical subject of Amos, luxury inside the palaces of the capital … is cited to prevent Judean readers from escaping the accusations of Hosea'.[35]

As for the Hosean influence on Amos, it is indeed to be felt in nearly every chapter. For this reason Jeremias believes there 'was never a book of Amos without a clearly discernible effect from Hoseanic texts'.[36] We have space for only one example here, involving the famous series of visions in chapters 7–8.

---

[32] 'Why does Hosea precede Amos? Perhaps length and unwillingness to interrupt the clear connections of Joel, Amos, and Obadiah explain the priority of Hosea' (Crenshaw, *Joel*, 22).

[33] Jeremias, 'Interrelationship', 175.

[34] Jeremias, 'Interrelationship', 176.

[35] Jeremias, 'Interrelationship', 176.

[36] Jeremias, 'Interrelationship', 177.

Amos receives two pairs of visions (locusts and fire in 7:1–3 and 7:4–6; plumb-line and ripe fruit in 7:7–8 and 8:1–2). His fifth and final vision can, for our purposes, be set aside. Many note that this was an original series of visions because of the symmetry and overall logic. The first two visions end in God's relenting at the prophet's bidding, while the second pair shows, tragically for Israel, a limit to God's patience: 'I will no longer spare them'.

The final form of the material seeks, however, to explain just why it is that God finally changed his view. The priest Amaziah forbade Amos to prophesy. He silenced him, and in so doing brought to an end his intercessory petitioning of God's favour. The first vision of the second pair links up with the narrative explanation by means of 7:9, wherein it is the high places and sanctuaries (Hoseanic terms) which occasion a decision of judgement against the house of Jeroboam, whose representative we see in the state cult official Amaziah. 'God's patience ends where the state represented by the priest tries to decide when and where God may speak through the prophet.'[37] 'The condemnation of guilt in worship and guilt by the state is especially characteristic of Hosea from ch. 1 through 14. Amos 7:9 sounds like a precise condensation of Hosea's general message.'[38] Because the final form of the text demands it as essential to its logic, it cannot be judged a late addition but is, rather, an integral moment in the original development of the Amos tradition. That is, the reader is urged 'not to perceive Amos as an isolated prophet but to relate his message to the message of Hosea'.[39] We need both Amos and Hosea to know where it was that God's patience came to an end. A second example of a programmatic text from Hosea finding its way into Amos is 3:2. 'To know' (*yd'*), 'to punish' (*pqd*), and guilt (*'awon*) occur only here in the book of Amos, but they are familiar terms in Hosea.

Further examples of this mutual influencing can be, and have been, adduced. It should also be noted that Schart sees as possibly significant the fact that in the letters from Mari a prophetic oracle is judged to have more authority if independently uttered by a different speaker. The fact that both Hosea and, after him, Amos, spoke judgement on the northern kingdom sealed its fate, as it were.[40]

I mention this because we must now turn to the question: why are Hosea and Amos not side by side in the order of the MT? It is understandable why the LXX has a series Hosea, Amos and Micah, because these are the three books with superscriptions locating them in chronological order, while Obadiah, Jonah and Nahum are three short, undated books. The sequence Hosea, Joel,

---

[37] Jeremias, 'Interrelationship', 179.
[38] Jeremias, 'Interrelationship', 180.
[39] Jeremias, 'Interrelationship', 181.
[40] Schart, 'Reconstructing'.

Amos requires interpretation. It is not enough to note that Joel refers to the Lord roaring from Zion, a theme which prominently opens the book of Amos (1:2). It is true enough, but what does that mean?[41]

Several explanations have been given. The threat of natural infertility is a clear one in Hosea ('Ephraim is blighted, their root is withered, they yield no fruit', 9:16), and this is an obvious, indeed relentless, theme in Joel. Instead of explicit national destruction, such as we see in Hosea and Amos, and especially in the major prophets and later in the Twelve, Joel speaks of locusts, a 'large and mighty army' (2:2) 'with a noise like that of chariots' (2:5). The Lord 'thunders' at this, 'the head of his army' (2:11). The threat of natural destruction and infertility in Hosea takes a concrete form in Joel.[42]

Related to this, the book of Joel describes this natural assault, not with martial metaphors only, but also as 'the day of the Lord' (2:11). The phoneme 'day' in the context of judgement rings across the opening sections (1:2, 15; 2:1, 2, 11), that is, until we come to the call for repentance in 2:12. Not only is the day of the Lord a concept presupposed in Amos 5:18 ('Woe to you who long for the day of the LORD'), Amos also uses the image of a locust plague in the first vision of the series referred to above (7:1). In Amos, we know that the prophet's entreaty meant that the Lord actually relented (7:2). Amos personally cries out in address to God: 'Sovereign Lord, forgive! How can Jacob survive? He is so small!' Joel urges the people to 'return', to 'rend your hearts', to 'return to the LORD … for he is gracious and compassionate', thus bringing to expression the formula uttered by God himself in the context of Mosaic intercession in Exodus 34. Joel urges this action in the spirit of Amos: 'Who knows? He may turn and have pity' (2:14).

Joel separates Hosea and Amos in order to signal that God is always in a position to relent, if the people turn back. Just as God relents before he utters his sentence of judgement through the speech of Amos reporting what he sees ('fruit', yes, 'end'), so it belongs to God's character to be 'slow to anger'. Amos seconds the word of judgement from Hosea, but God is also 'slow to anger'. Joel reinforces the point that is otherwise made in Amos alone and in the sequence Hosea, Joel and Amos.

---

[41] 'The ending of Joel confirms that Amos and subsequent books are to be read in the light of Joel' (Van Leeuwen, 'Scribal Wisdom', 41). Concerning the final verse (Joel 4:21 [ET 3:21]), 'Its status as final redaction in the Twelve is clear because it has no real function other than to link Joel and Amos in a manner that contrasts Judah (4:16–20) and Israel, the primary topic of Amos. It does this by alluding to the punishment formula of Ex 34:7: "He will by no means hold innocent [the guilty]". By these links Joel 4:21 reinforces and focuses the anticipation of Amos 1:2 found in Joel 4:16 (ET 3:16)' (Van Leeuwen, 'Scribal Wisdom', 41–42).

[42] Nogalski, 'Joel'.

Obadiah is a 21–verse description of judgement on Edom. The original accusation against Edom, found in Amos 1 ('because he pursued his brother with a sword'), is repeated in verse 10 of Obadiah. As the final chapters of Joel and Amos look ahead to a time of restoration after cleansing judgement, so too does the ending of Obadiah (19–21). The time frame for this appears to be set by Joel. The destruction potentially forestalled by repentance comes about in time, as Joel 2:25 makes clear. God speaks of repaying for the years eaten by locusts. Edom will be destroyed in that day (Joel 3:19). This oracle of judgement is seconded in Amos 9:12 and confirmed in the vision of destruction of Obadiah.

Most regard Jonah as a unique book, a late book and a strange book. Unique, due to genre (a book about a prophet, not a prophetic book); late, due to Aramaicisms, peculiar Hebrew idioms and history-of-religions issues (problems in unfulfilled prophecy; Israel and the nations); strange, because of its ironic character and final openness to rival interpretations (see the history of interpretation). Barry Jones, appealing to a very fragmentary collection of verses found at Cave 4 which appear to consist of Malachi and Jonah portions, also argues that Jonah was once the final book of the twelve-book collection, thus bolstering the 'strange book' perception. Jonah is a commentary on prophecy, according to Jones, and its 'original' position shows this. It is not one of the Twelve but an evaluation of the eleven from a late perspective.[43]

We agree that the book is patient of dating in Israel's later period. But what Jones's appeal to Qumran demonstrates is the widespread attestation of sequences which confirm the MT's order, and especially the location of Jonah after Obadiah (which concerns a foreign nation) and before Micah and Nahum (which, like Obadiah, is an oracle against a foreign nation – this time the major ancient Near Eastern power, Assyria). That is, we should view with great care an appeal to 'original' idiosyncratic order in the face of such a preponderance of standardized orders (in all the known LXX, ancient Greek and Hebrew and MT orders). If true, then obviously Jonah was intentionally and thoroughly repositioned, and this without loss of its remaining a singular witness to prophecy. The reason for this wide-scale uniformity in all other orders is probably the reference to a Jonah in 2 Kings 14. But it also belongs to the logic of the larger shape of the Twelve that Jonah appear after Obadiah and one book away from Nahum, as we shall briefly argue here.

Read in isolation, Jonah admits of a variety of interpretations. A quick glimpse at the history of ancient and more recent interpretation – Jewish, Christian and modern – bears this out (Elias Bickerman's *Four Strange Books of the Bible* provides an excellent summary).[44] Jonah is said to be about God's

---

[43] Jones, *Formation*, and 'Book of the Twelve'.
[44] Bickerman, *Four Strange Books*.

universal care for all nations. Jonah is about the problem of unfulfilled prophecy. Jonah is about Israel's hardheartedness and xenophobia. Jonah is a commentary on the unreliability of prophecy and the dissolution of the prophetic office.

Notable, too, is that all of these interpretations rely fairly heavily on an assessment of the proper context for interpretation being 'Israel's late history' – whether due to universalism as found in Israelite wisdom, or prophecy's coming to an end, or as a tract over against the 'narrow parochialism and exclusivism', as it is often termed, of Ezra-Nehemiah's vision of restoration. To date a book 'late' is to require the book to be fitted into an authorial intention congruent with the period, as this is inferred by hypothesis.[45]

An alternative is to view the matter of context as given by the work itself, and not by authorial location (whether late or not is irrelevant). That the book of Jonah has seized precisely on the figure of Jonah in 2 Kings 14 is strongly to be asserted (and here a later midrashic-type utilization is quite possible). That Jonah was a prophet remembered because he was associated with God's mercy towards the northern kingdom during the reign of Jeroboam is the likely context of association assumed by the author for his readers: 'And since the LORD had not said he would blot out the name of Israel from under heaven, he saved them' (2 Kgs. 14:27). Jonah was, moreover, a prophet of success: a true prophet, whose word had come true (v. 25).

With these interpretative parameters in place, we begin to rub up against the same sorts of concerns already spotted at work in the Hosea, Joel, Amos, Obadiah sequence. Not surprisingly, we run into the same divine formula used in Joel in a similar context of possible divine relenting (Joel 2:13–14 and Jonah 4:2). When Jonah complains that he knew about the character of God, that God could relent if people repented, thus making his prophets look a bit silly, whatever it means for Jonah to say 'he knew' that God was thus and so (4:2), the readers have a context for knowing about this as well: the context provided by the sequence Hosea, Joel and Amos.[46] That this perspective is intentionally drawn upon by the author of Jonah would be further strengthened if we had evidence of it to follow, and indeed we do, at Micah's close (7:18–19).

---

[45] Blenkinsopp treats Jonah in the very last chapter of his *History*, terming it 'a kind of sapiential critique of prophecy' (242) which emphasizes God's freedom over against prophecy and the prophetic word.

[46] Compare the remarks of Collins: 'The description of the fasting and repentance of the Ninevites is of course reminiscent of Joel 1:13–14; 2:15–16, which calls for fasting and sackcloth in Jerusalem. Even the animals are involved in both cases (Jon. 3:7–8 and Joel 1:20) … Its contribution comes both from the ideas it embodies and from its position after Obadiah to which it acts as a counterfoil in its attitude to the nations' (Collins, *Mantle*, 72).

Micah also names for the first time the national destroyer of Israel (Samaria-Jerusalem). Following the first explicit mention of Zion's death sentence in the Book of the Twelve (Mic. 3:12, a prophecy seconded in Jer. 26, where Micah's prophecy is explicitly brought into testimony on Jeremiah's behalf), we learn in chapter five that the Assyrians are that nation mustered for invasion (5:5ff.). But Micah also immediately delimits the Assyrian punishment, promising Assyrian defeat. God will not be angry forever, Micah consoles his people in the final chapter. He pardons sin and forgives the transgression of a remnant people (Mic. 7:18).[47]

Jonah shows that God has no mechanical attitude toward the nations. Edom's judgement is a function of her breaking laws that God has written into creation itself, just as Israel will be punished for knowing God's will as a people chosen. God can forgive, yes, even a Ninevite people – the negative associations of which are better known from Nahum or Kings or Isaiah than from a single act of repentance in Jonah. God insists he has a right to be concerned about a people who don't know their right hand from their left, even when it embarrasses his servants the prophets. But when Nahum opens with the same formula we have tracked in Joel, Jonah and Micah ('the LORD, slow to anger', etc.; see Nah. 1:2–3), it is clear that Assyria's day of judgement has come. God will by no means clear the guilty, the formula here emphasizes. For 'who has not felt your [Assyria's] endless cruelty?' (Nah. 3:19).

After Nahum, the movement from Habakkuk to Malachi is straightforward. I can only summarize here. Assyria's destruction is assumed by Habakkuk, but the prophet is bothered by a new reality (1:12–17). The judgement of Assyria is not prosecuted by angels, but by a more ferocious and more violent nation, whose deployment causes the prophet anguish. How can this be a just decision on God's part? Habakkuk takes his watch (2:1–5). The righteous shall live by faith, he is told. The book ends with the prophet modelling the proper behaviour required in the face of God's sovereign justice: with a prayer of confidence and firm resolve (3:1–17).

---

[47] '... nothing in Jon. 1.1–17 shows traces of revision in the light of Obadiah. Perhaps that is because with Jonah a new subject is introduced, namely, the fate of Assyria and its capital city Nineveh in particular. To be sure, Hosea had referred to Assyria ... but neither Joel, Amos, nor Obadiah mentioned it. In Jonah, Micah, and Nahum, Assyria is first pardoned, then threatened with subjugation by Judah's shepherds (Mic. 5.5–6), and finally condemned to undergo God's retributive vengeance (Nah. 1.2 and frequently). The clear contrast between the perspective of the book of Jonah ... and the book of Nahum is, thus, ameliorated by the presence of the book of Micah. The redactor's reading of history would seem to be something like this: repent though Nineveh might have done at the urging of Jonah, she apostatized by the time of Micah and deserved all the punishment Nahum envisioned' (Redditt, 'Zechariah', 264–65).

Zephaniah shows what is in store for Jerusalem at the hands of the Babylonians. The great day of the Lord is 'near and coming quickly' (1:14). But the book ends with a vision of a Zion cleansed by judgement, her exile removed and placed upon those agents who had done God's bidding. The patient resolve of Habakkuk is to see fruit in the restoration of Zion, which is the subject of Haggai–Zechariah. Temple and nature together are restored, in the spirit of Hosea's promises: 'From this day on, from this twenty-fourth day of the ninth month, give careful thought to the day when the foundation of the LORD's temple was laid. ... Until now, the vine and the fig-tree, the pomegranate and the olive tree have not borne fruit. "From this day on I will bless you" ' (Hag. 2:18–19). The temporal gap separating Zephaniah and Haggai is more than amply filled by the three major prophetic scrolls, and especially by Jeremiah and Ezekiel. Isaiah's panoramic view forms a parallel portrayal co-ordinated with that of the Book of the Twelve as a whole.[48]

This point has been established on two fronts. First, the similarity of themes in Malachi and Hosea (marriage and divorce; love and election; false worship) matches a pattern of similar themes in Isaiah 1 and Isaiah 65–66, whose linkages have been noted by many recent interpreters interested in Isaiah's unity.[49] And like Isaiah's final chapters, Malachi envisions a further division *within Israel itself*, between the righteous and the wicked (3:18; Isa. 65:13ff.). Those who question God's justice and unchangeable character are separated, in like manner to what we see in Isaiah 56–66. Those 'who feared the LORD and honoured his name' (Mal. 3:16) have their counterpart in him 'who is humble and contrite in spirit, and trembles at my word' (Isa. 66:2). The issues are similar to what we find in Habakkuk – patient obedience before God's sovereign timing – but here the negative example of those who lack patience and resolve is set out. Their names are not to be recorded in a 'scroll of remembrance' (Mal. 3:16).

To conclude: What lessons does a Book of the Twelve teach as a whole which are only sketched out – partially, in snapshots – in the case of individual books or individual prophetic figures?

(1) God's history is a providentially ordered whole. The various ingredients that lie at the base of Israel's historical experience from the eighth to the fifth century are brought into relationship with one another. Seen from

---

[48] 'The final composition of the Twelve Prophets has surprising structural and thematic parallels with the final form of the book of Isaiah, such as a common perspective centered in Sion and the vision of a universalistic future' (Trebolle Barrera, 'Qumran Evidence', 95). See also his further comments on p. 98. The editorial relationship between Isaiah and the Twelve has been explored in detail by O. Steck, *Abschluss*.

[49] See the discussion in Seitz, 'Isaiah'.

the perspective of individual prophetic snapshots, history could appear episodic and disconnected; but Israel's grasp of and presentation of history in the Twelve is an organic whole. The fate of the northern and southern kingdoms, of Zion–Jerusalem, of national entities in the region, of the Assyrian, then Babylonian, then Persian kingdoms, and beyond to a final eschatological tableau: these various ingredients are not sitting there demanding ancient Near Eastern reconstruction for them to make sense out of fifteen or more individual witnesses. The Twelve and the Three have linked these ingredients through the simple reality of their sequential presentation.

(2) Israel and the nations: more specifically, we learn that the nations have a different, but parallel and by no means neglected, place in God's economy. Whether they know their right hand from their left, as in Amos, or whether, as in Jonah, they do not, they are not outside God's larger plan or purpose. Repentance can be taken seriously. Hardness of heart as well. As with Israel, so too with the nations. The message of Jonah regarding Assyria is partial if kept apart from that of Nahum, and of them both if kept apart from Amos, Micah and Zephaniah. The sequencing of the Twelve makes a coherent total picture available.

(3) Models of obedience: Jonah, Habakkuk, Joel. Readers of the Twelve do not just hear prophetic words. They are also shown men of prayer. Jonah's prayer comes in the context of personal judgement and personal thanksgiving for deliverance. Habakkuk's prayer presents us with a model of patient obedience, as he confronts the mystery of divine justice. In this, he is the man after Malachi's heart. And Joel's plea for returning to God is as much directed to the reader confronting a history unfolding in Israel as it is to specific figures in that history itself. Hosea's final refrain is a motto for the whole collection, functioning as Psalm 1 does for the Psalter. 'Who is wise? He will realise these things. Who is discerning? He will understand them. The ways of the LORD are right; the righteous walk in them, but the rebellious stumble in them' (Hos. 14:9; Isaiah 1 ends similarly). The fact that Habakkuk's prayer is presented with the identical rubrics ('On *shigionoth*'; 'for the director of music. On my stringed instruments'), as in the Psalms, means to direct the reader to that 150-prayer book. This book seeks to inculcate, through prayer, the attitude of discernment necessary for comprehending the lessons of history, as God and no journalistic technique can reveal. The link beyond the Twelve to the Psalter is a form of canonical shaping as well.

(4) Tradition-history: the presentation of tradition-history is of necessity a partial historical portrait. The distinctive messages of the prophets must be related externally, as it were, one to another, through conjecture about tradition-historical affiliation (where it exists). How is Jeremiah related to Zephaniah, both as seventh-century prophets? This sort of investigation

must pursue such questions, and the answers provided are both speculative and partial. This inherent (literary and historical) gapping has no counterpart in the final form of the Twelve. However we may seek to relate the historical context of Joel to the historical context of Amos, it remains the case that for the canonical presentation, this is not at issue. As Deist puts it, 'I hope to show that the book [of Joel] was not intended to "refer" to any concrete event in history, but was rather compiled to serve as a "literary theology" of the concept of "The Day of the Lord".'[50] Joel's connection to Amos is historical in the context of the canon's final presentation, and that sort of 'historical reference' must be carefully handled as well by exegesis.[51]

(5)   The character of God: just but patient; patient, but not without limit. The use of the self-designation formula from Exodus 34 across the disparate witnesses of Joel, Jonah, Micah and Nahum is one of the strongest signs of a comprehensive editing of the Twelve. Even though the formula does not appear in full form, the call to return to God is strongest in Hosea, and most compellingly illustrated, under the narrative of human infidelity and God's abiding love. God is patient with his people and with the nations. But he will by no means clear the guilty. The path from Jonah to Nahum is clear on this. Malachi worries about those who question God's fidelity and unchanging character,[52] in the light of his capacity to forgive and alter a sentence of judgement, such as we see in Jonah. But this worry also becomes exhortation and stern instruction: 'you will again see the distinction between the righteous and the wicked, between those who serve God and those who do not' (3:18). The steadfastness of Habakkuk is required, and it is a gift of God

---

[50]   Deist, 'Parallels', 63.

[51]   Compare the remarks of Jeremias on Amos 9:12–13: 'Verse 12.13 (haben) … nicht nur das gesamte Amosbuch … im Blick, sondern das Zwölfprophetenbuch … V. 12 greift das Thema des Büchleins Obadja auf und bildet zu ihm eine Brücke, während V. 13 rückwärtsgewandt den Bogen zu Joel 4,18 schlägt und damit zugleich eine Inklusion zum Buchanfang Am 1,2 bildet, wo auf Joel 4,16 angespielt wird. Ohne dass hier auf das schwierige Problem der Priorität der Berührungen eingegangen werden muss, ist doch deutlich, dass die Bezüge den Leser des Amosbuches daran hindern wollen, das Buch in Isolation zur Kenntnis zu nehmen. Vielmehr wird ihm der lange Atem zugemutet, das Amosbuch zusammen mit den anderen Prophetenbüchern des Zwölfprophetenbuches zu betrachten. Er soll das Amosbuch mit dem Ernst der Verse 9,9f. lesen, die von der Lektüre des Buches Rettung oder aber Untergang des einzelnen abhängig machen, zugleich aber wissen, dass die Zeugenstimme des Amos mit den anderen Zeugenstimmen im Zwölfprophetenbuch zusammengehört' (Jeremias, *Prophet Amos*, 136–37).

[52]   'You have said, "It is futile to serve God. What did we gain by carrying out his requirements?" ' (3:14).

given to those who wait and trust in him. To forfeit this is to turn blessing on its head. It is to lose a place in the scroll of remembrance.

Final Remarks

The rationale and conceptuality within which my argument for the Twelve functions entails a combination of historical, literary and theological factors. All have their place. We know that as a *historical* datum, very soon after the final prophetic book took shape (Malachi?), the Twelve are regarded as a collection (Sirach; Qumran). Indeed, in Sirach the existence of the Twelve is something of a cliché: it is referred to as a given, without argument or assertion. The *literary* evidence for internal editorial affiliation, linkages and intentional juxtapositions is becoming increasingly clear as scholars turn to this sort of inquiry. And I have tried to probe into the *theological* coherence of the twelve-book collection which may be the intended consequence, or indeed, the originating engine, driving the historical and literary dimensions of canonical shaping.

But I should be very clear. There is also a *practical* consideration of exegetical treatment and, modest though it is, it cannot be set aside. A presentation of the prophets requires some sort of sequence. One has to start somewhere, move somewhere next, and so forth, until the entire corpus is handled.

We know how the matter of sequence has been handled in the genre of commentary and introduction and theology, since at least the middle of the nineteenth century. One makes a historical decision about chronology, and works from Amos through to 'First Isaiah', Micah through to Jeremiah, Ezekiel and 'Deutero-Isaiah', and from 'Trito-Isaiah' to a speculative end point, whether that be Jonah, or Malachi or Joel. There was a day when the theological justification for this was clearer: a genetic description of origins (and development) was required because that is where the inspiration was said to reside. And also, although this was rarely stated polemically, it was simply judged to be an empty observation that the canon presented the prophetic books in this or that arrangement. History, and theological interpretation derived from a historical reading, pushed the discipline away from any such consideration. Whatever theological rationale continues to animate the diachronic approach, the approach no longer requires it, strictly speaking. The developmental approach operates pretty much on 'autopilot'.

The problem is not, of course, the dated books, but the undated. As I have said, the dated books are in clear chronological order (Hosea/Amos is a special problem), and the obvious intention of the superscriptions is to relate these to the narrative world of 1 and 2 Kings. In the case of Hosea, the superscription means to situate the book as late as the Hezekiah period, and as such, anticipatory of the fall of Samaria. Hosea's signal position is tied up with an understanding of the range of its historical reference, as seen by the editors.

It is easy enough simply to date Joel, Obadiah, Jonah late and treat them in the history-of-Israelite-religion. My concern is to understand why they are not placed at the end of the Twelve where, strictly speaking, they 'belong' on a developmental model. These are the books that do not have the superscriptions linking them to Israel's history in Kings. That fact is also significant for interpretation.

It should be emphasized that my effort to read the Twelve as a whole is not aimed at flattening the notion of independent prophetic witnesses, or distinctiveness within individual books. Far from it. Rather, it is aimed against the notion of a historical-developmental approach being the only way to make sense of sequencing. That is, insofar as historical approaches assume that the canon's final arrangement is without significance, and that theirs is the only way to make sense out of sequential prophetic testimony, these approaches are, in my judgement, flawed.

I am seeking a way to understand sequentiality differently, by paying attention to the final shape of the Twelve in the MT orders (and, for that matter, also in an LXX ordering). There is nothing anti-historical in this approach, but it does assume that historicality is more than just pulling prophetic witnesses apart, determining what is authentic and secondary, and placing this all within a reconstructed history of traditions, or history of religion. In that sense, while the earlier history of interpretation may not have sought significance in the final shape of the Book of the Twelve, it is also true that they did not have to. They were not seeking to read books in the manner of modern historical approaches. They may have asked questions of historical reference, but these questions did not overwhelm the interpretative task. In that sense, my concern to read the Twelve in the order of their presentation belongs to the climate of modern historical reading, not premodern reading. But I also assume that my rejection of developmental, historical sequencing as the final index for proper interpretation means that the approach adopted here could well be open to insights from a former day, lost once the predominant model for reading became the developmental-historical one.

I suspect this approach to the Twelve and the Three ought to be called canonical-historical, to differentiate it from a strict diachronic analysis presently in vogue and tied to tradition-history or history-of-religions frames of reference. However, to the degree that the approach assumes a diachronic dimension not spotted in an earlier historical of interpretation, it is also a reading which belongs to its own day – and in that sense, so does every reading. There is a coherence and logic to the final arrangement of the Book of the Twelve, the character of which is such that it deserves to be called both intentional and theologically significant. It has been my concern to demonstrate this, for its own sake, and as a strong modification of the developmental approach now in vogue. That approach has not, to my mind, gone far enough in asking about historical matters. A canonical-historical reading will allow the distinctive message of each prophet to be heard. Yet these also form organic parts of a twelve-book presentation. This canonical presentation seeks to give a coherent, large-scale account of the history of the prophetic word in Israel and the world, under God's providential care and final purpose.

Bibliography

Allen, L.C., *The Books of Joel, Obadiah, Jonah and Micah* (Grand Rapids: Eerdmans, 1976)

Barton, J., *Joel and Obadiah: A Commentary* (OTL; Louisville, KY: Westminster/ John Knox Press, 2001)

Bauckham, R. (ed.), *The Gospels for All Christians* (Grand Rapids: Eerdmans, 1998)

Bickerman, E., *Four Strange Books of the Bible* (New York: Schocken, 1967)

Blenkinsopp, J., *A History of Prophecy in Israel* (Louisville: Westminster Press, 1996)

Childs, B.S., *Introduction to the Old Testament as Scripture* (Philadelphia: Fortress Press, 1979)

——, 'Foreword', in *Renewing Biblical Interpretation* (ed. C. Bartholomew, C. Greene and K. Möller; SHS 1; Carlisle: Paternoster; Grand Rapids: Zondervan, 2000), xv–xvii

——, *Biblical Theology of the Old and New Testaments* (Philadelphia: Fortress Press, 1993)

Collins, T., *The Mantle of Elijah: The Redaction Criticism of the Prophetical Books* (BibSem 20; Sheffield: JSOT Press, 1993)

Crenshaw, J., *Joel* (New York: Doubleday, 1995)

Deist, F., 'Parallels and Reinterpretation in Joel', in *Text and Context: Old Testament and Semitic Studies for F.C. Fensham* (ed. W. Claassen; JSOTSup 48; Sheffield: Sheffield Academic Press, 1988), 63–79

Gilkey, L., 'Cosmology, Ontology, and the Travail of Biblical Language', *JR* 41 (1965), 194–205

Jeremias, J., 'The Interrelationship Between Amos and Hosea', in *Forming Prophetic Literature: Essays on Isaiah and the Twelve in Honor of John D.W. Watts* (ed. J.D. Watts and P.R. House; JSOTSup 235; Sheffield: JSOT Press, 1996), 171–86

——, *Der Prophet Amos* (ATD 24.2; Göttingen: Vandenhoeck & Ruprecht, 1995)

Jones, B., 'The Book of the Twelve as a Witness to Ancient Biblical Interpretation', in *Reading and Hearing the Book of the Twelve* (ed. J.D. Nogalski and M.A. Sweeney; SBLSS 15; Atlanta: SBL, 2000), 65–74

——, *The Formation of the Book of the Twelve: A Study in Text and Canon* (SBLDS 149; Atlanta: Scholars Press, 1995)

Ludlow, M., 'Theology and Allegory: Origen and Gregory of Nyssa on the Unity and Diversity of Scripture', *IJST* 4 (2002), 45–66

Möller, K., 'Renewing Historical Criticism', in *Renewing Biblical Interpretation* (ed. C. Bartholomew, C. Greene and K. Möller; SHS 1; Carlisle: Paternoster; Grand Rapids: Zondervan, 2000), 145–71

Nogalski, J.D., 'Joel as "Literary Anchor" for the Book of the Twelve', in *Reading and Hearing the Book of the Twelve* (ed. J.D. Nogalski and M.A. Sweeney; SBLSS 15; Atlanta: SBL, 2000), 91–109

——, and M. Sweeney (eds.), *Reading and Hearing the Book of the Twelve* (Atlanta: SBL, 2000)

Peterson, D., 'A Book of the Twelve?', in *Reading and Hearing the Book of the Twelve* (ed. J.D. Nogalski and M.A. Sweeney; SBLSS 15; Atlanta: SBL, 2000), 3–10

Redditt, P.L., 'Zechariah 9–14, Malachi, and the Redaction of the Book of the Twelve', in *Forming Prophetic Literature: Essays on Isaiah and the Twelve in Honor of John D.W. Watts* (ed. J.D. Watts and P.R. House; JSOTSup 235; Sheffield: JSOT Press, 1996), 245–68

Rendtorff, R., 'How to Read the Book of the Twelve as a Theological Unity', in *Reading and Hearing the Book of the Twelve* (ed. J.D. Nogalski and M.A. Sweeney; SBLSS 15; Atlanta: SBL, 2000), 75–87

Schart, A., 'Reconstructing the Redaction History of the Twelve Prophets: Problems and Models', in *Reading and Hearing the Book of the Twelve* (ed. J.D. Nogalski and M.A. Sweeney; SBLSS 15; Atlanta: SBL, 2000), 34–48

Seitz, C.R., 'Prophecy and Tradition-History: The Achievement of Gerhard von Rad and Beyond', in *Prophetie in Israel: Beiträge des Symposiums 'Das Alte Testament und die Kultur der Moderne' anlässlich des 100. Geburtstags Gerhard von Rads (1901–1971), Heidelberg, 18.–21. Oktober 2001* (ed. I. Fischer, et al.; Altes Testament und Moderne 11; Münster: Lit-Verlag, 2003), 29–52

——, 'The Book of Isaiah 40–66', in *The New Interpreter's Bible*, VI (ed. L.E. Keck, et al.; Nashville: Abingdon Press, 2001), 538–50

——, *Figured Out* (Louisville, KY: Westminster / John Knox Press, 2001)

——, *Theology in Conflict: Reactions to the Exile in the Book of Jeremiah* (BZAW 176; Berlin: W. de Gruyter, 1989)

——, 'Historical-Critical Endeavor as Theology: The Legacy of Gerhard von Rad', in *Word Without End: The Old Testament as Abiding Theological Witness* (Grand Rapids: Eerdmans, 1998), 28–40

Steck, O., *Der Abschluss der Prophetie im Alten Testament: Ein Versuch zur Frage der Vorgeschichte des Kanons* (Neukirchen-Vluyn: Neukirchener Verlag, 1991)

Trebolle Barrera, J., 'Qumran Evidence for a Biblical Standard Text and for Non-Standard and Parabiblical Texts', in *The Dead Sea Scrolls in Their Historical Context* (ed. T.H. Lim, et al.; Edinburgh: T. & T. Clark, 2000), 89–106

Trobisch, D., *The First Edition of the New Testament* (Oxford: OUP, 2000)

Van Leeuwen, R.C., 'Scribal Wisdom and Theodicy in the Book of the Twelve', in *In Search of Wisdom: Essays in Memory of John G. Gammie* (ed. L.G. Perdue, et al.; Louisville, KY: Westminster / John Knox Press, 1993), 31–49

Von Rad, G., *Genesis: A Commentary* (Philadelphia: Westminster Press, rev. edn, 1972)

Ward, T., *Word and Supplement: Speech Acts, Biblical Texts, and the Sufficiency of Scripture* (Oxford: OUP, 2002)

Watts, J.D.W., 'A Frame for the Book of the Twelve: Hosea 1–3 and Malachi', in *Reading and Hearing the Book of the Twelve* (ed. J.D. Nogalski and M.A. Sweeney; SBLSS 15; Atlanta: SBL, 2000), 209–17

19

Divine Speaking as Godly Action in Old Testament Narrative[1]

The Metaphysics of Exodus 14

Neil B. MacDonald

Introduction

Prior to the Enlightenment, it could be said that the Judaeo-Christian tradition read the Old Testament narratives from Genesis through to Ezra for their plain sense and therefore as one continuous historical narrative committed to a sequence of events subsumed under a theological conception of history:

> In the beginning God created the world, humankind fell, Abraham was called, Isaac, Jacob, Joseph, the people of Israel in Egypt, Moses, exodus, wilderness, Sinai, settlement in the land of Israel, the time of the judges, the rise of the monarchy, David, Solomon, the united kingdom of north and south, the divided kingdom, the demise of the northern kingdom at the hands of Assyrian conquest in 722 BCE, the downfall of the southern kingdom in 587 BCE and the exile from Jerusalem signalling the end of the monarchy, finally the return from exile under the beneficence of Cyrus the great from 536 BCE onwards.

A modern commentator would typically take a different view of the narrative. First, he or she might simply reject the sequence of events narrated before Israel's subjugation to Egypt, especially the primeval history and most especially the mythical history of the genesis of human sin. Secondly, and more crucially for our purposes, he or she would eliminate the theological conception of history at work in later Old Testament narrative. Neither the biblical

---

[1] Scripture quotations in this chapter are taken from the New English Bible.

narrator's story of Israel's exodus from Egypt nor the account of the demise and downfall of Israel and Judah respectively should be attributed to a theological conception of history in which YHWH, the God of Israel, acted in Israel's history. Though the events might be said to have happened (though not necessarily exactly as described in the narratives), they came about without any intentionality on the part of any God of Israel. Hence, they can be explained in accordance with an entirely naturalistic set of assumptions.

In opposition to this view, I am going to argue that *God's speaking* in biblical narrative plays a crucial role in the theological conception of history in the Old Testament. Indeed, I would argue that it is divine speech in biblical narrative that marks out a theological conception of history (and the historical truth-claims in the narrative) from a non-theological one. It is divine speaking in biblical narrative that uniquely characterizes the theological conception of history therein as the history of YHWH. Robert Jenson asserts that YHWH in Old Testament narrative is identified as 'the one who rescued Israel from Egypt'.[2] I agree, but I want to add that this definite description becomes true of YHWH *in virtue of the divine speaking*. God speaking is God acting, because God speaking is a determining of himself to be a particular acting personal self, in this case precisely 'the one who rescues Israel from Egypt'. This is essentially a *philosophical* theory, and in particular a *metaphysical* theory, since it claims that the metaphysical identity of the divine speaking is precisely a divine acting.[3]

Ultimately, what my theory will juxtapose is what I take to be the two fundamental explanatory concepts in Old Testament narrative: on the one hand, YHWH's *divine speaking* and, on the other, the people of Israel's *historical experience* of YHWH. Crucially, I do not want to say that 'the people of Israel's historical experience of YHWH acting in her life' implies 'YHWH acted in the people of Israel's life'. I take it to be the case that one can understand oneself as experiencing something without it necessarily being the case that this something exists. Accordingly, I take the concept of divine speaking to be the more fundamental concept in that it provides for the greater rationality of the claim to historical experience of YHWH than does the concept of historical experience on its own.

Hence, as will be seen: in the context of Exodus chapter 14 – the deliverance at the sea (the 'parting of the Red Sea') – this means that, as the Priestly writer might have understood it, the J account on its own was not a complete account of 'the deliverance at sea' because it did not include the explanatory

---

[2] Jenson, *Systematic Theology*, I, 59.

[3] I employ the phrase 'divine speaking' in conscious distinction from the concept of 'divine speech', since the former embodies the notion of a personal identity in action.

reality of divine speech.[4] It was essentially an account of Israel's historical *experience* of YHWH – a narrative written from the perspective of the people Israel, rather than from the perspective of YHWH (as P seems to have it). As the J account has it, Israel saw the marvellous work that YHWH did against the Egyptians. The people feared YHWH and put their faith in YHWH and in his servant Moses. Crucially, it contains no narrative of God speaking. This is not to say that J did not know of Israel's speaking, and therefore personal, God; one only has to look at Exodus 3 to dispel that notion. But, still, it remains true that this God seems to be absent from the J narrative in chapter 14. And it is P who remedies this absence by placing the J account in the context of the speaking God who, I will argue, acts in his speaking.[5]

It should be noted also that, even though P introduces a more supernaturalistic account of the deliverance at sea, the writer is at pains to place even the realm of miraculous event in the context of the divine speaking. A world in which supernaturalistic events are possible is not in itself sufficient to deduce the

---

[4] When Brevard Childs focuses on the *canonical shape* internal to this narrative he means a specific composite nature he identifies as constituted of the individual contributions of the Priestly and Yahwist versions (and also the Elohist version) of the deliverance at sea. See Childs, *Exodus*, 23. This canonical shaping, he would argue, alerts one to the presence of different narrative viewpoints – of different layers of canonical shaping superimposed on one another – concealed, as it were, within the surface of the continuous narrative. Crucially, the fact that the Priestly writer redacts the Yahwist narrative – and not the other way round – means that our understanding of the final form of the text, the canonical text, has to be informed by this redactional history. This seems to me to be the fundamental difference between Childs's canonical approach and the pre-critical tradition of interpretation one finds in Augustine, Thomas and Calvin. I follow Childs's 'post-critical' orientation in stating my case in terms of the P and J sources and redactions. In that sense, my theory is resolutely 'post-critical'. Barth, too, was post-critical in his approach to the literary sources of the Old Testament. See my *Karl Barth and the Strange New World within the Bible*, ch. 7.

[5] It has to be said that J does not often posit Israel's historical experience of YHWH without also positing the presence of God's speaking as a potential means of explanation of this experience. It would have been a hypothesis of great simplicity had this not been the case. One could then assert that P provided the explanation of the historical experience of Israel affirmed by J. Nevertheless, what P does is to articulate in a much more determinate fashion God's speaking as a sufficient causal power – an efficient cause, if you will. P provides a theory (insofar as this concept is not anachronistic), connecting divine action with divine speech. The most important – indeed paradigmatic – example of this is, of course, the P creation narrative. That is, P understands the creation narrative as paradigmatic for the way that God acts in the world. Hence, in the cases where J has omitted (for whatever reason) to include God's speech in the narrative (as in the climactic events in Exodus 14), P will ensure that the narrative events are grounded in, and given their meaning by, the divine speaking.

presence of an acting God. A world with divine speaking is. This is why the Old Testament scholar Claus Westermann described the relation between the word of God and historical event, between the word of God and history, as 'the basic problem' in the then 'present search for understanding the Old Testament'.[6] James Barr, another Old Testament scholar, said much the same thing when he spoke out against G.E. Wright's account of divine action in the latter's *God Who Acts* on the grounds that Wright's God was essentially a speechlessly-acting God.[7] Gerhard von Rad also brilliantly characterized the Deuteronomistic history in terms of the relation between word and historical event.[8]

Brevard Childs is another biblical scholar for whom divine action coincides with divine speaking.[9] It is in this context that his distinction between 'divine action' and 'Israel's historical experience of YHWH', in his juxtaposition of 'ontic' (divine action) and 'noetic' (a concept designating the [intellectual] beliefs of the people of Israel as regards their experience of YHWH), should be understood. Speaking of the priestly creation narrative in his *Biblical Theology of the Old and New Testaments*, he writes:

> From a theological perspective it is significant to note that the present canonical shape has subordinated the noetic sequence of Israel's experience of God in her redemptive history to the ontic reality of God as creator. This is to say, although Israel undoubtedly first came to know Yahweh in historical acts of redemption from Egypt, the final form of the tradition gave precedence to God's initial activity in creating the heavens and earth.[10]

Following Childs, I would describe what follows as an attempt to evaluate the rationality of the noetic truth-claims of the people of Israel in the context of the ontic reality of God as creator and covenant-partner understood as essentially a speaking self. I might also describe the project as delineating the philosophical consequences of this canonical decision in that I would attempt to evaluate and affirm the rationality of the truth-claims emerging from inserting the experiential claims regarding YHWH's actions in Israel's life into the creational context of the priestly narrative.

It is von Rad who is to be credited with bringing to the fore the concept of Israel's historical experience of YHWH as a central methodological category for interpreting the Old Testament. Childs's main criticism of von Rad is not, in fact, the latter's commitment to the concept of 'the noetic experience of Israel' per se, but rather the fact that von Rad limited his theology in a fundamental

---

[6] Westermann, *Essays*, 4.
[7] Barr, *Old and New*, 43.
[8] Von Rad, 'Deuteronomic Theology'.
[9] Childs, *Exodus*, 204.
[10] Childs, *Biblical Theology*, 385.

way to this concept and sought to undergird the rationality of the concept of Israel's experience by taking recourse to what he thought was rationality's last refuge in this context – historical criticism. As Childs implies, there was something heroic yet tragic (and inconsistent) in von Rad's inability to break with the assumption that rationality proper could only be catered for by the critical-historical method – that the concept of experience on its own was not sufficient. When Childs criticized his esteemed teacher for failing to 'do justice to the final effect of the Priestly writer's editing of the Yahwist's material',[11] he intimated that one way von Rad could have moved the rationality of Old Testament theology without the historical-critical method would have been to understand the noetic experience of the people of Israel in the context of the 'ontic priority' of the creation history 'within the whole book of Genesis', and indeed beyond.[12]

I think Childs observed something of momentous importance when he perceived that the solution may lie in the priestly creation history and the priority canonical shaping has given it vis-à-vis Genesis, the Pentateuch, and indeed the rest of the Old Testament. This chapter takes its point of departure from Childs's observation and implicitly asks: Is it rational to affirm this particular canonical shaping and the consequences the ontic reality of the creation history has for the rest of the Old Testament?

My view is that the creation narrative underwrites the rationality of Israel's historical experience expressed throughout the Old Testament. But here I want to show how this is true in the particular case of the exodus of the people of Israel from Egypt, as narrated culminating in Exodus 14. I believe that the same analysis can be applied – *mutatis mutandis* – to the Deuteronomistic history, although I will not attempt to prove this in the space available here. I treat this historical narrative in a comprehensive and systematic exposition of the whole theory of divine action in Old Testament narrative in my forthcoming book, *Metaphysics and the God of Israel*.[13]

Divine Speech the Key to God the Self-Determining Self: Karl Barth on the Priestly Creation Narrative

Von Rad published a famous paper in 1936 entitled 'The Theological Problem of the Old Testament Doctrine of Creation', in which he argued that the doctrine of creation was ancillary to the doctrine of salvation in Israel's Scriptures and history. Israel first knew of YHWH as a saving identity and only

---

[11] Childs, *Biblical Theology*, 120.
[12] Childs, *Biblical Theology*, 120.
[13] MacDonald, *Metaphysics*.

later inferred that this God was the creator of all things.[14] But von Rad also noted that what was crucial to the identity of this God under both descriptions was that he was a God who *acted in his speaking*. Von Rad wrote: 'Just as this chapter [of Genesis] knows of nature as created by God's word, so the Old Testament knows history also as created by God's word. See Isa. 9:7; 55:10ff; Jer. 23:29, but also 1 Kings 2:27 etc.'.[15] If we put this observation in terms of the Priestly writer as the 'author' of the Genesis 1–2:4a creation narrative, it is not an untoward deduction to say that the Priestly writer can be imagined extrapolating backwards from the characteristic manner of YHWH's action in the world to that of the creation of all things. God's speech is the means by which God acts in the world; ergo, thought the Priestly writer, God's speech is the means by which God created the world. Divine speech in biblical narrative, and in Old Testament narrative in particular, is crucial to the identity of God. Without the reference to divine speech and intention in the Old Testament, what we have there – even with miracles – falls short of a theological conception of history.[16]

How is God's speech simultaneously his action? It is my view that Karl Barth saw the way forward in this matter in his doctrine of creation. For what Barth provided for in his doctrine was precisely a theory of a personal acting divine self that could be extrapolated to the plane of divine action in the world.

To be sure, Barth's doctrine of creation has confounded its many commentators, who seem to have been at a loss as to what to do with it. What should one do with a doctrine that seems to amount to no more than the advice 'believe in God the creator'? Speaking in the context of the Apostles' Creed, Barth wrote in *Dogmatics in Outline*:

> the confession does not speak of the world, or at all events it does so incidentally, when it speaks of [God, the creator] of heaven and earth. It does not say, I believe

---

[14] Von Rad, 'Theological Problem'.

[15] Von Rad, *Genesis*, 52.

[16] I am reminded of Thomas's claim in the *Summa* (Question 178, article 2) that the wicked cannot work miracles; the latter are the province of good and moral agents. One of Thomas's intentions may be to be able to move – as much as is possible – epistemologically from knowledge of miraculous event to knowledge of God as executor of this miraculous event. I take the view that this cannot be done. In the realm of possible-world semantics, it is surely possible to posit a world in which miracles happen without it being the case that this world was created by God (or that these miracles were done by God). What makes the difference is that God speaks in one world (the one he created precisely by speaking) and thereby acts in it, but doesn't in the other (even though this latter world does not exclude the miraculous). See Aquinas, *Summa*, XLV, 92.

in the created world, nor I believe, in the work of creation. But it says, I believe in God the Creator.[17]

Yet what Barth actually said in *Church Dogmatics*, III/1, amounted to a great deal more than this claim. In fact, Barth wanted to say that belief in God the creator was belief in God the one who determines himself to be the creator of all things. In Barth's mind this meant a doctrine which *in itself* was sufficient – rationally sufficient – for generating the conclusion that the world was created by God (a point to which we will return below).

If we put Barth's thesis in the form of a question asked in a catechism we get the following. Question: How did God create the world? Answer: God determined himself to be the creator of it. He determined himself to be the creator of all things. It is a highly counterintuitive theory. The paradoxical aspect to it is that it seems to put things the wrong way round. Our natural inclination is to say that God determines himself to be the creator precisely by creating the world. Barth's thesis is that God does not create the world *in order* for it to be the case that he determines himself as creator. God determines himself as the creator of the world; therefore, he is the creator of the world.[18]

Now crucially in Barth's doctrine, God determining himself to be the creator of all things is to be identified with God speaking.[19] Notwithstanding the presence of an older *Tatbericht* tradition in the narrative (in which creation is not derived from a divine word), Barth argues that the sole creative force by which God creates the world is divine speech. He thinks that this is in fact a rational interpretation of the final form of Genesis 1:1–2:4a. More importantly, he argues that God's speaking in the priestly creation narrative (as in 'let there be light') is precisely *identical with* God determining himself to be creator of all things (and, in the case of light, the creator of order or lawfulness in opposition to chaos). This is how God determines himself to be the creator. His speaking is a determining of himself as this personal self, as God the creator.[20]

---

[17] Barth, *Dogmatics in Outline*, 50.

[18] Counterintuitive Barth's doctrine might be – but in my judgement it is able to resolve some hitherto intractable doctrinal problems. I mention just two: the first is creation out of nothing, which Augustine perceived was still a problem late in the fourth century; the second is the problem of how a non-material creator can create a material world – a problem which worried the patristic fathers, and especially the Cappadocian father Gregory of Nyssa. How the doctrine in fact resolves these problems is discussed in my forthcoming book, *Metaphysics and the God of Israel*.

[19] God speaking in the context of Barth's doctrine of creation is God *revealing* himself to be the creator. Barth, *Church Dogmatics*, III/1, 110, 115. But God revealing himself in this way is also God determining himself to be the creator.

[20] I have given an extended account of Barth's doctrine of creation in my *Karl Barth*, 135–92.

Barth does not mean merely that God speaking is the *means* by which God determines himself to be the creator. He means that God speaking *is* his determining himself to be the creator (they are one and the same event). This means that the explanation of the creation of the world is not that God spoke per se, but that God's speaking is his determining himself to be the creator of all things. There is an intrinsic connection between speech and action. Goethe's reluctance to follow Luther's translation of the first verse of John's Gospel, 'In the beginning was the Word' (*Im Anfang war das Wort*), and his preference for 'In the beginning was the deed (or act)' (*die Tat*) has some credibility in this context. God speaking is, in fact, God acting. God speaking is an act because it is the act of God determining himself to be the creator. It is in fact an act in time, as against Augustine's 'eternalist' God the creator who creates outside of time. When God begins to determine himself as the creator of this or that, and ultimately determines himself to be the creator of all things, his creative acts are events, and these events occur in time.

'Let there be light'

Let me try to explain the import of Barth's doctrine with as illustrative an example as I can muster – the simple literal sense of Genesis 1:3. And God said, 'let there be light'. Let us suppose we switch the lights off in a windowless room and then utter the words, 'let there be light', in the fashion of the Creator. Were the room to be instantly bathed in light we would, I think, assume in good old Aristotelian fashion that we had been the efficient cause and our words the instrumental cause of the event of light coming into existence. That is how we would understand this event. For the developmental psychologist Jean Piaget, such a construal would function as an intrinsic part of our genetically programmed epistemological development as regards causing events to happen in the world. According to Piaget, the child throws a toy against the wall and concludes, rightly, that he or she caused the effect of the noise.[21] So far so good. But my point is this. What works as an explanation in the case of child development (assuming Piaget was right) does not work in the case of God speaking in the context of the doctrine of creation. Unfortunately, something like this assumption has been operative in the mainstream tradition of reflection on the biblical doctrine of creation throughout the centuries. We have been as children in the nursery! Aquinas is a pre-eminent example of this tradition. In his exposition of the Apostles' Creed it is clear that he deduced the doctrine of creation out of nothing from the premise that God created all things. In effect, Aquinas argued that, since God had created both the form of the world and the matter out of which it was formed, it followed that he had

---

[21] Piaget, *Genetic Epistemology*, 23.

created out of nothing (had he only created the form of the world, it would have followed that he had not created all things).[22] An integral part of this Thomistic conception of creation out of nothing was God the creator in terms of 'first cause' and his speech the instrumental cause of the creation.

My thesis is that we should not interpret divine speech after the Thomistic fashion. A much more fruitful way of understanding the priestly creation narrative is to construe divine speech in terms of God the self-determining self.

I submit that the correct interpretation of the event in the room is this: when we say 'let there be light', *we are determining ourselves as the creator of light* (in the room). We say 'let there be light', and there is light. The explanation of the happening of light is that *we have determined ourselves to be the creator of light (in the room)*. Given the self-determination, it must follow that there is light in the room. One cannot determine oneself as the creator of light – *and therefore be the creator of light* – and there not be light in the room. Given the premise, the conclusion that there is light in the room must follow.

To understand the validity of this thought, one has to appreciate that the conclusion follows as a matter of logic. It is exactly the same as saying that if you were to have determined yourself to be the person who won the Olympic gold medal in the hundred metres, then it would follow (logically) that you would have won the Olympic gold medal in the hundred metres. Analogously, *God's self-determining self is sufficient for it being the case that there is light in the room.*

Now of course we know, as a matter of fact, that when we say 'let there be light' in any windowless, and therefore dark, room, light does not come into existence in the room. We remain in the dark. And the explanation we give for this fact originates, as before, in something akin to our natural *a priori* 'Kantian' reaction as affirmed by Piaget. We argue that our failure to bring light into existence is because our saying 'let there be light' is not an instrumental cause of light coming into existence (as would, say, switching on a light switch). *But again, as before – in the context of the 'divine speaking' of the priestly narrative – this is not how we should understand the non-presence of light and our failure to bring it into existence.* We should say, rather, that when we say 'let there be light' *we are not determining ourselves as the creator of light.* And when we have finished uttering the words, we have not so determined ourselves. For counterfactually, were it the case that we had so determined ourselves then there would have been light. (This means that we have an explanation of why divine speaking explains the creation of the world and mere human speaking does not. If I, as a human being, say 'let there be light' I do not determine *myself* to be the creator of light. If God, as God, does, then he does so determine himself.)

---

[22] Aquinas, *Aquinas Catechism*, Article 1.101.

The significance of the above for the doctrine of creation is that there must be a subtle yet profound semantic shift from the traditional Christian apprehension of the literal sense of God's speaking toward the kind of theory Barth espouses. The traditional interpretation understands God saying 'Let there be …' almost as an instrumental cause in the Aristotelian sense bringing into existence, for example, order. This is so whether one understands this instrumental cause as personal and hypostatic in nature (as in the Son or Word of God) or as a merely impersonal causal creativity. While not in any sense rejecting a Trinitarian doctrine of creation, understanding God in terms of the concept of divine self-determination casts a new light on the matter of creation. In saying 'let there be light' God is determining himself as the creator of order or lawfulness, as opposed to the chaos described at Genesis 1:2.

Why should it be the case that when we say 'let there be light' we do not bring light into existence but, when God says it, he *does* determine himself as the creator of light? Or, putting it slightly more accurately, why is it the case that God saying 'let there be light' is his determining himself as creator and our saying it is not? The fundamental explanation is that God determining himself as the creator of light is *basic* – irreducible – in the sense in which mere human self-determination as this creator of light is not. What do I mean?

Human beings have to do something to create light in a room. They have, for example, to carry out the action of flicking a light-switch or turning on a torch (or activating a movement-sensitive lighting system). Human beings *do* things in order to determine themselves in this context. Human self-determination is not basic because it is precisely reducible to some other action that brings the self-determination to be, to come about. This is why divine self-determination implies a fundamental *disanalogy* with mere human self-determination. God does not *do* anything as a condition of self-determination (what he *does* is determine himself). He determines himself as the creator of light, ergo he is the creator of light, ergo there is light in the room.

In order fully to understand the point I am making it might be worthwhile uttering the words 'let there be light' and imagining, not – as one is wont to do in Piagetian fashion – that your words are the instrumental cause of light in the room, but that you are in the process of determining yourself to be the creator of light in the room, and that this is the reason there *is* light in the room. It is not merely that you intended to determine yourself as the creator of light, but that in so speaking you did determine yourself as the creator of light. Then you may have some sense of the mind of God – as it were.

If one were to describe the natural habitat of this model of divine creation, one might look to Enlightenment political theory or theory of government: the eminently Enlightenment concept of self-determination. (It would, I think, be a mistake to categorize Barth's doctrine along with the voluntarist views of God's will one finds in such as William of Ockam.)[23] The important thing for our present purpose is that when God determines himself, this is something that God does to himself. He does not determine anything or anyone else. Our proposition really says something solely about God and not about anything or anyone else. It is a statement solely about God determining his being or identity – not about God determining the existence of any other being or identity – or at least not directly. God is both the subject, and – crucially – the object, of his action.

To determine oneself *to be* this or that identity is not merely to do something to one or other of one's properties; it is to orientate one's whole identity. God determines himself *to be* the creator of all things. My first reaction when I initially reflected on the nature of divine self-determination was that it was a kind of self-reflexive action, similar in kind to the actions indicated in self-reflexive verbs such as 'I wash myself' or 'I shave myself'. But the similarity is only superficial. My washing myself is obviously merely to do something to one or other of my properties, in this case my body. Self-determination carries a connotation that mere self-reflexive action does not. So while determining himself to be the creator of all things may be something that God does to himself, it is something God does to his *whole* identity. He acts on himself to become an identity he was not before, though without becoming someone else. God remains God even as he becomes the creator of the world in the sense that he determines himself to be the creator of the world. When God determines himself to be the creator of all things he is acting on himself – more precisely, he is acting on his identity, orientating his identity.

A quick word on the logic of divine self-determination: One of the analytic philosopher's core strengths is that he or she will tend to view a proposition or a declarative sentence as alive with certain implications. In his or her eyes (or ears, for that matter), a proposition is not an inert thing which just says what it says; it is dynamic in the sense that if it is true then it generates other truths, entails other truths. Another way of saying the same thing is that *if the proposition under scrutiny is true, its truth is a logically sufficient condition for another proposition being true.*

In the case of God determining himself to be the creator of all things, two propositions follow in its wake. The first is that if God determines himself to be the creator of all things then he is the creator of all things. Philosophers

---

[23] For one thing, Barth has no objection in principle to the very 'unvoluntaristic' proposition that God could *only* have created this world. The catch in his position is that there could have been a world identical to the actual one in all respects except one: it wasn't created by God. To put it another way, this world is identical in every way except that it is not designated by the predicate 'created by God'. Clearly both deductive and inductive (probabilistic) natural theology fail under such conditions.

would say that God determining himself to be the creator is a logically sufficient condition of it being true that God is the creator. There is the premise that God determines himself to be creator and there is the logically deduced conclusion that God is creator. To put it another way, it is a simple logical truth that if God determines himself to be the creator or the one who creates all things, then he *is* the creator. Second, analytic philosophers would agree that if God is the creator of the world then it follows – again, logically – that the world was created by God. If God is the creator in virtue of determining himself to be the creator, then it follows that God determining himself as the creator of the world is *sufficient* for it to be the case that the world was created by God.

But God determining himself to be the creator of all things is also a *basic action*. His self-determination *explains* how God creates the world. This is not merely to argue a logical point but to make an actual claim about God's relation to the world and *how* God creates the world. In other words, God determining himself to be this or that identity explains how God created the world. It is to say that God's action here is something like *an efficient cause*.

'God said, "Let there be light." And there was light.' Meir Sternberg points out the pattern of repetition and, in particular, the laconicism of spoken word and fulfilment in the priestly narrative. God said 'let there be …' and there was – is indicative of the effortless manner ('God need not exert himself to work wonders' to quote Sternberg) in which God creates the world.[24] Could it be that the same is true of divine action in the world? Is it possible that God acts in the world in a formally identical manner to the way in which he created the world? Is it possible to say that the Priestly writer, in somewhat stylized fashion, was insinuating that the manner in which God creates the world is paradigmatic for the way in which he acts in it? In the context of von Rad's thesis of Israel's extrapolation back from God's soteriological identity to that of his creational identity – from the judging yet forbearing, saving God to God the creator of all things – this would mean that the way in which the soteriological identity acts in history is formally identical to the way in the creational identity creates the world. Let me set the context in which this theory will operate: the divine identity of YHWH the judging yet forbearing self in the exodus narrative.

From Exodus to Promised Land:
YHWH the Judging yet Forbearing Divine Identity

There is agreement among biblical commentators (von Rad, Noth, Childs, to name but three) that the traditions in the pentateuchal narrative after the

---

[24] Sternberg, *Poetics*, 101.

history of the patriarchs (inclusive of the creedal statements such as Deut. 26:5ff.) can be assigned to the following individual complexes of tradition: the exodus tradition, the wilderness tradition, the Sinai tradition and the settlement tradition. There is also a consensus that the most important tradition of the Pentateuch, and indeed the foundational tradition of the history of the people of Israel and its claim to be in historical relationship with the God of Israel, YHWH, is the exodus tradition. This explains why, as Noth puts it, 'the expression "Yahweh who brought Israel out of Egypt" very early became a *fixed formula* which occurs in widely differing contexts'. The theme of 'guidance out of Egypt' is, according to Noth, '*a primary confession* of Israel.' YHWH is 'the one who led Israel out of Egypt'.[25]

Intrinsic to the narrative presentation of YHWH 'guiding Israel out of Egypt' is God's action in delivering Israel from the Reed Sea – the miracle of the Reed Sea – one of God's 'great and terrible acts', one of his 'signs and wonders'. But though Noth argues that the activity of YHWH in this confessional formula originally seems in fact to have referred to 'the destruction of the Egyptians in the Sea',[26] there is also evidence in the final form of the text that the theme of deliverance at sea simultaneously functions as the thematic point of departure for the narrative that succeeds it: the 'wilderness' narrative culminating in the approach and occupation of the promised land. Indeed, this seems to have been its original context within the J (or JE) account.

As this latter narrative presents it, what we have, among other things, is *a saving history which is one and the same event extending from, and beginning with, the deliverance from Egypt at the Reed Sea and ending with the settlement tradition in the land of Canaan.*[27]

It is because of this fact that one can argue that the experience Israel has of YHWH acting in this history is precisely of a judging yet forbearing, saving God. The Reed Sea account becomes an act of God's faithfulness toward Israel in the face of Israel's lack of faith in her God. In this sense it can be argued that Israel's lack of faith – intensifying as it does into disobedience and rebellion right up to the approach to the promised land (Num. 21:4) – constitutes the primary hermeneutical context to God's saving action. This is the reason the 'murmuring' tradition against YHWH's action of 'leading them out of Egypt' is a central datum of the wilderness tradition. What begins as a thematic of faithlessness in God's provision becomes – after the golden calf incident – a thematic of disobedience and (repeated) rebellion against God.

Yet God desists from withdrawing his saving action. Though the wilderness is pictured as 'a series of very great crises' in which YHWH has to ponder the

---

[25] Noth, *History*, 23.

[26] Noth, *Exodus*, 104.

[27] Cf. von Rad, *Old Testament Theology*, I, 281.

nature and continuation of his relationship with Israel in the context of judgement and divine wrath (he refuses to lead Israel any further in person due to the fact that his holiness would result in annihilation for his sinful people), he does not abandon his saving history but sets up mediating institutions (the angel of the Lord, the holy tent, etc.) in order to remain in personal relationship with Israel.[28]

In the context of the 'murmuring' tradition in the wilderness, the occupation tradition – understood from the perspective of Israel's highly theological conception of history – testifies no less unambiguously than the deliverance phenomenon to the judging yet ultimately soteriological identity of the God of Israel. For, ultimately, even in the wake of Israel's disobedience and rebellion and God's reactive judgement, God remains faithful to his people. The crossing of the Reed Sea coalesces in the biblical imagination with the crossing of the Jordan River. In this way the 'guidance out of Egypt' theme and the 'guidance into the arable land' theme (the settlement or occupation) constitute the *terminus a quo* and the *terminus ad quem*, respectively, of the one saving

---

[28] Von Rad, *Old Testament Theology*, I, 284, 288. Von Rad argues that there are two different traditions present within the Pentateuch and the rest of the Old Testament, e.g., the difference between Jer. 2 and Ezek. 20. The first tradition puts the emphasis on God's marvellous signs and wonders succouring Israel in the desert. In contrast, the second puts the emphasis on Israel's faithlessness and sin (280–89). But, in this context, it is clear that the 'murmuring' tradition takes the form of two related but distinct stereotyped patterns (Childs, *Exodus*, 258–62). Pattern 1 takes the form of a genuine need (such as food or water) which is followed by a complaint, then by an intercession on the part of Moses, which issues in the need being met by God's miraculous intervention. Pattern 2 takes the form of an initial complaint (without the basis of a genuine need), which is followed by God's anger and punishment (judgement), then an intercession from Moses, and finally a reprieve of the punishment. The cry of the people of Israel narrated by Ex. 14:11–13 exemplifies the former pattern, while their behaviour as they approach the promised land (Num. 21:4) is indicative of the latter pattern. Further evidence of the stereotyped shaping of this material is the fact that the murmuring stories before the golden calf incident all follow Pattern 1; whereas the same stories after the great apostasy all follow Pattern 2. Both patterns are equally old. Hence the later commentary on the tradition, notably Jer. 2 (emphasizing Pattern 1 and God's marvellous saving actions); and Pss. 78, 106, 136; Ezek. 20 (emphasizing Pattern 2 and Israel's identity as 'a defiant faithless crowd' [von Rad, *Old Testament Theology*, I, 283]), are not in any sense incompatible. What we have is the narrators' focus equally on the human actions and the divine. Indeed, Ezekiel's take on the wilderness period as 'a type and pattern of the coming judgement' of the Babylonian exile of 586 BCE (von Rad, *Old Testament Theology*, I, 283), can be understood within the context of the theological conception of history identified in terms of YHWH's judging yet forbearing identity.

historical event in which Israel's experience of its God is an experience of the
one who shows gracious forbearance to her even in his judgement of her.

The Reed Sea Narrative

Nevertheless, as Noth points out, there is a tradition present in Exodus in
which the theme of 'guidance out of Egypt' does culminate with the 'deliverance at the sea' theme.[29] In effect, the latter theme is brought – and it is rational
to say that it is the work of the Priestly narrator – into closer relationship with
the exodus out of Egypt. The P narrative construes the deliverance theme as
the culminating event in Israel's exodus from Egypt, recapitulating the great
creative acts of redemption out of chaos in the priestly creation narrative, and
in this way placing the emphasis on YHWH's saving divine action at the heart of
Israel's earliest tradition. (It might be said that the priestly narrative puts the
emphasis more on the soteriological identity of God than on his judgement
per se.) Undoubtedly, however, this final form of the narrative affirms a theological conception of history in which God, and God alone, effects Israel's
release from Egypt.

   In the J account, the crossing of the Reed Sea is depicted as the effect of
'natural causes' (strong east wind, dry sea bed, panic among the Egyptians). By
comparison, the later P account is 'supernaturally' orientated (splitting of the
sea, wall of water, etc.). This has suggested to the modern critical reader the
theory that the original crossing was the result of 'a series of natural events, and
that the later writer sought to articulate the theological *meaning* of this event by
extending the imagery into the supernatural'.[30] But since the J account of the
crossing is embedded in the extended soteriological narrative of Israel's journey
toward the promised land, it is only *relatively* less concerned than P with putting
emphasis on the divine action in this event.

   The modern account, focusing as it does on a supposed historical development within the text from natural to supernatural, allows 'the modern biblical
theologian to speak of the great act of God at the exodus in delivering his
people while at the same time to regard the event historically as little more than
the accidental escape of some slaves across a treacherous marsh'.[31] In this
account, there is only one event which begins and ends in the realm of natural
causes, and which at best is identified wholly with 'God's act', and 'God's act'
wholly with it.

---

[29] Noth, *History*, 51.
[30] Childs, *Exodus*, 228.
[31] Childs, *Exodus*, 228.

This is not the witness of the final form of the text. It aligns the two levels of divine activity in the final form of the text in a way that combines 'ordinary and wonderful elements'.[32] As Childs puts it, 'there never was a time when the event was only understood as ordinary, nor was there a time when the supernatural absorbed the natural. ... Israel saw the mighty hand of God at work in both the ordinary and the wonderful, and never sought to fragment the one great act of redemption into parts'.[33] We might say that the P narrative is more concerned with narrating the event from God's perspective (from within the narrative context of 'God present within the constitution of the world'); whereas the J narrative gives an account of the divine activity from Israel's perspective, and her historical experience thereof.

The emphasis in the P narrative on God's perspective coincides with the locus of divine action, which in turn is to be identified with the divine speaking. Can the latter function as an explanation of divine action in the world? It can if something like Barth's doctrine of creation can be fruitfully employed in the realm of divine action per se.

Divine Speaking as Divine Action

How can something like Barth's doctrine of creation be *extended* into the theory of divine action in the world? Barth himself made some tantalizing remarks on the relation between divine speech and divine action in the world in *Church Dogmatics*, I/1. Although I think it would be difficult to argue that they constitute a fully developed theory, these remarks seem to me to point the way forward to the possibility of transposing Barth's conception of divine action from the plane of creation to that of divine action in the world. Barth writes:

> The Word of God does not need to be supplemented by an act. The Word of God is itself the act of God.[34]

Again, and perhaps most tellingly, he says:

> In human life, the distinction between word and act is that mere word is the mere self-expression of a person, while act is the resultant relative alteration in the world around. Mere word is passive, act is an active participation in history. But this kind of distinction does not apply to the Word of God. As mere Word it is act. As mere Word

---

[32] Childs, *Exodus*, 228.
[33] Childs, *Exodus*, 238.
[34] Barth, *Church Dogmatics*, I/1, 143.

it is the divine person, the person of the Lord of history, whose self-expression is as such an alternation of the world whose *passio* in history is as such *actio.*[35]

Finally:

> The fact that the Word of God is the act of God means thirdly that it is decision. This is what distinguishes an act from a mere event.[36]

What have we here? God's word is God's act? God's speech is God's act? There is no act beyond the speech? Note the proposition that says that God's word or speech is not mere event – it is act. Why would Barth want to distinguish the two? Because no one seriously doubts that God's speech is an event – of course it is, what else would it be? My speech, too, is an event – everyone's is. But God's speech is not just an event; it is also an *act*. It *does* something that my speech does not – and this *doing* something is to do with the concept of decision. It is the fact that God's speech is God's decision that makes the former God's act. And this means also that it is a historical act, and therefore history. God acts historically in his speech.

If we transpose Barth's thought on this matter to Childs's analysis of the exodus narrative, we find that Childs has similar strictures to make about exegesis that separates divine speech and divine action – at least in Exodus. Speaking of the Passover pericope in the context of Israel's exodus from Egypt, Childs writes:

> The biblical writer brackets the Exodus event with a preceding and a succeeding interpretation. He does not see the exodus as 'an act of God' distinct from the 'word of God' which explains it. In theological terms, the relation between act and interpretation, or event and word, is one that cannot be separated. The biblical writer does not conceive of the event as primary or 'objective' from which an inferential, subjective deduction is drawn (*contra* G.E. Wright, *God Who Acts*, SBT, 8). The event is never uninterpreted. Conversely, a theological interpretation which sees the subjective appropriation – whether described cultically or existentially – as the primary element from which an event can be reconstructed, is again introducing a theological scheme which has no warrant in the theology of the redactor.[37]

Two statements in this passage stand out for me. The first is that the narrator 'does not see the exodus as "an act of God" distinct from the "word of God" *which explains it* [emphasis mine]'. The second is that 'the relation between act and interpretation, or event and word, is one that cannot be separated'. The

---

[35] Barth, *Church Dogmatics*, I/1, 144.
[36] Barth, *Church Dogmatics*, I/1, 156.
[37] Childs, *Exodus*, 204.

first clearly echoes Barth's point that the answer to the question, 'whither God's act in history?' is 'in his speech'. This fact is the reason for the second statement: event – act – and word cannot be separated. Childs's theological exegesis can be explained in terms of God the self-determining self, who determines himself to be this historical identity in his speech.

The implications of Childs's exegesis are clearly at odds with a modern account which first separates word and event into two realms of event, linguistic and material, and then seeks epistemologically to evaluate each independently of the other. It is not that word and event are the same event, but rather that the word of God cannot occur without it being the case that the other – God's act – occurs.

This means that it is not natural or supernatural categories that make God's act *God's act;* it is God's speech that makes God's act *God's act.* Since the latter is sufficient, the former categories, especially the supernatural, are unnecessary: it is not the supernatural per se which makes God's act *God's act* (it is God determining himself, thus says the biblical witness). To have described the events of Israel's exodus from Egypt outside of the context of God's speech – without God's speaking to Moses as an intrinsic part of the narrative (and therefore being in personal relationship with Moses) – would have been literally to have described another event. In particular, it would have been to narrate an event that occurred outside of the ontic context of God's self-determination, outside of God's self-determining self. It would be to describe an event which, as was said, began and ended with the uninterpreted events, whether natural or supernatural.

If we put these comments in the context of Barth's doctrine of creation, we can extrapolate to the following thought. Just as God's speech as an act of self-determination is both basic and sufficient for it to be the case that the world was created by God, then so God's speech is both basic and sufficient for it to be the case that God acts in the world. There is the premise that God determined himself – in his speech – to be the one who delivered Israel from the bondage of Egypt, and there is the logically deduced conclusion that Israel was delivered from the bondage of Egypt by God.

In other words – as in the case of creation – God determining himself to be the one who delivered Israel from Egypt *explains* how God delivered Israel from Egypt. As in the case of creation, God's action here is something like *an efficient cause* of the fact that Israel was delivered from Egypt.

What I am in fact doing is transposing this understanding of God's action in creation to God's action within the constitution of the world. If the meaning of God's speech in the creation history is that he determines himself to be the creator of all things, why should it not be the case that divine self-determination provides the conceptual link between God's speech and God's action in the world? Why should it not be the case that God's self-determining act constitutes an efficient cause of his action in the world in the same way that it constitutes an efficient cause of the coming into being of all things?

God speaking is God acting because God speaking is God determining himself to be this or that personal historical identity. If God says to Moses in Exodus 6:2–9 'I will release you from your labours in Egypt. I will rescue you from slavery there' then – *given that this happens* – it can be said that he determines himself to be the one who will rescue them from their labours in Egypt, and so on. Therefore he *is* the one who will rescue them from their labours in Egypt, and so on. Therefore he *does* rescue them from their labours in Egypt (if it is true that one *will do* something, then it follows that one *does it*). Therefore YHWH *acts* in personal and historical relationship to the people of Israel. And he had done this merely by speaking – no more no less – since his speaking is his determining himself to be this historical-personal self. God's speaking is not mere event; it is also, crucially, action. And we can say that it is action because it is God determining himself to be this or that historical identity. The disanalogy with human speech is fundamental and complete. My speech can never be my action in God's sense since if I said what God said, for example, in Exodus 6:2–9 it would *not* be my determining myself to be the one who will lead Israel out of Egypt. And, without this implication in operation, my words are powerless by comparison.

I submit that the simple litmus test of this doctrine of divine action is that if it is a logically consistent explanation as regards the creation of the world, then there is no reason why it should not be equally so in the case of divine action within the world. Indeed, one theological benefit emerging from coupling God's divine action of creating the world through speech with that of his action within the world is that there is no conceptual distinction to be made as regards the power and might of God in his creation of the world over that of his soteriological history vis-à-vis the people of Israel. From our 'all too human' perspective we are naturally inclined to think that the power and energy involved in creating the world – the universe, all that is – is a great deal more than that involved in judging and saving Israel. But Meir Sternberg has drawn our attention above to the fact that God's speech in creation is indicative of the effortless manner ('God need not exert himself to work wonders') in which God creates the world. The implication to be drawn from this is that God's self-determination is as sufficient in one context as it is in the other. Accordingly, to say that the manner in which God created the world is qualitatively identical to the way in which he interacts with his people, the people of Israel, and humankind in general, is to say that concepts of might and power – which might well apply in a scientific context – are inapplicable in the context of the doctrine of God in a biblical context (except, of course, as a description of that very effortlessness).

Similarly, to place the deliverance at sea in the ontic context of divine self-determination through divine speech is to say precisely that God's word does explain God's act. God determined himself to be the one who delivered Israel from the Reed Sea; therefore he is the one who delivered Israel from the Reed Sea; therefore Israel was delivered by God from the Reed Sea. Or, putting it another way, the meaning in the narrative, of God speaking within the world, is precisely God determining himself to be – in this case – 'the one who led Israel out of Egypt'. Therefore, he *is* the one who led Israel out of Egypt. Therefore it is rational for the narrator of the final form of Exodus to affirm that God – YHWH – led the people of Israel out of Egypt. In other words, God's speaking *within the cosmos* is to be understood within the context of the efficacious power of his speech in the creation *of the cosmos*. Given the nature of God as divine agent, God's speaking is not meant to be construed as any ordinary human speaking. In this sense, there is no warrant in biblical narrative for positing an exact analogy between divine and human speech in the Bible in the context of a theory or doctrine of divine action.

Is the theory paradoxical? Decidedly, yes – but not, I think, contradictory. The brilliant physicist Richard Feynman once said of the celebrated double-slit experiment of quantum mechanics that, if you understood this experiment, then you understood the essence of quantum reality. Any difficulties in understanding and accepting the implications of quantum theory could, Feynman claimed, be tempered by reminding oneself of the paradoxical results of the experiment.[38]

Remember the suggestion earlier that it might be worthwhile uttering the words 'let there be light' and imagining, not that one's words are the instrumental cause of light, but that you are in the process of determining yourself to be the creator of light – and that this is the reason there *is* light in the room? Remember *that* suggestion for dispelling the sense of paradox? Well, in the case of divine action in the world it is exactly like that except that one imagines – not that your words are the instrumental cause of Israel's release from Egypt – but that you in your words are in the process of determining yourself to be the one who frees, or will free, Israel from Egypt, and that therefore you are the one who frees, or will free, Israel from Egypt, and that therefore – as a matter of logic – Israel has been delivered from Egypt by you. (You cannot be the one who delivered Israel from Egypt and it not be the case that Israel was delivered from Egypt by you.) Of course given your humanity you can only do it in your imagination. God can do it – and did it – in reality.

Conclusion

When I first mooted the idea that God created and acted in the world by respectively determining himself to be the creator of and actor in it, I had the

---

[38] Feynman famously made this point in his *Lectures on Physics*, III, 23–51.

sensation, or so it seems to me, of what the seventeenth-century poet Henry Vaughan called 'seeing eternity the other night'. Is this really how God created the world? Is this really how he acts in it? I also wondered, though not entirely seriously: is there an aspect of profaning the sacred in all of this? Of trespassing into the 'holy of holies'? I concluded not. First, the mystery is still intact. When I assert that God determining himself is a basic action – that God can and does act in this way – the question of how he is able to do this remains unanswerable. I submit that we have gone as far as we can toward grasping God's being in this respect. Beyond this point is the retention of mystery. Second, the act of discerning the 'mind of God' is not without precedent in the history of theology. To the modern mentality, the idea of mediaeval school philosophers constructing comprehensive systems proactively, and pedantically anticipating answers to potential objections, is the stuff of eccentricity, of faintly absurd comedy. 'How many angels can one get on the head of a pin?' is perhaps the most famous example of a scholastic curiosity taken to extremes. Yet it should be remembered that it was also a world in which the great thinkers of the time debated the actual mind of God and, in so doing, made it utterly real, present and alive to their audiences or their addressees. An example would be the intellectualist-voluntarist debate. Intellectualists such as Aquinas and Eckhart thought that choices of the will result from that which the intellect recognizes as good. In the case of God, this meant that God's will itself is determined by his reason, his intellect as it were. Voluntarists such as Duns Scotus and William of Ockam held that the will determines which objects are good. In the case of God, this meant that the divine will is the ultimate origin of the good. Did God reason before willing, or was will the ultimate origin of his action? These were all attempts to peer into 'the mind of God'.

There is also a modern precedent to this aspect of the mediaeval mind. It has found itself at home in no less a subject than fundamental theoretical physics. Physicists, in effect, are the minds who attempt to peer into the mind of God. Perhaps Stephen Hawking's *A Brief History of Time* is not a particularly good example; a better one might of course be Paul Davies' *The Mind of God*. But, even then, both examples are too secular in nature. It is time for a reappropriation of 'the mind of God' – as it were – on the part of the Bible and theology.

Bibliography

Aquinas, T., *The Aquinas Catechism: A Simple Explanation of the Catholic Faith by the Church's Greatest Theologian* (Manchester, NH: Sophia Institute Press, 2000)

——, *Summa Theologiae*, XLV: *Prophecy and Other Charisms* (2a2ae. 171–8) (ed. R. Potter; London: Blackfriars, 1970)

Barr, J., *Old and New in Interpretation: A Study of the Two Testaments* (London: SCM Press, 1982)

Barth, K., *Dogmatics in Outline* (London: SCM Press, 2001)

——, *Church Dogmatics*, III/1 (Edinburgh: T. & T. Clark, 1958)

Childs, B., *Biblical Theology of the Old and New Testaments: Theological Reflection on the Christian Bible* (London: SCM Press, 1992)

——, *Exodus: A Commentary* (London: SCM Press, 1974)

Davies, P., *The Mind of God: The Scientific Basis for a Rational World* (New York: Simon & Schuster, 1992)

Feynman, R.P., R.B. Leighton and M. Sands, *The Feynman Lectures on Physics*, III: *Quantum Mechanics* (Reading, MA: Addison-Wesley, 1965)

Hawking, S., *A Brief History of Time: From the Big Bang to Black Holes* (New York: Bantam Books, 1988)

Jenson, R.W., *Systematic Theology*, I (Oxford: OUP, 1997)

MacDonald, N.B., *Karl Barth and the Strange New World within the Bible: Barth, Wittgenstein, and the Metadilemmas of the Enlightenment* (Carlisle: Paternoster, 2000)

——, *Metaphysics and the God of Israel* (Carlisle: Paternoster, forthcoming)

Noth, M., *Exodus: A Commentary* (London: SCM Press, 1962)

——, *A History of Pentateuchal Traditions* (Englewood Cliffs, NJ: Prentice-Hall, 1972)

Piaget, J., *Genetic Epistemology* (New York: Columbia University Press, 1970)

Sternberg, M., *The Poetics of Biblical Narrative: Ideological Literature and the Drama of Reading* (Bloomington: Indiana University Press, 1985)

von Rad, G., 'The Deuteronomic Theology of History in 1 and 2 Kings', in *The Problem of the Hexateuch and Other Essays* (London: SCM Press, 1984), 205–21

——, 'The Theological Problem of the Old Testament Doctrine of Creation', in *The Problem of the Hexateuch and Other Eessays* (London: SCM Press, 1984), 131–43

——, *Genesis* (London: SCM Press, 3rd edn, 1972)

——, *Old Testament Theology* (2 vols; London: SCM Press, 1975)

Westermann, C., *Essays in Old Testament Interpretation* (London: SCM Press, 1963)

Wright, G.E., *God Who Acts: Biblical Theology as Recital* (London: SCM Press, 1960)

20

Inhabiting the Story

The Use of the Bible in the Interpretation of History

Stephen I. Wright

The cry for an interpretation of the human drama is a cry not for technical history but for something more like 'prophecy'. Those Christians who wish to have their history rich in values, judgments and affirmations about life, can find the clue and the pattern to its interpretation very easily; for they, of all people, ought to be the most inveterate readers and students of the Bible.[1]

Introduction

I have had the privilege and challenge of writing this essay *after* the consultation at which most of the other chapters in this volume were discussed. Privilege, because that means I have had first-hand access to the wide resources of wisdom brought by the other contributors. Challenge, because a much fuller wrestling with their ideas has been called for than if I had been writing concurrently with them.

In reflection upon both consultation and contributions, one thing has struck me with increasing force. The focus of our deliberations was almost entirely upon the way in which we understand the Bible as a text that *refers* in some way to the historical reality of its own epoch. In that context, the spectre of the 'historical-critical method' kept returning as a haunting presence, refusing to be exorcised. Hardly at all did we consider the question of how, in practice, the Bible is to be used today to *interpret* historical reality.[2]

---

[1] Butterfield, *Christianity and History*, 38.

[2] Though the chapters by Murray Rae, 'Creation and Promise: Towards a Theology of History', Ch. 12, and David Lyle Jeffrey, '(Pre) Figuration: Masterplot and Meaning in Biblical History', Ch. 16, are highly suggestive in this respect.

I think the reason for this is clear. Most of the participants work in academic fields in which either methods of studying the Bible and assessing its 'historicity', or the grounds for Christian faith itself, are deeply contested. This gives an urgency to the focus on the Bible's own reference to history which is understandable. The debate on this subject is vital and must be continued. Clearly, any project concerned with the renewal of biblical interpretation in the academy must address the questions that are burning in the academic sub-disciplines concerned.

And yet we ought not to think, either, that such questions are the only ones relevant to the issue of 'history and biblical interpretation', or that they can be considered in isolation from the wider issue of how the Bible is (so to speak) mobilized as an interpretative framework for history itself. The fact is that the Bible is a collection of ancient texts which is used today, many centuries after its original writing and assembly, as authority, source and resource for institutional churches and millions of individual Christians. Some focus on how it is right to use it as a key for understanding *our* history seems called for.

Here I declare my own current professional interest in homiletics, and the practical acts of interpretation involved in preaching which strives to help people make sense of their lives, individually and corporately. But also at issue here is the use of the very word 'interpret'. Different contexts, of course, allow for different meanings of the same word. However, I wonder if the Christian community in general allows the academy too much authority in dictating the meaning of this one.

In the discourse of much academic biblical criticism and theology – indeed, in the discourse often employed in these volumes – 'interpretation' seems to be normally used to refer to the attempt to determine the significance of the text in itself *without any necessary consideration of its applicability, meaningfulness or heuristic power for the world today*. To 'interpret' a text is taken as equivalent to 'discovering its meaning', where 'meaning' is generally understood in a historical sense (i.e., the 'original' meaning).[3] This is the case whether the specific *object* of interpretation is 'source' (how the text arose) or 'discourse' (its meaning and force as communicative act), to use Meir Sternberg's distinction.[4] But one

---

[3] Thus there is often more than a trace in such interpretation of the 'historicism' noted as one of the 'problematic tendencies of historical criticism' by Peter Williamson in his Ch. 10 in this volume, 'The Place of History in Catholic Exegesis'.

[4] Sternberg, *Poetics*, 15. A good example of the kind of usage I refer to here is to be found in Christopher Seitz's 'Scripture', where he distinguishes between 'serious' biblical interpretation as 'academic formulations and debates about Scripture' and the implicitly 'non-serious' kinds among which he lists preaching and hymns (43). One could equally argue that academic biblical interpretation which does not take into account the actual interpretative practices of the church and individual

might argue that for all practical purposes in the church, 'interpretation' of Scripture which just tries to explain how it arose or what it first meant is hardly 'interpretation' at all. It takes no cognizance of the current reading practices of the Bible's readers or of the issue of the use to which the Bible is put today.

At stake is much more than the question of whether we can *understand* an ancient text – that is, the question whether by imagination, sympathy and an intellectual grasp of our own context and the biblical one a 'meeting of minds' can take place. It is the question of whether, when we have understood, we can discern the ways in which that understanding could and should make a difference to the way we view the world and conduct ourselves within it today. Put another way, it is the question of whether we can extend the lines set down for us in Scripture, faithful to the direction they are taking, into all the dimensions of contemporary existence.[5]

'Interpretation', in this sense, by definition will *not* be carried on in an academy which insists on personal beliefs and practices being kept private, and on the rhetoric of academic discourse taking (quasi-) objective form. But scholars working in such an academic context must surely, at the very least, pay attention to 'interpretation' in this wider sense as a phenomenon. After all, most of the biblical and theological resources of the past come from those who have believed in the importance of 'interpretation' in the full sense. Such interpretation is a function of the Christian community as a whole.[6] One of the chief ways in which it comes to expression, and by which it is propelled, is in preaching – preaching which in various ways 'negotiates the distance'[7] between text and hearer so as to enable the active, meaningful and practical interpretation of Scripture by the Christian community.[8] Such interpretation ought to be the subject of intelligent conversation in a general academic milieu which does, after all, contain departments of 'practical theology' and 'homiletics', even if the latter in particular remains something of a 'Cinderella' subject in the UK (in contrast to North America).

Our particular concern in this volume is with *history* and biblical interpretation, and therefore a further word is necessary to underline the reason why a focus on our use of the Bible today, rather than on its historical origins and

---

Christians, but stays with the significance of the text 'in itself', is not only *not* 'serious' interpretation; it is not fully 'interpretation' at all.

[5] Compare Gadamer's insistence that application is integral to understanding: Thiselton, *Two Horizons*, 308.

[6] An excellent study of the way that community interpretation might work is found in Fowl, *Engaging*. Cf. Watson, *Text*.

[7] For this phrasing and an excellent discussion of how it works in practice, see Craddock, *Preaching*, 125–50.

[8] See the finely balanced discussion in Clark, *Preaching*, 67–75.

reference, is still closely bound up with the issue of history. If, as Murray Rae cogently argues, history is indeed the sphere of God's activity, and therefore not to be rejected as a medium of revelation,[9] then not only the history reflected in the biblical writings, but *all* history is to be taken seriously as a meaningful out-working of God's purposes. Without engaging in debate over the notion of revelation itself, and the sense in which it continues now, we must at least assert that the search for the meaning of the historical process as a whole, and that part of it in which we are most closely involved, is a thoroughly Christian and 'biblical' enterprise. And if we regard Scripture as in some sense mediating God's *definitive* revelation, Scripture will be our main source for seeking to interpret history. The question is *how* it should be used for this purpose.

I argue in this chapter that if we bring this dimension of biblical interpretation into the foreground we may be spared some of the anxieties concerning the relationship between the Bible and history that Christians wishing to continue to treat the Bible as their supreme authority have suffered since the Enlightenment. I wish, like my fellow contributors, to affirm both the veracity of the Bible's witness to crucial events and the central importance of that trust-worthiness for Christian theology and life. But I want to argue that in the church we move out from the defensive posture into which the attacks from negative historical criticism have often forced us and held us trapped. This is not just the essentially negative matter of escaping from anxiety. It is also the vitally positive matter of being liberated to use the Bible as the lens through which we interpret the world, rather than an object of contemplation on its own.

What follows falls into three parts: a brief look at the background of this approach in so-called 'postliberal' thinking, notably that of Hans Frei; a discussion of how four key co-ordinates of the hermeneutical debate, considered elsewhere in this volume in relation to 'history' as the object of scriptural reference, look rather different when considered in relation to 'history' as that which Scripture enables us to interpret; and an outline of what I believe to be essential features of a renewed 'figural' interpretation of Scripture in which its words and the events which lie behind them are allowed to form a framework for our understanding of world history and those parts of it in which we are caught up.

Inhabiting Biblical Narrative

Hans Frei has shown how one result of the Enlightenment was to throw Christian biblical interpretation on to the defensive.[10] This is a tale that has now

---

[9] See Rae's Ch. 12 in this volume, 'Creation and Promise'.

[10] Frei, *Eclipse*.

been rehearsed many times, and told from a number of angles in the present series of volumes. Here I offer merely a summary by way of relating it to my present argument.

From an earlier position of confident, trusting acceptance of Scripture as the lens or grid through which all of reality might be interpreted, the church found itself in the position of having to account for the veracity of Scripture in terms set by those for whom human reason was the fulcrum for knowledge and understanding of the world – even if many of these continued to acknowledge the existence of God. The net result was 'the eclipse of biblical narrative', a loss of the great story which made sense of the world, as Scripture started to be dissected and atomized. Partly this was a matter of its being divided up into those parts which could be accepted by natural reason (such as moral principles) and those parts which could not (such as miracles), with strategies being developed to deal with the latter – outright rejection, treatment as 'myth' (perhaps to be demythologized) and so on. Increasingly, it was a matter of letting Scripture be subject to minute scrutiny as an object of historical study like any other ancient text. The issue of Scripture's historical conditioning, and the extent to which its witness could be shown to correspond (or not) with what could be known of actual events from other sources and by the canons of reason, dominated biblical scholarship. The grand narrative *as narrative* fell out of view.

If this had been merely a matter of what those outside the church were doing with Scripture, it might not have been so serious. But the force of Frei's analysis is that the church itself was taken captive theologically by an outlook fundamentally alien to faith. It ceased to live restfully and confidently within its own story, letting the contours of that story describe and illumine all it saw and 'knew'. In Andrew Walker's words, 'there has been a hermeneutical oppression whereby the story – now fragmented and disconnected – has had to await authentication from the critics in order to be told'.[11]

The central thrust of Frei's thesis concerning the trend set in motion in the wake of the Enlightenment is difficult to dispute. Aspects of his work have been criticized,[12] but its main shortcoming seems to be that in one sense, Frei did not go far enough. That is, he so stressed the importance of taking the biblical narrative on its own terms as to give an impression of Scripture as a universe of meaning closed to the world itself.[13] For not only does he want the biblical narrative reclaimed from the alien frames of understanding imposed upon it; he also, paradoxically, seems afraid of opening it up to a conversation

---

[11] Walker, *Telling*, 51.

[12] See, e.g., MacDonald, 'Illocutionary Stance'; Sternberg, *Poetics*, 81f.; Prickett, *Words*, 194.

[13] Here I have found the critique of Frei in Watson, *Text*, 19–29, very helpful. Watson also discusses Frei's *Identity*.

with the world through which it might have a shaping influence on the world once again. Frei seems almost to seal off the Bible's power to communicate to that very world over which its authority is to be recovered.

The issue for Christians at our present juncture, therefore – and not least because so many aspects of the Enlightenment project and all that it spawned are now being so fundamentally questioned – is how we might 'inhabit' the great story once again: not as an enclosure sealed off from the world, but rather as the house through whose windows we look out onto the world. Without discarding genuine advances gained through the modern historical-critical study of Scripture, the theological moment is well overdue for such a new inhabiting of our founding narrative. This cannot simply be a return to premodern days in which such an inhabiting too often went hand in hand with the exercise of oppressive power.[14] Walter Brueggemann is helpful here in pointing to the value of the *small* narratives of which the great one is composed: as these little (often strange) stories are told, people may be wooed into a biblical world-view again – rather than being coerced by one particular individual's or institution's summary, totalizing version of the big story.[15] Garrett Green (like Brueggemann) calls for a renewal of Christian *imagination* as central to today's interpretative task, as we seek once more to fulfil our God-given mandate to make sense of the world through the lens of Scripture.[16] Green expresses it thus: for the believer, 'the only way to have the world – to apprehend it Christianly – is to imagine it according to the paradigm rendered in its classic shape by the canon of Scripture'.[17]

I suggest that we have *in nuce* the conceptual resources for this task in the ancient tradition of figural, typological reading of Scripture. Erich Auerbach has shown how central to biblical interpretation through the early and mediaeval periods was the conviction that the literal or historical sense of Scripture was to be held firmly together with its various non-literal senses.[18] Further, he makes clear that these non-literal senses found in Scripture were not fundamentally the product of any arbitrary, abstract or a-historical allegorization. They were, rather, precisely that which enabled Scripture to be the key to history beyond the immediate circumstances of its writing. The so-called 'allegorical' or 'spiritual' sense pointed to the partial historical fulfilment

---

[14] On reasserting the grand narrative as a liberating rather than a 'totalizing' story see Middleton and Walsh, *Truth*, 87–107.

[15] Brueggemann, *Bible*, 57–91.

[16] Green, *Theology*.

[17] Green, *Theology*, 175.

[18] Auerbach, 'Figura', 28–60. See esp. his comments on Tertullian (26–34) and Augustine (37–43). Origen is only a partial exception (36f.). On the continuation of a sensitive strategy of figural interpretation in Calvin, see Frei, *Eclipse*, 30–37.

of the text concerned in Christ and the new covenant; the 'anagogical' sense pointed to its ultimate fulfilment at the climax of history. Thus those in all the generations after Christ can find in Scripture texts which can unlock the meaning of their own phase of history as the time between the first and second comings of Christ.

Such figural interpretation may continue to serve well as the basis of a continuing productive use of Scripture in the church, precisely because it allows, indeed necessitates, *both* a strong emphasis on the rootedness of Scripture in historical events *and* a deep awareness of the continued meaningfulness of those events and the words which spoke of them. As corrective to the historical-critical method, figural interpretation functions within a community that seeks to inhabit its founding narrative, rather than one which seeks to dismember the narrative by unpacking its relationship to 'history'. But as corrective to Frei,[19] it functions to open the community and its sacred text up to the contemporary world in which they are set, allowing Christians to find in Scripture neither merely past reference nor impervious narrative, but the clue to history.

I shall now seek to sketch out, in somewhat preliminary and tentative fashion, how with such figural interpretation for our model, the sting of anxiety might be removed from four of the key dialectical conflicts which have troubled Christian interpreters throughout the era of historical criticism, and which are discussed elsewhere in this volume. These conflicts are those between, respectively, tradition and history; faith and knowledge; testimony and critical judgement; and the canonical and precanonical forms of the text.

Escaping the Anxieties of Interpretation

Tradition and history

The actual or potential conflict between the tradition of the church and the truth about Christian origins that may be uncovered by historical research is a familiar hermeneutical *topos*. In this volume, Stephen Evans has provided a very helpful discussion of the way in which the 'rule of faith' may appropriately be used in Christian interpretation of Scripture,[20] while Walter Sundberg has pointedly shown (with reference to Kierkegaard) that, real as the

---

[19] Frei seems to write with regret of the disrepute into which figurative interpretation fell following the Reformation and Enlightenment and the breakdown of the 'realistic' narrative reading of Scripture (*Eclipse*, 6–9), but I argue here that a renewed figural reading must go beyond the apparently closed 'narrative world' of Scripture posited by Frei as the conception from which we have fallen.

[20] Evans, 'Tradition, Biblical Interpretation and Historical Truth', Ch. 14.

tradition/history conflict has been, *both* 'tradition' and 'history' may at times become comfortable shields against genuine encounter with God, rather than mediating it.[21]

The conflict between 'tradition' and 'history' is something (in the nature of the case) peculiarly visible when we are looking *backwards* to Christian origins and seeking to decide the nature of 'genuine' Christianity. The relationship between the two looks quite different when we ask how tradition functions in our reading of Scripture as 'lens for history' today.

Tradition provides the context within which a present-day reader or group of readers takes the narrative of Scripture as the framework for 'reading' the world. It is not a body of belief, knowledge or custom that might sooner or later come into conflict with a reading of Scripture against its own historical background. It is, rather, the atmosphere – communal, liturgical, moral, aesthetic – in which the faith is passed on as a living flame.[22] It is indispensable as the catalyst for imaginative appropriation of Scripture by each generation.

This will be seen the more clearly when we recognize that the texts of homily and scriptural commentary which form one of the most tangible deposits of Christian tradition have been, for at least three-quarters of Christian history, predominantly concerned precisely with the applicability of Scripture in understanding the world, and not with 'Scripture in itself' as an object of historical scrutiny.[23] I have argued elsewhere with reference to the interpretation of Jesus' parables that the 'allegorical' treatment they have received for much of Christian history, and which modern criticism has so despised, was an integral part of the strategy of applying them to contemporary concerns, and (most of the time, at least) carried no claim to be representing their original intention.[24] The 'tradition' was precisely the tradition of *applying* Scripture. This tradition has never entirely ceased, though it has (so to speak) gone underground for much of the post-Reformation period, during which it has been suspected as the source of superstition and downright lies.

Understood as the living atmosphere of faith, there should be no danger of tradition becoming a hardened barrier against genuine encounter with God, for it is of its nature that it inspires *new* readings of Scripture as interpretations of the newly unfolding events of history. Christian tradition may be seen as analogous to the 'oral Torah' in Jewish practice, which insures 'that the written word never calcifies into a dead literalism'.[25] The danger occurs precisely when

---

[21] Sundberg, 'The Conflict of Tradition and History', Ch. 13.

[22] On this see especially Louth, *Discerning*, 73–95; cf. Walker, *Telling*.

[23] See Black, 'Augustinian Preaching', 608–609, on how appalled Augustine would have been at the notion that one ought to study Scripture for its own sake.

[24] Wright, *Voice*, esp. 62–112.

[25] Green, *Theology*, 178.

tradition is *lost:* in Augustinian terms, when love, interpretation's lodestar, is lost. In this sense, for example, *both* pre-Reformation interpretation that fossilized papal supremacy, *and* Lutheran interpretation, which demonized the Pope – not to mention the Jews – failed as Christian interpretation precisely because that heart of the tradition had been forgotten. The importance of tradition is not that any and every past interpretation of Scripture may be accepted as valid or true, which given their variety would be a very difficult position to hold, but that the communal life of the church centred on the gospel of Christ and permeated with his love continues, sparking off new ways of perceiving the world in a biblical light.

Historical research into the origins and background of Scripture, then, does not need to be at perpetual loggerheads with tradition. For tradition is not primarily a body of detailed information about 'what happened', but the life of the Christian community, bequeathed from one generation to the next, within which the Spirit enables the community's founding stories to speak to each new historical stage. Tradition, of course, assumes the historical basis for faith in Christ; if it ceased to do that, it would cease to be tradition. But communicating as it does a confidence in that basis, it has no need to be defensive about the labours of historians into the details of the events. For – paradoxically, given the connotations of 'traditionalism' – its orientation is to the *present* life of the community and the meaning of a scriptural outlook on our own history.

Faith and knowledge

If we are speaking about interpreting Scripture-in-itself as an ancient text which bears witness to the events which are foundational for Christian faith, then naturally the issue arises of how we can 'know' that those events actually took place. Granted that the claims to revelation which Scripture contains are not verifiable by modern canons of scientific and historiographical practice, are we yet able to claim true 'knowledge' of them? Or is it a matter of simply 'believing' them in a fideistic sense, without being able to give any rational grounds for that belief?

The issue has been pursued by Alvin Plantinga in the essay 'Two (or More) Types of Scripture Scholarship', which is included and discussed elsewhere in this volume.[26] Plantinga gives a well-argued philosophical case for the 'warranting' of Christian belief. Since all world-views, not only the Christian one, are grounded in basic presuppositions concerning God and the

---

[26] See Plantinga, 'Two (or More)', Ch. 1; Bartholomew, '*Warranted* Biblical Interpretation', Ch. 2; Gordon, 'A Warranted Version of Historical Biblical Criticism?', Ch. 3; and Plantinga, 'Reason and Scripture Scholarship', Ch. 4.

nature of the universe, presuppositions held prior to all rational thinking or empirical enquiry concerning them, Christians do not need to be on the defensive about their knowledge of the truths of revelation. If some historical critics are working from basic presuppositions different from the Christian ones, why should a Christian feel abashed about dissenting from their conclusions?

Without disputing Plantinga's thesis, I suggest that it remains an essentially defensive one. It aims to protect Christians from the charge that their faith is not and cannot be warranted. In this sense, it remains within the framework of Enlightenment handling of Scripture, as a masterly piece of apologetic reasoning – notwithstanding Evans's comment that Plantinga is not doing apologetics but simply giving an account of Christian 'knowledge'.[27] I see nothing wrong with such apologetic reasoning in itself. The faith has needed, and possessed, defenders in every generation. But it is important to restate that the position towards which Frei has pointed, and which many others have now stated from one angle or another, is that recovery of true biblical faith in our generation must *first* be a matter not of defence – a posture which has largely controlled hermeneutics for over three centuries – but of *inhabiting the story*.

What, then, of 'knowledge'? Do we simply yield it up as a category not central to faith or interpretative discourse? No, there is an alternative to this that does justice to the nature both of Scripture and of Christian experience. That is, that we reconceive 'knowledge' in its ancient biblical sense, which stresses participation and experience.[28] The Bible does not concern itself with 'knowledge' in any abstract sense. To know is to participate. The models for 'knowing' are supremely personal ones: the intercourse of man and woman (Gen. 4:1) and that of humans with God (Jn. 17:3). 'Knowledge' is intimately associated with 'wisdom' of a very practical kind (see the parallelism of Prov. 1:7).

In the mode of figural interpretation, 'knowledge' and 'faith' are fused into one. The interpreter 'knows', in faith, both that the central narrative of Scripture has true historical reference, and that it sheds light on history beyond its immediate sense. This is not to short-circuit the need to exercise literary and historical sensibility in discerning the particular kind of witness to historical reality that different sections of Scripture contain – a subject to which we shall return very shortly. It is, rather, to assert that we cannot separate 'knowledge' of the events at the heart of Christian faith and the sense that those events are crucial for the understanding of all history. Herbert Butterfield's comments are apposite here:

---

[27] Evans, 'Tradition', Ch. 14.

[28] At our consultation, Mary Healy helpfully pointed to Hosea as a fruitful source for a biblical epistemology. See also the comments on faith as appropriation of the deepest poetic truth, rather than as metaphysical opinion, in Shanks, *Truth*, 3–6.

It cannot be too strongly emphasised that, when we are confronted with historical writing of this kind [the Gospels], our attitude to it must depend primarily on the decision which we make in regard to its whole system of interpretation ... it is one's appropriation of the whole human drama ... that is in question, and our attitude on this essential point carries many of the other important issues along with it, for it represents our decision about the whole universe and our relation to it. It is at the same time our decision about ourselves – our answer to whatever challenge the Gospels may present to our personal life – for in choosing our attitude to the whole drama of world-history we are at the same time making the most intimate decision about ourselves.[29]

For the Christian, then, the everyday reality is not Cartesian anxiety about 'how can I know', though from time to time she may be called on to show Cartesian questioners a good Plantingan answer to that question. The everyday reality is that she *does* know. Christ incarnate, Christ crucified, Christ risen is not the object of abstract belief, but the Lord to whom she is vitally related. And she seeks to invest time and energy not in wondering how it can be, but in letting that knowledge inform and transform all her thinking about everything else.

Testimony and critical judgement

Closely connected to the issue of 'knowledge' is that of *testimony*. Iain Provan's essay very clearly demonstrates the actual dependence of all historiography upon testimony, and the folly of trying to evade this fact.[30] The truth that testimony is inevitably conditioned by the perspective and location of the testifier does not simply cancel out its value as testimony. The upshot is that Christians do not need to be fazed by radically revisionist accounts of Scripture (particularly the Old Testament) which evaporate the texts of most of their worth as accounts or reflections of historical reality. In many aspects of life, we depend for all practical purposes upon the testimony of others. Why, then, should the witness of Scripture be subjected to extreme suspicion?

As with Plantinga's account of 'warrant', this is a vital and reassuring truth in a context in which faith is under attack. Why, indeed, should the burden of proof lie with those who wish to trust the witness of the texts, rather than with those who wish to mistrust it? Provan's account of testimony aims to restore battered Christian confidence in Scripture, and I trust and expect that it will have the desired effect.

It is interesting, however, that the overall context of this account of testimony remains (like Plantinga's account of warrant) an essentially defensive one. It is a matter of showing how, when all around are growing suspicious, we

---

[29] Butterfield, *Christianity and History*, 165–66.
[30] Provan, 'Knowing and Believing: Faith in the Past', Ch. 11.

can go on trusting and remain perfectly reasonable in the process. I want to ask if in addition to this defence – whose validity and necessity I heartily endorse – we can, and need to, reach a deeper level of, as it were, non-defensive engagement with the testimony of Scripture as we seek to inhabit its narrative again and let Scripture shed light on *all* of history.

If we are to engage in this non-defensive manner with Scripture's testimony, we will be open about the need to exercise critical judgement concerning the nature of particular pieces of testimony. It is a commonplace of all study of texts that we ask what genre they belong to and what conventions they operate under, and that decisions on these issues bring the reader's personal insight into play alongside careful comparisons with other texts.[31] Provan's argument is not, of course, an argument for the *actual* historical value of *all* pieces of 'testimony' in Scripture. It is quite possible to assert the general trustworthiness of the biblical writers in both their statements and their intentions, by way of reaction to those who doubt it unnecessarily, and still allow that from time to time they might be mistaken. In other words, it is up to the reader to make up his or her mind – no doubt with the help of others – as to the nature of the individual pieces of testimony being offered, and the extent to which they point accurately to historical events.

Such critical judgement is not a matter of the pretence of detached objectivity and of the autonomy of the individual that characterizes scholarship influenced by the Enlightenment. It is, rather, the natural counterpart of the nature of testimony itself: testimony is assessed personally by the receiver on the basis of what can be known about the testifier and about the communicative conventions within which the testimony is given. Such assessment becomes naturally more complex as testimony is written down.

Just because the sophisticated techniques employed by historical critics in making such critical judgements were not available to the early practitioners of figural interpretation, or because some of the more elaborate methodological edifices erected by historical critics are rightly discredited,[32] is no reason to be coy about the need for critical judgement within a renewed figural interpretation today. We accept the testimony of the key witnesses to the central gospel events, because we trust in the tradition handed down in the church universal. But this does not mean that careful reflection on the nature of the biblical testimony to events of either Old or New Testament times is rendered pointless, unnecessary or even dangerous. On the contrary, even the testimony to the

---

[31] These twin requirements for interpretation were clearly formulated by Schleiermacher: see the account in Thiselton, *New Horizons*, 222.

[32] Such as the 'criterion of dissimilarity' in Jesus studies, popularized by Norman Perrin and others: see the critique by William Alston, 'Historical Criticism of the Synoptic Gospels', Ch. 8 in this volume.

death and resurrection of Christ calls for the profoundest critical engagement with its unique balance of reportage and theology. As a Christian, I believe that any serious reader of the New Testament is bound, sooner or later, to hear the ring of truth in the claim that Christ is risen; but her faith will be much deeper and stronger for having had to wrestle with the four gospel narratives and the apostolic claims for herself. Faith, in other words, comes from a real hearing of the word, not merely a submission to an authoritative pronouncement, whether from a Catholic, Protestant or Orthodox quarter.

Still it is natural to ask: will not the call for critical judgement inevitably conflict, at some point, with the call to trust the testimony? Here it is important to remember that the testimony on which contemporary Christian faith depends is the testimony of *human beings:* the living Christian tradition, oral as well as written. In our daily human relationships the elements of trust and critical judgement regularly and naturally go hand in hand. For instance, we may feel instinctively drawn to another person in friendship, and begin to exercise trust in them, but the relationship will not proceed far if we are not also able to observe their life and behavior on a regular basis in a quite detached way and see that their word can be trusted. Such critical observation is particularly necessary when they are physically absent and mediated to us only through written texts – which can *never* mediate human testimony in direct and uncomplicated fashion. The central point here is that to try to close down the space in our relationship to Scripture opened up from at least late mediaeval times onwards by critical examination of literary and historical questions is unnecessary and counterproductive. It is a maneuver of defensiveness that betrays a fundamental *lack* of trust in the testimony borne by our forebears and fellow saints of our own age. In other words, inhabiting the 'house' of the story, and looking out through its windows, is perfectly compatible with careful examination of the bricks and mortar of its walls; indeed, reluctance to do so would suggest that one was strangely ill at ease in one's own home.

Canonical and precanonical text

Christopher Seitz has shown in most interesting fashion how the arrangement of the canon itself – or at least a part of it, the prophetic books – seems to have functioned as an interpretation of Israel's history.[33] The ordering, connections, mutual links and patterns discernible within this section of Scripture bespeak a desire to see the divine purpose in Israel's turbulent years before, during and after the time of the exile. Variations in canonical ordering only strengthen the case for seeing such an intention at work in those who, in different contexts,

---

[33] See Seitz, 'What Lesson Will History Teach? The Book of the Twelve as History', Ch. 18 in this volume.

brought or kept these books together. The words of the prophets are brought into conjunction with one another not in order to flatten them out and make them say the same thing but to be mutually interpretative, and therefore interpretative of history.

Seitz thus argues that the final form of the text reflects the impulse to find divine meaning in history. In the context of the present chapter, we could say that on Seitz's reading, the arrangement of the prophetic books is itself a classic example of a figural reading of Scripture. The precanonical texts have been put alongside each other in such a way as to suggest the outworking of the plan of God in history. Their reference to, and rootedness in, actual historical events of the past is in no way obliterated by the ordering imposed by the shapers of the canon, yet they are shown as pointing to a yet unfulfilled future and helping to interpret an uncertain present. Thus there is no inherent conflict between a canonical text that tells the story we are to inhabit and a precanonical text that, in one way or another, reflects a historical past. The point of the canon itself is to interpret history; text opens onto world.

So once again we find that the heat is removed from a regular conflict zone. We are required neither to surrender an interest in 'history', as represented in the precanonical forms of the text, in order to inhabit the 'story', as represented by the canonical; nor to abandon the 'story' in the interests of pursuing 'history'. The canonical text offers an interpretation of history via its arrangement of the precanonical material. As such, it is the authentic precursor and inspirer of all subsequent figural interpretation.

Moreover, it is important to note the way in which those responsible for the canonizing process chose to do their interpretative work. The patterning arrangement of the prophetic books implies that the canonizers thought their history was to be interpreted not by the imposition of a monolithic intellectual grid but through disparate yet juxtaposed voices from the past which could be heard (as it were) bouncing off each other in mutually suggestive echo. Just as they refused to impose a tight connecting narrative, but let a sense of the strange sequence of God's dealings emerge through the juxtaposition of different voices from different periods,[34] so, we may argue, a Christian reading of wider history will not over-neatly systematize the two parts of the canon (the equivalent, for us, of the 'precanonical' texts inherited by the shapers of the canon) in a quest for ready (but too easy) access to history's 'meaning'. Similarly, just as the canon only emerged as such, and in a particular order, over time, and even then with a sense of provisionality about its reading of history ('What lesson *will* history teach?' being, as Seitz rightly says, the gently insistent

---

[34] We may compare the way in which even the overtly narrative parts of the Old Testament tend stubbornly to resist reduction to straightforward didactic purpose: on this see Sternberg, *Poetics*, 37–38.

question running through it), so it is right to be cautious and provisional about our reading of history in light of the two Testaments.

Figural Interpretation Today

What, then, might be the shape of a contemporary 'figural interpretation' in which Scripture, without losing its vital reference to a historical past, becomes the lens through which we view the continued unfolding of history? The question is huge and invokes centuries of Christian theologizing, philosophizing, Bible study and preaching, as well as attempts at 'Christian' historiography, all far beyond the scope of this chapter. I must concentrate on a few pointers.

I take for granted that an interpretation of Scripture through which we seek to interpret history will be Christ-centred and oriented by love.[35] That is the story we inhabit, and it calls for no argument. The aspects on which I shall comment can be identified from Christian history as the occasion of misunderstandings and blind alleys in the church's hermeneutical journey, and therefore in need of positive reclaiming. To focus attention at the outset on what we mean by 'figural interpretation', here is the opening of Auerbach's definition:

> Figural interpretation establishes a connection between two events or persons, the first of which signifies not only itself but also the second, while the second encompasses or fulfills the first. The two poles of the figure are separate in time, but both, being real events or figures, are within time, within the stream of historical life.[36]

This definition encompasses not only the 'fulfilment' of the old covenant in the new, but also the 'fulfilment' of both covenants in subsequent history and ultimately at the eschaton. It is the issue of how we understand the 'fulfilment' of Scripture in this interim period of history between Christ's first and second appearings which will concern us here.

Cosmic and personal

A renewed figural interpretation will, I suggest, be both cosmic and personal. That is, it will not confine itself to the application of Scripture to the course of individual lives; it will recognize the Bible as the key that unlocks

---

[35] On Augustine's dictum that love must be the goal of interpretation see Black, 'Augustinian Preaching'.

[36] Auerbach, 'Figura', 53.

understanding of the unfolding course of the universe.[37] Conversely, it will not neglect the life of the individual; for the Creator of the cosmos is also the Creator of each human being, who may learn through Christ to know him as Father.

So individuals must learn to interpret Scripture as having a bearing on infinitely more than their individual lives. Equally, those who discern in Scripture the clue to the cosmos must also discern and facilitate its transforming power on the personal level. There is no place for either private pietism or abstract intellectualism in figural interpretation. This much is required by the very content of Scripture, and by Christian testimony to a God who is both Creator and Father.

We must distinguish the idea that Scripture *interprets* the cosmos from the idea that Scripture constitutes an independent source of *knowledge* concerning the cosmos. When Scripture is treated as having the latter function, it is mistreated and becomes a hostage to every scientific advance. It is pressed into service to corroborate that which is known from elsewhere; conversely, archaeological finds (for instance) are pressed into service to corroborate that which is 'known' from Scripture. This is Frei's point when he comments on the way that Cocceius and Bengel saw in contemporary events the detailed fulfilment of scriptural texts: the ground had shifted from the days when the biblical narratives were the indispensable framework for *interpreting* the events of history, so that now the narratives only provided a kind of verification for events, which were perceived as constituting 'an autonomous temporal framework of their own under God's providential design'.[38]

A similar blind alley was trodden by nineteenth- and twentieth-century fundamentalism, which treated Scripture as a book which could and did give scientific answers to the questions which the age of science had thrown up.[39] The 'two books' of God's revelation, nature and Scripture, were put radically asunder.[40] If Scripture is basically an *interpreting* text, that implies that there are *data* to be interpreted. One cannot interpret the world and history in the light of Scripture if one looks only at Scripture. So Mark Noll comments that 'in their enthusiasm for reading the world in the light of Scripture, evangelicals forget the proposition that the Western world's early modern scientists had so successfully taken to heart as a product of their own deep Christian convictions – to understand something, one must look at that something'.[41]

---

[37] On the danger of an overemphasis on the individual appropriation of Scripture (as seen in one of Paul Ricœur's formulations of the goal of reading) see Watson, *Text*, 296, n. 13.

[38] Frei, *Eclipse*, 4.

[39] On this see Noll, *Scandal*, esp. 126–30, 177–208.

[40] Noll, *Scandal*, 183–84.

[41] Noll, *Scandal*, 199.

To make Scripture a book of 'knowledge' in the scientific sense is in fact to yield up its universal scope, for clearly there are vast areas of the cosmos and its history about which it gives us no knowledge whatsoever. It involves granting a certain 'autonomy' to those areas, even if God's overarching providence is still acknowledged. To treat Scripture as an *interpreting* book, however, means that its scope is indeed universal. The clearest illustration of this point is Genesis 1–3. To use these chapters simply as a source of information about the actual historical unfolding of the early stages of the universe is not only insensitive to their genre, but also relinquishes their power to continue interpreting the world, and throws us into contortions either defending a pre-scientific view of cosmic and human origins, or trying to reconcile biblical and scientific pictures on a literalistic plane. Treated as a figural text, however, these chapters speak not simply about the dawn of the world and of the human race, but also about its continuing history up to the present. They go on revealing the world as wondrously created and ordered by God, and humanity as the pinnacle of that creation, though disobedient and fallen. This, of course, does *not* mean that their reference to a primeval past is to be simply dismissed as being beside the point. If history and time mean anything, they imply a beginning. Genesis 1–3 interprets the world as God's world, and a world in time. It is therefore paradigmatic for a figural reading of Scripture which simultaneously affirms God's (and humans') past actions and sees those actions, and the words in which they come to expression, as giving meaning to all subsequent 'presents'. Considering 'Adam' makes this clear: there must have been an original human or humans, but 'Adam' is symbolic of the race.[42]

Spiritual, ecclesial and prophetic

Figural interpretation will necessarily be spiritual, ecclesial and prophetic.

Auerbach stresses that 'only the understanding of the two persons or events [connected by figural interpretation] is a spiritual act'.[43] That is, he emphasizes the historical character of the two poles themselves. Here it is worth stressing

---

[42] The gender-neutral *adam* in the majestic poem of Gen. 1 (v. 27) becomes, of course, the gender-differentiated man and woman of the narrative of Gen. 2 and 3. Both the poetic *adam* and the narrative man and woman partake of this symbolic quality. I owe to Dom Henry Wansborough ('Made', 2) the point that careful exegesis of Rom. 5:12–19 does not sustain the literalistic Augustinian view of original sin as something actually passed down from parent to child from an original 'Adam'. The *eph' hō* of v. 12 is to be translated 'insofar as' not 'because': death spread to all *insofar* as all sinned. Paul, like Genesis, assumes that there was indeed an original human, but that we are sinners not on account of literal descent, but simply by being part of the human race, for whom 'Adam' stands as a representative figure.

[43] Auerbach, 'Figura', 53.

the converse also. That is, such interpretation depends on the indwelling Spirit of God, promised by Jesus to guide the disciples into all truth, and to tell them 'what is yet to come' (Jn. 16:13). It is therefore far removed from a mechanical code-cracking exercise. Scripture must be allowed the freedom to shed shafts of light in unexpected ways upon the course of history, as the interpreting church remains open to the sovereign sway and insight of God. Fears about illuminism and eccentric readings should not be allowed to erase a sense of the importance of the spiritual dimension of figural interpretation. This dimension is defined not by the remoteness of the particular interpretation offered from the *sensus literalis*, but by the context of Christian fellowship and discipleship from which it springs.

Therefore such interpretation will also be ecclesial, arising in the community of the Spirit of Jesus, and especially focused on understanding the role of the church in the continuing purposes of God. This by no means negates the cosmic dimension discussed above, for the church is sent into the world by Jesus (Jn. 17:18) and the ultimate liberation of God's children will herald the ultimate liberation of the creation (Rom. 8:19–21). There should be nothing wooden about the process of letting Scripture illumine the role of the present-day church in history. Again, it is not a matter of cracking a code, as if (for instance) all the furnishings of the temple had to be made to speak of some aspect of God's present meeting with his people. It is a matter of dynamic inspiration, as we grasp that the church is not merely figured by, but continuous with, ancient Israel. So Israel's struggles and sin become ours. Her exile can speak eloquently of our contemporary marginalization.[44] Her hopes, fulfilled in Christ, are yet being realized and still await final consummation. We read Scripture, and we see where we are: we place ourselves on the map. Andrew Louth, discussing what I am calling figural interpretation under the general rubric of 'allegory', shows how allegory was one of the main means by which Scripture continued to be a channel of the life of Christ in the church, rather than a dead letter.[45] It especially helped maintain the identity of a people. It enabled Christians of the fourth, or seventh or fourteenth centuries to see themselves in the sacred text – and they can do so still today. It is a community-building manoeuvre, in which Christians of any 'present' are bonded with those of the past.

This brings us, however, to the prophetic dimension of figural interpretation. A perpetual danger for Christian interpreters, grasping the ecclesial significance of Scripture, is to interpret it in ways that simply support the status quo and bolster a dangerous and unchristian sense of superiority or exclusiveness in the Christian community. We need, rather, a prophetically figural

---

[44] On this see esp. the work of Brueggemann.

[45] Louth, *Discerning*, 96–131.

reading which finds 'us' not always in the places of favour in Scripture but, just like Israel of old, as the recipients of God's searing word of purgative judgement. Some allegorical interpretations of Scripture have become fossilized[46] along lines which allowed the church to become, in effect, deaf to the challenge of Jesus to which Scripture ought to have been continuing to bear witness. So figural interpretation as a life-giving bearer of tradition can easily turn into figural interpretation as the fossilizer of tradition in a way that brings death.

The example of this *par excellence* is the way in which the Scriptures have been used to heighten the church's sense of being an inviolate community over against a Judaism seen as irredeemably reprobate. In direct contradiction of Paul's warning to Gentile Christians not to be arrogant (Rom. 11:20), the Scriptures have been repeatedly used to reinforce a sense among Christians of being an 'in group' who, though once they needed to hear the penetrating word of challenge, need to hear it no longer. Happy to point to the 'hardness' of the 'Jews' (grossly generalizing, in the process – partly no doubt through the misuse to which the Gospel of John's terminology lends itself), as a chosen race who fell into presumption, we have with terrible deafness failed to hear the warnings of Scripture as addressed to *us*. In sad consonance with familiar human nature, we have been glad to take to ourselves Israel's honorific titles – a chosen race, a holy nation, as indeed in 1 Peter 2:9 – but slow to realize that precisely the same danger of presumption awaits us. The parable of the 'wicked tenants', especially in its Matthean version (Mt. 21:33–46), has been particularly susceptible to such misreading.[47] Given that the burning question for interpreters of the parables has always been 'who do these characters represent *now*', Matthew 21:43 ('Therefore I tell you that the kingdom of God will be taken away from you and given to a people who will produce its fruit') has tended to reinforce a sense that the wicked tenants 'are' – in a fixed sense – the 'Jews' who have 'rejected' Jesus.[48] The parable with this explanatory verse is then held to teach that the Jews *in toto* are excluded from the kingdom of God. This, of course, completely overlooks the challenge of the end of verse 43. If the 'nation' to whom the kingdom is now given similarly fails to 'bear fruit', why should they think that their end will be any less 'wretched' than that of the tenants in the story? This is but one example of very many that could be adduced where allegorical or figural reading has a tendency to make things black and white, and to iron out potentially uncomfortable details.

---

[46] On the general fossilization of allegorical method in the later Middle Ages, see Stuhlmacher, *Historical Criticism*, 31.

[47] Cf. Milavec, 'Analysis'.

[48] As in John Chrysostom, *Homilies on the Gospel of Matthew* 68.1, cited in Milavec, 'Analysis', 83.

We need, then, to find a way of maintaining that sense of continuity and community with the past which allegory has provided, often in a quite benign way, which avoids these more malign effects. We must continue to seek from Scripture a sense of our place in God's grand narrative without taming the prophetic challenge which God issues to his people by too comfortable an identification of 'us' with the chosen, the righteous. Here lies the true importance of seeking the 'moral sense' of Scripture: that we should allow it to indict and direct us, not simply confirm us in our accustomed ways. In preparing to preach, for instance, such openness to the prophetic word shows itself by a conscious avoidance of gravitating to what Craddock calls 'the choice places in the texts'.[49] And the 'choice places' may, of course, change from one generation and location to the next.

Provisional

If, as Scripture itself teaches, history is moving under God towards a final consummation, then to interpret any passage of Scripture as finding an *absolute* fulfilment in any events of the present is both to misinterpret it and to limit its power to *go on* interpreting history. Figural interpretation is always *provisional* interpretation. So, indeed, must be any interpretation of history, whether or not one draws upon Scripture. In Butterfield's words, '[history's] verdicts are an interim affair, and not a final judgement on anything';[50] or in Auerbach's, 'all history … remains open and questionable, points to something still concealed'.[51]

Elsewhere in this volume, David Lyle Jeffrey clearly indicates the danger of tying any one group in the present to the tag 'chosen people', and of identifying the 'promised land' of biblical hope with any aspect of the present world order.[52] Deeper still, this is shown to be the danger of letting Scripture interpret history in such a way as to imply that history itself is the ultimate datum. The future to which Israel, and now the church, looks (Jeffrey suggests), notwithstanding tangible earthly signs, is – if we are to understand Scripture aright – suprahistorical: history itself is but a figure, a trope (a powerful one, to be sure) for 'heaven'.[53]

So all attempts to see current historical events as in some sense 'fulfilments' of Scripture must be flawed *if* this gives to those events the finality which

---

[49] Craddock, *Preaching*, 120.

[50] Butterfield, *Christianity and History*, 78. Butterfield's entire chapter, 'Judgement in History', deals in a profound way with this subject.

[51] Auerbach, 'Figura', 58.

[52] Jeffrey, '(Pre) Figuration: Masterplot and Meaning in Biblical History', Ch. 16.

[53] Cf. again Auerbach: 'Thus history, with all its concrete force, remains forever a figure, cloaked and needful of interpretation' ('Figura', 58).

Scripture itself denies to all things earthly. If Scripture is to be allowed truly to interpret history, not only will it show history as something 'real', a dimension of God's creation and the locus of his incarnation, and therefore to be taken with great seriousness. It will also show that history cannot contain _ultimate_ reality.

Hence the misguidedness of all millennialism and of attempts to see in specific happenings the 'actual' fulfilment of biblical warnings and prophecies. As soon as the Bible is made to speak directly of subsequent historical events, it loses its power to reveal the tropical nature of history to which Jeffrey refers. It makes history into a closed system; effectively it robs it of its framework of meaning. The Bible itself ceases to be the overarching interpretative grid and becomes instead a mere book of codes. Moreover, history as a whole suffers a loss of meaning, as the 'true' application or reference of scriptural texts is concentrated solely on specific events.[54]

This caution is applicable to both Christian and Jewish perceptions of the 'fulfilment' of Scripture. It is a corrective to both Eusebius of Caesarea's hailing of Constantine's 'Christian' kingdom in the fourth century as 'an image of the heavenly one', and of Constantine's appointment of various 'Caesars' among his family as the fulfilment of Daniel 7:18, 'the saints of the most high will receive the kingdom';[55] and to modern Zionist excitement at the establishment of the state of Israel in 1948. But note that this caution does not negate the possibility of seeing in current events _glimpses_ or _foretastes_ of God's ultimate rule. Indeed, those who believe that Jesus did indeed usher in God's kingdom should be especially alert to such glimpses: not, to be sure, in the earthly trappings of power and pomp, but precisely where Jesus saw them – in the signs of divine love lifting up the poor, welcoming the outcast, healing the sick, forgiving the sinner. The Gospel stories, in particular, find a partial fulfilment wherever that surprising grace is to be seen – always only partial, for the reasons given – but real enough for us to be able to say of a tale of Jesus healing, or befriending the marginalized, that it not only refers to a historical person but also interprets contemporary examples of such activity, as signs of the kingdom. Such interpretation is provisional – because we do not have unmediated or infallible access to the inner character and dynamic of events, and also because only at the eschaton will these things be seen. Yet such interpretation is important, precisely as an act of faith that the eschaton is on its way.

A right application of Scripture to the events of history must, however, grasp the paradox that the more _absolutely_ one tries to tie the contemporary

---

[54] Noll (_Scandal_, 140), referring to responses to the Gulf War of 1991, writes tellingly of the 'evangelical predilection, when faced with a crisis, to use the Bible as a crystal ball instead of as a guide for sorting out the complex tangles of international morality'.

[55] _Oration in Honour of Constantine on the Thirtieth Anniversary of His Reign_, 3, in Wiles and Santer, _Documents_, 233.

'meaning' of Scripture down, the less meaningful historical events become. This is seen on a micro-level in some pietistic uses of Scripture to interpret the vicissitudes of personal life. The more precisely one ties a promise or a warning or a blessing to a particular event, the less meaningful other events in one's life may become, and at the same time the less Scripture is allowed to be an end-lessly new source of interpreting power. At an early stage of faith, a command such as that of God to Abraham (Gen. 12:1) to 'leave your country' may be used by God in an individual's life to call them, say, to overseas missionary service. But it would be a faith in a perpetual state of immaturity that tied that verse perpetually to that experience. It would lead to impoverishment both of the life (deprived of seeing the many ways in which that verse might continue to address him or her throughout their personal history) and of Scripture itself. If Scripture is to continue to function as an interpreting word, its fecundity as a perpetually renewable figural text must be acknowledged. As in psychological development, so in faith and Scripture reading: a grasp of symbol as symbol, of figure as figure, is central to growth.

Parabolic

The over-detailed and over-precise linkage of scriptural verses, prophecies and themes to events of subsequent history ends up absolutizing not only history, but also Scripture. It ceases to be pointer, figure, sacrament, window and inter-preter – and becomes instead a fixed datum beyond which one cannot see. I suggest that the vibrancy of a genuine figural interpretation, by contrast, lies in its *parabolic* treatment of Scripture.

Here I refer especially to the etymology of the Greek word *parabolē*, which means literally 'something thrown alongside'. This derivation leads to standard definitions of parable as involving a comparison of two things or situ-ations. However, the literal etymology is very suggestive. For what we find in Jesus' parables is, very often, no explicit comparison, but rather one situation simply 'thrown alongside' another: a story is told in a particular life setting, with little or no *explicit* links between them. It is left to the hearers of the origi-nal story, or the readers of the text in which story and situation are 'thrown together' like this, to meditate on the connections. The classic case in the Gospels is the story of the Prodigal Son, told (it seems) without a word of explanation, in the context of Jesus' socializing with the outcasts and the Pharisees' objection to it. Much of the power of the parable lies in the simple juxtaposition; labouring parallels would have killed it off as an effective rhetorical tool. Story on its own gets under the skin, and connections are grasped at an intuitive, precognitive level.[56]

---

[56] On the 'primordial' nature of parabolic discourse see Funk, *Language*, 236.

I suggest that, in a similar way, interpreters are called to 'throw' Scripture alongside historical occurrences in such a way as to provoke profound reflection and a sense of real, though provisional, meaning. This should not be taken as implying a lack of care – as we imply when we speak of 'throwing money' at a problem. Jesus surely took great care as to what story he told on what occasion! Nor does it imply that words of explanation and explicit connecting should always be missing completely; there are plenty of examples of these around the parables of Jesus – examples that are only arbitrarily attributed in their entirety to the early church. But it does imply that we should not always feel obliged to spell out every link or try to fasten down Scripture's contemporary 'meaning' in a tight fashion. Crude and rigid comparisons of scriptural *datum* with historical *datum* close down the possibility of ongoing interpretation. Parabolic juxtapositions encourage it.

An example can be taken from reflection on the meaning of the terrible events of 11 September 2001. It probably occurred to many Christians that a biblical passage that might speak to shed some light upon them was the story of the tower of Babel in Genesis 11. The similarity between the pictures in an ancient tale and contemporary news footage, of great towers symbolic of human endeavour coming crashing to the ground, is haunting. And yet to start to spell out connections too precisely would almost certainly diminish the power of the text to address those who in one way or another found themselves affected by the events. To speak directly and absolutely of judgement might prevent deep and challenging links being made, and might also prevent the Scripture from doing its work of provoking people to a reordered vision of the world. A parabolic style of figural interpretation, by contrast, brings Bible and history alongside one another and lets a fertile, transforming conversation among the hearers – or viewers – begin.

Imaginative

To choose how to juxtapose a passage from Scripture with an aspect of history, past or present, in a way that allows the former to shed continuing light upon the latter, demands an imaginative engagement with both. The imagination here is seen as the faculty which enables us to do three things: to penetrate beneath the surface of text and event, to perceive connections and to discern the way in which the juxtaposition can be made most meaningfully for one's hearers or readers.

Let us take these three things in turn. First, we look at penetrating beneath the surface of text and event. We return at this point, perhaps curiously, to the title of this book. For fundamentally it is *imagination* which takes us 'behind the text', beneath its surface. This fact at once both confirms the importance of historically-oriented study of the text, so that our imagination may be rooted in the life situations in which the text is grounded, and yet subverts the idea that historical criticism can be conceived as a purely 'objective' or 'scientific' enterprise, for imagination entails self-involvement.[57] And it is imagination, also, which takes us behind the scenes of the historical events that we wish to interpret – not, again, as a matter of mere fancy, but on the basis of careful observation, weighing the opinions of witnesses and commentators, and so on. In other words, superficial understanding of either text or event will not serve figural interpretation. We may take a rather extreme example to make the point clear. Old Testament passages recording 'holy war' cannot be used in a superficial sense as a framework for understanding contemporary conflict, so as to justify a nation's aggression. This is because of the basic need for a christological and love-oriented interpretation of Scripture which we noted above, but it is also on a still more fundamental level because to do so would be to fail to penetrate imaginatively the historical context of either the ancient text or the current warfare. We need to ask all kinds of questions about the motives, the players and the settings of these widely divergent contexts before the one can speak in any way coherently to the other.

Second, we look at perceiving connections. This presupposes the first stage. When, for example, we have penetrated beneath the surface of Israel's destruction of Ai in Joshua 7, we grasp the uniqueness of the historical period in which the event takes place, as God's chosen people enter the promised land. When we have penetrated beneath the surface of a present-day conflict, we grasp the fact that no party to it has any legitimate theological claim to be 'God's chosen people'. This does not, of course, solve our problems with the notion that the Lord should command such wholesale destruction – even by his chosen people at a crucial point in their history. These problems can only be addressed with reference to the christological and charitable criteria. But the very fact that this ancient band of aggressors was clearly in a different *theological* category from any we may observe today is sufficient to show us that the connection cannot lie on a superficial level. When, however, we recall all that is bestowed on and expected of those counted as God's chosen people in the New Testament, we may indeed perceive a connection that is deep and powerful. Those blessed with every spiritual blessing in the heavenly places (Eph. 1:3) do have warfare to engage in, but 'not against enemies of blood and flesh' (Eph. 6:12). In a situation of conflict, the paradoxical weapons of God's true children are truth, righteousness and peace. Note also that this does not arbitrate on the issue of the possible legitimacy of 'just war'. For the modern area of application is as carefully demarcated as the understanding of the ancient text. The connection made between text and contemporary world is not between ancient and modern international conflict, but between the calling of God's people then and now to battle.

---

[57] On this theme cf. Briggs, *Words*.

Once the connection is seen on that level, the true differences between ancient text and modern world are brought into sharp relief. And this is where the third imaginative stage comes into play. How does one so juxtapose *this* text and *this* contemporary situation that the right level of connectivity is mobilized, and the contrasts as well as the links between the two appropriately highlighted? To speak of imagination in this way is to stress, as I did at the outset, that 'interpretation' is never properly an activity abstracted from a particular human setting. It is always 'interpretation' *for* another, or others. Thus the story of Joshua 7 might be rendered 'parabolic' for contemporary conflicts in a variety of ways. Simply to tell the story on its own would not, in this case, be very helpful. Somehow, the emotional power of a tale of mass slaughter would need to be harnessed to evoke the deadly seriousness of the battle in which today's people of God are engaged; and then the spiritual nature and paradoxical weapons of that current battle would need to be revealed in such a way as to challenge head-on the validity of any contemporary 'crusade' 'against enemies of blood and flesh'. The biblical story must be taken seriously because of the historical rootedness of our faith, but also because interpretation is not well served by the unimaginative reduction of narrative and vivid imagery to abstract principles and points.[58] Narrative and imagery should rather spark new narrative and imagery, and the parabolic juxtaposing, interweaving and interlinking of material from Scripture and the contemporary world, so as to allow the former truly to address and transform perceptions of the latter. That is, Joshua 7 is still usable by a preacher, but only by one who is prepared to invest imaginative effort in a figural reading that is true to the historical settings of the text and of the present, who sees the real connections between them, and who presents them in such a way as to let the text live Christianly among God's people today.

Imagination, then, is the necessary complement to a parabolic style in figural interpretation. Spirit-inspired, it enables our parabolic juxtapositions of text and world to be truthful and fruitful.[59]

Conclusion

I have argued that an adequate engagement with the issue of 'history and biblical interpretation' in our time requires not only the defensive move of asserting our right to, or our reasons for, an essentially trustful attitude to the historical witness of Scripture, but also, and perhaps more deeply, the less

---

[58] On this cf. much of the contemporary literature on homiletics.

[59] Since completing this article I have discovered Wilson, *God Sense*, which explores the relevance for preaching today of the classical fourfold sense of Scripture.

self-conscious posture of simply 'inhabiting the story'. If indeed the Scriptures tell the story of the Christ who is the clue to history, we must allow them to go on illumining history. And I have suggested that the way, in practice, for that to happen is through a renewed figural interpretation in which the Bible's witness to something 'behind' is held together with its character as an *interpretative* text. There is no reason, it seems, why in the church we should not continue to engage simultaneously in exploration of that 'something behind', and in letting Scripture be the interpretative key to all our later history. On the contrary, there is every reason to do so.

Bibliography

Auerbach, E., 'Figura', in *Scenes from the Drama of European Literature* (New York: Meridian Books, 1959), 11–76

Black, C.C., 'Augustinian Preaching and the Nurture of Christians', in *The Lectionary Commentary: Theological Exegesis for Sunday's Texts (The Third Readings: The Gospels)* (ed. R. van Harn; Grand Rapids: Eerdmans, 2001), 603–14

Briggs, R., *Words in Action: Speech Act Theory and Biblical Interpretation: Toward a Hermeneutic of Self-Involvement* (Edinburgh: T. & T. Clark, 2001)

Brueggemann, W., *The Bible and Postmodern Imagination: Texts under Negotiation* (London: SCM Press, 1993)

Butterfield, H., *Christianity and History* (London: Fontana, 1957)

Clark, N., *Preaching in Context: Word, Worship and the People of God* (Bury St Edmunds: Kevin Mayhew, 1991)

Craddock, F.B., *Preaching* (Nashville: Abingdon Press, 1985)

Fowl, S., *Engaging Scripture: A Model for Theological Interpretation* (Malden, MA and Oxford: Basil Blackwell, 1998)

Frei, H., *The Eclipse of Biblical Narrative: A Study in Eighteenth and Nineteenth Century Hermeneutics* (New Haven and London: Yale University Press, 1974)

——, *The Identity of Jesus Christ* (Philadelphia: Fortress Press, 1975)

Funk, R.W., *Language, Hermeneutic, and Word of God: The Problem of Language in the New Testament and Contemporary Theology* (New York, Evanston and London: Harper & Row, 1966)

Green, G., *Theology, Hermeneutics and Imagination* (Cambridge: CUP, 2000)

Louth, A., *Discerning the Mystery* (Oxford: Clarendon Press, 1983)

MacDonald, N.B., 'Illocutionary Stance in Hans Frei's *The Eclipse of Biblical Narrative:* An Exercise in Conceptual Redescription and Normative Analysis', in *After Pentecost: Language and Biblical Interpretation* (ed. C. Bartholomew, C. Greene and K. Möller; SHS 2; Carlisle: Paternoster; Grand Rapids: Zondervan, 2001), 312–28

Middleton, J.R., and B. Walsh, *Truth is Stranger than it Used to Be* (London: SPCK, 1996)

Milavec, A.A., 'A Fresh Analysis of the Parable of the Wicked Husbandmen in the Light of Jewish-Catholic Dialogue', in *Parable and Story in Judaism and Christianity* (ed. C. Thoma and M. Wyschogrod; New York: Paulist Press, 1989), 81–117

Noll, M.A., *The Scandal of the Evangelical Mind* (Grand Rapids: Eerdmans; Leicester: Inter-Varsity Press, 1994)

Plantinga, A., 'Two (Or More) Types of Scripture Scholarship', *Modern Theology* 14.2 (1998), 234–78 = Ch. 1 in the present volume

Prickett, S., *Words and the Word: Language, Poetics and Biblical Interpretation* (Cambridge: CUP, 1986)

Seitz, C.R., 'Scripture Becomes Religion(s): The Theological Crisis of Serious Biblical Interpretation in the Twentieth Century', in *Renewing Biblical Interpretation* (ed. C. Bartholomew, C. Greene and K. Möller; SHS 1; Carlisle: Paternoster; Grand Rapids: Zondervan, 2000), 40–65

Shanks, A., *'What is Truth?' Towards a Theological Poetics* (London and New York: Routledge, 2001)

Sternberg, M., *The Poetics of Biblical Narrative: Ideological Literature and the Drama of Reading* (Bloomington: Indiana University Press, 1985)

Stuhlmacher, P., *Historical Criticism and Theological Interpretation of Scripture* (Philadelphia: Fortress Press, 1977)

Thiselton, A.C., *The Two Horizons: New Testament Hermeneutics and Philosophical Description with Special Reference to Heidegger, Bultmann, Gadamer and Wittgenstein* (Exeter: Paternoster, 1980)

——, *New Horizons in Hermeneutics: The Theory and Practice of Transforming Biblical Reading* (London: HarperCollins, 1992)

Walker, A., *Telling the Story: Gospel, Mission and Culture* (London: SPCK, 1996)

Watson, F., *Text, Church and World: Biblical Interpretation in Theological Perspective* (Edinburgh: T. & T. Clark, 1992)

Wansborough, H., 'Made and Re-Made in the Image of God: The New Testament Evidence' (unpublished paper, 2001)

Wiles, M., and M. Santer, *Documents in Early Christian Thought* (Cambridge: CUP, 1975)

Wilson, P.S., *God Sense: Reading the Bible for Preaching* (Nashville: Abingdon Press, 2001)

Wright, S.I., *The Voice of Jesus: Studies in the Interpretation of Six Gospel Parables* (Carlisle: Paternoster, 2000)

University of Gloucestershire

We are delighted that the fourth volume in the Scripture and Hermeneutics Series, *'Behind' the Text: History and Biblical Interpretation* is now published. This marks an important half way milestone in the Series, and the project as a whole. We thank the contributors and editors for their work for this volume, as well as the British and Foreign Bible Society and Baylor University for their indispensable partnership.

Although historical issues have dominated biblical interpretation for a long time, they continue to challenge scholars and are of importance and interest to Christians. Indeed, there is much at stake theologically in the whole debate about the Bible and history. The hope of the Scripture and Hermeneutics Seminar is that this volume will contribute towards fresh ways of wrestling with history and biblical interpretation.

In August 2003 the Scripture and Hermeneutics Seminar held a sixth consultation at the University of St. Andrews, Scotland. The theme was biblical theology and biblical interpretation and papers from that Consultation are being prepared for Volume 5 in the Scripture and Hermeneutics Series, to be published in November 2004.

Dr Fred Hughes

School of Humanities
University of Gloucestershire
Francis Close Hall
Swindon Road
Cheltenham
Gloucestershire GL50 4AZ
<www.glos.ac.uk/humanities/content.asp?rid=14>

The British and Foreign Bible Society

> History is not a text, not a narrative, master or otherwise; unfortunately history is what hurts and its alienating necessities will not forget us, however much we might prefer to ignore them.[1]

The above quote from the neo-Marxist postmodernist Fredric Jameson alerts us to the vigorous intellectual debate that still surrounds any current understanding and appreciation of the nature and importance of history for modern cultural theory. Not surprisingly, there is probably no area in contemporary theology that has been so racked by controversy and, at times, acrimonious discussion, than the way successive generations of biblical scholars have appropriated the science of historiography. Even the use of the term 'science' signals one of the key areas of dissent, simply because the early practitioners of historical-critical biblical scholarship in the eighteenth century largely borrowed their methodology from the natural sciences. The historicism that often accompanied their corporate endeavours was at least driven by the entirely laudable, if unfortunately mistaken, desire to get at the facts, isolate the sources and pinpoint the redactions that would supposedly allow the scholar to reconstruct the world that lay behind the text.

In the nineteenth and twentieth centuries successive theologians and philosophers, such as Schleiermacher, Dilthey, Heidegger, Gadamer and Pannenberg, introduced us to the quite crucial role played by our understanding of the nature of hermeneutics in this debate. To get behind the text was no longer regarded as merely an exercise in objective scientific historical research but much more an imaginative and empathetic engagement between the interpreter and the world that was *presumed* to inform the meaning *implied* in a particular text.

The advent of postmodernity, following close on the heels of the respective philosophies of language developed by Wittgenstein, Saussure and Derrida, initiated us into the peculiarities of a largely intratextual world-view. Reality, we were reliably informed, is largely encoded in texts. The task of the interpreter is consequently to break the code, deconstruct the text, defer or postpone meaning and leave us apparently exhilarated by the continual superfluity

---

[1] Fredric Jameson, *The Political Unconscious* (New York: Cornell University Press, 1981)

of meaning that cannot be constrained by any epistemological, hermeneutical or linguistic net.

It is not surprising, therefore, that the Scripture and Hermeneutics Seminar would produce a volume orientated to the quite crucial role exercised by the philosophy (or philosophies) of history that continually infiltrate the world of biblical interpretation. A contemporary understanding of the nature of historiography could not ignore any of the aforementioned developments in epistemology, hermeneutics and linguistics. The fourth volume in the Scripture and Hermeneutics Series, *'Behind' the Text: History and Biblical Interpretation*, demonstrates the importance of not cutting short any of these interdisciplinary conversations, if we are to understand what it is about history that continually bears down upon us when we engage with the biblical text.

The British and Foreign Bible Society remains committed to developing a new *modus operandi* endeavouring to re-engage the Bible as Scripture with important areas of public life. A central part of that task will be to construct a viable public theology that draws on the insights gained from inter-disciplinary biblical study and reflection. We warmly recommend this further volume in a series that is becoming increasingly aware of the complex nature of the issues that continually inform the world of biblical scholarship.

Revd Dr Colin J.D. Greene

Formerly Head of Theology and Public Policy
The British and Foreign Bible Society

Baylor University

Baylor University is honoured to be able to identify with the University of Gloucestershire and the British and Foreign Bible Society in supporting the Scripture and Hermeneutics Seminar as North American partner. As a university community with 157 years of commitment to Christian higher education and the largest Baptist University in the world, we are deeply interested in the kinds of issues the Seminar pursues. In particular we are grateful to the larger community of scholars whose purpose it is to situate the study of Scripture firmly in relationship to the intellectual life of a wide range of academic disciplines.

Interdisciplinary scholarship is an increasingly necessary and highly productive feature of academic life. Nowhere, perhaps, is it more necessary or productive than when the goal of biblical scholars is to make the full potential of biblical scholarship available to the life of the church.

We congratulate the editors and contributors to the present volume on the vigor and quality of their exchange of views. We look forward to working with the Seminar in the years ahead and to hosting a future Consultation here on the campus at Baylor University.

David Lyle Jeffrey

Distinguished Professor of Literature and Humanities

Provost
Baylor University
PO Box 97404
Waco, Texas 76798–7404
USA

Scripture Index

Names Index

Subject Index